Microcomputer
Troubleshooting & Repair

John G. Stephenson and Bob Cahill

SAMS

A Division of Prentice Hall Computer Publishing

11711 North College, Carmel, Indiana 46032 USA

WARNING AND DISCLAIMER

This book deals with subjects, and may involve the use of materials and substances, that are hazardous to health and life. Do not attempt to implement or utilize the information contained herein unless you are experienced. Although all possible measures have been taken to ensure the accuracy of the information presented, neither the author nor SAMS is liable for damages or injuries, misinterpretation of directions, or misapplications of information.

International Standard Book Number: 0-672-22629-4
Library of Congress Catalog Card Number: 88-60992

Acquisitions Editor: *James S. Hill*
Development Editor: *James Rounds*
Illustrator: *T. R. Emrick*
Compositor: *BMEP, Inc.*
Cover Illustrator: *Ned Shaw*

Printed in the United States of America

Trademark Acknowledgments

Contents

Preface

Since 1982, the world of microcomputers has experienced sweeping changes. The "hot" personal computers then in use were the Apple® IIs and the Commodore® 64s. The first IBM® PCs were just reaching the market. These computers were primitive by today's standards, but they introduced us to the world of personal computing.

In the following years, the trends seemed almost too good to be true—computing speed and memory increased while prices actually decreased. My first computer arrived with a paltry 48K of RAM, and I had to spend $100 to add another 16K. Today, manufacturers are experimenting with ICs that can store 1 Megabyte or more of memory on a single chip. The disk drive on that first computer could store 256K of data on a 5 1/4-inch floppy disk. Today, a smaller 3.5-inch disk can store 1 Megabyte or more. In 1982, hard disk drives were found only on large mainframe computer systems, and laser printers had not yet reached the market. Today, most "serious" PCs are sold with built-in hard disks, and laser printers are appearing on desktops all over the country. This rapid development shows no signs of slowing down. Just in the last year, we've seen the arrival of "desktop publishing." Out on the horizon, we can glimpse exotic new devices, including optical disks, 9600-baud modems, and color printers. Advances in basic IC technology will bring us computers that are even smaller, faster, and more capable.

In spite of these changes, some aspects of the field have remained the same. Even the most modern equipment still breaks down, so someone must still be able to make repairs. That brings us to the purpose of this book. In 1982, as I became familiar with my first computer, I wondered what I would do if it ever stopped working. When I began searching for material on computer servicing, I found that very little information was available. I collaborated with Bob Cahill and we produced *How to Maintain and Service Your Small Computer*.

As the time approached to update the book, we realized that we had to make a number of changes. Of course, we had to include material on the new technologies that had reached the microcomputer market. We also wanted to add information that would be helpful to the student beginning a career in computer servicing.

In this book, we've tried to give you a practical "down to earth" approach to computer troubleshooting and repair. In the real world, a knowledge of the "shortcuts" and "professional tricks" is just as useful as a deep knowledge of computer theory. We've tried to focus on the techniques which will actually help you to make repairs efficiently.

People tend to see computer equipment as mysterious, incomprehensible, and almost magical. We'd like to remove some of that mystery and show you the "nuts and bolts" reality of microcomputer equipment. To put it another way, we want to give you a start toward becoming one of the computer hardware "insiders." It's a long road, but this book should give you a good start. May the Force be with you.

JOHN G. STEPHENSON

*This book is dedicated to the friends who supplied the
moral support which made this book possible.*

Acknowledgements

The authors would like to thank the following persons and organizations for their generous help with this project:

American National Standards Institute
Thomas Barber, Pomona Electronics
James Buell, Xidex Corp.
Ken Burns, Windsor Technologies
Ben Calica, Boston Computer Society
Keith Comer, Toshiba
John Conroy, Jameco Electronics
Electronic Industries Association
John Hall, Hayes Microcomputer Products
Cynthia Harriman, Boston Computer Society
Ray Heineman, Seagate
Joan Henderson, Shugart

Steve Hiyashi, Epson America
Chad Ireland
Intel Corporation
Richard Lord
Jan Marciano, Epson America
Motorola Semiconductor Products
NCR Corporation
Y. Okada, Toshiba
Jeri Peterson, Hewlett-Packard
Martin Plude, B & K Precision
Jeff Wade, Boston Computer Society
Western Digital
Carl Ziter, IBM

Special thanks to Mr. Jim Rounds, Senior Development Editor at Howard W. Sams & Co., for his help and guidance.

Very special thanks to the experts who reviewed the manuscript:

Brian J. Daggett
Janice Farmer
Charles Liebau

J. Gregg Stephenson
Geoffrey Walsh, Northern Electronics

1

Introduction

Our world is full of microcomputer equipment. In the past five years, we have seen a whole generation of Americans learning to live with small computers. Not so long ago, the typical computer was a monster, made up of broiling hot vacuum tubes and miles of wiring, and filling several air-conditioned rooms. By modern standards, these dinosaurs were small-minded and slow-witted. It required a million-dollar budget to pay the legions of technicians needed to keep one of these things running. Computers were so rare and expensive that users had to battle each other for a few precious moments of computing time, and only Fortune 500 companies and the U.S. Government could afford to play this game.

Today, your plumber probably does his accounting on a microcomputer. In the schools, first-grade students are writing programs in BASIC. We have computerized coffee makers, computerized bathroom scales, and computerized autos that talk back to us. We've come a long way.

About This Book

We have designed this book to help several groups of readers. Computer servicing is, as they say, a "growth industry." With many new microcomputers reaching the market, there is a large demand for computer repair technicians. As a result, you may be interested in moving into the electronics repair field. Perhaps you are taking electronics courses at a university or technical school. Maybe you've had some training in the military, and want to make a transition to civilian electronics work. You may have had some training in basic electronics, or had experience servicing other types of equipment—television sets, stereo equipment, etc. One way or another, you have gotten a basic knowledge of electronics.

If you belong to one of these groups, this book will provide a solid grounding in the "basics" of computer repair work. In the early chapters of the book, we cover some practical "background" information on computer servicing. We deal with down-to-earth questions like "How can I find this IC on the circuit board?", "Where can I get a replacement for this burned-out part?", and "How can I replace this part without damaging it?" As a beginning technician, you must learn to deal with these practical details.

Throughout the book, we have tried to convey broad concepts, rather than describe specific details. This is really a necessity, because there are so many different kinds of microcomputers and peripherals. Once you understand the basic concepts, you can apply them to many different types of computer equipment.

Perhaps you don't plan to take up a career in computer servicing. Maybe you're a hobbyist or "hacker" and you tinker with computers and electronics in your spare time. Perhaps you're an end-user and you want to be able to do some of the repair work on your equipment. In this book, we will show you how to handle many servicing problems yourself. Sometimes, this knowledge can save you significant amounts of time and money.

For example, let's say that you press the "P" key on your computer once, yet you see two "P's" on the screen. At this point, most end-users would assume that something was seriously wrong with the computer. The average end-user would have to haul the microcomputer and peripherals down to the neighborhood service shop. If the shop was inefficient or dishonest, the repairs could be both time-consuming and expensive. However, if you can diagnose and repair your own equipment, you can handle this type of problem quickly and inexpensively.

In Chapter 9, we explain that this particular symptom—two characters from one keystroke—can be caused by dirty key contacts. If you follow the instructions in this book, you can clean a set of key contacts in two minutes and "repair" the computer for a total cost of about one cent. Of course, all computer repairs are not this simple, and the savings are not always so dramatic. However, even if you have your service work done at a shop, it is helpful to understand the equipment. As an "educated consumer," you will be able to judge whether the repair work is justified and whether the bill is reasonable.

Can *You* Really Repair Computer Equipment?

Many computer servicing operations are simpler than you may think. You will be surprised to learn that most service problems have simple causes—worn cables, dirty connectors, a screw loose in the works, and so on. Almost any end-user can check for this kind of problem. However, other problems are caused when a component fails in one of the circuits inside the equipment. If you can use a few simple tools, we can tell you how to track down many problems of this type.

If you are an end-user, we may have to convince you that it's possible for you to work on your equipment yourself. Over the years, the public has picked up some strange ideas about computers. We've been taught that computers are so "high-tech" that they can never be comprehensible to normal folks like ourselves. Thus, many of us are comfortable using computers, but are afraid to open the case and poke around inside.

This fear is a legacy from the "bad old days" of computers. As we said, the first computers were inefficient and obnoxious, and required constant pampering by teams of experts. It was in the interest of these specialists to make their work seem as mysterious as possible. That way, they could ask for larger raises. The specialists got their raises, and the public got the idea that computers were "big magic." Everyone was happy.

Today's microcomputers are smaller, of course, but they're also far more reliable and easier to understand. After all, each piece of computer equipment was designed by mere mortals like ourselves. If you stand back and look at a computer as a whole, it is indeed "big magic." But, if you look closely at a particular circuit or part of the system, you will find that it does its job in a logical, understandable way.

"But I can't do this," you may say. "I'm no expert in electronics." You may be surprised to learn that many "troubleshooting" jobs do not require much detailed knowledge of electronics. Even in a "professional" troubleshooting operation, the technician may not have a detailed knowledge of the circuitry.

Most computer dealers have some kind of servicing operation. Usually, the technicians in these shops depend on a two-step troubleshooting process. When faced with a faulty computer, they begin by running a diagnostic software program. The diagnostic program points out the circuit board or section of the equipment that is bad. Next, the technician replaces the bad circuit board or section of the equipment. This "board swapping" strategy does not require a lot of technical expertise. However, in this book, we will take you far beyond "board swapping." The point we're trying to make is that you do not have to be a technical wizard to service microcomputers.

Of course, the more technical knowledge you have, the better. To make full use of this book, you should have some basic knowledge of electronics and know how to use simple hand tools, such as pliers, soldering irons, etc. As a minimum, you should understand voltage and current theory, and know how resistors, diodes, transistors, and other electronic devices operate. You should also know how to use a *volt-ohmmeter* (VOM). This kind of information you can find in any basic electronics book. We've included plenty of reminders for those readers who were familiar with all of this material once, but who are now a little bit rusty.

It is also important that you understand something about "digital" circuits. Howard W. Sams & Company, the publisher of this book, sells two excellent introductory books: *Understanding Digital Electronics* (Cat. #27013) and *Understanding Microprocessors*

(Cat #27010). We strongly suggest that you read both of these books—they provide all the background you'll need. You can buy both books at local bookstores or can order them by mail from Sams.

A Look Ahead

We cover a lot of ground in this book. To begin with, we'll give you the basic "background" information we just described. We will also include specific troubleshooting information for each of the major parts of the system—the basic computer, printer, disk drives, and so on. Now, for the remaining part of this introduction, a quick preview of each of the chapters in this book.

Whenever you work with electronic equipment, there are certain dangers. Computer equipment uses 120-volt AC "house current," and this current can injure or kill you. If you understand the dangers and follow a few rules, you can work with this equipment safely. In Chapter 2, we have listed some important safety rules.

What parts of a computer system are most likely to fail? How often can you expect to have breakdowns? In Chapter 3, we present a "service profile" of modern microcomputer equipment.

Then, when a piece of equipment fails, does it really make sense to fix it yourself? Are you better off taking your equipment to a shop? How about "third-party servicing?" Chapter 4 discusses your options.

Next, there are many things you can do to make your computer equipment more reliable. By taking preventive steps and controlling the environment around your equipment, you can eliminate many service problems before they occur. We discuss "Environment and Operating Procedures" in Chapter 6. And, when a piece of equipment breaks down, where do you start? How do you "localize" a problem to one part of the system? What are the tricks and short-cuts that

technicians use to locate bad components quickly? In the first part of Chapter 7, we review some basic troubleshooting concepts. Then, in the second part of the chapter, we tell you how to test some simple electronic parts—resistors, diodes, transistors, and so on.

Next, in Chapter 8, we explain how to troubleshoot circuits that include *integrated circuits* (ICs). You must use some special tools and techniques to work with these complicated devices.

Finally, in the rest of the book, we tell you how to service a particular part of the computer system. Chapter 9 includes troubleshooting procedures for the main computer, while Chapter 10 covers floppy disk drives, and Chapter 11 deals with hard disk drives. Many hard disk drives use the SCSI high-speed serial port, so we have included a section on this port in Chapter 11.

In Chapter 12, we look at dot-matrix and daisy-wheel printers, and include some information on "parallel" ports. Chapter 13 discusses laser printers and modems are covered in Chapter 14. Since most modems are connected to an RS-232 "serial" port, we also cover this circuitry in Chapter 14. Chapter 15 deals with monitors. Chapter 16 is devoted to power supplies of all types. In Chapter 17, we have included some notes on advanced troubleshooting.

Servicing computers can be both fascinating and frustrating. Clients and customers can be very demanding. Sometimes the equipment can be stubborn and fight you at every turn. If you're working on your own equipment, it can be tough to think clearly when your system is down. However, there are compensations. If you become an efficient technician, you can make a good living. If you can troubleshoot your own equipment, you can often save large amounts of time and money. And, every time you repair a computer, you will feel that special satisfaction that comes from knowing, "I understand what's going on in that equipment. If it breaks down, I can fix it."

2

Safety

Introduction and Objectives

Whenever you're working on any microcomputer equipment, your own safety has to come first. Whether you're a "hacker" or you plan to work as a commercial technician, you must always take safety precautions. This is literally a matter of life and death.

Of course, it is possible to work with electronic equipment in complete safety. In this chapter, we'll help you understand the safety hazards and show you how to avoid them.

Shock Hazard

The most serious danger in servicing computer equipment is the threat of electric shock. We'll be blunt about this:

ELECTRIC SHOCK CAN KILL YOU!

Electric shock can be dangerous in several ways. A strong shock will often knock you out. Once you're unconscious, you have no control over your body. You may fall onto a sharp object, for instance. If you are unconscious, you can't protect yourself from other problems.

A serious shock may stop your heart. The heart is a very strong muscle. In order to keep beating, it depends on electrical impulses from the brain and the nervous system. These impulses tell the heart muscles when to contract and pump the blood. The heart muscles work like a team of rowers in a racing boat, all pulling their oars in the same direction at the right time.

If you receive an electric shock, this system may be disturbed. Instead of making large, regular pumping actions, the heart muscles may start to make short, disorganized contractions. This condition is called "fibrillation." It's as if each of the rowers were pulling on his oar at a different time. The heart stops pumping blood and you lose consciousness. Permanent brain damage can occur within a few minutes. Unless the heart is restarted quickly, you will die.

Shock can cause other problems as well. If a large electric current flows through your body, you can receive serious burns. Usually, these burns are concentrated on the parts of the body that make the electrical connections. For example, if you touch a wire, the current might enter through your hand and exit through your feet. The burns would be concentrated at these points.

When you receive a shock, the muscles in your arms and legs can contract. This can cause you to jump or fall. Sometimes, shock victims say they've been "thrown across the room." Keep this in mind if you ever have to help someone who is being shocked. Let's say that you're working with someone else, and he or

5

she accidentally touches a "hot" electrical wire. Because their muscles are contracted, they may not be able to move away from the wire and their whole body may be holding the same electrical charge as the "hot" electrical wire. This means that, if you touch the victim and try to pull him or her away from the wire, you may receive an electrical shock as well. Instead, try to turn off the power which is creating the shock at the source. Once the power is off, you can touch the victim. If you can't turn off the power, use a piece of insulated material to push the person away from the hot wire. A dry piece of wood is a good insulator for this purpose.

Finally, shock can interfere with your nervous system. After a serious shock, you may not be able to think clearly, or may have problems with your memory. You may have trouble controlling your arms or legs, or other parts of your body.

Are you scared yet? We hope so. You've got to treat electricity with great respect.

Factors Affecting Shock Hazard

The danger from a shock depends on three factors: the voltage of the source, the current the source can produce, and the path the current takes through your body.

The 120-volt alternating current found in house wiring has more than enough voltage to kill you. Even a voltage as low as 34 volts is strong enough to cause the heart muscles to "fibrillate" and cause death. If you create a short circuit, house wiring can supply current up to the limit allowed by the fuse or circuit breaker, usually about 20 amperes. This amount of current can be very dangerous.

When you shuffle across a thick carpet, you can build up a charge of static electricity. This charge might have a high voltage—5000 volts or more. However, the carpet can't generate much current at this high voltage. This combination of current and voltage is not very powerful. When you work on static-sensitive parts, you may wear a "grounding strap" attached to your wrist. While you're wearing this strap, you could conceivably touch a source of 120-volts AC. But since the strap includes a resistor with a high value (about 1 megohm), only a small current can flow through the strap. Again, this combination of voltage and current is not very powerful. *However, do not test the grounding strap by touching a "hot" conductor!* The grounding strap does not give you any protection against shock if you are also grounded through another path.

When you receive a shock, the amount of current that can flow through your body is limited by your body's electrical resistance and by the resistance in the connection between your body and ground. The human body contains a large percentage of water and is, unfortunately, a good conductor. You can't change that fact. However, you can protect yourself by avoiding situations where there might be a low-resistance path through your body. See Fig. 2-1A. In this example, the handyman is making a serious mistake. He doesn't know that the circuit breaker to the AC outlet is turned on, and he has touched the "hot" side of the AC line; his body offers a good low-resistance path for the electricity. To make matters worse, he's standing on a wet floor and the water provides an excellent low-resistance connection to ground. To sum up, the circuit through his body has a high voltage and low resistance. This combination causes a large current to flow. The poor guy could be killed or seriously hurt.

In Fig. 2-1B, the handyman is wearing rubber-soled sneakers and he's standing on an insulating pad. The sneakers and foam pad provide a higher resistance and, thus, limit the possible current flow. Even in this situation, the handyman might still receive a serious shock. The insulated shoes and pad only provide "back-up" protection in case he makes a mistake and touches something which is electrically "hot."

You can't predict the effects of a shock. In one situation, you might make a risky move and get away with it. You might do the same thing the next day and get a serious shock. Don't take chances.

Power Supplies

Most of the circuits inside modern computers use fairly low DC voltages. Almost all of the ICs on the circuit boards use +5-V DC. Some memory ICs, and the parts connected to RS-232 serial links could use +12-V and −12-V DC. Electromechanical parts, such as solenoids and motors, may use voltages of 25-V DC and higher.

Power-supply sections tend to be more dangerous. Refer to Fig. 2-2. In a typical micro-computer, the power supply is plugged into a 120-volt AC "house current" outlet. As we said earlier, house current can produce enough voltage and current to be very dangerous.

Normally, the 120-V AC will be carried just to the first stage of the power supply. Then, a transformer is often used to produce a lower AC voltage. "Downstream" of the transformer, there is less of

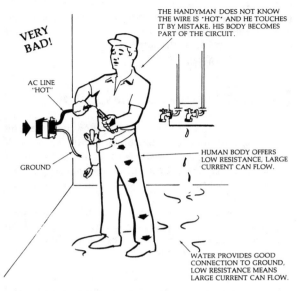

(A) Don't become a low-resistance path to ground.

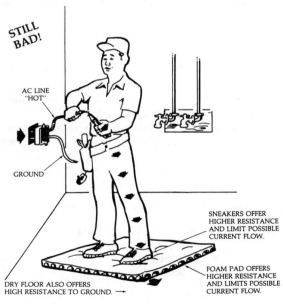

(B) Sneakers and foam pad form a high-resistance
insulation that limits current flow.

Fig. 2-1. Don't become part of the circuit!

a shock hazard since the voltage is lower. In a
"switching" type of power supply, the 120-volts AC
might go through several stages before it is converted to

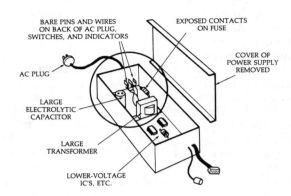

Fig. 2-2. Danger areas in a power supply.

low-voltage DC. At the point where the AC enters the
power supply, you will usually find a switch and a fuse
or a circuit breaker. Some of these parts may carry 120-
volt AC even when the switch is turned off. To protect
yourself, assume that the first few stages of any power
supply carry dangerous voltages. Chapter 16 discusses
power supplies in more detail.

The power supplies in most microcomputers are
shielded to limit the amount of radio interference they
produce. This means that the dangerous 120-V AC
areas usually are safely enclosed in a metal box. You
normally should not have to open the box around a
power supply, but if you do, remember that you're
entering a dangerous section of the computer. Be
careful not to touch any bare metal parts that might be
carrying 120-V AC. If you have good documentation
and you understand how the power supply is laid out,
you can determine whether a part carries 120-V AC or
not. If you don't have any service literature, or if you
don't really understand how the power supply is
designed, use this rule:

ASSUME ALL THE PARTS IN THE POWER SUPPLY ARE "HOT."

If a part is using 120-V AC or less, and you're not sure
whether a part is energized, you can always check it
with a voltmeter. Be sure your voltmeter can handle the
voltages you want to measure. Do not try to measure a
voltage that is higher than the voltmeter is designed to
handle.

In some older equipment, you may find high-
voltage capacitors. A typical high-voltage electrolytic
capacitor is contained in a metal can and looks a bit like
a salt shaker. In a power supply, capacitors are used

to filter any AC signal out of the desired DC voltage. If the capacitors are used in the part of the supply that handles 120-V AC, they can store quite a charge. Capacitors can retain this charge, even after you have turned off the equipment.

Before you work on a unit containing a large capacitor, be sure to discharge the capacitor. You can do this by creating a short circuit between the leads (see Fig. 2-3). Always turn off the power before you discharge a capacitor. Use a jumper wire and a 1000-ohm, 1-watt resistor to short-circuit the two leads on the capacitor. For a capacitor designed for very high voltage (400V or more), use a 10,000-ohm, 1-watt resistor. Hold the resistor with a pair of pliers that has insulated handles. Before you discharge the capacitor, be very careful not to touch either of the leads with your fingers. You don't want to become part of the circuit. Note that after discharge, the charge may build again. Leave the jumper in place until you are through servicing, or discharge the capacitor again after a few minutes.

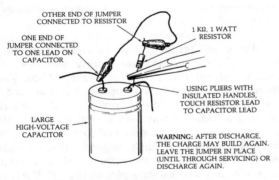

ONE END OF JUMPER CONNECTED TO RESISTOR

ONE END OF JUMPER CONNECTED TO ONE LEAD ON CAPACITOR

1 KΩ, 1 WATT RESISTOR

USING PLIERS WITH INSULATED HANDLES, TOUCH RESISTOR LEAD TO CAPACITOR LEAD

LARGE HIGH-VOLTAGE CAPACITOR

WARNING: AFTER DISCHARGE, THE CHARGE MAY BUILD AGAIN. LEAVE THE JUMPER IN PLACE (UNTIL THROUGH SERVICING) OR DISCHARGE AGAIN.

Fig. 2-3. Discharging a capacitor.

When a capacitor fails, it usually develops a short circuit. The short can allow a large current to flow through the part, generating heat, and causing the gases inside the capacitor to expand. If this happens suddenly enough, the case of the capacitor may explode. Keep this in mind when you energize a circuit you are working with. Move your face away from the capacitors when you first turn on the power.

Most power supplies are designed with self-protective devices. The typical power supply has a circuit breaker or a fuse. These devices are designed to cut off the power if the power supply is overloaded. However, circuit breakers and fuses do not act quickly enough to protect you from an electrical shock. These

devices are included to prevent damage to the equipment, not to protect you. Be sure the self-protective circuits are working correctly. When you replace fuses, always use a replacement fuse with the same current rating as the original.

Precautions Against Shock

Obviously, technicians work on computer equipment all the time, and most of them do it safely. They work carefully, understand the dangers, and avoid them. If you keep the equipment turned off as much as possible while you're working with it, you should minimize the shock hazard.

You also have little to fear from the low-power DC sections of the equipment, and this includes most of the circuitry. Here are some rules which should help you to avoid shock hazards:

1. Your safety always comes first. Do the job safely, even if this requires more time and trouble.

2. Always turn off the equipment and unplug it before you begin to work.

3. If you have to make tests while the equipment is operating, turn the equipment on, make your tests *carefully*, and then turn the equipment off again.

4. Be especially careful when working with those parts of the equipment that carry high voltage. Watch out for the 120-volt AC sections of power supplies. Large capacitors can be dangerous unless they've been discharged. In monitors, beware of the high voltage at the picture tube and in the horizontal circuits.

5. Don't work when you're tired or rushed.

6. Try to do the work with one hand, while keeping your other in your pocket. This "one-hand rule" reduces the chance that a current will flow through the main part of your body.

If you don't understand the nature of shock and the hazard it presents, or you're not sure what to touch and what not to touch—play it safe! Do not work inside the equipment. Use the information in this book to try to localize your problem, without probing around inside the equipment. Let a qualified service shop do the final diagnosis and repair.

Monitors and Television Sets

Monitors and television sets present special dangers (Fig. 2-4). Monitors have sections that use very high DC voltages. The circuitry in a monitor has to generate a very high voltage to pull the electron beam from the rear of the picture tube to the front surface of the screen. A small monochrome (B & W) monitor might require 12,000 V for this. On a larger color monitor, or a color TV, the voltage could be as high as 35,000 V.

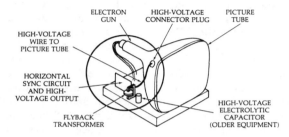

Fig. 2-4. Danger areas in a monitor.

The high voltage is usually created in the same part of the circuitry that generates the horizontal synchronization pulses. (We will discuss this circuitry in more detail in Chapter 15.) A part called a "flyback transformer" is often used to help generate the high voltage. The high voltage is then carried from the horizontal circuits, through a special high-voltage wire, to a plug near the front of the picture tube. The high-voltage circuits inside a monitor can give you a dangerous shock! As long as the monitor is enclosed inside its case, none of this high-voltage circuitry can hurt you.

Before you work on a monitor, you will have to de-energize the high-voltage circuits. The picture tube and other parts inside a monitor can hold a dangerous charge, even if the monitor has not been used for several days. (Always unplug the monitor before you discharge the high-voltage circuits.) Using a pair of pliers with insulated handles, carefully unplug the high-voltage connector on the side of the picture tube. Touch the metal tip of the connector to the metal frame around the front of the picture tube. This will eliminate most of the high voltage in the circuitry.

Even after you discharge the high-voltage charge on the picture tube, however, the charge may build up again. To prevent this, clip a jumper from the high-voltage connector to the metal frame around the front of the tube. Be sure to remove the jumper and reconnect the high-voltage plug to the picture tube when you are through working.

Some older monitors may include some high-voltage capacitors, and these can also hold dangerous charges. As we said earlier, before you work on this kind of equipment, discharge any large capacitors found in the equipment. Refer back to Fig. 2-3.

You can't measure very high voltages directly with a voltohmmeter and a standard set of test probes. When a standard VOM is subjected to a very high voltage, it will burn out in a flash. Instead, you'll have to use a high-voltage meter or a special high-voltage probe. A few standard voltmeters have connection points to allow the use of high-voltage probes.

There is another danger present when working on monitors. As we said, a monitor uses a very high voltage to accelerate an electron beam from the electron gun to the front of the screen. If this voltage is allowed to rise too high, the monitor can begin to produce X rays. Actually, *all* monitors produce a small amount of X rays. If the unit is operating normally, the output is very low. But as the voltage rises beyond specification, the output of X rays rises very quickly and X rays can damage your body. If you receive a large dose of X rays, you may face a higher risk of cancer and other medical problems. You can't see or feel X rays, so you cannot tell if you have been injured or not. Even if X rays do cause you damage, the medical problems affecting you may not appear for many years. A sloppy technician may take chances with X rays and may seem to "get away with it" for years, but he may have serious medical problems later.

In order to tell if the accelerating high voltage is within specification, you must measure it directly. If you find that the high voltage is much higher than specified, you have to assume that the monitor is producing X rays. Normally, monitors have protective circuits which keep the high voltage within design limits, and will shut down the set if the voltage rises above specifications. But, if a monitor is not working correctly, or if an inexperienced technician has changed the circuitry, the safety circuits may be bypassed, and the unit could be generating lots of X rays. If you suspect a problem like this, don't leave the unit turned on for very long. And, any X rays will pass through the front of the monitor, so don't stand in front of it. Get the high-voltage safety circuits working properly before you move on to other parts of the unit.

There is a vacuum inside the picture tube on a monitor or TV set. If you break the picture tube, the glass will "implode" (collapse inward) with a lot of force. An imploding picture tube can throw bits of glass all over the room. You should not have a problem as long as you leave the tube in the chassis. Be careful not to hit the rear end of the tube with a tool or part. If you must remove or replace a picture tube, handle it very carefully. Once the tube is free, place it face-down on a soft surface.

All Grounds Are Not Created Equal

Modern house wiring uses a three-wire system, as shown in Fig. 2-5. The "hot" and "neutral" wires carry the 120-volts AC. The same current is flowing through both the hot and the neutral wires. The neutral wire is supposed to be at the same potential as the rest of the world. To put it another way, there's not supposed to be any voltage difference between neutral and the earth outside your house.

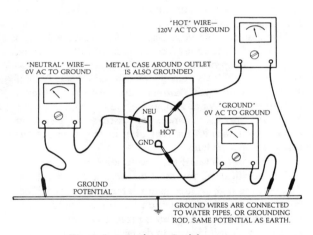

Fig. 2-5. A 3-wire AC wiring system.

The third wire to the AC outlet is a "ground." The ground is connected to the metal box around each outlet and wiring connection. What if something goes wrong and a "hot" wire is allowed to touch one of these metal boxes? In this case, the ground wire will provide a clear path directly to ground, a large current will flow, the circuit breaker or fuse will open, and the circuit will be protected.

You can never assume that an AC output has been wired correctly. Sometimes the hot and neutral wires are reversed, and sometimes the ground has not been connected. In Chapter 5, we will tell you how to check an outlet for correct wiring. Computer equipment

may not operate normally if the AC wiring is incorrect. We will cover this in more detail in Chapter 5.

Hot Chassis Problems

Safety problems can occur when you are using two pieces of equipment, and one of them has been wired incorrectly (Fig. 2-6). Let's say that you're working on unit A, a monitor. You plug the monitor's AC cord into an outlet. We'll assume that the AC cord for the monitor has only two wires, and is connected to a "polarized" plug. The side of the plug which is supposed to be connected to the "hot" side of the AC line will have a smaller prong. In this example, we'll say that the "hot" and neutral wires to the AC outlet have been reversed, but you do not know this. The wire which is meant to be "hot" is actually neutral, and the wire that is meant to be neutral is "hot." When you plug in the monitor, it still operates, because it is still receiving 120-V AC.

If you look closely at Fig. 2-6, you'll see that one side of the AC line has been connected directly to the chassis (the metal frame) of the monitor. This is called a "hot chassis" arrangement. The name is a bit misleading. The chassis is called "hot" because it is now tied to the hot side of the AC line. When the unit is wired as designed, the chassis is usually connected to the *neutral* side of the AC line. In our example, the chassis was designed to be connected to neutral. Since the wiring in the AC outlet has been reversed, the chassis is tied to the "hot" side of the AC line instead.

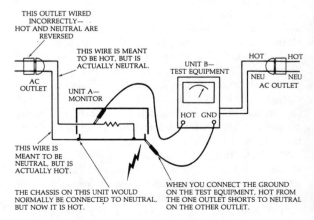

Fig. 2-6. "Hot chassis" conflict.

Nothing unusual happens until you start using your test equipment (unit B). Unit B is plugged into an outlet which has been wired correctly. The grounding lead on the test equipment runs back to the neutral side of the AC outlet for unit B. As part of your test setup, you'll usually want to attach the ground lead from the test instrument to a ground on the monitor. As soon as you touch the test unit's ground lead to the "hot" chassis, you've got a direct short circuit. The "hot" 120-V AC wire from one outlet is shorted to the ground wire on the other outlet. Sparks fly and fuses blow.

Now suppose that you don't know the chassis is "hot," and you touch it with your finger. You've made yourself part of the circuit. The effect is the same as if you'd shoved your finger into a light socket.

If all AC outlets and microcomputer equipment were wired correctly, you'd never have to worry about this problem. However, you can never trust AC outlets to be wired correctly until you have checked them. There may also be a problem inside the computer equipment which results in a "hot" chassis. Whenever you work on faulty equipment, you should be aware of this possibility.

You can protect yourself against problems of this type by using an "isolation transformer." Refer to Fig. 2-7. During servicing, the isolation transformer is connected between the monitor and the outlet. This is a 1:1 transformer, so it does not change the voltage. The transformer still produces 120-V AC at its outputs, but both sides of this AC line are independent of ground. If you were to accidentally touch one of these outputs, it would go to ground potential, and you would be protected. In the example shown in Fig. 2-6, if we had connected an isolation transformer between the monitor and the outlet, it would have prevented a short circuit.

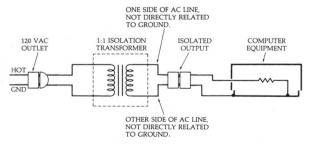

Fig. 2-7. Isolation transformer circuit.

Earlier equipment usually included a transformer in the power supply, and this eliminated the potential

for hot chassis problems. However, some modern units, especially monitors, are designed with a hot chassis. Professionals always use an isolation transformer when servicing this kind of equipment. If you don't see a large transformer in the power supply, or if you can't see inside the power supply, you have to assume that the unit has a hot chassis. You can't predict what problems you'll encounter inside faulty equipment, so an isolation transformer provides some valuable protection. Commercial units often include some overload protection and other features. B&K Precision sells a small isolation transformer for about $60.00.

Before you send a hot chassis unit back to a customer, you should be sure that an unusual amount of current is not leaking to ground. In Chapter 15 (Troubleshooting Monitors and Displays), we tell you how to check for this leakage current.

Laser Printers

The laser printer depends on a small laser to trace the page images on a photosensitive drum. The beam from this laser can damage your eyes. Some lasers generate a form of light which is invisible, so you may have no warning that you are being exposed. As long as the case of the laser printer is closed, you should be protected from any possible danger. Nevertheless, it is not wise to look into the paper-exit opening while the printer is operating.

When you open the case of the printer, an interlock switch will prevent the unit from operating. In this case, you are still protected from any danger, but there are a few servicing operations which require you to bypass the cover interlock switch. Once you do this, you are exposed to possible danger from the laser light. The path of the laser is usually encased in a series of panels and covers. Be particularly careful if you remove any of these interior parts. If you block the laser beam with a shiny tool, some of the light may be reflected upward into your eyes.

Because of these dangers, we advise the inexperienced technician not to bypass the cover interlock switch. If you reach a point in your troubleshooting where this must be done, take the printer to a shop, and leave the job to an experienced technician.

Laser printers present one other danger we must mention. The fusing rollers at the "downstream" end of the printer can become very hot. If you touch these parts by accident, you may be burned. Allow the printer to cool for a few minutes before you begin to work with these parts.

Lifting

Most microcomputer equipment is not very heavy, but be careful to lift it correctly. Keep your back straight and upright, and use your legs to supply the lifting power. Be sure each piece of equipment is set on a steady, secure base. Equipment that vibrates, such as a printer, can "walk" across a smooth surface and move right off the edge of a table.

Mechanical Parts

As you work on the equipment, keep your fingers out of any moving parts. The reason for this should be self-explanatory. Also, when a mechanism is operating, it can grab a piece of loose clothing and pull you into the machinery. This can happen very quickly. Be especially careful with powerful, fast-moving machinery.

Don't wear loose clothing which could be caught in the machinery. If you wear a necktie, take it off while you're working, or tuck it into your shirt. If you have long hair, tie it back. Throughout this book, we'll tell you to keep the equipment turned off as much as possible. If you absolutely must poke into a mechanism while it is operating, use a tool, not your fingers.

Other Dangers

Wear eye protection while working on electronic equipment. When you heat a solder joint, tiny balls of hot solder or flux may be thrown into the air. When you clip a lead on a part with wire cutters, the "waste" piece of wire may shoot across the room. The cheapest protective glasses are ugly and uncomfortable, and they scratch easily. Better-quality protective glasses, with screens at the side of the lenses, are available in hardware stores for about $10.00.

A soldering iron can give you a nasty burn! Inexpensive "pencil"-type soldering irons tend to be the most dangerous. A pencil iron usually has no switch, and it warms up slowly, so you tend to leave it plugged in while you're working. The cheaper pencil irons are often sold with a flimsy sheet-metal holder, which is meant to support the iron while it is not in use. The red-hot iron is left setting on your workbench, just waiting for you to lean on it with your hand, or touch it with something flammable.

It is much safer to use a battery-powered iron, or a pencil-type iron which has a switch. If you do use an iron having no switch, get a sturdy holder, and always place the iron in the holder when you're not using it. Do this whenever you're not using the iron, even for a moment. Also, remember that soldered joints remain hot for a while. Wait a minute before you touch heated circuit boards or parts.

If you are using a grounded-tip soldering iron, be careful not to touch the tip to any parts which may be electrically "hot." You can receive a shock. Turn off the equipment before making any solder repairs.

In service work, you'll use a number of chemicals, and some of these can be harmful. Some chemicals give off a vapor as they are sprayed from a can. Solvents and cleaners may produce vapors when they are heated. Try not to breathe these vapors. Be sure your work room has good ventilation, so the vapors can't collect.

For about $20.00, American Optical sells a respirator which will stop most "organic vapors." You can buy a respirator of this type in most hardware stores. If you are going to be using chemicals constantly, install a ventilating hood over your work bench.

Most solder includes lead. Your body can absorb the lead if you work with lots of solder over a long period of time, and this lead can damage your nervous system. This type of damage may not appear for a long time, so you may not know you have been exposed. If you do a lot of soldering, wear gloves so you don't touch the solder directly. You should also wear a respirator, or work under a ventilating hood, to reduce the amount of lead dust you breathe.

As you work with microcomputer equipment, you will encounter many protective devices. Fuses, circuit breakers, insulators, stand-offs, and shields—all of these have been included to protect both the user and the equipment. Replace all of the safety devices when you reassemble the equipment. Protective circuits may be troublesome to work with, but they've been included for good reason. Don't bypass these circuits.

Chapter Review

In this chapter, we have outlined the major safety risks that you will face when working on microcomputer equipment. Remember that your safety comes first, even if this means that a job will take more time or effort. Electrical shock can kill you or cause burns.

Shock is especially dangerous when your body is part of a low-resistance path to ground. Beware of "hot" parts inside power supplies. Watch out for very high voltages inside monitors. Be sure to discharge high-voltage capacitors before working near them.

Don't assume that an AC outlet has been wired correctly. On equipment without a transformer in the power supply, use an isolation transformer to prevent a "hot chassis conflict." Lift heavy objects carefully. Don't let your fingers or clothing be caught in mechanical parts. Soldering irons can burn you, so put them on a safe stand when they're not in use.

Review Questions

1. One morning you're shaving over the sink, where your wife's stockings are soaking in soapy water. You drop the electric razor in the water. What happens next? Do you pick up the razor?

2. How can an electric shock kill you?

3. Why is it a good idea to stand on a rubber pad while you're working at your service bench?

4. You are working on a disk drive which has its own power supply. Which parts are dangerous?

5. When can you get a hot chassis conflict? How do you prevent problems?

6. It's 4:56 on the Friday before Christmas, and a customer comes to your shop. He wants his monitor serviced on the spot. What do you tell him?

7. You have to make a field service call to fix a printer. Your boss wants you to wear a necktie because it "looks professional." Why could this be a problem?

3

Today's Equipment
–A Service Profile

Introduction and Objectives

In this chapter, we will discuss the different kinds of failures you're likely to encounter with microcomputer equipment. Some parts of the microcomputer system are more reliable than others. Within a particular section of the system, such as a disk drive, certain components will have a high failure rate, while others will have very few problems. When you've completed this chapter, you will be able to determine which parts in the system are most likely to fail.

Common Service Problems

What can go wrong with microcomputer equipment? What kinds of component failures are you most likely to face as you diagnose and make repairs? You might think that most of the breakdowns will occur in the computer itself, since it is the most complicated part of the system. Actually, most failures occur in the disk drives, printers, and other "peripherals" which are attached to the computer. The computer itself will probably be quite reliable.

Bob Cahill was service manager for five years at a dealership which sold Apple and Tandy computers. Fig. 3-1 shows his estimate of the kinds of service problems that he handled during that time. The largest share of

problems related to the floppy and hard disk drives. This category includes problems with the recording media—drop-outs on diskettes, damaged diskettes, and so on.

Disk drives and printers have many "electromechanical" parts that combine both electronic and mechanical action. Electromechanical parts are much less reliable than parts which are strictly electronic. Switches may get dirty or worn, and become unreliable. The coil in a solenoid can burn out. A motor can also have burnt-out coils, along with strictly mechanical problems, like bad bearings, bent shaft, etc. Simple mechanical devices can fail as well. Gears, pulleys, wheels—each of these can wear, change tolerance, break, lose lubrication, or become clogged with dust and dirt.

In Fig. 3-1, notice that many problems are caused by operator error and poor operating procedures. Consumers tend to blame these problems on the hardware, even though there is nothing wrong with the equipment.

The detail at the bottom of Fig. 3-1 shows the breakdown for failures in the computers themselves. There are two categories of problems here—"hard" faults and "soft" faults. When the equipment has a "hard" fault, the problem continues until the fault is identified and repaired. When the equipment has an intermittent "soft" fault, the problem can "come and go" by itself. Soft faults are usually harder to diagnose

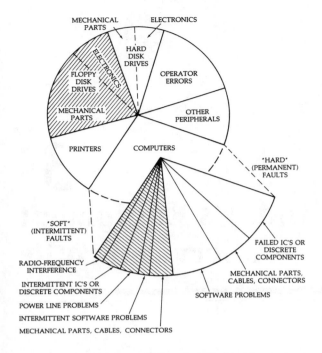

Fig. 3-1. Computer systems service problems.

and repair. About two thirds of the computer breakdowns are "hard" faults, and about one third are "soft" or intermittent faults. Consumers seem to think that most computer breakdowns are caused by "hard" failures of ICs, transistors, resistors, etc., in the computers themselves. As you can see by the illustration in Fig. 3-1, these actually account for a small percentage of all breakdowns.

Many faults in the computers, both "hard" and "soft," are caused by the software. These problems can't be blamed on the hardware. Many of the genuine "hardware" problems are actually caused by faulty cables and connectors. This is because these components are mounted outside the equipment, where they can be damaged. The pins inside a connector can be bent easily. The contacts may corrode. If a connector is attached to a circuit board, stress cracks can develop in the traces on the circuit board under the connector. A bad connection at any of these points can stop the computer from working.

Common Component Failures

Parts are more likely to fail if they handle relatively large amounts of power. A typical power supply has to take 120-V AC, and "rearrange" it into low-voltage DC. This means the components in a power supply are under a good deal of stress from relatively large amounts of voltage and current. By comparison, most of the ICs in the computer itself cruise along with a steady supply of +5-V DC. Power-handling components are more likely to fail.

You can also expect problems in devices that feed power to the electromechanical sections of the equipment. For example, in a printer, some of the parts may be moved by an electronic part called a "solenoid." Most solenoids will use a +12-V DC voltage or higher, and require a relatively large amount of current. This means the solenoid can't be powered directly by the usual +5-V DC signals inside the computer. Instead, the designers will use a low-voltage signal (+5-V DC) to turn on an output transistor. This transistor acts as a switch that provides the higher-voltage DC power to the solenoid. Because this output transistor is handling relatively large amounts of power, it is under more stress and is more likely to fail.

A transistor, resistor, or other component is called "discrete" when it stands alone on the circuit board. Computer equipment includes some discrete components, and these do fail from time to time. Transistors can short out and stop working. Resistors can fail and leave an open circuit, or can change in value. Capacitors can also change value with time. They can also short out or leave an open circuit. Diodes can fail and leave a short circuit or an open circuit.

Finally, there are the many transistors and resistors included in the "integrated circuits (ICs)." Each IC may contain thousands of separate devices, so you would expect the failure rate of these units to be relatively high, but ICs cause far less than their share of problems. Even when an IC does fail, the problem is likely to be caused by the pins and bonds that bring the signals into the IC, not by the IC devices themselves.

Some ICs are more vulnerable than others. The memory devices (RAMs especially) are among the most densely packed ICs you are likely to find in your equipment. Because space is so limited in these ICs, the physical size of each transistor and circuit trace must be as small as possible. These very small components are more sensitive to changes in temperature, voltage, and current. For this reason, memory chips and other densely packed ICs have higher than average failure rates.

Some ICs are especially vulnerable because they are used to "interface" parts of the computer to the outside world. For example, parts called "three-state buffers" are often located at a computer's input/output ports. These parts control access to the inner parts of the computer. When a high-voltage "spike" from the outside world tries to come into the computer, the first IC it encounters is often a three-state buffer. If the spike is strong enough, it can burn out the buffer. For this reason, these "interfacing" parts have a higher than average failure rate.

Disasters

A real "disaster" can affect many parts of the microcomputer system at once. One of the most common disasters, and the most preventable, is caused by removing an IC or circuit board while the equipment is turned on. This can damage many sections of the computer system at once. The equipment can also be damaged by inserting an IC in its socket backwards, by connecting power-supply leads backwards, or by disconnecting a cable while the power is on.

   Should lightning strike a nearby power line while your computer is plugged in, it can force its way inside your equipment and do considerable damage. Lightning can also enter through the telephone line and destroy a direct-connect modem.

   Liquids can damage computer equipment. Even plain water may carry enough salt that it can act as a conductor and cause a short circuit. Soft drinks, beer, etc., can cause even more serious damage.

   Disasters can come from unexpected directions. For example, in cool weather, some cats like to sleep on top of a nice, warm computer. If a cat is lazy enough, it may not move off the computer to relieve himself. Bob Cahill has seen several computers ruined by cat urine!

Typical Failure Patterns

Fig. 3-2 shows a typical failure pattern for computer equipment. Notice in the sketch that the failure rate is relatively high for the first two days of operation. It is during this time that defective ICs are most likely to fail. The manufacturers know this, so many of them "burn in" their equipment for at least two days before shipping. The high failure rate tapers off over the first 30 days of operation.

   After the initial burn-in period, the equipment generally has a long period of good reliability. All of the components are operating at or close to their rated value. As the equipment begins to age, problems become more frequent, and the equipment begins to show the kinds of problems we listed in Fig. 3-1. Electromechanical components start to malfunction,

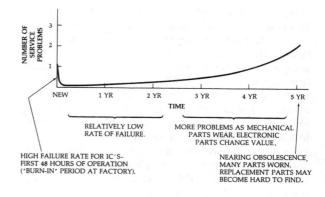

Fig. 3-2. Number of service problems versus time.

mechanisms wear, and electronic components start to fail or change value.

   Each kind of equipment will show a slightly different pattern of aging. The computer itself has no electromechanical parts, except for the key contacts and a few switches. Therefore, you can expect a computer to be relatively reliable for five to ten years or more. A printer or disk drive, on the other hand, has many mechanical and electromechanical components. These devices can be expected to show a much higher failure rate. At the end of the life cycle, the failure rate increases considerably. At some point, the manufacturer will stop producing a particular model, and this may make it hard to find parts. Finally, the equipment will become obsolete, and it may not pay to repair a problem.

   Computer equipment tends to have a long useful life. Often, a computer becomes obsolete before it wears out. On the other hand, most floppy disk drives have only a few years of useful life before they require overhaul or replacement. Of course, equipment used in full-time office service will begin to fail before equipment that is used only occasionally by a hobbyist.

   One measure of the reliability of microcomputer equipment is the "mean time before failure" (MTBF) rating. For example, the manual for one type of printer lists an MTBF of 5 million lines for all mechanisms in the printer except the printhead. The printhead is expected to have a life of 100 million characters. (Printing a standard size, double-spaced page, this would be equal to 83,000 pages for the printer and 52,000 pages for the printhead.) The MTBF rating for some kinds of equipment may be measured in "hours of operation." Remember that the MTBF rating is a "mean." Half of the units will fail before the rated time, and half will last longer. There's no way of telling how long any particular unit will last.

You might assume that, to arrive at the MTBF figure, the manufacturer would just turn on the equipment and run it until it failed. It's not always done that way. Instead, the MTBF may be an "estimate"—a mathematical abstraction cooked up using complicated formulas. For example, some manufacturers test their units in a harsh environment (high temperature, humidity, vibration, etc.) and note the failure rate. Then, the engineers calculate: If the units lasted x hours in this tough environment, they'll probably last y hours in normal service. Of course, there is a strong temptation to be overly optimistic. Consumers are beginning to pay more attention to MTBF ratings. A good rating is great for sales, and hard to verify.

Some computer designs have a characteristic "weak point." In all computers of a particular type, a certain component may be very likely to fail. For example, the engineers may have chosen a part which cannot handle enough voltage or current, or which tends to overheat. Sometimes, two parts of the computer system check out when used individually, but do not operate well together. Technicians quickly learn to recognize these characteristic problems. If you know about these "weak points," you can often go directly to the cause of a breakdown.

Our readers should be encouraged by the picture we've just painted. Many of the most common problems are within the capabilities of the beginning technician. For example, we already said that cables and connectors cause a large share of the operating failures. With just a little training, almost anyone can check these parts. Mechanical and electromechanical parts also cause many breakdowns, but these are also fairly simple to locate and service. Other faults are tougher to repair, of course, but with some help from this book, you should be able to deal with most of these.

Chapter Review

Most "computer" problems have simple causes. Bad cables and connectors cause a high proportion of failures. Mechanical parts wear out and cause many of the breakdowns. The actual electronics are fairly reliable. Power-handling parts fail more often because they're under more stress. Densely packed ICs, like RAMs, have higher failure rates. About two thirds of the actual computer problems are "hard" faults and about one third are "soft" faults. The "soft" faults are harder to find and repair.

Review Questions

1. Dealers usually offer an "extended warranty" which covers equipment repair during the first year of operation. What kind of failure rate can you expect during the first year?

2. You buy new equipment which has a 30-day warranty. Is there any advantage to leaving the equipment turned on continuously during the warranty period?

3. Which part is more likely to fail?
   (A) RAM memory.
   (B) Floppy disk memory.

4. Which part is more likely to fail?
   (A) RAM memory.
   (B) Simple ICs.

5. Which conditions can damage many parts of the computer at the same time?
   (A) Lightning strike on power lines.
   (B) Lightning strike on telephone lines.
   (C) Removing a circuit card while the power is on.
   (D) All of the above.

4

Servicing for Your Equipment–The Options

Introduction and Objectives

In the past, most new equipment was sold with a 90-day warranty. As competitive pressures have increased, many manufacturers have been forced to offer warranties of six months to one year. If your equipment fails after the warranty period, you must decide whether to repair it yourself, or have the servicing done by a dealer, manufacturer, or third-party organization. To make a decision, you'll have to balance the three factors of cost, time, and convenience. In this chapter, we will consider all of your options.

Servicing by a Local Dealer

Most microcomputer equipment is sold through local retail stores. Naturally, many computer owners take their equipment back to these stores for servicing. In fact, manufacturers' representatives account for about 85% of the servicing work performed in the United States. A local dealer represents the manufacturer of the equipment, and usually must follow the pricing and service policies set by the manufacturer.

Dealers usually encourage the new owner to buy a "service contract." For a flat yearly fee, the dealer will agree to make any necessary repairs on the equipment. Some dealers offer an "extended warranty" option, which is essentially the same as a ser-

vice contract. The precise terms can vary from one dealer to the next. Even among dealers handling the same brand names, the policies may vary. For example, an outlet which is owned as a franchise may have different service policies than an outlet which is owned directly by the manufacturer. It pays to shop around.

Radio Shack® charges 12% of the original retail price per year for "carry in" service. Apple® Computer, Inc., offers a 7-year "carry in" contract on the Mac SE, with a 20-Meg hard drive and a dot-matrix printer, for $438 per year. For a system consisting of an IBM PS/2 Model 30, with a 20-Meg hard disk, a color monitor, and a 24-pin dot-matrix printer, IBM® charges $340 per year for carry-in service. The IBM® technicians say they'll be able to repair the equipment in "a few days." If you want on-site "priority" servicing for this system, it will cost $535 per year. If you live more than 30 miles from the dealer's location, on-site service will cost even more. As you can see, a service contract can cost a substantial amount of money, because the owner must pay the rate this year, and next year, and on into the future.

Some dealers also offer insurance coverage against theft and physical damage. Many of these policies also cover damage caused by brownouts, power surges, and so on. For example, Apple® Computer, Inc. offers $5000 worth of coverage, with a $100 deductible, for $25.00 a year. Similar policies are also offered by mail.

Especially with new equipment, the value of a service contract is questionable. As we said earlier, digital equipment shows a relatively high rate of failure during the first few hours of operation, and then the rate tapers off during the warranty period. The first year or two of operation is probably the most reliable period in the equipment's life. The dealer and manufacturer know they have a relatively low probability of having to fix equipment during this period. The service contract is a high-profit "plum" that the dealer can add onto the original purchase price. A service contract can be a better value when the equipment has been operating for three years, and becomes more likely to fail.

However, even in the first few years of operation, a service contract may be called for in certain situations. If you use your equipment in business, perhaps time is more important to you than money. If you require maximum reliability from your equipment, and must have it repaired in the shortest possible time, then a "priority" service contract may be a good investment.

Most local dealers will service equipment even if you do not have a service contract. This is strictly a "carry-in" service, and many dealers will only repair equipment which they sold you. A shop will usually charge you a flat fee to check out each piece of equipment you bring in. This can cost from $20.00 to $50.00 per unit. If the shop's technicians find a problem, they will make a charge for their time in correcting the problem, usually $40.00 to $75.00 per hour, plus the cost of parts. You can also buy "on-site" servicing from a local dealer, but this can be much more expensive. One local IBM dealer charges $90.00 per hour for this service, which includes driving time to and from your location.

You can often get a substantial credit for trading in major components. For example, a replacement CPU board might cost $675, or so. However, a manufacturer might allow you to turn in your faulty board for a $500 credit. The manufacturer will then repair your board and put it back on the market.

Service policies vary greatly from one shop to the next. For example, if you're a regular customer, many dealers will give you a "loaner" to use while your unit is in the shop, and some shops will move your job to the head of the line for a legitimate emergency. However, dealers that have a franchise from a major computer manufacturer don't have to be so friendly. The world is beating a path to their door, so they can dictate some pretty touch policies. Some Radio Shack dealers, for example, will charge you double the basic rate and void your warranty if they discover that you have repaired your equipment yourself. One of the screws on the bottom of each unit is covered with a seal. To repair the equipment, you must break this seal before opening the

case. One type of hard-disk drive includes a small spring-loaded ball. If you remove the sealed case on the drive, the ball is forced through a barrier. This provides a permanent indication that the drive has been opened, and voids the warranty. At some Radio Shack dealerships, the technicians will remove all non-Radio Shack components from any of their computers in for repair, and charge you for doing this. Apple Computer also discourages users from repairing their own equipment.

Servicing Through a Mail-Order Outlet

Servicing can be more complicated when you buy equipment from a discount mail-order operation. You cannot depend on a local dealer to repair equipment which he did not sell. This means you will usually have to send your mail-order equipment back to the mail-order outlet for servicing, and the service rates are likely to be similar to the rates you'd pay at a local store. You can spend a lot of time shipping your equipment back and forth.

There are several different options for shipping your equipment—your choice should balance the factors of price and speed. The Parcel Post service of the U.S. Mail will carry a ten-pound package coast-to-coast for about $10.00. A one-way trip will take between ten days to two weeks. United Parcel Service (UPS) offers Ground Service delivery for the same package in five days for $5.53. UPS Next Day Air Service would cost $21.00, and Second Day Air Service would cost $11.50. If the mail-order outlet's shop works quickly, they can repair your equipment and ship it back in one to three days. In your calculation, remember to allow time for the return trip. Shipping times can be slightly less if you're not shipping all the way across the country. Realistically, your equipment will be gone for at least a week, but don't be surprised if this stretches to three or four weeks.

Whenever you ship computer equipment, be sure to package it carefully. It's best to save the original packaging and use this for shipping. If you don't have the original packaging, ship the equipment in a rugged cardboard box, and pad the equipment on all sides with a generous layer of plastic chips. Insure the equipment for its original purchase price.

What kind of service can you expect from a dealer, either local or mail-order? The quality of service can vary from good to terrible. Do a little research, and check out the reputation of each service shop in your area. Local computer clubs or user's groups are good sources for this type of information. Some of the technicians working in local shops are experienced electronics "pros," who learned their trade fixing hi-fi's and TVs. Most of these people have been able to make the transition to computers fairly well. Many of the newer technicians have graduated from vocational schools. However, these schools tend to give a good grounding in basic electronics, but sometimes lag behind in practical information on computers. Other technicians learned their trade in the military. These military repairmen and repairwomen are usually quite competent, although they may be more familiar with the larger computers. Note that a good dealer will keep his technicians up-to-date by sending them regularly to the various training sessions offered by the equipment manufacturers.

Dealers want to sell computers, *not* service them. They maintain a service department because the manufacturer says they must, and because customers won't buy equipment if they can't get servicing. To ensure good relations with the dealers, most manufacturers have set up a system that keeps the servicing operation as simple as possible. This is a system of maintenance levels.

"Level I" servicing is based on a strategy of "swapping" circuit boards. The dealer's service department stocks a spare of each important circuit board for the manufacturer's equipment. The technician troubleshoots until the bad board is identified, and then "swaps" the board for the correct spare. Usually, the technician depends on a diagnostic program to identify the faulty board. The bad board is sent back to the manufacturer, in return for a credit.

A "Level II" service operation can perform a much more detailed testing and troubleshooting of a faulty board. This type of shop can find the specific components on the board which are faulty, and then make repairs. A few large dealers have "Level II" facilities.

Some manufacturers also have highly automated "Level III" repair facilities. A facility of this type has a separate test setup for each type of circuit board. The technician simply places a suspect board in the test setup and then runs a very detailed diagnostic program. The diagnostic program identifies the specific component that has failed. Once the bad component has been replaced, the manufacturer will usually return the board to the dealer and put it back on the market.

Dealers like this "board-swapping" system because they can offer a service capability using personnel of limited ability. If the problem is simple, a customer can often get his job in and out quickly. Board-swapping has some disadvantages for the customer, however. The failure of a 59-cent part might make it necessary to buy a $175 board. As a result, repair costs can be unnecessarily high. If the problem is complicated or unusual, the local shop has to send the equipment out to a "Level II" shop, and the customer must wait while his equipment is shipped back and forth.

When you have your work done by a local shop, you must depend on the honesty of the people doing the servicing. This can sometimes be a problem, especially when a technician makes a mistake. We know of one case where a technician connected a power supply backwards, blowing out ICs throughout the equipment. In a situation like this, a technician has two choices. He can admit his mistake, look bad to his boss, and cost the company a lot of money; *or* he can simply tell the customer, "Your problem is more serious than we thought." In spite of the high shop fees, most technicians make only $8.00 to $20.00 per hour. But, in some shops, the technician also receives a percentage of the shop charges. This can encourage him or her to inflate the service bills.

Dealing with a Service Shop

As we said, Bob Cahill managed a dealer's service operation for over five years. He recommends these rules when dealing with a service shop.

1. *Bring in just the piece of equipment that has failed.* Many customers bring in their whole systems, and say, "Something's wrong somewhere. Fix it." Most shops charge a fixed amount to check out each unit, even if they can't find anything wrong. For this reason, you should always try to localize the problem to one or two parts of your system. The instructions in this book should help you to do this.

2. *Be specific.* Don't say "The printer doesn't work." Instead, say "The printer crumples up the paper and doesn't print the letter E." You can save time for the technician, and service charges for yourself, by describing the trouble carefully. At the same time, don't carry this too far. If you tell the technician to change transistor Q26, he might do just that and send the equipment back, whether it has been repaired or not.

3. *Don't mislead the technician.* Many people are too embarrassed to admit to some of the things they've done to their computers. If a customer has pulled a circuit card out of his IBM-PC computer while the power was on, the computer is probably damaged in many different places. Yet he may tell the technician, "I just bumped

into it and it stopped working." Before the repair is completed, the technician will have to locate and repair all of the damage, and he'll have a pretty good idea of what really happened. Because he had to start with misleading information, the repair bill is likely to be much higher than necessary.

Servicing by Mail

This is a common arrangement for equipment which is small, simple, or inexpensive. This may be your only option if your equipment is imported, or not widely distributed. Manufacturers of many modems, hard-disk drives, monitors, and accessories offer this type of service arrangement. If one of your units stops working, you can often send it directly to the manufacturer and have it repaired for a fixed price. Some manufacturers also have regional "walk-in" centers that serve the same purpose. A few of the large mail-order operations maintain their own service shops.

You can usually depend on good servicing from one of these operations. The technicians are likely to be very familiar with the manufacturer's product line. They know which parts are most likely to fail on any given model. The manufacturer's shop can afford to buy the expensive diagnostic equipment that can solve the really difficult troubleshooting problems. The "flat rate" pricing schedule is usually a good value. If the service center is nearby, you can drive there and drop off your equipment yourself. Otherwise, you'll probably have to mail in your equipment. If you're in a hurry, ship via United Parcel's Overnight Air service, and allow at least eight or nine working days for the round trip and repair. In some cases, it may be more convenient to ship via Greyhound Bus Line's freight service.

If the repair shop is particularly slow in responding, you may have to wait a month or more to get your equipment back.

Third-Party Servicing

About 10% of the servicing work being done is being handled by "third-party" service operations. Third-party companies make an agreement with a computer manufacturer to service certain makes and models of equipment, and then they sell service contracts to the consumers. Among the leaders in this line are TRW, Sorbus, Interlogic Trace, and CDC. Some of these companies have been servicing large mainframe computers for years, and are now expanding into the microcomputer market.

The terms of these third-party contracts are roughly the same as the terms you could expect from a local dealer. The charge can vary, depending on their estimate of the reliability of the particular equipment involved. Third-party servicing tends to be efficient, but expensive. Some third-party operations will come to your location to work on your equipment, others require you to bring the equipment to them, or they may offer a pick-up and delivery service. Some organizations have "loaner" equipment available.

TRW charges about $500 a year for a service contract on an IBM-AT computer with a color monitor. On-site service, without a service contract, costs $104 per hour, and you must pay the same rate for the technician's travel time.

Fix It Yourself or Take It to a Shop?

We've listed three possible service options. At the beginning of the chapters, we mentioned a fourth option—in many cases, you can fix the equipment yourself.

Self-servicing offers several important benefits. First, it can be less expensive than servicing done by a dealer. By tracking down a problem and fixing it yourself, you can often save substantial amounts of money. In the introduction, we described a case where dirty keyboard contacts were causing two characters to appear on the screen. You can fix a problem of this type in about ten minutes, using 1-cent worth of materials. In comparison, a dealer's shop might charge $50.00 for this same job. By doing the job yourself, you're "paying yourself" almost $300 an hour!

Troubleshooting does take time and effort. At the start of a job, you never know how much time will be required. Obviously, the more experience you've had with electronic work, the better are your chances of finding a solution quickly. With the right support, even a beginner has a good chance of locating and repairing many of the more common problems. What is your time worth? Think of yourself as an independent technician, competing with the dealer's shop. The typical shop rate is $25.00 per hour and up, and the shop's technician is likely to find the problem faster than you can. Unless your own time is particularly valuable, it is probably cost-effective to do at least some of the work yourself.

Servicing the equipment yourself does require some investment. To begin with, you will need a few special tools. The more equipment you have, and the better it is, the more successful you'll be. The cost of the tools required seems small when compared with the cost of a service call or service contract. Your initial investment can be repaid the first time you're able to fix a problem yourself.

Every time you start to work on a piece of equipment, there's a risk that you will accidentally damage something inside. Even experienced technicians sometimes make mistakes. As long as the circuits and mechanical parts are safely inside their case, you can't really do much damage. However, when the case is off, many of these parts are vulnerable. Readers with some prior electronics experience should be able to work on computer equipment with few problems. Even a beginner can do many diagnostic and repair jobs if he or she is prepared to work slowly and carefully, and follow the suggestions in this book. However, some people simply have bad luck with electronic and mechanical things. They're just not temperamentally suited to the careful, precise kind of work that is necessary to work on microcomputers. Readers who find themselves in this group should use this book to help localize and diagnose a problem, but they should probably avoid doing the actual repair work.

Turn-around time is an important consideration. You can often get your equipment back on-line much more quickly if you do the repair work yourself. As we said, a few top-notch shops will turn a job around in half a day, but most will make you wait one to three days. If the equipment must be mailed, it will be gone for two weeks or more. You can often track down a simple problem yourself in a relatively short time. If the necessary parts are available, you can often have your equipment working again very quickly.

Different service problems require different levels of expertise. You should match your repair work to your own level of knowledge and experience. As we explained in Chapter 3, the majority of computer problems have relatively simple causes—broken cables, corroded connectors, and jammed mechanisms. Almost anyone can spot and fix these problems quickly and easily. It is always worth the effort to check for this kind of problem yourself. Even if the problem is more complicated, it pays to try to identify the affected parts of the system. If you can localize the problem to a particular part or component, you can usually replace the part yourself. If you have to give up and take the

equipment to a shop, at least you can tell the technician where to start.

Since the technician doesn't have to start from scratch, the service bill may be lower. When you deal with the shop, you'll be an "educated consumer." You will have some idea of the complexity of the servicing job, so you'll be able to judge if the bill is reasonable.

Chapter Review

As a consumer of computer repair services, you have four options:

1. Have the equipment serviced by a local dealer.
2. Send the equipment to the manufacturer for servicing.
3. Contract with a third-party service operation.
4. Repair the equipment yourself.

How do you decide when to repair the equipment yourself? Perhaps we can sum up the answer like this: It always pays to do your own maintenance. It is always worth the effort to try and diagnose a problem. If the fault is relatively simple, and you can localize it to a particular component, it pays to repair or replace the part yourself. Take the equipment to a shop when you don't understand the section of the system that is affected, or you can't localize the problem past a certain point.

Review Questions

1. Why are dealers anxious to sell extended warranties and service contracts?

2. What is the likelihood that a microcomputer will fail during the first year of operation?

3. You buy a name-brand computer by mail from a discounter in another city. If it should break down, will the local dealer service it?

4. If you must have a piece of equipment serviced by mail, how long is this likely to take?

5. If you deal with a service shop, why should you be completely honest in describing the symptoms for the technician?

5
Reducing Potential Environment Problems

Introduction and Objectives

The environment around a microcomputer can affect the way the equipment operates. A computer may be affected by radio interference and power-line problems in the "electronic environment." Computers may also be affected by temperature, humidity, etc., in the "physical environment." In the first part of this chapter, we'll look at some of the problems that can be caused by the environment. After reading this section, you should be able to analyze any environmental problems that you may encounter, and know how to correct them.

You can prevent many problems by properly maintaining your equipment, operating it carefully, and planning for potential problems. If you take care of these "preventive" jobs, you can avoid a lot of "servicing" work altogether. In the second part of the chapter, we will discuss some good operating procedures.

The Electronic Environment

You might expect the power company to guarantee smooth, uninterrupted, electrical power. Unfortunately, the conditions in the power lines to your home or office are constantly changing. Momentary changes called "transients" and "surges" occur quickly on the line,

and then the system reverts to normal. Other changes can also take place over a longer period of time. Changes in the power-supply outputs were not as important in the past, when we were using simpler devices, such as motors and light bulbs. However, microcomputer equipment is much more sensitive to changes in the power grid.

The environment around us also includes high-frequency radio energy. When the local TV station runs an obnoxious commercial, the TV signal passes right through your house, your furniture, and your body. Radio signals are flowing around us all the time—signals from Top-40 radio, the BBC, Radio Moscow, truckers on CBs, and kids playing with walkie talkies. Generally, these signals have such low energy that they can't affect microcomputer equipment, but sometimes they can become troublesome. You can't see a power-line problem or a radio wave directly, but they're very real, and they can have bad effects on your equipment.

Early computers were particularly sensitive to power-line and other interference problems, but the industry has had time to work out some solutions. The manufacturers of the present generation of microcomputers were anxious to make their products as reliable as possible, so they included some effective defenses. Nevertheless, some problems are serious enough to get past the protective circuits and into the computers.

Complete Power Failure

The most severe kind of power-supply problem is the complete loss of power. Fig. 5-1A shows the waveform that occurs during a complete loss of power. The illustrations in Fig. 5-1 show the kind of displays you would get if you could check the power line with an oscilloscope.

Power may be cut off by the power company, by an accidental break in a line, or by a protective circuit in your home or office. The power grid is a tremendous system, with wires running all over the countryside. Unfortunately, most of this system of wires is suspended above the ground, exposed to such dangers as falling tree limbs, ice storms, lightning strikes, and so on. Other dangers are less spectacular—i.e., more than one power system has been shut down by a squirrel causing a short circuit in a transformer.

When wires are broken and fall to the ground, the electricity in the wires is allowed to short-circuit to ground potential. A short circuit has a very low resistance, so a very large current begins to flow (hundreds of amperes). This very large current can quickly overheat the wires and damage other parts of the system. The power grid is designed to protect itself by shutting down the damaged part of the system. In the old days, this job was handled by large fuses. Any large current would melt the fuse and open the circuit. Each time a fuse opened, a lineman would have to drive along the wire, find the bad fuse, and replace it. This was a slow process.

Modern power systems use a type of automatic circuit breaker called a "recloser." When the recloser detects an over-current condition, it opens automatically. It will wait a moment, then reconnect the power and see if the fault has passed. If the problem is still present, the recloser will cut off the power again. Some reclosers will make three or four attempts before they give up.

Normally, before you turn off a computer, you save all files, close them, and exit from any software you are running. By the time you actually turn off the switch, the computer makes sure that all of the important information in the system has been moved to safe storage locations.

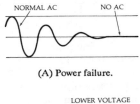

(A) Power failure.

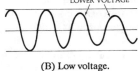

(B) Low voltage.

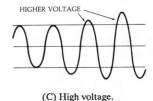

(C) High voltage.

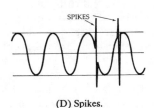

(D) Spikes.

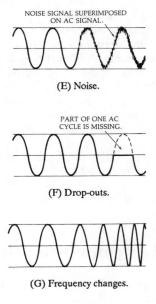

(E) Noise.

(F) Drop-outs.

(G) Frequency changes.

Fig. 5-1. Waveforms of various power-line problems.

What happens when the power is cut off while the microcomputer is running? Or what if you cause a "power failure" yourself by turning off the switch while the computer is operating? Remember that computers operate at very high speeds. A typical small computer might take two or three *millionths* of a second to process an instruction. During a power failure, all parts of the computer do not lose power at the same moment. For an instant, as the voltage drops, all of the components in the computer are "floating." During this "float," they can operate in strange ways. The computer is most vulnerable if it is reading or writing to a hard disk or floppy disk at the time of the failure. The controller in the disk drive may operate just long enough to write a few stray characters on the disk. If these stray characters appear in an important part of the disk, the disk may become unreadable.

A microcomputer can be designed to minimize problems during a power loss. Most small computers have some kind of power-sensing circuits. These circuits check the incoming 120-volts AC, or the low-voltage to the computer, and won't let the computer operate unless the voltage is adequate. Some of the more elaborate computers also have circuits which detect the dropping voltage caused when power is cut off. This gives the computer time to save some of the critical information before all power is lost. Computers with this feature are resistant to problems caused by power failures.

Low Voltage

Fig. 5-1B shows the AC waveform during a period of low voltage. Sometimes, when the power grid is overloaded, the power company will deliberately lower the voltage. During this "brownout" period, each customer receives slightly less energy from his AC line, but the loss is spread around evenly. Power companies resort to brownouts during periods of peak demand. Usually, these peaks are caused by changes in the weather, so beware of brownouts during the hottest parts of the summer when the power grid has to supply a large air-conditioning load. Brownouts may also occur in the coldest parts of the winter, when the system has to support a large heating load. Brownouts may occur several times a year, and may last up to a few hours in each case. It's unusual for the power company to cut the voltage by more than 5%, and most computer equipment can handle this drop with no problem. Most microcomputers will shut themselves down if the AC drops considerably; i.e., to 95 V or less.

When a large motor is started, it tends to draw down the line voltage for a moment. The motors in air conditioners, refrigerators, compressors, and some factory equipment can cause this effect. The resulting low voltage can cause computers to shut down or become unreliable. But even if a microcomputer stops working because of a brownout, the electronic components are usually not damaged.

High Voltage

High-voltage conditions occur less frequently than other problems, but they are more dangerous to microcomputer equipment. If the line voltage rises for a short period, it is called a "surge." A high-voltage condition can be created by switching errors, or by equipment problems at the power company. The power-distribution system inside your building may also cause problems. For example, in a new building, the power system may be set up to supply a large load. If big sections of that load are not yet installed, the line voltage may be higher than planned. In the same way, if large sections of the load are removed from an older system, the line voltage may be too high. Fig. 5-1C shows the waveform for a high-voltage condition.

High voltage can damage microcomputer equipment. When operating on high voltage, all of the parts in the computer's power supply (and perhaps in the rest of the computer) are handling more than the rated amounts of power. The parts are all running "hotter" than expected, so it is more likely that one of the weaker parts will fail.

Spikes

A "spike" is a very short burst of high voltage (Fig. 5-1D). Some small spikes are caused by switching equipment, including motor controllers. When lightning strikes the power system, it can cause very large spikes.

The effect on computer equipment varies with the size and power of the spike. A typical spike may have a fairly high voltage (5000 volts or more), but a very short duration (1 microsecond or less), so the total amount of power involved is usually small. These small spikes usually don't damage the components, but they can "confuse" the computer. Remember that computers are designed to process digital "1s" and "0s," and will interpret anything above +3 V as a "1." If a spike makes its way into the equipment and produces a false "1" or "0" at the wrong moment, it can interfere with the computer's operation. Let's say that the computer is writing to memory just as the spike arrives. We'll say that just one bit of the memory is changed by the spike, and this bit is part of a program instruction. We'll assume that the computer stores that incorrect instruction. When next it tries to run that program, the computer may write data to the wrong location, erase important information, or cause any number of other problems.

Spikes caused by lightning can be much more powerful. As a technician, you should have a healthy respect for the menacing power of lightning. Using a "high-voltage" transformer with an output of 15,000 volts, we can cause a tiny spark of electricity to jump a gap of 1 or 2 inches. Think of the power it takes to produce a solid bolt of electricity that can jump a half mile or more from the clouds to the earth. In one recent case, a bolt of lightning hit a tree, ran along the roots to a garage, came up through the floor, and moved a car about 10 feet. Windows were blown out, paint cans fell to the floor, and the garage looked as if it had been hit by a bomb. Incidentally, the lightning also erased a whole rack of audio tapes. The tapes were sitting in a house about 50 feet from the garage, so this effect was caused by minor disturbances running through the house wiring. The lightning could just as easily have erased a stack of floppy disks.

If a spike caused by lightning enters your equipment, it can cause a lot of damage. The precise effects depend on the details of the strike. A direct strike on your building can run through the AC wiring and turn your computer into a smouldering wreck. Even a strike a mile away can cause dangerous spikes on the power lines. The computer is more vulnerable if it is turned on at the time of the strike. The AC switch is turned on, giving the spike a direct path into your equipment. If the spike is powerful enough, it can even force its way past an opened switch. As it moves into the computer, the spike is most likely to damage the parts it encounters first—the components in the power supply. A very strong spike can get past the power supply and into the main section of the computer. This kind of spike can damage parts in many sections of the equipment. As you are troubleshooting, whenever you notice that many parts are damaged, in different parts of the equipment, suspect lightning damage.

Noise

Fig. 5-1E shows the waveform on a "noisy" AC line. Notice that the basic AC signal is still present, but a high-frequency signal with a smaller voltage has been added. If the noise is strong enough, it can get past the power supply and create false digital "1s" and "0s," and can confuse the microcomputer.

Noise is more likely to cause problems on the signal lines or data lines which run between sections of the computer system. Cables are used to connect the computer to printers, disk drives, remote sensors, and other parts of the system. If these cables run near a source of interference, they can pick up significant amounts of noise. The signals in these cables have a much lower voltage than the 120 volts on the AC lines. Between a computer and a modem, the voltage levels might be +12-V DC and −12-V DC. Between a computer and a printer, the signal levels might be +5-V DC and 0 V. If a 120-V AC line picks up some noise with an amplitude of 1 volt, this is less than 1% of the basic AC waveform. But if you put that same 1-volt signal on a line that is expecting +5 volts or 0 volt, it represents 20% of the signal range. When the line is prepared to work with a low-voltage signal, the noise signal is proportionately much larger.

Noise on signal lines can cause several different problems. Often, the noise can cause the computer to produce a bad bit of data. A few of the letters in a word-processing file may be incorrect, or some of the numbers in the spreadsheet may be wrong. If the noise causes the computer to record a program instruction incorrectly, the problem may be more serious. At best, the computer may "lock up," i.e., it may stop running the program and may not take any instructions from the keyboard.

If this happens, you may be able to reset the system with a "warm boot." (To try this on a computer using MS-DOS, press the "CTRL," "ALT," and "DEL" keys at the same time.) If this does not work, you will have to turn off the computer and then turn it back on again. This is called a "cold boot." At worst, the computer may start using that bad instruction, and begin writing "garbage" into your files. This is a nasty situation because the problems may be spread throughout your system, and it may be hard to catch up with all of them.

There are several different types of noise. *Radio-frequency interference* (RFI) is caused by radio or television sources, or even by other computer equipment. If your equipment is located near a radio or television transmitter, the power or signal lines may pick up enough of the radio or TV signal to cause problems. A weaker source, such as a wireless telephone, fluorescent lamp, lamp dimmer, or a car ignition system, can cause similar problems if it is close enough to your equipment. Radio energy drops off very quickly as you move away from the source.

Electromagnetic interference (EMI) can occur when computer wiring runs too close to equipment that produces an electromagnetic field. As the magnetic field changes, it can "induce" false pulses into nearby computer wiring. Again, this effect drops off sharply as you move away from the source of the EMI. EMI can be a problem when two wires run beside each other. A signal in one wire can create a changing field, which then induces a signal in the other wire. The effect is stronger when the wires are close together and when they are parallel for a distance. Large electric motors can create powerful electromagnetic fields and may cause EMI problems. Electric motors, which may cause EMI, are found in various kinds of equipment—refrigerators, air conditioners, washing machines, furnaces, copiers, elevators, machine tools, and so on.

Voltage Dropouts

Some conditions can cause the voltage to "drop out" for a very short time. In Fig. 5-1F, you can see that the AC waveform is missing for part of one cycle. This can be caused by the switching gear in the power grid. Dropouts may also occur when large loads are switched into the system. Because the amount of power involved is small, and because the normal AC signal resumes quickly, dropouts do not usually cause problems for microcomputer equipment.

Line-Frequency Problems

In the United States, our 120-volt AC "house current" has a frequency of 60 hertz (cycles per second). Some microcomputers use this frequency to operate real-time clocks and other devices. The 60-Hz frequency is generally very stable and reliable, but sometimes this frequency may change. We've shown a typical waveform in Fig. 5-1G. Frequency control can be a more serious problem if the computer is getting power from a source other than the power company. If the unit receives power from a private source, such as an uninterruptible power supply or a motor/generator set, frequency control is often less reliable.

Combined Problems

So far, we've listed several separate problems. In the real world, you'll often find that several different problems are combined in a characteristic pattern. For example, Fig. 5-2A shows the power-supply changes

you might see as a large motor is switched on and off. As the motor is first switched on, the switching equipment may create a spike. Next, the motor loads the circuit and tends to draw down the line voltage for a moment. An instant later, the voltage rises above normal as current surges in to supply the motor. Eventually, the line voltage stabilizes.

When the motor is first switched on, energy is stored in the windings of the motor. When the motor is switched off, this energy floods back into the supply line and causes the voltage to rise for a moment. Fig. 5-2B shows a pattern which might occur during a thunderstorm.

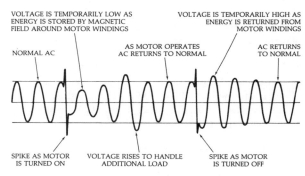

(A) Motor turned on and off.

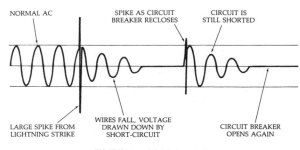

(B) Effects of lightning strike.

Fig. 5-2. Waveforms showing pattern of problem sequences.

Checking for Power-Line Problems

There are two parts to the process of checking power-line equipment. The first job is to check the quality of the power coming into your equipment. If you find any problems, you must determine whether they are caused by the power company or by equipment inside your home or building. The "history" of your power-line problem may give you some clues. Do you always experience a problem at a certain time of the day? Perhaps someone is turning a large motor on or off at that time each day. Do you have problems when it is especially hot or cold? Perhaps your equipment is sensitive to a "brownout."

Start by checking the AC wiring itself. Fig. 5-3 shows how an AC outlet should be wired. You can never assume that an outlet has been wired correctly, especially in older buildings. The "hot" wire should run to the shorter of the two vertical holes. Be sure the "ground" is actually connected. The "ground" line is important for safety, and some computers need the "ground" to run properly. You can check an outlet with a voltohmmeter set to read 120-V AC. Fig. 5-3 illustrates the readings you should see.

Warning! In making these tests, you will be working with 120-V AC. This voltage is dangerous. If you do not understand the dangers, leave this job to a qualified technician.

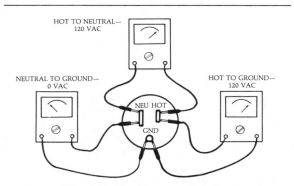

Fig. 5-3. Checking an AC outlet.

For about $5.00, Radio Shack sells a small plug-in device that you can use to test AC outlets quickly. This tester includes several LEDs. To use it, you simply plug in the unit and see which LEDs light up. Different combinations of LEDs indicate whether the outlet is wired backwards, the "ground" is disconnected, and so on. If you discover that the "ground" is not connected, you should correct this. "Ground" is normally tied to "neutral" and "earth ground" at the circuit breaker box.

All "grounds" are not created equal, and sometimes the standard ground in your AC wiring is not suitable. You can tie your computer to a separate

ground by using an "isolated" outlet (Fig. 5-4). In this kind of outlet, the third prong on the outlet is isolated from the normal ground system and from the metal case around the outlet. This allows you to run a special ground wire to another grounding point. If you want to install this kind of outlet, you should probably let an electrician handle the job, for safety reasons.

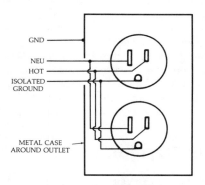

Fig. 5-4. An isolated outlet.

If you are concerned with spikes and voltage changes, you can do a certain amount of checking even without special equipment. For example, if a brownout is severe enough, you may see the image on your monitor shrink for a moment. The lights in the room may also flicker. Most power-line problems do not leave such obvious clues, however. If you really want to track down a problem, you will have to use a power-line monitor. Many types of monitors are available. A simple unit, costing about $150, might have LEDs to indicate "voltage spike," "high line voltage," and so on. Each time the unit detects a spike, for example, it will light the appropriate LED to indicate that fault. The problem is, when you discover that the LED is on, you don't know how many spikes have gone by, and when they occurred. A more complicated monitor, costing $1000 or more, might include a small printer, and might print out a record of the power-line conditions. The unit will note the type of problem, along with the date and time. This type is more useful for tracking down infrequent power problems.

You should install the power-line monitor as close as possible to your computer equipment. There can be significant differences at different points along the power lines, especially if you are checking for high-frequency noise. Before equipment is installed in large computer installations, the technicians usually check the power lines for at least a week. If a large electrical load is added to the system at your home or office, it may pay to recheck the power lines.

Once you've installed a power-line monitor, you'll be surprised at how many problems it detects. In one study done for IBM, the average computer installation had about 130 "disturbances" per month. Different forms of noise accounted for about 90% of these disturbances.

Defenses Against Power-Line Problems

Modern computers include some defenses against the most common power-line problems. Most microcomputers use a "switching" type of power supply. This kind of supply converts the 120-V AC to low-voltage DC by "chopping" up the AC and then smoothing out the resulting waveform. Switching power supplies are fairly resistant to low voltage and small spikes and noise signals. The older "linear" type of power supply is more sensitive to power-line problems. We will discuss power supplies in more detail in Chapter 16.

Cables, themselves, have some built-in resistance to very fast spikes. Every cable has some natural capacitance and inductance, and these can work together to hold down very fast spikes. Unfortunately, you can't count on these factors to protect you from powerful spikes, or from the other problems we've mentioned.

There are a number of things you can do to protect your equipment from power-line problems, and some of the steps are fairly simple. For example, during thunderstorms, it is wise to shut off your equipment and unplug all of the AC cords. Since you can't always predict thunderstorms, you may want to unplug your equipment at the end of each operating session. You can skip this precaution at those times of the year when thunderstorms are uncommon.

Be sure all of the AC power connections for your system are clean and tight. As you set up your equipment, run the power cables where nobody can trip over them. Keep the AC power cables as far as possible from any ribbon cables or other signal wires. When you must cross the two different types of cables, run them at a 90° angle, as shown in Fig. 5-5, to minimize any possible interference.

If your equipment seems to be affected when air conditioners, refrigerators, etc., are turned on and off, it may be easier to simply leave these units turned off while you're using the computer. If this is not practical, there are a number of possible ways to "clean up" a

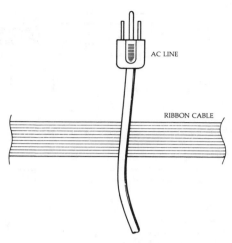

Fig. 5-5. The AC lines should cross ribbon cables at a 90° angle.

problem power source. The worst situation is when the computer is plugged into the same line as the motor (Fig. 5-6A). It's better if you can plug the computer into another circuit, as shown in Fig. 5-6B. The computer may still be influenced by the motor, however, since they are connected through the step-down transformer. In the ideal situation, the computer is supplied through a "dedicated line" using a separate transformer.

If your system is having problems with low or high voltage, you can sometimes correct this. The 120-V AC circuits in a building are usually powered by a step-down transformer located outside of the building, often on a power pole. Some of these transformers have several outputs or "taps," each providing a different output voltage. If the output voltage tends to be low, the power company may be able to connect your circuits to a different tap with a higher output voltage.

What if you're concerned with noise and spikes? As we said earlier, most small computers have some defenses against these problems, but you may want to add more protection. There are a wide range of protective devices on the market, costing anywhere from $10.00 to $2000.00, and providing different levels of protection. Most of these units are designed to be plugged into the AC line between the wall outlet and the computer.

The least expensive units, costing $5.00 to $20.00, protect only against spikes of high voltage. The key element of many of these circuits is the "varistor" (Fig. 5-7A). In common house wiring, the "hot" and "neutral" wires carry the 120-V AC current. The "ground" is part of a protective system. In the simplest

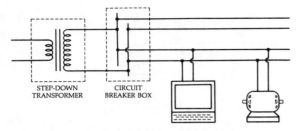

(A) Computer and motor on same circuit.

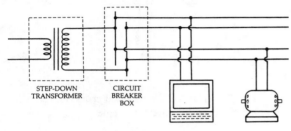

(B) Computer on separate circuit.

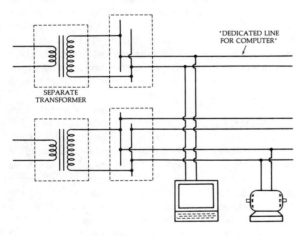

(C) Computer on separate transformer.

Fig. 5-6. Power-line arrangement.

"spike protectors," a varistor is wired between the "hot" side of the supply line and ground, as shown in Fig. 5-7B. As long as the supply voltage is normal, the varistor presents an open circuit. When a fault occurs, and the supply voltage climbs past a preset point, the varistor becomes a short circuit and passes the extra energy to ground. To put it another way, the varistor cuts off the voltage above a certain level. The highest voltage allowed by the varistor is called the "clamp" voltage. A clamp voltage of 250 volts is adequate for

systems that normally use 120-V AC. Better "spike protectors" have three varistors, which are connected between each of the three legs of the AC line (Fig. 5-7C). Radio Shack sells a similar device to protect phone lines.

(A) A typical varistor.

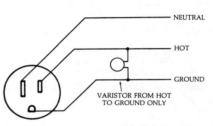

(B) Normal-mode spike suppression.

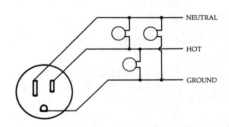

(C) Normal-mode and common-mode suppression.

Fig. 5-7. Varistor spike suppression.

Fig. 5-8 shows the waveform at a varistor when a spike reaches its clamp voltage. Varistors tend to lose their protective value as they grow older. When used to protect very valuable equipment, varistors should be replaced every few years.

More expensive units, costing about $50.00, also include filters which protect against noise. Each stage of a filter usually includes one or more capacitors and some coils or inductors, as shown in Fig. 5-9. The designer can choose the value of these components so that the filter will pass one group of frequencies and stop other frequencies. This type of filter is called a "low-pass" filter, since it passes the normal 60-Hz AC,

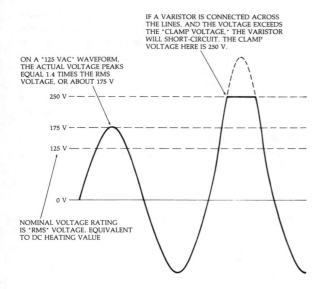

Fig. 5-8. Varistor operating principle.

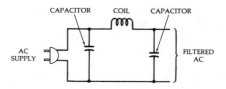

Fig. 5-9. An AC line-filter network.

but reduces the strength of those signals with higher frequencies. By adding additional filter stages, a designer can make a filter more effective. Filters of this type are rated by the speed of the fastest transients they can block. The better the filter, the higher the frequencies it can filter out. A filter that can handle transients of up to 20 MHz is adequate for most small computer installations.

The best filter units also include protection against very large power surges. Inmac offers a combination filter/surge protector unit which includes a gas-discharge tube. This unit costs about $70.00. Like the varistor, the gas-discharge tube is inactive until a very large spike or surge comes along. As the voltage rises, the gas inside the tube ionizes, creating an escape path for the excess current. This kind of device might save your equipment if lightning strikes nearby.

A "power conditioner" acts to smooth out the power supply to the microcomputer. For example, if the line voltage drops for a moment, a conditioner can boost the voltage for a moment. The conditioner may include filters and varistors for surge protection. A conditioner of this type costs $100 or more. A power conditioner will not help if all power is lost, however.

If you can't afford to have your system stop without warning, get an *uninterruptible power supply* or *UPC*. When the AC power fails, the UPC switches to a backup battery, and the computer never misses a beat. Inside the UPC is a type of battery called a "gel-cell." This battery is kept charged by a low-current "trickle-

charger" circuit. A small UPC might cost $300 or more. Each unit carries a wattage or volt-amp (VA) rating to indicate how much back-up power it can supply. A 400-watt system is designed to back up a computer like an IBM-XT, along with its disk drives, monitor, and printer. An 800-watt system is recommended for an IBM-AT system. These ratings assume that you will want to operate your system for 15 minutes or more after a power failure. Actually, you'll probably just want to save your files and then shut down the system. You can do this in 5 minutes or less, so even the smallest UPC will be fine for many users. A utility program called "Powerwatch" is available for use with a UPC. When the equipment detects a power failure, this utility program automatically shuts down the computer. This means the files will be saved, even if you are not present at the time of the power failure.

Large computer installations use even more sophisticated filtering and backup systems. An installation with a large load might have a motor/generator set. Normal AC is used to drive an electric motor, which then drives a flywheel. This flywheel will have enough momentum to ride out transients and spikes, and permit the automatic starting of a backup generator, which will supply clean power to the computer equipment.

You may decide to buy several of these protective devices, or none. Your decision will depend on the importance of your operation, and on the number of problems you have with the AC supply and with interference.

Defense Against Noise on Signal Lines

Most computer cables carry "TTL-level" signals. The digital "1s" and "0s" are represented by levels of +5 V and 0 V. In a parallel interface, the cable may carry eight or more bits of data at the same time. The signal levels in this type of cable will also be +5 V and 0 V. In a "serial" cable, the equipment will send a string of bits, one bit at a time. Serial connections usually use the RS-232 standard. RS-232-type signals use voltage levels of +12 V and −12 V to indicate the digital "1s" and "0s." For more on parallel interfaces, see Chapter 12 (Dot-Matrix and Daisy-Wheel Printers). For more on the serial interface, see Chapter 14 (Modems and Serial Interfaces).

If you are experiencing problems with induced noise, start by moving the cable to a different location. As we said, the power of the noise signal drops off very quickly as the cable is moved away from the source of the noise. If you must cross cables, try to cross them at right angles, as shown in Fig. 5-5. The longer the cable, the better a receiver it is for noise. Move your equipment closer together and use a shorter cable, if possible.

The next step is to try a shielded cable (Fig. 5-10). In an unshielded cable, the signal wires are bundled together and protected by an outer layer of insulation. Each of the signal wires also has its own insulation. In a shielded cable, the bundle is wrapped in a layer of metal foil or wire mesh. This "shielding" is connected to ground. If any noise signals reach the cable, they are intercepted by the shielding and drawn off to ground. Shielded cables are available from many equipment suppliers.

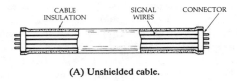

(A) Unshielded cable.

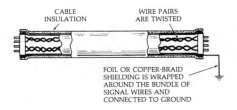

(B) Shielded cable.

Fig. 5-10. Shielded cable.

If the cable is using the RS-232 standard, you may want to buy a special surge protector for this interface. Radio Shack sells a unit of this type for about $60.00. Also, you may be able to convert RS-232 equipment to use the RS-422 standard, which is more noise resistant. In RS-232-type signals, the signal voltage is measured in relation to ground (single-ended transmission). In RS-422 configurations, one side of the signal is measured in relation to the other side of the signal, not to ground

(differential transmission). Any induced noise affects both transmission wires equally, so the noise does not distort the signal. Your equipment may be designed to allow you to make the conversion easily.

If the cable run is very long, and if the environment is very noisy, you may want to set up a fiber-optics link. At one end of the link, the electronic signals are converted to pulses of light. The pulses are passed through an optical fiber, and reconverted to electronic signals at the end of the link. The light pulses are completely immune to electronic noise, so this solution offers the best protection of all.

Static Electricity

A static charge may be built up when two surfaces rub against each other. As children, many of us have shuffled across a thick carpet and seen the spark jump from our fingertip when we touched a radiator or other grounded object. In our normal activities, we generate static charges all the time. Normally the air is humid enough to allow the charge to dissipate quickly. But when the air is dry, the charge has no escape route so it accumulates. You carry the charge until you touch a grounded object. This charge can have a voltage high enough (thousands of volts) to create quite a spark. Even though the voltage is high, the current is very low, so only a small amount of power is involved.

Some materials hold a static electric charge better than others. Some of the worst sources of static are carpets, synthetic fabrics, plastic materials, styrofoam coffee cups, and paper products. The outer surface of a monitor or TV screen can also build up a static charge.

When you develop a static charge and then touch an operating computer, the resulting spike can cause a variety of problems. The spike can stop a program from operating, or it may change a bit of data stored in memory. Usually, the problem passes quickly. You just reset the computer, reload the software, and find that everything operates normally again. Static is a leading cause of these minor, passing glitches. A really strong static discharge can permanently damage RAMs or other parts. Sometimes, the effect of the static is obvious right away and, sometimes, you don't notice the damage until much later.

The typical microcomputer is defended against static as long as its case is closed. When you touch a metal part on the outside of the case, the static charge is drawn off to ground. The story is different once you open the case and begin working inside the equipment. Some components are very sensitive to static, including

FETs (field-effect transistors) and one type of IC technology called "CMOS." On a typical CMOS device, the inputs are buffered by small capacitors. When the device is operating normally, these capacitors act to block the flow of DC from one stage to the next. If you touch a CMOS device while you are carrying a static charge, you can easily damage these input capacitors. The capacitors are mounted inside the IC, and since there is no way of replacing them, the whole IC must be replaced.

Defense Against Static Electricity

Static is always a problem when you are troubleshooting. You should take special precautions whenever you work on equipment which includes CMOS ICs. CMOS parts are widely used, so if you don't know differently, you must assume that CMOS parts are present. CMOS ICs are shipped in protective wrappers. Keep these parts in their wrappers until you are ready to use them.

Before you touch any parts inside the equipment, always ground yourself to get rid of any static charge. Many technicians wear a wrist strap which is connected to ground through a 1-megohm resistor. This safely drains off any static electric charges from their body.

Some suppliers sell "antistatic mats," which are intended to be placed under the equipment as you work on it. A mat of this type should be connected to ground, using a clip lead. Generally, these mats do not stand up well to the abuse they must take on the service bench. If you do use an antistatic mat, remember that the mat is conductive. If you allow exposed circuitry to touch the mat and then turn on the power, the mat may create a short circuit.

If the equipment has a three-prong plug, the case is grounded as long as the plug is connected. For this reason, it is convenient to have the unit plugged in, but turned off, while you are servicing. Once you have done this, you can always ground yourself simply by touching the bare metal part on the chassis.

When you connect your test equipment to a static-sensitive circuit, connect the ground lead first. When you disconnect the equipment, disconnect the ground lead last.

We think it is safer to actually unplug the unit. If you want to ground the chassis, you can run a jumper from the equipment to the screw in the center of the outlet plate. This screw should be connected to the

ground wire in the AC wiring (Fig. 5-11). Before you make this connection, double-check the system, by testing with a voltmeter, to see if the chassis is "hot." There should be no voltage difference between the chassis and the outlet-plate screw.

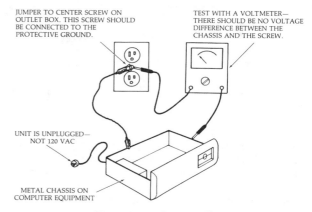

Fig. 5-11. Safe grounding arrangement during servicing.

Static can also be a problem in your day-to-day computer operations. If you suspect you're having problems with static, buy a device which measures the humidity of the air. For about $5.00, you can get a combination-type instrument that also includes a thermometer. During the humid days of summer, this instrument may show a relative humidity reading of 90% or more, and static won't be a problem. But during the winter, the humidity may drop to 30% or less. This is the time to be especially careful about static.

As we said before, some kinds of synthetic fabrics collect a lot of static as you move around. Avoid wearing these fabrics in dry weather. You may also want to buy an antistatic rug to use at your computer work station. Conductive threads are woven into the fabric of the rug, and a strap connects the rug to ground. As you shuffle across the rug, the conductive threads collect the static charge, and the strap draws the charge off before it can accumulate. A 4 × 5 foot rug will cost about $180. You can also buy an antistatic mat to place under the computer. Again, this mat includes conductive fibers and draws off any static charge to ground. A humidifier may also be helpful in fighting static. In dry weather, a humidifier can pump several gallons of water into the air per day. A slightly humid environment (above 50% relative humidity) is also more pleasant for the computer operator.

You might want to use antistatic sprays and wipes. Spray the carpet, furniture, and table top near the computer. Wipe down the outside of the equipment with an antistatic wipe. You don't have to soak these surfaces. If you're concerned about static on a stack of papers, lightly mist the outside edges of the stack. You may even want to spray your clothes.

Warning! Don't spray antistatic spray on the computer itself. Be especially careful not to spray liquid into the computer while it is operating. This can cause a shock hazard.

As the spray dries, it leaves a residue which allows static charges to dissipate. The effect lasts until the residue is worn away, so you'll have to repeat the procedure from time to time. Radio Shack sells a premixed antistatic spray. Bob Cahill uses a homemade spray made of equal parts of Downy Fabric Softener® and water.

The Computer Can Affect the Environment

Interference can be a two-way street. A computer can be a significant "noise generator" that can affect the signals received by nearby TVs and radios. The microprocessor inside a computer is running at a high frequency, usually measured up in the megahertz range. This is a radio frequency, and the computer radiates radio energy. Switching-type power supplies, clock circuits, and other parts of the equipment may radiate different frequencies.

The early microcomputers were particularly noisy, so in 1981, the Federal Communications Commission laid down a new set of rules. All computer equipment produced today must pass strict tests. In most cases, the power supplies and high-frequency sections of the circuit boards are shielded to prevent radiation. The new standards have reduced interference problems, but some of the early, noisy computers are still in operation.

A computer tends to generate noise across broad sections of the radio and TV bands. If you're experiencing interference in a very specific band, look for a different cause, such as, perhaps, a CB radio. On a radio, the noise from a computer may sound like a "buzz," "whistle," or "frying" sound. If a printer is operating, you may hear a rapid series of pulses on an AM radio. Computer-generated interference may create a series of lines or a cross-hatch pattern on a TV screen. It can also cause the picture to appear "fuzzy."

It may seem surprising that computers can cause so much trouble—after all, the interference signals generated by computers are relatively weak. But remember, a device like a TV set is designed to take very weak signals from the antenna, and amplify them many times. If some noise creeps into the system, the noise will be amplified also.

If you suspect that your computer is causing interference, you can make a check using a portable AM radio. Turn on both the computer and the radio, and hold the radio near the computer equipment. Tune the radio back and forth until you hear a strong signal from the computer. Use the computer to print a report from files stored on a disk. This will cause the computer to use the peripherals in your system. Now hold the radio near various parts of your equipment, and try to identify the components that are creating the most noise. You may be surprised to find that a lot of the noise is coming from the cables between the units.

There are two ways that computer-generated interference can reach another piece of equipment. Sometimes the interference travels along the power lines. If the computer and the affected equipment are both plugged into the same AC circuit, try plugging one of the units into another circuit. If this is not practical, you can put a line filter on the AC line going to the computer, on the line to the affected equipment, or on both pieces of equipment. A line filter prevents interference from getting out of the computer, as well as getting in. If these measures don't help, the interference may be radiating through the air directly to the antenna leads of the affected TV or radio. This effect drops off rapidly with distance, so try moving either the computer or the TV (or the radio). You may be able to minimize the problem by rotating the TV or radio a few degrees.

As we just said, computer cables can generate a lot of noise. If this is a problem, switch to shielded cables, as shown in Fig. 5-10. The shielding prevents the cables from radiating signals.

You can also attack the problem by changing the radio or TV's antenna system. Many TV antenna installations use flat 300-ohm "twin-lead" wire to bring the signal down to the set. You can replace this with a round 75-ohm coaxial cable. This is the same kind of cable used in cable TV installations. It is much more resistant to noise. At any point along the cable run, whenever you switch between 300-ohm and 75-ohm cable, you'll have to include a matching transformer or "balun."

Finally, you can buy or make a special filter and attach it to the antenna inputs on the TV to trap the unwanted interference before it gets into the set. Use a "high-pass" filter that will block any signals below 45 MHz. Legitimate TV signals have higher frequencies, so they will pass through the filter. Steve Ciarcia explained how to build an inexpensive high-pass filter in his "Ciarcia's Circuit Cellar" column in the January 1981 issue of *Byte* magazine. You may also want to check the *Radio Amateur's Handbook*, published by the American Radio Relay League (A.R.R.L.).

Other Environmental Factors

So far we've concentrated on factors that affect the electronic environment. Like any other equipment, microcomputers are vulnerable to mechanical damage. Try to place your equipment where nothing can fall on it. Run cables out of the way, where nobody can trip over them. A mail-order supplier of computer office supplies, like *Inmac®*, has a number of cable fittings that can protect cables as they run across open spaces on the floor. As long as electronic noise is not a problem, you may want to use wire ties to bundle the cables together. These are available in several lengths (3-inch to 8-inch), and a bag of 100 should cost about $5.00.

Be particularly careful to protect your equipment from water and other fluids. Make it a rule not to allow any liquids in the same room as the computer. You may want to get inexpensive vinyl covers for the computer, keyboard, and other peripherals.

Try to eliminate any sources of excessive vibration. It's best to mount a printer on a separate stand, where the vibrations can't affect the rest of the equipment. This is especially important if you have a hard-disk drive. A strong vibration from the printer could be carried through the desk and cause a "head crash" on the hard disk.

Microcomputers can also be affected by heat, cold, and other environmental factors. Most computer manufacturers list high and low temperature limits for their equipment. In general, if you can stand to stay in the room and operate the equipment, the computer will be fine.

Heat is bad for electronic components. Overheated parts fail much more quickly than components working at normal temperatures. An operating computer can give off a surprising amount of heat. To counteract this, some units have their own fans. Other units are designed with convective cooling

systems. On this kind of unit, the equipment's case has ventilation slots that allow warm air to escape. Other slots in the bottom of the case allow cool air to be pulled inside. If your equipment has this type of system, be sure to arrange the components so that all of the ventilation slots are clear.

It is possible to overload a convection system if you add a number of plug-in circuits or other equipment inside the computer case. Each of these boards creates more heat. The boards also block the flow of cooling air through the inside of the case. If your computer is starting to become overcrowded, you may want to buy an add-on fan.

We've already mentioned humidity in relation to problems with static. Setting the static question aside, most manufacturers don't want you to operate in an extremely high humidity. Very high humidity can cause moisture to condense inside the equipment, and the moisture can cause short circuits between the components.

Beware of any special environmental areas that include a high concentration of solvents or corrosive chemicals. Don't operate your equipment in a dusty or dirty environment. Dust can get into the mechanical parts of a printer or disk drive, and can cause jamming and premature wear. If a heavy layer of dust accumulates on the circuit boards, it can cause components to overheat and fail prematurely. Dust can also collect moisture, and the damp dust can cause short circuits. This is even more of a problem if you live near salt water. If your circuit boards are covered with a wet salty dust, you'll have all kinds of corrosion and short-circuiting problems.

Cover your printer and other mechanical equipment when it's not in use. This will prevent dust from settling on the components. Cooling fans draw a lot of air through the inside of the equipment. In the process, they also draw in a lot of dust, and some of this stays inside the case. Expect the dust to build up wherever your equipment has a fan.

Don't use a vacuum cleaner to get rid of dust. The vacuum can pull on components and perhaps pull something loose, or create a bad connection. Vacuum cleaners also produce large static-electrical charges, and these can be very dangerous to the CMOS components inside a computer. Some technicians use vacuums all the time, but we think this is too risky. Instead, we recommend you use the small cans of compressed air such as are available from computer supply and photo supply outlets to blow the dust away. These cans cost about $5.00 each. If you have to use a vacuum, use the air flow from the exhaust of the vacuum. Do not use the suction side.

Early hard-disk memory systems were particularly vulnerable to problems caused by dust. A tiny particle of cigarette smoke between the head and the surface of the disk could cause the disk drive to "read" or "write" an incorrect character. A bigger particle could cause a "head crash" and ruin the disk. The drives included filters which were supposed to catch all of the dust, but they were not always effective. Fortunately, most modern hard-disk systems are sealed. Floppy disk drives are not as sensitive, but they have a higher incidence of "soft" errors when operated in dusty, smoky environments.

Floppy disks, themselves, are very sensitive to the environment. Don't use a floppy disk that is extremely hot or cold. If a disk has been exposed to a temperature extreme, let it return to room temperature before you try to use it. Even then, you might not be able to read from the disk. As the disk changes temperature, it expands or contracts. This changes the relative spacing of the various bits of data stored on the disk. When the disk returns to normal temperature, these bits may not return to their original spacing. On a sunny day, disks can easily overheat if they are left in the glove compartment, in the trunk, or on the dashboard of a car. Sunlight can break down the plastic material used to make floppy disks.

Security

As computers become more common, more important, and more expensive, we all must take more precautions against theft and unauthorized use. A whole book could be written on this topic, but we'll just touch on the main points here. First, you can prevent someone from walking away with your equipment by locking it inside a sturdy cabinet. Some special computer cabinets are designed to let you lock up the computer quickly and easily. Some computers, such as the MacIntosh, are designed with fittings for the use of a locking cable. (You can attach one end of the cable to the computer, and the other end to something immovable.) Add-on kits are available for those computers which do not have cable fittings. Then, there is an accessory that allows you to lock the case of the computer so nobody can make off with the valuable add-on boards that are inside. Also, printers can be bolted down, or attached to the furniture with an adhesive pad.

Next, there are various ways of preventing unauthorized use of the equipment. You can buy key switches which cut off the power to the computer, or disconnect the keyboard. There is special software that requires the user to type in a password before it allows him or her to use the computer. If you are using floppy disks, or a "removable hard disk" like a Bernoulli drive, you can take your data home with you at the end of the day.

Finally, in some installations, the computer is left turned on and connected to a modem all day long. This is convenient for users who want to phone in and access the computer, but it is also an invitation to outside "hackers." If you have this kind of setup, you should be using a password scheme. The "call back" scheme offers even better protection. When a user calls in, the computer notes his phone number, disconnects, and then calls that number back.

Preventive Maintenance

Naturally, you want to be sure your system is as reliable as possible. One way to do this is to set up a regular program of preventive maintenance. The computer itself will not require much maintenance. Now and then, however, you might want to clean the outside of the case.

Warning! Always unplug your equipment before you begin to clean it. If you allow liquid to run inside the computer while it is turned on, you may receive a dangerous shock.

The computer's keyboard opens upward, and it can collect dust, crumbs, etc. If the debris begins to jam the key contacts, you may have to open the keyboard and clean it out.

Pay particular attention to sections of the system that include mechanical parts. Clean the heads on your floppy disk drives regularly. In an office where the disk drives are used all the time, you should probably clean the heads every 60 days. The home user or hobbyist should clean the heads once or twice a year. We explain how to clean the heads in Chapter 10. If you skip this step, you will begin to get "read" or "write" errors from the drives. If you use your equipment a lot, or if you move the floppy disk drives frequently, check the alignment of the heads about once a year. Over time, the head on a floppy drive can drift out of alignment. The misaligned drive may be able to read its own disks, but not disks written on other drives.

Hard-disk drives have mechanical parts, but they're sealed inside a metal case. The cases are sealed to keep out dust. Even a tiny bit of dust is enough to damage a hard-disk drive. For this reason, you really can't work on the mechanical parts in a hard-disk drive.

Clean and inspect your printer at least once a year as well. We've included the instructions for this in Chapter 12.

Software Maintenance

You should "maintain" your software as well. Use the write-protect feature on the floppy disks that carry your software. This protects the software from stray characters that may be written during a spike or other malfunction. You may have to unwrite-protect a disk for a moment to reconfigure a software package, but be sure to write-protect again as soon as you are done.

On 5 1/4-inch floppy disks, the disk is protected when the write-protect slot is covered. On the old 8-inch floppy disks, the write-protect arrangement was reversed. When the write-protect notch was exposed, the disk was protected. On the 3 1/2-inch disks, the disk is protected when the slider is moved out of the way, and the write-protect slot is opened.

Each software vendor should send you at least two copies of each program disk. You can then make more backup copies using a utility like "Copy II" or "Locksmith." Store at least one copy of each program in a safe place, in a different building from your working disks. We'll list some rules for safe disk storage in a moment. Most software manufacturers are willing to replace a "damaged" program disk for a nominal charge, once you return the bad disk to them.

Early versions of a commercial software package may contain a number of programming mistakes, or "bugs." The manufacturers don't discover these bugs until they begin to receive complaints from their customers. Eventually, they correct the problems by issuing an updated version. Some manufacturers don't like to admit their mistakes, so they don't advertise these updates. If you have sent in a warranty card, you may receive notice of updates, but you can't count on this. You should also watch for news about updates from dealers, user's groups, and trade magazines. Updates designed to repair "bugs" are usually available to registered customers for a nominal fee. Updates which include important improvements can be more costly.

Computer hardware is changing very quickly, and software publishers are struggling to keep up. One consequence of this is that operating systems seem to change every year or two. New versions of operating systems are usually designed so they will run all the software designed for earlier versions. Unfortunately, you can't count on this. If a particular program is incompatible with your current version of the operating system, it may not run at all. Sometimes a program will run well most of the time, but stop working when you try to use an unusual part of the software. Know which version of the operating system you are using. If you update the operating system, be sure each of your programs is compatible with the newer version.

Floppy Disk Handling Procedures

Floppy disks are one of the most vulnerable parts of the computer system, so they require special handling. Here are some rules:

1.   Don't bend or crease the plastic disk material. This will make it impossible for the disk to spin inside its case. Insert and remove the floppy disks from disk drives slowly and gently. Don't attach notes to the disks with paper clips. Never set parts, paperweights, etc., on top of floppy disks, or stack them more than ten high. The oxide layer on the surface of each disk is easily scratched or contaminated. Don't touch this surface with your fingers—the slight amount of oil present on your hands can cause problems. As we said earlier, ground yourself by touching the case of the computer before you handle disks in times of low humidity.

2.   Store the floppy disks carefully. Always return each disk to its paper container when it is not in use. Don't leave floppy disks exposed on a table or desk top. For longer-term storage, put the disks into some kind of container which protects them from dust. The disks should be stored standing on edge.

3.   Be sure to keep your disks at least six inches away from any device or wire that uses or carries electricity. The changing magnetic field present around AC wiring can erase a floppy disk. Keep the disks away from the section of the computer or other equipment that includes the power supply.

4.   Keep floppy disks at least five feet away from any magnets, since magnets can erase floppy disks. Don't use magnetic copy holders or

paper-clip trays in the computer room. Sooner or later someone will slip up and place one of these magnets near a floppy disk. The paper-clip holders are especially bad because they can magnetize items—like paper clips. Also, as a technician, remember that some screwdriver tips are magnetized. Even plain screwdrivers can become magnetized as you use them.

5. Don't store floppy disks near bottles of typewriter cleaner or other solvents. Given enough time, the solvent can damage a plastic disk, or loosen the oxide coating.

6. Label every floppy disk. Never write on the case of a disk with a ball-point pen. You can easily use too much pressure and score the disk material. Instead, use one of the various sizes of self-stick labels. A box of 1000 labels, measuring 3/4-inch by 1-inch, costs less that $5.00. Write on the labels with a felt-tip pen before you attach them to the disks. Don't use a pencil—graphite from the pencil tip can contaminate the surface of a disk. Be careful not to cover any of the openings on the disk. Remove any old labels before you add a new one—don't stack the labels.

7. Before you turn off the computer, remove all floppy disks from the drives. Don't turn off the equipment while the disks are still mounted. As the power is cut off, the drive may send some indeterminate signals that could change some of the data stored on one of the disks. When you leave the computer, close the doors on the disk drives. This will help extend the life of some of the springs inside the drives.

Handling Files

If you make a mistake in entering data, a few lines in a report may turn out to be incorrect. You can usually correct this very easily. But if you make a mistake in handling a file, you could easily lose the whole file. If you don't have a backup copy, you'll have to recreate the file, and this is very unpleasant work.

Let's be more specific. A particularly critical moment comes when you are through working with a file, and are ready to "SAVE" it onto a floppy disk. You can have a problem if the floppy disk does not have enough room for the new file. Under some older disk operating systems, the computer will begin copying the file, without checking the remaining space on the disk to see if there is enough room. When the system runs out of room on the copy disk, the copying action stops abruptly, and you may lose some of your data.

It is also possible to make a mistake in typing, and "SAVE" a file under the wrong name. If you include a control character in the file name (Control-D, Control-R, etc.), this character may not appear when you get a "catalog" of the disk. The file name may appear in the catalog as "FRD" while the computer reads it is "FR(Control-E)D." When you specify "FRD," the computer won't be able to find the file. (Some operators do this deliberately as a way of limiting access to a file.) In systems with more than one floppy disk drive, it is possible to send a file to the wrong drive, and lose some data.

"ERASE," "DELETE," and "KILL" are dangerous commands. If you're tired or not paying attention, it is very easy to delete the wrong file and lose hours of work. "COPY" and "BACKUP" are just as dangerous. If you're not paying attention, it's possible to copy the old version of a file over the new version, and lose all of your recent work.

You can avoid most of these problems by adopting some careful operating procedures. Whenever you're going to SAVE or ERASE something, stop and double check the operation. Ask yourself, "Is this what I really want to do?" On large or complicated jobs that involve many files, it is a good idea to keep a written index that lists the name of the current version of each file, its length, and the disk where it will be found. This saves time, and makes it less likely that you will delete the wrong file. For extra protection for a particularly important file, write-protect the floppy disk whenever possible.

It is possible to recover some files, even after they have been "erased." We explain how to do this in Chapter 11. If you want to recover an "erased" file, it is very important that you do not add any new material to the hard disk or floppy disk.

The best defense against all of these problems is to have a good system of backup disks. You just can't trust your equipment. Sooner or later, something will go wrong—you can count on it. When you suddenly lose a large file, you discover something interesting about your computer system. The real value of the system is not in the hardware, although this can be expensive enough. The really valuable part of the system is the information that you have stored there. If you have backup disks, a hardware breakdown is usually not a big problem. Without backup disks, the same hardware fault can be magnified into a major disaster. We'll repeat the message throughout this book:

BACKUP! BACKUP! BACKUP!

"Yes," you say, "that's very nice, and I'll get around to it real soon." Sorry, friend, that's not good enough. This is a serious problem, and if you're dependent on the information stored in your computer, you've got to take it seriously. Some day you'll thank us for insisting on this.

There are two different types of backups. As you work on the computer, you should make "running backups" every hour or so. These protect you against short-term problems, like power outages. At the end of the work session, you should make "archival backups." These help you to recover data if you lose your whole computer installation.

You should have archival backup copies of both your program and your data files. For your running backups, it's all right to copy just the data files. But, how often should you back up? This depends on the kind of work you're doing. If you make running backups every hour, then the most that you can lose is an hour's work. Archival backups should be fresh enough to be useful if you ever have to use them to rebuild your system. Backup procedures are different for floppy drives and hard disks. We have included some more information on backup procedures in Chapter 11.

Before you make a backup copy, be sure the file you're copying is in good shape. If something is wrong with the file on your work disk, and you copy the bad file onto your backup, you'll end up with two copies of the bad file, and no backup of the earlier file. One quick way to check a file is to get a CATALOG or DIRECTORY, depending on your system, and see how long the file is. If you know that the earlier version of the file was 30 sectors long, and you've recently added some material, yet the new version appears to be only 25 sectors long, you know that something is wrong with the new version of the file. To make this more complicated, some older disk operating systems don't always show you the true length of a file. Under Apple DOS, for example, the CATALOG function can only give a file length number up to 256. Above that number, the sector count starts over again. A file with 258 sectors would be listed as having 002 sectors.

Fire Protection

Inside a computer, electrical energy is carefully controlled and channeled so that it can do useful work. Very rarely, however, that energy can get out of line and a fire may result. Most electrical fires in computers are of the slow, smouldering sort. Should this happen to you, the *first step* is to unplug the equipment. Electrical fires tend to die out quickly once the power is cut off, because there is no more electrical energy feeding the fire.

Warning! Never use a propelled-liquid extinguisher on computer equipment that is plugged in. You may receive a dangerous electrical shock.

A propelled-liquid extinguisher will blast water inside the computer, and this water can cause short circuits and corrosion problems. Dry chemical extinguishers are not much better for use on computer equipment. The dry powder is not conductive, but it sticks to hot parts on the circuit board, and it can gum up mechanical parts. Once this powder has been sprayed on a board, you never really get rid of it. The best fire extinguishers for computer equipment use Halon®, a fire-suppressing gas. Halon does not damage the circuit boards. You can even breathe this gas, as long as it does not become too concentrated. You should be able to find a small Halon extinguisher for about $40.00 at a fire-extinguisher supply outlet.

Crisis Planning

You may not realize how dependent you've become on your computer equipment. If your main computing activity is playing "Space Invaders," you could probably do without your computer for a few weeks. But if you're using the computer equipment for business, or to handle important information, a computer crisis could be very costly.

What would happen if your computer were to break down without warning? How would it affect your operation? It's easy to give crisis planning a low priority. Because there's no immediate need, this is the type of job that's easy to shuffle to the bottom of the pile. If you're lucky, you'll never have a serious problem, and you will never need a crisis plan.

But what if you're not lucky? If you're using computer equipment in a business, you must take crisis planning seriously. To put it bluntly, if your computer is destroyed or seriously damaged, the resulting problems can put you out of business. For example, when a computer system is destroyed by a fire, the business will have to replace the computer equipment, and this can be expensive. Usually, however, this added expense doesn't threaten the basic existence of the company. The real dangers come from the business dislocations which occur as a result of the loss of the computer. Suddenly, it may be impossible to send out bills. With no bills going out, no money comes in. No checks are written, so the vendors cut off incoming supplies. Even if the business is able to keep some of these functions going, everything must be done by hand. All of the information must be reconstructed using roundabout, time-consuming methods. Everyone is distracted by the immediate demands of survival, so the customers get disgusted and shift their business to someone else. The whole operation grinds to a halt. We'll say it again: the loss of your computer, software, and data can threaten the survival of your business.

How should you approach this problem? The first step is to analyze your situation. Where are you vulnerable? In what ways are you counting on the computer? If the computer was down, would you still be able to send out bills? Would you still have access to the raw information that would allow you to send out bills? Would you lose track of inventory, employee files, and other important information?

It's best to assume that your computer equipment will be completely unusable. You should also assume that you'll lose all backup disks and printed information stored at your main location. The next step is to work out ways of protecting yourself from each of your possible losses. You've got to make arrangements for three categories: hardware, operating software, and data.

Many businesses arrange to have access to a backup computer, in case their main computer system is out of action. If your operation is small, you might just make an informal arrangement with a friend who has the same kind of equipment. If you're running a bigger operation, you might have to contract with an outside data-processing company or computer-leasing operation.

The next concern is the storage of backup copies of your software. Most software vendors will sell backup copies to registered users for a nominal cost. Even if the vendor is cooperative, this can take one or two weeks. If you lose all of your original disk copies, your operation can be paralyzed while you are waiting. If your software is noncopy-protected, you can make copies as easily as copying a data file. Even if the software is copy-protected, you should be able to make copies. Modern copy programs like "Locksmith" and "Copy II" are able to copy most software. You have a legal right to make copies as insurance against disasters.

It is very important that you store the backup disks at a remote location. Keep a set of backup copies at home, or downtown in a safe-deposit box at the bank. You may have a complete set of backup disks at your office, but this doesn't help if the whole office goes up in smoke.

The final concern is the duplication of your data files. This demands a lot of work, because the information is constantly changing. The extra work produces a big payoff, however, when measured in security and peace of mind. Your backup disks can be essential when you're trying to get back on your feet after an accident. They can protect you against the big disasters, as well as the smaller hardware problems and "glitches."

Chapter Review

Power-line problems are very common, and they can be dangerous to your equipment. Possible problems include power failure, low voltage, high voltage, spikes, noise, dropouts, and frequency changes. Noise can "confuse" a computer. A large spike from a lightning strike can burn out many parts on a circuit board. Before installing a computer, be sure the outlets are wired correctly. Most computers should be protected with a spike protector and filter, and perhaps an uninterruptible power supply.

Static electricity is always a danger when you work on computer equipment. It is very easy to burn out CMOS components, so you should always take precautions when working with them. Computers can radiate signals as well as receive them.

Computers, themselves, don't need much preventive maintenance. Concentrate on the units with lots of mechanical parts—the floppy disk drives and printers.

Floppy disks are easily damaged. Handle them carefully. Be very careful to SAVE and ERASE files correctly.

Plan ahead for the possible loss of your computer. Make regular backups. Arrange for the use of a backup computer. Keep backup disks of files and software in a remote location. Provide Halon fire extinguishers for use on the computer equipment.

Review Questions

1. Outdoors, the weather is very cold. You are inside in a heated room, and your computer begins acting up. Can you think of a possible cause?

2. You're troubleshooting a circuit board. It appears that several different ICs are not working. One of the parts is blackened. Can you suggest a possible cause?

3. You're operating a computer in a factory and every afternoon at 3:30, the computer crashes. What would you check first?

4. The tenant downstairs complains that he gets a fuzzy TV picture whenever you turn on your computer. What can you do about the problem?

5. A computer is installed in a factory, and it receives RS-232 signals over a long run of cable. From time to time, the computer locks up. Would this be a good place to install a fiber-optic link?

6. Why are CMOS parts so sensitive to static electricity?

7. Your boss has backed his computer up against a wall, and piled books and magazines on top of it. Why is this bad practice? Do you tell him about it?

8. What happens if you forget to clean the heads on your floppy disk drives?

9. A new worker is setting up his desk in the computer room. He puts a magnetic paper-clip holder on the front of the desk. What do you say?

10. You're using your computer to handle the billing, payroll, and inventory for your business. You have a fire at the office, and you lose the computer and all of the backup disks that were stored at the office. Is your system of backup disks and tapes good enough to allow your business to survive?

6

Documentation, Tools, and Parts

Introduction and Objectives

Before you can service computer equipment, you must collect adequate documentation, tools, and the parts you will need. In this chapter, we will discuss the preparations for such servicing work.

We start by discussing the state of mind required for this type of work, and, then, we suggest some good work habits. Next, we describe the types of service manuals which are available. It is very difficult to service computer equipment if you do not have the right documentation.

You will need several kinds of servicing tools—electronic test instruments, hand tools, software tools, etc. These basic tools are listed and described.

Finally, in order to make repairs, you will need replacement parts. In the last part of the chapter, we tell you how to choose replacement components and suggest some sources for the parts.

Preparation

The Boy Scout motto is "Be Prepared." This is also a good rule if you plan to service computer equipment. Computer problems have a way of happening with no warning. In fact, they always seem to come at the worst possible moment, just when you're rushing to finish a job. When your equipment stops working, you naturally want to get it operating again as soon as possible. That means that you must have your servicing system organized and in place before any trouble occurs. If you plan to make a living servicing computer equipment, it is even more important to be prepared. In the servicing business, "time is money," and you must use each moment efficiently. By collecting the required tools and the necessary information ahead of time, you can be ready to move quickly when trouble strikes.

In this first section, we'll list a number of useful tools. If you were to buy them all at once, they would be quite expensive. Fortunately, unless you plan to open a service shop, you won't have to do this. You will be able to handle many jobs with just a few simple tools: a voltohmmeter, a logic probe, a soldering iron, and some hand tools. Building on this base, you can collect any additional equipment gradually. The additional tools will allow you to diagnose problems more quickly and easily.

State of Mind

Start to develop the right state of mind for repair work. A computer repair problem requires mental discipline as well as a technical knowledge. The typical servicing situation includes many pressures that can make it difficult to think clearly. If you use the computer equipment yourself, just knowing that your equipment is "down" may put you in a bad mood, and if you really need the equipment to finish an important job, this adds an element of time pressure. If you are servicing equipment on a commercial basis, you face similar pressures. Your customers have problems and deadlines of their own, and, sometimes, they can be very demanding. The most intense pressures come during on-site service calls. As the technician, you have to deal with all of the technical problems. In addition, you may have an obnoxious client looking over your shoulder, making "helpful" suggestions. It can be hard to think clearly at times like this.

Repair work can be very frustrating. You may work for many hours to find a particular problem and make a repair, only to have the problem return a week later. In this kind of work, there's no "partial credit" for good intentions. Problems between people can be somewhat forgiving; often the parties can work out a compromise. But there's no way to "sweet talk" a faulty circuit; either it's fixed or it isn't.

Servicing computers is *work*. To make any progress, you'll have to attack the problem—the equipment won't repair itself. You'll have to poke and prod and try different approaches until you really find the cause of the problem. If one idea doesn't work, try something else; try yet another idea, and keep it up until you're successful.

Sometimes, you'll be sure that you've found the problem. For example, when you find a resistor that is burned and black, or a capacitor that has ruptured, you can be sure the part is bad. However, if the problem is "soft" or intermittent, you may not be quite sure that you've found the cause. You'll just have to put the equipment back into service and wait to see if it fails again.

As you get more experience with repair work, you'll begin to recognize the state of mind that brings good results. The experienced technician is cool and rational, and has a definite plan of attack. This gives him or her a big advantage over the amateur, who tends to work without a plan. Try not to work when you're tired or upset. Try to avoid working under the pressure of deadlines, although this isn't always possible. If a piece of equipment stops working near the end of the day, set it aside and "sleep on the problem." You'll come back in the morning in a much better frame of mind.

Work Habits

Practice good work habits. Here's another factor which separates the amateur from the pro. Start with a clean work area. Clear all papers, old parts, and other junk away from your workplace. If your workbench is cluttered, sooner or later you'll knock something over. It just takes a moment to clean up the work area, but it's well worth the trouble.

As you work, it is wise to leave everything in a "fail-safe" condition. Set up your work so that, if you are interrupted or not paying attention, you and your equipment will be safe. For example, let's say that you've plugged in a piece of test equipment, and you've left the power cord hanging over the edge of the workbench. If you trip over the cord, or pull on it by mistake, you can jerk the test equipment off of the bench. As long as you remember that the cord is exposed, you can avoid tripping over it. However, this is just one more thing to worry about. Will you remember the cord if you leave the job and return? What if your attention is diverted by something else? It is much simpler to place the cord in a safe position out of the way, so that you can forget about it. This is the "fail safe" way of working. If you "fail" to pay attention, you and your equipment will still be "safe."

Whenever possible, turn off the power to the equipment that you're working with. As you work inside the equipment, you can easily slip with a metal tool and give yourself a shock or cause a short circuit. The metal legs (leads) on an IC are very close together, and it's easy to create a short circuit between two of the leads. Sooner or later you'll make a mistake, but if the power is turned off, you won't cause any shorts.

Be sure to turn off the power before you unplug cable connectors or remove circuit boards. Never unplug or remove any part unless the equipment is turned off. Turn the equipment on only when you have to make measurements that require it to be operating (a "hot test"). When the measurements are finished, shut off the equipment again before you continue working. You can still measure resistance and make other tests ("cold tests").

As we said earlier, any time you open up a piece of equipment, you're taking a chance that you'll accidentally damage some parts. As you remove parts of the case, and undo connectors and circuit boards, you'll put unusual strains on the parts. If you work slowly and carefully, you can keep these strains to a minimum. For example, when you remove a circuit board from an edge-card connector, spread the pulling force over as much of the board as possible. Special circuit-board pullers are available. When you unplug a cable connector, pull on the connector, not on the cable. If you have to pull or pry too hard when removing a part, you're probably doing something wrong. Remember that each piece of microcomputer equipment has been designed to be repaired. Usually the designers have figured out a fairly easy way to remove the part that you want to work with.

Be especially careful as you remove tiny parts, including screws and spring clips. It is very easy for one of these parts to jump out of your grasp and disappear into the bottom of your computer or printer. If this happens and the power is on, shut off the power immediately, and retrieve the part. Many small parts are made of metal and can easily cause short circuits. If you're removing a small screw that could fall into the equipment, find a way to catch the part if it should slip loose. Put a paper towel under the screw, or hold the screw head with a piece of masking tape, or use a screwdriver that has a gripping mechanism. *Don't use a magnetic-tip screwdriver.*

Find a safe place to put parts as you remove them. Don't use a shallow box or tray. It's easy to hit the edge of one of these boxes in such a way that it throws your parts all over the room. The plastic film canisters that 35-mm film comes in are good containers for small parts. Ask for these at your local photo store. You can also store parts in an egg carton, or in a clean coffee can with a plastic lid.

Documentation and Advice

It is difficult to repair any piece of complicated equipment without some service literature. It is possible to repair computer equipment without the service manual, but it can be very time-consuming. A good manual will often point directly to the cause of a problem, saving you hours of troubleshooting.

As we said earlier, many computer service problems have simple causes—cables with broken wires, corroded connectors, etc. This book should help you deal with many of these simple problems. But what if the problem is more complicated? You'll need answers to specific questions: "How is this circuit supposed to work?", "How are the components laid out?", "Where are the test points?", and "What signals should I find at those points?" This is when a good manual can be very helpful.

Fortunately, others also need this information. Most computer manufacturers know they can expect a certain percentage of breakdowns in their equipment. The manufacturers must have a way of telling their own engineers and service people how to repair the equipment. Most manufacturers have learned that the best course is to document their equipment as completely as possible. To this end, many companies put out at least two kinds of documentation on every major piece of equipment.

Every purchaser receives a copy of the "User's Manual." This manual tells you how to set the unit up and get it running. If you're lucky, the appendix at the back of the manual will include some information which can be helpful in servicing. For example, you may find diagrams of the cable connectors describing the signals on each pin. The "Service Manual" or "Shop Manual" tells you how to troubleshoot and repair a particular piece of equipment. A really good service manual will include an extensive troubleshooting chart, a section on parts identification, a set of circuit diagrams, a list of adjustment procedures, and a number of tests to help you localize a particular problem.

The Shop Manual may also include a "Theory of Operation" section, which explains how the equipment is supposed to work. Usually, this section describes each major circuit or mechanism. This information is helpful in troubleshooting once you've localized the problem to a particular area of the equipment. Sometimes, the "Theory of Operation" discussion and the "Service Manual" documentation are printed as two separate manuals.

Whether you're a "home technician" or a pro, you should have a service manual for each major piece of equipment you own or expect to repair. If you're lucky, you'll be able to get the same documentation used by the manufacturer's own repairmen. On this point, you'll find a big variation from one manufacturer to the next. Some manufacturers try to control the market for servicing. They want to be sure all of the servicing business goes to their dealers, so they make it hard for "outsiders" to get manuals. This short-sighted policy is more common among the large manufacturers of microcomputers.

Apple Computer is probably the most militant—they won't release *any* servicing information to outsiders. In fact, they don't even release much information to their own people. Bob Cahill worked for several years for an Apple dealer, and he never saw any Apple schematics. Apple expected the technicians to handle all problems using diagnostic software and a "board-swapping" strategy. In spite of this policy, it is possible to get some information on Apple IIs and Macs from other sources. See the appendixes given in the back of this book.

IBM will gladly sell you the same manuals used by their own service people, but these books are expensive. The servicing information on the IBM PC, XT, and AT is included in two volumes, the "Hardware Maintenance Service" manual and the "Hardware Maintenance Reference" manual. At $195 and $150, these books are a bit expensive for the average user, but at least IBM makes them available. They are good books, and they're probably worth the investment for a dealer or someone setting up a repair shop.

Tandy Corporation (Radio Shack) puts out good technical references and service manuals at reasonable prices.

The smaller companies can't afford to have large networks of dealers and repair shops. As a result, they are a lot more open and helpful with service information. The shop manual for a computer might cost $50.00 or more, while the manual on a small dot-matrix printer might cost about $30.00.

The quality of these manuals varies. If you're working on a national name-brand product, the manual is usually very good. If you're repairing an add-on circuit board, the "manual" might be just a few mimeographed pages, covered with cryptic notes. Some of the manuals for Japanese products have been translated into "near-English" and can be hard to follow. If a product has just been placed on the market, you may discover that the manufacturer hasn't produced a manual yet.

Frequently, the documentation describes only an early version of a product. Many manufacturers make constant changes and updates in their products. Don't be surprised if the documentation is inaccurate for certain parts of the equipment. The manufacturers keep their service technicians up to date by sending out "Engineering Change Orders" (ECOs). Sometimes, you can arrange to receive these ECOs directly.

There is one other source of servicing information on computer equipment. Howard W. Sams & Company, the publisher of this book, puts out a complete line of service brochures called *COMPUTER-FACTS™*. Many of the most common computers, printers, disk drives, and monitors are included (see Appendix G). It is hard not to be biased, but we do feel that the COMPUTERFACTS packages are very complete and well done. The COMPUTERFACTS packages range in price from $20.00 to $30.00.

At first, you may be reluctant to spend $100 or more to assemble a set of manuals for your equipment. Those $30.00 and $40.00 manuals can certainly add up, but the expense seems less important when you compare it to the cost of commercial servicing. With the right information, you may be able to repair a problem very quickly by yourself, and this can pay for the cost of the manual(s).

Once you have an equipment breakdown, you won't want to wait two weeks for a manual to arrive. You should collect your manuals now, *before* you have problems. Don't put this off—it may be difficult or impossible to get manuals when your equipment is older. Write to the service department of the manufacturer for each piece of equipment you have, and ask what documentation is available. You should be able to find the manufacturer's address on a label somewhere on the equipment. If not, look up the office/factory address at your local library.

IC Identification Guides

You will need a way of identifying *integrated circuits* (ICs). Each IC is usually marked with the manufacturer's symbol, an identification number, and date code, and you'll need a way of deciphering these markings. Before you start working with an IC, however, you should know what the IC is supposed to do and what kind of signal to expect on each pin of the IC. If you're lucky, you'll be able to find a "truth table" for the IC. The truth table shows what kind of outputs to expect when different inputs are sent to the IC. For each pin, the table shows whether you should expect the signal to be "high," "low," or "pulsing."

How can you get this information? A list of manufacturers' symbols and logos is given in the appendices. This should help you to identify the manufacturer of an IC. If you have a COMPUTER-FACTS package for your equipment, it will give you some additional information on the ICs. For each important IC, the package usually includes a pin diagram and a truth table.

You can find the most complete information on ICs in a large master reference book, like the *IC Master*. These references contain the descriptions and pin-outs for most of the common ICs. The books are updated every year. You may be able to find a copy in a university library, or in the public library in a good-sized city. If you have a friend who is an engineer, he or she may be able to get you an outdated copy (just the newest ICs will be missing).

IC manufacturers send out data sheets which describe each of the ICs they produce. The very large manufacturers collect these data sheets into books. Many of the ICs in your equipment will be members of the 7400-series, with numbers like "74LS74," "74S00," etc. Many different manufacturers make these parts, so it is fairly easy to find information on members of the 7400-series. The *TTL Data Book* by Texas Instruments Incorporated lists the pin-out diagrams, truth tables, and other data for most of the 7400-series devices. The book is available in hardcover for $14.95 from Jameco

Electronics. The Jameco catalog also gives pin-out diagrams for many common 7400-series ICs.

Not all ICs are members of the 7400 series, however. *Linear* ICs, which include amplifiers, comparators, timers, and phase-locked loops, can be identified by a two-letter code, followed by a three- or four-digit number (for example, LM301N, LM741N). *Voltage-regulator* ICs use the same numbering system (for example, LM723CN). The Jameco catalog lists many of the common linear ICs, and also lists the purpose of each IC. Jameco also sells data books from National Semiconductor, Intel, and other manufacturers, which cover other types of ICs. Other data books are available direct from the manufacturers.

Radio Shack publishes a "Semiconductor Reference Guide" that lists a few of the most common ICs. For these ICs, the booklet shows pin diagrams and truth tables, and explains how the unit works. The booklet costs about $4.00.

You may not be able to identify all of the ICs in your equipment with these resources. Some ICs are made to order just for the computer manufacturer. You'll have to go directly to the manufacturer for information on these "custom" or "proprietary" ICs. Some manufacturers may be reluctant to give you much information on these parts.

As we said, it's wise to collect the information you need *before* you have a problem. Start by looking over your equipment, and making a note of the identification number of each unusual IC. (For this purpose, we'll say that an IC is "unusual" if it is not a member of the 7400 series.) Go through your references and identify as many of the ICs as you can. Make a note of any ICs that you can't identify. Using Appendix B, check the symbol on each of these ICs to identify the manufacturer. Next, write to the sales department at each manufacturer, and ask for a data sheet for each of your "mystery" ICs. Then, if a problem does occur, you'll have information on each IC in your equipment.

Advice via Telephone

Many manufacturers have a "technical support" line, often with a toll-free 800 number. You can check for this by calling long-distance information (1-800-555-1212). Sometimes, a company will have more than one "800" number, so be sure you've been given the right one.

It can be difficult to use the "tech support" lines. To begin with, the toll-free numbers are usually busy.

Many tech support offices will also have a second line, a non-800 number. Sometimes you can avoid a long delay by calling this second number. When you use an "800" number, expect to wait for half an hour or more once you get past the switchboard. You will spend this time listening to a recorded voice telling you how they will get to your call "any minute now." Sometimes we suspect that the manufacturers have included these long delays on purpose, hoping that many callers will become impatient and hang up.

Once your call is finally answered, however, you may either get some useful help or none at all. If a big computer manufacturer (such as Apple Computer) prefers that you have your equipment serviced by one of its dealers, you probably won't get any help at all. If you want to repair a piece of equipment that was made by a smaller company, the manufacturer may not have a large service network. But, when you call a smaller company, the technician you reach may be very helpful.

You can encounter a nasty situation when it is not clear which part of a mixed system is causing a problem. For example, let's say that your printer is not operating properly. When you contact the computer manufacturer, the technician says, "There's nothing wrong with our computer. The printer must be faulty." But, the printer manufacturer says, "The printer is fine. Your problem is caused by the computer." To deal with a "run around" like this, you will have to be very persistent.

Usually, the advice you receive from one of the "technical support" lines is free. However, some manufacturers do charge for this service. Technicians at some companies may not talk to you unless you have a service contract, and others will "start the clock" when you begin talking and charge by the minute, or by the fraction of an hour.

How do you contact a manufacturer to find out about these options? Start by checking the label on the back or bottom of your equipment. This will usually list the manufacturer's name and address. If the label just lists the company's name and a city, this address is good enough. Write a letter, addressed to "Service Department," and ask about documentation on your equipment and the availability of a "Technical Assistance" phone line. Most large libraries include industrial indexes that will allow you to track down almost any company or trade name.

There is usually no point is asking for advice from the technicians at your local dealer's shop. These folks usually have no interest in talking with "outsiders." They would prefer to service your equipment themselves.

User's Groups

Computer user's clubs are good sources of information. By going to a meeting, you can communicate in person. With a modem, you can communicate over the telephone lines, using a computerized "bulletin board." Whatever the problem you're facing, there's a good chance that one of the club members has dealt with it before. A user's group is a great source of "inside" information and straight answers. This is where you hear things that nobody can or will talk about publicly, such as:

> Brand X computers keep breaking down because the power supply is too small.

> Did you know you can refill the cartridges on your laser printer?

> Can you really use a hole punch to make a single-sided floppy disk into a double-sided one?

Books

Books can be among your most cost-effective servicing "tools." A few dollars spent on the right book can save you hundreds of dollars, or open up whole new fields of knowledge. Always be on the lookout for good books.

Books on microcomputer servicing fall into three categories. First are the general introductory books on servicing. We hope this book does a good job in this category.

Next are the books on servicing specific computers or peripherals. If you have a widely used brand of equipment, you should be able to find a detailed book on your unit. For example, if you have an IBM PC, you might be interested in the *IBM PC Troubleshooting & Repair Guide* (Cat. No. 22358) by Robert C. Brenner (published by Howard W. Sams & Company). Sams also publishes many other books on most of the common brands of microcomputer equipment. Books of this type are especially useful because they give *specific* information on the computer or peripheral; for example, indicating the ICs by part number and location. If a COMPUTERFACTS package has been published on your particular piece of equipment, and you can find a book specifically on that equipment, you'll have all the information you'll need.

The third category includes books that are directed toward computer users, rather than repairmen. These books tend to have more emphasis placed on the software. However, they sometimes include technical details which can be helpful to the technician. For example, a good book on a particular computer might include a listing of the addresses of the output ports. You might be able to use these addresses to write a BASIC program to use in testing the ports.

To find out what books are available, contact the larger technical-book publishers. Send a postcard to each publisher and ask for their latest catalog.

Service Records

This is one type of "documentation" that you can create yourself. It is good practice to keep a record of the service history for each microcomputer or peripheral. This type of record is helpful when you are planning routine maintenance. For example, with a good service record, you will know exactly when you last cleaned the heads on a floppy disk drive.

Some computer malfunctions develop gradually, over a long period of time. If you experience a "soft" error, but the system quickly returns to normal, you tend to forget the incident. However, let's say that you write down each "soft" error in the service record. In the future, you can look up this detailed information. You may discover that a number of "soft" errors form a recognizable pattern. In a case like this, the service record can be a valuable aid to troubleshooting.

Voltohmmilliammeters

The voltohmmilliammeter (VOM) will probably be your most useful troubleshooting tool. This analog meter can measure voltage, current, and resistance, and can test for continuity. Some of the better meters also have built-in circuits to test capacitors and transistors. The conventional VOM uses a meter to read out the test results. A digital voltmeter (DVM) performs the same functions, but it produces a digital display. DVMs are ranked by the number of digits they display. A "$3\frac{1}{2}$ digit" DVM will indicate three numbers for each reading. The "half digit" is reserved for characters like "+1" or "−1." The more sophisticated meters automatically choose the correct voltage or resistance range. This feature is called "autoranging."

All but the cheapest VOMs will be suitable for work on microcomputers, although the more expensive models are more accurate and easier to use. In many troubleshooting situations, you will want to know whether a certain point in a circuit is active. To put it another way, you will want to know whether the circuit is "dead" or "alive." In many cases, you will be less concerned with the exact voltage levels. In these situations, even an inexpensive meter is useful.

Each meter has an "impedance rating" which indicates how much the meter will "load" (interfere with) a circuit while you are taking a measurement. The higher the impedance rating, the less the meter will interfere with the circuit under test. An impedance rating of 20,000 ohms-per-volt is probably a lower limit for our purposes. The old reliable "vacuum-tube voltmeter" (VTVM) is still popular because it has a high impedance rating. A simple VOM can cost as little as $25.00. A good DVM may cost $60.00 or more.

We'll assume that all of our readers know how to take voltage readings with a voltmeter. This kind of information is available in any basic electronics book. In order for you to take voltage readings, the circuits being tested must be energized. *Be careful!*

Just as useful is the VOM's ability to check for continuity. When the meter is set to measure resistance (ohms), a small internal battery is switched into the meter circuit. When the meter's two test leads are shorted together, current flows out of the battery, through the shorted leads, through the meter, and back to the battery. A complete circuit results in a meter reading of zero resistance. If the current is somehow prevented from getting from one lead to the other, and the circuit is broken, the meter will show infinite resistance. Always be sure that all power is turned off when you use a meter to check for resistance or continuity. If the meter is set to read resistance, and you touch the test leads to two points having a voltage potential, the meter may be damaged. Once you are finished with your tests, set the selector switch on the meter to a position other than "OHMS." If you leave the selector switch in the "OHMS" position, the battery in the meter may run down.

Most VOMs can also test for small amounts of current, measured in milliamperes. In order to do this, the meter must be connected in-line with the other parts, and it becomes part of the circuit. VOMs can only measure very small currents. A VOM can test the small signal currents going through ICs and small transistors, but not the currents through parts which handle larger amounts of power. When you have finished testing for current, set the selector switch in the VOM to a different position. If a meter is set to test for current, and you connect the meter to a high voltage, the meter may be damaged.

Digital Logic Probes

A voltmeter can measure voltages that change relatively slowly, but it can't tell you much about the rapidly changing levels in a digital circuit. A digital logic probe can give you more information on the signals flowing through these circuits. The simplest probes include two or three indicator LEDs. These indicators light in various combinations to indicate whether the test point is "high," "low," or "pulsing." Better probes also indicate if the voltage at the test point is "floating" in the range between "high" and "low." The more expensive the probe, the higher the frequency of the signals it can test. Radio Shack sells a simple digital logic probe for about $20.00 (Fig. 6-1).

Logic Pulsers

Sometimes, you'll want a convenient way of supplying test signals to a circuit. One way to do this is with a logic pulser. You may set the pulser to generate either a constant "high" or a "low," or a series of pulses. In troubleshooting, you may use the pulser to inject signals at the inputs of a device, and, then, read the resulting pulses at the outputs with the logic probe.

A logic pulser has enough power to override any normal signal which may be on the line at the time you make the test. The pulser will not be able to overpower

Fig. 6-1. Digital logic probe. *(Courtesy Radio Shack, A Div. of Tandy Corp.)*

some fault conditions, however. For example, if a line is shorted directly to ground, the logic pulser won't be able to pull it "high."

Radio Shack sells a simple pulser for about $20.00. Models with more features may cost $60.00 or more. Like the logic probe, the pulser has two power leads which must be connected to a source of 5-V DC.

Current Tracers

The current tracer or "short detector" can detect the tiny amounts of current that pass through a circuit-board trace, without making direct contact with the trace itself. The tracer actually senses the changing magnetic field created by changes in the passing current. Some tracers flash an LED to indicate the presence of current, while other models turn on a buzzer. On tracers of the second type, the sound from the buzzer becomes louder as the tracer approaches the short circuit.

The current tracer can only detect a current when the current is changing rapidly. If the point being tested does not normally carry a changing current, you will have to inject a string of pulses with a logic pulser. The current tracer is very useful in cases where an IC or a trace has shorted to the +5-V DC source or to ground. The tracer usually operates on +5-V DC taken directly from the circuit under test. OK Electronics sells a simple current tracer for about $50.00.

Electronic Thermometers

When ICs and transistors fail, they often become unusually hot. Professionals sometimes use electronic thermometers to detect parts which have failed. A sensitive digital thermometer can cost $200. A special thermometer probe is available for some DVMs. This type of probe reads a temperature, and presents the result as a voltage on the DVM's scale.

For many types of troubleshooting, you don't really need to know the precise temperature of a part. Instead, you want to know which parts are relatively hot, when compared with the other components. "Thermoprobe®" by Metrifast is an inexpensive tool which can indicate relative temperature.

To use the Thermoprobe, unscrew the protective cap and touch the tip of the instrument to the part you wish to test. The Thermoprobe does not produce temperature readings in degrees. Instead, the indicator needle shows whether the part is unusually hot or cold. Projector Belt Co. sells the Thermoprobe for about $15.00.

Transistor Testers

You can make some simple tests on transistors using just a VOM. We will discuss this in detail in Chapter 7. However, you can test transistors much more easily using a special "transistor tester." Many different types are available. Radio Shack sells a simple unit for about $15.00. This type of tester allows you to make an in-circuit test, without removing the transistor from the circuit board. The tester indicates whether the transistor is working, and it also allows you to measure the "gain" or output of the part.

Transistors have three connecting leads called the "emitter," "base," and "collector." To use the simpler testers, you must know which of the three transistor leads handles each of these jobs. Sometimes this is indicated on the circuit board, but often it is not. The better transistor testers determine this automatically. A tester of this type will cost $100 or more. The best testers also allow you to check many of the operating characteristics of the transistor—gain, leakage current, and so on.

Oscilloscopes

An oscillopscope or "scope" can give you a "picture" of a changing electronic signal. Fig. 6-2 shows a typical "scope." The scope shows the changing value of a signal over a certain time period. When the signal has a higher voltage, the display line moves upward on the screen. A lower signal voltage moves the line down. The display moves from left to right to show the passage of time.

An oscilloscope is helpful because it can clearly show the digital "highs" and "lows." The scope is also very helpful for checking the "shape" of an electronic signal. If you know what kind of signal to expect, and the scope shows you a different signal, you know something is wrong. The scope may be used to check the operating characteristics of parts like transistors and capacitors. You can also use a scope to take voltage measurements, although this is easier with a VOM. Oscilloscopes have been used for many years to troubleshoot power supplies, amplifiers, and other analog devices.

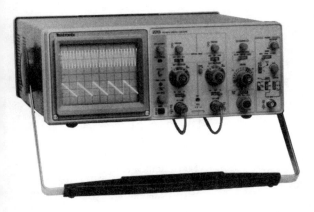

Fig. 6-2. A dual-trace oscilloscope.
(Courtesy Tektronix, Inc.)

1 VOLT/DIV   0.5 VOLT/DIV

(A) Vertical sensitivity adjustment.

1 SEC/DIV   2 SEC/DIV

(B) Horizontal sweep speed.

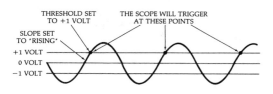

(C) Trigger.

Some "dual trace" scopes can display two signals at once. This lets you check the timing relationships of two related signals. The better the scope, the higher the frequency of the signals it can display. In the alignment procedure for floppy disk drives, some of the steps require a high-speed dual-trace scope, with a frequency response of 35 MHz. This type of scope costs about $600. It is an expensive piece of professional test equipment, and you probably won't have one lying around. You may, however, be able to borrow a sophisticated scope when your floppy disk drives need alignment. For most other digital servicing, a medium-priced scope will be fine. A good 10-MHz scope will cost about $200.

Using an Oscilloscope

As a quick review, we will mention some of the important controls on a typical scope. Refer to Fig. 6-3.

The "vertical" adjustment changes the voltage range displayed on the scope. The operator can set this so each vertical division on the display represents a given voltage (Fig. 6-3A).

The "sweep" or horizontal adjustment allows the operator to set the time period that will be represented by one sweep of the display. The time period is chosen so the scope can catch one or more cycles of the signal being displayed. This is shown in Fig. 6-3B.

The "trigger" adjustments let the operator choose the point on the changing signal where the scope will begin the display. The controls normally allow the operator to set the slope (rising or falling) and threshold for the trigger. In Fig. 6-3C, the scope is set to

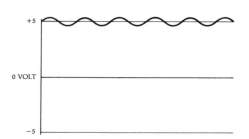

(D) DC coupling.

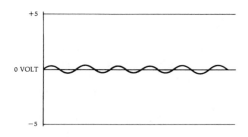

(E) AC coupling.

Fig. 6-3. Adjusting oscilloscope.

detect a threshold of +1 volt, on a rising signal. A scope can be set to trigger on a part of the signal being displayed (internal) or on part of a separate signal that is related to the signal being displayed (external).

When "DC" input coupling is used, the scope displays the complete signal, including the varying AC component, plus any DC voltage which may be present (Fig. 6-3D). When "AC" coupling is selected, only the varying AC component of the signal is displayed, as shown in Fig. 6-3E.

Many sophisticated scopes can display two signals at once, using two separate channels in the circuitry. In the disk-drive alignment process, it is necessary to invert the signal from one channel, and then add the two together. The resulting signal shows the differences between the two signals.

For more detailed information on scopes, you may want to refer to a book like *Know Your Oscilloscope, Fourth Edition*, by Robert G. Middleton. The book is available in paperback (Cat. No. 21742) from Howard W. Sams & Company, 4300 W. 62nd Street, Indianapolis, Indiana, 46268.

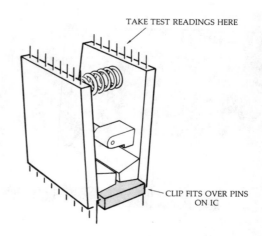

TAKE TEST READINGS HERE

CLIP FITS OVER PINS ON IC

Fig. 6-4. IC test clip.

IC Test Clips

As you work with digital equipment, you'll frequently have to take readings at the pins of various ICs. These pins are often difficult to reach. One solution is to use an IC test clip, as shown in Fig. 6-4. The test clip is designed to fit over the IC pins. You can then make your test connections easily at the top of the clip. A test clip of this type allows you to make an in-circuit test of an IC. Standard IC test clips (also called "DIP clips") come in sizes to fit 14-, 16-, 20-, and 40-pin ICs. The 16-pin size also fits 14-pin ICs in many situations. The smaller clips cost about $6.00 each; clips for the larger ICs are more expensive.

Breakout Box

This tool is used to diagnose problems in an RS-232C "serial"-type interface. The breakout box is designed to be connected in-line with the serial cable, so that all of the cable signals flow through the box. LED indicators show the state of each of the signal lines. By watching the indicators, the technician can determine whether the interface is working correctly. Some breakout boxes also include sockets for "jumper" wires. By inserting jumpers, the technician can reroute some of the signals.

The least expensive breakout boxes are powered by the RS-232C lines, and cost about $30.00. More expensive models may have separate power supplies, and may cost $100 or more.

DC Power Supply

In your service work, you will sometimes want to provide power to parts of a circuit board, without using the computer's main power supply. A small DC power supply will be helpful. The supply should be able to produce one or two amperes of current at +5-V DC, since this is the type of power used by most ICs. Some circuits also use other DC values, including +12-V DC and −12-V DC. If the power supply can produce these outputs as well, all the better. All of the outputs should be regulated so that the output voltage doesn't change as the power supply is loaded. A supplier, such as Jameco Electronics, sometimes sells small DC power supplies of this type for as little as $25.00.

Isolation Transformers

In Chapter 2, we explained the special problems presented by "hot chassis" equipment. To protect yourself from possible problems of this type, we recommend that you use an "isolation transformer." B&K Precision sells a small isolation transformer for about $60.00.

Variable Transformers (Variacs)

This tool is most useful when working on monitors. Many monitors include self-protective circuits which turn off the unit when a short circuit develops, or when the voltage to the picture tube becomes too high. The power supplies in some microcomputers have similar circuitry. When a customer brings you a monitor for servicing, the protective circuits may have prevented the set from operating. Without some help, you will not be able to operate the unit and find the cause of the problem.

A variable transformer allows you to reduce the input voltage to the monitor. Normally, the monitor operates on 120-V AC. Using a variable transformer, you can gradually reduce this to 60-V AC or less. At some point, the protective circuits will allow the monitor to operate, and you will be able to make your tests. Sometimes, the variable transformer also serves as an "isolation transformer." B&K Precision sells a combination variable transformer/isolation transformer for about $165.

Soldering Irons

ICs and transistors can easily be destroyed by overheating. For this reason, you must choose carefully when you select a soldering iron for use with digital circuits. The iron should deliver a limited amount of heat, quickly and efficiently. Even if an iron is underpowered, or the tip of the iron is dirty, the iron will still produce enough heat to melt solder. However, since the underpowered iron takes a long time to get up to temperature, the heat may have time to reach the IC and cause some damage. On the other hand, don't use a very high-powered iron, because it can easily overheat an IC or other part. If you overheat a trace on a circuit board, the heat can cause the trace to lift from the board.

Use a low-powered iron, with a rating of about 30 watts. An iron with a small, pointed tip is best for this type of work. Be sure to buy a grounded-tip iron with a three-prong plug on the cord. Because the soldering tip is grounded, it is safe to use this type of iron when working with static-sensitive CMOS components. Controlled-temperature irons are convenient because they can be set to reach and hold a particular temperature. A simple "pencil-type" iron costs about $5.00, and usually does not have a grounded tip, so

avoid this type. A heavy-duty controlled-temperature iron might cost $50.00 or more. This is a good value, since you will be using the soldering iron constantly.

Warning! If you work with a grounded-tip iron, be very careful not to touch any source of high voltage. Remember to turn off the equipment before you make any solder repairs.

A battery-powered iron is convenient to use for small jobs, and it removes all worries about static and grounding. A good battery-powered iron costs about $40.00. Be sure the battery is fully charged before you begin working.

Sponges

This is a soldering accessory that is never overlooked by the experienced technician. Always keep a damp sponge near your soldering station, and wipe the tip of the hot iron frequently while you're soldering. This will keep the tip clean and shiny for maximum heat transfer. Almost any type of sponge will work. Some technicians cut slits in the top of the sponge, and draw the hot tip through the slits.

Soldering Iron Holders

If you have an iron with no switch, it will remain hot all the time it is plugged in, so you'll need a safe place to set it down. We recommend that you use a sturdy wire holder with a heavy metal base. The holder is often formed into a spiral, with lots of air space to radiate the heat from the iron. The heavy base makes it harder to tip the unit over. Radio Shack sells this type of holder for about $5.00.

Solder

Use a good grade of solder. Solder is rated by the proportion of lead to tin. For example, "60/40" solder is 60% tin and 40% lead. Solder with a high tin content is best for electronics work. Use a solder with a small diameter—about 0.040 inch.

Most solder is manufactured with a hollow center which contains "flux." As the solder melts, the flux cleans the parts and prevents oxidation, helping to ensure a good connection. Always use rosin-core solder for electronics work—NEVER use the acid-core type! The acid flux can cause corrosion on electrical parts.

Heat Sinks

This handy tool keeps parts from overheating as you solder them. The typical heat sink is simply a pair of spring-loaded fingers that you can clip onto a wire lead, as shown in Fig. 6-5. In this illustration, we have shown someone soldering a transistor into place. Normally, heat from the soldering iron could travel up the leg of the transistor and damage the part. In our illustration, the heat sink is clamped onto the leg, so it diverts most of the heat. You can buy a set of heat sinks for less than $3.00.

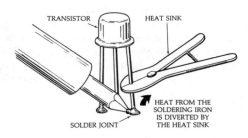

Fig. 6-5. Using a heat sink.

You may also use other metal tools as heat sinks. Technicians have used clamping tweezers, medical forceps, and even paper clips.

Solder Removal Tools

From time to time, you will want to remove parts from the circuit board, and this means you will have to unsolder some connections. You'll need a convenient way of melting and removing solder. The least expensive tool for this purpose is a roll of braided solder-wicking wire. Touch the braid to the soldered joint, heat it with a soldering iron, and the braid should "soak up" the melted solder. Some brands are impregnated with flux to soak up solder more easily. A roll of wicking braid costs about $1.00.

You may also select one of the vacuum-powered solder-removal devices. The least expensive device is a simple air bulb. Squeeze the bulb and hold the tip against the solder joint. Heat the solder, then release the bulb, and the excess solder will be sucked into the bulb. These bulbs are available for less than $3.00. For about $8.00, you can buy a soldering iron with an attached vacuum bulb.

Other vacuum devices are more complicated. Some kinds use a spring-loaded mechanism, as shown in Fig. 6-6. To use this device, cock the loading spring, then hold the tip of the vacuum pump against the solder joint. When the solder melts, press the trigger button and release the spring. This creates a powerful vacuum action, and pulls the solder up into the pump. Some pumps can generate a static charge—be sure to get an "antistatic" type. A vacuum pump of this type will cost about $12.00.

Fig. 6-6. Static-free desolder pump.
(Courtesy Ungar Div., Eldon Inds., Inc.)

After you remove the solder, reset the pump by cocking the loading spring again. As you do this, some bits of cooled solder may be forced out of the tip of the pump. Don't let these solder bits fall into your equipment—they are conductive, and can cause short circuits.

IC Removers and Inserters

Integrated circuits are delicate, so you must handle them carefully during removal and insertion. It is easy to remove and replace ICs if they're mounted in sockets. If you work carefully, you can pry up the ICs using a small screwdriver. The inexpensive removal tool shown in Fig. 6-7 makes the job easier. Fit the tips of the tool under the ends of the IC, and lift the IC out of the socket.

Fig. 6-7. IC removal tool.
(Courtesy Radio Shack, a Div. of Tandy Corp.)

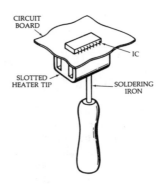

Fig. 6-9. IC heater tip.

It is possible to fit ICs into sockets without special tools, but the tool shown in Fig. 6-8 makes the job easier. A slot on the side of the tool allows you to align any bent legs on the IC. Use the bottom of the tool to grip the IC and press it into place. This tool is available from Radio Shack for about $7.00.

It is much harder to remove ICs if they are soldered in place. If the IC is a common 7400-series part, it may be easiest to cut the leads on the part, and then clean out the mounting holes on the circuit board with a desoldering device. Next, install a socket and then install a new IC.

There are ways of removing an IC without destroying the part. One sophisticated tool consists of a set of spring-loaded pliers that fit under the pins of an IC. When the pliers are closed, they exert an upward pressure on the IC. As you heat the other side of the circuit board and release the solder, the pliers pull the IC up and away from the board.

How do you release all of the IC pins at once, without overheating the part? An accessory is available for soldering irons that consists of a slotted bar, cut to fit over the IC pins (Fig. 6-9). When this tool is heated, all of the IC pins are released at the same moment. If you use a tool of this type, be very careful to use an absolute minimum of heat.

Pencil Eraser

This is a rather humble tool, yet you'll find it can be very handy. Many hardware problems are caused by corroded connectors. A layer of corrosion can act as an intermittent switch, rapidly making and breaking a connection. The microcomputer equipment can interpret this as a digital signal. If the connector is very corroded, the signal may be cut off entirely. Gold-plated contacts are supposedly immune to this, because gold does not corrode. However, some manufacturers use an alloy with such a low percentage of gold that even those contacts corrode.

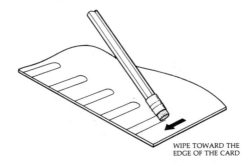

Fig. 6-10. Pencil eraser used to clean contacts.

Fig. 6-10 shows how to use an eraser to clean the contacts on the edge of a circut board. A pink pencil eraser is just abrasive enough to clear away the corrosion without wearing through the plating on the contacts. The layer of plating is very thin, so rub as little as possible. Always move the eraser toward the outer edge of the card—if you rub in the other direction, you may lift some of the contacts. Be sure to blow away the

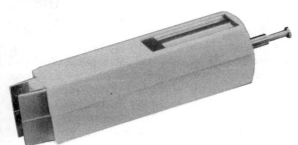

Fig. 6-8. IC Installation tool.
(Courtesy Radio Shack, a Div. of Tandy Corp.)

rubber "crumbs" when you're through. Rubber erasers become stiff after a while, so be sure you're using a fresh eraser.

Wire Strippers

Before you can make connections with a piece of wire, you must "strip" away the plastic insulation. Fig. 6-11 shows three common types of wire strippers. The scissors type (Fig. 6-11A) is the least expensive, but this type can nick the wire as it strips away the insulation. The nick creates a weak spot and allows the wire to break later.

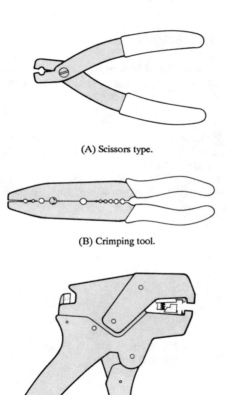

(A) Scissors type.

(B) Crimping tool.

(C) Automatic stripper.

Fig. 6-11. Wire strippers.

The crimping tool (Fig. 6-11B) and the automatic stripper (Fig. 6-11C) have slots of different sizes to accept different gauges of wire. These strippers are less likely to nick the wire. The automatic stripper does the job in one step. To use this tool, place the end of the wire in the jaws of the stripper and squeeze the handles. The tool will automatically strip off a length of insulation. You can buy an inexpensive stripper for about $2.50. An automatic stripper costs about $20.00.

Needle-Nose Pliers

"Needle-nose pliers" have very narrow tips. Thus, they are very useful for reaching into tight spaces inside the equipment. Many different styles are available. A good pair of needle-nose pliers will cost about $12.00.

Diagonal and Nippy Cutters

These tools are handy for cutting components free of a circuit board, or for disconnecting one or more legs of an IC. You may already be familiar with diagonal cutters (Fig. 6-12A). Inexpensive diagonal cutters cost about $4.00. More expensive cutters are made of better steel and will hold their cutting edges longer.

Diagonal cutters are useful for cutting leads on large parts, such as resistors and capacitors. However, you should not use diagonal cutters to cut the leads on ICs, transistors, and other delicate parts. When a lead is cut with diagonal cutters, the two pieces of the lead are forced away from the pliers. If you use diagonal cutters to disconnect a lead on a transistor, for example, the cutting action may force the lead up into the base of the transistor, and this may damage the part.

The cutting jaws on a pair of "nippy" cutters, however, are ground flat on one side (Fig. 6-12B). The special cutting blades force the leads in one direction, but not the other. Because the jaws are flat on one side, it is easy to cut very close to the body of an IC or transistor. Nippy cutters are available from Radio Shack or electronics stores for about $3.00.

Spring-Clip Pliers

Fig. 6-13 shows two kinds of spring retaining clips that you may find in microcomputer equipment. An

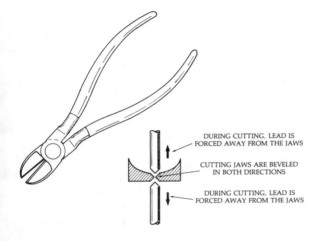

(A) Diagonal cutters.

DURING CUTTING, LEAD IS FORCED AWAY FROM THE JAWS

CUTTING JAWS ARE BEVELED IN BOTH DIRECTIONS

DURING CUTTING, LEAD IS FORCED AWAY FROM THE JAWS

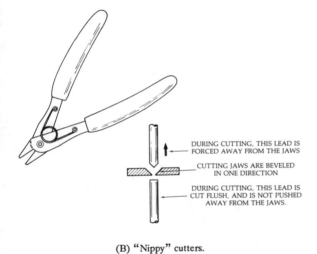

DURING CUTTING, THIS LEAD IS FORCED AWAY FROM THE JAWS

CUTTING JAWS ARE BEVELED IN ONE DIRECTION

DURING CUTTING, THIS LEAD IS CUT FLUSH, AND IS NOT PUSHED AWAY FROM THE JAWS.

(B) "Nippy" cutters.

Fig. 6-12. Diagonal and nippy cutters.

"inside retainer" clip is designed to fit into a slot in the inside diameter of a hole (Fig. 6-13A). An "outside retainer" clip is designed to fit into a slot around the outside of a shaft. It is not absolutely necessary to use special tools when working with these clips—you can usually work the clips free with either a small screwdriver or needle-nose pliers.

However, if you find yourself working on equipment which includes many spring clips, you may want to buy a pair of special pliers. To remove a spring clip, fit the tips of these pliers into the small holes at the ends of the clip. If the clip is an "inside retainer" type, move the ends of the clip closer together. This will make the clip a bit smaller in diameter and allow you to pull it out of the slot. On an "outside retainer" clip, make the diameter of the clip a bit larger to release the clip. Spring-clip pliers have interchangeable tips which allow you to work with many kinds of clips. An inexpensive set of spring-clip pliers will cost about $8.00.

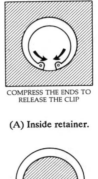

COMPRESS THE ENDS TO RELEASE THE CLIP

(A) Inside retainer.

SPREAD THE ENDS TO RELEASE THE CLIP

(B) Outside retainer.

Fig. 6-13. Spring clips.

Tweezers

When a tiny part disappears inside the equipment, it's time to reach for the tweezers. Self-clamping tweezers, shown in Fig. 6-14, are very handy. This type of tweezer includes a spring which holds the tips together. You can also use this tool to hold parts in place while you are soldering and you can use a self-clamping tweezer as a heat sink.

Remember that tweezers are made of metal and can conduct electricity. Be sure to turn off the power before you use tweezers inside a piece of equipment.

Fig. 6-14. Self-clamping tweezers.

Nut Drivers

When you repair printers and other electromechanical equipment, you'll have to remove and replace many various sized nuts and bolts. Professional technicians use *nut drivers* to speed up the work. To be completely prepared, you will need two separate sets of drivers—standard and metric—as you'll encounter metric parts in imported, foreign-made equipment. A good set of nut drivers costs about $20.00, and should never wear out. A cheap set costs about $8.00 or less.

Some inexpensive socket-wrench sets include a handle and a number of small $1/4$-inch-drive sockets. You can use various combinations of these parts instead of nut drivers.

Screwdrivers

Most screws can be turned easily if you use a screwdriver of the right size. Many people are in the habit of trying to turn a screw with whatever screwdriver that happens to be at hand. Screws are made in different sizes, and they're designed to be turned by screwdrivers of the corresponding sizes.

Conventional screwdrivers are designed with a straight flat area across the tip. The tip is meant to fit snugly into the slot in the screw, and actually touch the bottom of the slot. The edges of the tip should be sharp, to get a good grip on the screw slot. As you use a screwdriver, these edges will become worn. You should square the tip from time to time with a fine-tooth file.

In electronics work, you'll need three sizes of flat screwdrivers: medium (the flat on the tip is $1/4$-inch long), small ($3/16$-inch tip) and extra small ($1/8$-inch tip). Don't buy those 69-cent screwdrivers you find in discount bins—they will wear out quickly.

It is also helpful to have a small flat-tip screwdriver that is fitted with a mechanical gripping device, which is designed to hold small screws. Never use a screwdriver with a magnetic tip when working on computer equipment. You will also encounter two different types of screws with "X-shaped" slots in their heads. The true "Phillips-head" screwdriver has a blunt tip. The "Reed and Prince" screwdriver, used with a slightly different type of screw, has a sharply pointed tip. If you try to use a "Reed and Prince" screwdriver on a "Phillips head" screw, the screwdriver will not seat properly and will spin without turning the screw—possibly stripping the head of the screw or mangling the screwdriver tip. Most "cross-point" screwdrivers that are sold are actually a compromise between the two types, having a slightly blunted tip. You'll need medium, small, and extra-small sizes.

Finally, you may need a set of tiny screwdrivers to work on some mechanisms. A set of "jeweler's" screwdrivers with interchangeable blades will cost about $5.00. Be sure the set includes at least one blade that can handle small "cross-point" screws.

Special Wrenches

Fig. 6-15 shows three types of special screws, and the wrenches required to turn them. A set of Allen hex-key wrenches will cost about $3.00 at Radio Shack or a hardware store. You will probably need two separate sets of wrenches, for both metric and standard measurements.

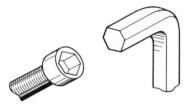

(A) Allen wrench.

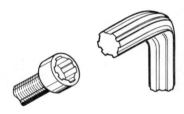

(B) Bristol wrench.

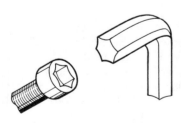

(C) Torx® wrench.

Fig. 6-15. Special wrenches.

Bristol or spline wrenches are less common. The newer Torx® screws are used to hold the outer cases together on some kinds of equipment. Bristol and Torx wrenches are available from Jensen Tools. Torx fasteners are becoming more popular because they can be handled easily by robots.

Cable-Tension Tester

Many printers use a wire cable to move the printhead carriage from side to side. A printer's manual will specify the required tension for this cable by saying that, when pulled to the side with a force of "x" ounces, the cable should deflect "y" inches. A cable-tension gauge will allow you to test this tension accurately.

You can make an approximate measurement using a postage meter. Form a piece of stiff wire into a hook and tape it to the top of the meter, as shown in Fig. 6-16. Run a string or wire between this hook and the cable you want to test. Push up on the base of the meter and you can read the tension, in ounces, on the front scale. A small postage meter costs about $10.00.

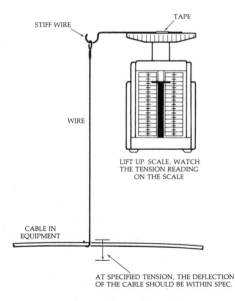

Fig. 6-16. Measuring cable tension with a postage scale.

Circuit-Board Vise

When you unsolder a part from a circuit board, you will need to hold the soldering iron with one hand, the desoldering device with the other hand, and the circuit board with the other hand. For those of us with only two hands, this maneuver is rather hard to do. It is much easier to use a circuit-board vise to hold the board.

One type of such a vise has two arms which grip the edges of the board. An adjustable head allows you to position the board at any angle. A good circuit-board vise can cost $20.00 to $80.00.

A "project holder" may also be used to hold circuit boards. This device is useful whenever you need a "third hand." It has two alligator clips which may be set in many different positions. A project holder from Radio Shack costs about $8.00.

Dental Mirrors

A small, adjustable dental mirror is helpful when you need to look into out-of-the-way places.

Heat Guns

You can often use temperature as a diagnostic tool. As part of this process, you'll sometimes want to heat a particular component. A home hair dryer works well if you use the lowest possible heat setting. You can create a narrow stream of hot air by holding a plastic funnel in front of the hair dryer. Never let a component get so hot that you cannot touch it. You can also use a heat gun to work with heat-shrink tubing.

Professional heat guns produce more heat. They also produce a more narrow stream of air than do home hair dryers.

Freeze Sprays

Freeze sprays can help you in locating "thermal intermittent" failures. The spray cools quickly as it is released from the spray can. Freeze sprays can generate a static charge, so buy a brand that is specified as "anti-static."

Alcohol

Use a good grade of isopropyl rubbing alcohol to clean the heads on a floppy disk drive. This is the main ingredient in most commercial head cleaners. Buy a solution that is about 90% alcohol. The remaining fraction is water, and you don't want this inside your equipment. Most drugstores sell this type of alcohol.

Platen Cleaners

Don't use alcohol to clean the rubber surface of the platen on your printer. The alcohol can damage the platen material and cause it to stiffen and crack. Instead, use a special chemical cleaner like "Fedron Platen Cleaner®" to clean the platen safely. You can order an 8-ounce spray bottle of Fedron for $7.95 from the Ames Supply Company, 169 Msgr. O'Brien Hwy., Cambridge, MA 02141. Another brand may be available from your local typewriter repair shop. Fedron has a nasty smell and, like other solvents, should be used in a room with good ventilation.

Spray Cleaners

Besides the key contacts on the keyboard, there are very few mechanical switches in most digital equipment. Most of the switches that are included are sealed, so the contacts can't get dirty. In the rare cases where you do want to clean switch contacts, be sure to use a nonresidue-type cleaner. Don't use TV-tuner type of cleaner; this type of cleaner contains abrasive particles that remain behind after the liquid has evaporated. Many brands of nonresidue cleaners are available. Check your local electronics store.

Epoxy and Thread-Lock Compounds

The mechanical equipment in a printer may produce a lot of vibration. This vibration can actually cause screws to work loose. Where this is a problem, the head of each screw will be locked in place with a drop of epoxy. When you disassemble equipment, you must sometimes break these epoxy seals. Be sure to replace the seals when you are through working on the equipment. Use only a small drop of epoxy on the side of the screw head. Don't cover the top of the screw with epoxy, or you won't be able to get the screw out again. Any type of epoxy will do.

Thread-lock compound is designed to be used down inside the screw hole. Place a *small* amount of the compound on the threads of the screw before you screw it in place. Just one small drop of thread-lock

compound is enough. Don't cover all of the threads on the screw, or you won't be able to unscrew the part.

Lubrication

Printers require regular lubrication. Usually, some points are lubricated with a light grease and others with a light oil. Both of these applications put special demands on lubricants. Most printer manufacturers specify and sell special grease and oil for their equipment. Buy the types specified by the manufacturers, even if you have to mail-order them directly from the manufacturer. As a general rule, use as little grease and oil as possible.

Special Tools for Surface Mount Devices

Some modern equipment includes special small parts called *surface mount devices* (or SMDs). The technology is called *surface mount technology* (SMT). We have shown some of these SMD parts in Fig. 6-17. As you can see, they are very small. The connecting leads are very close together and they are often positioned under the device. You will need some special equipment if you plan to work with these devices.

Fig. 6-17. SMD devices.

In production, many SMD devices are soldered in place using wave-solder equipment or infrared heaters.

The best way of soldering just a few SMD parts is to use a temperature-controlled hot-air gun. This is an expensive tool and a small service shop probably will not have one.

It is possible to solder and desolder SMD devices using hand tools. Because the parts are so small, you must work carefully to avoid overheating. To solder individual leads, use a low-powered pencil-type soldering iron with a conical tip. For simple SMDs with just two leads, you may use a soldering iron with special U-shaped tips (Fig. 6-18). The tips are interchangeable. Use a tip which matches the length of the part you wish to solder.

The larger SMD ICs are called *plastic leaded chip carriers* (PLCCs). The tool shown in Fig. 6-19 allows you to heat all four sides of the PLCC at once. This makes it much simpler to solder or desolder the part. Small diameter solder is best for this work—25 mils (0.025 inch) thickness is a good size.

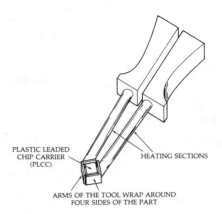

Fig. 6-19. Soldering iron for PLCC SMDs.

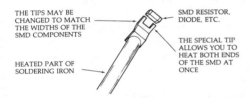

Fig. 6-18. Soldering iron for small SMD components.

Special conductive adhesives are available. Tiny dots of adhesive are placed in each lead on the SMD. The adhesive dots hold the SMD in place, and also complete the electrical connections. To release these adhesive joints, heat them.

You will also need a way of holding SMD parts in place while you make the solder connections. Use a temporary adhesive like "Stikki-Wax," "Fun-Tak," or "Plasti-Tak." These are available in department stores. Some parts are large enough to permit the use of ordinary masking tape.

Because SMD parts are so small, you will not be able to use ordinary test probes and DIP clips. Special probes and DIP clips for these devices are available from Pomona Electronics. One type of test clip is designed to fit around all four sides of a PLCC, and it gives you easy access to all of the leads.

Diagnostics

With the right software, a computer can often diagnose itself. Most computer manufacturers have written in-house diagnostics for the use of their production and service people. Unfortunately, the manufacturers often won't release this software to the public. You may be able to find similar software on the open market.

The IBM PC and other computers include diagnostic programs that run automatically each time you power up the equipment. This "POST" routine can help you localize the problem to a certain part of the computer system. For about $300, IBM will sell you a copy of their "Advanced Diagnostics." This package is more detailed than the POST which is supplied with the computers. It can often point out the individual component which has failed. Windsor Technologies sells a similar package for $295. Many computers are sold as being "IBM compatible," but IBM's diagnostics will often balk when they encounter non-IBM equipment.

A typical diagnostics package will include the following functions:

- ROM (read-only memory) test
- RAM (random-access memory) test
- disk-drive speed test
- other disk-drive alignment aids
- monitor tests

In addition, some packages include tests for specific interfaces, accessories, and modems. Diagnostic programs can vary widely in price and quality, so study them carefully before you buy.

Most diagnostic programs are loaded from a floppy disk drive. They will work only when the computer and disk drive are functional. However, they're no help when the computer is dead, or when the screen displays "garbage." To deal with this problem, Windsor Technologies produces a diagnostic program stored in ROM. The diagnostic program is available as soon as the computer is turned on, even if the floppy disk drive is not operating.

Floppy Disk Exerciser Programs

This group of programs may be included in a diagnostics package, or may be purchased separately. The programs are helpful when you align a floppy disk drive. A good exercise package will let you step the drive's read/write head in and out, specify the track you want to read, write test patterns onto a test disk, and test the motor speed setting. Vortron, Inc. sells an exerciser package for IBM PCs for about $25.00.

Alignment Disks

This is another tool used in aligning floppy disk drives. An alignment disk includes several tracks that carry precisely recorded tracks of signals. During the alignment procedure, you tell the floppy disk drive to read one of these tracks, and then you adjust the drive accordingly. Alignment disks are available from Dysan for $35.00 to $50.00. Some manufacturers will not release alignment disks to the general public.

Disk-Fixer Utility

This is a "software" repair tool. A good disk-fixer package can be a big help in recovering from disasters on disk drives. The same program can usually be used on both hard drives and floppy disk drives.

A good utility package will include these functions:

- A way to look at a disk that has a damaged directory.
- A way to look into a file that includes some bad data.
- A way to inspect and change specific bits of data so the directory or file is usable again.
- A way to recover a file when you accidentally erase it.

In addition, some packages include other functions—copying disks or files, listing directories, changing file names, and so on. Some programs are automatic, while others require the operator to know a lot of detailed information about the arrangement of the disk. A good utility package might cost $30.00 to $85.00.

In order to make full use of a disk-fixer package, you must have some detailed information about how your particular disk operating system works. For example, if you want to reconstruct a bad sector on a floppy disk, you will need to know how the sector is normally arranged. The better disk-fixer packages include some documentation. You may also want to get a book which describes the hard disk and floppy disk formats in detail. Several good books are available which include information on MS-DOS disk formats.

Choosing Replacement Parts

Sometimes, it can be more trouble to find parts than it is to identify the problem in the first place. In some cases, you must locate an exact replacement for the bad part; sometimes, you can get away with a "near match."

There are several things to consider when you choose replacement parts. Most important, the replacement should have the same operating characteristics as the original. To put it another way, the replacement should behave the same way in the circuit that the original did. If the faulty part is an IC, the replacement should process the inputs just the way the original did, and should produce the same outputs. Timing is sometimes an important consideration. The replacement should operate as quickly as the original. Inside a computer, the different circuits must work together. Often, one circuit must finish its work before another can operate. If a replacement part is too slow, it may interfere with the timing relationships between circuits. However, if the replacement is slightly faster than the original, this usually will not cause problems.

Next, be sure that the replacement can handle as much power as the original part. Components are rated to handle maximum amounts of voltage and current. If you install a replacement part which can't handle as much voltage as the original part, the replacement will probably fail. In the same way, if a replacement has a current rating lower than the rating on the original part, it probably will not last long. When compared with the original, the replacement part should be able to handle as much voltage and current (or more) as the original.

Finally, consider the physical size of the part. Be sure the replacement will fit into your equipment. This is usually not a concern when replacing resistors and other small parts, but, if you are replacing a circuit board, a power supply, or a disk drive, the physical size can be very important.

Resistors

A replacement resistor should have the same resistive value as the bad part. Resistors are identified by color code. Each resistor is marked with three or four color bands. The coding system used for resistors is explained in Appendix A.

The fourth band in the resistor color code, if it is present, indicates the tolerance. A resistor with no tolerance band can be within 20% of the specified resistance in either direction. This kind of resistor can have an actual resistance of 80 to 120 ohms. More accurate resistors have tolerance ratings of 10% and 5%. A replacement resistor should have the same tolerance (or better) as the original.

Larger resistors can handle larger amounts of power. A resistor with a diameter of $^1/8$ inch can handle $^1/4$ watt of power. A resistor with a $^3/16$-inch diameter is rated at $^1/2$ watt, while a resistor with a diameter of $^1/4$ inch can handle 1 watt. Always use a replacement resistor with a power rating that is equal to or greater than the original. It's a good idea to check the actual resistance with your VOM before you install the part.

Capacitors

In timing or oscillator circuits, use a replacement capacitor that is exactly the same type and value as the original. In circuits where the capacitor performs a filtering function, you can use a part that has the same or higher capacitance, and the same or higher voltage rating. Be sure that the replacement part is small enough to fit into the space available on the circuit board.

Fuses

Use a replacement fuse having the same current and voltage ratings as the original.

Transformers

Get a replacement transformer with the same input and output voltages, and the same current (or a higher) rating. If space inside the equipment is limited, you may have to get an exact replacement from the manufacturer. After you install a new transformer, recheck the output voltages—they may have changed slightly. You may have to adjust these voltages.

Transistors

Go out of your way to get an exact replacement—it's worth the trouble. If, for some reason, you can't do this, refer to one of the transistor substitution guides, and try to identify a "near replacement." Beware, however. A substitution guide will sometimes list a replacement for your part, even though the two parts are not very similar. Many local parts dealers carry Sylvania's "ECG" line of replacement transistors. MCM Electronics also carries a big selection of replacements.

Some important parameters are:

- *Power dissipation (in mW)*—The replacement part should be able to dissipate as much (or more) power as the original part.

- *Maximum collector current (I_C)*—The replacement part should be able to handle as much (or more) collector current as the original.

- *Maximum collector-to-emitter voltage (V_{CEO})*—The replacement part should have a V_{CEO} rating equal to or higher than the original.

- *Maximum collector-to-base voltage (V_{CBO})*—The replacement part should have a V_{CBO} rating equal to or higher than the original.

- *Maximum emitter-to-base voltage (V_{EBO})*—The replacement part should have a V_{EBO} rating equal to or greater than the original.

- *Gain (h_{FE})*—The replacement should have a gain equal to or better than the original and it should be as close to the original specification as possible.

Once you install the replacement part, you may have to make some adjustments to get the circuit working correctly. For example, if you install a replacement part with a higher gain than the original, the output current may be higher than intended. You can adjust for this by putting a trimmer pot in the output line to bring the current back to specification.

Integrated Circuits

Wherever possible, use a direct replacement for a bad IC. You should be able to find any 7400-series IC easily. Radio Shack carries many of these parts, as does MCM Electronics.

ICs having the same core number, but of different families (the TTL-logic "7474" and the low-power Schottky "74LS74," for example), are roughly equivalent. Each chip performs the same function, each can accept the same signal levels, and the pin connections are the same. In some applications, the two chips are interchangeable. In this example, the TTL type draws more power, so it may cause problems if it is placed into a circuit that is designed to use the low-power "LS" series ICs. The two types may also have slightly different timing characteristics, and this difference could cause trouble in a circuit with close timing tolerances. ICs of exactly the same type, but made by different companies, can also have slightly different timing characteristics. In many cases, these very slight differences won't matter.

RAM (random-access memory) chips are usually inexpensive and easy to find. RAM chips are rated by speed. The more expensive chips can store and retrieve data more quickly. The ratings are listed in billionths of a second (nanoseconds or nS). Be sure to use a replacement chip that is as fast as the original (or faster).

Most microprocessor chips are easy to find. If you have a common computer like an IBM PC or a clone, you should also be able to find most of the larger, more-important ICs. Some computers include custom ICs, used by just one manufacturer. You'll have to go to the original manufacturer for these. ROM (read-only memory) chips are used to store permanent instructions for the computer equipment. "Blank" ROM chips are inexpensive and easy to find, but they do not contain any instructions. Usually, you really want ROM chips in which instructions have been stored. Again, for these parts, you'll have to go to the manufacturer of the computer equipment.

Common 7400-series ICs cost as little as 20 cents each. At the other end of the scale, a manufacturer can charge $200 or more for a ROM or custom IC. Install a socket whenever you replace an IC. Use the type of socket that has gold-plated contacts.

Switches

You can usually find a replacement for a bad switch without too much trouble. Switches are identified by the number and arrangement of the contacts. For example, the abbreviation "SPDT" stands for "single pole, double throw."

The replacement switch should also be activated in the same manner as the original–push-on/push-off, momentary on, etc. The new part should fit within the available space, and should mate with any mechanical parts. Finally, the replacement should have voltage and current ratings equal to or higher than the original.

Solenoids and Motors

Always get an exact replacement part from the manufacturer.

Case and Cabinet Parts

Repair the original part with epoxy, or go to the manufacturer for a new part.

Small Parts

You can find a replacement for many kinds of screws, nuts, spring clips, and other small parts in any large, well-stocked hardware store. Look for a store that has trays or boxes of parts so you can check for the part yourself. Bring the original part for comparison, if possible.

Complete Assemblies

It is possible to buy complete assemblies, including the circuit boards and mechanical assemblies. For example, if many ICs in your computer are damaged by lightning, you may want to simply replace the whole "motherboard" (the main circuit board). This may be easier than trying to repair/replace each damaged IC on the original board. If the mechanical parts in a printer wear out, you can replace the mechanism and re-use the electronics. Replacement power supplies are available for IBM PCs, Apple IIs, and other common computers. When a floppy disk drive fails, it is often cheaper to replace the unit rather than repair it.

You can often get a credit by turning in the part. The manufacturer will then repair the part and put it back into circulation. Make this arrangement with the service department at your local dealer, or write the manufacturer directly.

Sources for Parts

There are several possible sources for replacement parts. It is wise to locate these sources before you need them, and find out what types of parts they can supply. This way, you can move quickly when you need to fix a piece of equipment.

Original Manufacturers

The manufacturer can theoretically supply you with a replacement for every single part in your equipment. Most U.S. manufacturers have a "parts department" that you can telephone from outside the plant. If the equipment is imported, you can usually get parts from the U.S. distributor. For example, Epson printers are imported from Japan, and parts are distributed through Epson America in California.

How do you get in touch with the manufacturer? Use the telephone—you'll probably have to make several calls before you contact the right person.

The manufacturer or distributor may have a toll-free "800" telephone number. Check this by calling long-distance information (1-800-555-1212). Some companies have more than one 800 number, so be sure you have been given the right one.

What if the manufacturer doesn't have a toll-free line? Sometimes, the manufacturer lists a telephone number in the documentation. If not, you can still get the number from the "information" operator. In the documentation, find the city and state where the manufacturer is based. Use the map in your White Pages to identify the area code for that state. If the state has several area codes, you can begin with any area code in that state. If the manufacturer's city is in a different area code, the operator will give you the correct code. Once you know the area code, you can dial the information operator direct (1-xxx-555-1212).

When the call is connected, explain that you want to buy parts, and mention the type and model of your equipment. The larger manufacturers have many plants in different parts of the country. Be sure you're dealing with the right division of the company.

The manufacturer can sometimes be your only source for odd items. Even a manufacturer may be out of some parts, particularly if your equipment is no longer in production.

Many manufacturers will gladly sell you parts, and others won't. Some companies, including Apple, do not encourage technicians who operate outside of their dealer network. Even if the manufacturer is opposed to selling parts, you may be able to get parts through a local dealer. If you are not working for a dealer, you will be operating outside of the routine parts-distribution system. Even if the manufacturer is willing, you can sometimes be caught in a "run-around." When you call the manufacturer, they may say "What's the matter with you? Call our local dealer." When you call the dealer, he may say, "I don't know anything about that part. Call the factory." You can usually get the part you need, but sometimes you have to be very persistent.

In some companies, the parts distribution system can be very complicated. Wang Computer has the most cumbersome system we know of. When you phone Wang and ask for the parts department, you are referred to the department which handles "consumables," such as paper and printer ribbons. When you explain that you're trying to buy replacement parts, they then refer you to the "hardware" department. Then, it turns out that "hardware" can't sell you a large assembly, such as a hard disk drive. Instead, you are referred to your local sales rep, who is supposed to call back and arrange to sell you the part. It took nine phone calls to discover all of this. Incidentally, the rep never called back, and we found another solution to our problem.

Dealing with manufacturers can be time-consuming. When you phone in an order, even if it is processed promptly and then shipped by UPS air service, you'll be lucky to get your part in a week. You may have to wait much longer.

Local Computer Stores

You may be able to buy some parts from a local dealer. Of course, choose a dealer who handles the brand of equipment you're servicing. Most local stores don't want to get into the retail parts business because it takes a lot of time, energy, and money to keep a parts inventory up to date. And, of course, most dealers would rather have their shops fix your equipment.

You can sometimes get a part from a local store if you know one of the technicians, if you have bought a lot of equipment at that store, or if the part itself is very common or inexpensive.

Local Hobby Stores

Your local hobby-type electronics store will stock many of the more common resistors, capacitors, switches, and so on. This type of store also carries the other supplies, like wire, solder, and connectors, that you need to finish the job. The largest store in this category is probably Radio Shack, a division of Tandy Corporation, with over 7000 outlets in the United States.

Radio Shack lists some of the most common 7400-series ICs in their catalog. They also carry a few standard replacement transistors. The local stores don't stock many of these parts, but they list many more in their catalog, and they can order these for you. If a part must be ordered, you can expect to wait two to three weeks.

Local Electronics Distributors

If you live in a large city or town, you may find that a local supply house has a selection of replacement transistors and ICs. This kind of outlet often does most of its business with electricians, but carries a few electronics parts on the side. Other outlets may specialize in electronics parts, and the inventory here may be quite extensive. These local distributors often hand out catalogs that list thousands of parts, but when you try to place an order, you sometimes discover that few of the parts are actually stocked. The local distributor can order out-of-stock parts for you, and you can expect to receive them in one to three weeks.

Central Electronics Distributors

This kind of operation is usually located in a large city. The distributor is really interested in selling parts in large quantities to manufacturers. However, some distributors will also sell small quantities to individuals. These distributors offer a huge off-the-shelf selection.

If the part you need is in stock, you can pick it up and get your equipment working the same day.

Mail-Order Outlets

In the back of the various computer and electronics magazines, you will find ads for mail-order parts houses. These offer a wide selection and good prices. A good mail-order outlet can supply most of the 7400-series ICs, and many of the CPU chips. You should also be able to find RAMs, blank ROMs, and many of the larger ICs which support the CPU. A mail-order catalog will usually include many smaller parts, such as capacitors, resistors, etc.

Mail-order houses are also good sources for the many larger assemblies. For example, if a power supply fails, check the mail-order catalogs. If you have a common type of computer, you should be able to get a replacement power supply for about $50.00. If you can get a part this cheaply, it does not pay to repair the faulty power supply. The part should be described as a replacement for your model. Be sure that the replacement fits into your equipment, and that the connectors match. Replacement floppy disk drives, and even hard disks, are also available at low prices.

Unfortunately, dealing with a mail-order house can take time. If the operation is first-rate, you can get parts within a week, but a wait of two to three weeks is more common.

A final note: When you ask, "How long will I have to wait for my parts?", take the answer you're given and double it. Everyone tends to give an optimistic estimate.

Chapter Review

In this chapter, we've covered the kind of preparatory work you'll have to do before you can begin servicing computer equipment. You may be surprised to see how much equipment and documentation is involved. You don't have to buy all of this equipment at once. Instead, you can build your collection gradually.

As we said earlier, your state of mind is important in servicing work. If you are emotionally "in tune" with the demands of the work, you will be happier and more productive. Servicing work is much simpler if you have good documentation. The right service manual can save you hours of testing. The same rule applies to tools. The better your tools, the more efficient you will be as a troubleshooter. You must choose replacement parts carefully. The replacement part should have the same operating characteristics as the original, and it should be able to handle at least as much power. It may often be difficult to get parts.

Review Questions

1. One technician's workbench is always a mess. Why is this bad practice?

2. In servicing a circuit board, you discover that a 100-ohm, $1/2$-watt resistor has burned out. The only part you have on hand is a 100-ohm, $1/4$-watt resistor. Can you use it?

3. You are repairing a piece of old equipment and you discover that a transistor is bad. The manufacturer has gone out of business, so you get a "near replacement" from an electronics parts dealer. Will the replacement work perfectly?

4. You discover that a 74LS74 IC has gone bad. Where can you get a replacement? Can you use a 74S74 IC as a replacement?

5. You suspect a short circuit in a wire that is meant to be carrying a constant DC current. You try to use a current tracer to find the short, but it will not give you a reading. Why?

6. You are repairing a printer and discover that one of the stepper motors is not working. Where do you get a replacement part?

7. The power supply in a computer fails. Can you get a replacement from a local dealer? Will you be able to buy the part from a mail-order outlet?

8. A screw vibrates loose on a printer and you want to hold it in place with thread-lock compound. How much compound should you use on the screw?

7

Troubleshooting
Strategy and Skills

Introduction and Objectives

When you're confronted with a piece of ailing equipment, what's your strategy? Where do you begin? Working in a strategic order is the key to making a repair as quickly as possible, and with a minimum of frustration. In the first part of this chapter, we will discuss some of the basic principles of troubleshooting. We will also reveal some of the troubleshooting "short-cuts" used by experienced technicians. When you have finished reading this chapter, you will know how to apply "chain troubleshooting" techniques in your own repair work. You will also know how to use a block diagram to plan your troubleshooting.

In the second part of the chapter, we will tell you how to test some of the simpler electronic components. We will describe test procedures for resistors, capacitors, and other parts. When you have finished reading this chapter, you will know how to determine whether these parts are operating correctly.

General Troubleshooting Principles

Localize the Problem

Your computer is only one part of a fairly complicated

system. Besides the computer itself, the system may include a monitor, several disk drives, and perhaps a printer and modem. Each of these units, in turn, consists of a series of smaller subsystems. Fig. 7-1 shows this "hierarchy." Inside the main computer, besides the main CPU chip, you will find subsystems for the power supply, data storage, program storage, and interfacing. At the bottom level of the scale, each of the subsystems is made up of individual components. The components in the power supply, for example, include a transformer, a fuse, a rectifier, a regulator, and various filters.

When you have a problem, you can work with this hierarchy of systems and subsystems to define the section of the equipment that is not working. To put it another way, you work your way along a "chain" of circuits, and try to locate the particular circuit in the chain that is causing the problem. Fig. 7-2 shows a simple chain. Let's say that a particular function starts in circuit A. The signal is then passed through circuits B and C, and the output appears at circuit D. You suspect a problem in this chain. What do you do?

First, check the output—the last step in the chain. What is happening at circuit D? If the output is abnormal, or missing altogether, you know that something is wrong somewhere along the chain. One strategy would be to start at either end of the chain, at either circuit A or D in this example. You could work along the chain and check each stage until you find the point where the normal signals stop and the abnormal signals begin. This technique is particularly suited to

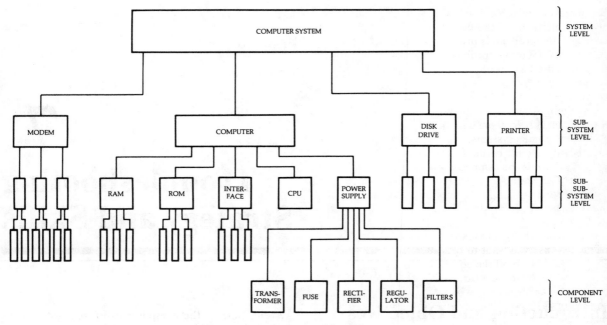

Fig. 7-1. System hierarchy.

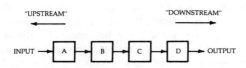

Fig. 7-2. Troubleshooting a chain.

those situations where you don't know exactly what kind of signal to expect at each stage.

A good technician may try to save time by cutting the chain in half. To use this method in our example, start by checking the output of stage B, because that is right in the middle of the chain. If the output at B is normal, you know that the circuits "upstream" of that point are operating normally, so both A and B are all right. If the output at B is abnormal or missing, you know that the problem lies in either A or B. It is not necessary to divide the chain exactly in half. In this example, if it is more convenient to take measurements at the output of circuit C, you might start there.

Sometimes the sections of a chain are arranged into branches. In Fig. 7-3, the system has four different outputs—C1, C2, C3, and C4. Let's assume for the moment that section A is working correctly. You can localize the problem by checking each of the outputs. If you detect abnormal signals on all four of the outputs, look for a problem at B, because that's the only point that all four outputs have in common. If B works

incorrectly, all of the output sections will be affected. If you have a problem at C1 only, check for a problem in C1 itself. You'll note that C3 is connected to C2. If you notice an abnormal output at C3, the problem could lie in either C2 or C3.

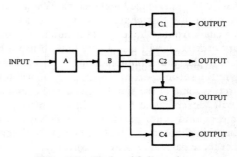

Fig. 7-3. Chain with branches.

Unfortunately, we have limited space in this book, and we can't give you complete details on every type of computer. What we can do, however, is give you a general idea of the functioning of each section of the system. To put it another way, we can show you how the "chains" are laid out. This is why we will put a lot of emphasis on block diagrams and functional descriptions.

One way to define the problem area quickly is to "strip down" the system. Disconnect as many peripherals as possible, leaving just the basic computer and the monitor. If the computer begins operating normally, the problem is probably located in one of the peripherals. (We say "probably" because the problem may be caused by an intermittent problem in a cable, connector, or other part. When you unplug the components, you may move this intermittent "part" enough to make the symptom go away.) Always turn off the equipment before you disconnect any peripherals!

On some systems, you can easily remove individual circuit cards from the computer. The principle here is the same—unplug all but the essential circuits. For example, if you wanted to strip down an Apple II computer, you would remove all of the plug-in cards, including the disk controller and printer interface cards, unless you specifically needed these to test the disk drive or printer. Leave the monitor adapter card in place, because you want to be able to read the screen. Remember to turn off the equipment before you unplug any cards! If you move a card while the power is turned on, you can easily short out two of the pins on the card connector. This can damage ICs both on the card and on the main "motherboard" on the computer.

The examples up to this point have all assumed that the signal flows in just one direction, as shown by the arrows in Fig. 7-2. There are some situations in troubleshooting where the signal flows in both directions. To put it another way, a problem "downstream" can work its way back "upstream" and cause abnormal readings all along the chain.

Fig. 7-4 illustrates one example. Let's say that you observe an abnormal output at C. You take a reading at A, and this reading is also abnormal. In this case, this really doesn't tell you much, because the signal can flow in both directions. The problem could still be in A, B, or C. You must "break" the chain, and see if the sections "upstream" of the break begin operating normally. In this example, you might disconnect the wire that runs between A and B, then check the output at A again. If A begins operating normally, you know the problem is farther "downstream." If A still shows an abnormal reading, you know the problem is in A itself. By disconnecting A from the rest of the circuit, you prevent the problem from working its way back up the chain.

You may encounter this two-way effect when a power-supply problem is involved. For example, you may discover that several points along a chain served by the power supply show abnormal readings. Since several points along the chain show the same reading, you can't tell exactly where the problem is. In a case like this, you must disconnect the power supply, at the beginning of

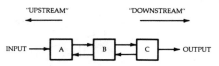

Fig. 7-4. Chain showing two-way effect.

the chain, from the components farther "downstream." If the supply still shows an abnormal output reading, you know the problem lies in the supply itself. On the other hand, if the supply begins to show a normal output, you know that the problem lies somewhere down the chain. A short circuit in a chain can "draw down" the voltage all along the chain so that you can't take meaningful readings. Before you can make any progress, you must disconnect the faulty part of the chain, so the rest of the units in the chain can begin operating normally.

One way to break a chain is to cut a circuit-board trace, but you should not do this except as a last resort. If a line runs into or out of an IC, and the IC is socketed, you can lift a pin of the IC, as shown in Fig. 7-5. Never remove an IC from its socket until you've shut off the equipment.

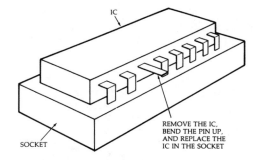

Fig. 7-5. Disconnecting an IC pin.

If the IC is difficult to reach, you may have to take a course that is a bit riskier. You can cut an IC lead with a small pair of "nippy" pliers, as shown in Fig. 7-6. After the test, be sure to resolder the pin, using a minimum of heat. You'll be working very close to the body of the IC, so be very careful not to overheat the part.

In some cases, you'll have no choice but to cut one of the traces on the circuit board itself. We recommend that you avoid this for two reasons. If you ever want to exchange the circuit board for credit, the manufacturer may not accept the part if you have cut and repaired traces. Secondly, it's all too easy to cut traces. This encourages the beginner to make cuts all

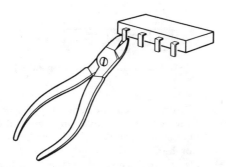

Fig. 7-6. Cutting an IC pin.

over the circuit board—a technique that can create more problems than the original fault.

If, in spite of these words of caution, you want to cut a circuit-board trace, use a sharp hobby knife. Draw the tip of the knife across the trace, as shown in Fig. 7-7. When the test is completed, repair the trace by soldering in a short wire jumper. Use a single-strand wire of approximately the same size as the trace itself. On some circuit boards, the traces may be covered with an insulating or solder-mask material. If necessary, scrape this material away so you can make a good solder connection.

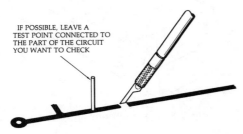

(A) Cutting a circuit trace with a sharp knife.

(B) Repairing a broken circuit trace with wire.

Fig. 7-7. Cutting and repairing a circuit trace.

Each time you disconnect an IC pin or a circuit trace, check it with a voltohmmeter to be sure that the connection has actually been broken. When you repair the connection, test it again.

Substituting Parts

Substitution is one of the most useful troubleshooting techniques. You will be able to come up with many variations on this same basic idea. Fig. 7-8 illustrates the idea.

Let's say that a customer tells you they have a "bad disk drive." What they really mean is that the disk drive is not operating normally. The disk drive is part of

(A) Don't know which part/section is bad.

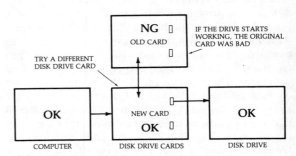

(B) Original card is bad.

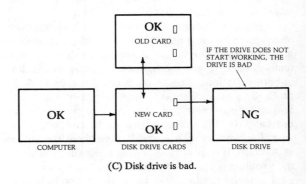

(C) Disk drive is bad.

Fig. 7-8. Check disk drives and the controller card by substituting parts.

a "chain" of components. The control signals are generated by the computer, passed through a disk-drive controller card, and sent on to the disk drive. When the disk drive stops working, the cause may be a problem in any of these three sections.

Now, let's find out which of the three sections is causing the problem. Earlier, we told you to start troubleshooting in the middle of a chain whenever possible. In the example shown in Fig. 7-8A, we'll substitute a new card for the disk-drive controller card. If the disk drive starts working, as shown in Fig. 7-8B, we can be pretty sure that the original card was faulty. In this case, the signals start at the computer (which is OK), go through the new replacement card (which, now, is also all right), and go to the disk drive (which was OK all along).

And, what if the drive does not start working when you substitute a controller card, as shown in Fig. 7-8C? The signals start at the computer (which is probably all right), pass through the new controller card (known to be OK), and pass to the disk drive. Re-install the original controller card and check out the disk drive.

In any kind of troubleshooting procedure, you have to find out which of many possible circuits is actually bad. By substituting, you can eliminate a big section of the circuitry in one step. In the previous example, with just one action (switching controller cards), we eliminated either the controller card or the disk drive. Notice that we did not have to make a detailed check of the operations of either section in order to do this.

Most professional service shops depend heavily on this "board-swapping" technique. They use diagnostic software to identify the section of the system which is faulty. Next, they substitute a spare part and see if the system operates normally. In order to work this way, they must maintain a large collection of spare parts. This is one of the major expenses of this type of operation.

When the system contains two identical circuits or sections, you can substitute in another way. To go back to our example, many disk-drive controller cards can handle two or more drives. This allows you to substitute without replacing the controller card. Fig. 7-9 shows what we mean. At the start of our test, let's say that we have a problem with Drive A. We substitute, this time, by connecting Drive A to the driver circuits for Drive B. If the drive starts working, you know that the driver circuits for Drive A were bad. In this case, the signal from the computer (which is all right) goes through the driver circuits on the Drive-B side of the card (which is also all right), and then to Drive A. The drive is working, so it is all right, and the A side of the controller card must be bad. (When you do this, you may have to tell the computer to start using the "Drive B" circuits.)

What if the drive does not start working? This suggests that there is a problem with the drive itself. The signals come from the computer correctly, and go through the driver circuits for Drive B (which are also all right). The disk drive does not respond to signals

(A) One controller card and two drives.

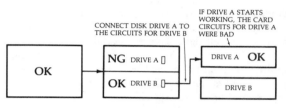

(B) Switching Drive A and Drive B (bad card).

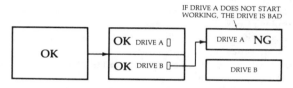

(C) Switching Drive A and Drive B (bad drive).

Fig. 7-9. Checking disk-drive controller card and two disk drives by the substitution method.

from either half of the driver card, however, because the drive itself is bad. Because the driver card has two identical circuits, we were able to substitute without removing the card.

Many computers use removable cards, including the IBM PCs and PC clones, the Apple IIs, the Mac II, and the Mac SE computers. Before you remove or replace one of these cards, be sure to turn off all of the power. As you remove a card, it is very easy to create a short circuit between two of the contacts on the card connectors. This cannot happen as long as the power is turned off. A short circuit can damage ICs throughout the equipment, and can cause problems much more serious than your original problem.

There are many variations on this basic idea of substitution. When you have a problem with a computer and monitor, try substituting another monitor. If you are suspicious of a power supply, plug in another power supply. Modern computer equipment tends to be "modular." This means that the circuits are arranged in distinct parts or sections. It is usually fairly easy to replace one of these parts or sections. Often, the parts are connected by cables and plug-in connectors. It is a simple matter to unplug the suspect part and plug in a part which is known to be good. *CAUTION:* Always turn off the power before you change any of these connections!

You can also substitute individual components. For example, if you are working with a circuit that includes a 74S74 IC (a common type), you have two choices. You can check the individual inputs and outputs for the IC. This can be a time-consuming process, and you must know something about the IC you're dealing with. As a faster alternative, you can simply "swap" the suspect 74S74 for a chip that is known to be all right. This is especially easy if the IC is mounted in a socket. You just pull out the suspect part, put in the replacement, and see if the equipment works. Again, always remember to turn off the power before you remove or replace any chips!

If you are working with a circuit that uses several ICs, and if you have enough spares, you can replace all of them. This is called the "shotgun" technique. Using this method, you won't know exactly which of the replaced ICs is faulty. Usually, it is more important just to get the circuit working. You can easily substitute other types of components—resistors, capacitors, transistors, etc. You can also substitute electromechanical parts, such as motors and solenoids.

It is also possible to substitute software. If a program won't run, try operating with a backup copy. If the computer seems to have trouble handling files, reload a different copy of the disk operating system (DOS).

In order to substitute, you must have spare parts on hand. If you are working for a dealer of name-brand equipment, this will not be a problem. In order to keep the franchise, the dealer must agree to stock a certain number of spares. For the small operator, or the technician working at home, this is more of a problem. One of the best ways of dealing with this is to have a spare computer on hand. With a second computer, you have a complete stock of every spare you will need, including circuit boards, electromechanical parts, and even individual ICs. However, you may not want to go out and buy a second computer just for this purpose. But, this is a good argument for standardizing. If you plan to get several computers, it will be very helpful if they are compatible, so the parts may be interchanged.

There are some cautions we should note here. You can't assume that a "known good" replacement part is actually working. A certain percentage of new parts, right off the shelf, do not work correctly. If you use a "known good" part in your troubleshooting process and that part is actually bad, the results of your tests can be misleading.

A problem in one part of the system can create problems in other parts of the system. Let's say that you're suspicious of Part B of the system, when the problem is actually being caused by Part A. If you substitute Part B, the problem in Part A may damage your substituted part. An inexperienced technician can burn out a whole string of replacement circuit boards this way. (To make matters worse, a dishonest service shop will sometimes charge the customer for all of the replacement boards.) Whenever you substitute a part, you run a risk of damaging the replacement.

Finally, board-swapping can be expensive. For example, on the Macintosh computers, a part for the monitor, called the "flyback" transformer, sometimes fails. This part costs about $30.00, and is fairly easy to install. However, the Apple technicians "aren't allowed" to replace just this one part. Instead, they have to sell you a whole circuit board, at a cost of $275. The "board-swapping" policy is convenient for the dealer, but expensive for the customer.

Understanding the Equipment

It's difficult to fix anything unless you understand how it works. In some cases, the operating principle is obvious and straightforward. For example, a cooling fan is a rather simple device. You can look at a fan, and understand how it works.

Some of the subsystems in a computer system are not much more complicated. For example, some circuits are based on a simple switch or photodetector. However, other circuits are quite complicated. All of the action is performed by tiny digitized pulses of electricity, so the workings of the circuits are invisible.

As a technician, you must develop just the level of understanding required to repair the equipment efficiently. Most beginners assume that this means you must understand every blip and bit in the system. This kind of detailed knowledge is helpful, of course, but it is not necessary. As a technician, you normally won't have to deal with all of the details of a circuit's functioning. You don't have to design the equipment—all you have to do is keep it working. Any piece of failed equipment was once working, so you can assume that all of the complex design problems have been taken care of by the engineers. All you must do is bring the equipment back to life.

If a digital circuit is working at all, it is probably working correctly. This means that you can perform a lot of your troubleshooting just by checking for activity of any type. There are exceptions, of course, but this is a good general rule. By applying a simple "go—no go" test, you can check whole parts of the system, the separate circuits, and even individual ICs. And what if you do have to get down to the component level? Even here, computer circuitry is relatively easy to work with. Most computer circuitry uses "digital" principles. Generally, this means that any point in the circuit is either "on" or "off." With the right test equipment, it is easy to tell whether a test point is "on" or "off."

The situation is different when you are working with the "analog" circuits used in power supplies, monitors, and other devices. An analog circuit may be "on," "off," or "in-between." To tell if an analog circuit is working, you must often know exactly where in this "in-between" range the circuit is operating.

There are some situations which call for advanced troubleshooting methods. Generally, this happens when the components are all working, but are not handling information correctly. As we said, most commercial operations avoid problems of this type by swapping whole circuit boards or assemblies. If you want to tackle a problem of this type, you may have to develop a detailed understanding of the circuitry. In a case like this, you must build up in your mind a model of the circuit, and try to understand how it is meant to work.

This book should help you to understand the general workings of many computer subsystems. For more specific information, you'll have to rely on the company that manufactured your particular piece of equipment. The "Theory of Operation" section in the manual for the equipment will usually explain in detail how each circuit is supposed to work. The manual may also show some test points, and list the voltages and signals you're supposed to find at these points.

Remember, all computer equipment must follow a very logical order of operations. The equipment is set up to follow a specific process: A leads to B leads to C leads to D. There's no other way of doing the job, no "magic" in the design. If you are persistent, you can get down to this "A-B-C-D" level of understanding, and follow each bit and byte through the circuitry. In service work, this is usually not necessary, but you should know that it is possible.

Check the Simplest Causes First

Service pros say that the largest proportion of problems are caused by simple "silly" things that someone has overlooked. A power cord with a bad connector, a paper clip stuck in the disk drive—these things can stop a computer just as easily as a complicated data-transfer problem. And as we pointed out in our "Service Profile," these simple problems occur quite often.

Always check for the simple causes of the problem first. If you can't find the problem, check the simple things *again* before you move on to more complicated possibilities. Start by investigating the components that are most likely to fail:

- connectors and cables
- electromechanical parts (motors, solenoids, switches)
- power-supply components
- high-density ICs (ROMs and RAMs)

Ask "How Did the Problem Begin?"

Sometimes, the circumstances suggest the cause of a problem. When you're confronted with a problem, ask yourself if something unusual happened just before the problem appeared. Did someone drop a screwdriver, or accidentally trip on a cable? Perhaps you noticed that the monitor display grew smaller for a moment. Each of these incidents can suggest a possible cause for a problem. For example, the momentary shrinking of the monitor display suggests a power-line problem.

Some problems are constant "hard" errors—part of the equipment does not work at all. With the "chain troubleshooting" methods we just described, you can often find a hard error without too much trouble, and you will usually be sure that you've found the cause of the hard error—a part may be burned or blackened, or an IC may not be working.

The really difficult problems are the intermittent "soft" errors. As you make your troubleshooting tests, you can never be sure whether the "soft" error is active or not. If the equipment is working all right at the moment you make your tests, all of your results will be normal and you won't be able to make any progress. Sometimes you must wait for a while for a "soft" error to reappear, and this can use up a lot of time. Even after you make a repair, you can never be completely sure that you've really found the cause of the problem. Instead, you must wait to see if the problem reappears.

Temperature as a Diagnostic Tool

Any computer system depends on energy to operate. If the equipment is to accomplish anything, this energy must be precisely channeled, controlled, and focused. When a short circuit develops, this focused energy escapes from its controls. As a result, the faulty parts often feel warm or hot. Sometimes, the fault is even more cataclysmic, and the bad component appears to be burnt or melted.

You can use your finger to make a quick "touch test" of components in a circuit you suspect. Pay particular attention to any part which is too hot to hold your finger on. Use the back of your finger to make the test, as shown in Fig. 7-10. This part of the finger is actually more sensitive to heat than the fingertip. If you suspect a component is very hot, wet your finger before you touch the part. In the last chapter, we described an inexpensive tool called a "Thermoprobe" which you can use to check temperature. Professional technicians sometimes use very precise digital thermometers to measure the temperature of a suspected component.

Some components are hot even when they're operating normally. If a transistor is attached to a large metal plate (a heat sink), you can expect the plate to be quite hot. A transistor with a smaller heat sink should be proportionally cooler. The printhead of a dot-matrix printer can become very hot in normal operation.

We'll add a note of caution here. Don't touch any parts of the computer that carry 120-V AC house current—this test is for the TTL-logic sections only. Before you touch any components, be careful to ground yourself by touching the case of the computer for a moment. If you don't do this, you can accumulate a static charge, which can damage delicate CMOS ICs.

Some kinds of component failures are directly related to the temperature of the component. In the most common case, the equipment works normally when you first turn it on. The problem doesn't begin to appear until the equipment has been operating for some time. The bad component begins to fail as it gets warmer. You can use this temperature effect to quickly locate the bad component. For this job, you'll need a can of aerosol freeze spray. When the spray is released from the can, it instantly cools to a very low temperature. You can use a narrow stream of spray to cool first one component and then another. When you cool the bad component, the equipment may begin to operate normally. If it does, you have found a "thermal intermittent." You can sometimes save time by spraying a row of ICs in one pass. If the problem disappears, check each of the ICs in that row individually.

In some cases, the results of the freeze spray test can be misleading. If a circuit-board trace has a hairline crack, a shot of freeze spray anywhere on the board may have enough of an effect to bring the two sides of the crack together, and re-make the connection. In a case like this, it seems that you can hit any IC and make the symptom disappear.

Freeze spray can also inject a static-electric charge into a circuit. For work with digital circuits, be careful to use a freeze spray that is marketed as "anti-static." Each time you spray a component, you subject it to a thermal stress. This can cause the part to fail

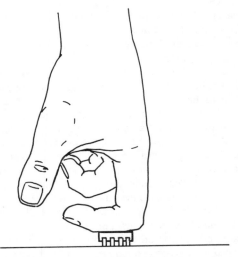

Fig. 7-10. Touch the IC with the back of your finger.

prematurely, so use freeze spray sparingly. Be careful to keep the spray away from your skin, and don't spray onto any electrolytic capacitors.

Some thermal intermittents work the opposite way—the equipment behaves abnormally at first, but stabilizes as it warms up. In this situation, you need a way to warm up a particular component. Don't use a soldering iron—it focuses too much heat on too small an area. A household hair dryer works well. You can focus the stream of hot air by holding a plastic funnel in front of the hair dryer. Professional technicians use heat guns that are similar to home dryers. With the professional tools, the flow of hot air is directed into a narrow stream.

When you use a hair dryer, use a low heat setting, if possible, and keep the dryer moving. The "touch test" is your guide here—don't heat any component to the point where you can't touch it. Test the equipment's outputs as you warm the various parts. The trouble symptoms should disappear when you warm the component that has the thermal intermittent. You may have to check your diagnosis by cooling the part with freeze spray, and then reheating it.

Some intermittent problems are not related to the temperature of the component. Intermittents may also be related to vibration or humidity, for example.

Find Good Test Points

As you service digital equipment, you'll have to take many test readings. Your work will go much more smoothly if you learn to take these readings in the most convenient locations.

All voltage readings require two test points—the source of the test voltage and ground. The term "ground" can have several different meanings, depending on the situation. One type is "chassis" ground. In earlier electronic equipment, components were assembled on a metal frame, or "chassis," and this frame was often grounded to the outside world through the power cord. You may still find a metal chassis in computer-type equipment. *Chassis ground* generally refers to a system that includes grounding traces on the circuit boards, ground leads on motors and solenoids, and, sometimes, the case of the equipment. Chassis ground is connected to the outside world through the third prong of the AC plug. Fig. 7-11 shows a typical chassis ground system.

You can attach a test clip to this ground at many locations. You will usually find a test pin dedicated to this ground. This pin may be located in the power-supply section, or you may find it on one of the circuit boards. Check the service manual for your particular piece of equipment.

In addition, traces on the circuit boards carry this chassis ground to all parts of the board. Frequently, these lines will run from a wider "ground bus," which runs around the outer edge of the board. On some boards, the trace may be insulated and you may have to scrape away some of the insulation to take a reading. Be careful to scrape away only the insulation, and not the trace itself. Be sure you have the right trace—the +5-V DC bus may run parallel to the chassis ground line.

Ground is provided to one pin on every IC in the system, as shown in Fig. 7-12. If you have narrow clips on your test equipment, you can take your ground (and also +5-V DC) directly from any IC.

There is one exception to this last case. In some equipment, the TTL logic circuits are provided with a "logic ground," which is isolated from the chassis ground. Fig. 7-13 shows this arrangement. This is done to prevent transients and noise from contaminating the power to the TTL ICs. In a system arranged this way, the logic ground may temporarily be at a slightly different potential from chassis ground. Your service manual will tell you if your equipment has this arrangement.

Another type of ground may exist in special situations. This is a dedicated, or "signal," ground. You may find this arrangement in a link between two pieces of equipment; for example, between a computer and a disk drive. The signals between these two points may be referenced to an independent "signal" ground.

Finally, some microcomputer systems use a separate grounding system for audio signals. For example, the output to the computer's speaker may be referenced to a special "audio" ground.

As a general rule, try to use a ground connection as close as possible to the component you're testing.

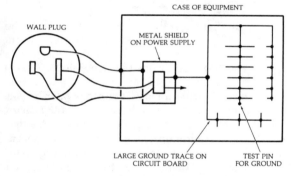

Fig. 7-11. Chassis ground network.

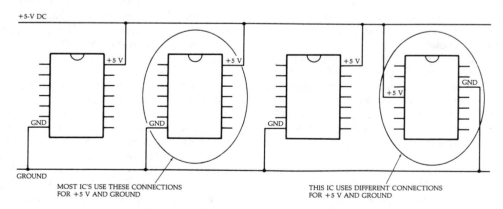

Fig. 7-12. Power and ground supply lines.

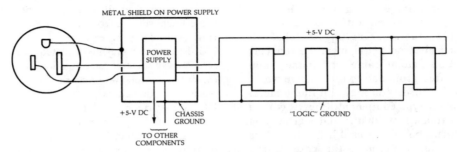

Fig. 7-13. Logic ground and chassis ground.

This will remove most of the confusion between the different types of ground. If you're checking an IC, for example, and you use a ground connection on the IC itself, you'll be sure to have the right type of ground. There's a second reason for this rule. If you take a ground reference at a location far from the point under test, various stray signals can creep into the reading. A reading taken using a ground close to the test point tends to be more accurate.

What about the other half of each reading–the positive or "signal" side? Whatever you're testing, it's a safe bet that other technicians have had to test exactly the same thing. In a computer, for example, among the first points you're likely to test are the various power-supply outputs. Every technician who works on your model of computer is likely to want to test those same outputs. For this reason, most manufacturers provide "test points" at convenient locations on the circuit boards. Fig. 7-14 shows a typical test point on a circuit board. A test point might take the form of a tall pin that rises above the other components on the board. Usually, this point will be identified by a label on the board, for example, "TP4." The service manual for your equipment should tell you what test points are included in your system, and what kind of signal you should find at each point.

If a specific test point is not provided, you'll have to take your reading from the circuit board itself. Try to find a stretch of bare wire to use as a connection. The best type of test probe for this job has a small tip, and a sharp point. The small tip is convenient when working with small parts. The sharp tip on the probe will cut through any corrosion and will permit accurate test measurements.

You can usually make connections at the pins of ICs, as shown in Fig. 7-15. Use small "clip on" test leads. This may be more convenient if you use an IC test clip.

When testing transistors, you may make connections to the legs (leads) under the case. Many circuit boards are not insulated so you can take a

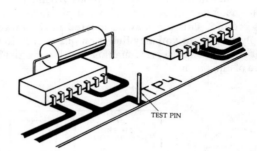

Fig. 7-14. A typical test pin (tie point).

reading directly from a trace. On other boards, you must scrape away a thin layer of insulation with a sharp knife. Be careful not to damage the trace itself. Another option, if the trace is insulated, is to locate a component that is connected to the trace, as shown in Fig. 7-16. Clip your test lead onto the leg of the component, on the side that is connected to the trace.

Plug-in connectors often offer good places to take readings. The connector pins themselves are usually well protected, but you can often take readings at the conductors behind the connectors, as shown in Fig. 7-17.

In each of these test situations, be careful to touch just one conductor at a time. If you allow your test probe to touch more than one conductor or IC pin at a time, you can easily create a short circuit.

You can take a reading from an insulated wire by piercing the insulation, as shown in Fig. 7-18. Carefully work a needle through the insulation and attach your test probe to the needle. You may have to insert the needle more than once in order to get a good connection. Be careful not to let the uninsulated needle touch any of the other parts inside the computer. When you're finished, repair the insulation with a piece of electrical tape, or a dab of silicone sealer.

Fig. 7-15. Taking test readings from ICs.

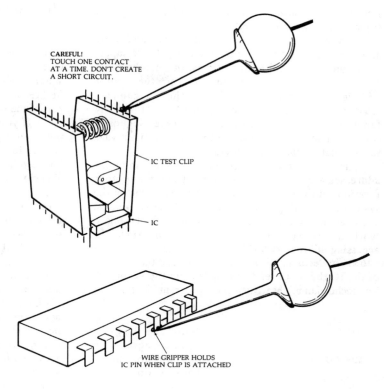

CAREFUL!
TOUCH ONE CONTACT
AT A TIME. DON'T CREATE
A SHORT CIRCUIT.

IC TEST CLIP

IC

WIRE GRIPPER HOLDS
IC PIN WHEN CLIP IS ATTACHED

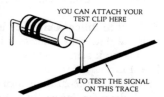

YOU CAN ATTACH YOUR
TEST CLIP HERE

TO TEST THE SIGNAL
ON THIS TRACE

Fig. 7-16. Taking test readings from an insulated trace.

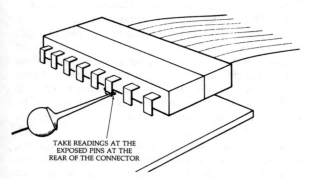

TAKE READINGS AT THE
EXPOSED PINS AT THE
REAR OF THE CONNECTOR

Fig. 7-17. Taking test readings from a connector.

If you cannot take test readings from any of these convenient test points, you can often take readings from

the underside of the circuit board. The leads on most ICs and other parts extend through the circuit board, so you can make your connections on the back of the board. In order to get access to the back of the circuit board, you may have to remove it from the chassis.

Stimulating Circuits for Tests

In the last chapter, we described the logic pulser. This tool allows you to stimulate a particular circuit directly.

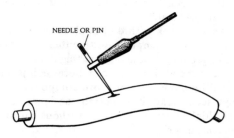

NEEDLE OR PIN

Fig. 7-18. Taking test readings from an insulated wire.

There are a number of other ways of stimulating a circuit so you can make a test.

In many cases, the most convenient and most accurate course to take is to tell the computer to supply the signals you require. Sometimes, this can be quite easy to do. For example, in order to check the "motor on" signal to a floppy disk drive, all that a technician must do is command the computer to perform any function that requires disk activity. Some diagnostic software packages include routines that can activate various parts of the computer system.

In many microcomputers, selected memory addresses are used to control output ports and other functions of the system. You can stimulate a part of the system by "writing" data to one of these addresses. Let's say that a technician wants to check the keyboard function in an Apple II Plus computer. In the Apple, the accessing address "C000" in hexadecimal notation, or −16384 in decimal, allows the CPU to read the contents of the IC that decodes the signals from the keyboard. The technician might write a short program like this:

```
10 A = PEEK (−16384)    Read the key-
                        board decoder.
20 GOTO 10              Set up an end-
                        less loop.
```

While it is running this program, the computer will continually ask to see the contents of the keyboard decoder IC, and will input these contents to the CPU. The technician will be able to spot the enable signals to the keyboard decoder, and the encoded keystrokes going back to the CPU on the data lines.

You can adapt this technique to many other troubleshooting situations. For example, you can use the computer to produce signals that will stimulate particular gates or other devices. Each gate is included in the equipment to perform a specific function. This means you can stimulate a gate by telling the equipment to perform a function in which the gate is active. In order to make use of this technique, you must know the important memory addresses used in your particular computer system. This information is often included in the "User's Manual."

As you work with digital circuits, you may be tempted to use a jumper wire to either the +5-V DC source or ground, to hold a point "high" or "low." We don't recommend this technique, because it is possible that you'll damage one or more components. Use a logic pulser instead—it is specially designed to supply digital "high" or "low" signals without harming the components in a circuit.

How to Locate Circuits

Let's say that you suspect a problem in a certain circuit. You've read about the circuit in the "Theory of Operation," and you know how it is supposed to work. When you turn to the back of the service manual, you find reams of schematic diagrams. How do you find the part of the schematic that relates to your circuit?

If you're dealing with a major subsystem—the power supply, for example—you may find that the circuit is detailed on a separate schematic. You can often locate other circuits in relation to the large CPU chip. The clock circuit, for example, is often pictured just to one side of the CPU. RAMs and ROMs are arranged in large fields of identical circuits. The buffers and interface ports tend to be arranged around the outside of the page.

Most parts are identified by number on the schematics. The schematic representation for a particular IC might show the logic symbol for the IC, and carry a label like "1/4 74LS02." The number "74LS02" identifies the type of IC. We'll tell you more about this numbering system later in this chapter. The note "1/4" means that this logic element takes up just one quarter of the IC chip. If the logic element is a NAND gate, for example, you could expect to find four separate NAND gates on the complete IC. Fig. 7-19 shows some other conventional symbols you may find on a schematic.

It can be difficult to follow a circuit trace across a schematic. Both the data and address buses include many parallel lines, so it's easy to lose the line you're trying to follow. Place a ruler under the line on the schematic, as shown in Fig. 7-20. The edge of the ruler will guide your eye along the line you want to follow.

Once you locate your circuit on the schematic, how do you find the actual parts on the circuit board? Sometimes, you can use the appearance of a component as a guide. The CPU chip is usually the biggest IC on the board. ROM ICs are usually larger than the rest. You'll usually find several identical ROM ICs. Most RAMs look like any other IC, but you can identify them because of the large number of identical chips. Other types of ICs are identified by part numbers. You will find the part number for the IC on the top of the component casing. The number may also be printed on the circuit board beside the IC.

The circuit-board positions for ICs, transistors, diodes, and other major components are usually labeled with the same numbers that are shown for the parts on the schematics. A transistor might be called "Q6," a capacitor, "C23," and so on. In some equipment, the part locations are keyed to a grid system on the circuit

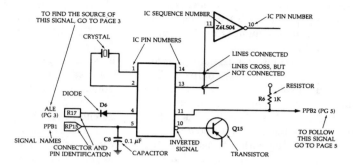

Fig. 7-19. Common schematic symbols.

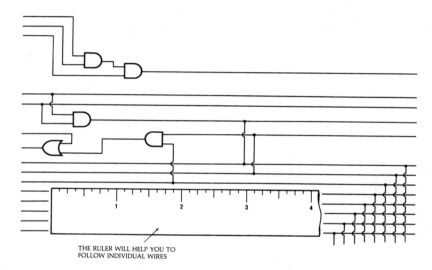

THE RULER WILL HELP YOU TO
FOLLOW INDIVIDUAL WIRES

Fig. 7-20. Use a ruler to follow lines on a multiline schematic.

board, as shown in Fig. 7-21. In the sketch, the CPU chip is located in the grid square identified as "B6." Often, the manufacturer will also list these locations on the schematic. For example, an IC might have the label "1/4 74LS02 B5." The last two digits give the grid location where you'll find the component.

To identify the specific connections on a component, you'll have to refer back to the schematic. On ICs, the schematic will usually identify the pin numbers for each connection. For the smaller ICs, the pin numbering system is quite logical, as you can see in Fig. 7-22A. The numbers start at the end of the chip identified by the notch or white dot. You'll find Pin 1 at the left corner of the chip closest to this notch. The numbers extend in a counterclockwise pattern around the IC. The pin carrying the positive voltage (+5-V DC for TTL ICs) is usually the pin with the highest number. This is the pin in the upper right-hand corner, as referenced to the notch or white dot. The ground connection is usually located in the lower left-hand

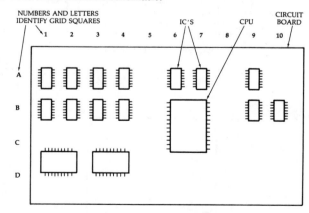

Fig. 7-21. A typical grid system used on some computer circuit boards.

corner. A few small ICs have +5-V and ground connections to pins in the center of the chip.

ICs using VLSI technology (very large-scale integration) have many connectors, so they use a different pin numbering system. Each pin is identified by an "address," consisting of a number or a number and a letter (Figs. 7-22B through 7-22D).

Identifying the connections to a discrete component can be more difficult. You must compare the schematic with the components you actually find on the circuit board. Sometimes, no grid numbers are included to help you find the part. You'll have to use the component number to locate the part on the board.

Let's say you're working with a transistor. On both the schematic and on the board, you see that the transistor has three leads. One of these is the "base," one is the "emitter," and one is the "collector," but which is which? One course is to identify the transistor

using the part number. Look up the transistor in a reference book—the manual should include a diagram that shows how the leads are arranged, as shown in Fig. 7-23. If you have a diagram like this, you can identify the legs by their positions relative to a tab or flat side on the case of the transistor. But be warned! Transistors with identical cases can have different assignments for each of the leads, so check carefully.

If no documentation is available, you'll have to use clues from the circuit board itself to identify each of the leads. For example, the schematic may show that a transistor's "collector" lead is connected to V_{CC} through a resistor. Associated parts will usually be located near each other, so you can expect to find this transistor near the resistor. By checking the circuit board visually, you should be able to identify the leg of a transistor that is connected to a resistor of the value shown in the schematic. Some transistor testers can

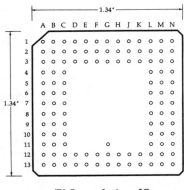

(A) Standard system for small ICs.

(B) System for large ICs.

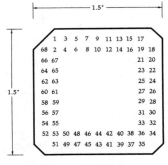

(C) Second VLSI numbering system.

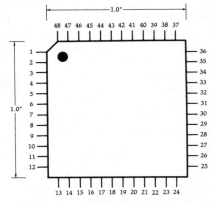

(D) Third VLSI numbering system.

Fig. 7-22. IC pin numbering system.

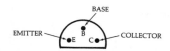

Fig. 7-23. Typical transistor base diagram.

determine the lead assignments automatically. It is also possible to determine the lead arrangement using a voltohmmeter. The procedure is described later in this chapter in the section on "Checking Transistors."

Frequently, it is not necessary to actually follow the traces across the circuit boards. Let's say that the schematic shows that the trace you're interested in runs from pin 3 on IC 28 to pin 9 on IC 33. You can simply take test readings at each of these points, and assume the trace between them is intact.

The exception to this is when you're interested in the circuit-board trace itself. For example, you may suspect that a trace has developed a short circuit to ground. In this case, you do have to follow the trace and inspect it. The ruler trick we just described may help. Now and then, a trace may go through the circuit board and emerge on the other side. Where this happens, you'll see the trace enlarged to form a circle, as shown in Fig. 7-24.

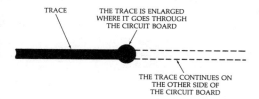

Fig. 7-24. Circuit trace passing through circuit board.

Checking Discrete Components

Once you have your test instruments conveniently located, you must know how to use them correctly to tell if a specific component is working properly or not. In the next section, we'll explain how to check out individual components. In this chapter, we'll concentrate on "discrete" components—parts that stand alone on the circuit board. We'll consider integrated circuits (ICs) in the next chapter.

Testing Circuit Boards and Traces

The circuit board is not exactly a "component," yet it is part of the assembly that makes up a working circuit. Many problems occur at the solder joints which attach components to the board. A "cold-solder joint" may intermittently disconnect a signal line. This type of joint can be difficult to spot, but, on a cold-solder joint, the solder may appear to be dull or "grainy." A correct solder joint should be clean and shiny, and the solder should make a smooth curve where it meets the component lead.

A solder joint may also develop a crack or break. If a heavy component has not been securely attached to the circuit board, one of the solder joints may break loose due to vibration. Then, you may see a small circular crack around one of the component's leads. You can correct any of these problems quickly by touching the suspect joint with a soldering iron and remelting the solder.

Circuit boards are also subject to cracks and other mechanical damage. Usually, the board itself is cracked, and this cracks one or more of the thin traces on the top and bottom of the board (Fig. 7-25). The crack may disconnect the trace entirely, or it may cause an intermittent fault that is sensitive to temperature or vibration. If a circuit has received too much current, one or more circuit traces may have burned away completely. Excessive heat may also cause the adhesive under the trace to loosen and allow the trace to lift. An inept technician can lift a circuit trace by overheating the circuit board during soldering.

You can check for cracks by inspecting the circuit board visually. Pay particular attention to the joints at the base of each connector, as shown in Fig. 7-25B. These points are subject to stress when the connector is plugged in or unplugged. Also inspect the connections at the base of each heavy component (transformer, large capacitor, etc.).

If circuit-board traces are broken, this may cause them to be sensitive to temperature and may cause intermittent errors. In that case, troubleshoot according to the procedure we described earlier in the chapter (Temperature as a Diagnostic Tool). Other intermittents could be sensitive to vibration. To check for one of these, turn the equipment on, and then tap or bend the circuit board and see if the fault appears.

Various conditions can cause a short between circuit-board traces. A short can be caused by any scrap of conductive material—a solder ball, a solder "whisker," stray piece of wire, loose screw, etc. A piece of metal shielding can slip out of position and cause a short. A component's leads can be bent so that they

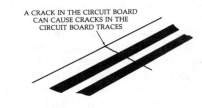

A CRACK IN THE CIRCUIT BOARD CAN CAUSE CRACKS IN THE CIRCUIT BOARD TRACES

(A) Broken circuit-board traces.

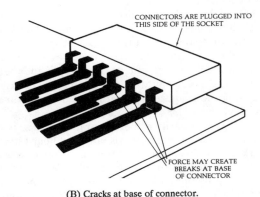

CONNECTORS ARE PLUGGED INTO THIS SIDE OF THE SOCKET

FORCE MAY CREATE BREAKS AT BASE OF CONNECTOR

(B) Cracks at base of connector.

Fig. 7-25. Bad connections on circuit boards.

accidentally touch each other and short out. In many cases, you can spot these conditions simply by looking carefully at the circuit board. When in doubt, double-check with a voltohmmeter set to read OHMS; take continuity/resistance checks.

Another problem that may afflict a circuit board is what is called a "cold solder joint." It is possible for a connection to appear to be soldered, yet not make a good electrical connection. This can occur when the solder is not heated enough to make a good bond. The solder in a cold solder joint will appear rough and grainy, rather than forming a smooth, shiny joint. You can check a cold solder joint by testing for resistance using a voltohmmeter. A good solder joint should show almost no resistance.

Some microcomputers use multilayer circuit boards. Special conductors or "planes" are included in the center of the board. If you hold the board up to a bright light, you can often see the conductors inside the board. The planes inside the board are often used to carry +5 V and ground. This arrangement reduces the radio-frequency emissions produced by the board. Circuit boards of this type are difficult to work with. Different leads on an IC or other component may be connected to different levels on the circuit board. If you

want to desolder parts on a multilayer board, you must work very carefully to avoid damaging the board.

Testing Cables and Connectors

Many "computer" problems are actually caused by faulty cables and connectors. Cables and connectors are most often mounted outside the equipment's case and are vulnerable to various kinds of mechanical damage. The small conductors inside a cable can break if the cable is pulled sharply or pinched. In some equipment, a cable is included to provide a "bridge" between a hinged part of a cabinet and a stationary part. On a "laptop" computer, you might find a flexible cable connecting the screen to the main part of the computer. This kind of cable is bent back and forth many times in about the same place. The cable is most likely to fail at the point where it flexes.

Faulty connectors can also cause problems. The delicate pins in a connector can be bent. If a connector is repeatedly plugged in and unplugged, the socket can wear, and it may not get a good grip on the plug. The contacts on edge-card connectors can corrode. This problem is more likely on older equipment having silver-plated contacts. Gold-plated contacts provide the best resistance against corrosion. However, some manufacturers use such a low percentage of gold in their "gold contacts" that some of these can corrode also. In Chapter 6, we described a way of cleaning edge-card connectors using a rubber eraser.

Whenever you're faced with a servicing problem, one of your first steps should be to check the parts we've just described. If you seem to be having problems with a cable, start by checking the connectors. Are all of the pins clean and straight? Does the connector seem to fit snugly in its socket? Next, check for continuity through each of the wires in the cable. Use a voltohmmeter (set to read OHMS) and use the test setup shown in Fig. 7-26. For each wire in the cable, the meter should show a very low resistance. A reading of high or infinite resistance indicates that one of the wires is broken. Be certain that you are measuring between corresponding pins (pin 1 to pin 1, pin 2 to pin 2). Fig. 7-26 shows two common pin-numbering systems.

Testing Resistors

This common component will be familiar to everyone who has ever worked with electronic equipment. Many of the resistors used in computer equipment are the cylindrical carbon-composition type. The colored bands around the outside of each resistor indicate its value.

to be pale. Sometimes a damaged resistor will grow a bit larger than it should be. When a resistor fails, it usually leaves an open circuit.

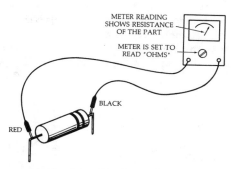

Fig. 7-27. Testing resistors.

You can make an in-circuit check of a resistor with your voltohmmeter. Turn the equipment off, and set the meter to read OHMS. Touch the red test lead to the wire at one end of the resistor and the black test lead to the wire at the other end of the resistor. Fig. 7-27 illustrates this procedure.

A reading of zero resistance indicates that the part has shorted. If the meter indicates an infinite resistance, the part is open. If the part is still working, the meter often will show you the resistance value of the part. An in-circuit test will sometimes give an incorrect reading for the value of a resistor, however. This is because of the influence of other components in the circuit. The in-circuit test should show whether a part is shorted or open, however. To get an accurate reading of the resistance value, you may have to disconnect at least one leg of the resistor from the circuit.

Testing Diodes

The diodes used in a computer applications are small cylindrical objects, similar in appearance to resistors. Instead of the series of colored bands found on resistors, however, diodes normally have just one band. A diode will often not give you any physical indication that it has failed. Sometimes, if a diode has been damaged, a tiny crack will develop around the part. When you touch the faulty diode with a probe, the body of the diode may fall apart.

A diode is designed to let current pass in one direction, but not the other. You can use this principle to make a quick check with the diode in-circuit. When the voltohmmeter is set to OHMS, a small battery inside the meter is connected to one of the test leads. Using this battery as a current source, you can use the VOM to test for continuity.

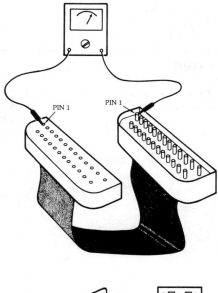

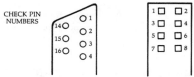

(A) Testing cable between plug and socket.

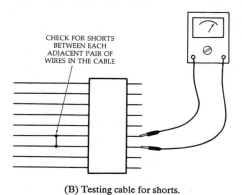

(B) Testing cable for shorts.

Fig. 7-26. Testing cables and connectors.

We've explained this color-code system in Appendix A. Other types include wire-wound resistors and resistors packaged in dual in-line (DIP) packages similar to those used for ICs. Sometimes you will find a row of resistors packaged in a single in-line (SIP) package as well.

When a circuit receives too much current, other parts usually fail before the resistors do. A damaged resistor may appear to be burned or discolored. The colored bands on the outside of the resistor may appear

To test a diode, turn the equipment off, and set the VOM to OHMS. Use the "R × 100" scale, if your meter has one. Touch the red test lead to the conductor at one end of the diode and the black lead to the conductor at the other end, as shown in Fig. 7-28. Note the reading on the meter. Now reverse the leads and note the meter reading again. In one of these positions, the meter should indicate a very low resistance, showing that the current from the meter's

single assembly, as shown in Fig. 7-29. The source sends a beam of visible or infrared light, which is picked up by the detector. The signal from the detector remains in one state as long as the detector "sees" the beam. If the beam is blocked, the output signal goes to the other state.

You can make an in-circuit test using your logic probe. You can also use a VOM, set to read a low DC voltage. The source side of the unit will include one lead

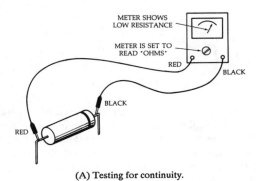

(A) Testing for continuity.

(B) Reverse leads and test again.

Fig. 7-28. Testing diodes.

battery is flowing through the diode. In the other position, the meter should show high resistance, to indicate that the current is blocked. When you're making an in-circuit test, the difference in reading between the two directions will be more subtle, because of the effect of the other components in the circuit. Reject a diode if it passes current in both directions, or blocks it in both directions. Before you remove a diode, note which end of the part has the band. Insert the replacement with the same orientation.

Testing a Light-Emitting Diode

LEDs are used as indicators in many types of computer equipment. Like conventional diodes, they pass current in only one direction. You can test an LED in-circuit, using the procedure described above. LEDs are usually wired into a circuit with an associated dropping resistor, to limit current flow. When you install a replacement LED, you may accidentally get the polarity wrong and the replacement LED will not light. Try reversing the leads.

Testing a Light Source and Detector

A light source and detector are often combined into a

that stays "high" and another that stays "low." The detector side will include one lead that stays "high" or "low," and another that changes when you block and unblock the beam.

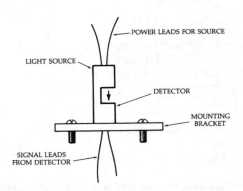

Fig. 7-29. Typical light source and detector.

Testing Capacitors

You may encounter several different types of capacitors in digital equipment. Some of these are illustrated and identified in Fig. 7-30. Ceramic disk capacitors are small flat disks ranging from $^1/_8$ inch to $^3/_8$ inch in diameter. Electrolytic capacitors are usually packaged in small cylindrical cans and electrolytics are usually "polarized." One of the leads on the capacitor (usually the negative one) is marked on the case. When you replace an electrolytic capacitor, match the alignment of the new part with the capacitor that is already in the circuit. Metalized-film capacitors are long and low, and usually have a shiny, colored, epoxy coating. Low-leakage tantalum types look like the end of a cotton swab, dipped in plastic. These are also polarized. Polystyrene capacitors often have a clear wrapping encasing a foil container.

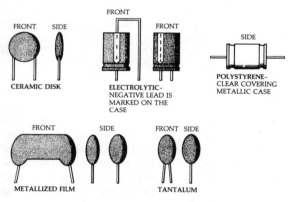

Fig. 7-30. Some popular types of capacitors.

To identify the value of a particular capacitor, start by checking the schematic. If the schematic does not list a value, you'll have to determine the value from the part itself. Without a capacitor checker, it is sometimes difficult to determine a capacitor's value. The capacitor probably has a number that identifies the value, but it may be difficult to determine exactly what the number means. Capacitance is measured in units called "farads." A "farad" is actually a very large unit, so most of the capacitors you will encounter will be measured in either *microfarads* ($1 \mu F = 0.000001$ F or 10^{-6} F) or *picofarads* ($1 pF = 0.000000000001$ F or 10^{-12} F).

Capacitors are generally made in any one of a number of standard values—1 pF, 2.2 pF, 4.7 pF, 6.8 pF, or a multiple of one of these. If the number on a capacitor is an exact multiple of one of these standard values, it probably represents a reading in picofarads. For example, on a capacitor carrying just the number "47," the number would represent 47 picofarads. A "100" would represent 100 pF.

If the number does not appear to be a multiple of a standard value, a different system may be in use. Let's say the number "104" appears on a capacitor. It would be unusual to manufacture a capacitor with the value of 104 pF, since the company probably also makes a part with the standard 100-pF value. In the numbering system used here, the first two numbers are the first and second significant digits of the value, and the third number represents a number of zeros. The whole number represents a value in picofarads. In this example, "104" would equal 100000 pF, or 0.1 μF.

At first, it may not be clear which system is in use. Use the size of the part as your guide. A capacitor with a value of 1 pF is a small part. A capacitor with a value of 1 μF is about the size of a typical 1-watt resistor.

When a circuit receives too much current, the capacitors are often the first parts to fail. A failed capacitor usually develops a short circuit. (The capacitance of a part may change over time.) The short can allow a large current to flow through the part, generating heat, and producing gas inside the capacitor. If this happens suddenly enough, the case of the capacitor may actually explode. Keep this in mind when you energize any circuit you are working with. Turn your face away from the capacitors when you first turn on the power to the circuit. If a capacitor has been damaged, you can sometimes see evidence of this. The top of the case on the device may be raised, indicating that pressure has built up inside. If an electrolytic capacitor has been damaged, you can sometimes see some leakage from the bottom of the part.

You can make an in-circuit check of a capacitor. First, turn off the equipment and touch a jumper wire

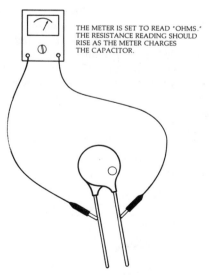

THE METER IS SET TO READ "OHMS." THE RESISTANCE READING SHOULD RISE AS THE METER CHARGES THE CAPACITOR.

Fig. 7-31. Testing a capacitor.

briefly to both leads on the capacitor. This will remove any charge remaining in the capacitor. Set the voltohmmeter to OHMS, and check the resistance between the legs of the capacitor, as shown in Fig. 7-31. As the battery in the VOM charges the capacitor, you should see the meter rise to a reading of infinite resistance. A low resistance means the part has developed a short circuit.

Other components in the circuit may interfere with this test. If a capacitor does not show an infinite resistance, clip one leg of the part and test again. Be sure to resolder the lead when you are through. When you replace a "polarized" capacitor, be sure to install the positive and negative leads in the correct positions.

Testing Fuses

Most digital equipment includes one or more fuses to protect it against current overloads. The most common device is the type of small fuse shown in Fig. 7-32. The

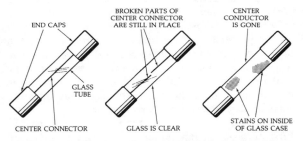

Fig. 7-32. Inspect fuses for an indication of the problem.

size of the center conductor (fuse element) is chosen to allow a certain amount of current to flow. When a larger current tries to cross, the conductor overheats and melts. This interrupts power to the equipment. The current rating for each fuse is engraved on one of the metal end caps. The notation "SB" (Slow Blow) means

the fuse was designed to take an overload current for a moment, rather than blow out immediately. If you are not sure whether a fuse is good, check for continuity with an ohmmeter.

A blown fuse can tell you something about your service problem. Often the glass case of the fuse appears clear, and you can still see the broken pieces of the fuse element. This means you have the kind of problem that causes a slow, gradual overload on the power supply. Some fuses even die of old age. But, if the inside of the glass tube is discolored, and there is no trace of the fuse element (the center connector), you know that the center connector was destroyed quickly and violently, using a lot of heat. The fault was a short circuit or other problem that caused a lot of current to flow very quickly. When you buy replacement fuses, get several—you can easily use all of them while you're troubleshooting an elusive problem.

Testing Transformers

You will often find a transformer in the power supply of a piece of digital equipment. You can make an in-circuit test of a transformer using the VOM as a continuity tester. Fig. 7-33 shows a simplified diagram of a transformer. To check a transformer, turn off the equipment, and set the VOM to read OHMS. Check for continuity through the primary winding. The meter should show a low resistance. Some transformers include a fusible link in the primary. If your test shows a very high resistance, this link may have opened. In this case, it is probably simplest to replace the transformer.

Check the continuity through the secondary winding as well. In rare cases, a winding can short to the frame of the transformer, so check for continuity from the primary to the frame and from the secondary to the frame as well. The meter should show infinite resistance in both of these tests.

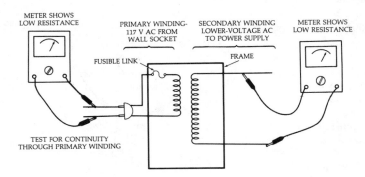

Fig. 7-33. Testing transformer for continuity.

Testing a Rectifier

The "rectifier" is a power-supply component that takes an AC input, and produces a rough DC output. Fig. 7-34 shows the input and output signals for a full-wave bridge rectifier. In computer equipment, the rectifying function is normally performed by a network of diodes, as shown in the sketch. In this type of rectifier, you can check each of the individual diodes separately. Test for continuity across each pair of leads in turn, and in both directions.

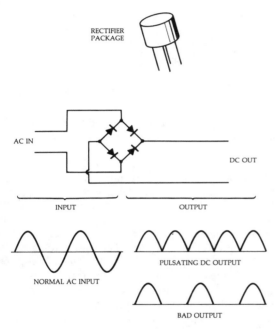

Fig. 7-34. A bridge rectifier, schematic symbol, and waveforms.

Testing Transistors

A transistor is an electronic device that amplifies current. Put a small current into the input side of the transistor, and the device produces a large current at the output side. *Field-effect transistors*, or FETs, are sensitive to voltage. A tiny voltage change at the input of an FET can control a large current through the output. The CMOS IC family uses the FET principle.

Digital equipment uses many, many transistors. For example, the MC6820 microprocessor chip contains over 190,000 transistors! Most of the transistors used in computer equipment are encased in ICs, and work in concert with each other, so you never see them. We're concerned here with "discrete" transistors—individual components that stand alone on the circuit board.

Discrete transistors are rather rare in most digital equipment. If a designer wants to use a transistor, it is usually cheaper to use a transistor that is inside an IC. Discrete transistors are used in power supplies, for switching, and to amplify current. You'll also find discrete transistors in printers and other electromechanical equipment, where current is amplified so that the digital circuits can actuate a solenoid or other mechanical device. A few transistors may be used in the conventional audio-amplifier role to drive a speaker.

Discrete transistors can vary in appearance, as shown in Fig. 7-35A. On schematics, transistors are usually identified with the letter "Q" and a number—for example, "Q26."

Transistors are made up of two basic materials—silicon and germanium. Silicon types are much more common in digital applications. In each material, there are two common configurations for the transistors—NPN and PNP. "N" and "P" refer to differently doped silicon or germanium materials, where N-types have an excess of electrons, and the P-types have a deficiency of electrons (are positive).

The order of the letters indicates the way these materials are arranged inside the transistor. An NPN transistor has a *collector* that is made of an "N-type" material, a *base* made of "P-type" material, and an *emitter* made of "N-type" material. As you can see in the schematic symbol for an NPN transistor (Fig. 7-35C), the arrow points to the emitter (one of the "N" sections); in a PNP transistor (Fig. 7-35D), the arrowhead points away from the "P" emitter section.

Transistors in digital equipment usually operate in the "saturation" mode. This means the transistor works as a switch and is usually either completely "on," or completely "off." This simplifies troubleshooting considerably. Other transistors handle "analog" signals and operate in the middle ground between "on" and "off."

Transistors can fail in a number of different ways. A bad transistor may short-circuit from the "base" to the "collector," or from the "base" to the "emitter." Sometimes a transistor is damaged so badly that short circuits develop between all three of the leads. A short circuit often allows a large current to flow, and causes the faulty transistor to heat up.

The first step in identifying a bad transistor is to check for signs of overheating. A bad transistor may appear to be burnt or melted. When the equipment is operating, you can touch the transistor to see if it feels unusually hot. The amount of heat you feel should be proportional to the size of the transistor's heat sink. If

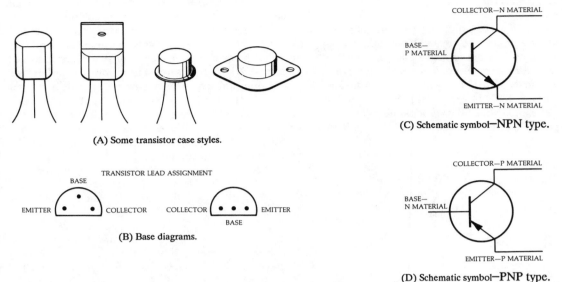

(A) Some transistor case styles.

(C) Schematic symbol—NPN type.

(B) Base diagrams.

(D) Schematic symbol—PNP type.

Fig. 7-35. Some common transistors.

the part has a large heat sink, you can expect it to be too hot to touch for very long. If the transistor has no heat sink, yet is very hot, you can suspect a problem. Don't touch a transistor if it is part of the circuitry that carries 120-V AC.

A good transistor checker can tell you which leg on a transistor is the "emitter," which is the "base," and which is the "collector." To use this type of tester, you simply clip a test lead to each leg, and the checker tells you whether or not the transistor is working. Many inexpensive transistor checkers are able to make an in-circuit check, but they are not able to identify the three legs on a transistor.

You can identify the leads, however, by using a voltohmmeter. Turn off the equipment, and set your voltohmmeter to OHMS. For testing purposes, you can think of a transistor as a network of two diodes, connected as shown in Fig. 7-36A. To identify the leads on the transistor, you can test each of these "equivalent diodes," just as if they were separate components.

The first job is to identify the "base" of the transistor. We have shown this step in Fig. 7-36B. With an ohmmeter, check the resistance between each pair of legs. Now reverse the test probes and check the resistance between each pair again. Between two of the legs, you should get a high resistance, regardless of which way you connect the probes. These two legs are the "emitter" and the "collector," but at this point you do not know which is which. The other leg is the base.

Now you must determine which leg is the "emitter," and which is the "collector." In the process, you can also determine whether the transistor is a PNP or NPN type. See Fig. 7-36C. Connect the negative probe of the ohmmeter to the "base" lead, and the positive probe to one of the other legs. If you get a low resistance reading, the device is a PNP type. If you get a high resistance reading, reverse the test probes. If you then get a low resistance with the positive probe connected to the "base," the part is an NPN type. (There is one final complication. If you are using a Japanese meter, these indications may be reversed. On some of these imported meters, the red lead does not carry the positive voltage during a resistance test, when the meter is set to read OHMS.)

These tests can also give some indication of a transistor's condition. If the transistor does not check out as described above, there may be something wrong with the part. For example, if the emitter-collector junction shows a low resistance in both directions, the transistor is shorted.

It is somewhat risky to make in-circuit checks on a transistor with an ohmmeter. The ohmmeter contains a power source, and, in some situations, it can produce enough current to damage the transistor. To minimize the risks, use the "R × 100" setting on your ohmmeter. When you make an in-circuit test, the test results will often be confused by the effects of other components on the circuit board. If you really want to be safe,

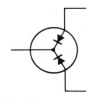

(A) Think of a transistor as two diodes.

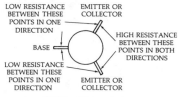

LOW RESISTANCE BETWEEN THESE POINTS IN ONE DIRECTION

EMITTER OR COLLECTOR

BASE

HIGH RESISTANCE BETWEEN THESE POINTS IN BOTH DIRECTIONS

LOW RESISTANCE BETWEEN THESE POINTS IN ONE DIRECTION

EMITTER OR COLLECTOR

(B) Identifying the base.

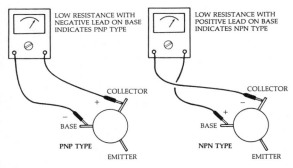

LOW RESISTANCE WITH NEGATIVE LEAD ON BASE INDICATES PNP TYPE

LOW RESISTANCE WITH POSITIVE LEAD ON BASE INDICATES NPN TYPE

COLLECTOR

COLLECTOR

BASE

BASE

PNP TYPE

NPN TYPE

EMITTER

EMITTER

NOTE: When using a Japanese ohmmeter these indications may be reversed.

(C) Determining device type—NPN or PNP.

Fig. 7-36. Testing transistors and identifying the leads.

disconnect one leg of the transistor from the circuit board. This will also eliminate the chances of other components interfering with your tests.

When you remove or replace transistors, remember that they are easily damaged. Always turn off power to the equipment before you remove or replace a transistor. Also, you can easily destroy a transistor by overheating it. When you solder and unsolder transistors, always clip a heat sink to the leg on which you're working, as shown in Fig. 7-37. The heat sink will draw off any excess heat before it can reach the transistor body. Use a low-wattage iron (30 watts), and don't allow the iron to either touch the part for more than 10 seconds, or come within $1/16$ inch of the transistor body.

Before you replace a transistor, bend the legs so they match the original hole pattern. Some transistors

come in cylindrical plastic packages, with a flat on one side. Transistors that use this package configuration can have several different leg arrangements. In the most common arrangement, with the flat side facing you and the legs are pointed down, the leads are arranged in the following order: "emitter" on the left, "base" in the center, and the "collector" on the right. However, some

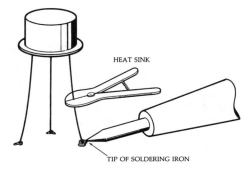

HEAT SINK

TIP OF SOLDERING IRON

Fig. 7-37. Use a heat sink when soldering transistors.

transistors do not follow this rule. If a transistor uses another configuration, this is usually noted on the packaging. It is easy to become confused—double-check the lead configuration carefully before you install a new part.

Large transistors can produce quite a bit of heat, so some are attached to heat sinks. The heat sink may be permanently bonded to the body of the transistor, or it might take the form of a finned plate which sits under or behind the part. If the original transistor has a heat sink, be sure the replacement transistor has a heat sink that is at least as large. If the part has a separate heat sink, smear the transistor body with a small amount of heat-sink compound before you fit it in place. This increases the heat-transfer rate between the transistor and the heat sink.

FET-type transistors are particularly sensitive to static. This family includes the CMOS group of devices. These components have a "high input impedance." The input is, in effect, a small capacitor, and it can be damaged by even a short burst of high voltage. Unfortunately, static electricity can cause just such a burst. We described this problem in Chapter 5.

FET components are usually shipped in a piece of antistatic foam. Leave the components in the foam until the last minute. Some components are shipped with a shorting wire between two of the transistor legs. Leave this wire in place until the transistor is installed, and then clip it. You can store an FET temporarily by setting it, legs down, on a piece of aluminum foil. Use a brand of foil that is not varnished or coated.

Be careful to ground yourself before you touch an FET. You can do this by touching the case of a computer, or another piece of equipment that is connected to ground. You may also use a grounding strap or grounding mat, as described in Chapter 5. When you solder FETs, be careful to use a grounded-tip soldering iron or an isolated, battery-powered, soldering iron.

Electromechanical Parts

Some parts combine a mechanical action with an electronic function. The mechanical sections of these parts are subject to wear, breakage, and corrosion. As a result, electromechanical parts have relatively high failure rates.

Testing Switches

A switch usually operates by moving one contact into position against another fixed contact to make a connection. After long use, the mechanical parts in a switch may bend or break, and the contacts may become burnt or corroded. Fig. 7-38 shows some common types of switches.

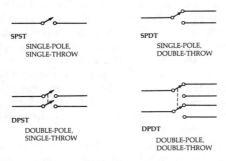

Fig. 7-38. Some common switch types.

You can use a voltohmmeter to make an in-circuit check of a switch. Turn the equipment off and set the meter to read OHMS. Touch the meter leads to both sides of the switch, as shown in Fig. 7-39. In a simple SPST switch, when the switch is set in the "off" or "open" position, the meter should show infinite resistance. When it is set in the "on" or "closed" position, the meter should show zero resistance. This indicates that the two sides of the switch are electrically connected.

You can also measure voltage to check the action of a switch when a circuit is working. Fig. 7-40

illustrates this idea. In this example, when the switch is open, current cannot flow through the circuit and there is a potential of 5 volts between the two sides of the switch. When the switch is closed, current can flow so the potential disappears, and the meter indicates zero volts between the sides of the switch.

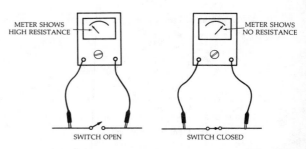

Fig. 7-39. Testing switches by measuring resistance.

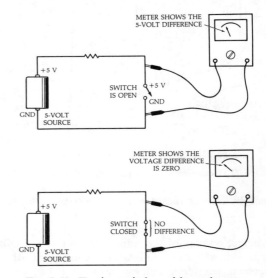

Fig. 7-40. Testing switches with a voltmeter.

Testing Potentiometers

A potentiometer, or "pot," acts as an adjustable resistor. One kind of "pot" uses a coil of wire as a resistor. A movable contact wipes against the wires in this coil, allowing an operator to change the resistance value of the potentiometer. Fig. 7-41 shows the arrangement.

You can test each side of a "pot" just as if it were a resistor. Use a voltohmmeter that is set to read OHMS. Measure the resistance between one of the side contacts and the "tap," or center contact. As you turn

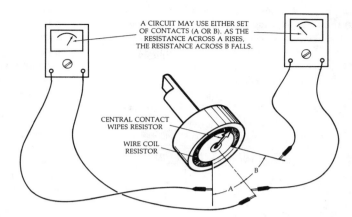

Fig. 7-41. Testing resistance of a potentiometer.

A CIRCUIT MAY USE EITHER SET OF CONTACTS (A OR B). AS THE RESISTANCE ACROSS A RISES, THE RESISTANCE ACROSS B FALLS.

CENTRAL CONTACT WIPES RESISTOR

WIRE COIL RESISTOR

the shaft of the pot, you should see the resistance change. As the resistance on one side of the potentiometer becomes higher, the resistance on the other side should become lower. If the resistance remains at zero as you turn the shaft, or stays at an infinite reading, replace the part.

The wiping contacts inside the pot can become dirty or corroded. Sometimes you can correct this by working some spray-type TV "tuner cleaner" into the unit. Most pots are enclosed in a metal case, so you'll have to spray the cleaner along the shaft, or into other openings in the case. Once the cleaner is inside, turn the shaft a few times to complete the cleaning action.

Testing Solenoids

A "solenoid" consists of a coil of wire surrounding a free-moving plug, as shown in Fig. 7-42. When current flows through the coil, it generates a force that moves the plug. You may encounter a solenoid in the head-loading mechanism of a disk drive, in the print-hammer mechanism in a printer, and in many other mechanisms.

The coil wires in a solenoid may either short-circuit or open-circuit. To test a solenoid, turn off the equipment and test for continuity through the coil using a voltohmmeter that is set to read OHMS. The meter should show a low, but measurable, resistance through the coil. An infinite resistance indicates an open circuit—a sign of a bad solenoid. Also test for continuity between the coil wire and the frame of the solenoid. A reading of zero resistance indicates a short circuit, and means that the part should be replaced.

Solenoids usually require a higher voltage and more current than the TTL logic circuits can provide. As a result, the solenoid is usually controlled by an output transistor, as shown in Fig. 7-42. The circuit is

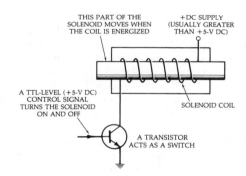

THIS PART OF THE SOLENOID MOVES WHEN THE COIL IS ENERGIZED

+DC SUPPLY (USUALLY GREATER THAN +5-V DC)

A TTL-LEVEL (+5-V DC) CONTROL SIGNAL TURNS THE SOLENOID ON AND OFF

SOLENOID COIL

A TRANSISTOR ACTS AS A SWITCH

Fig. 7-42. Solenoid operating principle.

usually wired so that the transistor acts as a switch to ground. The other end of the solenoid coil is connected to a continuous source of DC. When the transistor is turned on, it completes the connection to ground, allowing the current to flow through the coil. The output transistors may fail. If a particular solenoid is not working, check for an "input" and "output" at the appropriate output transistor.

Testing a Drive Motor

Fig. 7-43 shows a simple diagram of a drive motor. A "coil" consisting of many turns of wire is wrapped around the outer shell of the motor. The "rotor" in the center of the motor acts as a magnet. Sometimes this central part actually contains a permanent magnet. In other types of motors, the magnetic force in the center of the motor is developed by current flowing through another coil of wire. When current flows through the wire of the outer coil, it creates a force that pushes against the rotor, causing it to spin.

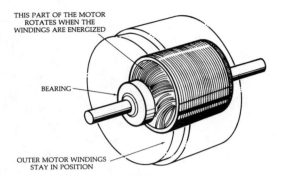

THIS PART OF THE MOTOR ROTATES WHEN THE WINDINGS ARE ENERGIZED

BEARING

OUTER MOTOR WINDINGS STAY IN POSITION

Fig. 7-43. Testing a drive motor.

To test a drive motor, check for continuity through the wire of the outer coil, using a voltohmmeter that is set to read OHMS. You should find a low, but measurable, resistance. An infinite resistance indicates an open circuit, and the motor should be replaced. Also check for continuity from the coil to the frame of the motor. A reading of zero resistance here indicates a short circuit.

If the motor is making an unusual noise, the rotor bearings may be worn or need lubrication. With the power off, try to turn the shaft by hand—it should move easily. If the motor bearings are worn or stiff, you usually must replace the motor.

Testing a Stepper Motor

A stepper motor is specially constructed so it can be moved in very precise increments. You may find one of these motors used in the head-stepping mechanism in a disk drive, or in the carriage-advance, paper-advance, or print-wheel mechanisms in a printer.

Fig. 7-44 illustrates the operating principles of a stepper motor. The motor has four independent sets of windings. In the sketch, and on schematics, these are identified as $\phi1$, $\phi2$, $\phi3$, and $\phi4$. (The character ϕ means *phase*.) The motor also has many poles, arranged around a permanent magnet that is free to rotate. Each pole is wrapped with wires from two of these windings—$\phi1$ and $\phi2$ on some poles, and $\phi3$ and $\phi4$ on others. When one of the windings is energized, the pole will behave as a "North" pole. When the other winding is energized, the pole will become "South." In Fig. 7-44, poles 2 and 3 are both North poles, so the

"south" end of the permanent magnet is attracted to a position between the two energized poles. On the other side of the motor, the two poles closest to the "north" end of the permanent magnet will be South poles at this moment. To move the magnet in a clockwise direction, you would make pole No. 4 a North pole, and pole No. 2 a South pole. This would force the magnet to move in the correct direction.

Fig. 7-45 shows the arrangement of the control circuits. The stepper motor is powered and controlled through four signal lines. A source of +DC voltage is provided at one end of each of the coils. At the other end is a transistor, which is turned on and off by the control circuits. Since stepper motors require a higher voltage and more current than TTL logic circuits can provide, designers often use discrete output transistors to provide the correct voltage and current. When the control circuits energize one of these transistors, it acts as a switch, connecting one end of the coil to ground. This causes current to flow through the coil, energizing it. Fig. 7-45B shows how the coils are actually wired. Each pair of coils is connected to a "common" line, which goes to the +DC source. Some motors have only one common line, wired to all four coils.

Many stepper motors include a "feedback" system that tells the control circuit how far the motor has turned. One arrangement uses one of the light-source and detector assemblies we described earlier in this chapter. The light source is aimed at a slotted wheel that is attached to the shaft of the motor. As the motor turns, the detector "sees" the slots and sends out a series of +5-V pulses. These pulses are counted and interpreted by the control circuit.

Fig. 7-46 shows some typical signals you might find on the four lines to the windings. Fig. 7-46A shows the signals you would find when the motor is using a "2-phase" excitation scheme. Fig. 7-46B shows the signals that correspond to a "1—2-phase" arrangement. Some steppers switch back and forth from one type of signal to another, depending on how fast they are turning.

To check a stepper motor, start by looking for signals on each of the four signal lines. The equipment will have to be turned on, of course, and you'll have to command the equipment to do something that activates the stepper motor. When the motor is active, you should see the signal waveforms we've shown in Fig. 7-46. You'll have to use an oscilloscope to do this, because the pulses on these lines will probably have too high a voltage to read with a logic probe.

If one of the signal lines is dead, check the discrete output transistor for that line. We described some simple in-circuit tests earlier in this chapter, in the section on "Testing Transistors."

Fig. 7-44. The operating principles of a stepper motor.

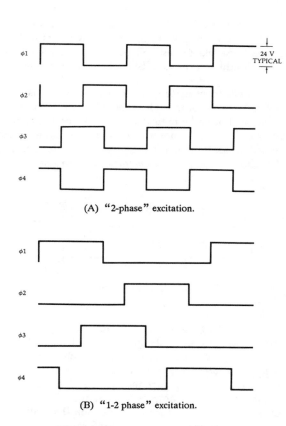

(A) "2-phase" excitation.

(B) "1-2 phase" excitation.

Fig. 7-46. Stepper motor signals.

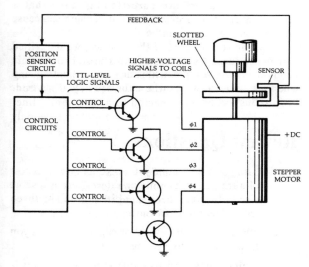

(A) Arrangement of the control circuits.

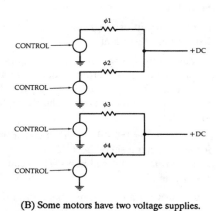

(B) Some motors have two voltage supplies.

Fig. 7-45. Stepper motor control circuits.

Of course, an output transistor could be inactive because it is not getting any input. Use your logic probe to check for a series of 5-V pulses coming along the input line from the control circuit. If one or more of these signals is missing, look for a problem in the control circuit.

If the signals into the stepper motor seem correct, check for a problem in the motor itself. Turn off the equipment and set your voltohmmeter to read OHMS. The test is similar to the test for a simple drive motor, but you have to check four separate sets of windings. As shown in Fig. 7-45B, you would start by setting one test lead on line $\phi 1$ and the other on the appropriate common line. The meter should show a low, but measurable, resistance. An infinite resistance indicates one of the windings has developed an open circuit. The correct resistance value is often listed on a label on the motor. Repeat the test for each of the other coils. Next, check the resistance through each pair of coils. This should be twice the resistance through one coil. Finally, test for a short from each common to the case of the motor. You should have a high resistance reading here.

Now and then, the feedback sensor may slip out of position or stop working. You may use your logic probe to check for pulses from the feedback sensor. You should see these pulses whenever the motor is turning.

Instead of a stepper motor, some mechanisms use a "servo motor." The type of motor, stepper or servo, will often be indicated by a label on the back of the motor. A servo motor can also be moved in precise steps, although the operating principle is different. Fig. 7-47 shows the essential elements of a servo system.

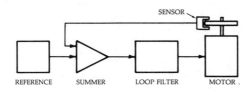

Fig. 7-47. A servo motor system.

In the servo, a feedback loop receives signals from a sensor that reads the position of the motor. As long as the voltage from the sensor and the voltage from the reference are in balance, the motor stays at rest. When the reference voltage changes, the "summer" circuit detects the change. The summer orders the motor to turn in a direction that will cause the voltage from the sensor and reference to equalize. When the two inputs are equal again, the motor stops.

The test for checking the motor, itself, is the same as that used for testing a drive motor (described earlier). The control signals for a servo motor can be complicated. If you have a problem with one of these units, refer to the manual for your equipment, or take the equipment to a service shop.

Chapter Review

In this chapter, we have covered most of the key principles of troubleshooting. The basic ideas we outlined in the beginning of the chapter are applicable to all types of troubleshooting. The idea of "chain troubleshooting" gives you a methodical way of localizing the cause of a problem. The concept of substitution will save you lots of time and effort.

As we explained, you do not have to understand every detail of the equipment's operation in order to make many repairs. We've shown you how to find and identify components on a circuit board. However, the more knowledge you have, the more efficient you will be. Many beginners are surprised to learn that a problem at the "downstream" end of a chain can cause problems at the "upstream" end.

In the second part of the chapter, we described test procedures for many of the simpler electronic components. As you practice your troubleshooting, and when you want to check out a certain part, you can refer back to this section.

Review Questions

1. Using an ohmmeter, you make an in-circuit test of a transistor. The meter shows there is a short circuit between each combination of the three legs. What does this tell you?

2. Why should you beware of capacitors when you turn on power to a circuit?

3. Which parts tend to fail first when a circuit is overloaded?

4. You are testing a motor, and you find a short circuit through the coil of the motor. What does this tell you?

5. Why should you use a ground connection that is close to your test point?

6. A customer brings you a computer which appears to be completely "dead." You check the outputs from the power supply and find no voltages. Does this mean you should replace the power supply?

7. You are having trouble with a printer which is driven through a serial port. You notice that the computer has two serial ports. How can you use this information?

8. You remove a burned-out fuse and notice that the inside of the glass case is blackened. What does this tell you?

8

Troubleshooting
Integrated Circuits

Introduction and Objectives

In a modern microcomputer system, the "integrated circuit," or IC, is the heart and soul of the microcomputer. Modern integrated-circuit technology has made the desk-top computer possible. Therefore, if you want to do "component-level" servicing on microcomputer equipment, you will have to learn how to troubleshoot ICs. In some ways, ICs are convenient to troubleshoot, because, for troubleshooting purposes, each IC can usually be thought of as a logical "block." Like other digital circuits, ICs use only two legitimate signal levels. Also, many ICs are mounted in sockets, making it easy to substitute one for one.

However, ICs do present some complications. To begin with, circuit boards often contain a large number of ICs and the ICs may be interconnected in very complicated patterns. Somehow, the technician must be able to identify the specific part that has failed. Remember that ICs exhibit the "two-way" effect (described in Chapter 7). A problem "downstream" in the chain of components can affect an IC which is "upstream." This complicates the normal "chain" troubleshooting techniques. Some ICs are very complicated, or handle many different inputs and outputs. This can make it hard to tell if an IC is doing its job correctly.

We will begin this chapter by explaining how to identify ICs—on a circuit board or a schematic. Next, we will tell you how to remove and replace ICs on a circuit board. In the following section, we will discuss the ways that ICs can fail. We will show you how to troubleshoot these parts in a number of different situations—broken input lines, broken output lines, output shorted to ground, and so on.

In the last part of the chapter, we'll look at several of the most common ICs. We will tell you how these parts operate, and give you some troubleshooting suggestions.

Identifying ICs

An IC may be indicated in two ways on a schematic diagram, as shown in Fig. 8-1. In one scheme an IC is represented by a rectangle. The pin numbers are shown, along with the signal carried on each pin. Often, an arrow will be used to indicate whether the signal is an input or output. A note on the schematic may list the IC's identification number. As we said earlier, some manufacturers use a grid system to locate components on a circuit board. If this system is in use, the grid location of the part will also be noted on the schematic.

Another notation is used when the IC contains simple logic elements, like gates. A typical IC chip might contain four simple gates, and these gates might be used in four different circuits. When one of the gates appears in the schematic, a note will indicate that this is only part of a complete IC, and then list the IC number and the grid location.

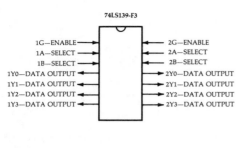

Fig. 8-1. IC schematic symbols.

Most ICs have identifying markings, similar to those shown in Fig. 8-2. Each manufacturer is free to use a different numbering system. There have been some attempts at standardization, but you will still find a wide variation in numbering systems. A well-marked IC has three important markings—the "logo," the core number, and the batch code.

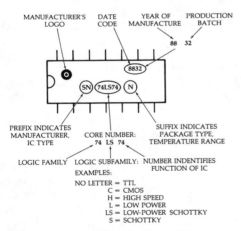

Fig. 8-2. Identification of ICs.

The "logo" or symbol identifies the manufacturer. We've given a chart showing some of the more common logos in Appendix B. The core number identifies the logic family and function of the IC. The numbering system is somewhat standardized for the 7400 series of ICs, as shown in Fig. 8-2. In our example, the core numbers are "74LS74." The first two numbers indicate that the IC is a member of the 7400-series IC "family." Many of the ICs you will encounter will be members of the 7400 series. There may be one or two

letters inserted in the center of the core number to indicate the logic subfamily. If no letters have been inserted, the part is a member of the "TTL" subfamily. These letters, TTL, stand for "transistor-transistor logic." A "C" in the center of the core number indicates the chip uses CMOS technology and requires especially careful handling. Table 8-1 shows how some of the other families are listed.

Table 8-1. IC Families

Core Number	IC Family
74xx	TTL
74ALSxx	Advanced Low-Power Schottky
74Cxx	CMOS
74Fxx	Fast
74Hxx	High-Speed
74HCxx	High-Speed CMOS
74HCTxx	High-Speed CMOS TTL
74Lxx	Low Power
74LSxx	Low-Power Schottky
74Sxx	Schottky

The last two or three digits in the core number identify the type of IC. By looking these up in a reference, you can discover what the chip is designed to do, and how the pin connections are laid out. For example, the number "7474" is assigned to an IC which contains a "Dual D-type Flip-Flop." This IC actually contains two separate D-type flip-flop circuits.

A "7474" chip does the same job as a "74LS74" chip or a "74C74" chip. All three types perform the same function and have the same pin connections. However, these three chips may not be interchangeable, because of differences in timing and power requirements.

Some ICs also carry a third marking which indicates the year of production and batch number for the IC. In our example, this code number is "8832." The first two digits represent the year of manufacture. The last two represent the production order of the batch that contained this particular chip.

There are plenty of ICs which do not fit into this neat numbering system. Sometimes an IC may be an analog component—an amplifier, for example—packaged in a "dual in-line" package (DIP) like an IC. Resistors may also be packaged in a DIP package. If the part is a custom IC, the chip may carry a "house marking" that is meaningful only to the manufacturer. Sometimes a manufacturer will black out the markings on an IC, so nobody can determine how the circuit has been designed.

In Chapter 6, we mentioned several possible sources for information on ICs. If you can find a listing for an IC in one of these sources, you can uncover a lot of useful information. For troubleshooting purposes, we're mainly concerned with the pin diagram and the truth table for the IC.

The pin-connection diagram shows the signals that are connected to each of the pins on the IC. As we explained earlier, the pin numbering system is consistent from one IC to the next (refer to Fig. 7-22). One end of each IC is marked with a white dot or a notch in the plastic of the IC. Pin number 1 will always be the upper left-hand pin at the end of the IC, when the IC is held so the notch is in the topmost position. The pin numbers run down the left side of the IC, and up the right side.

In the pin-connection diagram, the pin for the supply voltage will be indicated by the abbreviation "V_{CC}." In most of the ICs you will encounter, this voltage will be +5-V DC. The pin that connects to ground will be indicated by "GND." In general, the pin with the highest number will carry V_{CC}, and the pin with half that number will connect to ground, but this may not always be true.

In addition to the pin diagram, you'll usually find a truth table. On a digital IC, for every specified input, you can expect a defined, predictable output. A truth table is simply a list of all of the possible inputs and the resulting outputs.

Special Handling for ICs

ICs are delicate, and can easily be damaged by rough handling. All of the cautions we mentioned for discrete transistors apply to ICs as well. Don't drop ICs. Use the minimum possible amount of heat to solder and desolder connections. Note the orientation of an IC before you remove it. You might even make a sketch, showing the IC and surrounding parts and noting the position of the notch on the end of the IC. Always turn off the equipment before you remove or replace any IC!

Removing an IC can be troublesome unless you know how to do it. If you plan to discard the IC, you can simply clip each of the pins with a pair of "nippy" cutters. Remove the body of the IC, and then desolder and remove each of the legs. Clean out each hole in the circuit board by heating it until the solder is melted, and then push the point of a round wooden toothpick through the hole.

Removing an IC which you want to use again will be more difficult. Of course, if the IC is mounted in a socket, you can simply remove the IC. But, if the IC is soldered in place, you'll have to desolder and remove each of the pins. Many technicians will tell you never to put an IC back in the circuit once it has been desoldered and removed. They insist that the process of removing the IC puts such thermal and mechanical strains on the chip that it may be unreliable. If your technique is good and you can remove an IC quickly and cleanly, you can probably re-use it.

If you do want to try to remove and salvage a chip, work on one pin at a time. Heat the pin until the solder at the base of the pin melts. Draw off the solder with a vacuum device, or use one of the other methods we listed earlier. While the solder is still soft, grip the IC pin with a pair of needle-nose pliers and move it. You should hear the pin break free. Follow the same procedure with the other pins. Don't use too much force, or you may crack the circuit board or damage the traces.

Whenever you replace an IC, install an IC socket (one having gold-plated contacts). You can remove the new IC from the socket while you solder the socket into place. This eliminates any risk of heat damage during soldering. Don't mount a salvaged IC in an IC socket. The pins on the salvaged chip will retain some solder. When you fit a salvaged part into place, these enlarged pins may distort the contacts in the socket. Once the socket is installed, clean the back of the circuit board with a flux remover, like Freon TF Degreaser. Soldering tends to leave an area of flux on the back of the circuit board. This flux may be sticky, and can attract dust. The dust, in turn, can cause a slight leakage that can make the IC appear to be faulty.

Be sure the pins on the IC are straight before you fit them into the socket. Some insertion tools include a device which straightens the pins for you. Insert one row of pins first, and then the other row, as shown in Fig. 8-3. Be careful to align the IC so the notch is in the correct position.

ICs that use MOS or CMOS technology are particularly sensitive to static and require special handling. The inputs of a CMOS IC include some small capacitors. A quick shot of high voltage at the inputs can damage these capacitors and destroy the IC. The main danger is from static electricity. Circuit boards that contain MOS ICs are often marked with a warning label. CMOS ICs are identified by a "C" in the core number; i.e., 74C08, 74C150.

A replacement MOS IC is usually shipped in an antistatic tube or a piece of antistatic foam. Leave the chip in its protective material until the last moment. For temporary storage, you can also set a chip legs-down on a piece of aluminum foil. Before you pick up an MOS chip, be sure to ground yourself by touching the case of the computer or another piece of equipment that is grounded. Use a grounded-tip soldering iron, or a battery-powered iron, when soldering.

Working with Surface-Mount Devices

As you work with modern equipment, you will begin to find more "surface-mount devices" (SMDs). Surface-mounted parts are very small, and are mounted on one side of the circuit board. Several of these parts are shown in Fig. 8-4.

In your repair work, you may have to remove and replace SMD parts. As a first step, collect the tools we described in Chapter 6.

- Low-power grounded-tip soldering iron with a narrow tip
- Small-diameter solder (0.025 or 0.030 inch)
- Masking tape or a "tacky" adhesive
- Solder-wicking braid

To remove an SMD part, heat each solder joint with the soldering iron and draw away the solder with the wicking braid. Don't worry about overheating the part you are removing—you will have to throw it away in any case. Never re-use an SMD part that has been removed from a circuit board! Once you have removed

Fig. 8-4. SMD devices.

most of the solder, you can remove the part. SMD parts tend to stick, even after most of the solder is gone. In order to release the device, you may have to twist it slightly, using needle-nose pliers.

You can use a traditional "pencil-type" iron to solder SMD parts into place. In order to do this, you must have a way of holding the part in position. One simple way of doing this is to hold down one end of the part with masking tape, as shown in Fig. 8-5A. Solder one or two of the connections, and then remove the tape. You may also use a drop of one of the "tacky" adhesives mentioned in Chapter 6 (Stikki-Wax, Fun-Tak, etc.).

You must be careful to use just the right amount of solder. On a good solder joint, the solder should cover the connector on the SMD part (Fig. 8-5B). Begin

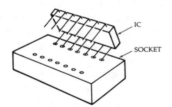

(A) Insert one row of pins.

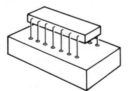

(B) Insert other row of pins.

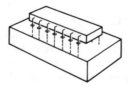

(C) Press IC into position.

Fig. 8-3. Mounting an IC in a socket.

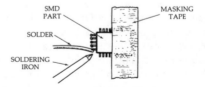

(A) Using tape to hold SMD part in place.

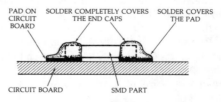

(B) Good solder connections (side view).

Fig. 8-5. Replacing SMD parts.

by heating the connector and the pad on the circuit board. When both parts are hot, touch them with the solder for just a moment. If you use too much solder, remove some of it with solder-wicking braid. Inspect each soldered joint carefully, using a magnifying glass! These joints are very small, and it is easy to make mistakes.

If you have some special soldering irons, you can use the "reflow" technique. Start by placing a small amount of solder on each of the connecting pads on the circuit board. Hold the SMD part in place, and touch the soldering iron to the terminals on the part. The solder on the pads will melt and "reflow," and then cool to form soldered connections. This technique will only work if you have a way of heating all of the soldered connections at the same time. The special soldering irons shown in Figs. 8-6 and 8-7 can do this.

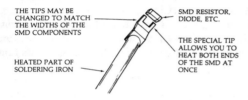

THE TIPS MAY BE CHANGED TO MATCH THE WIDTHS OF THE SMD COMPONENTS

SMD RESISTOR, DIODE, ETC.

THE SPECIAL TIP ALLOWS YOU TO HEAT BOTH ENDS OF THE SMD AT ONCE

HEATED PART OF SOLDERING IRON

Fig. 8-6. Soldering iron for small SMD components.

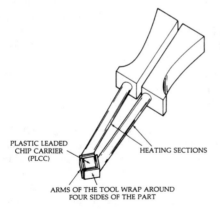

PLASTIC LEADED CHIP CARRIER (PLCC)

HEATING SECTIONS

ARMS OF THE TOOL WRAP AROUND FOUR SIDES OF THE PART

Fig. 8-7. Soldering iron for PLCC SMDs.

Troubleshooting ICs

We'll assume that many of our readers are already familiar with the basic concepts of digital technology. In addition, they should have done some troubleshooting work on analog circuits, using traditional tools—VOM, oscilloscope, and signal generator.

With analog circuits, it's possible to troubleshoot a circuit by testing one discrete component at a time, because it's possible for a technician to examine the input and output of each individual transistor, diode, etc. In an integrated circuit, whether digital or analog, the technician doesn't have access to discrete components. Instead, it is necessary to check a circuit as a whole, by observing the signals present at the inputs of an IC and then determining if the correct outputs result.

In analog circuitry, a technician is concerned with the way signals change—rise times, output levels, and so on. In digital work, there are only three possible levels—"high," "low," and "undefined." In this sense, digital troubleshooting work is simpler.

Fig. 8-8 shows a simplified model of an IC containing two digital devices. These don't represent any specific devices; we'll just use the illustration to make a few general observations about all IC devices. First, you'll note that both devices receive power from the same set of pins and neither device will work unless the IC is getting power. The supply voltage for TTL ICs can vary between 4.75 and 5.25-V DC. An input voltage above +6-V DC will probably burn out the IC. Reversing the V_{CC} and ground connections will also ruin the chip. Many CMOS ICs can operate on higher voltages, up to about 15-V DC.

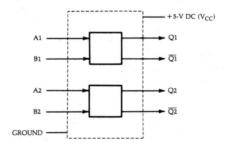

Fig. 8-8. Simple IC device.

In Fig. 8-8, you'll notice that each device has its own inputs and outputs. Thus, if you're troubleshooting an IC that contains several separate devices, you'll have to test each device individually. In digital notation, a bar above the letter means "the opposite of" or "not." In this example, each device has two outputs. The signal marked by the symbol "Q" with a bar above ($\overline{Q}$) will always be the opposite of the signal at Q.

Digital circuits can perform in ways that may seem surprising. Fig. 8-9 shows a simple digital device—an AND gate. You will note that input A is disconnected. What happens to the signals on the input and output lines of the device when one of the input lines breaks? In this case, the signal on line B is unaffected; it reaches the gate just as it did before. The gate itself is still working. It will perform its usual ANDing function on the inputs that reach it, and will place the result on output line C. But what happens on line A? The normal input signal stops at the point where the input line is broken. The remaining part of line A begins to "float." It assumes an "undefined" state, between logical "high" and logical "low." This is characteristic of digital circuits: when a signal line is broken or disconnected, the inputs of the device "downstream" will "float."

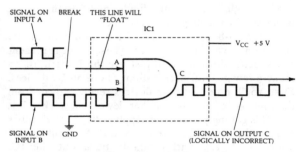

Fig. 8-9. Illustration of a floating input.

In TTL ICs, a floating line will show a voltage of about 1.5 volts with respect to ground. Even though this voltage is below the threshold required for a logical "high," many TTL circuits will accept a floating signal as a permanent "high." The effect of a floating input is less predictable for CMOS devices. A floating input may appear as either a logical high or a low, or it may change between the two.

How does this affect the output of the AND gate in our example? Line A is always high; so, because of the way the gate functions, the pulses from line B will be passed directly through to the output. There will be a signal at the output, but the ANDing function will be lost. The AND gate is a logical device, designed to condition and manipulate signals that contain logical information. From an electronic point of view, this AND gate is still active, inputting and outputting signals, but the gate has stopped performing its logical function.

There is a second complication that is caused by the "totem pole" output which is used in many ICs. Fig. 8-10 shows a second circuit which is not working. An input signal is clearly entering IC1, but no output is coming out. You may conclude from this that IC1 is bad, but you will not necessarily be correct. To be certain of what is happening at IC1, you must also be concerned with the next segment in the chain (IC2).

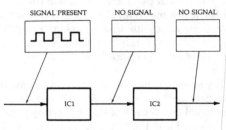

Fig. 8-10. Testing a chain of ICs.

As you can see, IC2 is also dead. Is this because of the problem with IC1, or is IC2 actually causing the problem? To find out, you might be tempted to introduce your own pulses at the input of IC2 to see if IC2 begins to operate normally. This idea is consistent with the "chain troubleshooting" techniques we explained earlier (Chapter 7). Unfortunately, this is one of those situations where the effects of a problem can be distributed through the chain in both directions. A problem "downstream" can affect components that are "upstream."

The "totem pole" output used in many TTL devices uses two transistors, as shown in Fig. 8-11. When the logic circuits in the IC decide they want to produce a "high" output, they switch on transistor Q1. This transistor connects the 5-V DC source to the output line, resulting in a "high" output. When the logic circuits want a "low" output, they turn on transistor Q2, which connects the output line to ground. This system works well as long as all of the ICs in the chain are operating correctly. A problem occurs when one of the ICs fails, so that one of its transistor outputs stays either "high" or "low."

Referring back to Fig. 8-10, let's say that you do try to put pulses on the line between IC1 and IC2. What happens next depends on what's happening at the output stage of IC1. This stage may have failed in such a way that it is trying to produce either a "high" or a "low" on the output line. If it is stopped in a "low" mode, the output line will be connected to ground. Any "high" pulses (positive voltage) you put on the output line will be drawn off to ground. They will never reach the inputs of IC2, so the test will be inconclusive.

A TTL IC which fails and holds a line "low" will usually overpower other ICs that try to pull the same line "high." To put this another way, most TTL ICs can "sink" more current to ground than they can "source." CMOS ICs may fail so that both transistors in the "totem pole" output switch on, causing the IC to overheat.

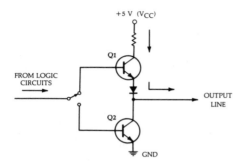

Fig. 8-11. TTL "totem pole" output.

In the example shown in Fig. 8-10, it might be simplest to replace both of the suspect ICs. The only way to tell which IC is faulty is to disconnect the output of IC1 from the input of IC2. You could do this using any of the methods we discussed earlier in this chapter. Once you've broken the chain into two separate subsystems, you can analyze them independently. You're then free to introduce pulses at the input of IC2 and see if IC2 behaves normally.

One likely cause of an IC failure is a broken "bond" between an IC pin and the actual circuitry inside the IC. Fig. 8-12 shows a partially assembled IC with the top part of the case removed. The circuit itself sits in the center of the case area. Very thin wires, about 0.001-inch thick, run from pads on the circuit to the IC pins. These wires, or "bonds," can easily be broken by rough handling or electrical stress. If a bond on an input line is disconnected, the input will not be able to reach the main part of the IC. If a bond on an output line is disconnected, that output will not be able to leave the

IC. A broken wire or circuit-board trace, or a cold solder joint outside the IC, can also cause problems similar to those caused by a broken bond.

The circuit symptoms may be different, depending on whether the break occurs inside the body of the IC or outside of the IC (Fig. 8-13). In Fig. 8-13A, the output bond is disconnected inside the body of IC1. To check this, you would take a reading at pin C. You would discover that the output signal is missing. In Fig. 8-13B, the break occurs outside the body of IC2. The output on pin C of IC2 will be normal. However, because the output line is broken, the signal still won't reach the next IC in line. The effect of the fault shown in Fig. 8-13A is the same as the effect of the fault shown in Fig. 8-13B. The first kind of failure is more difficult to diagnose because it occurs inside the body of the IC. For any suspect IC, start by checking for breaks in an

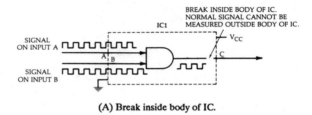

(A) Break inside body of IC.

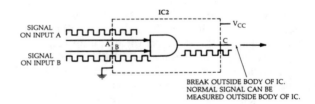

(B) Break outside body of IC.

Fig. 8-13. Effects of disconnected output lines.

output line. Remember that a break may occur inside the case of the IC, or at a broken circuit-board trace or cold solder joint outside the IC.

Fig. 8-14 shows another problem that may occur because of a break in an output line. The output may be directed to several ICs. In Fig. 8-14A, the inputs of ICs 2, 3, and 4 are deprived of a normal input, so they all "float." In TTL circuits, each floating input may be detected as a permanent "high." For this reason, a single broken output connection can affect a large number of ICs.

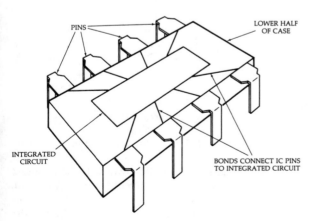

Fig. 8-12. Inside an IC (IC with cover removed).

The broken line may also appear at the input side of an IC. The break may occur inside the IC itself, or at a pin connection or wire outside the IC, as shown in Figs. 8-14B and 8-14C. The effects on the circuitry are the same, but the situation shown in Fig. 8-14C is easier to diagnose. In the example shown in Fig. 8-14B, if you take readings at the input pins on IC1, both inputs will appear to be normal, and the output line will show activity, although the signal will be logically incorrect.

In the example shown in Fig. 8-14C, the break occurs outside the body of IC2. If you check the signals on each of the IC pins, you will notice the "floating" value on pin A. As we said, many TTL circuits will accept this floating level as a logical "high," so the affected input will appear to be stuck in a "high" condition. As a result, the circuit will send out incorrect outputs which will cause errors in all downstream ICs.

A broken input line will not pass its effects "upstream." Fig. 8-15 illustrates this concept. IC3 is in a circuit which includes two other ICs. Because input line A is broken, the faulty IC is isolated from ICs upstream. This means these ICs are free to function normally, and send their outputs to separate circuits. The problem area will only extend downstream from IC3.

Less likely but easier to identify is a case where an input or output line is shorted to either the +5-V DC source, or to ground. Again, this kind of short can occur on the lines outside the IC, or inside the IC itself. In Fig. 8-16A, IC1 has developed a short from the +5-V DC line to one of its inputs, This particular short has occurred within the IC itself. This condition will hold line A permanently high. Note that you will find this high reading all the way from the output of IC1 to the input of IC2. Many circuits include small tantalum capacitors that are connected to the +5-V DC source. One of these can short and hold a line high.

Fig. 8-16B shows a similar problem. In this case, a circuit has developed a short from the output of IC3 to ground. This will hold the output line, and also the input of IC4, in a permanently low state.

When a signal line is shorted, the upstream IC driving the line may heat up. This is because the shorted condition overloads the output of the upstream IC.

A line that is shorted to V_{CC} or ground will appear to be permanently high or low. You should be able to detect this condition with a logic probe. Once you have identified a line that shows an abnormal condition, you must decide whether the problem is caused by the upstream IC, one of the downstream ICs, or by one of the circuit-board traces between them. You must disconnect the output pin of the upstream IC, or the input pins of each of the downstream ICs to be

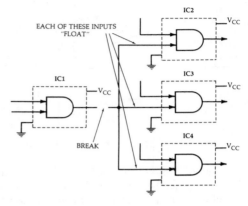

(A) Downstream effects.

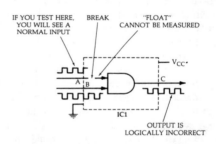

(B) Input disconnected inside IC.

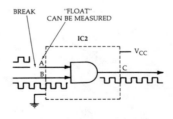

(C) Input disconnected outside of IC.

Fig. 8-14. Effects of broken input lines.

certain. Since there may be several ICs connected downstream of the one output, it is simpler to disconnect the output pin of the upstream IC. Use any of the disconnect methods described earlier in the chapter.

Some ICs use an "open collector" type of output. On this type of circuit, one of the totem pole transistors is missing. The output line is normally held high by a "pull-up" resistor to the +5-V DC source. When the transistor is turned on, the output line is shorted to ground, pulling the line low.

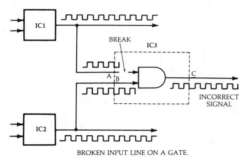

Fig. 8-15. When the input is disconnected, the effect is limited to ICs downstream.

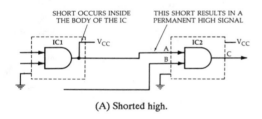

(A) Shorted high.

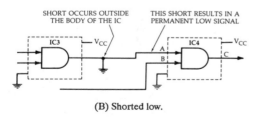

(B) Shorted low.

Fig. 8-16. Lines shorted high and low.

On this type of output, the transistor may short-circuit, holding the output line permanently low. This "low" can pull other parts of the system low as well, making it difficult to tell which IC has failed. One way of dealing with this is to use a current tracer. The tracer should lead you to the gate that is stuck in the low state.

Another kind of problem arises when an IC develops a short circuit between two pins (Fig. 8-17). A short may develop between two input pins or between two output pins. In some cases, the circuit will operate normally as long as the outputs feeding both pins carry the same signals. When the outputs feeding both pins are high, the shorted pins both display a high signal. When both outputs are low, the pins will show the correct low signals. It is only when one pin is low and the other is high that a problem arises. This is shown in the truth table of Fig. 8-17.

In a totem pole arrangement, the output producing a low is connected to ground. As we said earlier, most TTL devices can "sink" more current than they can "source," so in a contest between one device producing a low and another producing a high, the low will predominate. MOS and CMOS devices are less predictable. Note that this rule only applies when the lows and highs are generated by the devices themselves. A TTL device cannot pull a line low if the line is shorted to the +5-V DC source.

In the example shown in Fig. 8-17, we will assume that the IC is a TTL device. Because two pins are shorted, the output of IC1, which is trying to produce a high, is connected to ground through the output in IC2. The output in IC1 can't develop enough power to bring the signal up to high, so both lines show a low signal. You can't locate this type of problem by simply watching for outputs from each IC stage. Each IC does have an output, but the logical meaning of the signals is incorrect.

Another kind of IC failure occurs when the circuitry inside the IC fails. This usually results in an output that remains in either the high or low condition. Signals can't flow through the device and this normally stops all ICs downstream. If an IC has this type of problem, all of the inputs and outputs will have normal levels, but one of the outputs will be locked into one state.

There are other failure modes for ICs. We've already mentioned some of them. ICs may develop intermittent failures that are sensitive to temperature or vibration. Complicated ICs, including RAMs, ROMs, and CPUs, may develop problems with just a few of their functions. Any IC may develop a short circuit from the +5-V DC pin to ground.

Here's a review of the troubleshooting process used when working with ICs:

- Follow the signal until you find the point where the normal signals disappear. The bad IC is probably just upstream or just downstream from this point.

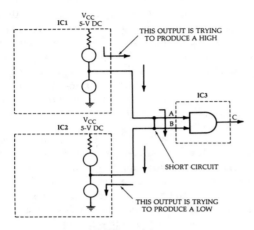

(A) Effects of short.

TRUTH TABLE (TTL IC'S ONLY)

OUTPUT IC1	OUTPUT IC2	PIN A IC3	PIN B IC3
H	H	H	H
L	L	L	L
L	H	L	L
H	L	L	L

(B) Truth table.

Fig. 8-17. Short between the IC's two input pins.

■ Disconnect the output pin on the IC just upstream, and see if the problems disappear. If they do, the upstream IC is bad.

■ Reconnect the upstream IC and start disconnecting the inputs of each of the downstream ICs. As you disconnect each input, check to see if the problems have disappeared. If they did, the chip you disconnected last is bad.

■ If you still do not find the problem, disconnect the output of the upstream IC again. This isolates a section of the circuit-board traces. Check for shorts to +5 V or ground.

■ When checking any particular IC, remember to test for +5-V DC to the chip.

Using a Logic Probe and Pulser

A logic probe allows you to check any test point for digital logic levels. The probe will indicate whether the signal at the test point is "high," "low," or "pulsing." Some of the better probes also show if a signal line is "floating" between high and low. On TTL-type ICs, a voltage below 0.8 V is defined as a low, and a voltage above +2.2 V is a high. A line is "floating" if it shows a voltage between these levels. Some CMOS ICs can use higher supply voltages. On CMOS ICs, a low is defined as a voltage less than 30% of the supply voltage. A high occurs when the voltage is greater than 70% of the supply voltage. Many probes have separate settings for testing TTL and CMOS ICs.

The logic probe is usually powered by the equipment being tested. Most probes operate on +5-V DC. A typical probe has two clip leads to supply power. The red lead should be clipped to a source of +5-V DC, and the black lead should be connected to ground. You will find two points that supply these voltages somewhere on the circuit board. You can also check the schematic for appropriate connection points. Most circuit boards include two large, wide traces for +5 V and 0 V. These traces often run around the outer edges of the board.

The logic probe should be connected to the same ground that is used as a reference for the signal under test. The probe should use a ground that is located as near as possible to the test point. If the ground used to supply power is too far from the test point, use an auxiliary grounding lead, as shown in Fig. 8-18. This allows you to choose a specific ground reference for the probe.

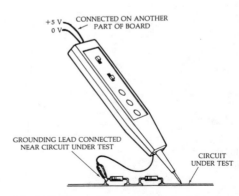

Fig. 8-18. Grounding lead for a logic probe.

Let's say that you want to check a simple digital device—an inverter. In an inverter, any signal which appears at the input is reversed, and produced at the output. A digital "high" at the input of an inverter will result in a "low" at the output. A "low" input results in a "high" output. Fig. 8-19 shows one way of testing an inverter, using just a logic probe. In Fig. 8-19A, the input of the inverter is receiving a high signal. In this case, when you touch the tip of the logic probe to the input on pin A of the inverter, the "high" indicator on the probe should light. When you check the output on pin B, the "low" indicator should light. In Fig. 8-19B, the inverter is receiving a low input. When you check the output side of the inverter, the "high" indicator should light.

A more complicated case is shown in Fig. 8-20. In this example, a series of positive pulses is flowing into the input of the inverter. When you touch the tip of the probe to the input pin and watch the display on the probe, the high indicator lights, and the pulsing indicator blinks. The high indicator lights because the pulses have longer high periods than low periods.

Now check the output side of the inverter. Here, you find that the low indicator is on, and the pulse indicator is still blinking. The output pulses have longer low periods than high.

When the pulses have equal high and low periods, both the high and low indicators will light, along with the pulse indicator. An inexpensive logic probe is not fast enough to track all of the high-speed pulses in computer equipment. When a train of pulses is too fast, a simple probe may light just the pulse indicator.

In troubleshooting work, the logic probe can reveal certain kinds of abnormal signals. If a signal line is completely dead, the probe will not light any of the indicators. Sometimes, digital circuits produce a value that is between the digital high and low. A line in this state is said to be floating—this should never happen, except on lines in a data bus. Different probes use different systems to indicate a floating line. On one type of probe, the high and low indicators may both glow dimly, for example. With a little experience, you'll learn how your probe displays the floating state. Sometimes, you may not be sure whether the probe is indicating a floating line or not. Touch the tip of the probe with your finger. If the line is floating, the probe will begin to show a solid "high" reading. Your finger injects some noise into the line, and this is enough to make the floating line read as a high—this trick applies only to TTL circuits.

A signal line may carry an occasional pulse that passes too quickly to light the LEDs. Many probes have a "memory" setting that will allow you to catch very fast pulses like this. When the probe is set on MEMORY, it will display the next pulse that passes, and will retain the display until you reset it. You can use this feature to spot an intermittent problem.

At times, you may want to run a jumper wire from the tip of the probe to the point under test, as

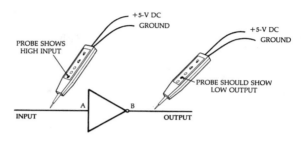

(A) When input is high, output is low.

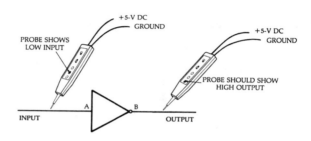

(B) When input is low, output is high.

INVERTER TRUTH TABLE	
A	B
HIGH	LOW
LOW	HIGH

(C) Inverter truth table.

Fig. 8-19. Testing an inverter with a logic probe.

shown in Fig. 8-21. This will allow you to keep both of your hands free to do other things.

You can use the logic probe to test any digital circuits which use +5-V DC, or 0 V. Be careful not to touch the probe to any part which carries 120-V AC, or any of the +12-V DC or −5-V DC lines used in the power-supply system. Be careful not to touch more than one IC pin at a time with the tip of the probe. If you touch two pins at the same time, you could create a short circuit and damage some components.

If the circuits inside your computer are accessible, you might want to try a few tests to familiarize yourself with the logic probe. Refer to the

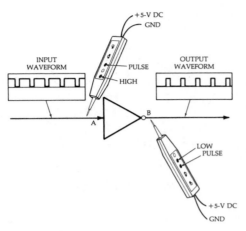

Fig. 8-20. Using a logic probe to test an inverter carrying changing signals.

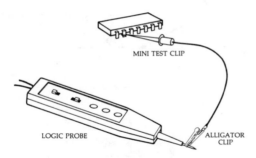

Fig. 8-21. Connect a jumper from probe to the test point.

documentation for the equipment, and find two source points for +5-V DC and ground. *Note*: The equipment will be turned on as you make these tests, so be sure you are familiar with the safety information given in Chapter 2.

You might want to check some of the signals around the CPU chip. Refer to the pin-out for the CPU in the documentation, and take the readings at the appropriate pins on the CPU. The tests should reveal the following:

1. The CLOCK line should show a constant string of pulses.

2. Each of the address and data lines should show constant activity.

3. The RESET line should pulse whenever you hit the Reset button, or boot the computer.

Using Pulser and Probe Together

The logic pulser can be used with the logic probe to check circuits that are more complicated than the inverter we described earlier. The pulser is used to generate specific test signals. Without the pulser, you must hope that the computer itself will generate the test signals you need.

Fig. 8-22 shows the test setup for an IC that includes an AND gate. The truth table shows that the output of this gate is high only when both of the inputs are high. How would you test a gate like this?

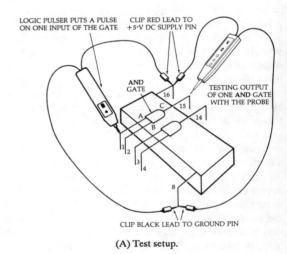

(A) Test setup.

A	B	C
LOW	LOW	LOW
LOW	HIGH	LOW
HIGH	LOW	LOW
HIGH	HIGH	HIGH

(B) Truth table.

Fig. 8-22. Testing part of an IC with a logic pulser and probe.

Before you begin, the circuitry which includes the gate should be turned on. The gate won't operate unless the IC is receiving power. Both the pulser and the logic probe require a +5-V DC power source. Locate two convenient take-off points in the power supply, or somewhere else on the circuit board, and clip on the power-supply lead for the pulser and probe. Now you're ready to check the gate itself.

Connect the top of the logic probe to pin 15, the pin that carries the output of the gate. You might want to use a jumper wire between the probe and pin 15, as shown in Fig. 8-21. The AND gate has two inputs. You can't supply both inputs at once with only one pulser, so how can you test this gate? If the inputs to the gate are not very active, perhaps you can use the existing input signals. For example, if one input is high, and the other is low, as shown in Fig. 8-23, you can test the gate easily. With the pulser, put a series of high pulses on input B, and watch the resulting output at C, using your probe. As indicated by the truth table, since one input is already high, you should see each of the pulses on input B passed through to the output.

This kind of test is not always possible. Frequently, the input signals change too rapidly for you to be sure what inputs are present at any given moment. And of course, many IC devices are more complicated than this AND gate.

A Pattern of Operations

We've explained how ICs fail, and we have reviewed the use of the logic pulser and logic probe. Now, let's look at a pattern of operations you can use when you open a microcomputer and see many, many ICs. You must have an orderly way of locating the precise IC that has failed. Your first job is to identify the section of the computer system that is affected, and then localize the problem further to a particular group of circuits. The troubleshooting chapters and flowcharts in this book should be helpful at this stage.

The next step is to identify the particular circuit that is causing the trouble. This is the place to apply the "chain troubleshooting" techniques described in Chapter 7. You can start at the beginning of the chain and work downstream until the trouble signals begin to appear, or you can start at the output of the chain and work upstream until the abnormal signals disappear.

Each IC becomes a convenient "block" for troubleshooting purposes. Start by looking for ICs that seem to be completely dead. In general, if an IC is receiving an input(s), but is not producing an output(s), it is probably not working correctly. The logic probe and pulser will be very helpful at this first level of troubleshooting. You will see characteristic signals at different points in the microcomputer. For example, pins connected to the data or address buses should always be busy. Pins carrying signals like CLOCK and STROBE should show a series of pulses. Other pins handle control signals that occur less frequently. The

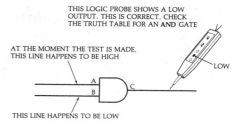

(A) One input high and one input low shows a low output.

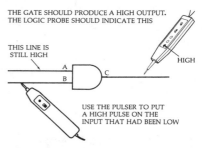

(B) Both inputs high shows a high output.

Fig. 8-23. Testing an AND gate with logic pulser and probe.

schematic should list the abbreviated name for the signal on each pin of an IC. By referring to the service manual for your equipment, you should be able to determine the kind of signal that should appear on each pin.

The "go/no-go" test will work for most simple ICs. However, there are cases where the results can be misleading. Earlier, we described a case where two signal lines were shorted together. If you simply checked the suspect IC for activity, you might not spot a problem of this type. The symptoms would not be evident unless both lines happened to receive the same outputs when the test was being made.

A more detailed test is required when an IC is producing outputs that are not logically correct. At this point, you need to know if each IC is working correctly and producing the correct outputs. The easiest way to do this is to simply substitute a new part. It is especially easy to substitute ICs if the IC is mounted in a socket.

Here's a trick that may help you in some cases. If you have a spare IC of the correct type, you can make a quick substitution while the original IC is still in-circuit.

If you bend the leads carefully, you can "piggyback" a substitute IC over the IC you suspect. Fig. 8-24 shows this arrangement. Turn off the equipment before you attach the top IC. Before you turn the equipment back on, be sure all the legs of the top IC are touching the legs on the bottom IC. Be sure the notched end of the top IC matches the notched end of the bottom chip. If you've done this correctly, the good chip may take over for the bad IC, and the equipment will begin to operate normally. If you try this technique and your troubles symptoms disappear, the bottom IC is bad.

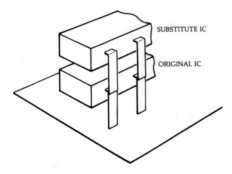

Fig. 8-24. Piggybacking an IC.

Sometimes you can't piggyback ICs. When you add the top IC, you're asking each input signal to drive twice the load. Another kind of problem arises with "counter" circuits. The original IC in the circuit may start counting from a different number than the piggybacked IC. Unless both counters receive a RESET pulse, they will not operate in synchronization. Finally, this trick won't work if the bottom IC is shorted. The top IC will not be able to override the short.

Sometimes, physical appearance will tell you that a particular IC is bad. Look for anything abnormal—a burnt case, a loose piece of solder, a bent component, etc. If the ICs are mounted in sockets, press the top of each chip in turn. If one of the ICs is loose, this will reseat it. If the problem is a "thermal intermittent," use freeze spray and a hair dryer to track it down (see Chapter 7).

If the IC is a simple part, and if the inputs to the IC change slowly, you may be able to make a detailed test using a probe and pulser. Begin by looking up the pin diagram and truth table for each IC you wish to test. Using the logic probe, check the signals present at each of the inputs of the IC. Refer back to the truth table—the set of inputs you observe should match one line of the table. Note the output predicted by the truth table and see if this matches the actual output you observe on the IC. If the predicted output and the

actual output match, the IC is probably working correctly. Move on to the next IC in the chain.

Some ICs are too complicated to test by simply checking for activity. On other ICs, the inputs are too active. If substitution does not reveal the cause of the problem, you will have to use more elaborate test equipment. Sometimes, the fault may be caused by a timing problem. A dual-trace oscilloscope is a big help in tracking down a problem of this type. Using the two traces on the scope, you can check the behavior of two signals at once.

An IC checker may also be helpful at this point. Many types are available, ranging from simple to very complex units. To use the simplest IC testers, you must remove each IC from the circuit. The unit produces a series of inputs for the IC being tested, and checks the resulting outputs. A tester of this type costs about $200. Some of the better testers are capable of making an in-circuit test.

Using the techniques we've described, you should be able to locate the point in the chain where the normal signals stop and the abnormal signals begin. The bad IC is probably the chip that marks the start of the abnormal signals, or one of the ICs directly downstream of this chip. Refer to Fig. 8-25. In this example, the trouble symptoms start just downstream of IC1. The faulty IC may be IC1, IC2, IC3, or IC4.

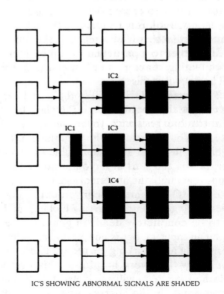

IC'S SHOWING ABNORMAL SIGNALS ARE SHADED

Fig. 8-25. A faulty IC can affect other ICs.

The next task is to identify the particular chip that is bad. On the upstream IC (IC1 in Fig. 8-25), disconnect the pin that shows the bad output. We described several ways of doing this at the beginning of the chapter. Double-check with a voltohmmeter set to read OHMS that the pin is really disconnected from the circuit. Once the pin is lifted, test the output on the pin itself. If this output is still abnormal, replace IC1. If the output becomes normal, you know the problem lies in one of ICs downstream (ICs 2, 3, and 4 in Fig. 8-25), or in the circuit-board traces that connect them to IC1.

Make a note of the signal that appears on the output pin of the IC1. Let's say that this signal is a constant "high." Now reconnect the output pin on IC1 that you disconnected earlier. The output signal will disappear, since the problem still exists. Go to the ICs directly downstream. One at a time, disconnect the appropriate input pin on each of these ICs. After you lift each pin, check the signal on the output pin of IC1. If you lift an input pin, and the output signal on IC1 becomes normal, you've located the problem. The bad IC is the chip whose pin you just disconnected.

If you disconnect all of the downstream ICs, and still haven't found the problem, look for a fault in the circuit-board traces. Disconnect the output pin on IC1 again. Now a small section of the circuit-trace system is isolated. No signals should be present on the isolated traces, because they are completely cut off from the rest of the system. Check for signals on these isolated traces, using a logic probe or VOM. If you detect a steady high, look for a short to the +5-V DC line. If one of the traces is low, look for a short to ground. A current tracer or short tester will be a big help at this point.

If the system passes this test, check for a short between two of the output lines. You can do this with a VOM, as shown in Fig. 8-26. Turn the equipment off, and set the meter to OHMS. The meter should show an infinite resistance between each pair of lines. If the meter shows zero resistance, you've located a short.

You can also make this test using a pulser and a logic probe, as shown in Fig. 8-27. Touch the pulser to

one output line, and the probe to the line beside it. Send out a train of pulses and watch the logic probe. If the logic probe detects these pulses, the two lines are shorted.

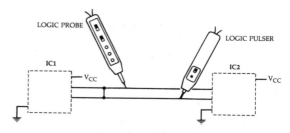

Fig. 8-27. Testing for a short using a logic pulser and a logic probe.

Troubleshooting Specific IC Devices

In this section, we'll look at some specific IC devices. We'll give you a basic idea of how each one works and suggest ways you can check for the correct operation of ICs that contain these devices.

AND Gates

This is one of the simplest of all digital logic devices. The AND gate produces a high output when both inputs are high. Fig. 8-28 shows the symbol for an AND gate and lists the truth table.

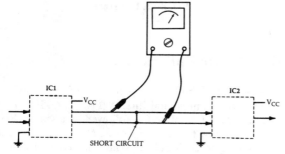

Fig. 8-26. Testing for a short using a VOM.

(A) Schematic symbol.

TRUTH TABLE

A	B	X
LOW	LOW	LOW
LOW	HIGH	LOW
HIGH	LOW	LOW
HIGH	HIGH	HIGH

(B) Truth table.

Fig. 8-28. The AND gate.

OR Gates

The schematic symbol and truth table for the OR gate are shown in Fig. 8-29. The output of the OR gate goes high whenever either of the inputs is high.

(A) Schematic symbol.

TRUTH TABLE

A	B	X
LOW	LOW	LOW
LOW	HIGH	HIGH
HIGH	LOW	HIGH
HIGH	HIGH	HIGH

(B) Truth table.

Fig. 8-29. The OR gate.

Here's a trick to help you remember which symbol represents AND, and which represents OR. The symbol for AND is rounded at the end, and is shaped like a closed hand. The symbol for OR is shaped like the blade of an oar. Fig. 8-30 illustrates what we mean.

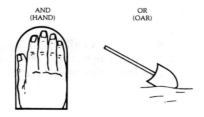

Fig. 8-30. Memory trick for remembering AND and OR symbols.

The "Exclusive-OR" gate, abbreviated XOR, is a variation of the standard OR gate. The schematic symbol and truth table for the XOR gate is shown in Fig. 8-31. For the first three possible input states, both the OR and XOR gates function in the same way, but when the XOR gate receives two high inputs, its output is low, where the output of an OR gate is high.

Inverters

An inverter takes the incoming signal, and reverses or "inverts" it. A high pulse on the input will result in a low pulse at the output. A low input will cause a high output. The symbol and truth table for an inverter are shown in Fig. 8-32. The circle at the tip of the triangle indicates that the device reverses the output signal. The triangle itself is a symbol for a buffer. Besides inverting the signal, this device also increases the number of devices that can be driven by the output.

(A) Schematic symbol.

TRUTH TABLE

A	B	X
LOW	LOW	LOW
LOW	HIGH	HIGH
HIGH	LOW	HIGH
HIGH	HIGH	LOW

(B) Truth table.

Fig. 8-31. Exclusive-OR gate.

(A) Schematic symbol.

TRUTH TABLE

A	X
LOW	HIGH
HIGH	LOW

(B) Truth table.

Fig. 8-32. Inverter.

Three-State Buffers

A TRI-STATE® buffer allows several different devices to share the same signal line. A TRI-STATE buffer behaves like a normal buffer, followed by a switch. Fig. 8-33 shows how this device works. Notice the control line running to each buffer. When this control line is high, the buffer is turned off and no signals flow through the device (Fig. 8-33A). When the control line is low, the buffer is turned on and the input signals are passed through to the output. This kind of device has three possible states—high, low, and disabled. (Some three-state buffers are active when the control line is high.)

Three-state buffers are often used at each outlet of a data or address bus. By turning various groups of buffers on and off, the control circuits can determine which devices will be connected to the bus at a given moment. Three-state buffers also help to isolate a circuit from extraneous electronic noise.

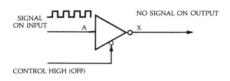

(A) Buffer turned off.

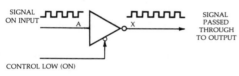

(B) Buffer turned on.

Fig. 8-33. TRI-STATE buffer operation.

Fig. 8-34 shows two possible arrangements of three-state buffers. In Fig. 8-34A, six buffers are arranged on a single IC chip. The first four buffers are arranged to control lines that run from the computer to the outside world. The last two buffers handle input signals. Fig. 8-34B shows an arrangement that allows two buffers to control a line as it passes signals in both directions.

A three-state buffer is frequently one of the first ICs a signal encounters as it enters the computer. This makes these buffers vulnerable and causes a relatively high rate of failure. The TRI-STATE buffers are often the first parts to fail.

You can use your digital logic probe to check out a particular three-state buffer. With the computer or other equipment turned on, check the control, input, and output lines for each buffer stage. When the buffer is enabled, the same signal should appear at both the input and output of the stage. If the line is very active, just check for activity on both sides of each stage. A bad buffer stage will show a good input but no output, or an output stuck in a high or low state.

Buffer stages are normally mounted in groups of

eight on a single IC. If one stage is faulty, you'll have to replace the whole IC.

The term "buffer" can have several different meanings, and this may be confusing. One type of buffer is an amplifying device, which is used to boost the number of inputs that can be driven by a certain output. This type of buffer is always turned on, so it is not TRI-STATE. The term buffer may also refer to a temporary memory space in RAM. A buffer of this type may be used to compensate for different operating speeds between different parts of the computer system.

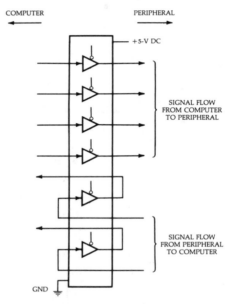

(A) Six three-state buffers in one IC.

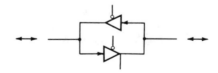

(B) An arrangement that allows three-state buffers to process signals in both directions.

Fig. 8-34. Three-state buffer configurations.

NAND and NOR Gates

In a NAND gate, an inverter has been combined with an AND gate in one device. The name of the gate reflects this—Not-AND. The schematic symbol and truth table for a NAND gate are shown in Fig. 8-35. Note that the symbol for the NAND gate looks just like an AND gate, but with a small circle at the tip. This circle is the symbol for "inversion." Compare the truth table of the NAND gate with the truth table of the AND gate. You'll notice that, for each pair of inputs, the outputs of the AND and NAND gates are opposite. The NOR gate is an OR gate with an inverter. Its schematic symbol and truth table are shown in Fig. 8-36.

(A) Schematic symbol.

TRUTH TABLE

A	B	X
LOW	LOW	HIGH
LOW	HIGH	HIGH
HIGH	LOW	HIGH
HIGH	HIGH	LOW

(B) Truth table.

Fig. 8-35. A NAND gate.

(A) Schematic symbol.

TRUTH TABLE

A	B	X
HIGH	HIGH	LOW
HIGH	LOW	LOW
LOW	HIGH	LOW
LOW	LOW	HIGH

(B) Truth table.

Fig. 8-36. A NOR gate.

In practice, simple gates like ANDs and NANDs are usually arranged in groups of four on a single IC. For example, the 7400 chip is a quad NAND gate. Fig. 8-37 shows some data you might find if you looked up the 7400 chip in a reference book of ICs. Each of the four gates is independent, except that they all receive power from the same V_{CC} and ground pins. Also, the four different gates may be involved in completely different circuits.

In troubleshooting, you'll probably be concerned with testing just one or two gates on a given IC. Your first concern is to make sure the supply voltage and ground are good. Once you know the chip is turned on,

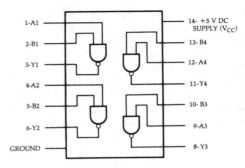

(A) Four NAND gates in one IC.

TRUTH TABLE

A	B	Y
LOW	LOW	HIGH
LOW	HIGH	HIGH
HIGH	LOW	HIGH
HIGH	HIGH	LOW

(B) Truth table.

Fig. 8-37. 7400 quad NAND gate.

you'll have to check each of the NAND gates separately. This is really no more complicated than checking one NAND gate several times. The inputs for the first gate are identified as "A1" and "B1," and the output will appear on pin 3 (Y1). The truth table lists all of the possible combinations of inputs, and predicts the outputs.

Flip-flops

When a flip-flop receives an input signal, it "flips" to one output state, and stays there. When it gets a second input signal, it "flops" back to the original output state, and waits for a new input. Because a flip-flop can remain in either output state, it is called a "bistable" device. Flip-flops have many uses in digital circuitry because they can temporarily store bits of information.

Flip-flops can be designed using discrete transistors, or can be wired up by using combinations of gates. In this section, we're concerned with flip-flops which are entirely contained in an IC chip. You will usually find two flip-flop circuits per chip. There are several different kinds of flip-flops, and they all work in slightly different ways.

R/S Flip-flops

Fig. 8-38 shows the inputs and outputs for the simplest type of flip-flop circuit–the R/S flip-flop. A high on input S results in a corresponding high on output Q, and a low on the other output. A high on input R causes the flip-flop to change states, resulting in a high on Q̄, and a low on Q. (The bar above a letter means "the opposite of.") By alternating high pulses between the two inputs, you can toggle the flip-flop back and forth. The signal on line S is called "Set," and the signal on line R is "Reset." As you can see, nothing changes when both inputs are low. Any circuit that uses this type of flip-flop should be designed so it can't deliver two high inputs at the same time.

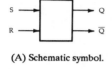

(A) Schematic symbol.

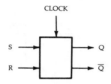

(B) Symbol shows flip-flop
has separate clock.

TRUTH TABLE

S	R	Q	Q̄
HIGH	LOW	HIGH	LOW
LOW	HIGH	LOW	HIGH
LOW	LOW	PREVIOUS STATE	PREVIOUS STATE
HIGH	HIGH	NOT ALLOWED	NOT ALLOWED

(C) Truth table.

Fig. 8-38. R/S flip-flops.

How would you check this particular circuit? The procedure is the same as for the simpler IC devices. Check the existing inputs with your logic probe, and see if the actual outputs match the outputs predicted by the truth table.

One variation of the R/S flip-flop uses a separate "Clock" signal, as shown in Fig. 8-38B. In circuits with this feature, the flip-flop doesn't do anything at all unless the clock line is high. In practice, this signal is used to ensure that the R/S circuit doesn't sample the input lines until the right moment. If the clock signal is somehow prevented from reaching the R/S circuit, the circuit will appear to be dead. Keep this is mind as you troubleshoot this kind of circuit.

D-type Flip-flops

The "D" in the name of this device stands for data, because this type of circuit is useful in the short-term storage of bits of data (Fig. 8-39). The input data enters the circuit on line D. However, the signal doesn't go any farther unless the CL (Clock) line is clocked high. If D is high, a high-going pulse on the CL line will cause a high on output Q. A low on the data line will cause a low at Q when the clock pulse arrives. The other output line always carries a signal that is opposite to the signal on Q.

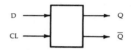

(A) Schematic symbol.

TRUTH TABLE

D	CL	Q	Q̄
HIGH	RISING EDGE	HIGH	LOW
LOW	RISING EDGE	LOW	HIGH
HIGH	LOW	PREVIOUS STATE	PREVIOUS STATE
LOW	LOW	PREVIOUS STATE	PREVIOUS STATE

(B) Truth table.

Fig. 8-39. A D-type flip-flop.

In practice, this kind of flip-flop can serve as a sort of *information gate* or *latch*. The equipment puts a series of "strobe" pulses on the CL line. As each of these pulses arrives, it momentarily opens the information gate. Whatever signal happens to be on line D at the moment is brought into the flip-flop. For a split second, as the strobe pulse passes through the "low" stage, the flip-flop is closed to new information. The bit that was brought inside is temporarily stored, where it can be read by circuitry farther downstream.

When checking a D-type flip-flop, start by watching for activity on the CL line. Nothing happens inside the circuit unless this line is clocked. Check the signal level on line D. When you put a pulse on the clock line, using a pulser, you should see this signal appear at Q.

Fig. 8-40 shows the schematic symbol for a 7474 dual D latch IC. The IC contains two separate D-type flip-flop circuits. These are very similar to the simple D-type devices we've just described. You'll notice two additional lines: Not-Preset and Not-Clear. These give a circuit designer a way to set the circuit to a given state during its operation. In this case, a low on the Not-Preset line sets output Q high. A low on the Not-Clear line sets Q low. Both Not-Preset and Not-Clear operate independently from the Clock signal. An IC circuit can always include refinements like this; that's why you must look up the IC in a data book before you test it.

truth table, even though they affect the way that the circuit works.

Test this circuit in the same way you would test the R/S circuit, but make allowances for the extra control lines. The circuit won't do anything unless you toggle the Clock line low. The Not-R and Not-S lines can stop the chip from operating if they remain low. If the chip appears to be "stuck," check each of these control lines.

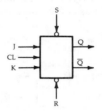

(A) Schematic symbol.

TRUTH TABLE

CL	J	K	Q	$\overline{Q}$
FALLING PULSE	HIGH	LOW	HIGH	LOW
FALLING PULSE	LOW	HIGH	LOW	HIGH
FALLING PULSE	LOW	LOW	PREVIOUS STATE	PREVIOUS STATE
FALLING PULSE	HIGH	HIGH	OPPOSITE OF PREVIOUS STATE	OPPOSITE OF PREVIOUS STATE

(B) Truth table.

Fig. 8-41. A JK flip-flop.

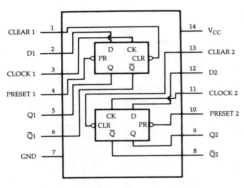

Fig. 8-40. A dual D-type flip-flop.

JK Flip-flops

The schematic symbol and truth table for this device are shown in Fig. 8-41. The basic JK flip-flop is very similar to the R/S device. A high on the J line brings Q high. A high on the K line brings the other output high. The JK flip-flop includes three extra control lines. Two of these lines, Not-S and Not-R, are used to set the starting point for the device (just like the Not-Preset and Not-Clear lines just described). A low on Not-S presets Q to high. A low on Not-R presets Q to low. The JK circuit also includes a Clock line. J and K signals will not pass through the circuit unless the Clock signal makes a high to low transition. Check the last line of the truth table. When both inputs are set high, the circuit toggles from one state to the other, following each Clock pulse. Sometimes a JK circuit can be wired to handle the Clock signal as if it were a data input. Several of these circuits can be used together to form counters. The R, S, and Clock functions may not always be listed on the

Counters and Dividers

A counter circuit simply counts the number of pulses that appear at its input. Each counter can handle a certain number of bits. It counts up until it reaches the maximum number that can be represented by these bits, and then it resets to zero. Some counters are designed to count down as well.

A binary counter interprets the count as a binary number. The output may be presented as a 4-bit (or larger) binary number, and then sent out along four (or more) different output lines. Fig. 8-40 shows how a 4-bit counter operates. When the first pulse appears at the input, the circuit counts it and produces four outputs: low, low, low, and high. This is the binary code for the number 1. After the second pulse, the outputs would read low, low, high, and low. Then, after the third pulse, the outputs would read low, low, high, and high, and so on.

Other kinds of counters can produce different outputs. A decade counter is a binary counter that has been designed to reset after every tenth input pulse. The output is still a binary number, but the highest number that can be represented is a 9. By combining several counter stages, large numbers can be represented.

A divider circuit is similar in design to a counter. A divide-by-10 circuit produces one output pulse for every ten input pulses. Divide-by-2, divide-by-5, and divide-by-12 circuits are also available.

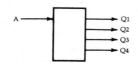

NUMBER OF PULSES ON A	BINARY 8 Q1	BINARY 4 Q2	BINARY 2 Q3	BINARY 1 Q4
0	LOW	LOW	LOW	LOW
1	LOW	LOW	LOW	HIGH
2	LOW	LOW	HIGH	LOW
3	LOW	LOW	HIGH	HIGH
4	LOW	HIGH	LOW	LOW
⋮	⋮	⋮	⋮	⋮
15	HIGH	HIGH	HIGH	HIGH
16	LOW	LOW	LOW	LOW ← RESETS TO ZERO

Fig. 8-42. A counter and its truth table.

You can make a quick check of a counter or divider using your logic probe. Simply check for activity at each of the inputs and outputs. Look for a problem in any chip that has active inputs, but inactive outputs. If the inputs to the device are not changing quickly, you can make a more detailed check. Check the existing outputs with your logic probe. These outputs should match one line of the truth table. Next, send a pulse to the input with a pulser, and check the outputs again. The outputs should change to match the next line on the truth table. Many counters and dividers have "enable" lines that must be high or low before the device will work.

Comparators

As the name suggests, a comparator is a device which "compares" the signals on two or more inputs. Fig. 8-43A shows one representation of a comparator. In digital applications, a comparator is used to compare digital highs and lows. The comparator may be wired to produce an output when both of the inputs are the same

($A = B$). The circuit may also be arranged to produce a "true" when one input is high and the other is low ($A > B$ or $A < B$).

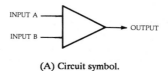

(A) Circuit symbol.

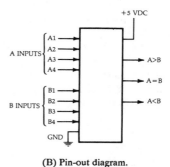

(B) Pin-out diagram.

Fig. 8-43. A comparator.

Fig. 8-43B shows a more complicated type of comparator. This device is designed to compare two inputs of four bits each. When the same signals appear on each set of input lines, the "$A = B$" output will be "true." Notice that there are also output lines for outputs that represent the conditions "$A > B$" and "$A < B$."

Optoisolators

Optoisolators may be used in the interface between the computer and the outside world. These parts are designed to protect or "isolate" the computer equipment from spikes and noise on the signal lines. Each optoisolator consists of a transmitter and a receiver, mounted together in a small DIP package. The transmitter converts the incoming signal to a beam of light. This light is then sent directly to the receiver, where it is converted back into an electrical signal. The transmitter and receiver are not connected electrically, so electrical spikes cannot travel directly between them.

Timers

This kind of IC may be used to generate a time delay. The delay period is usually very short, perhaps measured in microseconds. The 555 timer is the most common type of IC unit. The time-delay period is usually determined by an external capacitor.

Multiplexers

When a designer has two or more different input sources, but only one line over which to send the signals, he/she uses a *multiplexer* (Fig. 8-44). For example, sometimes a complete address is sent down an address bus in two parts. A multiplexer, or MUX, can be used to handle this. First, the MUX would put the first part of the address onto the bus. Next, the MUX would change state and place the second part of the address on the bus. In the same way, a multiplexer may be used to alternate between memory controlled by the CPU and memory controlled by the video display.

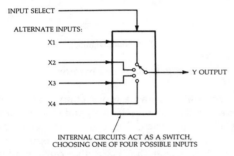

Fig. 8-44. A simple multiplexer.

In one type of circuit, data comes into the multiplexer along two sets of eight parallel data lines. A separate set of Data Select lines tells the chip which set of input lines to read. Each group of input signals is read in order, and put onto the output line. A series of pulses on an enable line can be used to synchronize the circuit's action with other circuits.

With your logic probe, you can tell if data are passing through a multiplexer. If the circuit is not very active, you should be able to check the state of each of the data input and data select lines. By comparing these inputs with the truth table, you should be able to tell if the correct outputs result.

Shift Register

A shift register translates between different data formats. One kind of shift register can read data from parallel input lines, and put this data onto a single

output line. Another type reverses this process and converts serial data to parallel data. A third type is the parallel-in, parallel-out register. Fig. 8-45 illustrates a serial-in, parallel-out shift register. This circuit takes a serial stream of eight data bits from the input, and stores each bit temporarily. Then, each of the eight bits is produced on a separate output line. At this point, the data have been converted from serial format to parallel. Each time a CLOCK pulse reaches the chip, the output bits all shift one place to the right. At any time during the cycle, the CLEAR signal can reset all the outputs to low.

Note that the circuit can be disabled by certain incorrect control signals. If the CLEAR line is stuck, the chip won't accept new data. If the CLOCK signal is missing, the outputs won't shift. Some IC shift registers have an AND gate on the input line. An additional "input enable" signal must be present on the gate before the IC will accept data. Some shift registers can shift in both directions.

Programmable Logic Arrays

You may think of a *programmable logic device* (PLD) as a collection of gates, wired to produce certain outputs in response to given inputs. This type of part may also be called a *programmable logic array* (PLA). Fig. 8-46 shows how this type of IC is arranged. (An actual PLA chip will have many more gates and inputs.)

The upper left-hand corner of Fig. 8-46 shows the inputs entering the IC. Each input is buffered, and inverters produce an inverted version of each input. Next, the inputs are routed to a series of AND gates. In the illustration, you'll note that different AND gates are turned on by different combinations of the inputs. The outputs from the AND gates are then sent to a "fuse array." You may think of this area as a series of intersecting wires. At each intersection, there is a "fuse." When stimulated by a special "programming" current, each fuse can be burned away, breaking one of the connections between the wires. During programming, most of the fuses are opened, leaving just a few connections. These connections determine the inputs for a series of OR gates, shown at the right side of the illustration. By using a single PLA, a designer can avoid using several simpler ICs.

A PLA chip must receive +5-V DC to operate. Some PLAs must receive a "chip enable" signal to produce an output. It is difficult to check the logic functions of a PLA without special test equipment. If you do not have this equipment, you can check a PLA by substituting a spare chip.

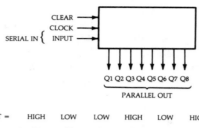

INPUT =	HIGH	LOW	LOW	HIGH	LOW	HIGH	HIGH	LOW
OUTPUTS	Q1	Q2	Q3	Q4	Q5	Q6	Q7	Q8
AFTER 1 CLOCK PULSE	HIGH	LOW	LOW	HIGH	LOW	HIGH	HIGH	LOW
AFTER 2 CLOCK PULSES	LOW	HIGH	LOW	LOW	HIGH	LOW	HIGH	HIGH
AFTER 3 CLOCK PULSES	LOW	LOW	HIGH	LOW	LOW	HIGH	LOW	HIGH
AFTER 4 CLOCK PULSES	LOW	LOW	LOW	HIGH	LOW	LOW	HIGH	LOW
AFTER 5 CLOCK PULSES	LOW	LOW	LOW	LOW	HIGH	LOW	LOW	HIGH
AFTER 6 CLOCK PULSES	LOW	LOW	LOW	LOW	LOW	HIGH	LOW	LOW
AFTER 7 CLOCK PULSES	LOW	LOW	LOW	LOW	LOW	LOW	HIGH	LOW
AFTER 8 CLOCK PULSES	LOW	LOW	LOW	LOW	LOW	LOW	LOW	HIGH

Fig. 8-45. A serial-in, parallel-out shift register.

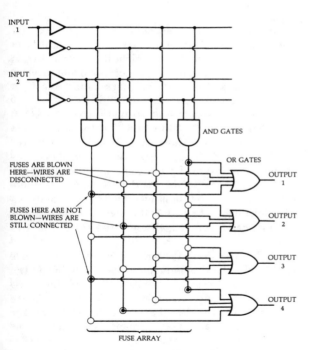

Fig. 8-46. A programmable logic array.

Interface Controller ICs

As you work with microcomputer equipment, you will find several types of "controller" ICs. Often, a controller chip is used as part of an interface between the computer and some other part of the system. Usually, the controller chip is the key component in an interface circuit. For example, the interface with a floppy disk drive is usually supervised by a "floppy disk controller" IC. The interface with a parallel printer is often controlled by an IC that is called a *Versatile Interface Adapter* (VIA).

There are many different types of controller ICs. We will cover some of them in more detail in the later chapters of this book. In this section, we will look at some of the features that these different controllers have in common.

Fig. 8-47 is the block diagram of a controller IC. Data will come into the chip on eight parallel data lines. Under control of the chip, the data are then passed through to the output lines. In this illustration, we have shown 8 output data lines. Sometimes the chip converts the data from one format to another. For example, a controller may take parallel inputs and produce a single serial output.

A number of control signals usually pass through the IC. Sometimes these signals pass directly through the chip, and sometimes they are modified inside the controller. The unit that is being controlled also generates some signals. The controller can use these "feedback" signals to supervise the controlled device. For example, in a floppy disk drive, the speed of the drive motor must remain constant. A sensor on the drive motor produces a signal that changes with the speed of the motor. This "feedback" signal is sent back to the control circuits. When the control circuits determine that the motor is turning too slowly, they act to speed up the motor.

The CHIP SELECT signal is used to enable the controller IC. Usually, a controller IC can perform several different functions. The IC, itself, is controlled by instructions stored in several "control registers." By changing the codes stored in these registers, a programmer can change the way the IC operates. For example, one type of controller chip is used to control the RS-232C interface used in most serial ports. One of the variables in the serial interface is the *bit rate*. ("Bit rate" is the speed at which the interface sends and receives characters.) A typical RS-232C interface can be set up to operate at several different speeds: 300 bps, 600 bps, 1200 bps, and so on. The programmer can change the bit rate of the interface simply by changing a few bits in one of the control registers. Usually, the registers are "initialized" with some basic information when the IC is first turned on. The initial data in the registers may later be changed. Usually, the control

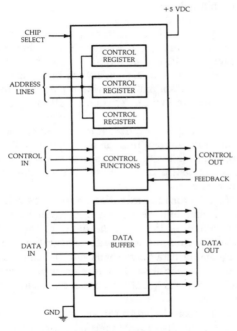

Fig. 8-47. Interface controller IC.

registers are enabled by signals received on two or three of the address lines.

It is difficult to check all of the functions of a controller chip without sophisticated equipment. Whenever possible, substitute a chip which is known to be working for the suspect chip. You can, however, check some of the functions of a controller with simple tools. Start by checking for the +5-V DC supply. None

of the other functions will work if the chip is not getting power. With a logic probe, you should be able to see data entering and leaving the chip. You should also be able to follow most of the control signals. If you have detailed documentation of the IC, you may be able to check the functioning of the control registers. You may be able to use the computer to write instructions to the control registers, and can then see if the IC functions differently.

Read-Only Memory

A *read-only memory* (ROM) device is usually used to hold a permanent set of instructions for a microcomputer. When the microcomputer is first turned on, the ROMs usually provide the "bootstrap" instructions which start the system operating. Each instruction is stored at a certain "address" in the ROM chip. In most ROMs, each instruction consists of 8 bits. When the computer wants to read one of the instructions, it places the correct address on the address lines. The ROM then recognizes this address, and places the instructions on the data lines. A typical small computer might include six or eight ROM chips. ROMs are also included in other devices, including printers and hard disk drives, if these are supervised by a separate on-board microprocessor.

There are some variations on the standard ROM. The abbreviation PROM stands for "programmable read-only memory." This type of ROM includes a large number of individual gates. By "fusing" various connections inside the part, the manufacturer can "program" the PROM. In the EPROM (erasable PROM), the programming can be erased by an ultraviolet light. The EEPROM (electronically erasable PROM) can be erased without exposing the part to light.

Fig. 8-48 shows the pin arrangement for a simple ROM chip. The various memory spaces inside the ROM are addressed by combinations of signals on address lines A0 through A10. These lines are connected to the address bus inside the computer. The data stored at each specified memory location in the ROM are output on data lines D0 through D7. These lines are connected to the data bus. This particular chip has three "enable" lines. Not-CS1 and Not-CS3 are active when they are low. CS2 is active when high. All three of these lines must be active if the chip is to accept an address and output data.

Testing a ROM is difficult without a sophisticated IC tester. With your logic probe, you can check for activity on the power supply, input, output, and control

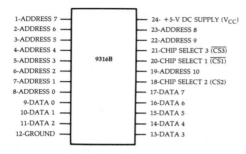

```
 1-ADDRESS 7 ─┤              ├─ 24- +5-V DC SUPPLY (V_CC)
 2-ADDRESS 6 ─┤              ├─ 23-ADDRESS 8
 3-ADDRESS 5 ─┤              ├─ 22-ADDRESS 9
 4-ADDRESS 4 ─┤              ├─ 21-CHIP SELECT 3 (CS3)
 5-ADDRESS 3 ─┤    9316B     ├─ 20-CHIP SELECT 1 (CS1)
 6-ADDRESS 2 ─┤              ├─ 19-ADDRESS 10
 7-ADDRESS 1 ─┤              ├─ 18-CHIP SELECT 2 (CS2)
 8-ADDRESS 0 ─┤              ├─ 17-DATA 7
 9-DATA 0    ─┤              ├─ 16-DATA 6
10-DATA 1    ─┤              ├─ 15-DATA 5
11-DATA 2    ─┤              ├─ 14-DATA 4
12-GROUND    ─┤              ├─ 13-DATA 3
```

Fig. 8-48. A ROM chip with pins identified.

lines of a ROM. This will tell you whether the chip is working or not. However, if the ROM is not "remembering" correctly, you won't be able to detect this. The microcomputer may show a number of unusual symptoms if a ROM is bad. We'll describe this in more detail in Chapter 9.

The most convenient way to test a ROM is to use a diagnostic software program. At the start of the test, the diagnostic program already knows what data are supposed to be stored at each ROM address location. The program simply checks the data stored in the ROM, compares this with data it is expecting to see, and tells you if it finds a difference. Of course, to use a diagnostic program, the computer must be running, and some ROM problems rule this out.

In equipment which includes IC sockets for each IC, you can remove individual ROM chips easily. Be sure to turn off the equipment before you remove any chips. Carefully remove half of the chips, and set them aside. Check the equipment, and see if it has begun to operate normally. If you see an improvement, you know the problem lies in one of the chips you removed. Replace them, one at a time, until the problem returns. This trick won't work if you have a problem in the ROM which controls the "Boot" routine that gets the equipment started.

If none of these techniques help you to localize the problem, you'll have to replace the complete set of ROMs, or take the equipment to a repair shop.

Random-Access Memory

Random-access memory (RAM) ICs provide temporary memory space for the microcomputer. RAMs are produced with many different internal arrangements. For example, the 6116 RAM uses a 2K × 8 arrangement. This means that this IC can store 2048 8-bit "words" of data. To store a 16-bit word, a micro-

computer would probably use two separate ICs, and would store half of each "word" in each chip. RAMs are also available in 4-bit and 1-bit configurations. To store an 8-bit memory word, the IBM PC uses an array of eight 1-bit RAMs, with an additional 1-bit RAM to hold a parity checking bit.

Fig. 8-49 shows the pin arrangement for a small RAM chip. The addressing procedure is the same, whether the equipment is reading from or writing to the RAM. The IC will not become active unless it is selected by two control lines at the same time. Memory space within a RAM IC is addressed using a system of "rows" and "columns." In the chip shown in the diagram, first the $\overline{RAS}$ (Row Address Select) line goes low, and the IC reads the first part of the address over the address lines. Next, the $\overline{CAS}$ (Column Address Select) line goes low and the IC reads the second part of the address.

In the illustration of Fig. 8-49, the signal on pin 3 determines whether the circuit is prepared to READ or WRITE. A high causes the RAM to READ, and a low causes a WRITE. During a READ, data comes in on the DATA IN pin and is stored at the addresses selected by the CPU. During a WRITE, data goes out over the DATA OUT line. Other RAMs may have eight or more data lines, used for both input and output.

Some RAMs require extra −5-V DC and −12-V DC voltages, in addition to the normal +5-V DC supply. Many recent RAMs require just the +5-V DC supply. Some RAM chips use circuits that are capable of "static" memory. This means that memory is retained as long as power is supplied to the chip. Chips designed for "dynamic" memory are more common. Data are stored in dynamic memory as a series of charges held in capacitors. These charges weaken over time, so they must be constantly "refreshed." In some RAM chips, this "refresh" function takes place each time a certain control signal ($\overline{RAS}$, for example) reaches the chip. The timing of this "refresh" function is important. If for some reason the "refresh" signal does not arrive on time, a dynamic RAM will become unreliable.

A RAM chip is one of the most densely packed ICs you will encounter. Because each RAM chip contains so many devices, these must be very small and densely packed. When compared with other ICs, RAMs have an above-average failure rate.

You can test for some aspects of RAM chip operation using simple instruments. Start by checking each of the supply voltages. As we stated, a RAM chip may use three or more different voltages—be sure to check them all. Next, use your logic probe to look for activity on the control lines. The address lines should show constant activity, and you should be able to watch

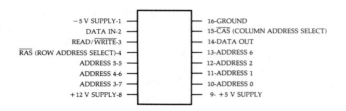

```
-5 V SUPPLY-1 ───        ─── 16-GROUND
     DATA IN-2 ───        ─── 15-CAS (COLUMN ADDRESS SELECT)
   READ/WRITE-3 ───        ─── 14-DATA OUT
RAS (ROW ADDRESS SELECT)-4 ───  ─── 13-ADDRESS 6
    ADDRESS 5-5 ───        ─── 12-ADDRESS 2
    ADDRESS 4-6 ───        ─── 11-ADDRESS 1
    ADDRESS 3-7 ───        ─── 10-ADDRESS 0
  +12 V SUPPLY-8 ───        ─── 9- +5 V SUPPLY
```

Fig. 8-49. A RAM chip with pins identified.

data flow into and out of the chip over the data lines. If a RAM appears to be inactive, try the "touch test." A bad RAM will often feel warm to the touch.

If all of the signals seem normal, you must next decide if the chip is storing the right information on cue, and reproducing it accurately. The easiest way to do this is to use the diagnostic software we described in Chapter 6. During the diagnostic test, the software writes a pattern into each memory space in each RAM. Next, the program checks these spaces, and sees if the correct information has been recorded. If the software notices a problem, it indicates which RAM chip is bad.

During a RAM test, a number of different test patterns may be used. Some RAM faults are intermittent. For example, a RAM might fail only when two digital 1s are written into two side-by-side memory locations. The RAM might function normally as long as any other combination of bits is written into these locations. Some diagnostics allow you to repeat the RAM test for a long time, as a way of detecting these intermittent faults.

Voltage Regulators

You will find the voltage-regulator integrated circuit in power supplies. As the name suggests, this component "regulates" an output voltage. As the circuitry adds more load to a power supply, the output voltage tends to drop. A regulator circuit keeps the output voltage steady, in spite of changes in the load.

Use a voltohmmeter to make an in-circuit test of a voltage regulator, as shown in Fig. 8-50. With the equipment turned on, check the voltage reading between the input leg and the center leg, and then between the output leg and the center leg. The output voltage should read close to the specified voltage, and the input voltage should be at least one-half volt higher. If the input voltage is present, but the output is missing, be sure the center conductor is actually connected to ground.

Some regulators include a "fold-back" feature. These units are designed to cut off the output when a short circuit or other problem causes an overload. To

check for this condition, you must disconnect the output of the regulator from the rest of the circuitry downstream. Use one of the disconnection techniques we described at the beginning of the chapter. Once you make the disconnect, measure the output of the regulator upstream of the break. If the output does not return to normal, replace the regulator.

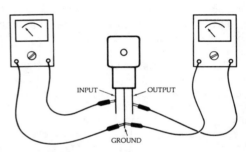

Fig. 8-50. Testing a voltage regulator.

Chapter Review

In this chapter, we've covered troubleshooting procedures for circuits that include ICs. As we have shown, ICs can behave in some surprising ways, and can make "chain" troubleshooting more complicated. Whenever an IC's input is broken, the line between that point and the IC will "float."

To troubleshoot a series of circuits, follow the signals until you find the point where the normal signals disappear. The bad IC is probably just "upstream" or just "downstream" of this point. Disconnect the output pin on the IC just upstream, and see if the problems disappear. If they do, the upstream IC is bad. If not, reconnect the upstream IC and start disconnecting the inputs from each of the downstream ICs. After you disconnect each input, check to see if the problems disappeared. If they did, the chip you disconnected last is bad.

If you still do not find the problem, disconnect the output of the upstream IC again. This isolates a section of the circuit-board traces. Check for shorts to +5 V or ground. When checking any particular IC, remember to test for +5-V DC to the chip.

In the second part of the chapter, we discussed test procedures for the common types of ICs. As you troubleshoot, you can refer back to this information.

Review Questions

1. You are troubleshooting a "chain" of ICs, and you locate the point where the normal signals stop. Is the bad IC just upstream of this point?

2. You want to use a logic pulser and probe. Where can you find points which carry +5-V DC and ground?

3. What is the effect on the signals in an IC when an output line is broken inside the body of the IC? What if the break is outside the IC?

4. How can you tell if a circuit trace is shorted to ground?

5. How can you tell if two circuit traces are shorted together?

6. How would you use a logic probe to test an inverter?

7. What is the easiest way of testing a complicated IC like an interface controller?

8. What is the easiest way of testing a RAM chip?

Troubleshooting the Microcomputer System

Introduction and Objectives

When a microcomputer system begins to malfunction, most beginning technicians assume the problem is in the main computer itself. A breakdown may actually be caused by any part of the whole microcomputer system. The complete system includes the main computer, plus the disk drives, monitor, printer, etc. The technician must determine which part of the system is faulty. In the first part of this chapter, we will discuss the steps you can take to troubleshoot the system as a whole.

We'll look at the main computer itself and begin by discussing some of the most important circuits inside a typical microcomputer. Then, we include some troubleshooting instructions for four common trouble symptoms. In the last part of the chapter, we give some test procedures for specific parts of the system. We will focus on the signals that are distributed to all parts of the system: clock circuit, reset system, address and data lines. This section also includes some troubleshooting notes on three common input devices: the keyboard, the game controller, and the "mouse."

Checking the Complete System

As explained earlier, in any troubleshooting situation,

the first job is to identify the sections of the system that are not working correctly. If you're troubleshooting a hand-held computer/calculator, the system is fairly small, so this job can be relatively simple. However, many microcomputer systems include a number of peripherals—monitor, disk drive, printer, modem, etc. Taken together, the computer plus peripherals add up to a rather complicated system.

The Hardware

Fig. 9-1 is a block diagram of a fully configured microcomputer system. Let's say that this system develops a problem that appears when the operator tries to use the printer. It's fairly safe to assume that the problem is caused by one of the three sections directly involved with the printer—the printer itself, the computer, or the interface between them. (The printer also has a separate power supply, but we'll assume that this is working. As soon as you make this assumption, you rule out many other sections of the system—the disk drives, keyboard, monitor, etc.)

At this point, you have determined that the problem lies in one of the units in the "chain" that controls the printer. Next, you must determine which of the three units is affected. The fastest way of doing this is by substituting various component parts of the chain. In this example, you might connect a different printer and

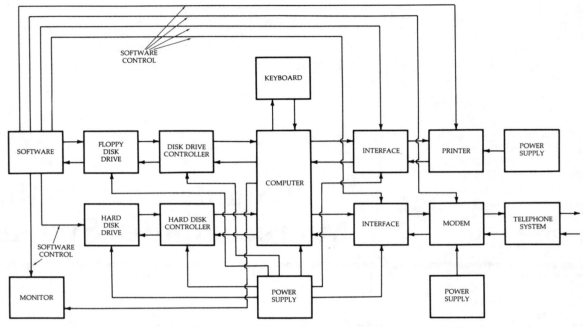

Fig. 9-1. Microcomputer with peripherals.

see if the substitute operates normally. If it does, the original printer is probably faulty. You might also try attaching the original printer to a different computer. If the original printer works, you would then suspect a problem with the computer or the printer interface. Remember that the cable is part of the chain. If possible, substitute another cable.

Circuit Cards and Substitution

In some systems, including the IBM PCs, many circuits are mounted on plug-in circuit cards. On computers of this type, it is possible to remove and substitute the printer interface circuits. This arrangement allows the technician to eliminate the interface as a cause of the trouble. Once you have the problem localized to a particular device in the chain, you can focus on that particular device.

Let's take another example. Suppose a problem appears when the operator tries to run a program that is stored on a floppy disk. As the diagram in Fig. 9-1 shows, this could involve four parts of the system—the floppy disk drive, floppy disk controller, microcomputer, and the software. (Again, we are ignoring the power supply.) In this case, you would start by substituting for

each part of the chain until you uncovered the faulty part. *Important!* Whenever you connect or disconnect any part of the computer system, be sure that all parts of the system are turned off. If you move a connector or circuit card while the system is turned on, you can cause extensive damage to the equipment.

Diagnostic Routines

At this point, you may also want to use a diagnostic software program. The diagnostic program will check the functioning of the main parts of the computer system. If any part of the system is seriously malfunctioning, the diagnostics should reveal this. The IBM PC will automatically run a diagnostic program called *POST* when it is turned on. This "POST" (Power-On Self-Test) program does a good job. When the program detects a problem, it presents an error code number. The user or technician can then look up this code number in the user's manual. Even more detailed "advanced" diagnostics are available from IBM and others. "Diagnostics" programs are available for many types of computers; we have listed some suppliers of these type programs in Appendix E.

The operating procedure for a typical diagnostic

package is fairly simple. To start, you place the diagnostic disk in the disk drive and "boot" the computer. The software displays a menu that offers a series of options. You simply choose an option, and the computer does the rest. Usually, one of these options is a general test of the whole computer system.

To test the ROMs (read-only memories), the software may run a "Check Sum" routine. In a routine like this, the program checks each memory location in ROM, and presents a sum that represents the integer value of the total number of bytes, with the overflow ignored. The program then checks this sum with a sum computed from an identical ROM that is known to be good. If there is a difference, the software will tell you which ROM IC appears to be bad. This check sum is used simply for error checking—the figure has no intrinsic meaning.

The RAM (random-access memory) test is a bit more involved. A RAM chip may fail in several different ways. A particular memory location may stop working completely. A memory location may also fail in such a way that it works most of the time, but will only fail when a certain pattern of digital bits is stored there. In fact, a memory location may not fail until a certain pattern is stored in one of the adjacent spaces. For this reason, any RAM test must be exhaustive. One test procedure involves copying an ascending series of numbers into each memory location. Other routines use random pattern tests. Most diagnostics allow you to leave the RAM test running for a long time, to reveal any faults that are related to temperature build-up.

Diagnostic programs do have some limitations, however. For example, they can't help you if the computer cannot read from a floppy disk. Some diagnostic programs are written into ROM chips, and these chips may be installed in a "sick" computer, allowing it to use the diagnostic program without reading from a disk. The diagnostics may not check all parts of the system. Also, diagnostics written for one brand of equipment may not work with the peripherals or circuit cards made by other manufacturers. For example, a diagnostic program written for a certain type of computer may not be able to handle a printer interface card made by another company. Because the card is not completely compatible with the original computer, the diagnostic routine may tell you that the card is not working, even if it is all right. Some diagnostics can troubleshoot down to the "component level," and can point out the individual IC that has failed. Most programs can do this for the RAM and ROM chips easily. However, the diagnostics are usually less specific when troubleshooting other parts of the system.

Software

Software programs control the action of each part of the computer system. For this reason, it's wise to consider the software as part of the chain, no matter which device you're having problems with. In our first example, the problems with the printer could be caused by a software fault. Software designers can leave mistakes or "bugs" in a program, and these can cause symptoms that suggest hardware problems. Also, perhaps the computer has not yet been set (by the software) to recognize the input/output port used by the printer.

Software problems can interfere with the computer's operations in many different ways. Some problems are severe enough to cause the computer to stop. Frequently, this kind of problem is caused by a "mismatch" of some sort. For example, the software might tell the computer to get a byte of information from a file with a certain file name. Because of a programming error, the software specifies the wrong file. The computer can't find the file, so it stops.

Another kind of mismatch may occur during an input/output operation, when the computer tries to communicate with a printer, a disk drive, or other peripheral. Let's say that the software tells the computer to prepare a report and send it to the printer. For some reason, the computer can't "find" the printer. Perhaps the printer is turned off, or the line/local switch is set to "local," or the printer cable is disconnected. Some computers will wait patiently for the printer to be connected. In other computers, a problem like this will cause a "crash."

Following a crash, the computer will not execute commands, and it may present an unusual display on the monitor. A crash can also be caused by hardware problems. To recover from a crash, press the "Reset" key. This will take the computer back to the start of the program that was being executed at the time of the crash. However, when you use "Reset," you often lose the data you are working with. Some computers allow you to try a "warm boot" procedure. For example, on an IBM PC or clone, if you press the control (Ctrl), alternate (Alt), and delete (Del) keys at the same time, the computer will reset. There are some cases where the "Reset" key will not start the computer operating again. If this happens, turn the computer off, wait about 30 seconds, and then turn it on again. This last procedure should clear the computer of any problems caused by the software. (You will also lose all data stored in RAM).

Some situations may cause a computer to appear

to have stopped, even though it is still active. Let's say that you tell the computer to execute a long, complicated routine. While it is doing this, the computer may present a blank screen on the monitor, and may ignore commands from the keyboard. You are most likely to encounter this when using software you write yourself. Commercial software usually presents a display or a blinking cursor to show that the computer is still active. In other instances, a wrong command will send the computer looking for an I/O port which is not connected. The computer will hang up and not return because it continues searching indefinitely.

When the computer stops because of a software problem, it will often tell you what happened by displaying an error statement on the screen. Sometimes this statement will tell you exactly what happened—for example, "Printer Not Connected." More likely, though, you will have to do a little decoding to discover the cause of the problem. Sometimes the error statement will include a reference number. By looking up this number in the owner's manual, you can find out what caused the problem(s).

At times, the computer will return an error statement that says something similar to this:

```
HALT AT 1020
```

The number "1020" refers to an instruction line in the program. You can find out what is contained in that line by using a command like "LIST 1020." The computer will display the specified line of instructions. It may read something like this:

```
1020 READ "DD$"
```

When the computer stops at a certain line in the program, it's safe to assume that it couldn't complete the instruction listed on that line. In this example, it didn't understand the variable "DD$." In any case, you now know that the problem was probably caused by a "bug" in the software, and you have an idea of how to correct the problem.

Other software problems are not as clear-cut. Some software may operate perfectly normally most of the time and fail only when a certain pattern of data is present. Because of a "bug," some software may compute an incorrect value now and then, or interfere with the instructions that tell the computer how to display the data. The result might be an unusual display on the monitor.

If you've written the software yourself, you probably know how to fix the problem. If you have trouble with a commercial software package, you'll have to check with the manufacturer. Some software houses are reluctant to publicize bugs in their products. If you press them, however, they may admit they've had to make an "update." On receipt of your original disks, they should be willing to give you copies of the update for a small fee.

Some computer systems are vulnerable to a new troublesome (and potentially dangerous) kind of software, called a *virus*. A "virus" is a short program that can reproduce itself and spread throughout a computer system. The virus program usually attaches itself to the computer's operating system. You can sometimes detect a system which has been "infected" by noticing that the operating system is longer than it should be. A computer system may become "infected" when a user downloads a file or program from a User group or other outside source.

A computer virus can have many ill effects. A benign virus may simply display a humorous message on the monitor, while a more destructive type may wait until a certain date, and then erase all of the files on your hard disk. Special "inoculation" programs are now becoming available to protect systems from this new threat.

Eliminate the possibility of software problems before you start to check the hardware. See if the problem occurs only when you run a particular program. If it does, this strongly suggests a software problem with that program. Make a copy of the backup version (a backup of the backup) of the program, and try running that. Don't use the "original" backup copy—if there is a hardware problem, you may damage the backup as well. If the backup copy operates normally, you know the problem was in the first version of the software. If you find the problem still occurs, even using the backup disk, try operating some other programs. If the symptom occurs when you're using a variety of software, suspect a hardware problem.

Sometimes, it is easy to localize the problem to one part of the system. In other cases, the system will not operate at all. In either of these situations, the best strategy is to strip the computer down to the "minimum" system. This minimum system includes the smallest number of components that will allow the computer to operate and still let you monitor the computer's operation. In most cases, the computer, keyboard, and monitor must remain connected to leave you with a workable system. In a computer with removable circuit cards, remove as many of the cards as possible. *Be sure to turn off the equipment before you disconnect any peripherals or cards*. If the problem disappears, you know that it was caused by one of the peripherals or circuit cards you just disconnected.

If the problem is still present, carefully check the units that are still connected. If the system still will not work at all, the problem is probably in the main computer. Look for a problem in the power-supply system. Also, make the other checks outlined in the next section of this chapter.

Each type of computer goes through a slightly different start-up process. During this process, several parts of the system will interact. A malfunctioning computer will often "hang up" at some point in the start-up process. If you know the details of the process, you can often tell how far the computer was able to go before it stopped. This can point to the faulty part of the system. For example, when you first turn on an Apple II computer, the unit is controlled by instructions stored in ROM. These instructions cause the computer to "beep" and display a cursor on the screen. Next, the ROM tells the computer to read from the floppy disk in Drive 1. On this floppy disk, the computer reads the instructions for the "Disk Operating System" (DOS), and stores them in memory. Once this has happened, the computer can move on to normal operations.

The preceding sequence may be interrupted at several points. For example, what if you turn on the switch and the computer does not produce a "beep" or a screen display? This means that the unit was not able to get through even the first few steps of the start-up process. A symptom like this would point to a problem in the power supply. It may also be that the microprocessor is completely "hung up" and can't execute any instructions.

Let's take another example. We'll say that the computer gets to the point where it is meant to read from the floppy disk. In this case, we'll say that the disk drive just continues to turn (run), and you must press the "Reset" key to stop it. This means that the computer was able to execute only the first few steps in the start-up process. The problem occurred when the unit tried to read the floppy disk. Perhaps the instructions on the disk were unreadable, or the drive may have been looking in the wrong place. Either way, by knowing the details of the start-up process, you would be able to "localize" the problem.

The start-up process in an Apple II is actually more complicated than this, and in some computers, the start-up process is really quite involved. A computer may present several "cues" as it goes through the start-up process. For example, a unit may "beep" in different ways at different points in the process. It may also display cursor marks with different shapes, to indicate whether the computer is under the control of the instructions in ROM, the disk operating system, or the application software. Various LEDs may light to indicate different stages in the process. As we said, on start-up, the IBM PCs automatically run the "POST" program. If a part of the system does not pass the tests, the computer will not be able to continue and operate normally.

Here's a review of the steps required to "localize" a problem to a certain part of the system:

- Identify the device which is not working.

- Identify the chain of components that drive that device.

- Substitute parts of the chain, and see if the problems disappear.

- Try the diagnostics program.

- Eliminate software as a cause. Try different programs.

- If you still haven't found the problem, strip the computer down to the minimum system.

- If the system still won't operate, look for a problem in the main microcomputer.

The remainder of this chapter covers troubleshooting instructions for the main computer system.

The Main Computer and Keyboard

As we pointed out in Chapter 3, hardware problems in the main computer account for a relatively small percentage of the faults in microcomputer systems. Many problems actually have other causes—failure in disk drives and printers, problems with cables and connectors, software and operator errors, and so on. For this reason, many "computer" problems cannot be blamed on the main computer itself.

This part of the chapter deals with problems inside the main computer unit. If the problem is elsewhere in your system, and you still haven't localized it, re-read the beginning of this chapter. If you're having trouble with a specific peripheral—disk drive, printer, etc.—start with the chapter discussing that unit.

In the first part of this section, we will review the major subsystems in a microcomputer. Next, we will discuss three common trouble symptoms, and suggest a troubleshooting sequence for each. After that, we will describe some tests for specific parts of the computer. Finally, troubleshooting and repair routines for the keyboard will be discussed.

Inside a Microcomputer

In any microcomputer system, the *central processor unit* (CPU) does just what its name suggests. The CPU acts as a central processor, interpreting control signals and data, and transferring data from one part of the system to another. We won't go into all the details of CPU operation here. For troubleshooting purposes, we're most interested in just a few key functions of the CPU. Fig. 9-2 is a simplified block diagram of a microcomputer. Let's take a quick look at some of the other areas that interact with the CPU.

The *math coprocessor* is a special chip designed to handle calculations with large numbers. The coprocessor can operate at the same time as the CPU, and can work on a different part of a problem.

The *ROM* (read-only memory) chips store permanent instructions for the CPU. The data stored here tell the CPU how to start up or "Boot" the computer, how to transfer and process various types of data, how to read the keyboard, and so on. In some computers, these ROMs also store a computer language, like BASIC.

The *RAM* (random-access memory) ICs contain memory locations that can temporarily store bits of data or pieces of a program. The computer can read from these memory locations, and can also write into them.

The *keyboard* allows the operator to communicate with the computer. Signals from the keyboard are processed by a decoder and passed on to the CPU.

Several *input/output* (I/O) interfaces allow the computer to communicate with the outside world. One interface might be connected to a printer, another to a disk drive, a third to a modem, and so on.

A *reset system* starts the CPU operating upon receipt of a specific set of instructions, at the "known starting point," when the system is first turned on. When it receives the Reset signal, the computer will begin executing the instructions it needs to get the system running. This Reset system may be used at any time to return the computer to the known starting point.

A *clock* provides a train of timing pulses that regulates the CPU's operation. Although it is not shown in the diagram, a network of lines carries the CLOCK signal to many other parts of the computer system. In this way, the operations of the various parts of the system are synchronized.

A separate *video-driver circuit* handles signals to the monitor. On some computers, each screen display is stored temporarily in a special "video RAM" section.

A central *power supply* provides the right voltage and current for each section of the microcomputer. Although it is not shown in Fig. 9-2, power-supply lines extend to every part of the microcomputer. A problem in this central power supply or distribution system can disable the whole computer. (Some of the peripherals, including the printer or hard disk drive, may have separate power supplies.)

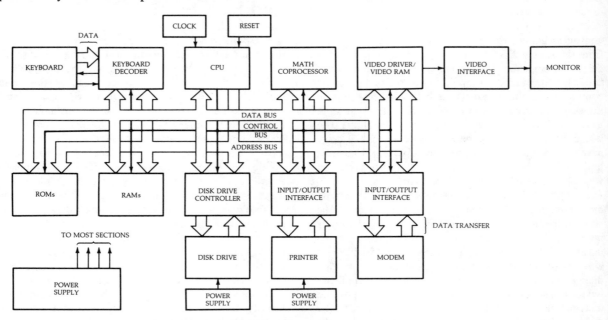

Fig. 9-2. Simplified block diagram of a microcomputer.

A *data bus* extends from the CPU to each part of the system that handles data. As illustrated in Fig. 9-2, the data bus extends to every ROM, every RAM, and to each of the I/O interfaces. The device is called a "bus" because the common group of lines is shared by many different devices. This particular bus is used to carry information in both directions. Many smaller computers, including the IBM PC, have eight lines in the data bus. More advanced computers may use sixteen or more lines in the data bus. The data bus in the IBM PS/2 Model 50 has 16 lines. A control line called "read/write*" determines the direction of data on the data bus. When this line calls for a "Read," the CPU will input data from a memory device. When the control line calls for a "Write," the CPU will send data in the other direction, and will store the information in one of the memory devices.

Many different devices are connected to the data bus. This means that the CPU must have a way of being sure only the correct devices are connected to the bus at any one time. At each point where the bus is connected to a device, the designers will include a "buffer." The part used here is usually a three-state buffer (described in Chapter 8). As you will recall, a three-state buffer can be "turned off" so that it does not allow signals to pass. The CPU uses the buffers to connect or disconnect devices from the bus. When it wants to connect a device, the CPU turns on the appropriate buffer. The CPU turns off the buffers when other devices are using the bus.

An *address bus* runs from the CPU to all of the sections that store or handle data. Unlike the data bus, the address system works in only one direction. The address bus carries address signals from the CPU out to each of the other devices. The CPU uses these addresses to "enable" or "turn on" various parts of the system. The address system may consist of from eight to twenty-four or more signal lines. The IBM Model 50 has 24 lines in the address bus. All of the address lines are not carried to all parts of the system. Sometimes, just one or two address lines may be used to enable a part of the system.

Let's say the CPU wants to retrieve a certain instruction which has been stored in memory. To start the process, the CPU generates the address for the desired instruction, and places the address on the address bus. The memory IC then recognizes the address, and places the instruction on the data lines. Once the instruction is on the data lines, the CPU will be able to read it.

The system will include several input/output devices. In some systems, the CPU uses the address lines to turn different parts of the system "on" and "off." For example, when the CPU wants to turn on one of the output ports, it might produce a certain address on the address bus. The IC controlling the output port can then recognize the address and go into action. The data on the data bus at this time will be output through the output port. This is called *memory-mapped I/O*. When the address system is used to enable parts of the system, only a few of the address lines may be used. For example, two or three of the address lines may be used to control one of the output ports. Other microcomputer systems use I/O ports which are not "mapped" into the memory. These are turned on and off by a set of I/O control lines.

Sometimes the data and address lines may be used in ways which may seem surprising. For example, the IBM PC has an address bus which includes 20 lines. However, inside the CPU chip, only 16-bit "words" are used. To create a 20-bit address, the CPU produces two separate 16-bit addresses—a "segment" address and an "offset" address. The CPU then combines these two to create a 20-bit "physical address," and it places this address on the 20 address lines.

The IBM PC has another surprise in store. Some of the lines are used, at different times, to carry both data and addresses. Eight of the address lines are designated "AD0" through "AD7." The rest of the lines are called "A8" through "A19." The lines listed as "AD0" to "AD7" may carry either data or addresses. Control signals ensure that the correct signals are on these "dual-purpose" lines at the correct times. This process of alternately putting different signals on the same set of lines is called "multiplexing." Sometimes, the designers may extend some of the lines in a bus, run these lines to a particular part of the system, and use them for a special purpose. For example, a data line used in this way might have a label such as "XD1" (extended data line 1). Watch for special arrangements like this as you work with microcomputers.

A set of control signals run to all parts of the system. We have already described one of these control signals: the Reset signal. Other signals help supervise the activity of the memory, and tell the CPU what is happening in other parts of the system. *Interrupts* are special control signals which interrupt the operation of the CPU. Each time the CPU receives an interrupt, it stops what it is doing and goes to a special programmed routine. The CPU follows the instructions in this routine, and then goes back to the job it was originally doing. The name "interrupt" suggests that the system will only generate this type of signal when something unusual is happening. This is not the case, however. An interrupt signal may be used to tell the CPU to take care of many routine jobs. For example, a keyboard may be set to generate an interrupt whenever the operator presses a key. When this happens, the CPU will stop executing its regular program, and will process the keystroke from the keyboard.

What if two devices generate an interrupt at the same time? Computer systems use many different levels of interrupt signals, and they give some signals priority over others. An IC called an *interrupt controller* may be used to determine which interrupt signal is to be processed first. A *non-maskable interrupt* (NMI) takes precedence over all others.

Let's take another look at the way the CPU communicates with the memory areas. Let's say that the CPU wants to read some data from a disk drive and store it in memory. In the normal sequence, the CPU will read the data and hold onto it temporarily. Next, the CPU will send this data to the memory ICs for permanent storage. To put it another way, the data must "pass through" the CPU chip. We have shown this in Fig. 9-3A.

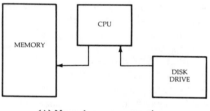

(A) Normal memory operation.

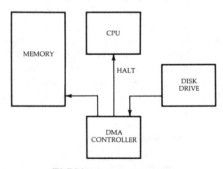

(B) DMA memory operation.

Fig. 9-3. Direct memory access (DMA).

Many modern microcomputers use a principle called *direct memory access* (DMA) to speed up this process (Fig. 9-3B). When the CPU wants to move large blocks of data, a separate device called a "DMA controller" can take control of the address and data buses. Let's go back to our example. You will recall that the CPU wanted to move data from a disk drive to

memory. We'll assume that the system has a DMA controller. At the start of the data transfer, the DMA controller will tell the CPU to "halt" for a moment. Next, the DMA controller will read a "word" of data from the disk drive. Finally, the DMA controller will pass this data on to memory. To put this another way, the data "pass through" the DMA controller, rather than through the CPU. For a number of reasons, this makes the data transfer much faster.

When a DMA system is used, some of the control of the memory is taken away from the CPU and given to another part of the system. Some modern microcomputers take this idea even further. Fig. 9-4 shows the block diagram of the IBM PS/2 Model 50 microcomputer. This computer is designed around a bus structure called the "Micro Channel™." As you can see, the Micro Channel is used to connect all parts of the microcomputer system. This system is an advancement because many of the devices on the bus have some "intelligence" of their own. They do not simply follow instructions issued by the CPU. For example, devices located along the bus can request the use of the bus, to transfer data from memory or for other purposes. "Arbitration" logic decides which device can use the bus at any given moment. You can expect to see similar "distributed intelligence" arrangements as microcomputers become more complicated.

Of course, any working computer system is more complicated than the system we've described here. However, this explanation includes the systems that are most important for troubleshooting purposes and most easily checked. We will concentrate on the sections that extend to all parts of the microcomputer: the address and data buses, the Clock and Reset lines, and the power-supply system. Faults are most likely to appear in these sections, since they are connected to so many of the ICs in the microcomputer.

The CPU is the central connection point for all of these various systems, so it is a logical place to start checking. By watching a few key signals at the CPU, you can quickly check the overall health of the whole computer. In Fig. 9-5, we have shown the signals that appear on the pins of a 8088 CPU IC. There are many different types of CPU chips, but this illustration will give you an idea of the types of signals that are available on the CPU pins.

Many microcomputers have slots which allow the use of plug-in circuit cards. Generally, the connectors for these cards carry all of the important signals used by the computer, including all of the lines of the data and address buses. This means these connectors offer a convenient place for checking all of these key signals. In

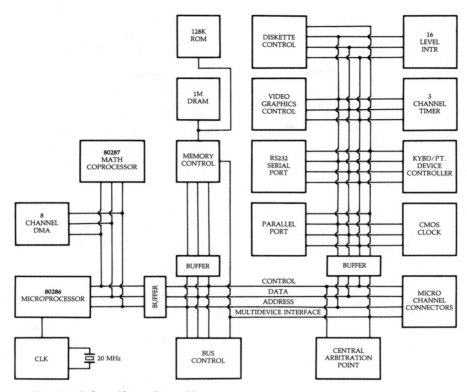

Fig. 9-4. Micro Channel™ Architecture. *(Courtesy of International Business Machines Corp.)*

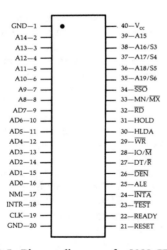

Fig. 9-5. Pin-out diagram of a 8088 CPU IC.

Fig. 9-6, we show a card connector used on many "PC-type" computers. As you can see, all of the most important signals are present, including the Clock signals, Reset, and the data and address signals. Of course, other computer systems will have different types of card connectors. In order to take test signals at the connector, you must know which signals are carried on each of the pins. If the connectors are located down inside the body of the computer, it may not be convenient to make your test connections. However, an "extender card" may be available. To use an extender card, you plug it into an empty connector slot. Each of the signals is brought up to a pin on the top edge of the card, so you can take test readings easily.

The Main Microcomputer

In the next part of this chapter, we'll cover four separate kinds of symptoms that can be related to problems in the main microcomputer. In each of these sequences (throughout the rest of this book), we'll use a system of index numbers (i.e., 9.1.2, 9.2.3, etc.) to refer to specific sections of the text.

One most common problem is the computer that starts operating correctly, but later "crashes." We

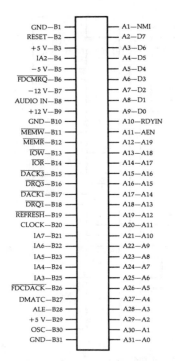

GND—B1	A1—NMI
RESET—B2	A2—D7
+5 V—B3	A3—D6
IA2—B4	A4—D5
−5 V—B5	A5—D4
FDCMRQ—B6	A6—D3
−12 V—B7	A7—D2
AUDIO IN—B8	A8—D1
+12 V—B9	A9—D0
GND—B10	A10—RDYIN
MEMW—B11	A11—AEN
MEMR—B12	A12—A19
IOW—B13	A13—A18
IOR—B14	A14—A17
DACK3—B15	A15—A16
DRQ3—B16	A16—A15
DACK1—B17	A17—A14
DRQ1—B18	A18—A13
REFRESH—B19	A19—A12
CLOCK—B20	A20—A11
IA7—B21	A21—A10
IA6—B22	A22—A9
IA5—B23	A23—A8
IA4—B24	A24—A7
IA3—B25	A25—A6
FDCDACK—B26	A26—A5
DMATC—B27	A27—A4
ALE—B28	A28—A3
+5 V—B29	A29—A2
OSC—B30	A30—A1
GND—B31	A31—A0

Fig. 9-6. Pin-out arrangement of a card connector slot.

discuss this type of symptom in Section 9.1.1. Then, Section 9.1.2 discusses the computer that makes mistakes, presenting incorrect data, etc., while Section 9.1.3 covers the computer that displays "nonsense" on the screen when you first turn on the power. Section 9.1.4 considers the computer that seems to be completely dead when you turn on the switch.

9.1.1 Problem 1

Symptom: Computer starts operating correctly, then stops. Screen is blank.

The customer's complaint runs something like this: "I turned on my computer and it ran perfectly for a while. Then suddenly it 'crashed,' for no apparent reason." Or, "I've used this program every day for the last month. Suddenly, part of it won't run. When I try to use the program, the computer just sits there."

Both of these symptoms are "intermittent." Unlike a "hard" failure, the cause of the intermittent problem might be absent when you make your tests. This means it will be more difficult to be sure that you've found the cause of the problem. Intermittent

faults are the most demanding and most frustrating kind to find and repair.

When you encounter a problem like this, leave the computer alone, with the power still turned on, for five or ten minutes. Even though the screen is blank and the computer appears to be inactive, it may still be processing a particularly time-consuming problem. A slow program in BASIC, such as a prime number search, may take several minutes to produce a result. This kind of situation is most likely to occur when you're running a program that you've written yourself. Well-designed commercial software will usually display a blinking cursor or some other indication that the computer is active.

A few computers run a "garbage collection" routine to rearrange available space in memory. The computer may start this routine on its own, without a command from you. While the computer is executing the routine, the screen will go blank and the computer will appear to be inactive. If your system has this feature, you can minimize delays by cleaning out the "garbage" yourself. A command will be provided for this.

Let's say that you wait for a few minutes and the computer still does not return to life. What next? Try pressing the "Reset" key. If the computer does not respond, turn the unit off, wait about 30 seconds, and then turn it on again. This should start the computer operating again, but it doesn't tell you what caused the problem in the first place. There are several possibilities.

As we said earlier, it is possible that the computer was in the middle of processing a very long program and you interrupted it. If this is the case, the computer should operate normally as long as you avoid that particular program.

It is also possible that the computer was disturbed by a "transient" on the power line, or by some other form of interference. Several kinds of interference were described in Chapter 5. If the incident was caused by a transient, the computer should begin operating normally as soon as you press "Reset." By the time you do this, the transient will be long gone. On the other hand, if the problem was caused by interference, the interference problem may still remain, causing the computer to stop again shortly after you press "Reset." It is also possible that the level of interference varies slightly from one moment to the next. Most of the time, the interference is not serious enough to cause problems, yet, from time to time, it becomes stronger and stops the computer. Crashes caused by transients do occur from time to time, but interference problems serious enough to stop a computer are rare.

Another possibility is that a problem with the software is causing the "crash." The only way to determine which of these possibilities is the actual cause is by running a series of tests. What program were you using when the computer stopped? Try running the same copy of the program again. If it works correctly this time, you may have had a brush with a transient. If the computer crashes again, try running a backup version of the program. If the backup runs correctly, perhaps your original copy of the program is bad. If the backup crashes also, try several different programs. If these run correctly, perhaps your original program has a programming mistake that causes the problem. If you see a pattern of problems that is consistent across different copies of several different programs, begin suspecting a hardware problem.

As you check out the software, remember to substitute a backup copy of the disk operating system (DOS) as well. If the DOS copy the computer is trying to use is a faulty copy of DOS, it may "hang up," or even Read or Write data incorrectly.

Perhaps a problem between the computer and one of the peripherals is causing the system to crash. Strip the system down to the smallest possible number of components. On computers like the IBM PC, with removable circuit cards, remove as many cards as possible. In most systems, the minimum system will include the main computer, plus the keyboard and the monitor. For some tests, you can even eliminate the monitor and driver circuits. You can use the "beep" and other start-up cues to tell you if the computer has started normally. Remember to turn off the equipment before you unplug anything.

Once you have stripped down the system, run some tests on the remaining parts. If the system seems to work correctly, turn off the equipment, plug in one of the peripherals or circuit cards, and test the system again. If you reconnect a unit and the trouble symptoms reappear, look for a problem with that unit. Turn to the chapter in this book that deals with that specific peripheral.

We'll assume that none of these suggestions reveal the problem. How did the computer crash? Did it happen right away, as soon as you turned on the machine? If this happened, suspect the ROMs. The ROMs supply instructions for the computer when it is first turned on, before the other programs take over. In many computers, some of the space in RAM is also set aside for use during this start-up phase. If the computer crashes on start-up, perhaps one of these critical memory locations is faulty. If the computer failed later, during execution of the program, you might focus your suspicions on the RAMs, although a ROM might still be involved.

At this point, try using the diagnostic programs for your computer. If this test shows a problem with either a ROM IC or a RAM IC, replace the suspect chip and try running the program that caused the crash. Run several others also. If the diagnostics show a problem with a large number of RAMs, it is possible that one of the data or address lines is faulty. Refer to Section 9.2.3.

Your computer's power supply is meant to deliver clean, smooth power to all parts of the computer. If any of the power-supply voltages are low, the computer could operate erratically. (Chapter 16 explains how a typical power supply is arranged.) Take voltage readings at each of the output stages. If the voltage at any output stage is incorrect, troubleshoot the power supply, as instructed.

Even if the voltage levels seem correct, you still may have a power-supply problem. If the filters in a particular section of the supply are inefficient, the supply could be passing some electronic "noise" from the AC power line through to the computer. Use an oscilloscope to check for noise at each output stage of the power supply.

If the power supply appears to be operating correctly, check for normal signals at key points on the CPU or the card connectors. Check the Clock signal (see Section 9.2.1), the Reset signal (see Section 9.2.2), and the data and address lines (Section 9.2.3).

There is a possibility that a problem like this could be caused by a faulty CPU chip. Depending on the type of CPU used in your computer, it may be more convenient and less expensive to just replace the CPU. This should be done only as a last resort, and only after you've checked out each of the possibilities we've described above.

If you haven't located the problem at this point, it's time to take the computer to a shop.

9.1.2 Problem 2

Symptom: Computer makes random errors.

The complaint used to describe the equipment problem may be, "The computer is printing incorrect values in the balance sheet," or, "The word processor inserts an incorrect character now and then." These are intermittent problems. Unlike a "hard" failure, the cause of the intermittent problem might be absent when you make your tests. This means it will be more difficult to determine if you've found the cause of the problem. Intermittent faults are the most demanding and frustrating kind of breakdown to find and repair.

If you find only an occasional error, start by

checking for a problem in the software. Try running the original version of the program again. If this still produces errors, try a backup copy of the program. If the errors continue, run some other programs. If you find that the errors occur in only one program, the software program probably has a "bug" or programming error. Contact the software manufacturer and describe your problem. The company may have produced an update which will correct your problem.

If you find a pattern of errors that seem to appear in many different programs, you'll have to do some more checking. If the intermittent problems occur seldom enough, it may not be practical to run the tests all at once. Instead, operate your system normally and keep a record of each time that you notice a problem. Try to find some common factor that relates the errors. Did they always occur at about the same time of day? Were you always running the same general type of job (sorting a file, printing a long file from disk, etc.)? In Chapter 5, we described a number of possible problems that are present in the environment around the computer. One of these conditions could be the cause of your problem.

It is also possible that a bad "memory" IC is the cause of the problem. As we explained in Chapter 8, a bad RAM can produce a confusing pattern of intermittent failures. A program instruction written into a bad memory space in RAM can be garbled when it is read back, causing the program to work incorrectly. A bad RAM can result in incorrect totals, incorrect characters, etc. A bad ROM can also cause intermittent problems.

If the computer will allow it, run a diagnostics program. The diagnostics will check the RAMs and ROMs, and will tell you if an IC appears to be bad. If the diagnostics points out a particular IC, replace that part and test again. This kind of test reveals most RAM and ROM problems, but not all of them. Even if the memory ICs pass the diagnostics test, don't rule out a memory problem entirely.

Some kinds of power-supply problems can cause intermittent failures. One of the filters in a power supply may fail, and the supply may start to pass electronic "noise" through to the computer. Check for noise at each output stage of the power supply, as described in Chapter 16.

It is possible that the main CPU IC has developed an intermittent fault. Depending on the CPU chip used in your computer, it may be less expensive and more convenient to just replace the CPU. This should be done only as a last resort, and only after you've checked out all of the possibilities we've mentioned above.

At this point, we've eliminated all of the possible causes that are easy to locate. If you can afford to operate your system with an occasional fault, you may want to study the problem further and see if you can discover a common factor that seems to relate to all of the intermittent faults. If you can't afford to live with the problem any longer, take your unit to an electronics/computer service shop.

9.1.3 Problem 3

Symptom: At power on, "garbage" is displayed on screen.

The complaint from the customer is this: "One day I turned on the computer and the screen seemed to be filled with random characters." Technicians call this kind of display "garbage on the screen." A symptom like this means that the computer is "lost." For some reason, the computer couldn't execute one of the instructions in its program, and began executing instructions at random. This process continued until the computer filled the screen with "garbage," and then it stopped. The whole process probably took a fraction of a second. You must find out why this has happened.

If you're lucky, the problem was caused by some kind of "transient" fault. If this happened, the transient will be long gone. Press the "Reset" key. This will take the computer back to a known starting point in its chain of instructions. If this doesn't work, turn the computer off, wait 30 seconds, and turn it on again. The computer may start to operate normally. If this problem happens often, look for a problem in the environment around the computer (see Chapter 5). For now, we'll assume that you've tried the "Reset" key, and the computer immediately produces "garbage" again.

Disconnect all of the peripherals, one by one. As you disconnect each unit, try the "Reset" key again and see if the computer begins to operate normally. If it does, look for a problem in the unit you disconnected just before the problem disappeared. Refer to the chapter in this book that refers to *that* particular unit. Remember to turn off all power to the system before you disconnect any peripherals or circuit cards.

Check the power supply next. Obviously, part of the power-supply system is working, since the computer is partially active. It's possible that the power in one section of the computer is shut off. For example, the 5-V DC supply may be operating normally, so all of the ICs are powered up and ready to work. Yet, if the −12-V DC supply is out of action (on computers that require this voltage), the computer won't be able to use any of the RAMs. When the CPU asks for an instruction stored in memory, it will get no response. At this point, the CPU may begin to drift, causing the "garbage" to appear on the screen.

Check the voltage at each of the output stages in the power supply. We've explained how to do this in Chapter 16, so if you discover a problem, troubleshoot it according to the procedure described there.

If this doesn't turn up the problem, check the key signals at the CPU chip, or at one of the card connectors. Check for the correct Clock signal (Section 9.2.1), check the Reset system (Section 9.2.2), and check the data and address lines (Section 9.2.3).

It is possible that the "garbage" on the screen could be caused by a problem in the driver circuits associated with the monitor. Refer to Chapter 15.

A faulty CPU could be causing the problem. Many replacement CPU ICs are common and inexpensive. If this is the case, you might want to replace your CPU chip. This should be a last resort, though, after you've checked each of the possibilities mentioned above.

At this point, you've checked out all the simple causes for this symptom. If you have plenty of time, you should be able to locate the cause of the problem. If you're in a hurry, take your equipment to a service shop.

9.1.4 Problem 4

Symptom: Computer seems dead when you turn on the power; there is no response to commands.

Here's a typical complaint: "I sat down to work, and I turned on all of the usual switches, but there was no response. The computer seemed to be completely dead." In many ways, this is one of the easier problems to troubleshoot. The problem is clear-cut; part of the computer is not working at all. In addition, the problem is static—it will sit there and wait while you track it down.

First, be sure the computer is really dead. Does your computer have a "Power On" indicator? It'spossible that the light bulb or LED has failed. Some computers "beep" on power-up. Perhaps the monitor is not working, so you can't see any indication that the computer is operating. For the moment, assume that the computer is working and tell it to read (load) something from either a floppy disk or the hard disk. Is there any activity at the disk drive? You might discover that the computer is more "live" than you thought.

Next, "strip down" the system. One by one, disconnect each of the peripherals attached to your computer—the printer, modem, disk drive, etc. On an IBM PC and other computers with removable circuit cards, unplug as many cards as possible. Turn off the computer, unplug one component, and then turn the computer on again. If the computer suddenly appears to work correctly, look for a problem in the unit you just disconnected, or in the cables and connectors that run to that unit. Refer to the chapter that discusses the affected peripheral.

Whenever any device seems to be completely dead, check the power supply. It is possible that the power supply, itself, has failed and is not producing any output. It is also possible that a problem somewhere in the power-distribution system has caused the power supply to turn itself off. A power supply will "foldback" like this to protect itself. The power supply may be all right and may be protecting itself as it was designed to do. Chapter 16 includes some detailed troubleshooting instructions for power supplies.

A faulty CPU could be causing the problem. Replacement CPU ICs for many computers are common and inexpensive. If this is the case, you might want to replace your CPU chip. This should be done as a last resort, after you've checked each of the possibilities mentioned above.

If none of these procedures reveals the problem, it's time to take the computer to a service shop.

Checking Key Signals

If the power supply appears to be working correctly, check for key signals at the CPU or a card connector. Check the Clock signal (Section 9.2.1), the Reset system (Section 9.2.2), and the data and address lines (Section 9.2.3).

9.2.1 Test 1
Checking the "Clock" signal.

The heartbeat of every computer is provided by a "Clock" circuit. This type of clock doesn't tell you the time of day (although your computer may have a second unit that does that too). The clock we're talking about provides a series of precise pulses. These pulses are carried to every part of the computer and are used to synchronize many of the computer's functions. If the signal from this clock stops, or is weak, or if the pulses begin to vary, the computer might show intermittent

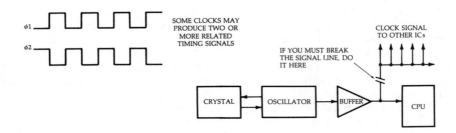

(A) Simple clock circuit with timing signals.

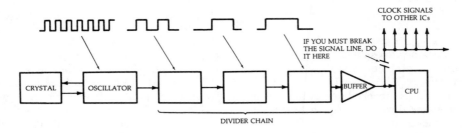

(B) High-frequency clock circuit.

Fig. 9-7. Clock circuits

faults or might stop altogether. Fig. 9-7 shows two kinds of clock arrangements.

The heart of the Clock circuit is an "oscillator." This type of circuit switches back and forth between two states. This happens very quickly. For example, one of the clocks in the IBM PC-AT oscillates at a frequency of over 14 MHz (14 million cycles per second). The operating frequency of the oscillator is stabilized by a "crystal." Crystals are produced so that they tend to resonate at a very precise frequency, and engineers use a crystal to keep the frequency of the clock from drifting. In some computers, the original clock operates at a very high frequency, far above the frequency used by the CPU. This high frequency is then routed through a chain of "divider" circuits (divide-by-2, divide-by-10, etc.), which bring the high frequency down to a frequency that can be used by the CPU and other parts of the microcomputer.

The clock signal always goes to the CPU chip, so check the schematic for your computer and locate the CPU. Look for a pin having an input with a label of something like "CLK." You should also be able to find

this signal on one of the pins of a card connector. When you've identified the right pin, and with the computer running, check the pin with your logic probe. The probe should show a continuous series of pulses. (Some clock signals may be too fast to be picked up by an inexpensive probe.)

If you get a good signal at this point, you can assume that the Clock oscillator and divider are working. Skip the rest of the following material on the clock, and go to Section 9.2.2, which discusses the Reset system.

For the moment, we'll assume that the clock signal at the CPU pin is not correct. In the diagram of Fig. 9-7, you will notice that both of the clock circuits shown include a buffer "upstream" of the CPU. Take another reading just "upstream" of this buffer. If you detect a normal clock signal here, you can assume that the clock itself is working correctly, and the problem is in one of the distribution lines downstream. If the clock signal is missing "upstream" of the buffer as well, look for a problem in the crystal or the oscillator. We'll discuss this possibility in a moment.

Some computers do not have a buffer in the clock distribution system. In a case like this, you don't know whether the problem is caused by a bad crystal or oscillator, or by a fault in the distribution system. This is one of those situations where a problem "downstream" of the measuring instrument can produce incorrect readings throughout the distribution system. We described this type of problem in Chapter 7.

To progress further, you must disconnect the clock circuit from the distribution system. The CPU should remain connected to the clock circuit—make the break downstream of the point where the clock system branches off to the other ICs. There are several ways to disconnect part of a circuit. We discussed them in Chapter 8. In this case, you might identify the last IC in the clock chain, and then lift the pin that carries the clock output. Once you make this disconnection, test the "upstream" side of the break with your logic probe. If the clock signal is now normal, look for a problem in the distribution system. If the clock signal is still abnormal, look for a problem in the clock circuits themselves. We'll consider this case first.

Most clock circuits are pretty simple, and you should be able to locate a problem here without much trouble. As we said, all of these circuits use some kind of oscillator, stabilized by a crystal. The result is a regular waveform with a precise frequency. There may be a few other components in the circuit. The two most likely causes for a failure here are: (1) a bad crystal, or (2) a timing capacitor which may have failed. Try replacing the capacitor first, because it is cheaper. If that doesn't work, replace the crystal.

We also mentioned a different type of circuit, using a high-frequency clock and string of divider circuits. One step in the chain might be a "divide-by-4" circuit. The circuit counts the pulses coming into its input. For every four pulses coming in, the circuit sends out one pulse. It is possible that one of these divider-chain ICs may have failed. Use your "chain troubleshooting" skills here. We explained this technique in Chapter 7.

What if the problem is not in the clock circuit itself, but in one of the ICs which receive a clock signal, or in one of the lines running to those ICs? Various clock signals may run to twenty or thirty ICs. This means that a lot of ICs, and a lot of circuit board traces, must be checked.

Earlier, we told you to break the clock line "downstream" of the buffer. Test the "downstream" side of the break with your logic probe. With TTL circuits, you should detect an undefined or "floating" state. We described this effect in Chapter 8. A steady "high" suggests that somewhere in the distribution system, there is a short to the +5-V supply. A steady "low" suggests a short to ground. NMOS and CMOS circuits don't tend to float, so we can't be so specific about circuits which include these devices.

Inspect the whole circuit board visually, looking for obvious faults. Check for stray bits of solder, mechanical damage to the board, etc.

With the computer turned on, try testing the temperature of each IC with your finger. We described this technique in Chapter 7. If your problem is caused by a bad IC, one chip may seem warmer than the rest.

If you have instruments that have a current-tracing capability, you should be able to find the cause of the short. Without special tools, however, you can't go much further. Take the computer to a service shop.

9.2.2 Test 2
Checking the Reset system.

If the Clock appears to be operating, check the Reset function next. "Reset" is one of the first signals the CPU receives when the computer starts up. You can generate a "Reset" signal yourself by pressing the "Reset" key on the keyboard. Whenever you hit this key, the computer will go back to a known starting point in its series of instructions. If you are running a commercial software package, the "Reset" key will probably take you back to the software's main menu. However, you may lose any data on which you were working.

Fig. 9-8 shows a typical Reset network. To troubleshoot this system, check the schematic for your computer and locate the pin on the CPU which receives the "Reset" signal. (Actually, this signal should usually be called "Not-Reset," because it is active when it is

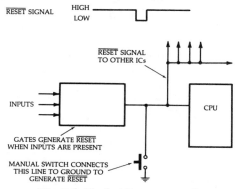

Fig. 9-8. Typical Reset network.

"low.") With the computer running, check this pin with your logic probe. On most computers, the pin should go "low" when you hit the "Reset" button, and then return to "high." If you don't see any activity on the "Reset" pin, look for a fault in the network of lines that carry the "Reset" signal. One of these lines may be shorted to +5-V or ground. In Chapter 8, we tell how to deal with this type of problem.

In some computer systems, the "Reset" line is not allowed to operate until some other conditions are checked. For example, the Reset circuits may detect a low-voltage output from the power supply, and will hold the "Reset" line to "false." The "Reset" line may be inactive because of a problem elsewhere in the system.

9.2.3 Test 3
Checking the data and address lines.

Assuming the Reset system is working correctly, check the lines in the data and address buses. On most computers, these are two separate systems. Fig. 9-9 shows the two bus systems. Lines from both systems run to all parts of the computer.

When the computer is operating normally, you should see plenty of activity on each of these lines. If you suspect a problem in either system, you should look for two possible kinds of problems: (1) a short circuit or other problem with one of the data or address lines, as they run across the circuit card, or (2) a problem in one of the ICs served by the data or address lines. Most of these ICs are memory devices—ROMs and RAMs.

You can make a quick check of the data and address lines using your logic probe. On the schematic for your computer, identify the pins on the CPU that carry the data lines. With the computer running, touch each of these pins with the tip of the logic probe. Each line should show lots of activity. Take a closer look at any line that appears to be stopped in a steady "high" or "low" state. A continuous high suggests that the line is shorted to the +5-V DC power supply. A steady low suggests the line is shorted to ground. Check each address line in the same way.

TTL-compatible digital equipment is designed to receive a signal that is either high (above 3.5 volts) or low (below 0.5 volt). If an address or data line shows a value between these two states, it is said to be "floating." This situation will give you a strange readout on your logic probe. Perhaps the high and low indicators will both glow at the same time, but dimly. Your probe may indicate that a line is floating, but TTL logic circuits in the computer will often interpret a "float" as a constant "low." A "floating" reading on an address line definitely indicates a problem. A data line may float temporarily between data transmissions. A data line that floats continuously is suspect.

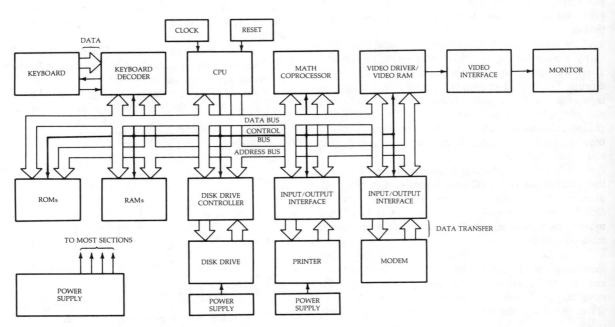

Fig. 9-9. Block diagram showing microcomputer bus lines.

You may also notice an unusual reading from two lines that run side by side. Because the lines in a data or address bus are so small, and because they run so close together, it is possible for two adjacent lines to short together. However, it is possible to check for two lines shorted together. One method is to use a pulser to put signals on each line, and see if the pulses appear on adjacent lines. You can also shut off the equipment, and test the resistance between each pair of lines with a voltohmmeter set to read OHMS. There should be a high resistance between each pair of lines. A low resistance indicates a short.

Many different devices share the use of each bus. Between the bus and each of these devices, you will find a series of three-state buffers. A three-state buffer can act as a switch to either connect or disconnect a device from the bus. By supervising the action of these buffers, the CPU can be sure that the correct devices are connected to the bus at the correct moments. However, these buffers can fail. We described a test procedure for three-state buffers in Chapter 8. Note that each address or data line is connected to many buffers.

Let's say you've localized a problem to a certain line. The line itself appears to be all right—no obvious breaks or shorts. The three-state buffers associated with the line also appear to be all right. Perhaps the line is shorted to +5 V or ground inside of one of the other ICs to which it is connected. Both the data and address systems run from the CPU to all the ROMs and RAMs, plus the interface ports and other locations as well. (The data and address systems are illustrated in Fig. 9-9.) When so many ICs are connected to each data and address line, how can you tell which IC is faulty?

Diagnostic software may be helpful at this point. The diagnostic programs are usually stored on a floppy disk, so they will only be useful if the computer can read from a disk drive. A good diagnostic program will be able to test the computer's ROMs, RAMs, and, perhaps, other components as well. If the software detects a problem, it will indicate which IC to replace.

The diagnostics may indicate that ten or twenty ICs are bad. It is unlikely that so many ICs would fail at the same time, unless the computer experienced a disaster of some sort. It is more likely that one of the address or data lines is faulty, and this is making it appear that many of the ICs are bad. Tests included in a diagnostic package may not be conclusive. For example, a diagnostic program may miss some types of RAM problems, and diagnostics may not be able to diagnose problems in devices which were not made by the original manufacturer of the computer.

If the problem is so serious you can't load the diagnostics, you must use other methods to try to locate

the bad IC. As we said, the problem may be caused by a short circuit inside one of the ICs. You can try the "touch test" we described in Chapter 7. The bad IC may seem warmer than the rest. If you have instruments with current-tracing capability, you should be able to find the cause of the short. Without these instruments, it is difficult to make much progress beyond this point.

Another possibility is that one of the ICs is processing signals incorrectly. It is difficult to determine which IC is bad without special instruments. We described some basic tests in Chapter 8 (refer to the material on ROMs). A bad ROM will often cause a problem with one of the "housekeeping" functions of the computer. For example, the computer may forget the meaning of a command, repeat a line in a program, or insert information you never typed in. ROMs are usually replaced as a set. This can be expensive, so you should be certain this is the cause of the problem. Let a service shop determine this.

We also described some basic tests in Chapter 8 for RAMs. One or more memory locations in a RAM may fail. A computer with this condition may garble a line in a program or miscopy a bit of data. Some sections of the memory are used before others. If the bad memory space is located in one of these less-used parts, you may not see the problem until you run a program that uses nearly all of the available space. Thus, a problem that appears to be intermittent can really be constant. If the RAM is shorted, the "touch test" we described in Chapter 6 may detect it. You may also be able to locate the bad RAM with this method: check the manual for your computer, and identify the RAMs that contain the memory space essential for the "housekeeping" functions of the computer (RAMs used as stack space for the ROMs). Leave these RAMs in place. Turn off the computer, and remove four of the other RAMs. Turn on the machine again, and make the checks we've described above. If the computer is still behaving abnormally, turn it off again, and remove four more chips. If the computer suddenly begins to work normally, you know the bad IC is one of the four you removed last. Now replace these four ICs, one at a time, being sure to shut off the equipment each time. You should see the trouble symptoms reappear after you replace the bad IC. RAMs should be handled carefully. Reread the section pertaining to the special handling of ICs given in Chapter 8.

Dynamic RAMs must receive a "refresh" pulse regularly if they are to retain data. If this refresh signal is absent or delayed, all of the RAMs may become unreliable. Check the manual for your computer to find out if your system includes dynamic RAMs. Determine which line handles the refresh function, and check for the correct signal on any suspect ICs. We described this "refresh" system in a bit more detail in Chapter 8. (Refer to the section on RAMs.)

9.2.4 Test 4
Checking the keyboard.

The keyboard is the "interface" between the computer and the operator. Fig. 9-10 shows a typical keyboard system. The keyboard circuits consist of a matrix of crossing wires. Whenever the operator presses a key, a switch under the key connects two of these wires. In our simplified example, if the operator were to press the key for "B," he would short lines "2" and "X" together. The keyboard decoder detects the two lines that are shorted together, and decides which key has been pressed. Of course, the operator may want to use an uppercase character, or one of the special or control characters. In this case, he or she would press a letter, plus "Shift" or "Control" at the same time. The decoder is designed to detect this. "Shift," "Control," and other control keys each have a separate line into the decoder.

As the operator presses each key, the decoder produces signals on the outgoing data lines. Often, there are a number of output lines, operating in parallel. The characters are coded onto these output lines, using the "ASCII" scheme of coding. (The ASCII coding system is discussed in the Appendix D.) Each of the output lines passes through a three-state buffer on its way to the data bus. Each buffer amplifies the signal. The CPU controls the switching function of each three-state buffer to make sure the signal from the keyboard is on the data bus at the correct moment. Data are clocked into the CPU by a "data strobe" signal. The CPU will only accept data from the keyboard when the data strobe signal is "true."

Some of the more recent computers use a different arrangement. On units of this type, the keyboard is designed around an on-board microprocessor. The microprocessor system has all of the basic components you would expect to find with any microprocessor—CPU chip, ROM, RAM, etc. The data are sent from the keyboard to the main computer over a single data line, using a "serial" format. At the other end of the link, the computer may use a UART or similar device to convert the serial signals back to a parallel format. (We describe this device in Chapter 14.)

There are a number of trouble symptoms that will suggest a problem in the keyboard. The most obvious is the case where you press a certain key, but the character doesn't appear on the screen. This does not always indicate a hardware problem. The computer may not respond to a keystroke if it is processing a long program. During this process, the computer is not expecting input from the keyboard, so it ignores most

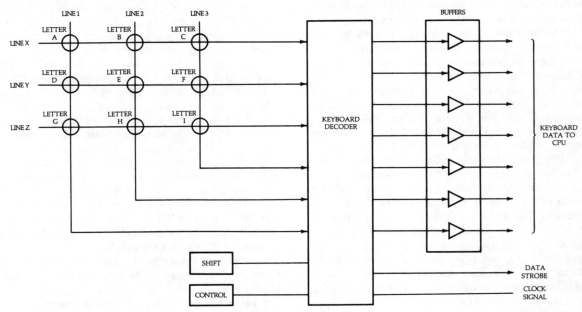

Fig. 9-10. Keyboard circuits.

keyboard signals. However, one signal that the computer can't ignore is the Reset signal. Press the "Reset" key and see if the computer responds. If you don't get any response, the keyboard is dead.

Sometimes, you may press a key once and get two characters on the screen. This symptom is caused by dirty contacts in the key switches. Dirty or corroded contacts can cause a poor connection that actually "makes" and "breaks" several times when you press a key. The key decoder is fast enough to detect each of these contacts as a separate request for a character. If the contacts on a keyswitch are dirty enough, the key won't work at all.

On most microcomputers, each key switch is a separate unit. You can disassemble the keyboard, open up the affected switch, and check the switch contacts directly. However, you may have to remove the whole keyboard circuit board in order to get access to the one faulty switch. On some microcomputers, the separate switches are sealed. Sealed switches are much less sensitive to dirt and corrosion. However, if one of these sealed switches does fail, you'll have to remove it and solder in a new part. Some computers use a calculator-type keyboard, with free-floating plastic keys, held in place by springs. You can disassemble one of these keyboards and clean the individual contacts. However, it can be difficult to assemble this kind of keyboard again. You must line up each of the keys before you reassemble the keyboard, and the springs under the keys may make this difficult. Some inexpensive computers use a "membrane" keyboard in which all of the key contacts are sealed in a single flat unit,

protected on both sides by a flexible plastic sheet. If some of the switch contacts fail, you must replace the whole unit.

There are many different types of key mechanisms. On mechanical switches, you will always find some sort of switching mechanism. There will be two contacts—one for each side of the switch. Somehow, when you press the key down, these contacts will be brought together. In order for a mechanical switch to work, the contacts must meet, of course. The contact points should be clean and shiny. You can test a mechanical keyswitch, using a voltmeter (Fig. 9-11) or an ohmmeter (Fig. 9-12).

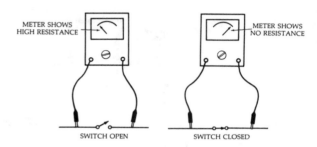

Fig. 9-12. Testing a switch with a ohmmeter.

One common type of key mechanism is shown in Fig. 9-13A. Other switches have more mechanical parts, as shown in Fig. 9-13B.

In the past, keyswitches have been among the most unreliable parts of the microcomputer system. Manufacturers have been trying to find a way of avoiding mechanical switch actions. Fig. 9-14 shows one alternative. This type of switch uses a change in capacitance to indicate a keystroke. One of the sensing plates is fixed; the other can be moved. When the key is pressed, the upper plate is moved close to the lower plate, but not touching it. This changes the capacitance of the assembly. This capacitance change is used to alter the frequency of an oscillator circuit. A phase-lock loop circuit detects the frequency change. A comparator takes the output from the phase-lock loop and compares this with a reference. When the output from the phase-lock loop passes a certain "threshold," the comparator detects this and produces a "true" output. This output indicates to the CPU that a key has been pressed.

Fig. 9-15 shows another type of mechanism that has been used to avoid mechanical contacts. Two coils of wire are arranged as shown in the sketch. These coils may be thought of as the "primary" winding and the

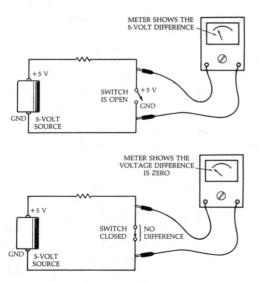

Fig. 9-11. Testing a switch with a voltmeter.

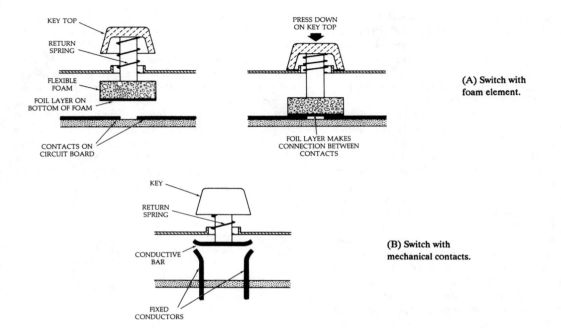

(A) Switch with foam element.

(B) Switch with mechanical contacts.

Fig. 9-13. Keyswitch mechanisms.

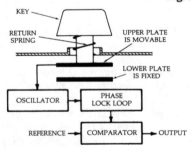

Fig. 9-14. A capacitive keyswitch.

"secondary" winding of a 1:1 transformer. You may also think of the "primary" as the input to the switch, and the "secondary" as the output. At the bottom of the keyswitch mechanism is a small magnet. As long as the key is not pressed, the two windings do not interact. However, when the key is pressed, the magnet is moved so that it is close to both of the windings. The magnet "couples" the two windings so that signals can pass between them. There is no direct connection—the "coupling" is caused by induction. When the magnet is in place, a rapidly changing signal on the primary winding is "coupled" to the secondary winding, producing an output from the key.

If you are working on a unit with mechanical contacts, and you notice any dirt or corrosion on the contact points, this is probably the cause of the problem. Clean the contacts with a TV-type contact cleaner. If a particular switching unit gives you much trouble, it is best to replace it. Replacement switches cost about $5.00 each. If you must replace more than five or six switches, it often makes sense to simply replace the whole keyboard.

If one key contact is dirty enough to cause trouble, the others are probably almost as dirty, so you should plan to clean all of the contacts. Work on one row of keys at a time. Turn off the computer before you work on the keys. Carefully pry up each key top, as shown in Fig. 9-16, and set it aside. This is a two-hand operation. Support the key top with one hand, and pry it away from the base with a small screwdriver using your other hand. As you set down the key tops you've removed, keep them in order.

In the type of switch shown in Fig. 9-17, the connection is made at the tip of the two key contacts. These contacts must be clean if the keys are to work smoothly. It is best to clean this type of switch with a "burnishing tool" and some burnishing fluid. These are available from computer supply houses. Moisten the burnishing tool, and then place the end of the tool between the key contacts. With a small screwdriver, depress the center of the switch mechanism, so that the tips of the contacts pull together lightly against the burnishing tool. Move the burnishing tool up and down a few times to clean the contacts. You don't need a lot

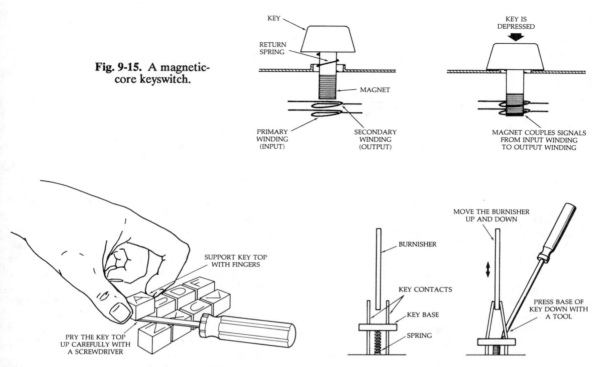

Fig. 9-15. A magnetic-core keyswitch.

Fig. 9-16. Removing key tops.

Fig. 9-17. Cleaning key contacts.

of force—count on the chemical to do most of the cleaning. Wait until the chemical evaporates before you replace the key tops.

Carefully check any cables associated with the keyboard. This is particularly true if your keyboard is contained in a separate unit that sits in front of the computer. A bad cable connection usually results in intermittent, erratic operation. The computer may refuse to display several different characters, or may substitute characters. In other cases, a damaged cable can cut off all the signals from the keyboard.

If you suspect a cable problem, refer to Chapter 7, and check the cables and connectors according to the instructions given there. Type a variety of characters, while moving the cable and while tapping on the connectors. Watch the screen on the monitor and see if the fault occurs while you're doing this.

One of the other components in the keyboard system may fail, in particular, the decoder chip. A faulty decoder chip can generate multiple characters for one keystroke, or can cause a number of other problems. Be sure the chip is getting adequate power, of course. You should be able to spot the inputs from the key contacts, using your logic probe. You should see the decoded

outputs as well. Check the schematic for your equipment. If the chip requires a clock signal, check for this with your logic probe. The CPU won't accept any data from the keyboard unless the decoder is producing a "data strobe" signal. Check the three-state buffers according to the instructions given in Chapter 8.

Keyboards are very vulnerable to mechanical damage. They are set in just the right position to catch falling objects. If only a few switches are damaged, you can often replace just the affected switches. If a keyboard is soaked by a corrosive liquid, such as beer or soda pop, you can try to rinse out the unit with distilled water. However, you will probably have to replace the whole keyboard.

9.2.5 Test 5

Checking the game controllers.

Game controllers take a lot of physical abuse, so they present more than their share of servicing problems. The most common type of controller uses a single "joystick" to signal to the computer. The joystick is often connected to four switches, as shown in

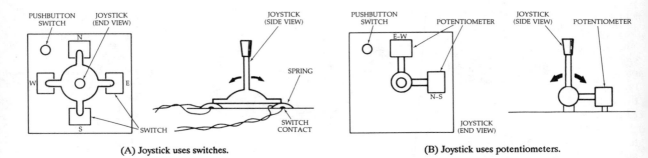

(A) Joystick uses switches.

(B) Joystick uses potentiometers.

Fig. 9-18. Typical game controllers.

Fig. 9-18A. Many inexpensive controllers use sealed switch contacts that are molded right into the case material, as shown in the sketch. When the joystick is tilted toward one of the switches, an arm presses down on the top of the switch spring, making a contact between the two parts of the switch. (In our explanation, we'll use the points of the compass to indicate the different signals generated by the controller.) Referring to Fig. 9-18A, if you were to tilt the joystick toward the upper right-hand corner of the controller, in a "northeast" direction, you would close switches "N" and "E." This would signal the computer to move the cursor or aim the "spaceship" in a diagonal direction toward the upper right-hand corner of the screen.

Another arrangement is shown in Fig. 9-18B. In this kind of controller, the joystick is connected to two "pots" (short for *potentiometer*). One pot sends signals that express the joystick's position in the "east-west" direction, and the other pot produces signals for the "north-south" direction. Each pot acts as an adjustable resistor. This means that the controller can produce graduated outputs to the computer, rather than simple "on" or "off" outputs. Inside the computer, the interface circuits must have a way of changing these graduated "analog" circuits to digital "1s" and "0s." Timing circuits may be used to accomplish this. The resistive input from each pot is routed to a timer. This timer is constantly cycling "on" and "off," and the CPU is constantly checking to see which state the timer is in at the moment. The length of time that the timer stays "on" is set by the resistance across one side of the control pot. By comparing the number of "on" samples with the number of "off" samples for each potentiometer, the CPU can calculate the setting of the joystick. Most controllers also include one or more separate push-button switches for firing "photon torpedoes," etc.

People tend to get excited when they play video games. As a result, the game controllers take a lot of abuse. Most of the problems are strictly mechanical. Many joystick mechanisms are surprisingly flimsy, and the plastic parts break after a period of hard use. Sometimes, the shaft of the joystick breaks, but more often, it is the supporting section of the joystick assembly that fails.

If a joystick won't move normally, open the case of the controller and inspect the mechanical parts. Undo the screws on the back of the controller to open the case. Be sure to turn off the computer and unplug the controller before you do this.

If you have an intermittent problem, check the connectors and cables between the controller and the computer, as described in Chapter 7. The connectors can wear out quickly, particularly if children plug and unplug the controllers several times a day. The female part of the connector opens up a bit and doesn't allow a good contact. You can check this by turning off the computer and using a voltohmmeter to check the continuity through the connector. Move the connector. If you see the OHMS reading on the meter jump back and forth, replace the connector.

The various switches can also wear out. If you suspect a problem, turn off the computer, unplug the controller, and check for continuity through each of the switches, using a voltohmmeter as instructed in Chapter 7. If your controller has sealed switches that are molded into the case and a switch fails, you'll have to buy a new controller. However, if you can remove the bad switch, you can probably get a replacement part from the manufacturer.

If your controller includes potentiometers, test them according to the procedures listed in Chapter 7. Perhaps the pots are just dirty. Try to work some spray-type "TV-tuner" cleaner into each pot. This won't be easy, because most pots are enclosed in a metal case. Try to "leak"some of the cleaner down along the shaft, and squirt some into any holes in the casing. Once you get the cleaner inside the casing, turn the shaft back and forth a few times to complete the cleaning action.

If one of the push-button switches fails, you should be able to find a replacement easily at any local electronics store. Some of these switches are the "push-on/push-off" type, but most are the "momentary on" type. Any replacement switch will do, as long as it is of the right type and it fits the space available inside the case of the controller.

It is possible for a problem in the game controller to cause damage inside the computer. For example, if an overzealous game enthusiast pulls too hard on the joystick, he can push one of the pots past its stops, and cause a short circuit. On some computers, the same kind of connectors are used for the game controllers and for other peripherals. This makes it easy to plug the game controller into the wrong socket. Either of these mistakes can cause damage inside the computer. You will usually find buffers on the signal lines from the joystick, just as they come into the computer. If you suspect a problem, check the buffers, following the instructions given in Chapter 8.

Once you diagnose the problem, you can usually get replacement parts from the manufacturer. This may not be practical, however, because of the time or expense involved. It may be simpler and less expensive to buy a new controller.

9.2.6 Test 6
Checking the mouse.

The "mouse" or "pointing device" is a helpful accessory for some microcomputer applications. In Fig. 9-19, we have shown one typical mechanism used inside a mouse. The mouse rides on a rubber ball. As the ball turns, the motion is picked up by two rollers. One roller detects motion along the "X" axis, and the other detects changes along the "Y" axis. Each roller is connected to a "chopper" wheel. Each of these wheels includes a number of slots. A light source is positioned on one side of the chopper wheel, and a detector is placed on the other side. When the slot passes, the light is allowed to reach the detector, and the detector produces a digital pulse. By counting the pulses along the "X" and "Y" axis, the CPU can tell which direction the mouse is moving. In addition to these parts, a "mouse" will usually include one to three switches.

Another type of mouse uses a different principle. This type of mouse must be placed on a special pad. The pad is marked with a number of lines, aligned along the "X" and "Y" axis. An optical sensor is

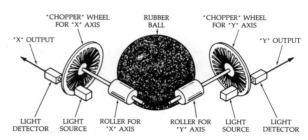

Fig. 9-19. A typical "Mouse" mechanism.

mounted on the underside of the mouse. As the mouse is moved, the sensor detects the number of "X" and "Y" lines crossed and produces a series of digital pulses.

When a mouse fails or becomes erratic, it is usually because the mechanism is dirty. Eventually, the rollers can collect quite a bit of dirt. This can make the rubber ball move unevenly as the mouse is moved across a desk top.

To clean the mouse, start by turning the unit over. There is usually a simple way of removing the rubber ball. Once the ball is out, you have access to the rollers. With a small screwdriver, scrape off any hard deposits on the surfaces of the rollers. Pull away any dust which may have become wrapped around the roller shafts. Finally, clean the surfaces of the rollers with a cotton swab dipped in alcohol. If you use a "mouse pad," the mouse will not pick up as much dust, and will not require cleaning as often.

It is possible that some of the other parts in the mouse may fail. Whenever you experience a problem, always check the cables and connectors first. Also, the light source and detector arrays sometimes fail. (Refer to the material in Chapter 7 on Testing a Light Source and Detector.") Possibly, the switches may fail.

9.2.7 Test 7
Checking other circuits.

Each computer will include many more circuits than what we've discussed here. A problem in one of these circuits can stop the computer as easily as a problem in the data or address bus. We will cover some of these circuits in other chapters of the book. For example, in Chapter 10, floppy disk drives are discussed, and we cover the interface circuits between the drive and the main computer, while monitors and other display circuits are the subject of Chapter 15, and we take a detailed look at power supplies in Chapter 16.

Each microcomputer system is different, so we can't be too specific in this book. Hopefully, in these first few chapters of the book, we've given you the skills and background to help you track down an elusive problem by yourself. Regardless of which circuit develops a fault, the procedure is roughly the same. Use the "chain troubleshooting" techniques described in Chapter 7 to localize the problem. Next, read the owner's manual, and find out how the circuit is supposed to work. Use the general information on ICs, and the specific IC tests we've listed, to determine if one of the ICs or other components is bad.

Chapter Review

We began this chapter by looking at the complete microcomputer system as a whole. In any troubleshooting situation, your first job is to determine the section of the system that is faulty. "Strip down" the system as much as possible. Substitute when you can. Use diagnostic software to locate the faulty section.

We reviewed some of the main systems inside the microcomputer: the Clock system, Reset system, and address and data lines. These systems are especially important to the troubleshooter, because they are so extensive. A fault anywhere in one of these systems can stop the whole microcomputer from operating. A short circuit in the power-supply system can also stop the computer.

Once you've localized the problem to the main computer, you can take a more detailed approach to your troubleshooting. We listed four common troubleshooting symptoms, and suggested some tests you can make. In the last part of the chapter, we told you how to check out the important systems which we mentioned earlier. We also included some troubleshoot-ing notes on keyboards, game controllers, and pointing devices. These units all contain switches. When they fail, you can usually trace the cause to a faulty switch.

Review Questions

1. A client enters your shop and tells you, "My computer is not working. The printer produces incorrect characters." What is your next step?

2. Should you consider the software when trouble-shooting a complete microcomputer system?

3. A microcomputer "hangs up," and won't respond to commands from the keyboard. How can you start the computer operating again?

4. A diagnostic software program tells you that sixteen of the RAM ICs in the computer have failed. What are the possible causes for this diagnosis?

5. In troubleshooting work, why do we emphasize the Clock system, the Reset system, and the address bus and data bus?

6. Name two convenient test points where you can check for most of the signals in the computer.

7. A computer is not operating. You check for the "Reset" signal at the CPU chip, but it is not present. What does this tell you?

8. A key pressed on the keyboard does not produce an output on the screen. What is the likely cause?

9. What is the most common cause of trouble when using a "mouse?"

10. Why do game controllers have such a high failure rate?

10

Floppy Disk Drives

Introduction and Objectives

The floppy disk drive offers the user a convenient way of storing large amounts of information. We'll start this chapter by taking a quick look at the mechanical parts in a typical disk drive (Fig. 10-1). We will also explain how information is recorded on a floppy disk. Next, we'll discuss some of the things that can go wrong with floppy disks and disk drives.

Then, we will discuss alignment procedures for floppy disk drives. Experienced technicians often "troubleshoot" a faulty drive by performing a complete alignment. We'll list some common disk drive problems and suggest a troubleshooting sequence for each. The final part of the chapter will be devoted to service routines for specific circuits and mechanisms in the drive. Throughout this chapter, as in the previous chapter, we'll use a system of index numbers (10.2.1, 10.3.5, etc.) to refer to different sections of the text.

Fig. 10-1. A typical floppy disk drive. *(Courtesy Micro-Sci.)*

Floppy Disk Construction

Let's take a quick look at the floppy disk itself. Fig. 10-2 shows two common types of disks. Fig. 10-2A shows the 5¼-inch disk assembly. The case on this type of disk measures 5.25 inches on each side. The disk itself is made of Mylar®, and is coated on both sides with a

metal-oxide material. A reinforced hub at the center of the disk allows the drive mechanism to get a good grip on the disk. Inside the flexible plastic case is a liner made of a synthetic fabric material. This liner reduces friction as the disk turns, and also catches any dirt or dust which may get into the case of the disk. The control circuits use the index hole to generate an important timing signal. The user can keep the drive from writing onto the disk by "write protecting" it. On a 5¹/4-inch disk, this may be done by covering the Write-Protect notch.

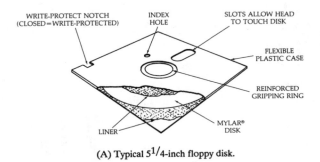

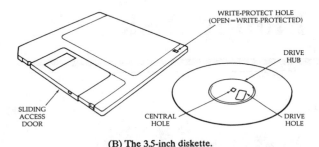

Fig. 10-2. Floppy disks.

The more recent 3.5-inch diskettes show some improvements in design (Fig. 10-2B). The case of a 3.5-inch diskette is made of a rigid plastic. The earlier disks could be bent or creased, but the new design is much more rugged. The 3.5-inch disk itself is still made of Mylar and, as before, is coated with oxide. The earlier disks were designed with open slots, to allow the heads to touch the surface of the disk. This allowed dirt into the case of the disk. On the newer 3.5-inch disks, the surface of the disk is protected by a spring-loaded sliding metal door. When the 3.5-inch disk is inserted in the drive, the door slides to one side, allowing the heads to touch the surface of the disk. The drive arrangement has also been improved for the 3.5-inch disks. The central part of the disk is gripped by a rigid metal hub. When the drive mechanism engages, a pin fits into a hole in the center of the hub and centers the disk. Then, a drive tooth engages a second hole, spinning the disk.

These are the two most common types of floppy diskettes, but there are others. Early microcomputers used 8-inch floppy disks. Some special units use 2.5-inch disks, similar in construction to the 3.5-inch disks we have just described. Each of these types has a different

arrangement for providing Write Protection (Table 10-1).

Table 10-1. Write-Protection Systems

Disk Type	Write-Protection Indication
2.5 inch	Tab in place = Write enabled
	Tab removed = Write protected
3.5 inch	Door open = Write protected
	Door closed = Write enabled
5.25 inch	Slot open = Write enabled
	Slot closed = Write protected
8 inch	Slot open = Write protected
	Slot closed = Write enabled

Inside a Floppy Disk Drive

Let's examine the mechanical components and the circuits inside a floppy disk drive. Fig. 10-3 shows a single-sided 3.5-inch drive. A single-sided floppy disk drive has a single head that handles both the "read" and "write" functions. The read/write head is built around a core of soft iron, as shown in Fig. 10-4. A coil of wire is wrapped around this core. The coil is actually tapped in the center, so that it behaves as if it were two separate coils. When the control circuits want to write something on the diskette, they send a current through these coils. This creates electromagnetic lines of force in the soft iron material. The "air gap" at the bottom of the core acts to "focus" this force on the oxide layer on the surface of the diskette. This creates a magnetized spot on the oxide layer.

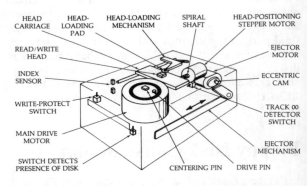

Fig. 10-3. Illustration of a 3.5-inch disk drive mechanism.

When the control circuits want to read from the disk, the process is reversed. As the magnetized spots

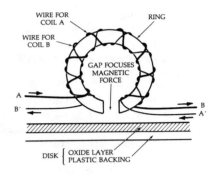

Fig. 10-4. Illustration of a read/write head.

pass under the head, they induce lines of force in the soft iron core, which then create tiny currents in the coils of wire. Other circuits then amplify this weak signal.

There are several different methods of storing information on a disk. The *frequency modulation* (FM) recording format is shown in Fig. 10-5. A series of zeros would be recorded as a series of pulses that appear at a certain frequency, which we'll call "F." A series of ones would be stored as a series of pulses at twice that frequency, or 2F. If you look at the pulse train for the series of zeros, you can think of each unit in the train as being a *marker* or *clock* pulse, followed by a "slot" or storage space. In the train of 0s, each of these slots is empty. In the train of 1s, each storage space is filled with an extra pulse. The space between markers is called a *bit cell*. If the "read" circuitry detects a pulse in one of these bit cells, it registers a "1."

Higher-density floppy disk drives use a *modified frequency modulation* (MFM) format, as shown in Fig. 10-6. In this scheme, each bit cell can begin as either a high or a low. If the bit written in that bit cell is a "0," the level will stay the same. If the bit for that cell is a "1," a transition will be recorded in the cell. The "read" circuitry detects these transitions.

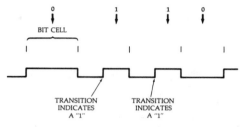

Fig. 10-6. MFM data storage.

A drive that uses double-sided disks will have two read/write heads. On some drives, a separate section of the Read/Write head erases the edges of each track as it is written. This prevents signals from one track from overlapping onto another track.

A "Write-Protect" system prevents the drive from writing to a disk when the disk is write-protected (see Table 10-1). Usually, the drive includes a switch which can sense the status of a write-protect opening on the case of the disk.

A "head loading" mechanism is used to move the head into contact with the surface of the disk. In a drive that uses single-sided disks, a head-load pad pushes the disk into contact with the head (Fig. 10-7A).

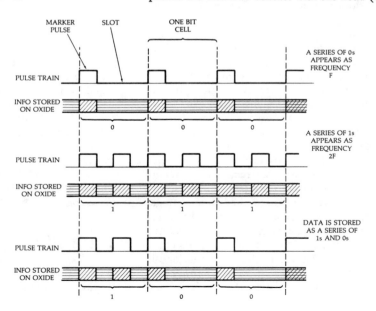

Fig. 10-5. Format of data storage.

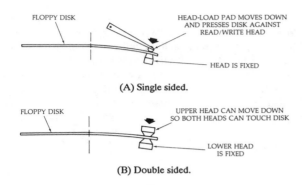

Fig. 10-7. Disk drive head configurations.

In double-sided drives, one of the heads can move, usually the upper head. When this upper head is "loaded," it pushes the disk into contact with the lower head (Fig. 10-7B).

Once the 3.5-inch disk has been inserted into the drive, the hub of the disk sits directly over the main drive motor. Fig. 10-3 illustrates the location of the centering pin and the drive pin. The drive pin is spring loaded. The disk assembly may be inserted into the drive without aligning the drive pin with the drive hole. When the drive starts, the drive motor will spin once or twice until the drive pin and drive hole align. The pin will then pop up and begin driving the disk. The main drive motor turns the floppy disk at about 300 rpm. On most disk drives, the speed of the main motor is constant. Some disk drives do use drive motors with variable speeds. On this type of drive, the disk is turned faster when the drive is using the outer parts (edge) of the disk, and slower when the drive is working with the inner parts.

The 3.5-inch-type of drive uses an interesting clamping mechanism to hold the disk assembly firmly in position. First, the user slides the disk assembly into the drive. A metal plate is suspended above the disk assembly. When the disk is inserted, this plate is lowered, clamping the hub of the disk against the top of the drive motor.

A motor-control circuit turns the drive motor on and off. As the motor turns, a sensor detects its speed and reports back to the control circuit. The controller uses this "feedback" to make corrective adjustments and keep the drive motor speed constant.

The read/write head is attached to a carriage, which can move both toward and away from the center of the disk. By moving the head carriage in and out, the drive can position the head to read different parts of the disk. On this particular drive, the head carriage is moved by a stepper motor which drives a spiral shaft. As the shaft turns, the carriage is forced in or out.

The rotary motion of the stepper motor causes the carriage to move with a linear motion.

The drive illustrated in Fig. 10-3 has an automatic ejection system. When the control circuits want to eject the disk, they turn on a small ejector motor. This motor drives an eccentric cam, which moves a lever. When this lever is moved, it triggers a series of mechanical actions, and the disk assembly is forced out of the drive.

The drive also includes several switches, which act as sensors for the control circuits. The Write-Protect switch is activated when the disk is write-protected. The Track 00 detector switch is tripped when the head is reading the outermost track on the disk. The index sensor generates a pulse each time the disk rotates. Another switch may also be included to tell the control circuits when a disk assembly has been inserted in the drive.

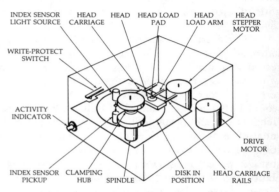

Fig. 10-8. Illustration of $5^1/4$-inch disk drive mechanism.

Fig. 10-8 shows a drive for the $5^1/4$-inch floppy disk. With this drive, the disk is held in position by a clamping assembly. Two cone-shaped clamps are positioned above and below the hub on the disk. When the door to the disk drive is closed, these clamping hubs grip the center of the disk.

The lower clamping hub is supported on a free-spinning spindle assembly. Notice that the drive motor is not connected directly to the spindle. Rather, the motor drives a rubber belt, which then drives the spindle.

An activity light on the front of the drive lights whenever the head is loaded, or whenever the motor is turned on.

Data Storage Formats

A large amount of information can be stored on a single floppy disk. Somehow, the drive must have a way of locating and recovering specific bits of information. As we said earlier, the data are stored on the floppy disk on concentric rings called "tracks" (Fig. 10-9). The outermost track is always numbered "00." The next track is numbered "01." The track with the highest number is closest to the center of the hub.

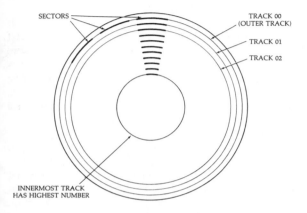

Fig. 10-9. Disk tracks and sectors.

The drive does not write data along the whole length of a track. Instead, each track is divided into a number of "sectors," which radiate out from the center of the disk. The drive can access any section of the disk by listing its track number and sector number. However, the term "sector" can be confusing. A "sector" may refer to a segment of the whole disk, including parts of many tracks. Some people also use the term "sector" to refer to just one of the memory areas, on just one track.

Fig. 10-10 shows how data are actually stored on one of the tracks. As you can see, the format is quite complicated and much of the available space is used for various "housekeeping" functions. Earlier, we men-

tioned the *index sector detector*. The signal from this detector is used to indicate the start of a track. A moment after the index hole in the disk passes over the sector detector, *index* characters are written on the disk. The index characters (often the hexadecimal number "FC") set the timing for the rest of the track. The "gaps" before and after the index characters are filled with spacing characters.

Information for each of the *sectors* is stored in two blocks. The *ID block* allows the drive to identify the sector being read. The *data block* contains the data being stored in that sector. Fig. 10-10 shows the format for each of these blocks. The *ID address mark* is a pair of characters (often the hexadecimal number "FE") that indicates the beginning of the ID block. The next characters in the ID block include information about the sector—track number, side of disk, sector number, and sector length.

The last two characters in the ID block are used for error checking. The abbreviation "CRC" stands for *cyclic redundancy check*. To generate the CRC characters, the computer analyzes the other characters in the ID block. Using a mathematical formula, the computer calculates values for the two CRC characters. When reading back the ID block, the computer compares these CRC characters with the characters in the rest of the block. If the CRC characters do not agree with the information in the rest of the block, the computer knows that something is wrong, and can rewrite the information.

The data being stored are written into a separate block. Together, the ID block and the data block make up a complete sector. On a $5^1/4$-inch double-density drive, the data block can hold 256 bytes. The data are stored on the disk as a series of digital "1s" and "0s." Letters and numbers are coded into ASCII format before they are sent to the disk drive. Using ASCII coding, each character is represented by a series

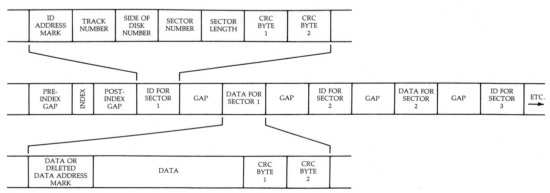

Fig. 10-10. A typical track format.

of "1s" and "0s." For example, the letter A would be represented by the sequence 0100 0001. The complete character is stored as a series of 8 bits. (If you are not familiar with ASCII codes, refer to Appendix D for further explanation.) Notice that the data block also has two CRC error-checking characters.

A floppy disk can store many files, and each file may be stored on tracks in a large number of sectors. The computer must have a way of finding each file, and must have a way of finding the sectors that contain that file. In the type of DOS used by the IBM PCs, the information on the sectors is stored in a separate *file allocation table*, abbreviated as "FAT." A list of the files stored on the disk is located in a section of the floppy disk called the "directory." On some computer systems, the directory also tells the computer how to find the sectors which make up each file.

Over the years, engineers have been able to pack more and more data onto a floppy disk. Every year seems to bring a new format, offering more data storage in the same space. As you work with floppy disks, you will find many differences. However, the arrangement we have just described applies to most of the floppy disk drives built to date.

The Disk Operating System

The *disk operating system* (DOS) is a set of instructions stored in the computer and used to control disk operations. The DOS controls the activity each time the disk drive reads or writes to a disk. The DOS also allows the user to change file names, move files from one place to another, and so on. The DOS handles the "housekeeping" chores that are involved in disk operations—assigning track and sector locations for files, for example.

While the disk drive is operating, the DOS is constantly interacting with the memory areas on the disk. For example, let's say that the computer wants to "read" part of a particular file. As a first step, the DOS must tell the drive to read the directory and file allocation table on the disk. Using the information from the directory, the DOS then tells the drive to refer to the correct sectors for that file. To put it another way, some of the memory used by the DOS is stored on the disk itself.

The DOS includes some functions which make the system more reliable. We already mentioned the CRC error-checking bits, which are included at the end of each ID block and data block. The DOS can use these CRC bits to check each read and write operation, and will display an error message if it detects a mistake.

The DOS may also display other error statements to indicate mechanical problems associated with the drive—"Drive can't find track 00," "Disk is write-protected," etc.

Control Circuits

The control circuits inside a floppy disk drive are very busy. A typical floppy disk drive handles countless thousands of data bits every day. The read/write operations take place in fractions of a second, and all of these countless transactions must be accurate or the output from the drive is no good. This is a complicated task, so the circuitry that does the job must also be complicated.

The drive control circuitry is usually designed around a large IC called a *floppy disk drive controller* or FDC. Many of these controllers are made by Western Digital, and may be identified by the prefix WD. Fig. 10-11 shows the inputs and outputs of a typical FDC chip. Two or more "address" lines (A0, A1) are used to select control registers inside the IC. By storing

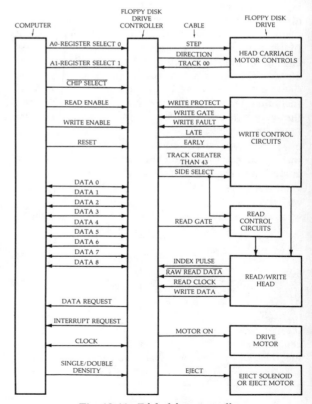

Fig. 10-11. Disk drive controller.

commands in these registers, the computer can control the operation of the IC. The "Chip Select" line is used to enable the IC.

The FDC is connected to the data bus of the main computer. In this example, eight of the data lines are connected to the FDC. When the computer wants to write something onto the disk, it places the data on the data bus and strobes the "Write Enable" line. The FDC converts the 8-bit parallel data to a stream of serial bits on the "Write Data" line. The computer strobes the "Read Enable" line when it wants to read from the disk.

The "Reset" line clears the registers in the FDC. This line is connected to the Reset system in the main computer.

The disk drive generates a "Data Request" when it is ready to write data, or when it has completed a "Read" operation. This signal allows the drive to tell the computer, "I'm ready, let's do something else." The FDC chip can use the "Interrupt Request" line to break into the main routine executing on the main computer.

Some FDC chips are timed by a "Clock" signal from the main computer. Some chips also have a switch input, which allows the designer to specify whether the drive is single density or double density.

Now, let's look at the signals passing between the FDC chip and the floppy disk drive, itself. We've already explained how the Read/Write head can be moved in and out by a stepper motor. The "direction" signal tells the stepper motor which direction to move. Each time the "step" line is pulsed, the motor moves the head one step. The "Track 00" sensor signals the FDC chip when the head has reached the outermost track on the disk. The "Write-Protect" signal is "true" when the floppy disk has been write-protected. This inhibits the writing circuits in the drive.

The "Write Fault" line is a bidirectional line which can serve several purposes. The line is "true" when a Write fault is detected at the Read/Write heads.

When the drive is operating normally, the data to be written appear in a serial stream on the "Write Data" line. Each time the "Write Gate" line is pulsed, a bit of data is written by the Read/Write head.

As the drive begins to use tracks near the center of the disk, the data bits are written more closely together. When two bits are written very closely, they tend to "spread" a bit. A "precompensation" circuit can compensate for this by moving the bits more closely together, writing one bit a little late and the next a little early. The FDC uses the "early" and "late" lines to accomplish this.

On a double-sided drive, the "Side Select" line determines which set of Read/Write heads will be active. The "Read Gate" signal is used to synchronize a data separator circuit outside of the main FDC chip. The data separator conditions the raw signal coming from the Read/Write heads.

A pulse is generated on the "Index" line each time the index hole passes over the index detector.

The signal from the Read/Write head is returned to the FDC chip over the "Raw Read Data" line. The matching Clock signal appears on the "Read Clock" line.

The "Motor On" line is "true" whenever the main drive motor is turned on. The "Eject" line is "true" when the computer wants to eject a disk from the disk drive.

The example we have shown here uses a fairly complicated FDC IC, so the FDC is doing most of the work. On a working disk-drive controller, you will find a number of other circuits. For example, the circuits in the Tandy 1000SX computer include an FDC and two large "motor controller" ICs. These motor controllers generate the outputs for the stepper motors. They also handle miscellaneous tasks, including interpreting the signals from the Index Detector and the Write-Protect switches. A single "read/write amp" IC handles the signals associated with the Read/Write heads. You may also encounter a computer with a "data separator" IC. This IC conditions the raw signal from the Read/Write heads, and produces a clean digital signal for the computer.

Some disk drives have an on-board microprocessor. For example, the Commodore 1541 disk drive is supervised by an 8-bit 6502 microprocessor. The CPU is supported by two ROMs, a RAM IC, and two interfacing chips (VIAs). This type of drive contains a complete computer system that is dedicated to the job of supervising the other sections of the disk drive.

Some disk drives are powered by the main computer, via the connecting cable. Other drives have a separate, on-board power supply. Most drives seem to use +5-V and +12-V DC power.

Service Problems with Diskettes and Floppy Disk Drives

One common problem occurs when the Read/Write heads becomes covered with oxide from the disks. This oxide layer can interfere with the read/write action of the head, and cause intermittent errors. As we said, the DOS often includes a routine that automatically checks for errors during reading and writing. A DOS might try to read a sector ten times before it gives up and produces an error statement. On a dusty disk, or a drive with a dirty head, the DOS might have to try to read each bit of data two or three times. Sometimes this can slow down the rate of data transfer enough for you to notice the effect. If you notice that your drives seem to be working more slowly, it may be time to clean the heads. Cleaning the heads is certainly called for if you begin having intermittent errors from a disk drive.

Diskettes

Rough handling can damage a floppy disk. The surface of the disk may be scratched at a certain point. Floppy disks are not really very tough. If you bend a floppy disk sharply, it won't flatten out again. As a result, the disk won't be able to spin inside its plastic case, and you will not be able to read from it. You can also ruin a disk by writing on the case with a ball-point pen. Never do this. Also, never write on a disk with a pencil. Graphite from the pencil tip can interfere with the Read/Write head. Don't use a rubber pencil eraser near a floppy disk either.

You can ruin a disk by touching the oxide surface directly. The oily coating on your skin can stick to the surface of the disk and can attract dust. Even the slightest touch is sometimes enough to make a disk unreadable. On single-sided disks, the critical oxide coating is on the underside of the disk.

Some disk operating systems allow you to use a disk, even though part of it is unreliable. The DOS will make a note of the sectors that are affected, and will not use them. Don't use one of these disks to store any important data.

Magnetism

Sometimes it is possible to rescue and reuse a bad disk by erasing it with a "bulk eraser." The bulk eraser contains a powerful magnet which neutralizes the magnetic orientation of all of the magnetic particles on the floppy disk. This has the effect of erasing all of the writing on the disk. Generally though, a "hard" error means the disk should be retired.

If a magnet gets too close to a floppy disk, it can cause serious damage. Normally, the disk drive's read/write action is accomplished through a carefully controlled series of magnetic impulses. If a magnet passes near the disk, it can disturb the data stored on the oxide layer. A magnetic paper-clip holder is particularly dangerous. Never use this type of holder around a computer and never fasten notes to a disk with

a paper clip. Incidentally, remember that home loudspeakers contain powerful magnets.

Transformers can have the same effect. Almost any piece of electronic equipment with a power supply contains a transformer. In most computer equipment, the power supply is surrounded by a metal shield that restricts the magnetic field radiating from the transformer. The power supplies in peripherals—TV monitors, for instance—are often not as well shielded. A two-wire line carrying AC house current probably won't cause any trouble, however, unless you set a disk very close to it. A good general rule is to keep your disks at least six inches away from anything electrical, and five feet away from any type of magnet. Keep this in mind when you choose a place for the long-term storage of your disks.

Temperature and Humidity

As mentioned earlier, floppy disks can be affected by both temperature and humidity. Disk manufacturers recommend disks be used in a temperature range of 50 °F to 125 °F and a humidity of 8% to 80%. For storage and shipping, this range can be extended a bit—40 °F to 127 °F. Disks may be unreliable outside these limits. Also, the expansion and contraction of the disk itself may change the spacing of the various bits of data stored on the surface of the disk. Thus, when the drive tries to read the disk, some of the bits may have moved out of position and the disk will be unreadable.

If one of your disks has exceeded one of these temperature or humidity extremes, you may still be able to read from it. Allow the disk to return to room temperature before you try to work with it. Don't use any artificial means to heat or cool the disk to normal temperature.

All of the preceding problems can be minimized or eliminated by careful disk handling. A series of disk-handling instructions were given in Chapter 5.

Worn Disks and Soft Errors

After long use, a floppy disk can simply wear out. Each time you use a floppy disk, the read/write head actually touches the surface of the disk. In particular, the part of the disk that holds the directory is constantly in use. Over a period of time, the oxide layer on the disk gets thinner. Eventually, the coating may become so thin that the disk drive can't read the information stored at a particular location on the disk. The information is still stored on the disk, but the signal from that part of the disk is so weak that the disk drive can't pick it up. This situation can change from day to day, so you may be able to read the disk successfully at a later time. You certainly shouldn't put any new work on a very worn disk. Use the best-quality disks you can afford. Top-grade disks will give long service with a minimim of problems.

The most mysterious and frustrating of all floppy disk problems is the so-called "soft error." This is the Read or Write problem that is present one minute and gone the next. For example, you might find that the computer is unable to find a file, even though you are sure that file has been stored on the disk. A moment later, you try to access the file again and the computer finds the file with no problem. Something interfered with the drive's ability to read that file name for just a moment.

A "soft error" of this type may be caused by a bit of dirt or dust. If a particle of dust gets between the disk and the head, it can interfere with the head's Read/Write action. Particles of cigarette smoke can have the same effect. The first time the drive tries to read the file, the dust interferes with the reading and you get an error statement. When the drive tries to access that particular part of the disk again, the dust particle is gone, and the Read/Write operation is successful. The more dust in the environment around the disk drive, the greater are the chances of encountering a "soft error."

A "soft error" may also be caused by a problem in the power supply. An electrical transient from the power source can be powerful enough to force its way into the computer and interfere with the Read/Write operation. (This was explained in greater detail in Chapter 5.) A transient normally lasts for a fraction of a second. When you try to use the disk again, the transient is long gone, and your Read/Write operation is successful.

A single miscopied bit of data can have different effects, depending on where it ends up on the disk. If your drive has written an incorrect character onto a disk, and this character falls within a text file, one letter of the text will be incorrect. It is easy to correct a problem of this type. But what if the altered character falls within a program? The program may not run, or it may "run away" in an uncontrolled manner and may even change some of the data stored on your disks. The most serious problems occur when the mistake falls within the disk's directory or file allocation table. If this happens, you may not be able to access any of the files on the disk.

Even though the directory on a floppy disk has been damaged, you may still be able to "rescue" most of the files. Several software houses offer utility programs that let you inspect a damaged disk and make

repairs. We will discuss this in more detail in Section 10.6.16 of this chapter. The process is similar on hard disk drives and we will cover this in Chapter 11. These heroic recovery efforts are not necessary, however, if you have a backup of the disk. We discussed backups in some detail in Chapter 5.

Disk Drives

Now, let's consider some possible problems with the disk drive mechanism. Over time, floppy disk drives can drift out of alignment. For a drive to function correctly, a series of electronic and mechanical functions must take place in a precise order. The head that does the reading and writing must move to the correct track on the disk, and must Read or Write a particular bit of information at the correct moment. As the disk drive continues to be used, various mechanical settings can gradually change. Finally, one of the adjustments may get so far "out of spec" that the drive begins to be unreliable. However, the electronics in the drive are probably still working correctly. The drive can often be brought back to life by correcting each of the mechanical adjustments.

Whenever you take an ailing disk drive to a service shop, the technician is likely to begin troubleshooting by doing a complete alignment. This procedure will probably fix the problem that caused you to bring in the drive for repair, and will probably also clear up other questionable adjustments that you are unaware of. Bob Cahill estimates that an alignment will clear up 90% of the service complaints for disk drives.

The main drive motor is designed to turn at 300 rpm. If the speed of the main motor varies by more than ±4 rpm, the drive may begin to produce intermittent errors.

As the drive is used, the head load pad will wear and will require periodic replacement. Eventually, the Read/Write head will also wear, and will produce a weaker signal. Disk drives contain motors and other mechanical parts and these also wear out. The eject mechanism often takes a lot of abuse, and some of the parts can be bent out of shape. On a drive with an electronically controlled auto-eject mechanism, electronic or mechanical parts can fail.

The Read/Write heads are delicate. They are often made of a ceramic material which is somewhat brittle. On a double-sided drive, the heads can be damaged if they are allowed to bang together when the drive is moved. When you move a floppy disk drive, insert something into the drive to hold the heads apart. Some manufacturers supply cardboard or plastic inserts for this purpose. If you do not have an insert, you can use an old floppy disk.

Disk drives also have cables and connectors that can fail. A problem could be caused by a bad component in the control circuitry. Disk drives depend on conventional IC technology, so you can expect the same kinds of failures here that you will see in the main computer—bad ICs, faulty transistors, burnt-out resistors and diodes, etc.

An operator can ruin a disk drive interface card by removing the card while the power is turned on. This can burn out many ICs on the card.

In the last few years, prices for floppy disk drives have dropped rapidly. For example, Jameco Electronics sells a replacement floppy disk drive for the IBM PC-AT for about $90.00. A replacement controller card costs about $30.00 With prices this low, you may decide that it is not cost-effective to realign or repair a floppy disk drive.

Maintaining Floppy Disk Drives

Most floppy disk drives are designed to be "maintenance-free." This doesn't mean that they will never wear out. It just means that you can't do much to slow down the wear.

Cleaning the Heads

Over time, the Read/Write heads tend to collect some of the oxide material from the surfaces of the floppy disks. The heads also collect some of the dust and dirt from the outside world. If the drive is used by a heavy smoker, the heads will become dirty very quickly.

There is a wide range of advice available on the question of cleaning the heads. The people who make the head-cleaning chemicals suggest you clean the heads every week. The disk drive manufacturers tell you to clean the heads as seldom as possible. We advise you to clean the heads whenever you begin experiencing intermittent errors. But, even if you never have intermittent errors, clean the heads two or three times a year. If the equipment is in constant use, clean the heads about once a month. You may have to clean the heads much more often if the computer is used by a heavy smoker.

You can sometimes tell if the Read/Write heads need cleaning by inspecting them. You may have to remove the drive's case to get a clear view. Turn off power to the drive and the computer, set the drive on its side, remove the screws on the bottom of the case, and slide the case away. If the heads are dirty, you may be able to see a build-up of the brownish oxide material. If

this layer is very thin, the heads will appear to be slightly yellowish. The heads should be cleaned even if they show just a light coating. The oxide build-up will be slightly sticky. You must use a solvent to release the build-up, so you can wipe it away.

It is possible to clean the heads in a floppy disk drive by hand, without removing the case, and using alcohol and cotton swabs. Use a grade of isopropyl "rubbing" alcohol with a low water content. The type of alcohol most commonly sold in drugstores contains 70% alcohol. The other 30% of this mixture is water, and you don't want much water inside the drive. Try to get a mixture that is 80% to 90% alcohol.

Open up the door of the drive so you can get a clear view of the head. Be sure to turn off power to the drive. Dip a swab into the alcohol and wipe it against the rim of the bottle. You want the swab to be moist, but not dripping. Gently rub the swab across the top of the Read/Write head. Wipe a second moistened swab across the head to clear away all of the dissolved oxide. Wait about 15 minutes before you use the drive. This will allow time for the alcohol to evaporate.

It is much more convenient (and much more expensive) to use one of the prepared head-cleaning disks (Fig. 10-12). To use one of these disks, you insert the disk, and then send the computer a command that will activate the disk drive. For example, you may ask for a "directory" or "catalog" of the cleaning disk. The drive will run for a moment or two, until the DOS determines that it cannot read the disk. In the meantime, the cleaning disk cleans the heads.

Some inexpensive head-cleaning disks contain an abrasive material that quickly wears away the accumulated oxide on the head. This results in a clean head, but the abrasive can also wear down the head. Never use a head-cleaning disk unless it is specified as "nonabrasive."

Some head-cleaning disks are premoistened with a solvent. This type of disk is usually wrapped in a moisture-proof envelope. The disk is designed to be used once and then thrown away. Other brands come with a separate bottle of solvent. You're asked to pour a little solvent on the cleaning disk, assemble the plastic carrier around the disk, and then insert the disk in the computer. We prefer this method. Even though the manufacturers don't tell you this, the cleaning disks can be used many times. When the solvent runs out, you can substitute the 90% isopropyl alcohol we mentioned earlier. If you use this type of cleaner, be careful not to pour too much solvent onto the cleaning disk. The disk material should be damp, but not dripping. Again, remember to wait about 15 minutes before using the disk drive.

You should never have to demagnetize the heads

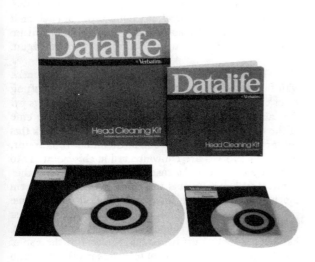

Fig. 10-12. Head-cleaning disks. *(Courtesy Verbatim Corp.)*

on your disk drives, as you might have to do with the heads in some kinds of audio recording equipment.

Cleaning the Drive Mechanism

Operate the drive in a clean environment, and keep the unit as clean as possible. If your drive does get dusty, remove the case and blow out the dust with low-pressure compressed air.

Periodic Inspection

If you have a single-sided disk drive, inspect the head-load pad every six months. The load pad is made of fabric. Replace the part if it appears to be worn or frayed, or if it becomes discolored with oxide (Fig. 10-13). On 8-inch drives, the load pad may be covered with a layer of red material. Replace the pad when this layer wears through.

SIDE VIEW

NEW LOAD BUTTON-
SMOOTH SURFACE,
SHARP EDGES

WORN LOAD
BUTTON

Fig. 10-13. Inspecting the head-load pad.

Lubrication

Follow the manufacturer's recommendations with regard to lubrication. In most cases, the manufacturer

will tell you not to lubricate the drive at all. If any oil or grease is put inside the drive, it tends to end up on the Read/Write head. Even a tiny amount is enough to interfere with the drive's operation. Most drives are designed to operate without lubrication, and critical parts, like the bearings, are permanently lubricated and sealed.

10.1 Troubleshooting Floppy Disk Drives

In this section, we'll list some common problems and suggest some solutions. We'll use the same system of index numbers (10.2.1, 10.3.3, etc.) to refer to specific sections of the text as used in earlier chapters.

10.1.1 Problem 1

Symptom: Disk drive has intermittent Read or Write failures.

This is the most common type of disk drive failure, so we'll consider it in some detail. Always start by cleaning the drive's Read/Write heads. Over a period of time, a sticky layer of oxide and dust can build up on the heads. This layer can interfere with the Read/Write action. Refer to the "maintenance" section given earlier in this chapter.

If the computer displays an error statement, refer to the manual for the disk operating system (DOS) for your equipment, and see if that helps to identify the problem.

If the drive can read disks that it has written, but can't read disks that were written on other drives, you have an "interchange" problem. Refer to Section 10.1.4.

Some intermittent problems can be caused by poor operating procedures. You can damage a floppy disk by turning the power on and off while the disk is in the disk drive. When you first send power to a disk drive, it takes a few microseconds for the various circuits to initialize. During the short time it takes these components to stabilize, the drive may be "floating" out of control. During this period, the drive may write strange bits of data onto your disk. The same thing can happen when you cut off power to the drive. The best procedure is to turn on the computer and the drive first, and then put the disk into the drive. When you shut down the computer, reverse the process. Remove the disk first, and then turn off the power.

Some computers do not follow this rule, however. On these computers, the system disk should be inserted before the computer is turned on. On power-up, the disk drives on these computers execute a time delay before reading from the disk. Even on systems of this type, it is still wise to remove the disk before you turn off the equipment.

Perhaps the floppy disk itself is causing the problem. Remove the disk and inspect it for signs of damage—bends, creases, fingerprints, scratches, dirt inside the case, etc. If the disk appears to be all right, substitute a backup or a different disk, and try again. You can use a disk-fixer utility program to make a quick check of a disk that is giving you trouble. Most of these utilities will test a particular disk and will report any bad or unusable sectors. The utility program will also list all of the files stored on the disk, and will verify that each of the files is complete and usable.

Many of the problems that are blamed on disk drives are actually caused by the software. For example, you may find you can't access a certain file. Even though the file name appears on a catalog, the computer can't find the file. You may suspect a hardware problem is causing this, but the real cause could be quite different. In this case, you may have inadvertently typed a control character as you entered the file name (i.e., Ctrl-S, Ctrl-D, etc.). The control character won't appear on the screen, yet it will remain part of the file name, so the computer will look for the "wrong" file. Even though this problem involves disks and disk access, you can't blame it on the hardware.

Other disk-related software problems can occur when the computer tries to look for a file on the wrong disk drive, or on a floppy disk that does not include the desired file. There are many possible variations. Noncommercial software is very likely to include "bugs." Even commercial software can include "bugs" that can cause a disk drive to behave strangely at certain times. To eliminate the software as a possible cause of the problem, try using a backup copy of the software. If this is successful, you will know the first copy of the software is bad. If the backup shows similar symptoms, try a completely different program. If the symptoms persist, you can start to suspect a hardware problem.

The disk drive system actually includes a long chain of components. The chain begins with the control circuits inside the computer, and includes both the cable and the logic circuits inside the drive itself. The floppy disk, the DOS, and the program software are also parts of the chain. Each of these sections must work correctly if your computer is to read and write correctly.

You've already eliminated two parts of the chain—the floppy disk itself, and the software. Next, check the cable that runs between the computer and the disk drive. Carefully check the connectors at each end of the cable. Do the connectors fit tightly? Are the contacts clean? Do you notice any bent or damaged pins?

There is one problem which occurs frequently with floppy disk drives: Someone knocks the drive off of a desk or table, and, for a moment, the drive hangs by the cable. Be sure to check the connections at the end of the cable that terminates inside the drive. Check the solder joints where the connector meets the circuit board. The forces are concentrated at this point. You may have to remove the case of the drive to look at this connector. Next, inspect the cable itself. Has it been pinched or bent sharply anywhere along its length? The conductors inside the cable are very thin and they can be broken if the cable is bent sharply. Again, if the drive has been knocked off of a desk, the end of the cable may be damaged, and some of the wires may be broken.

If you're at all suspicious of the cable, substitute a cable that you know is all right for it, and see if the symptoms disappear. Use a cable from one of your other disk drives, or borrow a cable from a friend. If you can't find an extra cable, you'll have to check out the suspect cable using a VOM. Set the meter to read OHMS, and use it as a continuity tester. We described the procedure in Chapter 7. Check out one conductor at a time. The contacts should be numbered at each end.

Some computers, including the IBM PC line, use disk drive interface cards that plug into the main computer. This is very convenient for troubleshooting, because it lets you eliminate most of the control circuitry in one step. If your system has one of these plug-in interface cards, borrow a replacement, and switch cards. Run the computer through its paces and see if the problem has disappeared. If the computer operates normally, you have localized the problem to the control circuits on the card. Refer to Section 10.3.15.

If you have two disk drives, or if you can borrow a spare, you can substitute by switching drives. If you unplug your drive and connect a spare and the symptoms disappear, you know that the problem is in the original drive. If the symptoms persist, however, you can suspect a problem in the control circuits in the computer. Refer to Section 10.3.15.

Still haven't found the problem? Then it is time to localize the symptoms a bit. Think carefully—can you find any rule that seems to tie the problems together? Do they always seem to happen during a "Read" or "Write" operation, for example? If the problems occur only during a "Read", refer to Section 10.1.2. If the problems occur during a "Write" operation, go to Section 10.1.3.

Could an environmental problem be causing the symptoms? Perhaps your system is being affected by transients on the power line. Do you tend to have problems at a certain time of day, or when it's hot, or when the refrigerator or air conditioner switches on? Do a little detective work and see if you can discover a pattern. We discussed environmental factors in Chapter 5.

Check the power supply that feeds the drive, as described in Chapter 16. A bad ground may cause intermittent problems in a disk drive. Check the motor speed of the drive, as described in Section 10.2.1.

At this point, many technicians would do a complete alignment. This procedure will correct a number of possible problems. Refer to "Alignment and Adjustment Procedures" discussed in Section 10.2

If the alignment does not help, check the signals running through the cable, as described in Section 10.3.1. If any of these signals are abnormal, check the control circuits, as described in Section 10.3.15.

10.1.2. Problem 2
Symptom: Drive operates, but will not read.

Start by cleaning the heads, as described earlier in the chapter.

If the drive will not boot, you may have a bad copy of the disk operating system. Try a backup copy. But if the computer displays an error message, check the manual for your disk operating system, and see if you can locate the problem.

Then, eliminate the floppy disk itself as a possible cause of the problem. Remove the disk from the drive, and check it for signs of damage—bends, creases, fingerprints, scratches, dirt inside the case, etc. Eliminate the software also. Try operating with a backup version of the software you were using at the time of the fault. Next, try a different program.

Check the cable that runs between the computer and the disk drive as there is one problem that occurs frequently with disk drives: Someone knocks the drive off of a desk or table, and for a moment the drive hangs by the cable. For this reason, pay particular attention to the end of the cable that terminates inside the drive. You may have to remove the case of the drive to look at this.

Next, inspect the cable itself. Has it been pinched or bent sharply anywhere along its length? The conductors inside the cable are very thin, and they can be broken if the cable is bent sharply. Carefully check the connectors at each end of the cable. Do the connectors fit tightly? Are the contacts clean? Are there any bent or damaged pins?

If you're at all suspicious of the cable, substitute a cable that you know is all right for it, and see if the symptoms disappear. Swap it for a cable from one of your other disk drives, or borrow a cable from a friend. If you can't find an extra cable, you'll have to check the cable out, using a VOM. Set the meter to read OHMS, and use it as a continuity tester. The procedure is described in Chapter 7. Check out one conductor at a time (the contacts should be numbered at each end).

Some computers, including the IBM PCs, use disk-drive interface cards that plug into the main computer. This is very convenient for troubleshooting, because you can eliminate most of the control circuitry in one step. If your system has one of these plug-in interface cards, borrow a replacement card and swap it for yours. Run the computer through its paces and see if the problem has disappeared. If the problem does disappear, check the control circuits. Refer to Section 10.3.15.

If you have two disk drives, or if you can borrow a spare, you can substitute drives. If you connect a spare drive in place of your drive and the symptoms disappear, you know then that the problem is in your drive. If the symptoms persist, however, you can suspect a problem in the control circuits. Refer to Section 10.3.15.

Check the condition of the head load pad, as described in Section 10.3.7. Check the head-loading logic as well.

Check the "Drive Select" signals through the cable, as described in Section 10.3.1. If these signals are missing, look for a problem in the control circuits, as described in Section 10.3.15.

Check the "Read Data" signals through the cable, as described in Section 10.3.1. Then, check the "Read" circuits, as described in Section 10.3.9.

At this point, many technicians would do an alignment. The alignment procedure is described in Section 10.2. If you still haven't found the problem at this point, check the control circuits (described in Section 10.3.15).

10.1.3 Problem 3

Symptom: Drive operates, but will not write.

If the computer displays an error message, check the manual for your disk operating system, and see if you can locate the problem.

Is the disk write-protected? Check for this.

Eliminate the disk itself as a possible cause of the problem. Remove the disk from the drive and check it for signs of damage—bends, creases, fingerprints, scratches, dirt inside the case, etc. Try operating with a blank disk.

Eliminate the software also. Try operating with a backup version of the software you were using at the time of the fault; then, try another kind of software program.

Next, check the cable that runs between the computer and the disk drive. Carefully check the connectors at each end of the cable. Do the connectors fit tightly? Are the contacts clean? Do you notice any bent or damaged pins? Pay particular attention to the end of the cable that terminates inside the drive. You may have to remove the case of the drive to look at this. Next, inspect the outside of the cable itself. Has it been pinched or bent sharply anywhere along its length? The conductors inside the cable are very thin, and they can be broken if the cable is bent sharply.

If you're at all suspicious of the cable, try substituting a cable that you know is all right, and see if the symptoms disappear. Swap it for a cable from one of your other disk drives, or for a cable borrowed from a friend. If you can't find an extra cable, you'll have to check out the cable using a voltohmmeter. Set the meter to read OHMS and use it as a continuity tester. The procedure is described in Chapter 7. Check out one conductor at a time. The contacts should be numbered at each end of the cable. Be sure you're checking the right pair of contacts.

Some computers, including the IBM PCs, use disk-drive interface cards that plug into the main computer. This is very convenient for troubleshooting, because it lets you eliminate most of the control circuitry in one step. If your system has one of these plug-in interface cards, find a replacement and install it. Run the computer through its paces and see if the problem has disappeared. If the symptom does disappear, look for a problem in the control circuits (refer to Section 10.3.15.)

If you have two disk drives, or if you can borrow a spare drive, you can substitute by switching drives. Unplug your drive and connect the spare drive, and if the symptoms disappear, you know the problem is in the original drive. If the symptoms persist, however, you can suspect a problem in the control circuits (refer to Section 10.3.15).

At this point, many technicians would do a complete alignment of the drive. The alignment procedure is described in Section 10.2. If the alignment does not help, check the "Write-Protect" circuit, as described in Section 10.3.8. Then, check the "Write"

logic circuits and drivers, as described in Section 10.2.10.

If both of these circuits seem all right, check the "Write Gate" and "Write Data" signals through the cable, as described in Section 10.3.1. If these signals are absent, look for a problem with the control circuits (Section 10.3.15).

10.1.4 Problem 4

Symptom: Drive can't read a disk written on another drive.

This is called an "interchange" problem. One of the drives is out of alignment. This out-of-line drive can read any disks that it wrote, but it cannot read disks that were written on other drives. Also, other drives cannot read disks written on the out-of-line drive.

If you have two drives in your system, it may not be readily apparent which drive is out of alignment. Test both drives by trying to read from disks that were recorded on other systems. You might also try to use some commercial software—this is usually recorded fairly accurately.

We describe the alignment procedure later in the chapter. Before you do an alignment, be sure to make copies of all the disks that were recorded on the bad drive. Read these disks using the bad drive, and make copies onto a drive that is in alignment. (Once you've finished making an alignment, the drive that was formerly out-of-line may not be able to read the out-of-line disks.)

10.1.5 Problem 5

Symptom: Drive won't operate; motor is dead.

Check to be certain that the floppy disk is not jammed inside the drive. See if you can remove the disk freely.

Listen to the drive. If the drive motor is jammed, you may be able to hear a low buzzing sound. Turn off the drive and the computer. Turn the drive on its side and remove the screws on the bottom of the case. Slide the case away. Inspect the drive mechanism for any loose screws, broken mechanical parts, or any other foreign particles that could be jamming the drive.

Your drive may have a drive belt between the drive motor and the spindle. While the drive is open, check the drive belt, as described in Section 10.3.4.

Is the motor getting power? Check the drive motor as described in Section 10.3.3. If the motor is not getting power, check the power connections to the computer. If the drive has its own power supply, check this according to the procedures described in Chapter 16.

Next, check the connectors at each end of the cable that runs between the computer and the disk drive. Do the connectors fit tightly? Are the contacts clean? Do you notice any bent or damaged pins? Pay particular attention to the end of the cable that terminates inside the drive, because there is one problem that occurs frequently with disk drives—someone knocks the drive off the desk, and for a moment the drive hangs by the cable. You may have to remove the case of the drive to look at this problem.

Next, inspect the cable itself. Has it been pinched or bent sharply anywhere along its length? (The conductors inside the cable are very thin, and they can be broken if the cable is bent sharply.) If you're at all suspicious of the cable, substitute a cable that you know is all right for it, and see if the symptoms disappear. Swap a cable from one of your other disk drives for it, or borrow a cable from a friend. If you can't find an extra cable, you'll have to check the cable using a VOM. Set the meter to read OHMS, and use it as a continuity tester. The procedure is described in Chapter 7. Check out one conductor at a time (the contacts should be numbered at each end of the cable).

Some computers, including the IBM PCs and clones, use disk-drive interface cards that plug into the main computer. This arrangement is very convenient for troubleshooting, because it lets you eliminate most of the control circuitry in one step. If your system has one of these plug-in interface cards, borrow a replacement card and install it. Run the computer through its paces and see if the problem has disappeared. If the problem does disappear, look for a problem in the control circuits (refer to Section 10.3.15).

If you have two disk drives, or if you can borrow a spare drive, you can substitute drives. Unplug your drive and connect the spare, and if the symptoms disappear, you know the problem is in the original drive. If the symptoms persist, however, you can suspect a problem in the control circuits (refer to Section 10.3.15).

Check for the "drive motor on" signal through the cable. If this signal is missing, refer to Section 10.3.15.

10.1.6 Problem 6

Symptom: Drive turns slowly; there is noise from the drive.

Can the disk turn freely in the drive? Open the drive door, and see if you can remove the disk easily.

Turn off the computer and the drive. Turn the drive on its side and remove the screws on the bottom. Remove the drive's case. Inspect the drive mechanism for any loose screws, broken mechanical parts, or any other foreign objects that could be causing the problem.

Your drive may have a drive belt that runs between the drive motor and the spindle. While the drive is open, check the drive belt, as described in Section 10.3.4.

Test the power connections to the drive, as described in Section 10.3.1. Some drives have their own power supplies. If the voltages for the drive motor are out of "spec," refer to Chapter 16 (Troubleshooting Power Supplies).

The problem could be caused by a bad connection in the cable that runs between the computer and the disk drive. Do the connectors fit tightly? Are the contacts clean? Do you notice any bent or damaged pins? Pay particular attention to the end of the cable that terminates inside the drive. The connections may have been stretched or strained and broken. (You may have to remove the case of the drive to do this.)

Next, inspect the cable itself. Has it been pinched or bent sharply anywhere along its length? (The conductors inside the cable are very thin, and they can be broken if the cable is bent sharply.) If you're at all suspicious of the cable, substitute a known good cable for it, and see if the symptoms disappear. Use a cable from one of your other disk drives, or borrow a cable from a friend. If you can't find an extra cable, you'll have to check the suspect cable out with a voltohmmeter. Set the meter to read OHMS, and use it as a continuity tester. The procedure is described in Chapter 7. Check out one conductor at a time (they should be numbered at each end). Be sure you're checking the right pair of contacts.

Check the motor-speed adjustment procedures, as described in Section 10.2.1. If you're using diagnostics software, run the motor-speed test for a while, and note any variations in speed.

If this is possible on your drive, run the "raw data test" described in Section 10.2.7.

Test the drive motor and spindle, as described in Section 10.3.2.

10.1.7 Problem 7

Symptom: Disk won't slide in or out of drive.

If you can't insert a disk easily, don't force it. With the disk safely out of the drive, try opening and closing the drive door a few times. This repositions the mechanical parts inside the drive.

Now and then, you may find that the head-load mechanism inside the drive stays in the "loaded" position, even though no disk is in the drive. This can prevent you from inserting and removing disks. If this happens, "boot" the computer—or use the "Reset" key. The head should unload, and you should be able to change disks.

On drives with a manual eject system, various parts of the mechanism may become bent or jammed. Turn off the drive and the computer. Turn the drive on its side, and remove the screws on the bottom of the case. Slide the case away from the drive. Inspect the eject mechanism, as described in Section 10.3.13.

On drives that include auto-eject, the eject mechanism may stop working. This is probably a mechanical problem. Shut off power to the computer and the disk drive, and remove the drive's case. Inspect the mechanism, as described in Section 10.3.13.

10.1.8 Problem 8

Symptom: Drive won't format a disk.

This problem may be caused by a slow drive motor. Try the motor-speed adjustment procedures described in Section 10.2.1.

This symptom could also be caused by other alignment problems. The complete alignment procedure is described in Section 10.2.

10.1.9 Problem 9

Symptom: The head won't step in or out.

Check the "Stepper Logic and Stepper Motor" procedures discussed in Section 10.3.6.

10.1.10 Problem 10

Symptom: The head oscillates at Track 0.

Check the "Track-Zero Detector" procedures discussed in Section 10.3.11.

10.1.11 Problem 11

Symptom: The head will not load.

Check the "Head-Load Mechanism" procedures discussed in Section 10.3.7.

10.2 Alignment and Adjustment Procedures

A full alignment procedure will correct many of the problems that a floppy disk drive may have. You can perform some of these adjustments with simple tools, but to do a complete alignment, you will need a few special tools, including an "exerciser disk," an "alignment disk," and a good oscilloscope.

The exerciser disk includes special programs that allow you to test a disk drive. For example, one of the programs allows you to move the Read/Write head to a particular track. Using another program, you can write a series of digital pulses (1s and 0s) onto a test or "scratch" disk. The exerciser program may also help with other alignment functions. Vortron, Inc. sells an exerciser disk for IBM PCs for about $25.00. Allow the exerciser disk to sit at room temperature for at least 20 minutes before you begin an alignment. A floppy disk changes dimensions slightly as the temperature changes. This time delay permits the temperature of the disk to stabilize.

Service shops which must repair many disk drives may have a professional tool called a "disk drive exerciser." This tool makes it unnecessary to use a computer and software to operate a disk drive. Instead, the technician can simply plug in the disk drive directly into the exerciser. Using the exerciser, it is possible to step the heads in and out, check the motor speed, check the head alignment, and so on.

You will also need an "alignment disk." This kind of disk includes several tracks of very accurately prerecorded test signals. These are "analog" signals, and can't be processed by the computer. When the drive is made to read one of these test tracks, the output from the heads can be analyzed with an oscilloscope. Each different disk-drive format requires a different alignment disk. For example, to work with 48-tracks-per-inch (TPI) drives, 96-TPI low-density drives, and 96-TPI high-density drives, you would need three different alignment disks. (You could use the same exerciser program, however, as long as the same computer could operate all three drives.) Dysan sells alignment disks for the types of drives used with the IBM PC and clones. An alignment disk used with a single-sided drive costs about $35.00, and a disk for a double-sided drive costs about $50.00 It may be difficult to find an alignment disk (and it may be expensive) for a computer from a different manufacturer.

One note of caution should be inserted here. When you are using the alignment disk, you will have scope probes and other devices connected to parts and components inside the drive. If you are not careful, you may slip with a metal-tipped tool and create a short circuit between two parts of the circuitry. This can put the disk drive in a "Write" mode, and cause it to write over one of the tracks of the alignment disk. If this happens, you have ruined a tool worth $50.00 or more. The alignment disk is usually write-protected, however, and this will give you some protection. But if you create a short between two legs of an IC and cause the "Write Gate" line to go "true," you could bypass the write-protection circuits. Work carefully.

For many of the steps in the alignment process, you will also need an oscilloscope. Even the simplest scope will be useful for many of the steps. You will need a dual-trace scope in the 20-MHz range to make the "head radial alignment" adjustment. The "index sector adjustment" is even more demanding—for this, you will need a dual-trace scope that can handle signals with frequencies up to 30 MHz or more. It will be necessary to add the two channels and invert one, so get a scope that is capable of doing this.

10.2.1 Adjustment 1

Motor speed adjustment.

Check the speed of the main drive motor at least twice per year. On most disk drives, the drive motor should turn at 300 rpm, ±5%. If the speed falls outside of this range, the drive may begin to experience intermittent Read/Write errors.

You may be able to use a software routine to check the motor speed. Many of the general "diagnostics" packages include this feature. When you use this type of software, the display on the computer will indicate the speed of the drive. You will quickly be able to tell if the speed of the drive is within tolerance. Some diagnostics allow you to run the speed check continuously over a long period of time. This kind of software displays the variation in speed during the test period.

On some disk drives, the floppy disk is mounted on a "spindle," which is turned by a drive belt. The belt is driven by the main drive motor. This type of drive may have a "strobe" test pattern etched onto the bottom of the spindle assembly. To check the motor speed on a drive of this type, start by turning off the power to the computer and the disk drive. Take off the drive case and set the drive on its side. Turn on the computer and the drive, insert a disk in the drive, and "boot" the computer. Fig. 10-14 shows the pattern of radial lines on the bottom of the drive pulley. Hold a fluorescent light above the disk drive and watch the pattern of lines. When the motor speed is correct, the

lines will seem to stand still. If the speed is either too slow or too fast, the lines will appear to rotate one way or the other. Many drives will have two sets of strobe lines—one for operation with 60-Hz AC (for use in the U.S.) and a second set for European 50-Hz operation. Be sure that you are watching the right set of lines.

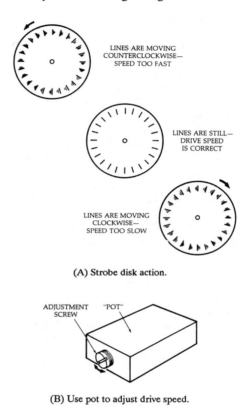

(A) Strobe disk action.

(B) Use pot to adjust drive speed.

Fig. 10-14. Motor-speed adjustment.

Some of the more recent drives do not have a strobe test pattern. On drives of this type, you will have to use a frequency counter to check the motor speed. The documentation for the drive will tell you where to connect the probe for the frequency counter. The frequency at this test point should fall within a specified range. For example, on the Shugart Model SA-455, the frequency should be 5 Hz ±0.05 Hz.

Once you have tested the speed of the drive motor, you may have to make adjustments. Consult the manual for your drive. The manual will indicate the motor-speed adjustment potentiometer, or "pot." This is usually a small square unit (part of the drive) that includes a small brass screw. Turn this screw a few degrees one way, then the other, and watch the effect on the motor speed. If you are using the strobe test pattern, adjust the screw until the lines appear to stop turning. You should not have to adjust this screw more than one full turn either way. Fig. 10-14B shows this adjustment pot.

10.2.2 Adjustment 2

Head radial alignment.

For best Read/Write performance, the head of the disk drive must be positioned directly over the center of each track that it is reading. If the head is allowed to drift to one side of the track, the output from the drive may be unreliable. Work carefully as you make this adjustment. It is possible to overdo the adjustment, so the drive actually reads a track that is to one side or the other of the track that it is meant to be reading.

Let's assume that one of your drives is quite far out of alignment. As long as you do not correct the alignment, the out-of-line drive will be able to read any out-of-line disks that it has recorded. Once you correct the alignment, the drive may not be able to read these out-of-line disks. If you suspect that a drive is significantly out of alignment, be sure to copy each disk before you change the alignment of the drive. Copy from the out-of-line drive onto a drive with a better (correct) alignment.

Set up a dual-trace scope. For this test, many manufacturers specify a scope which can handle signals having a frequency of 20 MHz. Set the "vertical" and "sweep" controls; typical settings are 50 millivolts and 20 milliseconds—check your manual. Set the scope to add channels A and B, and invert channel B. Set the trigger switch to "external," if the scope has this option.

Fig. 10-15 shows the setup for this test. Refer to the manufacturer's manual, turn off the power to the computer and drive, and remove the cover from your drive. You must locate four test points on the circuit card inside the drive. Locate the two "head" test points, and connect the probes for channels A and B. Make sure both probes are also grounded to the circuit card, as shown in Fig. 10-15A. Connect the external trigger probe to the test point that carries the "sync" signal.

Turn on the computer. Insert the exerciser disk in the drive and boot the computer. Remove the exerciser disk, and put the alignment disk in the drive. Using the programs that you loaded from the exerciser disk, tell the Read/Write head to step to one of the tracks that is recorded with alignment test signals. Normally, you will use a track near the center of the disk.

You should see a "cat's eye" pattern, as shown in Fig. 10-15C. The signals from channels A and B should be equal. Fig. 10-15C shows the ideal situation—both patterns are of equal size. In Fig. 10-15B, the signal represented by the right shape is stronger than the other signal. In Fig. 10-15D, the opposite is true. Most manufacturers say that the weaker signal should be within 75% of the value of the stronger signal. If your scope trace does not look like the trace shown in Fig. 10-15C, the head is out of alignment.

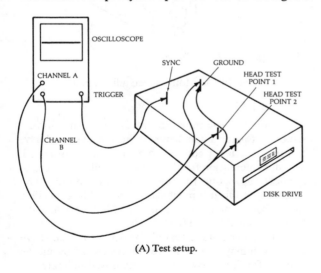

(A) Test setup.

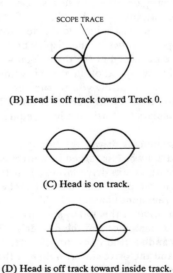

(B) Head is off track toward Track 0.

(C) Head is on track.

(D) Head is off track toward inside track.

Fig. 10-15. Head radial alignment.

The next step depends on the type of disk drive that you have. There are several different kinds of mechanisms which allow you to change the head radial alignment. In each case, you adjust the mechanism while the drive is spinning and watch the result on the scope. If the two lobes on the test pattern become the same size, you know the head is reading the center of the test track. If the test pattern becomes more uneven, move the mechanism in the other direction.

In one type of drive, the head position is set by a small pulley or cam at the end of the shaft of the stepper motor. Fig. 10-16 shows this arrangement. On some drives, the position of the pulley or cam is adjustable. The pulley or cam is attached to the shaft with a small setscrew. If your drive has this setup, loosen the small setscrew that holds the pulley in place. Slowly turn the pulley while watching the trace on the scope. When the two patterns are equal, retighten the setscrew. On other drives, the pulley is intended to remain in place, while the base of the stepper motor is turned. The base of the stepper motor is held in position by several small screws. To adjust this type of drive, loosen the screws, turn the motor slightly, and then retighten the screws.

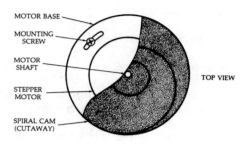

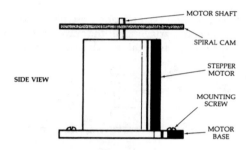

Fig. 10-17. Head radial alignment adjustment No. 2.

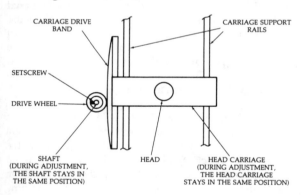

Fig. 10-16. Head radial alignment adjustment No. 1.

In another possible arrangement, the stepper motor is mounted with two or more screws on its base plate. The head is moved via a round plate with a spiral cam pattern. Fig. 10-17 shows this mechanism. If your drive is built like this, loosen the screws, and gently turn the stepper motor. Watch the trace on the scope and stop when the patterns are equal. Now, retighten the screws. Hold the motor securely as you retighten the screws—it tends to move a little as you make that last turn.

Your drive may use a spiral shaft to serve the same purpose, as shown in Fig. 10-18. The adjustment

procedure is the same. Loosen the screws that hold the motor in place, adjust the shaft until the two patterns on the scope are equal, and retighten the screws.

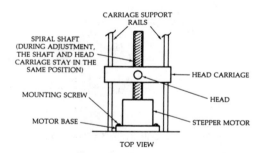

Fig. 10-18. Head radial alignment adjustment No. 3.

After you make the adjustment, step the head three tracks closer to the center of the drive, and then step it back. Now recheck the alignment. Next, step out three tracks and back again, and recheck. The head may stop in a slightly different position when it is moving in or out. The final setting should be a compromise that takes this drift into account.

When you change the head radial alignment, be sure to check the Track-zero sensor adjustment and carriage stop adjustment.

10.2.3 Adjustment 3

Track-zero sensor adjustment.

The Track-zero adjustment will not change with normal use. This mechanism signals the control circuits when the head has reached the outside track on the disk. On some drives, the circuit actually signals when the head passes between tracks 2 and 3.

Turn off power to the computer and the disk drive. Remove the cover from the drive, check your manual, and identify the Track-zero sensing mechanism. One common system uses a simple microswitch. When the head carriage is all the way out, toward the rear of the drive, it trips this switch (Fig. 10-19A).

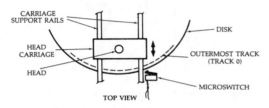

(A) Circuit with microswitch sensor.

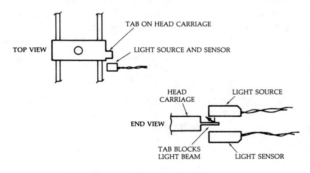

(B) Circuit with light source and detector.

Fig. 10-19. Track-zero mechanism.

Another type of Track-zero sensing mechanism uses a photodetector switch, as shown in Fig. 10-19B. This type of switch consists of a light source and a photocell, separated by a small space. Normally, the light source sends out a beam of light and the photocell detects the beam. When the head approaches the Track-zero position, however, a small tab on the head carriage blocks this beam.

You can check these types of switches with a VOM or a logic probe. Connect the two leads on your logic probe to the +5-V DC and ground sources on your disk drive. On drives that use a microswitch, test the switch as described in the section on "Switches" in Chapter 7. On drives that use a light source and photocell, check these components as described in the material on "Light Source and Detector" in Chapter 7.

Turn on the computer, insert your exerciser disk in the drive, and "boot" the computer. Instruct the computer to step the Read/Write head from Track 0 to Track 5, and back again. Watch the results with your logic probe. If the output on your test pin is "high" when the head is at Track 0, it should drop to "low" as the head passes between Tracks 2 and 3. If the output is normally "low," it should go "high" at this point.

If the Track-zero switch does not work, refer to the instructions given in Section 10.3.11.

It is possible that the detector switch is working correctly, but the head is not over Track 0 when the switch is tripped. One way of checking this is to use an alignment disk that includes a test pattern on Track 0. The manual for the drive will tell you where to connect an oscilloscope to read the output from the Read/Write head. When the head is positioned directly over Track 0, the output from the Read/Write head should appear on the scope.

10.2.4 Adjustment 4

Carriage stop adjustment.

On most drives, the Read/Write head is supported by a carriage that moves the head forward and back along a pair of rods. Normally, there is an adjustable stop at the outer end (Track 0) of these rods. This stop is an emergency device, designed to keep the carriage from slamming into the rear of the disk drive if something goes wrong with the control circuits. When the drive is operating normally, the stepper mechanisms will position the head over Track 0, and the stop will not be necessary. You should not have to readjust this setting. If you do find it necessary, check your manual for specific instructions. In most cases, the stop is set so there is a very small clearance between the stop and the carriage, as measured when the head is over Track 0.

10.2.5 Adjustment 5

Head load adjustment.

The disk drive has to read and write to very specific

locations on the spinning disk. On some drives, the index timing circuitry gives the disk a "hard" reference point once during each revolution of the disk. The drive can use this reference to lay out the "sectors" on a particular track. Using this arrangement, the drive can tell which part of the disk is under the head. Some drives do not use an index sensor, so the index timing adjustment may not be necessary for your drive—check your manual.

The index timing mechanism is quite simple, as illustrated in Fig. 10-20. An LED or infrared light source is mounted on one side of the disk. A photocell is mounted to detect the beam from this source. Both the disk and the disk case are provided with a hole. As the disk rotates, the hole in the disk lines up with the light source and the photocell. On most drives, this happens once during each revolution of the disk. Each time the beam reaches the sensor, the index circuit sends out a pulse.

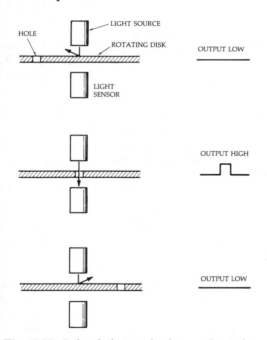

Fig. 10-20. Index timing mechanisms and waveforms.

For this alignment, most manufacturers require a scope that can handle signals having a frequency of 30 MHz. A typical setting for the "vertical" control is 0.2-volt per division, and for the "sweep" setting, 50 microseconds. Set the scope to add channels A and B, and invert channel B. Set the trigger switch to EXTERNAL.

Turn off the power to the computer and drive,

remove the cover from your drive. Refer to the manufacturer's manual—you must locate four test points on the circuit board inside the disk drive. Use the same test connections that you used for the "head radial alignment." (These connections are described in Section 10.2.2, and illustrated in Fig. 10-15.) Connect the leads for channels A and B to the two "head" test points. Be sure that the ground connection for each probe is attached to a good ground. Connect the trigger probe of the scope to the "sync" test point on the circuit board.

Turn on power to the computer. Insert the exerciser disk in the drive and "boot" the computer. Remove the exerciser disk, and insert the alignment disk. Using the programs that you loaded from the exerciser, instruct the computer to read the track on the alignment disk that carries the test signal for this test.

The scope trace should look like the trace shown in Fig. 10-21. The important measurement here is the time delay between the time the drive (and the scope) gets the index pulse, and the time the pulses from the test track begin to appear. A typical delay would be 200 microseconds. With a typical "sweep" setting, each horizontal division on the screen would represent 50 microseconds, so a distance of four divisions would represent the ideal time delay.

If the time delay is not correct, you can make an adjustment by moving either the light source or the photocell. Normally, one or the other of these components will be mounted with screws and slots, so you can slide the part from side to side. Loosen the screws and move the part gently, until the time delay is correct. Fig. 10-22 shows the adjustment.

10.2.6 Adjustment 6

Head load adjustment.

On some drives, the clearance on certain parts on the head load arm and loading mechanism are adjustable. These settings should not change with normal use. Refer to your service manual to see if your drive has these adjustments.

The head load pad will eventually wear and require replacement. Some drives allow you to adjust this pad to compensate for wear. Refer to Section 10.3.7 for instructions on inspecting the head.

10.2.7 Adjustment 7

Raw data test and adjustment.

This function is not available on all floppy disk drives.

Fig. 10-21. Scope trace during index timing test.

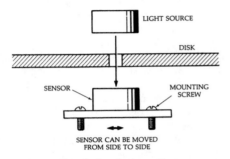

Fig. 10-22. Index timing adjustment.

The *raw data test* checks the stability of the Read circuits and the motor drive. It is something like the "wow and flutter" test for an audio turntable. To make this test, you will need an exerciser disk that includes the appropriate software.

Set up the scope and connect the test leads using the same setup as the test used for the "head radial alignment." Section 10.2.2 describes these connections, and Fig. 10-15 illustrates the setup. Refer to the manual for your drive for the correct "vertical" and "sweep" settings on the scope.

Once the test equipment is connected, insert the exerciser disk, and boot the computer. Remove the exerciser disk and replace it with a "scratch" disk. The computer will write onto this disk, so do not use a disk that contains anything important. Instruct the computer to begin the raw data test.

The computer will write a pattern onto the scratch disk, and will read it back again. The scope should show a trace similar to the trace shown in Fig. 10-23. Watch the leading edge of the third pulse. This leading edge may seem to blur as it moves within a certain time range.

Refer to the manual, and locate the "pot" that makes the raw data adjustment. (Some drives are not adjustable.) By adjusting the screw on this pot, you can minimize the blurred area.

The manufacturer of the drive will specify an acceptable tolerance. If, after adjustment, the blurred area is still larger than the specs allow, there is something wrong with the disk drive. Look for a

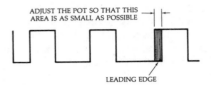

Fig. 10-23. Scope trace during raw data check.

mechanical problem. Pay particular attention to the drive motor and the bearings on the main spindle (see Section 10.3.2).

10.2.8 Adjustment 8

Azimuth check.

Fig. 10-24 shows what we mean by the word "azimuth." When the Read/Write head is positioned correctly, the center of the head should lie at an angle of 90° to a line drawn to the center of the disk. If the drive is dropped, it is possible for the head to be knocked out of this ideal position. The word "minute" is used to indicate a very small angle. A full circle has 360 degrees, and one degree has 60 minutes. The azimuth setting of the head must be accurate within ±15 minutes. There is no way of adjusting the azimuth, so if a head is out of alignment, the head assembly must be replaced. This usually costs just a bit less than a new disk drive.

The manual for your drive will specify the setup for the azimuth test. Use the alignment disk for this test. The test track for the azimuth test is prerecorded with a special test signal. This test track actually includes four signals, each recorded by a Write head that has been turned slightly from the correct azimuth. For example, two of the signals may correspond to 10 minutes clockwise from the correct position, and 18 minutes clockwise. The other two signals might be 10 minutes counterclockwise, and 18 minutes counterclockwise. If the head is out of alignment, it will read one of these test signals more strongly than the others. For example, if the head is aligned 10 minutes clockwise from the correct position, the strongest signal it will pick up will be the signal recorded when the record head was turned 10 minutes clockwise.

Fig. 10-25 shows how to interpret the test results. When the azimuth setting is correct, the Read/Write head will read the center of the test track (Fig. 10-25A). The two test signals at the center of the track (10 minutes clockwise and 10 minutes counterclockwise)

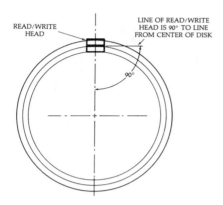

Fig. 10-24. Correct azimuth position.

will appear to be equally strong. Fig. 10-25B shows the situation when the head has been turned clockwise a bit. Now the head picks up the signal that was recorded at 18 minutes clockwise. Fig. 10-25C illustrates a head that has been turned the other way.

10.3 Checking Individual Circuits and Mechanisms

In this next section, we will discuss the procedures for troubleshooting specific sections of a floppy disk drive.

10.3.1 Test 1

Checking connecting cables.

Connectors and cables tend to be vulnerable in any system, and this includes the cables that run between the computer and the disk drives. To check a cable, start by checking the continuity of each wire in the cable with a VOM. Inspect the connectors for corrosion, bent pins, etc.

You may check the signals flowing through a disk drive cable with a logic probe. This should reveal any missing signals or dead lines. This test can be a useful step in troubleshooting the control circuits or other logic circuits in the drive. Note: Several wires in the cable may carry voltages that can damage a logic probe (i.e., +12 V DC). Refer to the manual and identify these wires before you begin to use the probe.

You will have to consult the manual anyway, to

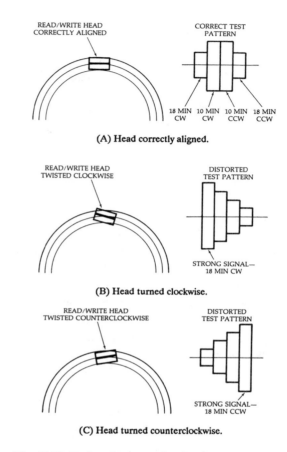

(A) Head correctly aligned.

(B) Head turned clockwise.

(C) Head turned counterclockwise.

Fig. 10-25. Azimuth test results showing test patterns.

learn the assignments for each wire in the cable. Chart 10-1 shows the signals that you can expect to find. The cable used in your system may not carry all of these signals.

10.3.2 Test 2

Checking drive motor and spindle.

Start by making all of the troubleshooting checks listed in Section 10.1.6. You may find that you cannot adjust the drive to run at the correct speed, or that you need to use most of the adjustment range to get the drive to run at the correct speed. If this is the case, you have not yet found the problem.

It is possible that a mechanical problem is creating a drag and slowing the drive motor. If you have

Chart 10-1. Signals in Cable to Disk Drive

Step Direction	Should be constantly pulsing. A "true" tells the stepper-motor circuits to prepare to move the head in one direction. A "false" tells the circuits to prepare to move the head in the other direction.
Step	Should be constantly pulsing as the head moves from one track to another.
Drive Select 0 and Drive Select 1	Should remain constant while one drive is in use. Combinations of "highs" and "lows" on these lines enable the disk drives.
Write Gate	Should be pulsing while the drive is writing. Write gate enables the drive to write.
Write Data	Should be pulsing while the drive is writing.
Write-Protect	Should be "true" when the disk is write-protected.
Write Fault	Multipurpose line. See the manual for your drive.
Late, Early	Should be constantly pulsing when the drive is reading the inner tracks of the disk. These are "precompensation" signals.
Side Select	Should be "true" when the computer is using one side of the drive, and "false" when using the other.
Read Gate	Should be constantly pulsing when the drive is reading.
Read Data	Should be constantly pulsing when the drive is reading.
Read Check	Should be constantly pulsing when the drive is reading.
$\phi 1, \phi 2, \phi 3,$ $\phi 4$ (some drives)	These are the signal lines to the stepper motor.
Index	Should be constantly pulsing. This is the train of pulses from the index detector circuit.
Track 0	Should be "true" when the head is parked over Track 0 (outermost track).
Eject	Should be "true" when the computer tells the drive to eject the disk.
Motor On	Should be "true" when the drive motor is on.
+5-V DC, +12-V DC, −12-V DC, GND	Some of the wires may carry power-supply voltages.

a drive with a separate spindle, turn the spindle gently by hand. It should turn smoothly, with no catching or resistance. One manufacturer says that, with a gentle push, the spindle should spin one half turn to three turns.

You should check for resistance in the motor bearings as well. These bearings are permanently lubricated and sealed. If they feel "gritty" or rough, or if they produce a scratching or grinding sound as you turn the motor shaft, the bearings have gone bad. If it is not clear whether the motor or the spindle is causing the problem, remove the drive belt and test again. Refer to Section 10.1.4.

If the bearings in the motor fail, you will have to replace the whole motor. You can replace the bearings

in the spindle yourself. Fig. 10-26 is a side view of the spindle mechanism. If the disk drive is worn enough to require new spindle bearings, you should probably retire the drive. You may also want to consider swapping the core of your faulty drive for a replacement core, and install this in the drive yourself.

One particular power-supply problem can cause the disk drive to turn slowly. Most power supplies include a device called a voltage regulator. This component is supposed to keep the voltage from the supply constant, regardless of the load put on the supply. If the voltage regulator fails, the disk drive will tend to start normally, but will then slow down. If your drive shows these symptoms, check out the power supply according to the instructions given in Chapter 16.

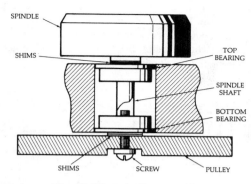

Fig. 10-26. Spindle assembly.

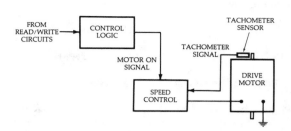

Fig. 10-27. Block diagram of drive motor circuits.

Let's say that you adjust the speed on your disk drive, but quickly begin to have problems again. You recheck the speed adjustment and find that it has changed. This suggests that the speed-control circuitry is drifting. A block diagram of this circuitry is shown in Fig. 10-27. Most small disk drives use a tachometer device to detect how fast the disk is turning. In some drives, a tiny magnet is mounted in the spindle. Each time this magnet spins past a pickup, the pickup generates a pulse. The speed-control circuit uses these signals to keep the disk speed within narrow limits. If the tachometer tells the logic circuit that the disk is turning too slowly, the control circuit increases voltage to the motor, which begins to spin more quickly. If you suspect a problem with the speed-control circuit, check the pickup to be sure that it is generating a series of pulses. If you have a problem in the control circuitry itself, use the general troubleshooting procedures outlined in Chapter 8.

10.3.3 Test 3

Checking stopped drive motor.

Start by making all of the troubleshooting checks listed in Section 10.1.5. If you cannot locate any mechanical problem, check to be sure that the motor is getting power. Turn the computer and disk drive on, and check for a DC voltage, 10 volts or more, between one of the input lugs on the motor and ground. If this voltage is missing, track down the power source that is supposed to supply power to the motor. In some cases, the drive receives its power from the main computer through the disk-drive cable. In a system like this, check the cables and connectors as described in Section 10.3.1. In other systems, the disk drive has its own power supply. Check this power supply as described in Chapter 16.

If the voltage to the motor is present and the

motor is still not turning, the motor itself may be faulty. Shut off the drive and the computer, and using a VOM set to read OHMS, test the continuity of the windings inside the motor. Use the two input lugs on the motor as your test points. The meter should show a very low resistance between these two points. If the resistance is high or infinite, the motor windings are probably burned out.

If you have ruled out a mechanical problem, if the power supply seems all right, and the motor appears to be good as well, begin to suspect the motor drive circuitry. This circuitry turns the motor on whenever the computer wants to read or write something onto a disk. The circuits can be rather complicated because they incorporate time delays and other refinements to help the system run smoothly. In most disk drives, the motor drive logic is mounted on a circuit board inside the disk drive. In the other computers, this logic may be mounted on a plug-in interface card. If you have a problem here, follow the general troubleshooting techniques outlined in Chapter 8.

10.3.4 Test 4

Checking drive belt tension.

Some disk-drive mechanisms are turned by a drive belt made of rubber or plastic. After two or three years, the belt may begin to loosen or slip. The service manual for your drive may list a tension specification for the belt. As a general rule, the belt should be snug, but not too tight.

On many drives, you can loosen the mounting screws at the base of the drive motor and rotate the motor, or move it away from the spindle. This changes the relative position of the drive shaft and allows you to adjust the belt tension. If a drive belt has stretched enough to require a significant adjustment, replace it.

At the same time, clean the drive pulleys if they appear to be dirty or sticky to the touch. Use a cotton swab, moistened slightly with alcohol. Let the alcohol evaporate before you replace the belt.

10.3.5 Test 5

Checking the drive select system.

Fig. 10-28 shows a block diagram of the drive select system. In a typical microcomputer system, there will be two drive select lines. Each line may be either "high" or "low," so the system can be used to address up to four different disk drives ($2^2 = 4$). Each drive is set up to respond to a unique combination of "highs" and "lows" on the select lines.

The drive select signals begin in the disk-controller circuits. From there, the select lines run to each drive in the system. Each drive has its own Read/Write logic circuits. The input and output for a particular drive are inhibited unless the correct combination of drive select signals is present.

You can check this system quickly by using your logic probe to check for activity on each of the select lines. You should see the signals change each time a new drive is selected. If one of the drive select signals is missing, check the cables and connectors that lead from the computer to the drive (see Section 10.3.1). If the cables and connectors are good, the problem may be in the Read/Write circuits inside the drive (see Section 10.3.9).

10.3.6 Test 6

Checking the stepper logic and stepper motor.

This system causes the Read/Write head to move toward and away from the center of the disk, so the head is positioned over the correct track. A small stepper motor moves the head assembly in precise increments. The control circuits produce the signals that drive the motor. The logic communicates with the motor by sending related signals along four separate lines. Stepper motor operating principles were explained in Chapter 7. Basically, a mechanism converts the rotational motion of the motor shaft to a lateral motion of the head.

To check the stepper motor, start by turning off the disk drive and computer. Remove the cover from the disk drive. Then, turn on the computer and disk drive again. Next, use an exerciser disk, compatible with the DOS used on your system, to tell the drive to step in and out. If the Read/Write head does not move, shut off the drive and the computer and check to see that a screw, paper clip, piece of dirt, or other foreign object is not jamming the mechanism.

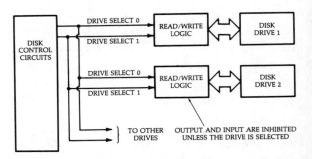

Fig. 10-28. Block diagram of the drive select system.

Next, check the lines that carry signals from the control circuits in the computer to the stepper logic circuits in the drive. The "direction" signal specifies whether the head will step in or out. When this line is "true," the stepper is prepared to step in one direction. When the line is "false," the drive should be prepared to step in the other direction. The "step" signal actually tells the motor when to step, and when the motor receives this signal, it steps in the direction specified. Use your exerciser software to step the drive both in and out, and, using your logic probe, watch for activity on the "step" and "direction" lines. Check for these signals at the cable, as described in Section 10.3.1. If the signals are missing, look for a problem in the control circuits (Section 10.3.15).

If you still have not found the problem, check the stepper logic circuitry. Fig. 10-29 is a simple block diagram of these circuits. Use the exerciser disk to command the disk drive to step in and out. With an oscilloscope, watch for activity on each of the four signal lines that run to the motor. As you step past a series of tracks, each of these lines should show activity. The presence of one or more inactive lines suggests a problem with the stepper logic circuits. Check the output transistor for each inactive line, using the procedures described in Chapter 7.

The logic circuits use a "feedback" system to tell how far the stepper has turned at any given moment. Check for a train of pulses from the feedback sensor, as described in Chapter 7. The stepper motor itself is not likely to fail, but you can test it according to the instructions given in Chapter 7.

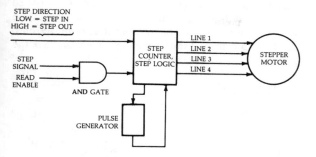

Fig. 10-29. Stepper motor logic.

Fig. 10-30. Inspecting the head load pad.

10.3.7 Test 7

Checking the head-load mechanism.

If the Read/Write head was continuously in contact with a spinning floppy disk, both the head and the disk would wear out quickly. Instead, the head only contacts the disk when the computer specifies a Read or Write operation. The head normally loads when the drive is selected, but some drives are wired so the head loads when the drive receives the "motor on" signal.

If you have a single-sided disk drive, begin by checking the head-load pad. This is a small button made of fabric that actually touches the back of the disk, opposite the head. The surface of the button should normally appear smooth and rounded. If you notice that the edges of the button appear rough or frayed, or if the button is discolored by oxide from the disks, replace the button (Fig. 10-30). On some 8-inch drives, the load pad is covered with a thin layer of red material. When this layer is worn away, the pad should be replaced. In normal use, a load pad should last one or two years.

In some drives, you can rotate the load pad 90°, or can make other adjustments to compensate for wear. This adjustment should be just a temporary solution. You should still plan to replace the pad. To replace the pad, shut off the disk drive and the computer and remove the drive case. Gently pry the old load pad free, and press a new pad into place. Be careful not to bend the load pad arm as you do this.

The loading mechanism may also fail. To make a test, turn on the disk drive and the computer. Use your exerciser disk, or operate one of your other programs, and watch the head-loading mechanism. See if it moves whenever the computer specifies a Read or Write operation. On most drives, the red LED activity indicator will light to show a Read or Write. If the

mechanism does not move at all, or if it moves just a bit, check for a loose screw, paper clip, dirt, or other foreign object which may be jamming the mechanism.

The loading mechanism uses a "solenoid." This is a small electromechanical device that moves the loading arm. The troubleshooting procedures for electromechanical devices and solenoids are given in Chapter 7. If the solenoid appears to be good, perhaps the head-load logic is not receiving signals from the control circuits. Check the cables and connectors between the disk drive and the computer. In particular, look for the "drive select" signals. (Refer to Section 10.3.1.)

10.3.8 Test 8

Checking the Write-Protect system.

The Write-Protect system is very simple. Refer to the block diagram given in Fig. 10-31. On a 5¼-inch disk drive, the sensor for this circuit is a simple switch. The switch is positioned to line up with the left edge of the disk as it sits in the drive. When the disk is pushed into the proper position, the switch will sit directly under the Write-Protect notch in the side of the disk cover. This notch allows the arm of the switch to swing upward. If the Write-Protect notch on the disk is covered, the arm will be prevented from swinging up and the switch will remain closed, sending the drive a signal that disables the Write circuits. However, this convention is reversed for 8-inch disk drives. On these drives, a disk is write-protected when the notch is uncovered.

On a 3.5-inch disk drive, the arrangement may be slightly different. This type of drive is likely to use a photodetector, rather than a mechanical switch. One part of the detector unit is a light source and the other part is a light sensor. The two parts are separated by a small space. When the 3.5-inch floppy disk is write-protected, a small "window" on the side of the disk is opened. When this window is open, the light from the source is allowed to reach the sensor. The signal from this sensor inhibits the Write circuits.

A write-protect problem can keep a drive from writing at all. This can happen when the write-protect circuitry fails in the "true" state. Sometimes, write-protection can also be controlled by a signal from the main computer. A problem in the main computer can cause this line to be permanently held in the "true" state.

Most of the problems in the Write-Protect system are caused by a faulty Write-Protect switch. If you suspect a problem here, start by turning off the computer and the disk drive, and removing the drive cover. Insert a floppy disk in place in the drive and watch the action of the switch. Does the Write-Protect notch on the disk line up with the arm on the sensor switch? Can the arm move freely? If the mechanism appears to be operating normally, check the switch itself. Use the troubleshooting sequence described in the section on "Testing Switches" in Chapter 7. If the drive has a photodetector, see the section on "Testing a Light Source and Detector" given in Chapter 7.

If all of the components appear to be working properly, look for a problem in the cable that runs to the computer (Section 10.3.1) or in the control circuits (Section 10.3.15).

10.3.9 Test 9

Checking the Read circuits.

If you suspect a problem with the "Read" circuitry, start by making all of the checks listed in Section 10.1.2. Next, inspect the head for score lines or scratch marks. If the head shows visible signs of damage, it should be replaced.

After a long period of use, a Read/Write head will begin to wear. A badly worn head will fail the fol-

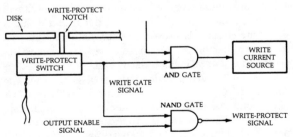

Fig. 10-31. Write-Protect logic diagram.

lowing "head output test": Set up your oscilloscope, using the test points for the "head radial alignment" adjustment described in Section 10.2.2. The test setup is illustrated in Fig. 10-32. "Boot" the computer and load the programs from your exerciser disk. Next, insert a

"scratch disk." The computer will write on this disk, so do not use a disk that contains anything important. Use your exerciser program to write a series of pulses onto the scratch disk, and then have the drive read back the pulses.

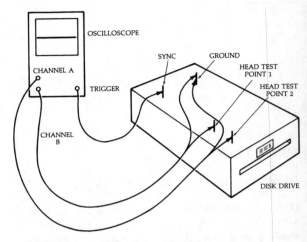

Fig. 10-32. Test setup for radial head alignment.

Note the amplitude of the signal displayed on the scope. Gently place a one-half ounce weight on the load arm, directly above the load pad or the upper head. (One quarter or four pennies will weigh about one-half ounce.) Watch the scope trace. The amplitude of the output pattern should increase only slightly. If the signal amplitude increases more than about 10%, the head is worn and should be replaced.

Fig. 10-33 shows a simple block diagram of a typical Read circuit. As shown in the diagram, the original signal coming from the drive is not the clean series of pulses you might expect. Rather, it is a lumpy pattern with worn edges, and it must be cleaned up by a series of amplifiers, filters, and wave shapers before it is fit to go back into the computer. One of these stages may stop working completely, and may block the train of signals coming out of the Read circuitry. A stage may also fail in such a way that it passes signals through but it does not do the job it was meant to do. This can result in weak or undefined pulses being fed into the computer. Use your oscilloscope and apply the "chain" troubleshooting techniques described in Chapter 7. Some of the parts of this system deal with "analog" signals, so digital troubleshooting methods may not help you here.

If the Read circuits do not seem to be getting any signals at all, turn off the drive and test the continuity of

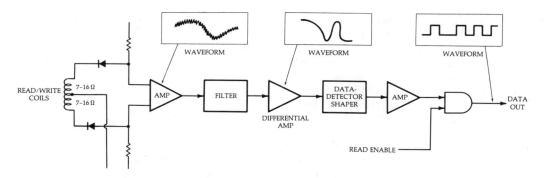

Fig. 10-33. Block diagram of a typical Read circuit.

the coil in the head with a VOM. There should be a very low resistance across the coil—about 5 ohms to 10 ohms. If the resistance is infinite, the coil wire is broken.

The Read circuits could also be disabled because the drive is prepared to Write. Check the "Write Gate" signal at one of the cable connectors, as described in Section 10.3.1.

10.3.10 Test 10

Checking the Write circuits.

Let's say that your problem occurs only during a "Write" operation. Start by making all of the checks described in Section 10.1.3. Fig. 10-34 shows a simple block diagram of the circuits associated with the "Write" function. Check the control signals that have to do with writing—"Write Data," "Write Gate," and "Write-Protect."

If the write-related inputs seem to be good, look at the logic and driver circuits. Most drives use two "Write Driver" circuits—one for each side of the head coil. The best way to check the Write function is to try the head output test described in Section 10.3.9. Since this test causes the device to first write some data and

then read it back, you can check both functions at once. Use the chain troubleshooting techniques described in Chapter 7.

Some disk drives include a separate "Erase" coil in the head. The Erase system seldom fails. If the Erase coil is inoperative, some of the magnetic signals on adjacent tracks may overlap. The disk drive may operate very well most of the time, and will just show an occasional error. The checks for the Erase system are very similar to the checks for the Write system (just described). The Erase head is built into the Read/Write head assembly. Start by inspecting the head and checking the head coil for continuity. You should find a very low resistance, usually around 3 ohms. One of the leads to the Erase head should show an intermittent voltage with respect to ground whenever the drive is writing. Use the chain troubleshooting techniques to localize the problem from there.

10.3.11 Test 11

Checking the Track-zero detector.

As shown in Fig. 10-35, the Track-zero detector circuitry is very simple. The component most likely to

Fig. 10-34. Block diagram of the Write circuits.

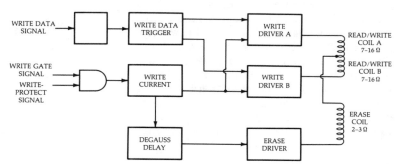

cause problems is the switch. To check the switch, turn off the computer and the disk drive. Set your VOM to read OHMS, and connect a test lead to each side of the switch. The mechanism will use a button or arm to activate the switch. Gently depress and release this arm. The meter should cycle between readings of high resistance and very low resistance as the switch makes and breaks the connection. Some drives may use other components, such as debouncers and inverters, to condition the Track 0 signal. If you encounter a problem here, use the chain troubleshooting techniques described in Chapter 7 to further check out the circuitry.

10.3.12 Test 12

Checking the index detector.

A simplified block diagram of the index detector system is shown in Fig. 10-36. To operate, a light source is lined up to shine onto a light detector. Normally, the beam is blocked by the surface of the spinning disk. Once each revolution, however, an index hole in the disk moves past the detector. For a moment, the light beam is able to shine through to the detector, and the associated circuitry generates a pulse. The drive control circuits use this pulse as a "hard" reference to mark the beginning of a track, and to lay out the other sectors on the track.

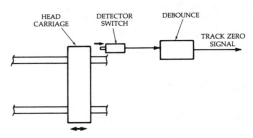

Fig. 10-35. Track-zero detector.

The light source and detector cause most of the problems with this system. First, be sure the source and detector are correctly aligned. We explained how to do this in Section 10.2.3. If the index detector system seems to be completely dead, be sure the source, detector, and the ICs in the system are getting power. These components all require a low-voltage DC source.

Next, check the source and detector themselves, using the procedure described in "Testing a Light Source and Detector" in Chapter 7. The light source

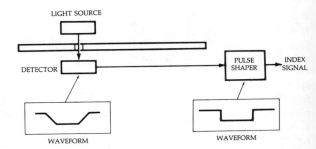

Fig. 10-36. Block diagram of the index detector circuitry.

and detector are usually part of the same assembly and should be replaced as a unit.

10.3.13 Test 13

Checking the ejector mechanics.

Many disk drives have a mechanical linkage which ejects the floppy disk when you open the door on the front of the drive. A common arrangement is shown in Fig. 10-37. As you push a disk into the drive, the mechanism is cocked. The rear edge of the disk contacts the ejector block and pushes it back,

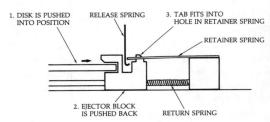

(A) Loading disk into ejector.

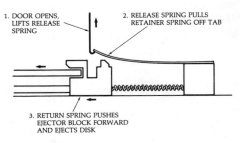

(B) Disk being ejected.

Fig. 10-37. Ejector mechanism.

compressing the main spring. The tip of the retainer spring has a hole that fits over the tab at the rear of the ejector block and holds the ejector block in place.

When the drive door is opened, the release spring is lifted. This spring catches the end of the retainer spring, and lifts it off the tab on the ejector block. The force of the compressed main spring pushes the ejector block forward and ejects the disk. Your drive may contain a different mechanism, but it will work in roughly the same manner.

When one of these mechanical ejectors stops working, it is usually because a part has been bent. Turn off power to the drive, remove the case, and you should be able to see the working parts.

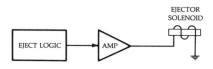

Fig. 10-38. Electronically controlled ejector mechanism.

Some ejectors are controlled electronically, using a solenoid. As shown in Fig. 10-38, this system is also simple. The ejector logic is included with the control circuits on the disk controller. When the computer is through with a disk, it sends a signal along the "eject" line. This sends current through the solenoid coil, causing the plunger to move and activate the eject mechanism.

If you have trouble with this kind of system, start by turning off the computer and drive, and remove the drive case. Look for a loose screw or bent part that could be jamming the mechanism. This is the most common cause of problems with this type of ejector.

Next, check the solenoid, using the procedure described in "Testing Solenoids" in Chapter 7. If the solenoid is working, use your logic probe to check for activity on the "eject line." Absence of this signal may mean a problem in the cable (Section 10.3.1) or in the control circuits (Section 10.3.15).

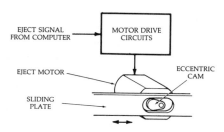

Fig. 10-39. Ejector system with motor.

Some 3.5-inch disk drives use an auto-eject mechanism driven by a motor (Fig. 10-39). The motor drives an eccentric cam, and this cam causes a sliding plate to move back and forth. Through a mechanical linkage, this sliding plate causes the disk to eject. If you experience problems with the mechanical linkage, check for bent parts and foreign objects. Some of the parts of the linkage are mounted outside of the main frame of the disk drive. It is all right to lubricate these parts with a small amount of grease.

There may be times when you will want to eject a disk without using the auto-eject mechanism. There is usually a way of ejecting the disk mechanically. For example, on the disk drives used on the MacIntosh computer, there is a small hole located near the right end of the slot for the floppy disk. If you poke a stiff wire into this hole, the disk will eject. (A straightened paper clip works well.) You should only do this as a last resort, however, since it may confuse the computer. The computer will have no record of the disk having been ejected, since it did not do this itself. Never eject the disk while the drive is trying to Read or Write. This will certainly scramble the directory on the disk, since the drive will not have time to close the file it is working with.

10.3.14 Test 14

Checking the activity indicator LED.

Most disk drives use a single LED to indicate activity. Normally, this LED will light whenever the drive is reading or writing. One common arrangement is to supply this LED from the head-loading circuits.

If the LED does not light, yet the disk drive appears to work correctly, the LED has probably failed. Replace the faulty part with another LED of the same size and color. Most single-color LEDs are interchangeable, so you can get a replacement at almost any electronics supply store. Since an LED is a type of diode, it will only conduct current in one direction. If your replacement LED does not light, try reversing the connections.

10.3.15 Test 15

Checking the control circuits.

Besides the circuits that process specific control signals (Write-Protect, Write Gate, etc.), the disk-drive system includes circuits which supervise the overall functioning of the drive. These circuits take signals from the computer and, under the supervision of the disk operating system, produce the control and data signals that go to the drive. Usually, most of this work is handled by a large "disk-drive controller" IC, or "FDC." Many of these chips are made by Western Digital, and may be identified by the prefix "WD."

In the IBM PCs, the Apple IIs, and some other microcomputers, the control circuits are mounted on a disk-drive interface card. This simplifies trouble-shooting considerably. You can interchange a suspect interface card for a card that is known to be good. If the problem disappears, you know you have a problem on the first card. It may not be cost-effective to repair a bad adapter card. For example, Jameco Electronics sells a replacement floppy disk adapter card for the IBM PCs and clones for about $35.00.

Most computers can handle more than one floppy disk drive. This means that you may have a "spare" interface circuit already installed in the computer. Let's say that you have two drives, and Drive A is faulty. Simply interchange the cables for Drive A and Drive B. Let's say that Drive A begins to work correctly, now that it is driven by the circuits used by Drive B. We'll also say that Drive B now begins to show the trouble symptoms. This tells you that the circuits which normally operate Drive A are faulty, and the Drive A mechanism is probably all right.

The floppy disk control circuits in your computer may not be mounted on a removable card. In this case, you will not be able to take a "shortcut" and substitute the whole interface circuit. Check each of the inputs and outputs around the FDC chip. We discussed these inputs and outputs in the first part of this chapter. They are illustrated in Fig. 10-11. If you want to go much farther, you will have to find an accurate schematic diagram for the unit.

A few computers use "intelligent" disk drives. A drive of this type has an on-board microprocessor, along with the supporting RAMs, ROMs, etc. This arrangement allows the main computer to spend less time supervising the disk drives. If you have a problem with an intelligent drive, you may troubleshoot the microprocessor, using the instructions given in Chapter 9.

Recovering Data from a Damaged Disk

It may be possible to recover data from a damaged floppy disk, depending on the exact nature of the damage. If the disk has been frozen or overheated, allow it to return slowly to room temperature before you attempt to read it. If the disk can be read on one disk drive but not on other drives, you may have an "interchange problem" (see Section 10.1.4).

Sometimes, a floppy disk will simply wear out. The layer of oxide on the surface of the disk may become too thin to produce a strong magnetic field. As a result, the output from the Read/Write heads will be marginal. You may be able to read the disk one day, and not the next. A disk that is wearing out will usually, as a warning, begin to give you intermittent errors. In this case, copy as many files as possible onto another disk. You may have to make several attempts.

If you scratch the surface of the floppy disk, you may be able to read most of the rest of the disk. Some disk operating systems can identify bad sectors on a disk and take them out of use. As long as the scratch appears in a noncritical part of the disk, you should be able to access the rest of the disk.

What if you erase a file by mistake? You may be able to recover the file if you have a disk-fixer utility program. When DOS "erases" a file, it does not eliminate all of the recorded "1s" and "0s" that made up that file. Instead, it alters the directory on the floppy disk. The "erased" file used one or more "sectors" of memory. When "erasing" a file, the DOS simply marks these sectors as available for use. With the disk-fixer program, you can find the "erased" sectors and reclaim them.

There is one caution here. Once the DOS marks the sectors as available, it may use those sectors to store parts of other files. The new files may overwrite some of the sectors to the old file. If you erase a file by mistake, set the disk aside immediately, and don't use it for any other purpose until you have recovered the lost file.

The most serious problem occurs when you lose one of the "housekeeping" files on a floppy disk—the directory or the file allocation table (FAT). When one of these files is damaged, the rest of the disk may be unreadable. You can sometimes reconstruct the housekeeping files, but this can be a big job. You will need a disk fixer program, and you must also have some very detailed information about the way that the information has been stored on the disk. In the first part of the chapter, we explained how a typical track was arranged. The directory and file allocation table have similar structures. You will have to reconstruct the missing housekeeping file, bit by bit. If you are persistent enough, it can be done.

In Chapter 11, we'll discuss the recovery procedures used on a hard disk drive. The procedures are very similar for a floppy disk drive.

Chapter Review

By now, you should understand the important mechanisms and circuits in a floppy disk drive. We have explained how the Read/Write head records data on a magnetic disk. We also described the signals around the key part of the control circuit—the FDC chip. You should have a general understanding of the steps in the alignment process. With some specific information and a bit of help, you should be able to perform a disk drive alignment. The last part of the chapter covered a number of common problems, and suggested some solutions for each. Using these instructions, you should be able to localize a problem to a particular section of the drive, and then locate the faulty part.

Review Questions

1. A customer brings in a computer and the floppy disk drive does not work. You test for signals on the adapter card and discover that several of the ICs seem to be dead. How could this happen?

2. A disk drive is giving you intermittent errors, and it seems to make a strange noise each time the drive motor is turned on. What is happening?

3. You are not getting a signal on the "index" line. Can you suggest a cause?

4. The "Write-Protect" line is "true" even though the Write-Protect switch is not activated. What is happening?

5. A floppy disk drive does not show any signs of activity. The LED on the front of the drive does not light, and you do not hear the drive motor. Where do you start?

6. You determine that a floppy disk drive needs a new head. What is the next step?

7. On a single-sided drive, the door mechanism is loose. Why could this be a problem?

8. You accidentally erase an important file. Will you be able to recover it? Did you make a backup?

11

Hard Disk Drives

Introduction and Objectives

In this chapter, we will take a look at the hard disk drive, also called the "Winchester" drive, "nonremovable" disk, and "fixed" disk. A hard disk manages to support a huge amount of memory in a very small space. As you might suspect, this is not a simple matter, so a hard disk drive is a fairly complicated piece of equipment. The mechanical parts of the drive are important, of course, but the controlling software is just as important. The disk operating system (DOS) handles all of the "housekeeping" details.

For the technician, the rules are a bit different when working on hard disks. The mechanical parts of the hard disk are sealed inside a metal case. For practical reasons, you can't open this sealed case, so you can't work on the mechanical parts. We will begin by looking at the physical construction of the hard disk drive. We will also take a quick look at the control circuitry. In many ways, the control circuits for a hard drive are similar to the circuits for a floppy disk drive, so we will concentrate on the differences between the two.

Many hard disk drives are interfaced to the computer via a high-speed "SCSI" bus. We will explain how this bus operates. Then, we will discuss the servicing problems you are likely to encounter with hard disk drives. As we said, your servicing options are limited. We will discuss the steps you can take yourself,

and the procedures which must be done by the manufacturer.

Backup procedures are very important whenever you depend on a hard disk drive. Therefore, we will examine the different combinations of hardware and software you can use to handle your backing-up chores.

When a hard disk fails, you often cannot read a particular file. If the problem is very serious, you may not be able to retrieve anything on the hard disk. Fortunately, you can often recover from this type of problem. So, we will take a quick look at the procedures required to recover from several types of disk errors. Also, when you try to recover data from a damaged disk, you will need to know how the "directory" of the disk is organized. We will take a quick look at the arrangement of a typical directory.

At the end of the chapter, we have listed some common problem symptoms and suggested some solutions.

Inside a Hard Disk Drive

Let's start by looking at the mechanical parts of a hard disk drive (Fig. 11-1). The disk platter itself is made of aluminum, and is coated with a very thin layer of nickel-cobalt or ferromagnetic material. This ferromagnetic material can store signals recorded by a Read/Write

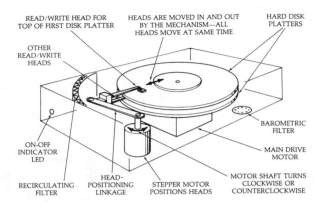

Fig. 11-1. Illustration of a hard disk drive.

head. On the larger capacity drives, several of these platters are stacked together. A separate head is provided for each side of each disk. For example, a drive with two disks would have four separate Read/Write heads.

The Read/Write heads are moved by a stepper motor, which drives a mechanical linkage. All of the Read/Write heads move at the same time, but only one of the heads is activated at a time. Some drives use a faster "voice coil" device instead of the mechanical linkage. This is the same principle as the "solenoid" arrangement we described in Chapter 7.

The stack of disks is turned at 3600 rpm by a drive motor. (Note that this is twelve times faster than the 300-rpm speed of a floppy disk.) The spindle braking/locking mechanism acts as a brake to slow the disks when the drive is switched off. Once the disks stop, the spindle lock holds them in place.

A typical hard disk might hold 20- to 40-million bytes of information. Each of these bytes requires 8 digital bits. Much of the space on the disk is used for "housekeeping" functions. On a drive that can store 20 megabytes of user data, the disk must be able to handle over 200 million digital "1s" and "0s." To fit this much information on a small disk, each of the digital storage spaces must be very small. The recorded tracks must be very close together, and the disk itself must be very rigid. The motor bearings must hold the disk assembly very firmly, with no sign of free play. Most drives may be operated with the disk turning either horizontally or vertically.

When the drive is operating, the Read/Write head never touches the surface of the disk. Instead, the head "flies" above the disk on a very thin layer of air. This layer of air keeps the head 10 to 50 microinches (0.00001 to 0.00005 inch) above the surface of the disk.

The drive mechanism is enclosed in an air-tight metal case, as hard disk drives can be damaged by the smallest particle of dust. The case is sealed to keep these dust particles out of the drive. A "recirculating filter" is provided inside the case. As the disks turn, they create an air flow inside the case. This air is routed through the recirculating filter, which then catches any dust particles that may be present. The recirculating filter typically catches any particles bigger than 0.3 micron (10 microinches or 0.00001 inch).

A hard disk drive also has an opening through the case, which is protected by a "barometric filter." This opening provides a way of equalizing the air pressures inside and outside of the case. Consider what would happen if the case was completely sealed, and you took the drive up in an airplane. The case would tend to expand, since the air pressure outside the case would decrease but the pressure inside the case would be the same. The barometric filter allows a small amount of air to leak into or out of the case, so the pressures can equalize.

The disk itself is arranged into a system of "tracks" and "sectors" similar to the arrangement on a floppy disk. On a hard disk, however, the tracks are much closer together. As a result, the hard disk can hold much more data. A hard disk might have 300 tracks or more. The sectors used on hard disk systems also tend to be larger than those on floppy disks. Hard disks usually have 256 bytes or 512 bytes per sector. The format of a track is similar to the format we described for a floppy disk and illustrated in Fig. 10-10. Track 000 usually holds the "housekeeping" files, which tell the computer where to find the various files and sectors. As on the floppy disk, these are called the *directory* and the *file allocation table* (FAT). Before the drive can read a particular sector, it must first refer to the directory and the FAT. This means the drive is constantly using Track 000.

Since many hard disk drives have more than one disk platter, a special system is used to address a particular sector. This is illustrated in Fig. 11-2. Let's start by accessing a particular track, say Track 50. One track, labeled Track 50, is located on top of the first platter, and another is located on the underside of the platter. A third Track 50 is located on the top of the second platter, with still another Track 50 found on the underside of that platter. We could group all of these "Track 50" tracks together and say that they formed a "cylinder." Thus, "Cylinder 50" includes any "Track 50" that is included on any of the platters.

Now let's say we wanted to read the "Track 50" that is written on the top of the first platter. The Read/Write head that would be used for this job would

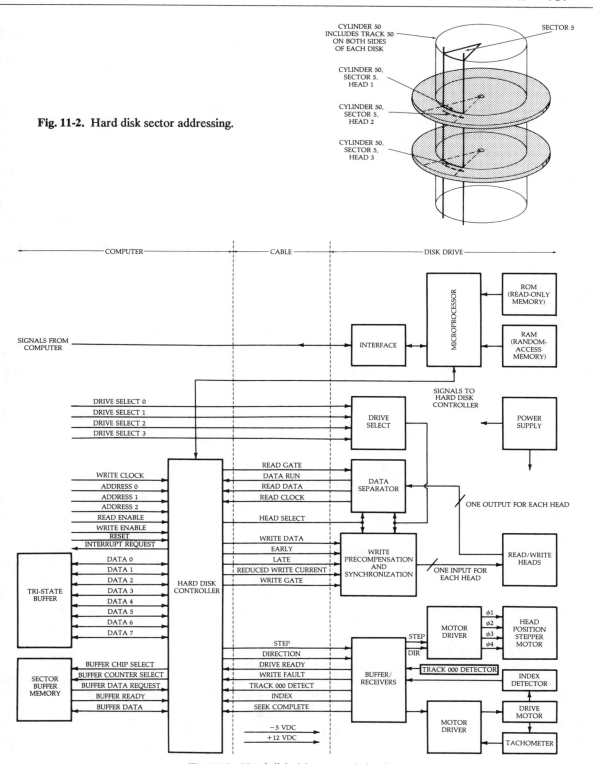

Fig. 11-2. Hard disk sector addressing.

Fig. 11-3. Hard disk drive control circuits.

be "Head 1." If we wanted to read "Sector 5" on that track, the complete address would be "Cylinder 50, Head 1, Sector 5."

The whole surface of each disk is not used for memory storage. Some of the inner tracks of the disk are left "blank," and are not coated with oxide material. The Read/Write heads may be "parked" over these blank tracks when the drive is not in use.

The control circuits for the hard drive are very similar to the circuits for the floppy drive that were described in Chapter 10. Of course, the hard drive operates at much higher speeds and can hold much more data. The large part of the interfacing work is handled by a hard disk controller IC that is similar to the floppy disk controller described earlier. Fig. 11-3 shows the signals entering and leaving this hard disk controller. Many of these signals are similar to signals you would find in a floppy disk drive controller, but some of them are different. We will focus on the differences.

In the illustration of Fig. 11-3, the system uses four different "drive select" lines. The computer uses a combination of "highs" and "lows" on these lines to turn on a particular disk drive. With four lines, the computer can specify any one of 16 disk drives. The system also uses three "address" lines (A0, A1, and A2). These are used to select the "registers" in the controller IC. By changing the contents of the registers, the computer can control the action of the IC.

The *Reset* line is connected to the master reset system in the main computer. When the controller IC receives the "Reset" signal, it initializes all of its internal registers. The controller IC can use the *Interrupt Request* line to break into the software routine executing on the main computer. Some hard disks generate an interrupt whenever the drive is ready to read or write a character.

The "Read Enable" and "Write Enable" lines are "true" when the computer wants to read from or write to the controller. The controller IC is also connected to eight of the computer's data lines. When the computer wants to write something on the disk, it places the data on these eight lines. The controller IC then converts this parallel data to a serial format that can be written by the Read/Write head.

Hard disk drives can handle very large amounts of information, and the transfer speeds are much higher than for floppy disk drives. Because of this, when the drive is reading, it may not return the data directly to the main data lines on the computer. Instead, it may write to a special memory area called a *Sector Buffer* (Fig. 11-3). The buffer is large enough to store at least one whole sector of data. Using this arrangement, the disk drive can write to the buffer at a very high speed.

The main computer can then access this information when it is needed. During a writing operation, the disk drive may also read from this buffer area as well. This "sector buffer" space may be part of a *Direct Memory Access* (DMA) arrangement.

The *Buffer Chip Select* line allows the controller IC to determine which sector buffer IC will be used. The *Buffer Counter Reset* is pulsed whenever the controller IC begins working with a new buffer IC. The *Buffer Data Request* line is "true" when the main computer is accessing the buffer. This keeps the disk drive from writing to the buffer during this time. The *Buffer Ready* line informs the controller that the buffer is empty and ready to receive data. Data move into and out of the buffer along the buffer data line.

Now let's look at the signals which run between the controller IC and the disk drive itself. Again, some of these signals will be familiar from our discussion of the floppy disk drive.

The *Read Gate* line is held "true" when the drive is reading from the disk. The *Data Run* line is used to indicate that the drive has detected a string of "1s" or "0s." This is part of the system used to search for address marks. The *Read Data* line carries the data from the Read/Write head back to the controller IC. The *Read Clock* line carries a reference clock signal, which is derived from the data being read.

The *Head Select* lines determine which of the Read/Write heads is active. When the drive is writing, the *Write Data* line carries the incoming data to the Write circuits. The *Early* and *Late* lines carry "precompensation" signals. When the drive is using the inner tracks of the disk where the bits are packed more closely together, the bits tend to "spread" a bit as they are written. These two lines give the controller a way of compensating for this. On these inner tracks, the current used by the Read/Write heads during writing may be reduced. This occurs when the *Reduced Write Current* line is "true." The *Write Gate* line is held "true" while the head is writing a sector of data onto the disk.

Sometimes the Read Data and Write Data lines may be identified by titles such as "+read data," "−read data," "+write data," and "−write data." This type of interface uses a "differential" arrangement to handle the Read Data and Write Data functions. The signal on the "+write data" line is referenced to the "−write data" line, rather than to ground. This gives the system some extra immunity to electronic "noise." If some noise does get into the system it tends to affect both the "+write data" and the "−write data" lines equally. The voltage difference between the two lines remains the same, so the noise has no effect.

The Read/Write heads are moved from one track to another by a stepper motor. The *Direction* line prepares the stepper motor to move in one direction or the other, depending on whether the line is "true" or "false." Once the direction has been set, pulses on the *Step* line tell the motor how far to move the heads. The *Track 000* line goes "high" when the heads are positioned over the outermost track on each disk. When the heads have moved to the assigned track and stopped, the *Seek Complete* line becomes "true."

The *Drive Ready* line tells the controller IC that the drive is up to speed and is ready to read or write. The *Write Fault* line is held "true" when the drive detects a problem with the writing action. The *Index* line is pulsed once each time the disks turn. The detector circuits see the beginning of a new sector. (Most hard disks use a "hard sector" arrangement.) The beginning of each sector may be marked by a signal from a magnet on the disk's hub. On another type of hard disk, each new sector is marked by a hole drilled through the platter.

In the remainder of the block diagram of Fig. 11-3, we have shown the other important parts of the disk-drive control circuits. The *Data Separator* extracts the "read clock" signal from the data stream, and is also used to condition the signals coming from the Read/Write heads. The Separator takes the "analog" signals from the heads, and produces a clean train of "digital" pulses for the main computer. The *Motor Drive* circuits generate signals for the head-positioning stepper motor and the main drive motor. The input for the stepper motor consists of four parallel signals ($\phi1$, $\phi2$, $\phi3$, and $\phi4$).

Sometimes the operation of the disk drive will be supervised by an on-board computer. The microprocessor chip will be supported by some ROMs, which hold a permanent set of instructions. One or more RAMs may provide space for temporary memory. The communication with the computer may be handled by one or more interfacing chips similar to the *Versatile Interface Adapter* (VIA) described in Chapter 12.

The tracks and sectors on a hard disk are identified during the "formatting" process. Most hard disks use a "hard sector" arrangement. The beginning of each sector is marked by a small hole or other physical indicator on the disk. On IBM-type hard disks, the formatting process is a two-step process. The first step, *physical* formatting, usually takes place at the factory. Next, the *logical* formatting is handled by the DOS "FORMAT" command. But, FORMAT cannot perform the physical formatting. The program that handles this is available on the IBM Advanced Diagnostics disk, which retails for about $175 from

IBM. Many of the other hard disks are supplied with formatting programs which can handle the whole process in one step.

The Bernoulli Drive

A "Bernoulli" drive has some characteristics in common with a traditional hard disk drive, but it uses a different operating principle. This principle is illustrated in Fig. 11-4. Fig. 11-4A shows the drive at rest. The data are stored on a flexible disk. When the drive is turned off, this disk sags (hangs downward), away from the Read/Write head. A fixed plate is mounted above the flexible disk. The Read/Write head can move from track to track along a slot in the fixed plate.

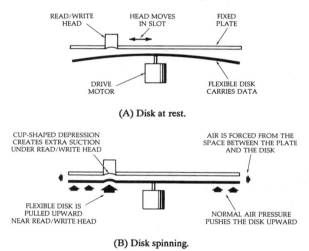

(A) Disk at rest.

(B) Disk spinning.

Fig. 11-4. A "Bernoulli" drive.

Fig. 11-4B illustrates the drive in action. When the drive is turned on, the disk begins to spin. Because of Bernoulli's principle, any air in the space between the flexible disk and the fixed plate is forced outward. As a result, the air pressure drops in the space between the flexible disk and the fixed plate. The back of the flexible disk is still exposed to normal air pressure. The flexible disk is lifted upward, and the surface of the disk moves close to the Read/Write head. The head itself includes a cup-shaped depression, and this creates an extra suction action. This pulls up the section of the flexible disk which is directly under the head. The clearance between the head and the flexible disk is about 10 microns (0.00001 inch). A double-sided drive has two flexible disks. When the drive is turned on, one disk will move upward, toward the upper head, and the other disk will move downward. The flexible disks are mounted in a removable cartridge. The operator can exchange these cartridges, much as he or she would change floppy disks.

The control circuits on a Bernoulli drive are similar to the controls in a hard drive. The flexible disk is marked with some special "servo tones." The drive can read these signals and determine how fast the flexible disk is turning. This is used as part of a "feedback" scheme to control the speed of the drive motor.

This type of disk drive has some "fail safe" features which rule out a "head crash." When the drive is turned off, the flexible disk automatically moves away from the Read/Write head. If a bit of dirt does get between the disk and the head, the air flow moves the dirt out of the way, and the disk is flexible enough to cooperate.

The manufacturer recommends that you clean this type of drive about once a month. A cleaning cartridge is available to handle this job. A Bernoulli drive will include a filter, and this should be replaced about twice a year.

The SCSI Parallel Port

Some hard-disk drives are interfaced to the main computer via a high-speed "SCSI" parallel port. The term "SCSI" is pronounced "scuzzy" and it is an abbreviation for "Small Computer System Interface." This type of interface can handle data at very high speeds—up to 4 megabytes per second. The bus usually operates in an "asynchronous" mode, meaning that the various SCSI devices are not synchronized by a clock signal.

The SCSI system is designed around a "bus" structure. Each of the wires of this bus runs to each of the SCSI devices. Eight of the wires carry 8-bit data signals in parallel. The other lines carry control signals, power-supply voltages, and ground.

Several SCSI devices may be "daisy-chained" together. The bus system includes an *arbitration* procedure to decide which device uses the SCSI bus first. Each device may operate as an *initiator*, a *target*, or both. We will assume that the computer is operating as the *initiator*, and the hard disk drive is the *target*.

The SCSI system is so efficient and adaptable because it depends heavily on software control. During a data transfer, the bus passes through eight different phases of operation:

bus free phase
arbitration phase
selection phase
reselection phase
command phase
data phase
status phase
message phase

During the arbitration phase, the various SCSI devices compete for access to the bus. The winner is selected during the selection phase. "Reselection" gives the computer and disk drive a chance to resume an earlier operation which was interrupted. Command signals are sent down the SCSI data lines during the command phase. The actual data bits are sent next, during the data phase. Then, the disk drive reports its status to the computer during the status phase. The message phase may be used to send information in either direction along the bus.

At present, the SCSI bus is most often used for hard disk drives, but it may also be used to interface to printers and other devices. Fig. 11-5 illustrates two types of SCSI connectors you may encounter. The 50-pin connector shown in Fig. 11-5A is standard. This type of connector may use two different types of pin-outs. Table 11-1 shows the pin-out used when just one wire is dedicated to each of the SCSI data signals.

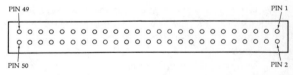

(A) Standard 50-pin connector.

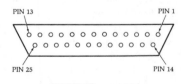

(B) DB-25 connector.

Fig. 11-5. SCSI connectors.

Another arrangement is used when each data signal is carried on two lines in a "differential" scheme. This differential system also uses the 50-pin connector shown in Fig. 11-5A. On this interface, the data signal "DB1" is actually carried on two separate lines: +DB1 and −DB1. The circuitry measures the voltage difference between these two lines to determine the

Table 11-1. SCSI Port—Single-ended
50-Pin Pin-out Assignments

Pin Number	Signal Name
2	−DB0
4	−DB1
6	−DB2
8	−DB3
10	−DB4
12	−DB5
14	−DB6
16	−DB7
18	−DBP
20	GROUND
22	GROUND
24	GROUND
26	TERMPWR
28	GROUND
30	GROUND
32	−ATN
34	GROUND
36	−BSY
38	−ACK
40	−RST
42	−MSG
44	−SEL
46	−C/D
48	−REQ
50	−I/O

Table 11-2. SCSI Port—Differential
50-Pin Pin-out Assignments

Pin Number	Signal Name
1	SHIELD/ GROUND
2	GROUND
3	+DB0
4	−DB0
5	+DB1
6	−DB1
7	+DB2
8	−DB2
9	+DB3
10	−DB3
11	+DB4
12	−DB4
13	+DB5
14	−DB5
15	+DB6
16	−DB6
17	+DB7
18	−DB7
19	+DBP
20	−DBP
21	DIFFSENS
22	GROUND
23	GROUND
24	GROUND
25	TERMPWR
26	TERMPWR
27	GROUND
28	GROUND
29	+ATN
30	−ATN
31	GROUND
32	GROUND
33	+BSY
34	−BSY
35	+ACK
36	−ACK
37	+RST
38	−RST
39	+MSG
40	−MSG
41	+SEL
42	−SEL
43	+C/D
44	−C/D
45	+REQ
46	−REQ
47	+I/O
48	−I/O
49	GROUND
50	GROUND

state of signal "DB1." This differential scheme makes the SCSI bus more resistant to noise. For example, when noise affects the +DB1 line, it also affects the −DB1 line in the same way. The voltage difference between the lines remains the same, so the noise has no effect. Table 11-2 shows the pin-out arrangement used for the 50-pin connector with this differential arrangement.

Some computers route the SCSI signals through a 25-pin DB-25 connector, as shown in Fig. 11-5B. Table 11-3 shows the pin-out arrangement for this connector.

The BSY (busy) signal indicates that the SCSI bus is in use. SEL (select) is a signal used by the computer to select the disk drive to be used. The state of the C/D (control/data) line determines whether the data lines will carry data or control signals. "True" indicates the lines will be used for control signals. The I/O (input/output) line is used to indicate whether signals will flow from the computer to the drive, or from the drive to the computer. A "true" on this line will call for input to the computer. A signal on the MSG (message) line indicates that the bus is in the message

**Table 11-3. Single-ended DB-25
Pin-out Assignments**

Pin Number	Signal Name
1	−REQ
2	−MSG
3	−I/O
4	−RST
5	−ACK
6	−BSY
7	GROUND
8	−DB0
9	GROUND
10	−DB3
11	−DB5
12	−DB6
13	−DB7
14	GROUND
15	−C/D
16	GROUND
17	−ATN
18	GROUND
19	−SEL
20	−DBP
21	−DB1
22	−DB2
23	−DB4
24	GROUND
25	TERMPWR

phase of operations. To initiate handshaking, the disk drive sends a REQ (request) signal to the computer. The computer answers with an ACK (acknowledge) signal. When the SCSI bus enters the "attention" phase of operations, the computer holds the ATN line "true." The RST (reset) line resets the devices on the bus. Lines DB7 through DB0 constitute the data bus. These lines may carry data or commands, depending on the states of the other signal lines. An extra line, DBP, is provided to carry a *parity* bit. Some systems do not use this last line.

Inside the SCSI device, the interface circuits are usually designed around a large IC called an "SCSI controller." For more detailed information on the SCSI bus, get a copy of the original design standard from the American National Standards Institute (ANSI X3.131-1986).

Service Problems with Hard Disk Drives

Hard disk drives tend to be quite reliable, especially when you consider the huge number of bits they handle. A typical MTBF (mean time before failure) for a hard disk is 15,000 hours or more. A typical hard disk will read or write an incorrect character once in every 1,000,000,000,000 operations, so we really can't complain too much about reliability.

The most common type of problem is the Read/Write error. This happens when the drive writes some data, but cannot read it back as written. Sometimes the information has been changed—a "1" may become a "0," for example. Sometimes a bit is missing, or the drive writes an extra bit. A bit may also be "shifted" to one side, so that the data separator cannot interpret it correctly. Errors often are grouped together in a "burst."

There are several possible causes for this type of error. The oxide layer on the disk surface may include an imperfection, or may be scratched. Even when brand new, many drives have one or more bad sectors. The bad sectors are often noted on a sticker on the back of the drive. Depending on the design of the DOS, the computer may stop using the whole track on which the bad sector appears. The outermost track (Track 000) usually carries the directory and the file allocation table (FAT), so this track is usually certified to be 100% usable.

If the surface of the disk has an imperfection, this usually results in a "hard" error. This means the drive cannot read or write to a particular sector, and this error happens consistently, each time the drive tries to use the sector. A bad sector is generally not a big problem. When the drive is first formatted, the DOS can usually identify bad sectors and take them out of use. When a disk drive is new, it begins by using the outer tracks of the disk drive. Sometimes "new" bad sectors may appear as the drive fills these outer tracks and begins working toward the inner tracks.

The oxide layer at a particular point on the disk may be thin. This can cause a weak signal output when that point is read. If the output is marginal, the head may be able to read that location at one time and not at another. At first, this can produce a "soft" or "intermittent" error. As the location produces a weaker output, it can become a permanent or "hard" error. Over a period of time, the Read/Write heads also wear, and this can also cause a weaker signal. If the heads are out of alignment, and reading slightly to one side of the center of the track, the Read/Write action will be less efficient.

Because the Read/Write head operates so close to the surface of the disk, hard disk drives are very sensitive to contamination by dust and dirt. Fig. 11-6 shows why this is so. We said earlier that the head is normally about 10 to 50 microinches above the surface of the disk. A particle of cigarette smoke is much larger than this, at about 250 microinches. On this scale, a human hair is a huge object, almost 600 times larger than the gap between the head and the disk.

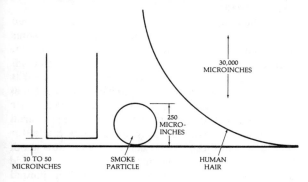

Fig. 11-6. Contaminants on a hard disk surface.

This means that almost any foreign matter in the drive will be large enough to cause problems. Fig. 11-7 shows what can happen when the Read/Write head hits a smoke particle. When the head hits the foreign object, it tends to bounce upward. Next the head falls back and "crashes" into the surface of the disk. The head is "flying" over the surface of the disk at more than 70 miles an hour, so the crash can involve a lot of force. The head can scrape off some of the oxide coating on the disk surface, making that part of the disk unreadable. The head itself may become covered with oxide, or may be damaged in other ways. It can be expensive or nearly impossible to repair these conditions, so it is usually not cost-effective to fix a drive after a head crash.

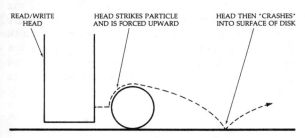

Fig. 11-7. Diagram of a head "crash."

A hard drive is particularly vulnerable to a head crash when the drive is just starting or stopping and the disks are not turning at full speed. However, serious damage can occur whenever the drive is moved while the disks are turning. Always mount a hard disk drive in

a secure place. Some printers can create quite strong vibrations. Don't mount the hard drive on the same desk or table with a printer of this type—the vibrations from the printer can damage the drive if it is operating.

The heads are less vulnerable when the disks are not operating. When the disks stop turning, the Read/Write heads settle back down to the disk surfaces. The disks are no longer moving in relation to the heads, so less energy is available to cause problems. Many drives are made with special "parking tracks." These tracks are not coated with the oxide material. When the drive is shut down, the heads can be "parked" over these blank tracks, reducing the chances for damage even more. Many drives now offer an automatic parking feature. The heads automatically park over the blank tracks when the drive is turned off. If the drive does not have this automatic feature, then you must "park" the heads manually by running a short program. The drive should be turned off, and the heads should always be parked before you move a hard disk drive!

Manufacturers often list ratings for the amount of force a drive can accept and continue working. A typical rating is 15 G's when the drive is operating, 30 G's at rest. The abbreviation "G" refers to an amount of force equal to the force of gravity. 15 G's is quite a bit of force, but you should try to avoid giving a hard disk *any* mechanical shock.

We explained earlier why the disk platters must be so rigid, and why the bearings must hold the platters firmly. Over time, the bearings may begin to loosen up. This can allow the platters to "wobble" a bit. If the problem becomes severe enough, the tracks may begin to drift away from the Read/Write heads, and the drive may begin producing intermittent errors. However, worn bearings often give you some warning before they fail completely. Sometimes, a high-pitched "whine" develops as the bearings wear.

Most external disk drives have separate power supplies. However, most internal drives depend on the microcomputer's power supply. Depending on the model of computer, adding a hard drive may overload the power supply, or make the system "marginal." If a microcomputer system is drawing more power than the power supply can provide, the +5-V output tends to drop. If this occurs in your system, install a power supply that can handle more power.

An internal drive may also block the normal flow of cooling air. This can cause parts of the system to overheat and can increase the failure rate. If you install an internal drive, you may also want to install a fan.

We have already explained why hard disk drives are so sensitive to dust and dirt. Because of this, hard disk drive mechanisms are assembled in "clean rooms." The air in a clean room is specially filtered and is kept at a positive pressure, so dust will tend to drift out of the room and not in. All of the workers are vacuumed off before they are allowed to enter the room.

You really cannot work on a hard disk drive unless you have access to one of these clean rooms. The air around us contains millions of micron-sized dust particles. Unfortunately, there is no practical way of filtering the air in your workshop. When a hard disk drive develops a mechanical problem, the drive must be returned to the manufacturer. You won't be able to work on any of the parts contained inside the sealed case of the disk drive. This means you will not be able to do many of the tests and alignments that you could do on a floppy disk drive. For example, if you suspect a drive has experienced a "head crash," you won't be able to look at the head and disk directly. When a problem occurs inside the sealed case, you must depend on the manufacturer to repair your unit quickly, and at a reasonable price. This should be an important consideration when purchasing a hard disk. (Remember that when a manufacturer repairs a hard disk, the data on the disk is usually lost.)

There are many parts of the hard disk drive that you can work with, however. The control circuits on the drive are mounted outside of the sealed case. You can also check the signals flowing between the hard drive and the computer. Even if the problem is located inside the sealed case, you can usually localize the problem. For example, let's say that the heads in a particular drive have become worn and are producing a low output. You won't be able to inspect the heads visually. However, you can check the outputs from the heads with an oscilloscope. The results of these tests should tell you whether the heads are working correctly. You cannot see whether the heads are positioned over Track 000, but you can check the signal from the Track 000 detector switch.

On the IBM PCs and some other computers, the control circuits for the hard disk are mounted on a removable adapter card. This is handy for trouble-shooting, because it is possible to substitute a suspect card for a card which is known to be working. This can eliminate a large part of the circuitry in one step. In addition, most controller cards can handle two or more disk drives. This makes it possible to "swap" cables between the driver circuits for the first drive and the second, and see if the problem symptoms disappear.

Some hard disk drives have some built-in diagnostic capability. For example, the Shugart 706 drive has an LED which may be used to indicate certain problems. For example, if the LED blinks 3 times, it indicates that "spindle failed to start." Special jumpers must be installed on the circuit board to enable this LED. To use these special diagnostic features, you must have the service manual for the drive you are working with.

The control circuits can often run some routines which may be helpful in servicing. For example, some drives automatically move to Track 000 and calibrate themselves each time they are turned on. This means the drive always knows the exact location of Track 000. On start-up, some drives automatically move the heads in and out a few times. This routine is designed to warm up the lubricating grease on the head actuator arm. Also, other provisions may have been made for servicing, and these can be helpful if you know about them. For example, a servicing jumper may be installed in the circuitry for the Shugart 706 drive. This jumper enables a special "exercise" routine. During this routine, the Read/Write head will randomly seek different tracks, thus covering the entire surface of the disk. To find out about these service routines, you will have to have the manual for your particular kind of equipment.

Most "disk fixer" utilities will work on either floppy or hard disk drives. Many of the diagnostics packages include tests for both hard drives and floppy disk drives. You will probably need an "exerciser" program written specifically for your hard drive, however.

When a file or sector on the disk is damaged, you may be able to save the information it contains. We cover this in some detail later in this chapter, in the section on "Recovering Data from a Hard Disk."

Before working with a hard disk drive, try to save as many of the files on the disk as possible. When you remove the disk drive and run tests, you can easily erase some of the files on the disk. Also, you may want to reformat the hard disk. You can sometimes save a disk that is not working correctly by just reformatting. (Remember, however, that all data will be lost when you reformat.)

Backup Procedures

If you really depend on a hard disk drive, it is very important to make backup copies of all of the important data on the disk. We don't say this because hard disk drives are especially unreliable—the service record for most hard disk drives is fairly good. The problem is that users tend to become very dependent on their hard disk drives. If a hard drive is used on a business system, the business may "grow around" the hard disk. You do not realize how important the hard disk has become until it suddenly stops working. You can defend yourself against potential problems by maintaining a regular system of backups. At best, backing up is boring work, and, at worst, it can be very time-consuming. It's the type of job that is very easy to overlook.

You can use several combinations of hardware and software to handle this job. Some methods are quick and efficient, but require more of your time and effort. The choice depends on your particular situation. How important is your computer data? If you spend most of your computing time playing "Space Invaders," then backing up the hard disk is not a high priority. On the other hand, if you use the computer in your business, you should be very serious about backing up the disk. How much information do you work with, and how quickly do you change it? If you work with just a few small files and you do not change them frequently, you may be able to use one of the "low cost/labor intensive" options. But what if you are handling large amounts of data, and make frequent changes? You will probably choose a back-up option that is quick and convenient, even if the equipment is more expensive.

The least expensive way of backing up a hard disk is to copy the disk contents onto floppy disks. If you have a hard disk drive, you probably already have some type of back-up software. Sometimes the software is part of the DOS, and sometimes it is provided with the disk drive.

MS-DOS and PC-DOS provide several programs which may be used as part of a back-up scheme. You can use the "COPY" routine to copy individual files. This solution may work if you do not change large amounts of data in each work session. If you are copying program files or other files which must be letter perfect, you can use the "verify" option (/V). This tells the computer to check each section of the copy before it moves on. "Verify" makes the copy much more reliable, but it also takes twice as long to use. Later versions of MS-DOS include the program "XCOPY," which is faster and more convenient to use.

The designers of MS-DOS intended for you to use the programs, "BACKUP" and "RESTORE," to back up the hard disk. "BACKUP" copies the files you specify onto floppy disks, but it uses a different format than "COPY." The files created by "COPY" can be read directly by the DOS. The files created by "BACKUP" are different, and can only be read by the corresponding program, "RESTORE." At the start of the process, "BACKUP" copies as much of the first file

as possible to the first floppy disk. If the program is too big to fit on the first disk, "BACKUP" puts the rest of the file on the next floppy disk. This process continues until all of the selected files have been copied. If the hard disk fails, and you ever have to depend on the back-up copies, you will use the program, "RESTORE." This program takes the selected files, converts them back into a form that can be read by DOS, and places them back onto the hard disk. The combination of "BACKUP" and "RESTORE" is effective, if you do not have to copy too many files. However, if you have to copy all of the contents of a 20-megabyte hard disk, it can take an hour or more. You can also run into problems if you do not have enough formatted floppy disks on hand. To format more disks, you must abandon your "back up in progress."

Faster back-up programs are available. One of the best is "Fast Back" from Fifth Generation Systems. Using "Fast Back," you should be able to back up a 20-Meg hard disk in about 20 minutes, using unformatted floppy disks. This program also uses some data-compression schemes, so the back-up copy requires fewer floppy disks.

No matter which back-up program you use, it is very time-consuming to copy all of the contents of a hard disk. This means you will probably use a system of "master backups" and "incremental updates." Fig. 11-8 illustrates this idea. Once a week (or month), you make a "master" backup of all of the contents of the hard disk. Every day, as you make changes to some of the files, you make fresher backups of just those files. Then, if you ever have to depend on your back-up disks, you start by restoring your "master" backup. Next, you restore all of the files that were changed since the "master" backup. When you are finished, you will have brought the hard disk up to date.

The BACKUP program offers you two ways of specifying which files will be included in these incremental backups. For example, if you add the switch, "/D", at the end of the BACKUP command, the DOS will save copies of all files that were changed after a certain date. If you specify the date on which you made the master backup, the BACKUP program will save all files altered after that date.

You can also use the "/M" switch. This will save all files marked by the DOS as "modified" during the current work session. If you use "/M", be sure to also use the "append" switch, "/A". When you use "append," the DOS constructs a long string of backups, with the most recent files at the end. Within the string, there may be several versions of a particular file. If you ever have to reconstruct this string of files, the DOS may overwrite a particular file several times. This does

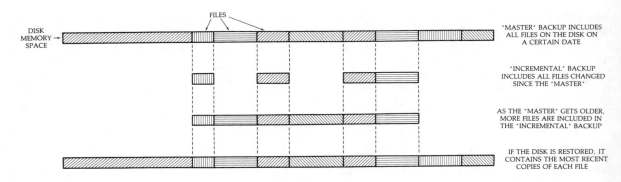

Fig. 11-8. Master and incremental backups.

not matter to you, as long as the most up-to-date version of the file is written last. This is the version which will appear on the hard disk.

You can save back-up copies on media other than floppy disks. For example, units are available which use magnetic tape to store back-up copies. A tape unit can back up a large hard disk in one pass, without attention from the operator. Some tape units use tape cassettes, similar to audio tape cassettes. You can also find back-up units which record on video cassettes. A single video cassette tape can hold 50 to 150 megabytes of data.

As the prices of hard disks drop, there is another option which is becoming cost-effective—backup to a second hard disk! You can make backups from one hard drive to the other very quickly. The odds are very slim that both hard disk drives will fail at the same time.

Recovering Data from a Hard Disk

One dark day, you turn on the computer and the monitor says "Disk Drive Error." You get a sinking feeling as you realize that you can't read *any* of your megabytes of hard-won data. We hope this day never arrives for you, but if it does, you should be prepared.

When a hard disk fails, your course of action depends on the details of the problem. The simplest problems occur when a part of a file is bad. For example, a sector may be damaged, so that the DOS cannot read or write that sector. In other cases, the DOS may be able to read a sector, but the sector contains incorrect information. There are many possible causes for these errors. The drive itself may not be working correctly, as we explained earlier. This could be caused by a flaw in the disk surface, by weak output

from the Read/Write heads, or by a number of other causes.

One problem may lead to other problems. For example, if the drive begins using a faulty copy of the DOS or a program file, it can write incorrect data in many places and "corrupt" some of your files. Fortunately, you can often recover from these problems—at least partially. Many utility programs are available to deal with different hard disk problems. Of course, you must have the correct program on hand when trouble arrives.

Some programs require very little input from the user. To use a program of this type, you simply start the program, and hope that it recovers your data. Other utilities require more of a "hands on" approach. Either way, the process is not foolproof—you often end up losing at least one sector of data. This can amount to 512 bytes or more, but it is much better than losing a whole file.

We will try to give a quick overview of the possible problems and solutions, but to actually perform the recovery operations, you may need some more detailed information. To use one of the "hands on" utilities, you will need to know exactly how your DOS uses the space on the disk. You should have a reference which lists the "housekeeping" characters at the start and finish of each sector. To recover from some problems, you may also have to know how the directory and FAT sectors are arranged. For background information, it will be very helpful to have a book that describes recovery procedures for your particular DOS. For MS-DOS computers, including the IBM PCs, a good book is "Managing Your Hard Disk" by Don Berliner (published by Que Corp.).

There is one other option that we should mention here. Some repair services will recover the data on a hard disk for you. A few operations specialize in just this function. This service is available in most large cities—check the Yellow Pages of your telephone book.

In this section, we will describe nine different problems. The prescription is different for each:

- Bad data in a readable file sector
- Sectors cut off from file by "End Of File" character
- Unreadable file sector
- Sectors lost from the directory
- Bad master boot record or DOS boot record
- Bad root directory
- Recovering an erased file
- Recovering an accidentally formatted disk
- Recovering an erased directory

For this explanation to make sense, we will have to explain a bit more about the "housekeeping" files contained on the disk. Fig. 11-9 is a simplified diagram showing how Track 000 might be arranged. (The details may vary, depending on the type of DOS used.) The first sector on Track 000 contains the "Master Boot Record." When the drive is first turned on, it reads this sector first. The Master Boot Record includes enough information to get the system started. Next, the drive reads the "DOS Boot Record" (or "Disk Partition Table"). The disk operating system is recorded on another part of Track 000, and this DOS Boot Record tells the system where to find the first sector of the DOS files. In the third step, the drive reads in the DOS files. From this point on, the system is controlled by the DOS.

When the drive wants to retrieve a certain file, it searches for the file name in the "Root Directory." The Root Directory refers the drive to an entry in the "File Allocation Table," or "FAT." The FAT then tells the drive which sectors on the disk hold the desired file. The FAT is so important that two copies are recorded on the disk. As you can see, during normal Read/Write operations, the drive must constantly refer to Track 000.

When the DOS opens a file, it does not assign that file just one sector. Usually, the smallest memory area the controller can specify is a "cluster" consisting of several sectors. If the file is too large to fit in the first cluster, the DOS assigns a second cluster and makes another notation in the FAT. On the disk surface, this second cluster may not be anywhere near the first. To read a complete file, the heads may have to jump to many different locations on the hard disk. The DOS follows a chain of instructions, beginning with the Root Directory, leading to the FAT, then to a cluster, then back to the FAT, then to another cluster, and so on.

Of course, the Read/Write action would be faster if the clusters from a given file were always located side by side. The more a hard drive is used, the more the files tend to become fragmented, and the slower the Read/Write speed tends to be. To cure this problem, you must copy everything off of the hard disk, reformat the hard disk, and then reload the disk contents.

On many drives, even sectors with consecutive sector numbers are not actually located side by side. For example, let's say that the control circuits identify the sectors on a certain track as Sector 1, Sector 2, etc. From a "logical" point of view, Sector 2 follows directly after Sector 1. However, if you were to look at the physical locations of those sectors on the disk, this might not be true. As the sectors are actually arranged on the track, between the sectors labeled Sector 1 and Sector 2, you might find two or three other sectors. This is called "interleaving." This allows time for the control circuits to interpret the signals from one sector before they must deal with the signals from the next sector. Many hard disk drives insert two or three sectors between those sectors which the DOS thinks are located side by side.

Some problems occur only within a certain file, while the rest of the directory structure is all right. The easiest problem of this type is a damaged sector in a word-processing file. If the DOS can read the damaged sector, you can use a text editor to correct the altered characters. If the DOS cannot read the bad sector, use a utility like "RECOVER." This utility is provided as

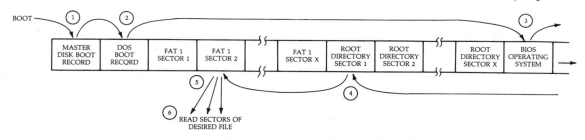

Fig. 11-9. Arrangement of Track 000.

part of the DOS on many IBM-compatible systems. "RECOVER" will read as much of the file as possible, and will mark any bad sectors as "unusable." Try to make a copy of the file before you begin working on it. This will protect you if you make a mistake during your rescue attempt. Be sure to specify a file name when you use "RECOVER," or the DOS will rearrange the whole hard disk.

If you have to change a few characters in a readable sector, you can use a byte-editing utility like the "NU" program offered by Norton Utilities. This type of program allows you to look through the file, byte by byte, and change the incorrect characters. Fig. 11-10 shows a typical screen display, which might be used by one of these programs. The program shows the exact contents of the file, listed in both hexadecimal numbers and conventional letters and numbers. To make a change, you can edit a pair of hexadecimal numbers, or can change one of the regular letters or numbers.

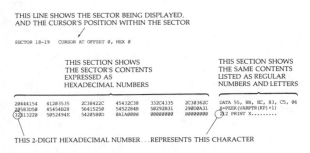

Fig. 11-10. Typical screen display for a byte-editing program.

"NU" will work on an ASCII text file or a data file. If the whole program will fit into the computer's memory, you can also use the "Debug" routine, which may be included with the DOS. It is much more difficult to repair a non-ASCII data file. In order to do this, you will have to have some detailed information on the format of the file.

When you are through working with a file, the DOS "closes" the file. Normally, the DOS inserts an "End Of File" (EOF) character at the end of your data. The character used is often "Control-Z" (decimal 26, hex 1A). If the DOS is not allowed to close a file normally, the EOF character may be written in the middle of the file. The DOS will not be able to find any "clusters" of file sectors written after the EOF character. You can use an editing program such as "NU" to solve this problem. Use the "search" feature to find the EOF character. Next, change the EOF to

another character. You can use the "Space" character (decimal 32, hex 20). The DOS should then be able to read the rest of the file.

A problem with the "housekeeping" structure may be minor or serious, depending on where the problem occurs. If the drive finds it can't read a certain sector, it may give you an error statement. If that sector is in a section of the disk which is not being used, this is a minor problem. You can mark the sector as "unusable," and the DOS will avoid that sector in the future. Normally, however, a sector should not go bad after the disk has been formatted. This may be a symptom of another problem.

Another problem can occur when sectors have been written correctly, but the directory "loses" them. The DOS utility, CHKDSK, is designed to deal with this. CHKDSK makes sure that each active sector is listed correctly in the FAT. If CHKDSK finds sectors that contain data, but are not listed in the FAT, it can give them file names and make them readable by the DOS.

The problem is much more serious if the drive can't read one of the sectors in the disk boot record, DOS boot record, or FAT. If the drive can't read one of these files, the computer may say Disk Boot Failure or Drive Not Ready. You may not be able to read anything at all from the drive. If the master boot record or DOS boot record is damaged, you can use the DOS "FDISK" utility to restore them.

If the root directory is damaged, use the "RECOVER" utility, with no file name specified. RECOVER will not save the file names, but the file data will be recovered. You will have to check each file, determine the contents, and assign a new file name. You can use programs like TYPE, DEBUG, and NU to inspect the file contents.

If you act quickly, you should be able to recover a file which has been "erased." When the DOS "erases" a file, it leaves most of the bits of the file in place. The DOS does change the first letter of the file name in the directory. The character inserted here is not a normal letter or number, and it indicates to the DOS that the file name is no longer valid. The DOS also goes to the file allocation table, and marks each of the sectors used by the file as "unused." If you continue to use the disk, the DOS will begin to overwrite these "unused" sectors, and you will begin losing the data permanently. Using the "NU" program from Norton Utilities, you can change the first character in the file name, and recreate the entries in the directory and FAT, and read the file again. Since it it is dangerous to edit the directory and FAT yourself, try one of the automated recovery programs, which are available on the market.

You face a similar situation when a disk has been accidentally formatted. Many disk operating systems do not really erase all of the files when they reformat a disk. Instead, the DOS rewrites the directory and the FAT. Again, most of the files are still in place on the disk. Without some special help, you will not be able to access them, however. A utility, like "UNFORMAT" from Mace Utilities, can recreate the directory structure for you. You will lose the file names, but the data in the files will be saved. (The formatting process does not always work this way, so check your specific version of DOS before proceeding.) If a subdirectory has been erased by mistake, the "UD" utility from Norton Utilities can recreate it.

11.1 Troubleshooting Hard Disk Drives

In this section of the book, we will list some common trouble symptoms for hard disk drives. We'll suggest some tests you can make. Also, in this discussion, we will use a system of index numbers (11.1.1, 11.2.3) to refer to specific sections of the text.

11.1.1 Problem 1

Symptom: Disk drive has intermittent Read or Write failures.

When an error occurs, the computer may display an error statement. Check the documentation, and see if the explanation of the error statement is helpful. Also, many drives have some self-diagnostic capability. The documentation for the faulty drive will tell you whether the drive has this feature.

If the drive is not mounted inside the main computer, check the connecting cable. Inspect the connectors at both ends of the cable. Check the cable itself to see if any wires have been pinched. The procedure for making these checks is described in Chapter 7 (see "Testing Cables and Connectors" subsection). Section 11.2.1 describes the signals you should find in the cable.

If the drive is mounted on a plug-in card, check the card connector. Be sure the card fits firmly in the socket and the connectors are clean and shiny.

On the IBM PC and some other computers, the hard drive is controlled by circuitry on a plug-in card. If possible, remove the suspect card and install a replacement card. If the problem disappears, you know the original card is bad.

Many controller cards can handle more than one hard disk drive. If this is the case in your situation, reverse the cable connections so the control circuitry normally used for one drive operates the other drive. If the problem disappears, you know the drive itself is all right, and the problem lies in the driver circuitry.

If the drive has a separate power supply, check the supply according to the instructions given in Chapter 16. If the supply voltage is low or if the power is very "noisy," the drive may become unreliable.

When you add an internal hard disk to a computer, it can sometimes overload the power supply. Add up the wattage ratings of the computer, the disk drive, and other components, and see if the power supply can deliver that much power. An internal hard disk drive can also cause the inside of the case to heat up. The drive itself creates some heat, and it also blocks the flow of cooling air to other components. You may want to install a fan.

A drive can become unreliable if the bearings are worn. This can allow the platters to "wobble" a bit, moving the tracks away from the Read/Write heads. If this is the case, you can often hear a high-pitched "whine" from the drive. If the bearings are bad, you must send the drive to the manufacturer for repair.

The drive may be unreliable because the Read/Write head is worn, or because the reading or writing circuits are weak. The best way of checking the efficiency of the Read/Write system is with the "Bit Shift Test" we described in Section 11.3. This will have to be done by the manufacturer or a service representative.

As a last resort, you can sometimes bring a hard disk back to health by reformatting it.

11.1.2 Problem 2

Symptom: Drive operates, but will not read.

This symptom points directly to a problem with the Read circuits, but we will check the obvious causes first. When the error occurs, the monitor may display an error statement. Check your documentation, and see if the explanation for this error statement is helpful. Also, many drives have some self-diagnostic capability. Check the documentation for the faulty drive to see if it has this capability.

If the drive is not mounted inside the main computer, check the connecting cable. Inspect the connectors at both ends of the cable. Check the cable itself to see if any wires have been pinched. See the section in Chapter 7 that describes the testing of cables and connectors. Be sure the following signals are present: "Read Gate," "Read Data," "Read Clock," and "Read Enable." Section 11.2.1 describes the signals you should find in the cable.

If the drive is mounted on a plug-in card, check the card connector. Be sure the card fits firmly in the socket and the connectors are clean and shiny.

On the IBM PC and some other computers, the hard drive is controlled by circuitry on a plug-in card. If possible, remove the suspect card and install a replacement card. If the problem disappears, you know the original card is bad.

Many controller cards can handle more than one hard disk drive. If this is the case in your situation, reverse the cable connections so the control circuitry normally used for one drive operates the other drive. If the problem disappears, you know the drive itself is all right, and the problem lies in the driver circuitry.

The problem may lie in the Read control circuits. Check Section 11.2.4

The Read/Write head may be worn, or the Read circuits may be producing a low-amplitude signal. The best way of checking the efficiency of the Read/Write system is with the "Bit Shift Test" we describe in Section 11.3. This will have to be done by the manufacturer or a service representative.

11.1.3 Problem 3

Symptom: Drive operates, but will not write.

When this error occurs, the computer may display an error statement. Look this error statement up in the documentation—it may be helpful. Also, many drives have some self-diagnostic capability. Check the documentation to see if the faulty drive has this capability.

If the drive is not mounted inside the main computer, check the cable. Inspect the connectors at both ends of the cable. Check the cable itself to see if any wires have been pinched. See the section in Chapter 7 that describes the testing of cables and connectors. Section 11.2.1 describes the signals you should find in the cable. Be sure the following signals are present: "Write Gate," "Write Data," and "Write Enable."

If the drive is mounted on a plug-in card, check the card connector. Be sure the card fits firmly in the socket and the connectors are clean and shiny.

On the IBM PC and some other computers, the hard drive is controlled by circuitry on a plug-in card. If

possible, remove the suspect card and install a replacement. If the problem disappears, you know the original card is bad.

Many controller cards can handle more than one hard disk drive. If this is the case in your situation, reverse the cable connections so the control circuitry normally used for one drive operates the other drive. If the problem disappears, you know the drive itself is all right, and the problem lies in the driver circuitry.

The problem may lie in the Write control circuits. Check Section 11.2.5.

The Read/Write head may be worn. The best way of checking the efficiency of the Read/Write system is with the "Bit Shift Test" we describe in Section 11.3. This will have to be done by the manufacturer or a service representative.

11.1.4 Problem 4

Symptom: An unusual noise is heard in the disk drive.

The spinning disk platters must be held firmly in position by a set of strong bearings. When these bearings wear, they may begin to make a high-pitched "whining" noise. The drive may also emit an unusual noise if the head is damaged, if there is a problem in the mechanism that moves the head, or if the disk has slipped loose from its clamping arrangement on the spindle. All of these mechanisms are located inside the sealed case of the drive. Since you cannot open this sealed case, you will have to send the drive to the manufacturer for repair.

11.1.5 Problem 5

Symptom: Head won't step in or out.

When the error occurs, the computer may display an error statement. Check the explanation for this error statement in the documentation—it may be helpful. Also, many drives have some self-diagnostic capability. Check the documentation for the faulty drive.

If the drive is not mounted inside the main computer, check the connecting cable. Inspect the connectors at both ends of the cable. Check the cable itself to see if any wires have been pinched. Refer to the section in Chapter 7 that discusses the testing of cables and connectors. Section 11.2.1 describes the signals which you should find in the cable. Be sure the "Step" and "Direction" signals are present.

Table 11-4. Signals in Cable to Hard Disk Drive

Signal Line	Activity
Read Gate	Should be constantly pulsing when the drive is reading.
Data Run	Should be constantly pulsing as the drive detects address marks.
Read Data	Should be constantly pulsing as the drive is reading.
Read Clock	Should be constantly pulsing as the drive is reading.
Head Select 0 and Head Select 1	The combinations of "highs" and "lows" on these lines should change as the drive uses different Read/Write heads.
Write Data	Should be constantly pulsing when the drive is writing.
Early	Should be constantly pulsing when the drive is writing on an inner track of the disk.
Late	Should be constantly pulsing when the drive is writing on an inner track of the disk.
Reduced Write Current	Should be "true" when the drive is writing on an inner track of the disk.
Write Gate	Should be constantly pulsing when the drive is writing.
Step	Should be constantly pulsing when the head is moving in or out.
Direction	Should be "high" when the head is moving in one direction, "low" when the head is moving the other way.
Drive Ready	Should normally be "true."
Write Fault	Should normally be "false."
Track 000 Detect	Should be constantly pulsing as the drive accesses the directory and FAT on Track 000.
Index	Should be constantly pulsing as the drive motor turns.
Seek Complete	Should show a pulse each time the heads arrive at a new track.
+5-V and +12-V DC	Power-supply voltages.

If the drive is mounted on a plug-in card, check the card connector. Be sure the card fits firmly in the socket and the connectors are clean and shiny.

On the IBM PC and some other computers, the hard disk drive is controlled by circuitry on a plug-in card. If possible, remove the suspect card and install a replacement card. If the problem disappears, you know the original card is bad.

Many controller cards can handle more than one hard disk drive. If this is the case in your situation, reverse the cable connections so the control circuitry normally used for one drive operates the other drive. If the problem disappears, you know the drive itself is all right, and the problem lies in the driver circuitry.

If the heads are positioned by a stepper motor, check the four signals for this motor (ϕ1, ϕ2, ϕ3, and ϕ4) among the driver circuits. Refer to the discussion in Chapter 7 pertaining to stepper motors. In Section 11.2.3, we describe a procedure for checking the stepper circuitry which lies outside the sealed case. If the heads are positioned by a "voice-coil" arrangement, check the

signals to the coil, and check the resistance through the coil. See the discussion of solenoids in Chapter 7.

If the stepper motor or voice coil is receiving the correct signals, but the heads are still not moving correctly, you probably have a mechanical problem inside the sealed case. You will have to return the drive to the manufacturer.

11.1.6 Problem 6

Symptom: Head oscillates at Track 000.

This problem can happen if the Track 000 detector system is faulty. (We described the device in the first part of this chapter.) On a hard disk drive, the Track 000 detector switch may be activated by a part of the arm that positions the heads. You can check this switch indirectly by watching the signal on the "Track 000" output. The switch itself is mounted inside the sealed case, so you will not be able to check it directly. If the switch is faulty, you will have to return the drive to the manufacturer.

In Section 11.2.6, we describe a procedure for checking the rest of the Track 000 circuitry.

11.2 Test Procedures

11.2.1 Test 1

Checking signals at the cable.

The hard disk drive is usually connected to the controller IC via one or more cables. All of the signals for the drive pass through these cables, so this is a convenient place to check the overall health of the control circuits. You must know which signal to expect on each of the wires in the cable, so refer to the manual for your particular drive. The drive must be active as you make these tests. You can activate the drive for short periods by calling for a CATALOG or DIR (directory) of the drive's contents. If you have an exerciser program, you can also use this to activate the drive.

You can use a logic probe for most of these tests, since most of the wires carry voltage levels of 0 V and +5-V DC. However, some of the wires in the cable may carry power-supply voltages that are greater than +5-V DC—be sure to avoid these wires with your probe. Check the signals at the connector at one end of the cable. You may be able to make your connections at the rear of the connector, where the pins are connected to the circuit board.

When the drive is installed in the computer, you may not have access to the ends of the cables. However, you may be able to operate the drive outside of the main computer. If so, disconnect the cables, remove the drive and place it on top of the main computer, and then reconnect the cables. Be sure to turn off the computer before you disconnect the cables or move the drive!

If a signal is present at the input end of the cable, but not at the output, one of the wires inside the cable itself may be broken. Disconnect both ends of the cable. Check for continuity through the cable wires with a VOM (set to read OHMS). Also, check the adjacent wires for shorts. Table 11-4 lists the signals you should expect to find on each line in the cable.

11.2.2 Test 2

Checking the drive select circuits.

Most hard-disk controllers can handle more than one hard disk. The controller will use a series of "Drive Select" lines to activate the different hard disks. Each hard disk will respond to a specific set of signals on these "select" lines. For example, let's say that the controller has 3 select lines, and each of these may be either high or low. This type of control arrangement can handle up to 8 different disk drives ($2^3 = 8$). One drive might respond when the 3 select lines are carrying the signals "0-0-1." Another drive might respond to the combination of "0-1-0," and so on.

The select lines will show the same signals as long as a particular drive is active. You can check them with a logic probe. You should find TTL-level signals (+5-V DC and 0 V).

11.2.3 Test 3

Checking the stepper logic and stepper motor.

The stepper logic and motor system causes the Read/Write heads to move to and from the center of the disk, so the heads are always positioned over the correct track. A small stepper motor moves the head assembly in precise increments. An arm mechanism converts the rotational motion of the motor shaft to a lateral motion of the heads. The control circuits produce the signals that drive the motor. The logic communicates with the motor by sending related signals along four separate lines ($\phi1$, $\phi2$, $\phi3$, and $\phi4$). We explained the principles of stepper motor operation in Chapter 7.

To check the stepper motor, use an Exerciser program that tells the drive to step in and out. You can then move the heads onto and away from Track 000. By watching for a signal on the "Track 000 Detect" line, you can tell if the heads are actually moving.

Next, check the lines that carry signals from the control circuits in the computer to the stepper logic circuits in the drive. The DIRECTION signal specifies whether the head will step in or out. When this line is "true," the stepper is prepared to step in one direction. When the line is "false," the drive should be prepared to step in the other direction. The STEP signal actually tells the motor when to step. When the motor receives this signal, it steps in the direction specified. Use your Exerciser software to STEP the drive both in and out, and watch for activity on the STEP and DIRECTION lines, using your logic probe. Check for the signals at the cable, as described in Section 11.2.1. If the signals are missing, look for a problem in the interface circuits at the computer's end of the cable.

If you still have not found the problem, check the stepper logic circuitry. Fig. 11-11 is a simple block diagram of these circuits. Use the Exerciser program to command the disk drive to step in and out. With an oscilloscope, watch for activity on each of the four signal lines that run to the motor ($\phi 1$, $\phi 2$, $\phi 3$, and $\phi 4$). As you step past a series of tracks, each of these lines should show activity. The presence of one or more inactive lines suggests a problem with the stepper logic circuits. Check the output transistor for each inactive line, as described in Chapter 7 (see discussion of stepper motors).

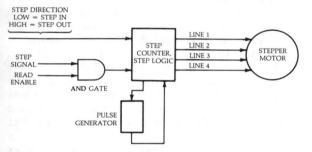

Fig. 11-11. Stepper motor logic circuitry.

The logic circuits use a "feedback" system to tell how far the stepper has turned at any given moment.

Check for a train of pulses from the feedback sensor(s), as described in Chapter 7.

Some disk drives use a "voice-coil" mechanism to move the heads in and out. The voice coil consists of a coil of wire, wound around a hollow core. A magnet is placed inside the core. When a current is sent through the coil, the magnet is forced forward or backward. This provides the force required to move the heads in or out. The principles used in this action are described in the discussion of solenoids given in Chapter 7. You can check the resistance through the voice coil using an ohmmeter. You should find a very low resistance, not an open circuit.

If any of the mechanisms inside the sealed case are faulty, you will have to return the drive to the manufacturer.

11.2.4 Test 4

Checking the Read circuits.

Refer to the schematic for your particular drive, and apply the "chain troubleshooting" techniques described in Chapter 7. The block diagram shown in Fig. 11-12 may be helpful. At this point, the manufacturer's technician would use the "Bit Shift Test" described in Section 11.3.

11.2.5 Test 5

Checking the Write circuits.

You will need a schematic for your particular drive in order to make much headway here. The block diagram

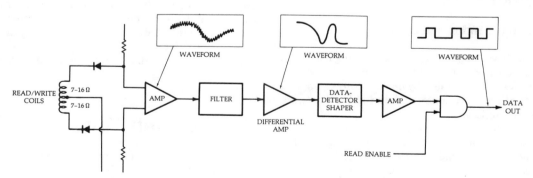

Fig. 11-12. Block diagram of "Read" circuits.

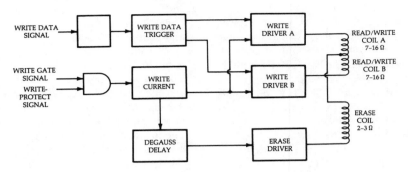

Fig. 11-13. Block diagram of "Write" circuits.

shown in Fig. 11-13 may provide some help. At this point, the manufacturer's technician would use the "Bit Shift Test" described in Section 11.3.

11.2.6 Test 6

Checking the Track 000 detector.

The Track 000 signal is generated by a switch, which is activated by the arm that moves the Read/Write heads. This switch is located inside the sealed case, so you cannot check it directly. However, you can use the Exerciser program to move the head to Track 000, and, then, you can check the output from the detector switch. The signal may be routed through a "debounce" circuit.

    If the switch is faulty, you will not be able to open the sealed case and make a repair. Send the drive to the manufacturer for servicing.

11.2.7 Test 7

Checking the index detector.

While the drive is operating, check for a regular series of pulses on the INDEX line. On some drives, the INDEX signal is generated by one or more sensors on the shaft of the drive motor. Often these sensors are Hall-effect transistors.

    Some drives do not have an actual index detector switch. Instead, the "index" signal may be generated each time the heads read a special index mark on one of the disks.

    The basic index signal may be "debounced" and buffered before it is passed on to the control circuits.

11.2.8 Test 8

Checking the power connections.

Most hard disk drives are powered by the power supply in the main computer. If the drive is mounted on a plug-in card, it receives +5-V DC and +12-V DC from the card slot. If this is the case, check for the correct DC voltages on the conductors along the sides of the slot.

    If the drive is separate from the computer, it receives its DC voltages through a connecting cable. Check the DC voltages at the point where this cable is connected to the hard disk drive. The conductors may be exposed at the back of the connector, and you may be able to take your readings there. The documentation for the drive will list the test points for these DC voltages.

    Some hard disk drives have separate power supplies. In this case, check the separate power supply, using the instructions given in Chapter 16.

    There are two concerns when you test these DC voltages. The DC voltage must be quite close to the specified voltage. Be sure to check the voltages when the drive is operating. A voltage may appear to be correct when the drive is at rest, but will drop a bit when the drive begins working. If one of the DC voltages is more than ±10% of the rated voltage, something is wrong.

11.3 Bit Shift Test

Disk-drive manufacturers use this test as a quick way of checking the overall health of a disk drive. Unfortunately, you cannot perform this test yourself without special equipment. The test measures the "bit shift" as data bits are written on the inner tracks of the drive. When bits are written on these inner tracks, they tend to "spread" a bit. Normally, the "precompensation" circuitry adjusts for this. On a drive with worn heads, or with Read/Write circuits producing low-amplitude signals, more than the normal amount of "bit shift" will occur. Experience has shown that, if a drive shows a large degree of bit shifting, it has a high probability of failure.

Chapter Review

In this chapter, we have discussed the mechanical parts and control circuits in a typical hard disk drive. As you have discovered, these are similar in many ways to the parts and circuits in a floppy disk drive. We explained why hard disk drives are so vulnerable to damage from dust and vibration. We also described the precautions you can take to avoid these problems.

We reviewed the options you have for backing up the data on the hard disk. We also covered the basics of recovering data from a damaged hard disk drive. In the last part of the chapter, we described some common hard-disk problems, and suggested some possible solutions.

When you are troubleshooting a hard disk drive, your options are limited because so many of the parts are mounted inside the sealed case. We have tried to concentrate on the steps you can take, working with the parts and circuits that are outside the sealed case.

Review Questions

1. You visit a client's office and notice that a computer system, including the hard disk drive, is assembled on a movable cart. The computer is plugged into a long extension cord. While the computer is operating, a secretary moves the system to another desk. Do you have a comment on this practice?

2. You remove a hard disk drive from the computer and (gently) shake the unit. You hear a metal part rattling around inside the sealed case. What is the next step?

3. An old drive begins to give you intermittent Read/Write errors. Can you suggest a likely cause?

4. You hear that the company which manufactured your disk drive is going out of business. What would be a good move on your part at this point?

5. You are having trouble with a hard disk drive. The computer says "Directory Damaged" or something similar, but you can still read all of your files. Can you suggest a reason? What should you do?

6. You are working with a word-processing file. The computer can read all of the sectors of the file, but some of the information has been recorded incorrectly. How do you recover?

7. The files of your DOS are recorded incorrectly onto Track 000 of the drive. Why is this bad?

8. A client is using the "BACKUP" program to backup. He is using the "/M" option, but is not adding the "/A" switch as well. Why is this bad practice?

12

Impact Printers

Introduction and Objectives

A modern printer is a complicated device. The electronics inside even a simple printer may be almost as complicated as the electronics in the computer. In fact, a typical printer (Fig. 12-1) is supervised by a separate microcomputer system, complete with a CPU, ROMs, and RAMs. In addition, each printer includes a number of electromechanical systems that must work very quickly and precisely if the printer is to do its job. Fig. 12-2 is a simplified block diagram of the major subsystems in a small dot-matrix printer.

We'll begin by reviewing the mechanisms and electronics you are likely to find inside a dot-matrix or daisy-wheel printer. Next, we'll discuss the kinds of problems you are likely to encounter with these machines. We'll include a short section on periodic cleaning and maintenance, and then we'll list a troubleshooting sequence that should help you to localize most printer problems. Finally, we'll discuss repair and adjustment procedures for each of the major subsystems, starting with the electromechanical subsystems.

Fig. 12-1. A dot-matrix printer.
(Courtesy Epson America Inc.)

Printer Mechanisms

Dot-Matrix Print Mechanism

Dot-matrix characters are created by a printhead containing one or two vertical sets of print-wire mechanisms. Vertical lines of dots are printed as the printhead moves across the page. Some typical dot formats are 5×7, 7×9, and 9×9. These three formats use a single vertical line of print wires, as shown in Fig. 12-3. Thus, a letter is processed in vertical "slices" as the print mechanism moves across the page. As the printer prints each "slice," the control circuits tell each print wire whether to print or not. The resulting pattern of dots represents readable letters.

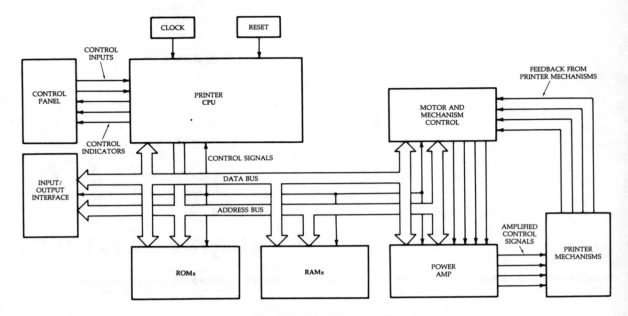

Fig. 12-2. Simplified block diagram of a printer.

The printhead moves across the page to print a single line of characters. Then, the printer advances the paper to begin a new line (line feed). On inexpensive printers, the printhead usually returns to the "home" position on the left side of the page before beginning a new line. On the faster *bidirectional* or *logic seeking* printers, the head may start the new line from the right side of the page, without returning to the "home" position.

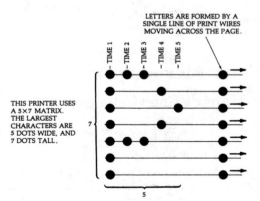

Fig. 12-3. Printing dot-matrix characters.

Even a simple dot-matrix printer can print "near letter quality" (NLQ) characters by making more than one "pass" over the characters (Fig. 12-4). In this example, the second set of dots has been moved a bit to one side to fill in the horizontal spaces between the first set of dots. Next, the paper has been advanced a bit, and another set of dots printed to fill the vertical spaces and complete the character.

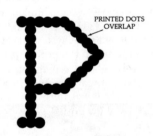

Fig. 12-4. Near letter quality (NLQ) type of printing.

Fig. 12-5 shows two typical dot-matrix printheads. In Fig. 12-5A, the printhead has 7 individual print-wire mechanisms. On a "near letter quality" printer, the printhead might have 21 or more print wires, as shown in Fig. 12-5B. Notice that the two rows of print wires are offset. A printer with this type of printhead can print overlapping dot patterns without making multiple passes.

On some printers, the print wires are driven directly by solenoids. This is illustrated in Fig. 12-6A. On other printers, the end of each print wire is struck

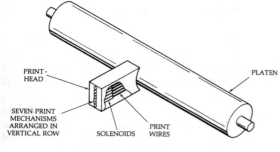

(A) Printhead with 7 print wires.

(B) Printhead with 21 print wires.

Fig. 12-5. Dot-matrix printheads.

print wire. The other end of the print wire hits the ribbon, and makes a dot on the paper. The rebound action of the print wire, aided by a small return spring, resets the mechanism.

These print mechanisms operate at very high speeds. A printer with a 7×9 dot matrix, printing at 120 characters per second, must process over 1000 vertical lines of dots per second, or almost 65,000 vertical lines per minute! If the printer is operated for a long time, the printhead may become very hot, so cooling fins are mounted on the outside of the head.

On many modern printers, you can easily remove the printhead and snap in a replacement.

Daisy-Wheel Print Mechanism

The "daisy-wheel" printer offers a better print quality, at the sacrifice of speed. Fig. 12-7 shows a daisy-wheel print mechanism. Each print arm is formed in two parts. A rigid section at the end of each arm carries one letter. The center section of each arm is flexible. When the printer wants to print a certain letter, it spins the daisy-wheel until the print arm (petal) for the desired character is in position in front of the print hammer. (This type of printer has a single print hammer, which is driven by a solenoid.) At the right moment, the print hammer hits the back of the arm, pushing the character forward against the ribbon. On many printers, the hammer has a notch that mates with a projection on the back of each print arm. This system helps align the type during the striking action.

The daisy-wheel print wheel is turned by a "stepper motor" which moves the wheel in precise steps. A sensor near the shaft of the stepper motor

by a hammer, which is powered by a solenoid, as shown in Fig. 12-6B. (A solenoid is simply a coil of wire wrapped around a metal core, with a movable shaft mounted inside the core. When a current is sent through the coil, it creates an electromagnetic field, which causes the shaft to move.) The two different types of print-wire drive mechanisms are shown in Fig. 12-6.

When the printer wants to produce a dot, it sends a current through a solenoid to drive the appropriate

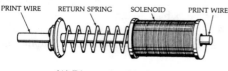

(A) Direct solenoid drive.

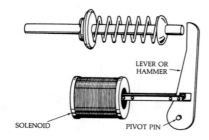

(B) Lever-driven wire drive.

Fig. 12-6. Print-wire drive mechanisms.

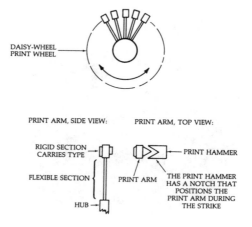

Fig. 12-7 Daisy-wheel print mechanism.

sends out a series of pulses as the motor turns. The printer's CPU uses this "feedback" system to keep track of the position of the print wheel.

As the printer begins each line, the print wheel is spun around to a known or "home" position. When the printer CPU decides to print a letter, it calculates which direction the print wheel must spin, and how far it must turn, to bring the print arm for the correct letter under the hammer. The control circuits communicate with the stepper motor over four signal lines. The signals on these lines cause the motor to spin in the correct direction, with the correct speed. When the print wheel begins to get close to the desired position, the printer CPU tells the stepper to slow down, and then stop. When the desired arm of the print wheel is in position, the printer CPU sends a current through the solenoid in the print hammer, causing the hammer to strike. All of this happens in a fraction of a second. During the printing action, most of the other mechanical functions in the printer are inhibited, including both Line Feed and carriage motion.

The print wheel does not spin back to the "home" position before printing the next character. Instead, the CPU calculates the direction and velocity that the wheel must turn to move directly to the next letter.

Some printers made by NEC use a similar system. Instead of a daisy-wheel, however, this kind of printer uses a "thimble," as shown in Fig. 12-8. Each arm of the thimble carries two letters. A stepper motor rotates the thimble into the desired position, as it did for the daisy-wheel print wheel. A solenoid then shifts the thimble up or down so the correct character is positioned in front of the print hammer.

Instead of a stepper motor, some printers use a *servo motor*. Like the stepper motor, a servo motor can move a mechanism in precise increments (and it employs a feedback circuit), yet the operating principle is different. Servo motors were described in Chapter 7.

Paper-Feed Mechanisms

Paper-feed mechanisms are much the same from one dot-matrix or daisy-wheel printer to the next, regardless of the type of printhead. Fig. 12-9 shows a typical arrangement for a friction-feed system. The paper is carried around a typewriter-type platen. The vinyl covering on this platen is designed to give just the right amount of resistance to the print wires or print arms as they strike. The paper is supported both above and below the print area by spring-loaded pressure rollers.

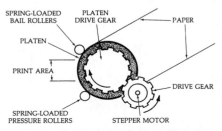

Fig. 12-9. Friction-feed mechanism.

When the printer CPU wants to advance the paper a line, it signals a stepper motor, which drives the platen using a set of gears. As in the daisy-wheel mechanism described earlier, the printer communicates with this stepper motor through four signal lines. The motor is capable of moving the platen in small increments—one type of printer moves in increments of $1/48$th of an inch. To advance the paper a whole line, the stepper on this printer actually moves through a number of positions. A sensor near the stepper motor counts the number of increments that the motor moves and then reports back to the printer CPU.

A "pin-feed" mechanism works in essentially the same way. The platen on a pin-feed machine is fitted

Fig. 12-8. Thimble printer wheel for a NEC printer.

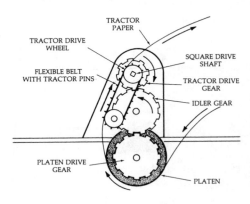

Fig. 12-10. Tractor-feed mechanism.

Impact Printers **211**

with two rows of pins. These pins fit into rows of holes at each edge of the pin-feed paper and allow positive paper positioning.

A "tractor-feed" mechanism is offered on some printers. Fig. 12-10 shows a typical tractor-feed mechanism. The mechanism includes two flexible belts. Each belt has pins that grip holes along the edges of the tractor-feed paper. Each belt is driven by a drive wheel, which is turned by a shaft that is connected to a train of gears. These gears mesh with one of the drive gears that drive the platen.

Carriage-Drive Mechanisms

A moving carriage supports the printer's printhead and ribbon-feed mechanism. Fig. 12-11 shows the top view of a typical carriage mechanism. A stepper motor and a cable-and-pulley arrangement provides the power to move the carriage. On some printers, the stepper motor is mounted to one side of the printer, and drives a toothed belt (Fig. 12-12). The carriage is also attached to this belt.

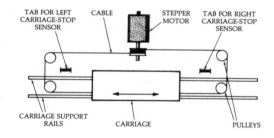

Fig. 12-11. Top view of printer carriage mechanism.

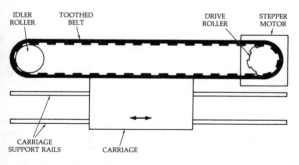

Fig. 12-12. Belt-drive system used on some printers.

The carriage moves from side to side on two or more support rails. In one common arrangement, the carriage is actually carried by small wheels that ride

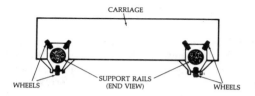

Fig. 12-13. Printer carriage support wheels ride along support rails.

along the sides and bottom of the support rails, as shown in Fig. 12-13.

The control circuitry for the carriage stepper motor is similar to the circuitry described for the daisy-wheel stepper motor. A sensor near the shaft of the stepper motor sends out a series of pulses as the motor turns. The printer CPU uses these pulses to calculate the position of the carriage. When the printer CPU wants the carriage to move, it communicates with the stepper motor through four signal lines. The signals on these lines tell the motor in which direction to turn. The stepper motor usually can move the carriage in small increments—as small as $1/120$th of an inch. This allows the printer to move the carriage less than a whole character width. To move one character width, the stepper will move through several of these increments. When the CPU decides the carriage has reached its intended position, it tells the stepper motor to stop. Some printers use a servo motor here instead of a stepper motor.

When the printer is first turned on, the printer CPU tells the carriage stepper motor to move the carriage to the extreme left end of its range. This is the "home" position for the carriage. A tab mounted on the bottom of the printer marks this point. Under the carriage, a light source normally sends a beam to a pickup. When the carriage moves over the tab, the beam is blocked. The signal from this sensor tells the CPU that the carriage has reached "home," and the CPU stops the stepper motor (Fig. 12-14). A similar tab marks the right edge of the carriage range.

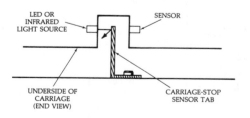

Fig. 12-14. Carriage stop sensor.

Ribbon-Feed Mechanisms

The ribbon-feed mechanism is normally mounted on the carriage. Sometimes the ribbon is mounted on the main frame of the printer, and a length of ribbon is stretched across the whole width of the printer. The ribbon itself is usually contained in a plastic cartridge, for easy installation and replacement.

Sometimes, the ribbon is advanced by a stepper motor. The printer CPU tells this motor to advance the ribbon whenever the printer prints a character. The driver circuits are similar to the circuits for other stepper motors. However, other printers don't use a stepper motor. Instead, they may use a gear that is driven by a "rack" on one of the carriage support rails. As the carriage moves down the rails, the rack turns this gear and advances the ribbon.

Some printers use a toothed drive belt to move the carriage from side to side. The power from this drive belt may be transferred, through a train of gears, to the ribbon-feed mechanism. The carriage can be, and is, moved back and forth, but the ribbon must be advanced in only one direction. Because of this, there are really two sets of gears—one set is used to drive the ribbon while the carriage is moving in one direction, and another is used to drive the ribbon when the carriage is moving in the opposite direction. When the carriage switches direction, one set of gears disengages and the other engages.

Many printers are designed to use a two-color ribbon. In printers with this feature, a solenoid moves the ribbon mechanism up and down, so the hammer strikes either the top or bottom half of the ribbon.

Printer CPU and Control Circuits

The control system of a dot-matrix or daisy-wheel printer is usually designed around a small CPU IC. This system operates in much the same way as any other microcomputer system. At the heart of the system is a microprocessor chip. This "printer CPU" uses an address bus to address the inputs, memories, and outputs of the system. Data flow from one part of the printer to another along a data bus. (Actually, there may not be a separate data bus. Some of the address

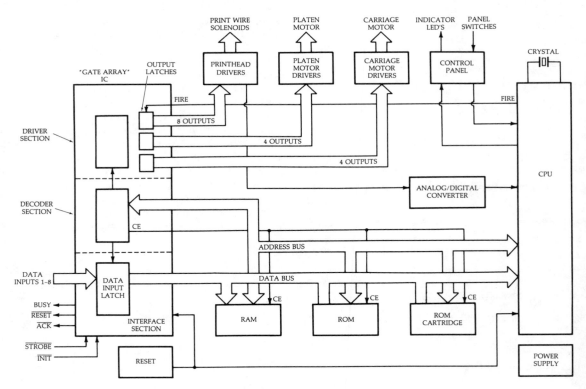

Fig. 12-15. Block diagram of a printer's control circuits.

lines may be used at different times to carry either data or addresses.)

A set of ROMs contain the operating instructions for the printer CPU. In dot-matrix printers, additional ROMs tell the printer what combination of dots to print to produce each letter. For example, when the printer is asked to print the letter "P," it will look up this character in the ROMs. The ROMs will then tell the microprocessor, "Hit print wires 1 through 7 for the first line of the P, wires 1 and 4 for the second line . . .," and so on. Some printers allow you to plug in cartridges containing other ROMs, which contain instructions for printing special characters.

RAMs provide temporary storage for characters that are waiting to be printed. The RAM storage space used for incoming characters is called the "input buffer."

Over the years, printers have been designed using fewer and fewer ICs. The functions of many simple ICs have been combined into a few larger ICs. For example, in the Epson FX-86e, most of the "thinking" is done by just two complex ICs. We have shown a simplified block diagram of a printer's control circuits in Fig. 12-15. We will use the Epson FX-86e printer as a model for our discussion. Other printers will perform similar functions. They may require more than two main ICs to do the job, however.

The large IC on the right of the diagram in Fig. 12-15 is the printer CPU. This is an 8-bit microprocessor, similar to the CPU you would find in any small 8-bit computer. When the printer is turned on, this CPU executes a program that tells the printer how to input data and then convert data to printing instructions.

In many ways, the printer CPU is just like any other microprocessor IC. For example, the CPU requires timing signals from a crystal-controlled oscillator. The CPU uses the "Reset" signal in the same way as any other microprocessor. When the CPU wants to access some memory in RAM or ROM, or wants to input a new character for printing, it places an address on the Address bus. The other circuits respond, and return the data on the Data bus. The CPU produces a "Write" output when it wants to write to RAM, and a "Read" signal when it wants to read.

There are some CPU functions that are different, however. As we said earlier, the printer includes a number of switches to detect conditions such as "out of paper," and so on. The signals from some of these switches are carried directly to inputs on the CPU chip. The printer is always checking itself to be sure that it is sending the correct amount of power to the print mechanisms. An "analog/digital converter" circuit

analyzes the printing action, and reports back to the printer CPU. The CPU uses this "feedback" to modify the next set of printing commands.

The printer CPU also produces some outputs that you would not see on a computer's CPU. For example, to energize the print wires in the printhead, the CPU sends out a timing signal called "Fire." Other outputs turn on the indicator LEDs on the control panel.

Epson America Inc. calls the second large chip in Fig. 12-15 a "gate array." This chip provides most of the support functions required by the CPU. One part of the chip forms part of the "driver" circuits. On command from the CPU, these circuits send trigger signals to the printhead mechanisms, the platen drive motor, and so on. For example, the printhead on this printer has 8 print wires. Each of the print mechanisms has a separate input line, as described earlier. The "gate array" chip takes inputs from the CPU, and produces pulses on each of these output lines. The "gate array" also produces outputs for the platen drive motor and the carriage drive motors. For each motor, the array produces four outputs, as described earlier.

Another part of the "gate array" acts as an address decoder. This section takes addresses from the address bus, and activates different RAMs and ROMs. For example, if an address falls within the range of memory carried on a particular RAM IC, the decoder generates a "Chip Enable" signal (CE) for that IC.

The third part of the "gate array" acts to handle the interface between the printer and the computer. The data from the computer are carried on eight parallel data lines. The array includes a *latch* (temporary memory space), which holds each incoming data "package" until the printer CPU is ready to use it. This section of the array also handles other interfacing signals such as STROBE*, BUSY, and so on. We will take a more detailed look at the interfacing arrangement in a moment.

Since this type of printer uses two ICs to handle so much of the "thinking," troubleshooting is fairly simple. If you eliminate these two ICs, the rest of the printer consists of fairly simple parts–RAMs, ROMs, switches, print-wire drivers, and motor drivers. It is relatively easy to check these simple parts.

On a typical small printer, the important ICs are usually mounted on one or two circuit boards. The manufacturer's own service people will usually just use a "board swapping" strategy, rather than try to identify the specific part which has failed. Let's say that you can localize a problem to a particular board. The dealer or manufacturer may allow you to turn in the bad board for a credit, when you buy a replacement board.

Interface to Computer

The connection between the computer and the printer is called the "interface." For each combination of computer and printer, this interface must be carefully planned so the two units understand each other. Several different kinds of interface formats are in use. One of the most common is the "Centronics" parallel format, which uses eight data lines. IBM, Epson, and many other companies use variations of this format. In this type of parallel interface, the data are broken down into a series of "packages" of eight digital bits each. Each "package" represents a character that the printer will print, or a "control code" which tells the printer to do something. To send a message, the computer sends the first package of eight bits of digital information, followed by another package of eight more bits, and so on, until the transmission is complete. We have illustrated this idea in Fig. 12-16. We'll take a detailed look at the parallel interface later in the chapter in the section on troubleshooting.

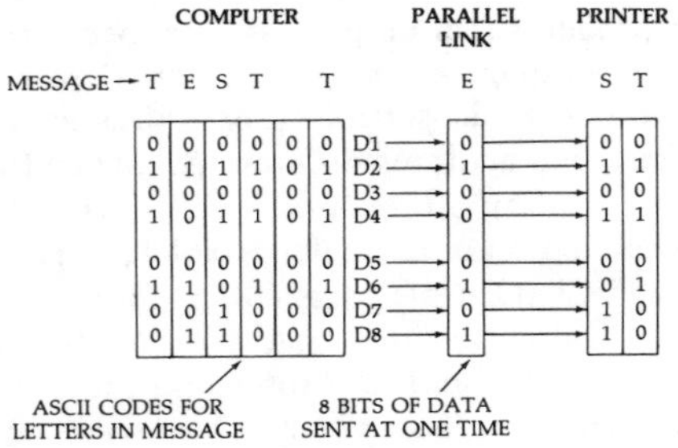

Fig. 12-16. Parallel data transmission.

Another common interface uses the RS-232C "serial" format. This interface uses just one data line (although it includes many control lines), so it can only handle one bit of information at a time. The data are sent, one bit after another, until the transmission is completed. We will cover the RS-232C serial interface in detail in Chapter 14.

The printer CPU reads the data coming into the printer, and interprets it. Some of the input data represent control signals to the printer—line feed, carriage to "home," and so on. The printer CPU recognizes these signals and sends them to the appropriate control mechanisms. The rest of the signals represent characters to be printed. The printer CPU sends these to the input buffer, where the characters are stored temporarily. Then, when a simple printer wants to print a character, it chooses the character at the "bottom" of the stack in the input buffer—the character

that has been stored there longest. More complicated printers may use their "logic seeking" capability to check the characters in the buffer, and then determine the most efficient way to print them.

Protective Circuits

The printer CPU is usually programmed to protect itself if something goes wrong. For example, while the print hammer is operating, the print wheel, paper advance, and carriage mechanisms are often disabled. If the hammer were to operate while the print wheel was still turning, it could hit the wrong part of the print wheel.

When a dot-matrix printer operates for a long time at high speed, the printhead may overheat. To prevent this, many dot-matrix printers include a temperature sensor. The sensor signals the printer CPU to slow down the printhead if the head starts to overheat.

Many printers also include circuits that watch over the important power supplies. When a supply voltage drops below specification, the printer CPU will disable the printhead. Many printers will also stop operating when the printer CPU detects something wrong with the input data. If the CPU detects an "unprintable" character or a bad control code, it may shut down. Most printers have at least one "alarm" or "error" indicator that lights when one of these problems occurs.

A printer may also stop for more routine causes. For example, most printers have switches that detect "paper out" and "cover open" conditions. Any one of these conditions can cause a printer to stop operating.

Ink-Jet and Thermal Printers

Ink-jet printers and thermal printers have some features in common with dot-matrix and daisy-wheel printers. In each case, the systems that move the platen and carriage are similar. All of these printers have similar interface circuits. However, each kind of printer uses a different principle to print on the paper.

There are several different types of ink-jet printers. The "continuous-stream" type uses magnetic ink. This special ink can be attracted or repelled by a magnetic force. In this type of printer, the ink is forced from the printhead in a continuous stream. As long as the printer does not want to make a mark on the paper, the stream is deflected downward into an "overflow" or

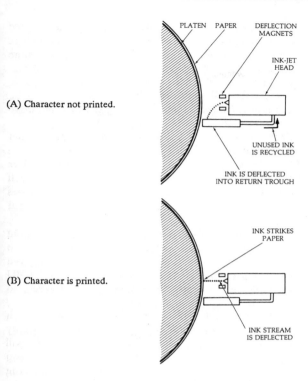

(A) Character not printed.

(B) Character is printed.

Fig. 12-17. Continuous-stream ink-jet printer.

"return" trough. The ink is then filtered, pumped back up to the printhead, and reused. This is illustrated in Fig. 12-17. When the printer does want to make a mark, it energizes the deflector magnets, and the ink stream is allowed to reach the paper.

A second type of ink-jet printer produces a dot of ink only when the printer wants to make a mark. These printers use the "dot-on-demand" principle. Printers of this type do not need magnetic ink. One dot-on-demand mechanism uses a "piezoelectric cell" to pump the ink (Fig. 12-18). The piezoelectric element changes shape when it carries an electric current. Thus, when the printer wants to create a dot, it sends a current to the piezoelectric cell. The cell then changes shape, which forces a drop of ink out of the printhead.

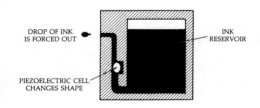

Fig. 12-18. Piezoelectric ink-jet printer.

In another type of dot-on-demand printer, a very small hole is drilled in the side of the ink reservoir. Surrounding this hole is a heating plate, containing an electric heating element. When the printer wants to produce a dot, it sends a current to the heating plate. The plate heats a small amount of the ink, creating steam, which forces a dot of ink toward the paper (Fig. 12-19).

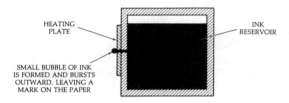

Fig. 12-19. Heating-type of ink-jet printer.

Thermal printers use heat to make marks on specially prepared paper. The thermal printhead includes one or more tiny electric heaters. When the thermal printer wants to create a dot, it sends a current through one of the heaters. This heat affects the paper directly under the heater.

In a similar type of printer, the printhead creates tiny sparks which arc from the printhead to the surface of the paper. This type of printer uses aluminum-coated paper. The sparks burn holes in the metal layer on the top surface of the paper, creating an image.

Possible Service Problems

Many of the problems in printer operation are caused by the interface between the computer and the printer. The control signals sent by the computer must match those expected by the printer. The cable that runs between the printer and the computer must carry the right signal on each wire. Often, you must set switches inside the printer to reflect the particular input format you're using. You should solve most of these interfacing problems when you first set up the printer. In this discussion, we'll assume that your printer has been set up correctly, has worked well for a while, and suddenly starts to have a problem. In this case, there may well be a fault or failure in one of the components involved in the interface, but the problem is probably not caused by a mistake in the basic interfacing setup. Many of the problems with interfaces are caused by corroded connectors and broken cables.

In printers that have been set up correctly and have been operating for a while, the electromechanical mechanisms are the cause of a large share of the problems. Dirt, dust, and paper chips can jam the mechanisms. Metal parts may be bent. Plastic parts can break or wear out.

Among the electronic components, the parts that are most likely to fail are those that handle the power. For example, on a daisy-wheel printer, the control circuitry that drives the print hammer uses low-power TTL logic. The last part of the chain, the print-hammer mechanism, requires a higher voltage and current than the TTL circuits can provide. When the control circuitry wants to drive the print hammer, it sends a signal to an output transistor which produces the current required by the solenoid. The output transistor and solenoid can handle relatively large amounts of power and are more likely to have problems than the TTL logic circuits.

Most printers have an independent power supply. These circuits can have all of the usual power-supply problems—shorted transformer, bad filtering capacitor, bad voltage regulator, etc.

Finally, something can go wrong with the printer CPU and the TTL logic circuits. As in other types of computer equipment, the circuits themselves will probably be quite reliable. Start by checking for problems among the mechanical parts.

Ink-jet printers are subject to a special problem. Because the ink-jet orifice is so small, it can become clogged. Usually, the orifice can be cleared if the pressure on the ink is increased for a moment. Sometimes the printer is designed with a "purge cycle," which does this automatically. For some printers, a syringe or "plunger" is available. To clear a clog, fill the plunger with ink and connect it to the ink reservoir. Next, press down on the handle of the plunger. This will increase the pressure inside the reservoir and should clear the orifice. On some printers, the ink supply is contained in a flexible bladder. By pressing slightly on this bladder, you can increase the ink pressure and can clear the clogged orifice.

Cleaning and Maintenance

Printers start to become troublesome if they are neglected. Because printers include so many mechanical parts, periodic cleaning and maintenance are very important.

At least once a year, give the printer a really complete cleaning. Start by unplugging the printer and removing the case. Wipe down the carriage support rails with a clean soft cloth. Use a source of clean, low-pressure, compressed air to blow away any dust or paper chips that may have accumulated on the carriage or inside the case. Be sure not to blow dust into other nearby equipment. If you can't dust off some of the mechanisms, wipe the parts with a cloth moistened with alcohol. Be careful not to use alcohol on rubber parts, as alcohol will dry out the rubber and cause it to stiffen and crack. Check the pulleys along the carriage drive cable, and be sure the groove around each pulley is clear. Clear any dust and dirt away from the rollers that support the carriage.

Blow out any dust that may have accumulated on the circuit boards. You may want to remove the circuit boards for more complete cleaning. If you do this, clean the edge connectors with a pencil eraser, as described in Chapter 6.

If the printer's cover is dirty, clean it with a mild detergent. Don't use any kind of solvent that could lift the paint. Use a small amount of Windex® or diluted ammonia to remove any finger marks around the switches on the front panel. Next, remove the platen. You can usually do this by releasing two spring-loaded clips at each end of the platen. Once the platen is free, wipe down the rubber covering with Fedron® platen cleaner. Do the same with the pressure rollers and bail rollers. Fedron is best for this purpose because it won't dry out the rubber. We listed a source for Fedron in Chapter 6. Read the cautions on the bottle and handle the Fedron carefully. Fedron will damage some kinds of plastic.

If you have a daisy-wheel printer, clean the print wheel carefully with a paper towel moistened with alcohol. Be careful not to break the delicate print arms. Sometimes in heavy use, some of the characters can "fill in" with dirt. You can clean out these letters with a pin.

On a dot-matrix machine, clean the tip of the print mechanism with a cotton swab moistened with alcohol. Work very carefully so you don't catch any of the print wires with the swab and bend them.

The next task is lubrication. If you skip this step, some of the mechanisms may wear prematurely, or may start to stick and jam. Printer manufacturers usually specify their own brand of oil and grease for lubricating their equipment. Try to get the exact brand and grade specified. Printer mechanisms put special demands on a lubricant. The grease and oil must be viscous enough to do their jobs, yet they must stay where you put them and not "migrate" around the printer.

When you first start the printer, the lubricants must go to work right away, so the low-temperature characteristics are important. You can probably find off-the-shelf lubricants that will match the specified lubricants, but do you really want to compare all of the specifications? You should be able to get the specified lubricants directly from the printer manufacturer. If, for some reason, you can't get lubricants from the manufacturer, you'll just have to use off-the-shelf products. You'll need a light grade of white grease and a light oil.

Use very small amounts of grease and oil. If you use too much, the lubricant will attract dust, and a lump of oily dust can cause more problems than the original lack of lubrication.

The service manual will list the specific lubrication points for your printer. Be especially careful to lubricate any mechanisms that are in use all the time. These include the platen drive gears, the platen bearings, the rollers that support the carriage, and the pulleys that guide the carriage drive cable.

Use grease to lubricate the larger mechanisms that handle power. The lubricant in grease is made into a thick formula, so it can stand up to heavy loads, stays where you put it, and works well where the spaces between parts is relatively large. Use grease on all gear teeth, and on mechanisms that slide or rotate against a cam. Fig. 12-20 shows what we mean.

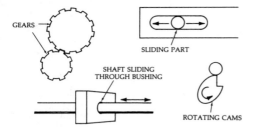

Fig. 12-20. Use grease when lubricating these parts.

Use oil for mechanisms with smaller spaces between parts, and for parts which move only a short distance. See Fig. 12-21. Machine oil is light enough to penetrate into tight spaces. If a space is small enough, the oil will be held in place by surface tension. Use oil for bearings and bushings that carry rotating shafts.

Many motors have permanently sealed bearings and cannot be lubricated. If the motor can be

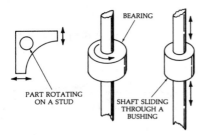

Fig. 12-21. Use oil when lubricating these parts.

lubricated, you will often find a felt wick positioned above the part, as shown in Fig. 12-22. If a unit has a reservoir of this type, moisten the top of the wick with oil. The wick can supply oil to the part over a long period of time. Some bushings have built-in reservoirs, as shown in the sketch. The felt wicks are protected by seals, so you can't lubricate them directly. Spread some oil on the shaft that runs through the bushing, and then move the device up and down along the shaft. As the bushing passes over the oil, the felt will soak up the oil and retain it. You may find a similar wick arrangement on other mechanisms.

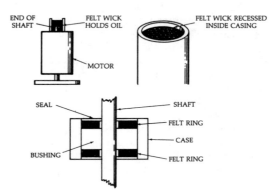

Fig. 12-22. Oil reservoirs.

On dot-matrix printers, don't lubricate the solenoids, armatures, or print wires in the printhead. These parts operate too quickly—oil will just gum up the works. Many top-quality ribbons include a lubricant. Inexpensive off-brand ribbons do not have this lubricant. If you try to operate the printer with these off-brand ribbons, the printhead may wear very quickly. It is important to use the type of ribbon specified by the manufacturer.

The final step in your equipment checkup is a complete inspection of the printer. Run off a print sample, using a good ribbon. On many printers, you can use a "self-test" mode that will print every character, and will also print across the full width of the paper. Next, unplug the printer and remove the case. Check the whole machine for bent or broken parts, or signs of wear. Try to move the ends of the platen. The platen should sit firmly in its bearings, with no sign of free play. The carriage should sit firmly on the support rails. The surface of the platen should be smooth. As the rubber material gets older, it may lose its resiliency and become too hard. The platen surface should have just a little bit of "give," and should not feel stiff or glazed. Remove the platen assembly and inspect the pressure and bail rollers.

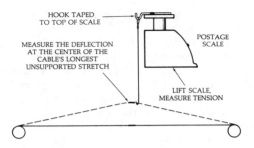

Fig. 12-23. Measuring cable tension with a postage scale.

The carriage drive cable or drive belt should be tight. The manufacturer may list a specification for the cable tension. This will state that it should take "x" ounces of force on the center of the cable to deflect the cable "y" inches. You can use a postage meter to make a rough check of this tension, as shown in Fig. 12-23. If you must readjust the tension, see the instructions given later in the chapter. Replace the cable or belt if it is worn or frayed.

Check the switches for the "paper out" and "cover open" functions for mechanical damage. If you're suspicious of a switch, test it with an ohmmeter as described in the section on "Switches" in Chapter 7. If your printer uses removable circuit boards, be sure each of these is firmly seated. Inspect all cables and connectors carefully, including the interface cable connections at the rear of the printer and the internal cable connections between the circuit boards. Be sure all of the connector contacts are clean and the connector pins are straight. The cables themselves should not be bent or pinched.

Check for wear on the various gears in the machine. When one gear is stopped, you should not be able to rock the other gear back and forth. This movement is called "backlash" (Fig. 12-24). If the backlash becomes too great, the gears won't be able to position the mechanism accurately. Check each set of gears to see that they turn smoothly, without much backlash.

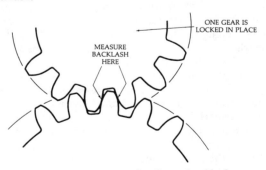

Fig. 12-24. An example of gear backlash.

If your printer has a tractor-feed mechanism, check the flexible belts that carry the tractor pins. Replace the belts if they seem frayed or worn, or if the segments that hold the pins are loose.

Now check the test printout you made earlier. Each character should be uniformly black. If the bottom of each letter is too light, the platen is too high in relation to the printhead (Fig. 12-25). If the top of each letter is too light, the platen is too low. Refer to Section 12.2.3. If the line of type gets progressively lighter as it nears one edge of the page, the platen is out of square. See Fig. 12-26 and Section 12.2.3.

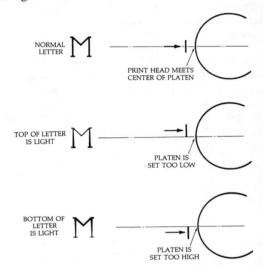

Fig. 12-26. Platen out of alignment.

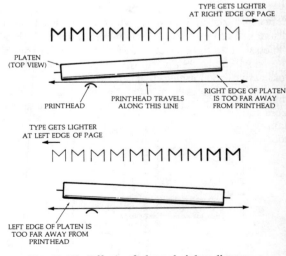

Fig. 12-25. Effects of platen height adjustment.

On daisy-wheel printers, if the top or bottom or one of the edges of a character is weak, the printhead is out of alignment. See Fig. 12-27 and refer to Section 12.2.6. While the printer is at rest, check to be sure that the proper print arm is positioned directly in front of the print hammer. Most manufacturers make a "jig" that fits in front of the hammer so you can check the alignment. If possible, you should get one of these. The service manual for your equipment will specify which character should be in front of the hammer when the printer is in the "home" position. Check the daisy-wheel itself. Look for signs of wear or deformation of the print characters. Be sure none of the flexible arms are permanently bent out of position.

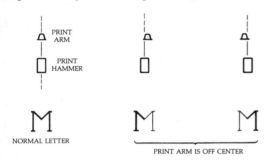

Fig. 12-27. Effects of print hammer being off-center.

On dot-matrix printers, inspect the solenoids, armatures, and springs on the printhead. Watch for signs that some of these parts are bent, or are working loose. Fig. 12-28 shows two problems that can occur at the printhead. Sometimes, the openings for the print wires become worn, and begin to widen out a bit. In the illustration, the opening for the upper print wire is worn. This can allow the end of the print wire to move out of alignment. A worn printhead will print fuzzy or indistinct characters. Sometimes the print wires may jam as a result of this wear. In the illustration, the lower print wire demonstrates yet another problem. The end of the print wire has been pushed back, causing the shaft of the wire to thicken. This keeps the print wire from retracting completely into the head. This type of damage can also cause the print wire to jam. If you notice either type of damage, replace the printhead.

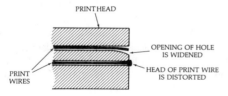

Fig. 12-28. Damaged printhead.

12.1 Troubleshooting Dot-Matrix and Daisy-Wheel Printers

Each brand and model of printer is different, so all we can give you here are some general comments. For specifics, refer to the manual for your particular printer. Most printer manufacturers put out fairly complete manuals for their products.

As we said earlier, most printers have a "self-test" option. This test lets you check out most of the electronics and mechanisms in the printer very quickly. During the "self-test" run, the printer is isolated from the computer. Any printer problems that are caused by the computer or interface should not appear when the printer is running in "self-test" mode.

In addition, some printers have auto-diagnostic capabilities. Inexpensive printers may have a single "Alarm" indicator that can mean many things. The alarm may trip when the printer is out of paper, when the cover is opened, when the printer CPU detects a problem with the input data, or for any number of other reasons. More sophisticated printers may have separate alarm indicators for many of these functions. Check the manual for your printer.

In this section, we'll list some of the most common printer trouble symptoms, and will suggest some possible causes. Then, we'll discuss repair and adjustment procedures (Section 12.2) for the most important subsystems. A system of index numbers (12.1.3, 12.2.5, etc.) will be used to reference specific parts of the text.

12.1.1 Problem 1
Symptom: Printer produces one or more wrong characters; an intermittent problem.

Sometimes a printer will operate correctly most of the time, but, now and then, will print one or more incorrect characters. In a case like this, start by eliminating the software as a possible cause of the problem. Even commercial software can include "bugs" that will cause an abnormal printout now and then. Does the problem occur only when you are running a certain program? Try using a backup copy of the program. If the problem does not disappear, try other programs, and see if the problem is consistent from one program to another. If the fault continues to appear, you should begin looking for a hardware problem.

When the printer prints normally, and then suddenly produces a whole group of incorrect characters at once, look for a problem with the interface. This would also be the place to start if the printer "loses" a number of characters. This can happen when the input buffer "overflows." See Section 12.2.9.

A printer that occasionally prints one or two incorrect characters may have a different kind of problem. There may be a bad connection in one of the cables, or the cable may be picking up some "noise." Start by checking the cables and connectors between the printer and the computer. Refer to the discussion of testing cables and connectors given in Chapter 7. Use the computer to send some characters to the printer. During the test, jiggle the printer cable and both connectors. If the printer starts to malfunction, the problem is probably caused by a bad connection. (Don't pull on the cable so hard that you create another problem, however.)

Check inside the printer as well. Are all of the printed-circuit boards firmly seated? Are the internal cables and connectors all right? Routinely clean the edge-card connectors on the circuit board, using a pencil eraser. We illustrated this procedure in Chapter 6.

Check inside the printer for any loose paper clips, screws, staples, solder particles, etc., that could be moving around and shorting out various circuits.

Inspect the mechanical parts. If one of the mechanisms is jammed, the printhead will stop in one position, creating a black smear on the paper. If the head is no longer making a side-to-side motion, check for a problem with the carriage-drive mechanism (Section 12.2.1). If the paper is no longer advancing at the end of each line, check the platen drive mechanism (Section 12.2.3). Check the mechanical parts carefully. Are any of the parts bent or binding? When the printer is operating, do you hear any unusual scraping or rubbing sounds? An unusual noise suggests a mechanical problem.

Various power-supply problems can cause intermittent faults on a printer. Bad filtering or low voltage from the power supply in the printer can cause problems. Check the outputs of the printer's power supply for correct voltage levels and lack of electronic "noise." If you suspect a power-supply problem, refer to Chapter 16.

An intermittent problem might also be caused by environmental factors. "Noise" or transients from the power line, or radio-frequency interference coming directly through the air, can affect printers. Refer to Chapter 5.

Perhaps the problem is not in the printer at all. Maybe the printer is printing the characters correctly, and the error is creeping into the system from somewhere else. Perhaps the disk drive is not writing and reading characters correctly, or the computer is inserting a few errors of its own. Eliminate these possibilities by substituting the suspect unit for one that is known to be good. If you have two disk drives, reverse the cable connections temporarily. Try operating the printer with a different computer.

An intermittent fault could be caused by a failure of one of the components connected with the interface. Check the interface circuits inside the computer, and the corresponding input circuits in the printer (Section 12.2.9).

Check the printer CPU and control circuits (Section 12.2.10).

12.1.2 Problem 2

Symptom: Printer starts printing, and then stops prematurely.

Perhaps the printer stopped to protect itself. Are any of the "Error" or "Alarm" indicators on? Check for simple conditions that could stop the printer— "paper out," "ribbon out," "cover open," and so on.

There may be a problem with the connections or the interface circuits between the computer and the printer. Before the printer begins printing, the computer sends a series of characters and control signals to the printer. In this case, the printer began printing these characters, but it encountered something it didn't like and stopped.

Set the printer on "local" or "off-line" and try to run a "self-test." This will isolate the printer from the computer. If the test results appear to be normal, you know that the problem lies in the connections or in the interface circuits. Check the cable and connectors carefully, as described in Chapter 7 (Testing Cables and Connectors). Also refer to Section 12.2.9 of this chapter.

If the self-test run is not successful, or if you rule out an interfacing problem, check the printer's power supply (see Chapter 16). A low voltage from one of the sections of the supply could cause the printer to shut itself off. Measure the voltages at each output stage of the supply. Bad filtering could allow "noise" to reach the printer's logic circuits, causing an intermittent error. Use an oscilloscope to check for "noise." If you find a problem, troubleshoot the power supply according to the instructions given in Chapter 16.

Is there any environmental factor that could be causing electrical noise on the 120-V AC line or is there extreme radio-frequency interference? (Refer to Chapter 5.)

If you still cannot find the problem, refer to Section 12.2.10, and read the discussion on "Printer CPU and Control Circuits."

12.1.3 Problem 3

Symptom: Printer is completely dead. No fan noise. Indicators on front panel do not light.

This is most likely caused by a power-supply problem. Start by checking for voltage at the wall plug or the power distribution strip. If the printer is plugged in, check the fuse. If the fuse is burnt out, replace it and turn the equipment on again. If the fuse burns out quickly, you know you haven't found the problem yet.

Check the voltage at each DC output in the power supply. To troubleshoot further, refer to the discussion on power supplies in Chapter 16.

12.1.4 Problem 4

Symptom: No print action, yet front panel indicators light.

Is the "On-Line/Local" switch set to "On-Line?" Some of the indicators light up, so you know the printer is getting power, although this power may not be reaching all parts of the machine. It is possible that the printer has disabled the print mechanism to protect itself. Is one of the "Alarm" or "Error" indicators on? If you find an alarm, check to be sure that the printer has a paper supply, that the printer cover is securely in place, and that the ribbon has not run out.

The print mechanism will not operate if the carriage moves beyond the normal limits of its range. Special sensors detect the carriage as it passes and cuts off power to the print mechanism. Check to be sure that the carriage has not moved unusually far to the left or to the right. Sometimes you can move the carriage by mistake as you load a new print ribbon. If the carriage does seem to be out of its range, turn off the printer and push the carriage by hand toward the center of the printer.

If you still haven't found the problem, set the printer to "Local" and try a self-test print. If the self-test works normally, look for a problem with the cable and the connectors between the computer and the printer, or with the interface circuits in the computer

and the corresponding input circuits in the printer. Start by checking the cable and connectors, as described in Chapter 7 (Testing Cables and Connectors).

If the cable appears to be all right, double-check the arrangements for the interface. If the interface is not correctly wired, it is possible for both the computer and printer to be inactive, each waiting for the other unit to do something. You may also have a hardware fault in one of the interface circuits (refer to Section 12.2.9).

If the self-test is not successful, you know the problem is in the control circuitry inside the printer. Check the voltage at each of the DC outputs in the power supply. Refer to Chapter 16 for instructions. Many printers will disable the print mechanism if one of the supply voltages drops too low.

If you still have not found the problem, check the printer CPU and control circuits (Section 12.2.10).

12.1.5 Problem 5

Symptom: Carriage does not move.

Shut off the printer, open the case, and look for any mechanical problem that could jam the mechanism. Inspect the underside of the carriage, where the carriage wheels roll along the support rails. Examine the carriage drive cable or drive belt where it goes around each of the pulleys to be sure that the cable is not jammed.

Check the stepper motor and driver circuit for this mechanism. Refer to Section 12.2.1 (Carriage-Drive Mechanism).

12.1.6 Problem 6

Symptom: Carriage moves, but there is no printing action.

Check for a mechanical problem that could jam the printhead. Is there a paper clip or dust ball interfering with the action of the printhead?

Check that the printhead is getting signals from the printer CPU. Is the flexible power cable still connected to the underside of the carriage?

Check the printhead mechanism itself. For dot-matrix printers, see Section 12.2.5. For daisy-wheel types, refer to Section 12.2.7. Sometimes, the printhead may be turned off because of problems in other parts of the printer. Check the DC voltages at each output stage of the power supply. See Chapter 16 for more detailed instructions.

If you still can't find the problem, refer to Section 12.2.10 (Printer CPU and Control Circuits).

12.1.7 Problem 7
Symptom: There is printing action, but no printed characters on the page.

Look for a problem with the ribbon. Is the ribbon cartridge mounted correctly? Does the ribbon appear to be advancing, or is the hammer striking repeatedly at the same spot on the ribbon? In some ribbon cartridges, the ribbon can jam. Remove the cartridge, and try to turn the knob that advances the ribbon. If the cartridge is jammed, replace the unit. Also, refer to Section 12.2.8.

It is possible that the ribbon advance mechanism itself has stopped working. Remove the ribbon cartridge, and check the mechanism for a loose screw, paper clip, etc., that could be jamming the mechanism.

12.1.8 Problem 8
Symptom: Printer operates slowly.

When a dot-matrix printer operates continuously at high speed, the printhead can overheat. Some dot-matrix printers have a temperature sensor that tells the printer CPU when the printhead is getting too warm. The CPU then slows down the print action until the head cools down. If the printer has been operating continuously for a long period of time, this condition is probably normal.

If the printer works slowly at all times, check for a problem with the temperature sensor. Also, check for a mechanical problem that could be causing one of the mechanisms to drag or slow down.

12.1.9 Problem 9
Symptom: Paper does not advance.

Shut off the printer and remove the case. Look for any foreign objects that might be jamming the platen drive mechanism. Spin the platen by hand to be sure it is free to turn.

Check the platen drive circuits (refer to Section 12.2.3).

12.1.10 Problem 10
Symptom: Print wheel won't stop spinning (on daisy-wheel printers).

Check the head driver circuits. Refer to Section 12.2.7.

12.1.11 Problem 11
Symptom: The print density is uneven.

There could be several possible causes for this symptom. Fig. 12-25 illustrated some typical print problems. If the top of each letter is too light, the platen is mounted too low in relation to the printhead. If the bottom of each letter is too light, the platen is too high. Refer to Section 12.2.3.

Sometimes each line of type becomes progressively lighter as it nears one edge of the page. This symptom is caused by a platen that is out of square with respect to the printhead, as shown in Fig. 12-26. Refer to Section 12.2.3.

On daisy-wheel printers, the left or right edge of each character may be too light, as illustrated in Fig. 12-27. This can occur when the print hammer strikes off-center on the print arms. Refer to Section 12.2.6.

12.1.12 Problem 12
Symptom: Printed characters are incomplete.

Dot-matrix printers can print incomplete characters when one or more of the print wires is not working (Fig. 12-29). If you have this problem, start by inspecting the printhead carefully, and check for dust or other foreign particles that could be jamming the mechanism. If you can't find a mechanical problem, check the circuit that drives the affected print wire. Refer to Section 12.2.5.

On daisy-wheel printers, you may find several problems. The left or right edge of each letter may be

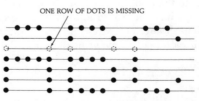

Fig. 12-29. One bad print wire.

too light, as shown in Fig. 12-27. In a case like this, each print arm (petal) is stopping in a position that is off-center in relation to the print hammer. Refer to Section 12.2.6. Also, some characters may appear to be "filled in," as pictured in Fig. 12-30. In this instance, dirt or dust has become packed into the enclosed spaces of the characters on the print arms. Remove the daisy wheel, and clean the letters very carefully with a pin. Finish by wiping the daisy wheel with a paper towel soaked in alcohol. Be careful not to bend the arms on the print wheel.

Fig. 12-30. Filled-in letters.

With either type of printer, you may find that the bottom of each letter is chopped off, as illustrated in Fig. 12-31. This is caused by a problem with the ribbon mechanism. Is the ribbon cartridge firmly seated? Does the ribbon move smoothly through the various guides? If your printer can handle a red/black ribbon, it is possible that the solenoid that lifts the ribbon is faulty. Refer to Section 12.2.8.

12.1.13 Problem 13
Symptom: Printed letters are part red, part black.

Many printers use a two-color ribbon, and can print in either red or black. A mechanism moves the ribbon up or down, so that either the red or black section is in front of the print mechanism. Sometimes the ribbon-adjusting mechanism can slip out of adjustment, so the print mechanism hits right on the division between the red and black sections of the ribbon. Refer to Section 12.2.8.

12.1.14 Problem 14
Symptom: Weak printing. The printed characters are faint.

Start by checking the ribbon. Is it fresh enough to make a dark impression? Is the ribbon jammed? Can it move

Fig. 12-31. Bottom part of letters are cut off.

freely through the various guides? If the ribbon is jammed, or if the ribbon advance mechanism does not seem to be working, check Section 12.2.8.

Most printers have an "impression" control that lets you specify just how hard the print mechanism will strike the ribbon. You normally set this control for a hard strike when you're printing several carbon copies at once. The control switch may have been set to a light setting.

Perhaps the printhead has slipped out of alignment. For a dot-matrix printer, see Section 12.2.4. If you have a daisy-wheel printer, refer to Section 12.2.6. Also, it is possible that the platen has worked loose, and is too far away from the printhead. Check for this; refer to Section 12.2.3.

On a daisy-wheel printer, the print impression can be weak if the daisy wheel is worn. Remove the wheel and check the printing surfaces. You should see clean, sharp edges on all the characters. You can also get a weak impression if the print hammer is not working correctly. Check the mechanism carefully for any dust or foreign matter that could be interfering with the hammer action. Be sure the print-hammer solenoid is getting the right signals. Check Section 12.2.7.

The solenoids in the printhead on a dot-matrix printer also require pulses of a specified voltage level and duration. Check for the presence of correct signals. Also, refer to Section 12.2.5.

12.1.15 Problem 15
Symptom: There is one missing letter; it does not print.

This symptom will occur on a daisy-wheel printer when one of the print arms is damaged. Replace the daisy wheel.

12.1.16 Problem 16
Symptom: There are paper-feed problems.

On friction-feed machines, the paper is drawn between the platen and the pressure rollers at the lower front of the platen (Fig. 12-32). Most printers have a lever that allows you to release the pressure rollers to insert a fresh piece of paper. Check this mechanism and be sure it is working correctly.

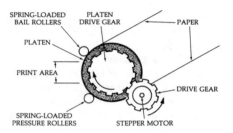

Fig. 12-32. Friction-feed mechanism.

One or more springs force the pressure rollers against the platen. Make sure the pressure rollers are exerting enough force against the platen to get a good grip on the paper.

Other problems can occur when the paper sheets drag against the various guides on top of the printer. These guides should be set so that they sit just beyond the edges of the paper.

On some machines, the printhead can catch on the left edge of the paper as it begins to print each line. The easiest solution is to set the paper slightly farther to the left, so the printhead is always positioned over the paper.

Tractor-feed printers can have different problems. Make sure the paper is lined up correctly with the drive pins, as shown in Fig. 12-33. Make sure the paper sits squarely on the drive pins. You can check this by counting the number of drive pins that lie above

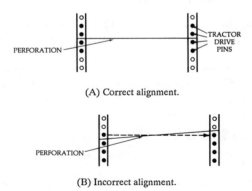

(A) Correct alignment.

(B) Incorrect alignment.

Fig. 12-33. Mounting tractor-feed paper.

or below one of the perforations. In Fig. 12-33B, the paper is mounted incorrectly.

On most machines, the tractor mechanisms are adjustable to take various widths of paper. For each kind of paper, the spacing between the tractor mechanisms must be just right, to hold the paper with the right tension. Refer to Fig. 12-34. If the tractor mechanisms are too close together, the paper will be held loosely. If the mechanisms are too far apart, they will put too much tension on the paper. The mechanisms should be set so that they hold the paper firmly, but without pulling on the outer sides of the holes in the paper.

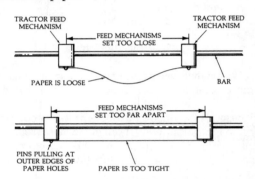

Fig. 12-34. Setting width of the tractor mechanism.

Tractor-feed machines can use a lot of paper very quickly. If the paper jams up, it can create a mess. Be careful to ensure that the paper can feed smoothly, with no catches or hang-ups. Be particularly careful to check the way that the paper feeds out of the box or tray in which it is stored.

The tractor mechanism itself can develop mechanical problems. For example, the tractor drive pins can be out of phase, as shown in Fig. 12-35. A bent drive rod can make the mechanism work unevenly.

On machines that can handle both tractor-feed and friction-feed paper, be sure to release the pressure rollers before you run the tractor-feed mechanism.

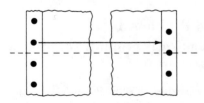

Fig. 12-35. Tractor pins out of phase.

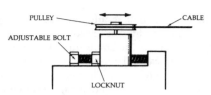

Fig. 12-37. Adjusting cable tension.

12.2 Troubleshooting and Adjusting Specific Subsystems

Many printer manufacturers don't encourage customers, or even dealer service personnel, to repair bad components in their printers. They base their troubleshooting on a "swap the circuit board" strategy. This is often the fastest way to localize a problem, but since most of us don't have a rack of spare circuit boards, this method is not very practical.

Fortunately, many printer problems are relatively simple. With this in mind, we've listed some key signals to check and adjustments to make. These procedures should help you to fix many of the more common problems.

12.2.1 Adjustment 1
Adjusting the carriage-drive mechanism.

The carriage-drive mechanism is usually activated by a stepper motor, as illustrated in Fig. 12-36. For this motor to move the carriage accurately, the drive cable or belt must be tight. Refer to Section 12.2.2 if the cable or belt appears to be loose. All moving parts along the cable path should be cleaned and lubricated.

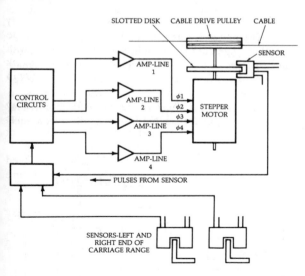

Fig. 12-36. Block diagram of carriage-drive mechanism.

If the stepper motor is inactive, check for the correct signals on the four lines to the motor. Refer to the discussion of stepper motors in Chapter 7. If signals are absent from one or more of the signal lines, check

the discrete output transistors. When the motor is supposed to be active, you should see a train of TTL-level pulses inputting into each transistor, and a train of higher-voltage pulses outputting on the other side. If one or more of these input pulses is missing, look for a problem in the control circuits. Check for correct functioning of the sensor on the motor's shaft, as described in Chapter 7.

Two detectors mark the left and right ends of the carriage travel. If the carriage somehow gets outside this range, or if one of the sensors fails, the carriage-drive mechanism could be inhibited. Check the current position of the carriage and test each sensor, as described in the discussion on "Testing a Light Source and Detector" in Chapter 7.

12.2.2 Adjustment 2
Setting the carriage-drive cable tension.

Earlier in the chapter, in the section on "Cleaning and Maintenance," we described how to check for the correct tension on the carriage-drive cable or belt, using a postage scale. (This was illustrated in Fig. 12-23.) Over a period of time, the cable or belt will stretch and may need to be tightened. Fig. 12-37 shows one possible cable-tightening arrangement. To tighten the cable, you loosen a lock nut, turn an adjustable bolt until the cable is tight, and then retighten the lock nut. However, many printers use a toothed drive belt. On this type of mechanism, the idler pulley may be moved in or out to loosen or tighten the belt (Fig. 12-38).

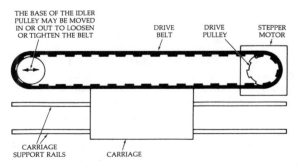

Fig. 12-38. Adjusting belt tension.

The cable or belt should be quite tight, since the printer depends on this tension for accurate positioning of the printhead. At the same time, be careful not to over tighten the cable, because this may cause wear or damage to the pulleys and other parts. Try to meet the specification listed by the manufacturer for belt tension.

12.2.3 Adjustment 3
Adjusting the platen and platen drive.

In many printers, the platen is easily removable; it is secured by clip mechanisms at each end. The service manual will sometimes specify a clearance between two parts on these clip mechanisms. If the clearance is correct, you know that all is well at these points. The manual may point out some setscrews you can adjust to make small changes in the way that these parts sit. In general, if the platen is held firmly in place, the platen supports are all right.

Many manufacturers also list an adjustment for the platen drive gears. You should not have to worry about this unless the gears wear and develop significant backlash. See Fig. 12-24 for an illustration of backlash. One possible adjustment scheme for the gears may be made by referring to Fig. 12-39 and loosening the screws that hold the stepper motor in adjustment. Adjust for zero backlash between the platen drive gear and the idler gear by undoing the locknut and turning the eccentric cam on the idler gear. Next, adjust the position of the stepper motor for zero backlash between the motor drive gear and the idler gear. Retighten the screws on the base of the stepper motor.

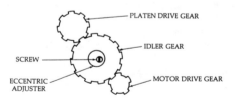

Fig. 12-39. Gear-train adjustment.

In Fig. 12-25, we illustrated how the printed character would appear if the platen was too low or too high. Fig. 12-40 shows how you can adjust the platen to correct for this. Printer mechanisms vary, but each end of the platen is often mounted on a plate that can be adjusted vertically. Usually, this plate is locked in place by one or more screws. You must loosen these screws, and adjust an eccentric screw, or setscrew, to change the vertical setting. Adjust each end of the platen

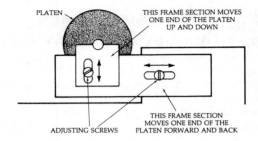

Fig. 12-40. Platen adjustments.

separately. Retighten all the screws, and run a test print to check the result.

A similar mechanism allows you to set the distance between each end of the platen and the printhead. You can use this adjustment to correct for the problem that was shown in Fig. 12-26.

The pressure rollers beneath the platen should not give you any trouble unless the supporting rod is bent, or unless the rollers themselves wear out. The manufacturer should list the clearance that appears between the rollers and the platen when the paper pressure lever is released. Normally, the pressure rollers should retract enough to allow four or five pieces of typing paper to fit between the rollers and the platen. Each of the rollers should make solid contact with the platen when the lever is set in the normal position. The spring-loaded paper bail rollers located on top of the platen should also make a solid contact.

The platen is often driven by a stepper motor. A typical arrangement is shown in Fig. 12-41. If the motor appears to be dead, start by checking for normal signals on each of the four signal lines for the motor. (Refer also to the discussion on "Stepper Motors" given in Chapter 7). If one or more of these signals is missing, check the output transistors in the amplifier on each

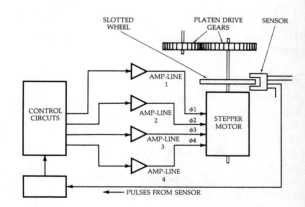

Fig. 12-41. Diagram of the platen drive mechanism.

signal line. You should see a train of TTL-level pulses entering each transistor, and higher-voltage pulses exiting from the output. If one or more of the input signals are missing, look for a problem with the control circuits.

You might also check the sensor that detects the position of the motor's shaft. Sometimes the sensor will fail or slip out of position. Refer to the material in Chapter 7 on "Testing a Light Source and Detector."

12.2.4 Adjustment 4
Adjusting the head mechanical alignment (dot-matrix printers).

The tip of the printhead should sit very close to the surface of the platen, as shown in Fig. 12-42. One manufacturer suggests a clearance of 0.018 inch, or 0.45 mm. This is about the thickness of three sheets of typing paper. The clearance might be slightly different on your machine. Use a feeler gauge to make the measurement.

The printhead should also be square in relation to the platen. The printhead may be adjusted side-to-side by releasing the two screws shown in Fig. 12-42. The center line of the printhead should line up with the center of the platen. (This was illustrated in Fig. 12-25. The sketch also showed the symptoms noted when the adjustment is incorrect.)

On many printers, the platen is adjustable, as well as the printhead. Before you change the setting of the printhead, however, try to determine if the platen has moved. If the platen is loose, adjust the platen rather than the printhead. (Refer to Section 12.2.3.)

Most manufacturers make a "jig" that can help you align the head quickly and accurately.

12.2.5 Adjustment 5
Checking the head driver circuits (dot-matrix printers).

Fig. 12-43 shows the driver circuits for two of the print wires in a dot-matrix printer. Set the printer in "self-test" mode, or use the computer to send some characters to the printer. Watch the solenoids and the print wires in the printhead. If a particular print wire does not move, turn the printer off. Use a voltohmmeter to check for continuity through the solenoid coil, as described in Chapter 7. Also check for a short from a coil wire to ground.

If the solenoid seems all right, turn on the printer

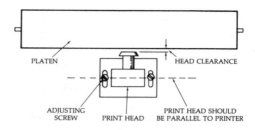

Fig. 12-42. Head mechanical alignment for a dot-matrix printer.

and check for a train of pulses at the input of the inactive solenoid. Use a VOM or an oscilloscope to check for this signal—the voltage level will probably burn out a logic probe. If the signal is missing, check the amplifier for that solenoid. Pay particular attention to the discrete output transistor, if the amp includes one.

Each print signal originates as a series of 5-volt pulses from the control circuits. You can check for these with your logic probe.

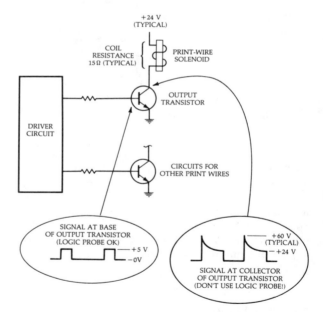

Fig. 12-43. Driver circuits for a dot-matrix printer.

12.2.6 Adjustment 6
Adjusting the head mechanical alignment (daisy-wheel printers).

Most manufacturers make a "jig" that will allow you to

do this alignment quickly and accurately. If you don't have a jig, you can make a visual inspection. Be sure the platen is in good shape and is in alignment before you change the settings on the printhead. (See Section 12.2.3.)

Fig. 12-44 shows a side view of a daisy-wheel print mechanism. The center of the print hammer should line up with the center of the platen roller. You can change this setting by using the adjusting screws on the hammer assembly. One manufacturer says that the front edge of the daisy wheel should be about $1/10$th of an inch, or 3 mm from the surface of the platen. Sometimes you can change this setting by using the adjusting screws at the base of the head assembly.

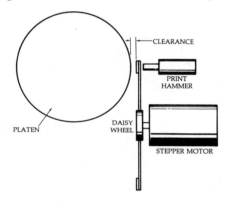

Fig. 12-44. Head mechanical alignment for a daisy-wheel printer.

Fig. 12-45 shows the top view of a daisy-wheel mechanism that is in the "home" position. A specified character is positioned in front of the print hammer. (Fig. 12-27 illustrated what would happen if the hammer strikes the print arm off-center.) By setting the position of the "home" character, you center all of the other characters as well. If necessary, you can make an adjustment, and rotate the daisy wheel relative to the print hammer.

12.2.7 Adjustment 7
Checking the head driver circuits (daisy-wheel printer).

Fig. 12-46 shows a typical arrangement for the head driver circuits. If the stepper motor appears to be inactive, start by checking for normal signals on the four signal lines. (Refer to the discussion on stepper motors given in Chapter 7.) You'll have to use a VOM or an

oscilloscope here—the pulses on these lines would probably burn out a logic probe.

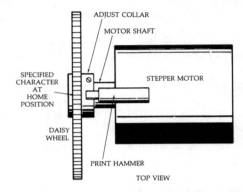

Fig. 12-45. Daisy-wheel printer in home position.

Each of the signal lines passes through an amplifier that takes 5-V TTL signals and boosts them up to the higher voltage and current levels needed to drive the motor. The last stage of each of these amps often uses a discrete transistor. Check out the amplifier for each inactive line, and pay particular attention to this output transistor.

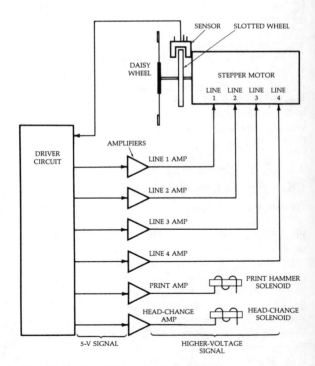

Fig. 12-46. Head drive circuits for daisy-wheel printers.

If the amp seems all right, check the 5-V input signal from the control circuits. You can use your logic probe here.

If the control circuits are not producing any stepper motor commands, check the sensor mechanism. You should be able to pick up the sensor pulses with your logic probe. If the pulses are missing, the sensor mechanism may have slipped or stopped working.

A separate circuit controls the print hammer. If you have a problem here, start by checking the solenoid. Use a voltohmmeter to check for continuity through the solenoid's coil, as described in the discussion on solenoids in Chapter 7. Check also for a short from the coil wires to ground.

The print-hammer control also passes through an amplifier stage. Use a VOM or an oscilloscope to check for a signal going into the print solenoid. If the signal is missing, check the TTL-level output from the control circuits. If the amp has an input, but no output, be sure to check the discrete output transistor in the last stage.

NEC-type printers have two rows of type on the print arms. A solenoid moves the print thimble up and down so the print hammer can strike either one set of characters or the other. The basic circuit is similar to the print-hammer circuit we described above. If you have a problem with this mechanism, check it using the procedure we've just described.

12.2.8 Adjustment 8
Checking the ribbon-adjustment mechanisms.

The height of the ribbon as it passes in front of the print hammer can usually be adjusted. Fig. 12-47 shows one kind of mechanism. The service manual will specify how the ribbon should be positioned.

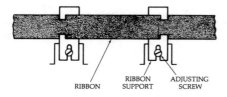

Fig. 12-47. Adjusting ribbon height.

On printers that use a ribbon cartridge, you will have to change the height of the ribbon by changing the way the cartridge sits. On printers designed for a red/black ribbon, you may have to change the stops that set the upper and lower limits of travel as the cartridge tilts up and down. On some printers, the ribbon is driven by a gear that rides down a rack on one of the

carriage support rails. The main concern here is backlash between the drive gears. (Fig. 12-24 illustrated how to measure backlash, and Fig. 12-39 illustrated how to make an adjustment on a typical gear train.)

Some printers use a stepper motor to advance the ribbon. Fig. 12-48 shows the signals involved. If the stepper motor appears to be inactive, start by checking for normal signals on each of the signal lines. Refer to the discussion in Chapter 7 on stepper motors. Use a VOM or oscilloscope to check these signals. The voltages on these lines may burn out a logic probe.

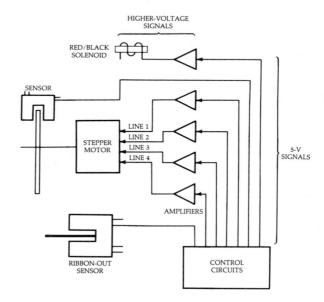

Fig. 12-48. Ribbon drive circuits.

If one or more of the signals are absent, check the amplifiers on each of the signal lines. You should detect TTL-level pulses going into each amp, and higher-voltage pulses on their outputs. If the input signals are missing, look for a problem in the control circuit.

Some printers have a sensor that detects the ribbon-out condition. This is usually a typical LED-and-detector arrangement. A piece of clear plastic is attached to the end of the ribbon. When this clear section passes through the sensor, the LED beam can reach the detector and the device sends a signal to the printer CPU. You can check for the output from the detector using your logic probe. Refer to the discussion on testing a light source and detector given in Chapter 7. If the output is missing, the sensor may have slipped out of position or stopped working.

Printers that use a red/black ribbon include a solenoid that causes the ribbon to be raised or lowered in front of the print hammer. Check for continuity through the coil of the solenoid using a voltohmmeter. Refer to the discussion on solenoids given in Chapter 7. Check also for a short from the coil wire to ground.

One of the two possible positions for the solenoid and the ribbon is what is considered as "normal" or "at rest." You won't see a signal to the solenoid when the printer is calling for this position. When the printer wants another position, the solenoid should receive a signal. Check for this with a voltmeter or oscilloscope. If the signal is missing, check the amplifier. Pay particular attention to the discrete output transistor.

The amplifier should receive 5-volt inputs from the control circuits. Check for these using your logic probe.

Continuous-loop fabric ribbons may eventually jam up. Fig. 12-49 shows a typical cartridge. This kind of cartridge usually jams because the ribbon is caught between one end of the drive wheel and the case, as shown in the sketch. You can usually pry off the case, unwind the extra ribbon from the drive wheel, and reassemble the cartridge. Be sure the parts of the case are pushed tightly together, leaving no space at either end of the drive wheel.

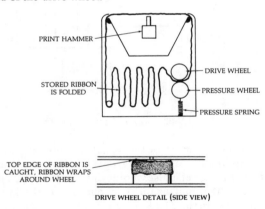

Fig. 12-49. An endless-loop ribbon cassette.

12.2.9 Adjustment 9
Checking the interfacing circuits.

Some printers receive signals from the computer over a "serial" interface. This kind of interface handles data one bit at a time. The interface has a single line for data, although it may have many other lines for control signals. The most common type of serial interface uses the RS-232 standard. (Refer to Chapter 14 for details on the RS-232 interface. Since it is also the most common standard for modems, we've discussed it in detail in Chapter 14.)

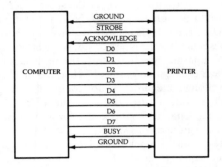

Fig. 12-50. Centronics-type parallel interface.

The alternative is the "parallel" interface. In this kind of system, the interface transfers several bits of data at the same time, using several parallel data lines. Many small printers use the Centronics® parallel interface, which has eight data lines and handles eight bits of data in each data "package." Fig. 12-50 illustrates the idea of this parallel format. Fig. 12-51 shows the data and control-line signals. IBM, Epson, and other companies use variations of this interface.

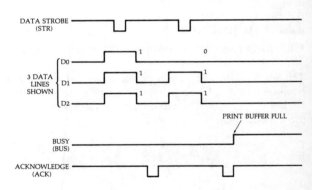

Fig. 12-51. Centronics interface data and control signals.

Each 8-bit data "package" represents either a character to be printed or a "control code" that tells the printer to do something. The printer is always sorting through the characters as it receives them. The codes that represent printed characters are stored for printing. The control codes are stripped out and processed by the printer's CPU. Many printers can use "escape" codes. Whenever the printer receives an "escape" character (ESC), it knows that the next few characters will make up a command.

Most printers use characters coded in the standard ASCII format. (ASCII stands for *American Standard Code for Information Interchange*, and is pronounced "as-key." Appendix D lists the ASCII codes.) For example, let's say that the computer wants to command the printer to print the capital letter "A." In the table given in Appendix D, you can see that the decimal code for "A" is "65." (Notice that a different code is used for the small "a.") Notice also that the ASCII set includes uppercase and lowercase letters, numbers, special symbols, and control codes.

Each code number may also be translated into the *hexadecimal* numbering system. A decimal code of "65" could be expressed as a hexadecimal code of "41." The hexadecimal system is based on the number 16. Our normal decimal system is based on the number 10. To indicate the decimal numbers 10 through 15, the hexadecimal system uses the letters A through F. Hexadecimal values often are marked with a dollar-sign symbol ($). The number written as "$12" in the hexadecimal system represents "16 +2," rather than "10+2." If you are not familiar with this system, refer to Appendix D.

The hexadecimal code tells you how a particular letter or command is coded on the eight parallel data lines. Two-digit hexadecimal numbers can easily be expressed as a series of binary "1s" and "0s" on eight data lines. The first four lines carry the binary code for the first digit, which in the previous example is the number "$4." The binary code for "$4" is "0100." The second four lines carry the second digit code, or "0001" for "1." The complete hexadecimal number $41 would be expressed as binary 0100 0001. These binary codes can easily be placed on the eight parallel data lines. In this example, line 1 would be "low," line 2 "high," line 3 "low," and so on.

Each time the computer wants to send data to the printer, it sends out a pulse on the *data strobe* (STR) line. As you can see in Fig. 12-51, this line is normally held "high," and the pulse is a temporary "low" state. The printer may actually load the data on either the rising edge or the falling edge of the pulse. The eight data lines carry up to eight bits of binary data from the computer to the printer, with the eight bits being loaded into the printer at one time, each time a STROBE pulse is present.

Each time the printer receives an 8-bit byte of data, or a printer control signal (line feed, bell, etc.), it answers with an *acknowledge* (ACK) signal. As you can see in the diagram of Fig. 12-51, this is a positive pulse.

In many cases, the computer sends characters more quickly than the printer can print them. The printer usually has an "input buffer" to help make up for the difference in speed. The printer can temporarily store a few characters in this buffer, and can hold them until it is ready to print them.

If a fast computer were to constantly send a stream of characters to a slower printer, this buffer would quickly overflow. In an overflow situation, some of the characters are lost from the buffer, and are never printed. To prevent this, the printer sends a "busy" signal. As the name suggests, the BUSY line signals whenever the printer is too busy to accept new data. This line will normally signal when the print buffer is full, and will stop the computer from sending characters until the buffer is empty. When the buffer is empty again and ready to accept new data, the BUSY line will change and allow the computer to send more characters. The "true" state for the BUSY line can be either "high" or "low," depending on the printer.

The BUSY signal is not used on some interfaces. Some computers look for a signal from the printer called *acknowledge* (ACK), which is similar to BUSY. Some computers expect to see both BUSY and ACK. When the DATA STROBE, ACKNOWLEDGE, and BUSY signals work together to supervise the data transfer, the process is called *handshaking*.

One set of interfacing problems is usually caused by a failure of this "handshaking" system. For example, let's say that the computer gets ahead of the printer, and the handshaking system doesn't stop the computer from sending more characters. The printer will store as many characters as possible in the input buffer, and then, any other characters will simply be lost. The printer may continue to print, but several characters will be missing. Also, the remaining characters may appear in incorrect locations on the page.

Another kind of interfacing failure occurs when the computer and printer are both waiting for each other. The computer says, "I'm ready to send data, how about you?", and the printer says, "OK, I'm ready to print." If the signal from the printer never gets back to the computer, both units will wait patiently for a control signal that never arrives.

Both of these interfacing problems should be corrected when you first set up your printer. As we said earlier, we're assuming that your printer has been working correctly for some time, and that the problems have just recently begun to appear.

A hidden interfacing problem may also appear when you tell the printer to perform an unusual function. For example, a printer may work well until you ask it to print boldface characters. As some printers take more time to print boldface characters, the printer may fall behind the computer, the printer's input buffer may be overloaded, and the printer may start to print erratically. In a situation like this, the interface may be set up incorrectly. Double-check all of the connections and switch settings on the computer interface circuits and on the printer.

To correct a problem with an interfacing setup, you need specific information on the interface circuits in both the computer and the printer. Is the computer expecting to see BUSY, or ACK*, or both? When the printer is busy, is the BUSY line supposed to be "low" or "high?" In most cases, you can set switches in both the printer and the computer to control these functions. To be certain that the interface is set up correctly, you must understand the function of each of these switches. The owner's manuals for the units may discuss the switch settings in detail. If not, you will have to refer to the service manuals for each unit. To solve a particularly tough problem, you may have to phone the computer manufacturer, the printer manufacturer, or both.

Whenever you have an interfacing problem, check the connections in the cable that runs between the computer and printer. In some cables, each pin in one connector is wired to the pin of the same number in the other connector. But in some special cables, the designers may scramble these pin assignments. For example, pin 2 on the first connector may be deliberately wired to pin 3 on the other connector. These "custom" cables must be wired by hand and, sometimes, someone makes a mistake in wiring or sends you the wrong cable. The only way to be sure that the cable is wired correctly is to test each connector and see if the correct pins are wired together. You will need pin diagrams for each of the connectors. Turn off the equipment and unplug both ends of the cable. Use a voltohmmeter, set to read OHMS, to see which points are connected. Refer to the section on cables and connectors in Chapter 7.

The activity of the interface is under the control

Table 12-1. Signals on Centronics Interface

Signal	Description
STROBE*	"Data strobe" signal from computer to printer. This line will be "high" until a character is sent to the printer. The line should normally show a series of pulses.
DATA 1 to DATA 8	"Data" lines from computer to printer. These lines carry ASCII characters coded into binary "highs" and "lows." Each line should normally show continuous pulses.
ACKNLG or ACKNLG* (ACK or ACK*)	"Acknowledge" signal from computer to printer. If the computer is configured for this, the ACK signal will prevent the computer from sending more characters to the printer. Depending on the printer, this may happen when ACK is high (ACK) or ACK is low (ACK*). Some computers ignore the ACK signal—check the manual. If ACK is used, this line should show continuous activity.
BUSY or BUSY*	"Busy" signal from printer to computer. When the printer is occupied, it makes the BUSY line active to stop the computer from sending more characters. Depending on the printer, this may happen when BUSY is high, or when BUSY* is low. Some computers ignore the BUSY signal—check the manual. If BUSY signal is used, this line should show continuous activity.
PE	"Printer error" signal from printer to computer. This line is normally low unless something is wrong with the printer. Depending on the printer, this can be triggered by any of the sensors on the printer—out of paper, cover open, low voltage, etc.
GND	Logic "ground." Always 0 V.
CHASSIS GND	"Chassis ground" on the printer. Always 0 V.
RETURN GND	"Return ground" for each of the data lines. Always 0 V.
INIT*	"Initialize" signal to the printer. This line will remain "high" until the computer wants to initialize the printer. When INIT* goes low, the print buffer is cleared. This line should normally be "high."
ERROR*	"Error" signal from printer to computer. This line is normally high unless something is wrong with the printer. Depending on the printer, this can be triggered by any of the sensors on the printer—out of paper, cover open, low voltage, etc.

Note: All lines on the parallel interface should show TTL-level signals (+5-V DC and 0-V DC). Use a logic probe or oscilloscope for these tests.

of the software. A typical problem occurs when the software has a "bug" that causes the computer to look for the interface at the wrong address. In other cases, you can make a mistake that misleads the software. For example, in an IBM PC, the printer interface may be handled by one of several adapter cards. When you start running a commercial software package, the computer will ask you which card slot holds the printer interface adapter card. If you specify the wrong card slot, the system will not be able to contact the printer, and it may stall or "hang up."

When you have an interface problem that does not appear to be caused by the setup, start troubleshooting by eliminating the software as a cause. Does the interface stop working when you use a certain program? Try a backup copy of the program. If you still have a problem, try running other programs that activate the interface. If the problem appears when you're running several different kinds of software, you can begin to look for a hardware problem.

Next, you might check the signals on each line of the interface. On a "Centronics" interface, you can use your logic probe. Fig. 12-52 shows the pin-outs for a typical Centronics-type connector. Table 12-1 lists the types of signals you should expect to find. The computer should be sending characters to the printer as you make your tests. To do this, you can use a word-processing program to print a long file, or you can use a short BASIC program. The program may be written in a continuous loop. Program 12-1 is a simple BASIC program you can use. (End the program by pressing "Reset.")

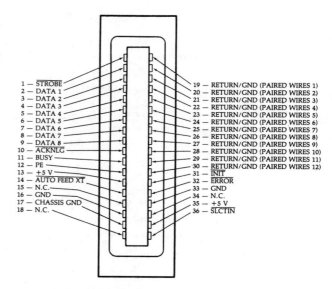

Fig. 12-52. Signals on a Centronics-type connector.

In a Centronics interface, STROBE* is generated by the computer. The printer won't do anything if the STROBE* signal is missing. If this signal is missing at the printer, and the cable and connectors are all right, look for a problem in the computer itself. It is important to know whether the computer is generating the first STROBE* signal in the sequence. If the computer is generating a STROBE* pulse, but the printer is not responding, you know that the problem lies in the printer. If the computer never generates even

```
Program 12-1. Printer Test Program No. 1.
10   PR#1                     Future output will be sent to printer.
20   PRINT "THIS IS A TEST"   Test characters sent to printer.
30   PRINT "QWERTYUIOP[]\"     Test characters sent to printer.
60   GOTO 10                  Set up a repeating loop.
```

You may discover that the signals you find don't match the pattern we've just described. For example, one of the data lines might show no activity. Check the cable and connectors between the computer and printer, as described in Chapter 7. The conductor for the missing signal may be broken, or one of the connectors may be damaged.

At each end of the cable, inside the computer and inside the printer, you will probably find a set of TRI-STATE® buffers (Fig. 12-53). Check for correct activity at these components. Also, refer to the material in Chapter 8 on "Three-State Buffers."

Perhaps the computer is not sending data because some of the "handshaking" signals are missing.

the first STROBE* pulse, look for a problem in the circuits in the computer. (This is a good assignment for the "memory" feature on your logic probe. The STROBE* pulse passes very quickly, and the normal "high/low" indicator on the probe may not be fast enough. By setting the probe to the "memory" mode, you can see whether that first STROBE* pulse ever arrives.)

The ACK* and BUSY signals are both generated by the printer. On many computers, the interface will not work if ACK* is missing or if the BUSY line is always "true." Check to see if these handshaking lines are "hung up."

Inside the computer, one or more ICs will

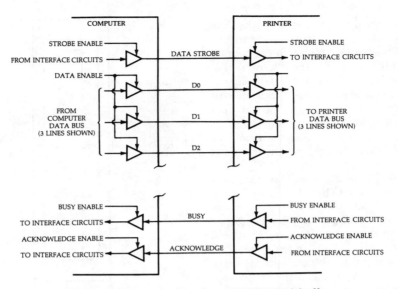

Fig. 12-53. Centronics interface–TRISTATE® buffers.

generate the signals going out to the printer. Often, this job will be handled by a single IC called a *peripheral interface adapter* (PIA). Fig. 12-54 is a simplified block diagram of this device. The PIA in Fig. 12-54 has two interface ports, A and B, and each port has eight lines. Each of these may be set up to operate as either an input or an output.

As stated, within a particular port, some of the lines may be used as inputs and others may be outputs. These assignments are made when the PIA is first turned on, or "initialized." At this time, the computer stores some "control bits" in the data direction registers, and these registers determine whether a line will work as an input or an output.

In a printer interface circuit, one of the ports will be used to handle the 8 data lines to the printer. All 8 lines on this port will be set up as outputs. The second port will handle the control signals, such as STROBE*, INIT*, and so on. Some of the lines on this second port will be configured as inputs to handle the signals coming back from the printer—BUSY, ACK*, RESET*, and so on.

The PIA operates as a complicated latching device. As we said, 8 lines are used as data outputs to the printer. When the computer wants to enable these output lines, it selects the PIA chip. The read/write pin (R/W) is set to "write," and any data on the computer's data bus are passed through to the 8 outputs. Other lines are used as inputs. The PIA is selected, R/W is set to "read," and any inputs on these lines are connected to the computer's data bus.

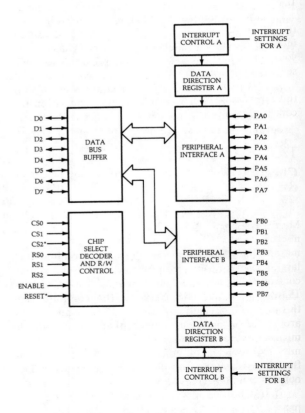

Fig. 12-54. Peripheral interface adapter (PIA) block diagram.

You can make a quick check of the PIA if you know which lines are configured as inputs and which are outputs. As the printer operates, you should be able to see the data coming to the data inputs of the PIA, and data going out along the 8 output lines. This is easier if you command the printer to continually print the same character. You might use a short program like Program 12-2. (End the program by pressing "Reset".)

```
Program 12-2. Printer Test Program No. 2.
10    PR#1                   Future output will be sent to printer.
20    PRINT"XXXXXXXXXXXXX"    Test characters sent to printer.
30    GOTO 10                 Set up a repeating loop.
```

Some computers do not use a single PIA chip to handle the parallel interface. The functions are the same as those shown in Fig. 12-54, but each of the "blocks" in the diagram might be handled by one or more separate ICs. The input and output lines are usually buffered at each end of the link, as shown in Fig. 12-53.

In some computers, including the Apple II series, the IBM PC and its clones, and the Mac II, the interface circuits are mounted on removable cards. If your computer allows this, substitute another card and see if the problems disappear.

If all appears to be well with the signals through the interface cable, check the printer CPU and the control circuits, discussed in the next section.

12.2.10 Adjustment 10
Checking the printer CPU and control circuits.

Many printers are controlled by common microprocessor chips—an 8080, 6502, etc. Besides the main CPU chip, these printers usually have several large supporting ICs. Some of the newer printers are controlled by just two or three "smart" ICs. In Fig. 12-15, we gave a simplified block diagram of a printer of this second type. The basic components of the system are similar to the components you would find in any microcomputer. The difference is that this particular microcomputer is dedicated to one particular function—receiving and translating digital data and outputting it as printer characters.

In Chapter 9, we described a troubleshooting procedure for the main computer's CPU and associated circuitry. With a few additional comments, these instructions will serve just as well for troubleshooting the printer's CPU. All of the basic steps are the same. Start by checking for Clock and Reset signals. If these are all right, check the control lines and the data and address buses.

The circuitry in a printer can be inhibited by a number of control signals from the various printer mechanisms. These can include the "paper out," "ribbon out," and "carriage out of range" signals.

Other functions are inhibited only at certain times. For example, when the printhead is actually printing, the line feed and carriage mechanisms are usually inhibited. These are all designed to protect the printer if something goes wrong. The problem is, if any of these signals is stuck in the "warning" state, it may prevent some of the printer circuitry from operating. Therefore, if the printer CPU seems to be operating normally, track down these various "warning" signals and be sure they are working correctly. You may have to do some research in the manual for your printer to understand exactly how these circuits are meant to work.

Any interfacing problem can cause the printer to stop. The printer may also stop if it detects an incorrect character or signal in the incoming data (Section 12.2.9). In addition, the printer can stop working if one of the power-supply outputs drops below a certain specification. If the printer CPU seems to be inactive, check for a low voltage using the procedure described in Chapter 16.

Chapter Review

As you have learned, printers are complicated devices. In this chapter, we reviewed the operating principles of dot-matrix and daisy-wheel printers. Next, we discussed some of the considerations in servicing these units, and learned that because printers have so many mechanical parts, they should be cleaned and lubricated regularly. We also reviewed a typical "parallel" interface between the printer and the computer. Finally, we offered some troubleshooting suggestions for each type of printer.

Whenever you experience problems with a printer, start by checking the mechanical parts, but remember that cables and connectors also create more than their share of problems. The electronic circuits themselves tend to be quite reliable.

Review Questions

1. Your printer stops working. You set the printer to "off line" or "local" and tell the printer to start a "self-test." The printer still does not print. What does this tell you?

2. You are servicing a printer, and you suspect a problem in the parallel interface with the computer. With your logic probe, you determine that the BUSY line is always "high." What does this tell you?

3. One of your clients tries to save every cent possible. His dot-matrix printer seems to be wearing out printheads very rapidly. Can you think of a reason why this might happen?

4. On a dot-matrix or daisy-wheel printer, the characters are half red and half black. Why?

5. On an older daisy-wheel printer, the printed characters are starting to look "fuzzy." Can you suggest a reason why this might happen?

6. You are working with a parallel interface and you notice that it includes a large IC called a "VIA." Can you tell where the 8 data lines for the interface are likely to be connected to this IC?

7. On a dot-matrix printer, you notice that in each line of type, one row of printed dots seems to be missing. You look at the front of the printhead and you notice that one of the print wires is extended from the head. Why has this happened?

8. Your ink-jet printer stops printing characters. What is the most likely cause?

9. On a dot-matrix printer, you notice that the carriage drive belt is quite loose. Why is this bad?

10. On a dot-matrix printer, one of the print wires has stopped working. When you swap connections with the next print wire, the first wire begins to operate. The resistance through the solenoid coil on the first mechanism is about 18 ohms. Where do you look next?

11. You have a dot-matrix printer. In the middle of a long printing session, the printing speed seems to slow down. Can you suggest a reason?

13

Laser Printers

Introduction and Objectives

In this chapter, we will examine how the laser printer operates. This new type of printer offers a very high resolution, and has the ability to handle both text and graphics. We expect the laser printer to become increasingly common in the years ahead.

Since a laser printer is quite different from the other types of printers we have discussed, we will need to go into some detail. A laser printer is a very complicated device. To begin with, a laser printer includes many mechanical parts and these must function smoothly together. This type of printer must also include quite a bit of computing power. The typical laser printer includes a complete microcomputer system, including a sophisticated CPU, plus ROMs and other supporting circuits. This type of printer is often designed to "remember" the image of a whole page of type, and this requires large amounts of RAM. For example, the Personal LaserPrinter, produced by General Computer, includes a 68000 microprocessor chip and 2-megabytes of on-board memory. A laser printer often has more computing power than the computer that is driving it.

We will base our discussion here on the Hewlett-Packard 33440A. The "print engine" in this printer is made by Canon USA Inc. Many other laser printers use the same print engine.

Later in the chapter, we will discuss some of the common service problems you may encounter with a laser printer, and then, we will include some troubleshooting instructions for some common trouble symptoms.

The Laser Printer Mechanism

Many of the most important parts in a laser printer (Fig. 13-1) are mounted in a *removable cartridge*. This cartridge is intended to be replaced when it runs out of *toner powder*. The replacement cartridge will have a fresh supply of toner, but it will also include a new *photosensitive drum* and *developing cylinder*. This arrangement eliminates most of the need for any servicing by a trained technician.

Fig. 13-2 is a side view of the interior of a laser printer. The print image is formed on the large photosensitive drum in the center of the cartridge. Then, a dark toner powder is transferred to the drum by the developing roll. Next, the toner image is then transferred to the paper. Finally, the toner is "fused" to the paper by the hot fusing rollers.

The photosensitive drum must turn several times in order to print one page. The drum cannot hold enough "dots" to print a whole page during one turn. During printing, different processes are taking place on

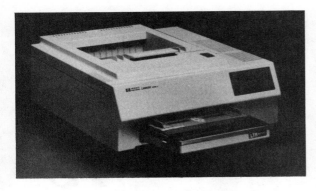

Fig. 13-1. Hewlett-Packard LaserJet II printer.
(Courtesy Hewlett-Packard Co.)

is coated with a light-sensitive layer of *organic-photoconductive material* (OPC). The inner part of the drum is made of a thin aluminum sheeting. This aluminum tube is connected to ground.

Normally, the OPC layer is a fairly good insulator. If negative charges are deposited on the outside of the drum, they tend to stay here until they are removed. However, when a section of the drum is exposed to light, it becomes conductive. If the outside of the drum at that point is charged, and the drum is struck by a bright light, the charge on the drum will be drained off to ground. However, other sections of the drum, which are not exposed to light, will remain charged.

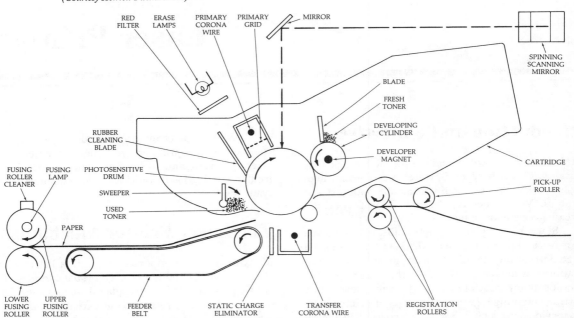

Fig. 13-2. Inside a laser printer.

different parts of the drum at the same time. One section of the drum is picking up toner while another part is placing toner on the paper. As the drum turns, each point on the drum moves through each of these processes. Let's follow one point on the drum as it goes through each of the different phases.

Conditioning the Drum

Fig. 13-3 illustrates how the printer transfers an image to a piece of paper. The key to the printing process is the photosensitive drum. The outer surface of the drum

At the start of the printing process, the surface of the drum is given a uniform negative charge. This process is called "conditioning." The *primary corona wire* is mounted inside a long narrow enclosure. See part A of Fig. 13-3. This wire is given a high-voltage negative charge of about −6000 V. This high voltage causes the air molecules around the wire to break down or "ionize." The air around the wire no longer acts as an insulator, but becomes able to transfer charged particles, called "ions."

Below the primary corona wire is the *primary grid*. Circuitry in the printer can change the charge on this grid. Normally, it is about −690 V. This is a strong

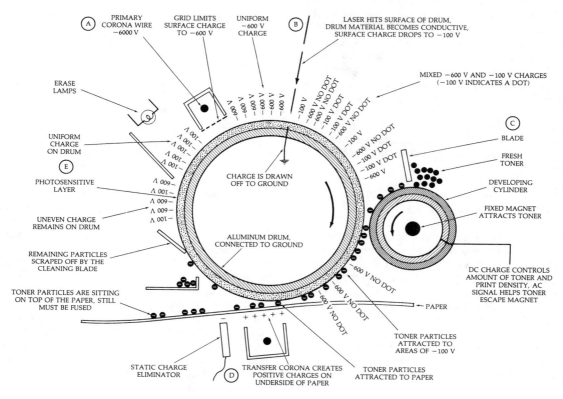

Fig. 13-3. Laser print cycle.

negative charge, but it is less negative than the −6000 V at the corona wire. The grid attracts charged ions from the corona wire. The negatively charged ions move toward the surface of the drum. As they pass, the grid limits the negative charge on the ions, and the ions give the surface of the drum a uniform charge of −600 V.

Writing the Image on the Drum

Whenever the printer wants to print a black dot, it turns on a small "laser diode." See part B of Fig. 13-3. The beam from this laser diode is reflected by a series of mirrors, and aimed onto the surface of the print drum. When the beam reaches the OPC material on the drum, the OPC becomes conductive. The strongly negative charge of −600 V is reduced to a less negative charge of about −100 V. The printer then paints an image of the page on the drum, using tiny "dots" of −100-V charges. At this point, these charges are invisible, and will not leave any marks on the paper.

Developing the Image

To make an image, the printer uses a black powder called "toner." The *toner* consists of a powdered black plastic, with the particles of plastic bound to tiny particles of iron. The iron particles can be attracted by magnets and, when this happens, the black plastic material is carried along. This means that the mixed toner powder can be moved and controlled by magnets. A supply of this toner is available at the top of the developing cylinder. See part C of Fig. 13-3.

A fixed magnet is mounted inside the developing cylinder (part C, Fig. 13-3). As the cylinder turns, the magnet attracts toner powder. A blade levels off the toner, so the surface of the developing cylinder carries a uniform layer of toner. The developing cylinder is given a negative charge, and the toner particles take on this negative charge. The amount of negative charge, or "bias," on the developing cylinder can be changed to change the amount of toner picked up, and, thus, the density of the print can be changed. An AC current of up to 1600-V AC is placed on the cylinder to help the toner particles break free from the attraction of the fixed magnet.

The photosensitive drum and the developing cylinder are mounted so that they almost touch. As we said earlier, when a part of the photosensitive drum has been exposed to the laser, the charge at that point will be −100 V. When one of these points passes the developing cylinder, the highly negative toner is attracted to the less-negative photosensitive drum. This causes the toner powder to jump across to the surface of the drum. At this point, the invisible image of −100-V dots has been turned into a visible image of toner dots.

Transfer of Image to Paper

The photosensitive drum turns a bit more and comes into contact with the paper. See part D of Fig. 13-3. Beneath the paper is a second corona wire. This wire generates positive charges, which attach to the back of the paper. These positive charges are strong enough to pull the negatively charged toner dots off of the photosensitive drum. At this point, the toner dots are sitting loosely on the top surface of the paper.

A negative charge is created by the *static charge eliminator*. This unit weakens the attractive force between the paper and the photosensitive drum, and allows the paper to pull away easily.

Fusing the Image

To make a permanent image, the toner dots must still be joined or "fused" to the paper. The fusing section consists of two rollers, as shown in Fig. 13-2. The upper roller contains a very hot lamp. As the paper passes through this section, the heat from the lamp melts the plastic material in the toner, and the pressure from the two rollers forces the toner into the fibers of the paper.

The fuser rollers are normally in a "standby" mode at about 165 °F (74 °C). When they are processing a sheet of paper, the rollers heat up to about 180 °F (82 °C). A special type of resistor called a "thermistor" senses the temperature at the fusing rollers and reports back to the control circuits. Based on the "feedback" from this thermistor, the circuits adjust the voltage to the fusing lamp, and keep the fusing temperature constant. A protective switch called a "thermoprotector" is included to prevent the fusing rollers from overheating. If the rollers ever reach 210 °F (99 °C), the thermoprotector switch will open and cut off power to the lamp. Fig. 13-4 illustrates these parts.

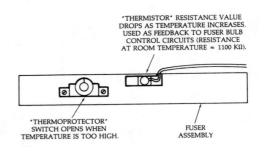

Fig. 13-4. Fusing section temperature sensors.

The fusing rollers are coated with Teflon® so the hot toner will not stick to them. A cleaning pad clears the upper roller of any extra toner or dust. The pad also applies a thin coat of silicone oil, which helps keep the toner from sticking to the roller.

Cleaning the Drum

Meanwhile, the photosensitive drum continues to turn. A rubber cleaning blade scrapes off any remaining toner. See part E of Fig. 13-3. The used toner drops into the bottom of the cartridge. From time to time, a "sweeper" blade swings around and brushes away the pile of used toner.

As the drum continues to turn, it passes under five "erase lamps." These lamps bring the whole surface of the drum back to a uniform −100 V. At this point, this section of the drum is ready to go past the primary corona and begin the cycle again.

Laser Scanning

If the printer has only one small laser, how can it make dots across the whole width of the photosensitive drum? The secret lies in the scanning system, shown in Fig. 13-5. A small laser diode creates the beam of laser light. This laser beam is focused by a series of lenses. The beam is aimed at a rotating six-sided mirror. Think of each of the six sides as a separate mirror. As each mirror turns, it causes the beam to sweep across the surface of the photosensitive drum. At the start of a scan, each mirror is positioned so it aims the beam at the left edge of the drum. At the very beginning of the scan, a small mirror deflects the beam into an optical fiber. A sensor on this fiber generates a "beam detect" signal which is used by the control circuits.

The turning mirror causes the beam to sweep toward the right edge of the drum. As the beam moves

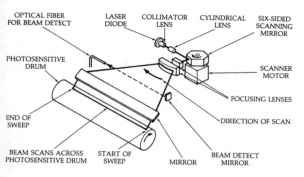

Fig. 13-5. Laser scanning system.

across the drum, the laser is switched on and off. When the beam reaches a point where the printer wants to produce a dot, the laser is energized. When the printer wants to leave a blank space, the laser is turned off. Once the beam finishes the sweep, the photosensitive drum moves forward (turns) a bit. Now the drum is ready to accept a new line of dots. The next surface of the six-sided mirror swings into position, and the laser begins a new scan.

Paper-Feed System

The paper-handling system is very similar to the arrangement you might find in a photocopy machine. The paper is carried through the printer by a series of rollers. Some of these rollers are powered, and some are not. Usually, all of the powered rollers are driven by the same electric motor. This motor is connected, by a series of gears, to each of the powered rollers.

The main drive motor is usually a stepper motor, and is energized through four input lines ($\phi1$, $\phi2$, $\phi3$, and $\phi4$). We described stepper motors in some detail in Chapter 7. Even when the main motor is turning continuously, some of the powered rollers start and stop independently. This is achieved by using a clutch for each powered roller. Normally, each clutch is disengaged—the motor drive gears are turning, but this power is not transferred through to the roller. When the printer CPU wants to turn a roller, it energizes the clutch for that roller. The power from the drive gears is then transferred through the drive gears, causing the roller to turn.

Fig. 13-6 shows the pick-up and registration rollers at the entrance to the printer. Notice that the bottom of the pick-up roller is flattened. When the printer wants to feed a sheet of paper, it rotates this roller. Actually, the control circuits energize a clutch, which then transfers power from the main drive motor.

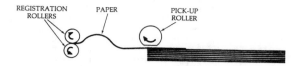

Fig. 13-6. Registration rollers.

At the start of the printing process, the leading edge of the paper presses forward against the registration rollers. Notice that the leading edge of the paper is "bunched up" a bit. This maintains a bit of forward pressure on the leading edge of the paper. The lower registration roller is also connected to a small motor. When the printer wants to feed a sheet of paper, it energizes the clutches for both rollers. The timing of this action is important. The leading edge of the paper must arrive under the photosensitive drum at just the right moment. This must happen just when the photosensitive drum brings the first part of the image into position.

The rest of the paper-handling system is fairly straightforward. Sensor switches are included to tell the printer CPU when the feed tray is out of paper, and when the paper level is too high or too low. Another switch notifies the CPU when a finished page reaches the delivery section. These sensor switches allow the CPU to follow each sheet of paper as it goes through the rollers. The CPU's program allows a certain amount of time for each sheet to pass through each of the stages. If the paper takes too long to move through a certain stage, the CPU assumes the paper has jammed.

Control Circuits

A simplified block diagram of the control circuits in a laser printer is shown in Fig. 13-7. As you can see, a typical printer includes an extensive microcomputer system.

At the start of each printing cycle, the printer receives data from the main computer. In some printer/computer systems, these data carry the coded image of a page of type to be printed. To put this another way, the computer has already compiled the page image before the data are sent to the printer. Many printers of this type use a page-description language called "PostScript®." In other systems, the computer sends information on individual characters, much as it would interface with a conventional dot-matrix printer. In this type of interface, the computer might send signals telling the printer to "Print an A," "Print a d," and so on. Sometimes, the job of

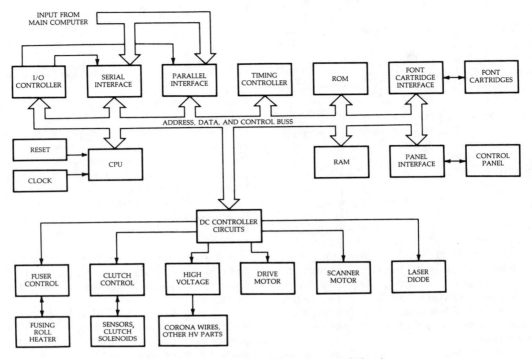

Fig. 13-7. Block diagram of printer control circuits.

assembling the page image is split between the computer and the printer.

However this activity is handled, at some point, the printer assembles a digital image of the page to be printed. Some simpler printers do not assemble a whole page at one time, but rather work on the page in sections. This digital image is then stored in the printer's memory. Many laser printers have a resolution of 300 dots per inch, so a square inch of page area may contain 90,000 possible dots. In order to store a whole full page of dots, therefore, the printer must have a large amount of on-board RAM.

As we said earlier, the laser printer contains a small "laser diode" which can quickly be turned on and off to create dots on the page. When the printer begins to print a page, the control circuits begin to "scan" through the stored characters. At each point in the scan, the circuits decide whether the printer should produce a black dot or not. When the control circuits call for a dot, the laser is turned on.

Power-Distribution System

A laser printer uses several different voltages, and the power-distribution system is more complicated than the system in a simpler printer. The first stage of the power

supply takes 120-V AC and converts it to a lower-voltage DC. See Chapter 16 for details on this stage of the power system.

In the Hewlett-Packard HP33440, the power supply produces outputs of +5-V DC, −5-V DC, and +24-V DC. The +5-V DC is used to power all of the logic ICs, as you might expect. This voltage is also used to operate the paper-sensing switches. If the +5-V DC is present, the printer will be able to "boot," accept inputs, and light the indicators on the control panel.

The +24-V DC voltage is routed to the cooling fans, the scanner motor, the erase lamps, and the clutch controls. The +24-V DC also is the input to the high-voltage power supply. An interlock switch is included in the cover of the printer. This switch cuts off the +24-V DC if the printer's cover is opened.

A high-voltage supply generates the special high voltages required by the laser printing process: −6000 V for the corona wires, −690 V for the corona grid, and the AC and DC bias for the developing cylinder. Many of these high voltages are routed to parts inside the toner cartridge. Since the cartridge can be removed and replaced, the high voltages can't be "hard-wired" directly to the corona wire, developing drum, and other parts. Instead, these voltages are carried to a set of contacts inside the printer, and these match up with contacts on the cartridge.

The power supplies are arranged in a chain: 120-V AC to +5-V DC and +24-V DC; then +24-V DC to the high voltage. You will find fuses or circuit breakers at various points along the chain. You may also find a number of safety interlock switches, and these may be wired to interrupt the power-supply chain.

Switches and Safety Devices

A typical laser printer includes many switches. The control circuits use these switches to tell what is happening in various sections of the printer. Many of the switches are included as safety devices, to prevent injury to the operator or damage to the printer. Table 13-1 lists some typical switches and their functions.

Possible Service Problems

Laser printers are very complex, and they include many electromechanical parts. Generally, mechanical parts cause a relatively high proportion of service troubles. In spite of this, laser printers seem to be quite reliable.

Most laser printers use toner cartridges which can be replaced by the user. Not only does each new cartridge include a fresh supply of toner, but it also has a new photosensitive drum and developer wheel. This means that all of the most critical parts are replaced when the cartridge is changed. You may not appreciate this unless you have had to work with photocopy machines, which are very similar. Earlier photocopy machines were not designed to use cartridges. As a result, they required constant adjustments by a service technician.

From time to time, a laser printer may jam as it tries to feed a sheet of paper. Usually, the printer will detect this, and will either light an LED on the control panel or send a warning signal back to the computer. Clearing the jam is simple—just open the lid of the printer and pull out the crumpled piece of paper. Be sure to pull the paper in the direction it would have been moved by the printer. Don't pull the paper "upstream" and turn any of the rollers backwards.

If you have many problems with paper jamming, check the way the paper is loaded into the printer. The leading edge of the stack of paper should be pressed right up against the metal stops. Some printers can also jam when the level of the paper in the feed tray is too low.

All cartridges are not created equal. One cartridge might create indistinct letters, and the next cartridge might work well. The organic photosensitive coating on the drum is a complicated material. Even brand-new cartridges, fresh off the production line, have different properties. In fact, on Hewlett-Packard printers, each cartridge is rated for sensitivity. When a cartridge is installed, projections on the bottom of the cartridge tell the printer how sensitive the cartridge is, and the printer circuitry adjusts for this.

The way the cartridge has been stored can affect its performance. The material on the photosensitive drum can be damaged by strong light. For this reason, a cartridge should be stored in a dark place until it is ready for use. The toner powder is also sensitive to the environment. A cartridge may be stored for 2 years or more, as long as the foil wrapper around the cartridge is unbroken. Once the wrapper is broken, the storage time drops to 6 months.

Table 13-1. Laser Printer Switch Functions

Switch	Function
Paper tray inserted.	Reports to CPU when paper tray is present.
Paper tray type.	Three switches indicate type of paper tray that has been inserted.
Paper level low.	No paper in paper tray.
Toner cartridge inserted.	Reports to CPU when toner cartridge is present.
Toner cartridge sensitivity.	Three switches indicate sensitivity of OPC layer on toner cartridge.
Toner level low.	Antenna in cartridge senses toner level.
Paper at delivery.	Signals CPU when paper reaches delivery point. If paper does not arrive in time, CPU assumes paper has jammed.
Cover interlock.	Safety switch—cuts off +24-V DC and high voltage when printer cover is opened.
Thermoprotector.	Safety switch—turns off printer if fuser rollers overheat (210 °F/99 °C)

Handling can also affect a cartridge's performance. Some good rules are usually listed in the owner's manual for the printer. Don't stand the cartridge on end. This can cause all the toner to slide to one end of the cartridge. The cartridge is sealed with a tape, which keeps the toner from escaping. Don't remove the tape until you are ready to install the cartridge. This will keep the toner inside the cartridge and will also protect the drum and toner from light and humidity. Before installing the cartridge, hold it horizontally and rock it back and forth. This distributes the toner evenly inside the cartridge.

The manufacturer's specifications will tell you how long you can expect a cartridge to last. On the earlier laser printers, the cartridges were rated for 3000 images. Newer printers get much better "mileage" from a cartridge. When a cartridge is nearing the end of its life, the printed characters will begin to fade. Some types of printers have indicators which tell you when to change the cartridge. Even when the indicators tell you to change the cartridge, if the cartridge is still producing clean black characters, you can continue to use it for a while.

As a cartridge is used, the supply of fresh toner is used up. Some of the toner is deposited on the printed pages. The rest of the toner is scraped up by the cleaning blade and dropped into a compartment in the front of the cartridge. The greater the amount of fresh toner originally in the cartridge, the longer the cartridge will last. If you are printing many pages with large black areas, the toner will be used up more quickly. Operating the printer with the "contrast" control turned up will also speed the use of the toner. Our experience is that cartridges seem to last about 50% longer than the manufacturer's specs.

Sometimes you can bring a "tired" cartridge back to life. Remove the cartridge and rotate it gently to redistribute the remaining toner. Keep using a cartridge as long as the image quality is acceptable. You can't damage the printer by using a "tired" cartridge. When you start using a new cartridge, save one of the first few pages it produces. After the cartridge has been used for a while, you can use this page as a reference to judge how much life the cartridge has left.

It is possible to refill a used cartridge with fresh toner. Some mail-order shops will refill your cartridge for about half the cost of a new one. You can also do the job yourself. This involves melting two holes in the used cartridge—one hole for placing fresh toner in the cartridge, and the other for draining out the used toner. You can use a soldering iron. Do not use a drill for this process, since the resulting plastic chips may damage the printer. The holes must be made at points in the

cartridge where they do not interfere with any switches or mechanical parts in the printer, and where the hot iron "drill" will not damage anything inside the cartridge. The replacement toner must be the special type required by laser printers. (Most photocopy machines use a different kind of toner.) At the end of the process, block the holes with pieces of tape, and the cartridge is ready to go back into service. Don Lancaster described this process in more detail in the February 1987 issue of *Modern Electronics*. In his article, he also listed sources for replacement toner powder.

If you wish to refill cartridges, be careful to use the correct type of toner. If you somehow use the wrong type of toner, it could stick to the rollers and cause other problems. When you buy a genuine replacement cartridge, you also receive a new fusing roller cleaner (Fig. 13-2). This cleaner removes stray bits of toner from the fusing rollers, and also lays down a thin layer of silicone oil. If you use a refilled cartridge, and do not replace the fusing roller cleaner, the old cleaner will eventually become clogged with debris and will run out of oil. This can result in dirty fusing rollers, which can cause smudges on the paper. Always replace the cleaning roller when you change cartridges.

The most serious problem has to do with the photosensitive drum. As we said, the photosensitive layer is delicate, and it deteriorates over time. Even if a cartridge is recharged with fresh toner, this photosensitive material will eventually wear out. However, some users report that a cartridge does not deliver the best performance until it has been refilled three or four times.

Most types of bond or photocopy paper seem to work well in laser printers. Office-supply dealers are beginning to sell special "laser papers" which are supposed to offer better image quality. Some of these papers have a thin coating of white clay. This coating holds the toner dots on the top surface of the paper. Avoid very shiny paper or paper with a textured surface. These papers should not damage the printer, but they will not take the toner image well.

Some letterhead paper is printed with raised characters, using a process called "thermography." This kind of printing is easy to recognize because the printed letters appear to be thick, and raised slightly above the paper. Don't use this kind of paper in a laser printer! At the end of the laser printing process, the finished sheets pass between the fusing rollers. These rollers are very hot, and they can melt the raised lettering on the stationary.

There are some special dangers involved in servicing laser printers. As we explained, some very high voltages are used inside a laser printer. The corona wires use voltages as high as −6000 V. Other parts of the printer use voltages in the −600-V range. These are dangerous voltages.

Most printers are designed with safety switches which turn off the high voltages when you open the equipment's cover. Generally, printers also include the normal fuses and circuit breakers for various parts of the power supply. Some printers may include other safety devices as well. For example, the Hewlett-Packard 33440 includes a "thermoprotector." This unit is designed to turn off the printer if the fusing rollers become too hot. (The fusing rollers are located in the delivery end of the printer, as shown in Fig. 13-2.) Even in normal operation, these rollers become very hot. Be careful not to touch them. The safety devices protect the printer, and they can also help you in your troubleshooting work. When one of these safety devices operates, the printer usually lights an LED or gives you some other indication. This points out the section of the printer that has failed.

The laser in the printer presents some special dangers. The beam from this type of laser is invisible, but it can damage your eyes. When the equipment is operating normally, the laser is enclosed. Generally, if you do not open the case while the printer is operation, the laser can't hurt you. You can never be sure of how a printer is designed, however. To be safe, don't look through the paper slot into the printer while it is operating.

Most laser printers include safety switches that turn off the laser when you open the printer's case. If you open the case and the printer is still operating, be careful not to deflect the beam of the laser. For example, if you block the beam with the shiny tip of a screwdriver, the laser light might be reflected upward into your eyes. For these reasons, laser printers are more dangerous than the simpler printers, and this means that you must take special precautions. In fact, one group in Germany insists that, when servicing a laser printer, as least two technicians should be present.

Often, you first learn of a problem when the printer begins to produce unusual-looking pages. The printed characters may begin to become lighter, or you may notice smears or smudges on the page. These signs can be very helpful as you try to troubleshoot the problem. For example, if you notice a vertical smear near the left edge of the page, you can assume that one of the parts on the left side of the printer is dirty.

Some problems tend to "repeat" several times as you move vertically down the page. You can use this effect to help you find the problem. Let's say that one point on the photosensitive drum has been damaged and, every time that point touches the paper, it leaves a mark. When you measure the distance between marks on the paper, you find that they are "x" inches apart. Next, you check the rollers in the printer until you find the one which measures "x" inches in circumference.

Most laser printers have the ability to print a "self-test" pattern. The Apple LaserWriter prints a test page every time it is turned on. The Hewlett-Packard 33440 has two different self-test modes. The self-test allows you to tell quickly whether the printer is faulty. During self-test, the printer uses self-generated test routines, and is not handling signals from the main computer. If the printer operates normally in the self-test mode, you can suspect that the problem is in the main computer.

Cleaning and Maintenance

A laser printer has some special maintenance requirements. Usually, the user's manual will show you how to perform these steps, so we will just mention them briefly here. On most printers, you are asked to clean some of the parts whenever you change the cartridge. If a roller or other part is dirty, it often leaves a mark or smudge on the paper. This calls for a cleaning, even if the cartridge is still fresh.

Clean the transfer corona wire (shown in Fig. 13-2). Use a 90% solution of isopropyl alcohol and a cotton-tipped swab. The swab should not be dripping wet. Don't break the fine wires above the corona wire and don't drip alcohol on any of the rollers or plastic parts.

The primary corona wire can be reached through a slot in the top of the cartridge. Clean this wire with a cotton swab, or with the special cleaning tool supplied with the printer.

Downstream of the transfer corona wire is a metal plate called the "transfer guide." Wipe down this part with a cloth dampened with water. Watch for a buildup of dust or toner on the other parts, and clean them as necessary.

As we said earlier, it is important to handle the toner cartridges carefully. If the wrapper around a cartridge is opened, or if the cartridge is exposed to bright light, it may not work well. Store the cartridges carefully, and think of this as part of your "maintenance" routine.

Troubleshooting Laser Printers

There are many different types of laser printers. We can give you some general guidance here. However, for specific information, you will have to get some documentation from the printer's manufacturer.

As we said, most laser printers can run a "self-test" program. During this testing mode, the printer ignores signals from the main computer and depends on instructions stored in on-board ROM. If a laser printer operates correctly during self-test, you can assume that most of the circuitry in the unit is working properly. In this case, the problem probably lies somewhere in the link with the main computer.

Many laser printers also have some self-diagnostic capability. For example, some printers present error codes by lighting different combinations of the indicators on the control panel. A printer may also produce error codes which appear on the computer's monitor.

At the end of this section, we have included two test procedures you may use. The *image development check* (Section 13.2.1) allows you to check most of the steps in the development process. The *fusing check* (Section 13.2.2) tests the functioning of the fusing rollers.

13.1.1 Problem 1

Symptom: No printing–page is white.

The developing cylinder may not be picking up toner. This can happen if the DC bias for the cylinder is absent. Also, the photosensitive drum may have become disconnected from ground. Since the charges have no way of draining off to ground, the laser has no effect and the printed page remains white.

If the photosensitive drum is not turning, no image can be created and transferred to the page. Be sure the drum is turning. Turn off the printer before you make this check! Remove the cartridge, open the slot at the top of the cartridge, and make a mark on the nonprinting part of the photosensitive drum. Reinstall the cartridge and operate the printer for a moment. Remove the cartridge again and see if the drum has moved.

Check to be sure the cartridge is not out of toner. Be sure the cartridge has been installed correctly, and the sealing tape has been removed.

A white page can result if the laser beam is blocked on its way to the drum. Check the beam path for obstructions. Be sure the printer is turned off as you do this! The laser beam can damage your eyes.

The transfer corona wire may be broken, or the corona high voltage may be absent.

13.1.2 Problem 2

Symptom: The page is black.

This symptom can occur when the primary corona is not working. Check the corona wire to be sure it is not broken. Be sure the corona voltage is present.

The control circuits may have failed, leaving the laser permanently on. Also check the beam detector at the edge of the beam path.

13.1.3 Problem 3

Symptom: The printing is very light.

The cartridge may be out of toner. Remove the cartridge and gently rock it forward and back, as described earlier in this chapter. If this does not improve the print quality, replace the cartridge.

Light print may result if the transfer corona is not working. Check the corona wire to be sure it is not broken. Be sure the corona voltage is present.

The developing cylinder may not be getting the normal DC bias. The toner particles may not be charged by the cylinder and, therefore, won't transfer well to the photosensitive cylinder.

13.1.4 Problem 4

Symptom: The printing is slightly light.

The printer may begin producing very light pages when the cartridge begins to run out of toner. If the cartridge appears to be near the end of its life, replace it.

All photosensitive drums do not have the same sensitivity to the laser light. Perhaps this cartridge is not very sensitive. Sometimes, the manufacturer grades the cartridges for sensitivity. A series of tabs on the bottom of the cartridge press onto sensor switches, which adjust the laser power to match the sensitivity of the cartridge. Maybe the sensitivity switches are not working correctly.

The erase lamps may not be working correctly. Perhaps the bulbs are not producing full output. Over time, the laser may also begin to produce a weaker signal. The laser output must be measured with special tools. Don't try to do this job yourself.

13.1.5 Problem 5
Symptom: Dark blotches occur on the paper.

This problem can occur when the primary corona is not putting a uniform charge on the photosensitive drum. Areas which do not receive a strong negative charge (about -600 V) will behave as if they had been struck by the laser. You will recall that when the laser strikes a point on the drum, it leaves a less-negative charge (-100 V). The areas with the less-negative charges will attract dots of toner.

13.1.6 Problem 6
Symptom: The paper has vertical white streaks.

White streaks can be caused by dirt on the long mirror that is mounted above the photosensitive drum. The laser light is not reflected off of the dirty spot on the mirror. At just that one point in the scan, the light does not reach the photosensitive drum. This can cause narrow white streaks in the printout.

The transfer corona is mounted under the paper path, and it can pick up dust and debris. Part of the corona assembly may be dirty or blocked. This may prevent the toner from transferring from the photosensitive drum to the paper.

The toner cartridge may be "tired." This usually causes wider areas of light type. Remove the cartridge and gently rock it forward and back, as described earlier in this chapter. This may redistribute the toner. If this does not improve the printout, replace the cartridge.

13.1.7 Problem 7
Symptom: The left or right side of the page is blank.

For some reason, the laser beam is scanning to one side of its normal path. The large mirror above the photosensitive drum may be out of position. This symptom can also occur when the toner cartridge is getting "tired," and the remaining toner is concentrated on one side of the cartridge.

Remove the cartridge, and rock it gently forward and back as described earlier in this chapter. This may redistribute the toner. If this does not improve the printout, replace the cartridge.

13.1.8 Problem 8
Symptom: The page is out of registration, with distorted print.

When this symptom occurs, it appears that the whole page image has been shifted in one direction or another. The margins on one side of the page may be too large; on the other side, the margins may be too small. This can happen when the drive rollers are worn or dirty, so that they do not give an even "push" to the paper. Also check the gears that drive the paper-handling mechanisms.

13.1.9 Problem 9
Symptom: Horizontal black lines occur on the page.

This symptom could be caused by a problem with the *beam detect signal*. The beam detect signal is generated when the laser is turned on at the beginning (left edge) of a scan. If the CPU does not receive a beam detect signal, it turns the laser on continuously to "search" for the signal. When the laser is on continuously, it generates a horizontal line.

This problem can also occur when the DC bias to the developing cylinder is not stable.

13.1.10 Problem 10
Symptom: Random dot patterns are printed.

This symptom can occur when the laser is randomly turning on and off. The printer's control circuits can be causing this, or the problem may be coming from the main computer. Run a "self-test" program and see if the problem disappears.

13.1.11 Problem 11
Symptom: The print is smeared.

The fusing rollers may not be doing their job. For some reason, the rollers may not be heating up. Check the fusing lamp and any temperature controls. Also, the fuser cleaning pad may be dirty or clogged.

Check the static-charge eliminator teeth. If one of the teeth is bent, part of the paper may be sticking to the photosensitive drum and this can cause smearing.

The paper you are using may not be suitable for laser printers.

13.1.12 Problem 12
Symptom: Repeating marks on the paper.

As a sheet of paper goes through the printer, each of the rollers in the printer turns several times. The large photosensitive drum might turn two or three times per sheet, while a smaller feed roller might turn a dozen times. When a mark appears at regular intervals along the page, it may have been made by a dirty or damaged roller.

Let's say that a bit of dirt has become attached to one place on the roller. As the roller turns, each time that the dirty spot touches the paper, it leaves a mark. If the mark repeats in a very short distance, it was probably made by a small roller. If the distance between the marks is longer, check for dirt on a large roller. In fact, you can measure the distance between the marks and use this to figure out which roller caused the problem. Use the formula:

$$\text{Diameter of roller} = \frac{\text{Distance between marks}}{3.1}$$

For example, in the Hewlett-Packard printer, the distance around the photosensitive drum is 3.75 inches (95 mm). The circumference of the developing cylinder is 2 inches (51 mm), and the fusing rollers measure about 3 inches (75 mm) around. If you find a mark on the paper which appears every 3.75 inches, start by checking the photosensitive drum.

13.1.13 Problem 13
Symptom: Black page with white horizontal lines on it.

This can happen when the optical fiber for the beam detect signal is damaged. Most of the time, the laser is left continuously on, causing the black areas. Then, when the printer discovers that it cannot find the beam detect signal, it turns the laser off, causing the white horizontal lines.

Test Procedures

13.2.1 Test 1
Run an image development check.

Use this test when the printer is not forming an image correctly. To start the test, tell the printer to print a test page. When the printer is about halfway through the page, turn it off. Open the printer and gently pull out the cartridge. Look at the photosensitive drum inside the cartridge. (There should be a shutter on the bottom of the cartridge that will allow you to do this.)

Can you see the toner image on the surface of the drum? If you can see the toner image, you know that the first stages of the process are working correctly—conditioning by the primary corona, image formation by the laser, and transfer of toner by the developing cylinder. You can now concentrate your troubleshooting on the remaining steps—transfer of toner to paper, static-charge elimination, and fusing.

13.2.2 Test 2
Run a fusing check.

The toner particles are bonded to the paper as the paper passes through the fusing rollers. To test the fusing action, run off 10 copies of a test page. Choose the first and tenth pages. On each page, try to rub off the printed characters. The toner should be firmly bonded to the page.

A thermistor is used as part of a "feedback" system to control the fuser temperature. The fusing rollers may not be holding a constant temperature because of a problem with this part. The thermistor may simply be dirty; check the part and clean it, if necessary. The resistance of the thermistor should drop as the part is heated.

On the Hewlett-Packard HP33440, the resistance of the thermistor at room temperature is about 1130 kilohms.

Chapter Review

As you complete this chapter, you should have a basic understanding of the operating principle of a laser printer. As you have learned, the printing process is complicated and involves six separate steps:

1. Drum is charged by primary corona.

2. Charged spots on drum are released by laser.

3. Toner is transferred to drum.

4. Toner is transferred to paper.

5. Toner is fused to paper.

6. Drum is cleaned and recharged for next cycle.

We explained how the control circuits supervise the different sections of the printer. We also pointed out the special safety hazards in working with this type of equipment. Then, we listed some of the service problems you may encounter working with a laser printer.

In the last part of the chapter, we listed some troubleshooting symptoms and probable causes. You can troubleshoot many problems by examining the pages that are produced by the printer. If a printer has a self-test function, you can check most of the system in one step. We also described the *image development check* and the *fusing check* procedures. These tests allow you to check specific parts of the developing system.

Review Questions

1. A customer brings in a faulty laser printer. You run the "self-test" routine, and the problem is still present. What does this tell you?

2. Why is it important not to bypass the safety interlock switch on the printer's cover?

3. You are servicing equipment in an office and you notice a row of spare laser cartridges in a closet. The cartridges have been unwrapped. Why is this a bad practice?

4. You are troubleshooting a printer and you run the image development check. When you open the shutter on the cartridge, you do not see a toner pattern on the drum. What does this tell you?

5. You want to refill a toner cartridge. Can you use any type of toner powder?

6. You are working with a faulty printer. You notice that the toner seems to come off of the page easily. What does this tell you?

7. A faulty printer seems to be getting the correct power outputs, but does not respond to any inputs. It also does not print during the self-test routine. What is your next step?

8. A printer is producing pages containing lightly typed characters. You remove the cartridge, rock it from side to side, and then replace it. Now the type quality is better. What does this tell you?

14

Modems and Serial Interfaces

Introduction and Objectives

In this chapter, we'll discuss the circuitry that allows a computer to communicate over telephone lines. This is a two-step process. Data are usually carried from point to point inside the computer using a "parallel" format. Then, as the data leave the computer, they are converted to a "serial" format by the interface circuits, and fed to a *modem* (Fig. 14-1). Most "serial" interfaces use the RS-232C standard, and we will discuss this standard in some detail.

Fig. 14-1. A typical direct-connect modem.
(Courtesy Hayes Microcomputer Products, Inc.)

In the second step of the process, the "modem" circuits take the data in "serial" form and produce

signals that can be sent over telephone lines. Different "modem" circuits may be used, depending on the operating speed of the interface.

For an incoming signal, the process is reversed. First, the incoming signal is received by the "modem" circuits and converted to RS-232C "serial" format. Next, the "serial" data are converted to a "parallel" format and sent to the computer. After you read this chapter, you should understand how these two sets of circuits operate.

Finally, we will discuss some possible problems with these circuits. We will also discuss some test techniques. The "breakout box" is a very useful tool for diagnosing problems with RS-232C serial circuits. Most modems can be made to "self-test" using "loopback" connections.

Modems

The term *modem* is an abbreviation for "*mo*dulator/ *dem*odulator." In this chapter, we'll discuss the type of modem that allows a computer to send signals over a telephone line. (The "modulation/ demodulation" principle is also used in other parts of the computer system.)

As you can see in Fig. 14-2, there are actually two kinds of signals associated with a typical modem. The computer talks to the modem through an RS-232C interface. In the modem circuitry, the data from the computer are converted into pulses of +12-V DC and −12-V DC. (Notice that the pulses in the RS-232C link are still "digital," but the voltage levels are not TTL-compatible +5-V DC and 0 V).

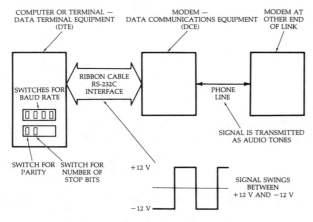

Fig. 14-2. Signals through a modem.

The RS-232C link is a "serial" interface. This means that the computer sends or receives just one bit of data at a time. Fig. 14-3 illustrates this idea. The RS-232C serial interface has just one data line in each direction, although it has many other lines for control and timing signals.

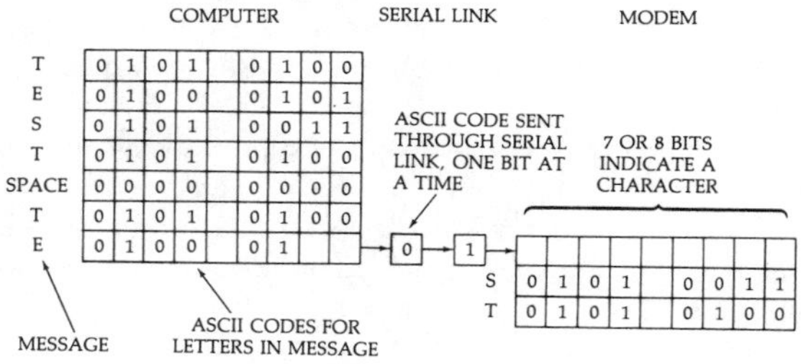

Fig. 14-3. Serial data transmission.

A modem communicates with the outside world over a telephone line. However, the telephone system was designed to carry human voices, not digital information, so a modem must produce a type of signal that can be handled by the phone system. As an output signal, the modem circuits produce a series of audio tones which can be carried over the phone lines. To summarize, there are really three different data formats in use in a complete modem system. First, *parallel* data are converted to the RS-232C *serial* format. Next, the

digital RS-232 signal is converted to an *analog* signal for handling by the phone system.

The RS-232C Interface

Let's take a more detailed look at the RS-232C interface. The term "RS-232C" refers to a set of specifications for this type of interface. The RS-232C standard was designed by the Electronic Industries Association (EIA) in the early days of computing. The engineers at EIA were not sure what types of equipment would be developed in the future, so they provided many different signal lines so that the RS-232C standard would be as flexible as possible. Most of these signal lines are not used in modern microcomputer equipment.

Fig. 14-4 shows the pin assignments for an RS-232C connector. Shown is a "DB-25" connector, the most common type of connector used with RS-232C circuits. The DB-25 has 25 pins, but some serial interfaces use the smaller DB-9 connector, which has 9 pins. Often, only seven of these lines will be used. Actually, an RS-232C system can operate using only three lines, as shown in Fig. 14-5.

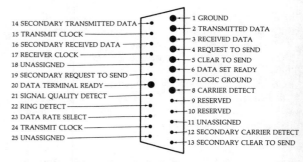

Fig. 14-4. Pin assignments for an RS-232C connector.

In any RS-232C system, one end of the link is designated as the *Data Terminal Equipment* or *DCE*, and the other is called the *Data Communications Equipment* or *DTE*. The signal and control lines are named according to their relationship to the computer. For example, line 2 is named TRANSMIT DATA because it carries the signal that is transmitted by the computer. In a computer/modem system, the computer is the *terminal* (DTE) or *data terminal*, and the modem is the *communicator* (DCE) or *data set*.

In the simplest possible interface, the three key lines are connected to pins 2, 3, and 7 on the RS-232C connector. This is shown in Fig. 14-5. Line 2 carries "transmitted data" from the terminal to the communicator. Line 3 carries "received data" from the communicator to the terminal. Line 7 is a ground for the other two lines.

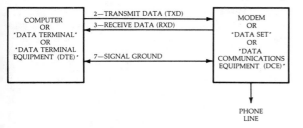

Fig. 14-5. Minimum number of lines used in an RS-232C system.

Handshaking

Fig. 14-6 shows a more complicated RS-232C interface. This diagram is typical of the type of interface that may be used to connect the computer to a modem. This interface includes the three lines shown in Fig. 14-5—GROUND (line 7), TRANSMIT DATA (line 2), and RECEIVE DATA (line 3). Most of the other lines are used to control "handshaking" between the computer and the modem.

The designers wanted to be sure that the computer would not send characters until the modem was ready. For example, line 20 is "Data Terminal Ready" (DTR) and line 6 is "Data Set (or Communicator) Ready" (DSR). At the start of the "handshaking" process, the computer will hold the DTR line "high" to signal to the modem, "I'm ready to send. How about you?" When the modem is ready, it will answer by holding the DSR line "high." The computer will not send data until both lines are "true."

Another type of handshaking uses Request To Send (RTS), line 4, and Clear To Send (CTS), line 5. To start this "handshaking" cycle, the computer will hold the Request To Send line high. If the modem is ready, it will hold the Clear To Send line high.

Some RS-232C links do not use this "hardware-controlled" handshaking; the handshaking is controlled by software. Special control codes are sent back and forth over the *data* lines. (You will recall that, with "hardware-controlled" handshaking, the control signals were sent over separate *control* lines.) One common handshaking scheme is called "X-ON/X-OFF." The computer and DCE exchange the characters "DC1" and "DC3." On some ASCII tables, DC1 is listed as CTRL-Q (hex code 11) and DC3 is listed as CTRL-S (hex code 13). Each time these special characters appear in the data stream, the computer or modem detects the characters and acts on them.

Whenever data are sent over phone lines, transmission errors can creep in. Another handshaking system called "X Modem" uses the ASCII characters "ACK" and "NAK" to supervise transmission and error-checking. In this scheme, a long file is sent as a series of "blocks." Each block is preceded by a "Start of Text" character, and ended by an "End of Text" character. The Start of Text character is abbreviated STX, but it may also be listed as CRTL-A or hex code 02. The End of Text character is abbreviated ETX. It may also be listed as either CTRL-B or hex code 03. At the end of each block, a special error-checking code is included. For each block, the computer calculates this error-checking code, based on the data sent in that block. The error-checking code is transmitted, along with the rest of the block. If there are no transmission errors, the error-checking code matches the information received in the block, and the modem knows that the block has been received correctly. If all is well, the modem sends back an "acknowledge" code (ACK, CTRL-F, or hex 06). Whenever the error-checking code does not match the information in the block, the modem sends the "not-acknowledge" code (NAK, CTRL-O, or hex 15). This tells the computer to retransmit that block.

Some of the other RS-232C lines may be used on some interfaces. Line 8 is CARRIER DETECT. When the modem makes a connection to the phone line, it should detect the "carrier"—the signal that is always present when the phone line is active. By holding line 8

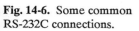

Fig. 14-6. Some common RS-232C connections.

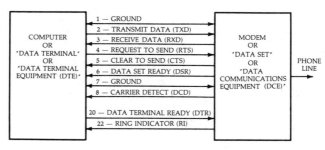

true, the modem can signal the computer that it has detected the carrier. Line 12 may be used as a *speed indicator*. The modem may hold this line high when it switches to high-speed operation. Line 22 is a "ring detect." Some modems use line 22 to indicate they have completed the telephone connection, and the phone on the other end of the line is ringing.

RS-232C Signal Coding

RS-232C lines do not carry the familiar TTL-level signals (+5 V and 0 V). Typical voltage levels are +12 V and −12 V, but RS-232C lines can carry signals as high as +25-V DC, and as low as −25-V DC. Don't try to check these lines with your logic probe—the probe will be destroyed by the high voltages. Use an oscilloscope instead. A sensitive VOM, set to a low AC range, should be able to detect the activity on the data lines, but you won't be able to "read" the signals. The control signals change more slowly than the data signals, so you can measure the control signals with a voltmeter.

Fig. 14-7A shows how data are coded on the RS-232C link. Notice that the coding system (signal levels) is different for the data lines and the control lines. On the data lines, a positive DC voltage greater than +3 V indicates a logic "0." A negative voltage lower than −3 V indicates a logic "1." Note that the signal levels are the same on the control lines, but the meaning is reversed. A positive voltage indicates "true," and a negative voltage represents "false."

Most of the modems used with microcomputers use an *asynchronous* interface. This means that the activities of the computer and modem are not synchronized by a series of "clock" pulses. Instead, the modem circuits are ready to process data whenever they arrive. Using this asynchronous interface, the modem circuits see a constant string of characters moving in or out. Thus, the circuits must have a way of identifying the beginning and end of each "package" of data. Each "data package" consists of a *start bit*, the *data bits*, and one or two *stop bits*. A complete package usually

represents just one letter or character. The character itself is usually represented as being 7 or 8 data bits. We say that the character is "framed" by the start bits and stop bits. For the transmission to be successful, both ends of the link must be expecting the same kind of framing.

Fig. 14-8 shows the series of signals an interface might use in sending the letter "C." To mark the start of the data "package," the computer sends one "start bit" (positive voltage, logic 0). Then it sends a series of "1s" and "0s" (usually seven) to represent the character itself. Like many other parts of the computer system, the RS-232C link uses ASCII coding to represent the letters and characters. An ASCII conversion table is included in Appendix D.

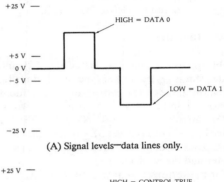

(A) Signal levels—data lines only.

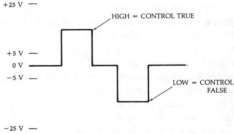

(B) Signal levels—control lines.

Fig. 14-7. RS-232C signal levels.

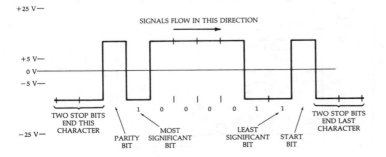

Fig. 14-8. Passage of one character through the RS-232C link.

The ASCII coding for the letter "C" is "1000011," reading from the most significant bit to the least significant bit. (In the decimal number 156, the "1" is the most significant digit because it represents "hundreds." The "6" is the least significant digit.) In the sketch of Fig. 14-8, we have shown how the RS-232C circuits would send the letter C. The end of the data package is identified by one or two stop bits (low). These are followed by a start bit (high) for the next data package. The circuits recognize this combination, and know that an ASCII-coded character is following. The ASCII code is sent "backwards," starting with the least significant digit, and ending with the most significant digit.

If the system is using 7-bit ASCII codes, an eighth data bit may be included as a "parity" bit. The parity bit is an error-checking device. This bit may be sent "high" or "low," depending on the coding of the data bits. When the data package is transmitted, the parity bit is sent along with the data bits. The modem uses the parity bit to be sure that none of the data bits have been changed. If the parity bit does not match the data bits, the modem can ask the computer to retransmit the character.

To calculate the setting for the parity bit, the interface circuits add up the total number of "1s" in the data bits, and determine if the total is odd or even. In the example above, there are three "1s" in the ASCII code for the letter C, and three is an "odd" number. We'll say that the circuits are prepared to expect "odd" parity. They will only write a "true" parity bit when the parity is different from the parity being expected. In this example, the parity sum is "odd," and the circuits are expecting an "odd" bit, so the circuit will use a negative signal to mean "not different from odd parity." This "error-checking" scheme allows the receiving computer to check each incoming character.

Note that the start bit, stop bits, and parity bit all use a different coding system from that used for the data bits. As we explained earlier, for the control bits, a positive signal is "true," while for the data bits, a negative signal represents a "1."

A serial interface can be set up to operate with one or two start bits, one or two stop bits, and odd parity, even parity, or no parity bit at all. Both ends of the link must be set to expect signals of the same type.

Other Uses for the RS-232C Standard

An RS-232C link may be used between a computer and a serial printer, or between one computer and a second computer. In fact, anywhere you encounter a "serial" interface, it is likely to be based on the RS-232C standard. The serial interface to a printer is quite similar to the interface we have just described. One difference is that, with a printer interface, you will have a larger choice of transmission speeds. The interface must be able to handle a wide range of printers, from slow to fast, so the designers usually include a wide range of speed options (150 bps, 300 bps, 600 bps, etc., up to 19,600 bps or faster). Choose a transmission speed that is slightly slower than the fastest speed your printer can handle. To put this another way, the printer should be able to handle characters a bit faster than the computer is allowed to send them.

When an RS-232C link is used to connect two computers, which is the "terminal" and which is the "communicator?" One solution is to change the switch settings on one of the computers to designate it as the communicator (DCE). You may also decide to use a device called a *null modem*. See Fig. 14-9. A "null modem" allows the interface to operate, even though both ends of the link are designated as terminals (DTE). In the sketch, you can see that lines 2 and 3 (TRANSMIT DATA and RECEIVE DATA) are reversed (cross-connected). The information transmitted from one computer is sent to the receiver of the other computer. The DATA TERMINAL READY signal from one computer is used to drive some of the handshaking inputs on the other computer. On another type of null modem, lines 4 and 5 (REQUEST TO SEND and CLEAR TO SEND) are reversed.

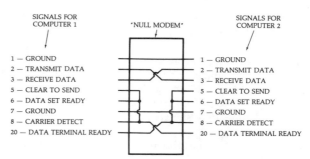

Fig. 14-9. Diagram of a "null modem" connector.

Don't confuse the null modem with another device called a "gender changer." The gender changer is used to match different types of plugs and connectors (male-male, female-female, etc.). The signal lines pass straight through a gender changer, with no crossovers.

The RS-422A Standard

Over the years, designers have found a few disadvantages with interfaces using the RS-232C Standard. The RS-232C interface had a built-in speed limitation, which began to be a problem as faster equipment was introduced. Also, the RS-232C system did not work well when the transmission lines were longer than about 50 feet, and the RS-232C lines were also sensitive to electrical "noise." In order to deal with these problems, EIA introduced the RS-422A Standard.

In many ways, an RS-422A interface is similar to an RS-232C type. Most of the control lines are the same, for example, and the signal levels are the same. The key to the RS-422 Standard lies in the way the "transmit" and "receive" signals are handled. You will recall that in an RS-232C interface, there are two signal lines—TRANSMIT DATA (TXD) and RECEIVE DATA (RXD). Both of these signals are compared to a single reference—the GROUND on line 1.

The RS-422A Standard uses a "balanced" arrangement for the transmit and receive lines. Both the transmitted signal and the received signal are actually handled by two lines rather than one. The signal voltage is measured across these two lines, rather than from one line to ground. The advantage of the "balanced" design is that both lines are affected by noise in the same way, so the noise does not distort the signal. For example, if a noise pulse induces a change of +1 V on one of the balanced lines, it will also induce +1 V on the other line. The voltage difference between the two will remain the same. RS-422 circuits often use DB-37 connectors, with 37 pins.

Interface Circuits

During the conversion to RS-232C signals, the parallel data on the data bus of the computer must be converted to a string of serial data. What is more, the TTL-level signals (+5 V and 0 V) inside the computer must be converted to the +10-V and −10-V signals used in the RS-232C link.

Let's examine the first step of this process—the conversion from parallel data to serial data. Most of this work is usually handled by a single large IC called a *Universal Asynchronous Receiver/Transmitter* or *UART*. There are many variations of this basic device. A similar IC is called an *Asynchronous Communications Interface Adapter* or *ACIA*. In the Apple IIe computer, the IC that handles this job is called an *Input/Output UART (IOU)*. Sometimes, one IC may handle two separate serial ports.

Fig. 14-10 is a simplified block diagram of a UART. At the left of the drawing, the bus buffers on the UART are connected to eight of the data lines in the computer. When the computer wants to send a character out through the UART, it selects the IC using the CHIP SELECT lines. The READ/WRITE* line is held low, and the computer is allowed to "write" a character into a temporary memory space in the UART called a "register." The seven or eight bits of this character are loaded into the register in parallel, in one step. The character is then coded into a series of "high" and "low" bits, using the ASCII coding system. When all of the handshaking signals are correct (Request to Send, Clear to Send, etc.), the transmitting circuits will send out the character, one bit at a time.

The process is reversed when the UART receives a character. The bits of the incoming character are stored, one bit at a time, in another register. When the ACIA is selected, and when the READ/WRITE* line is high, the bits will be sent, in parallel, onto the eight lines of the computer's data bus.

The UART is a very versatile IC. For example, it can be programmed to operate at many different bit rates—300 bps, 600 bps, 1200 bps, and so on. The bit rate is controlled by a number stored in a memory space inside the UART, called a "register." In order to change the bit rate, the computer enables the IC and writes a new value in this register. Other registers control other functions, such as word length, type of parity, number of stop bits, and so on.

Signals on Telephone Lines

After the UART has done its work, a second set of "modem" circuits convert the RS-232C signals to a series of audible tones that can be sent over the phone line. These circuits also accept the incoming audio signals on the telephone line, convert them into RS-232C signals, and send them on to the computer.

Today, most modems have connectors that plug directly into the phone network. These are called "direct-connect" types. On earlier modems, you had to fit the handset of a telephone into a pair of cups on top of the unit. These modems were "acoustic coupled."

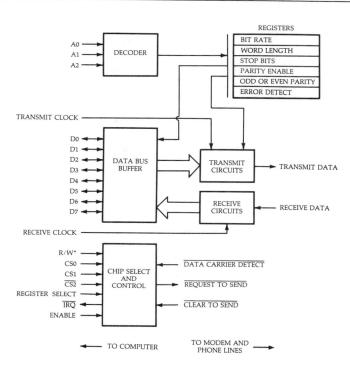

Fig. 14-10. Simplified block diagram of a UART.

The telephone system was originally designed to carry human voices, and the basic standards for the phone system were set down at the turn of the century when nobody had any idea that computers would be using the system. As a result, the telephone system is not exactly ideal for use by computers. To begin with, most of the existing equipment is set up to handle analog signals, because the human voice can be expressed easily as an analog signal. The existing phone system also has a limited "bandwidth"—it can handle only a certain range of frequencies. In addition, the phone lines are subject to "noise." When digital data are sent down a phone line, some of the characters can be changed by the noise on the lines.

Computer engineers had to come up with a way of sending digital information over this analog-based telephone network. The system had to be as fast and reliable as possible. As computers began to speed up and demand more and more data, the engineers evolved ever more ingenious ways of doing this.

Frequency-Shift Keying (FSK)

The telephone company's Bell 103 Standard was the earliest system of this type. A modem using this standard can process data at about 300 bits per second (or 300 baud). Since each character requires 10 or more bits, this works out to about 30 characters per second.

The digital data are converted into a series of audio tones, and these tones are sent down the phone line. The circuitry indicates the difference between a "1" and a "0" by changing the frequency of the outgoing signal (Fig. 14-11A). Thus, the frequency is "shifted" to indicate a change from a "1" to a "0," earning the name of "Frequency-Shift Keying" or FSK.

Under this standard, the modem uses different sets of tones, depending on whether it is playing the role of the "originating unit" or the "answering unit." Here are the frequencies used in this standard:

originate:	transmit	mark	1270 Hz
		space	1070 Hz
	receive	mark	2225 Hz
		space	2025 Hz
answer:	transmit	mark	2225 Hz
		space	2025 Hz
	receive	mark	1270 Hz
		space	1070 Hz

In this notation, "mark" indicates a logical 1, and "space" represents a 0. These tones all fall within

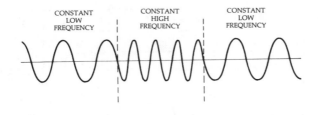

(A) Frequency-shift keying (FSK).

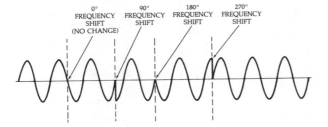

(B) Phase-shift keying (PSK).

Fig. 14-11. Modem transmission methods.

the range of 1070 to 2225 Hz, which means you can hear them if you can listen to the phone line.

Differential Phase-Shift Keying (DPSK)

Computers quickly outgrew this slow transmission method, and the engineers had to find a faster way of sending data. The next development was "Differential Phase-Shift Keying" or DPSK. Under this standard, the telephone line has a constant-frequency carrier signal. As long as no data are being sent down the line, the sine-wave waveform of the carrier signal is allowed to continue undisturbed. When a data bit is to be sent, the circuitry "interrupts" the waveform, and begins it again at a new "phase" in the cycle. The circuitry at the other end of the link compares the phase of the original waveform and the phase of the altered waveform, and notes the phase shift.

Fig. 14-11B shows four possible phase shifts. The DPSK circuits are actually set up to recognize eight different phase shifts. Table 14-1 shows that, using eight options, you can represent any possible combination of three data bits. The DPSK circuits use each of the eight possible phase shifts to represent one of the data bits combinations. Each time the phase shifts, the DPSK circuits are able to send three characters at once.

The term "baud" refers to the number of frequency-shifts per second, while "bits per second"

represents the actual number of data bits transmitted. Under the old Bell 103 standard, 300 frequency-shifts per second (baud) resulted in a transmission rate of 300 bits per second (bps). But, under this new standard, a carrier with a frequency of 600 frequency-shifts per second (baud) has a resulting transmission rate of 1200 bits per second.

Table 14-1. DPSK Coding

Data Bit 1	Data Bit 2	Data Bit 3	Combination Number
0	0	0	0
0	0	1	1
0	1	0	2
0	1	1	3
1	0	0	4
1	0	1	5
1	1	0	6
1	1	1	7

Quadrature Amplitude Modulation (QAM)

However, even 1200 bps was not fast enough, and yet another standard evolved. The system called Quadrature Amplitude Modulation (QAM), uses the phase-shift scheme just described, but with yet another twist. The strength or "amplitude" of the carrier signal may be changed. At any point, the carrier may be set to one of two amplitude levels. This means the total number of options is:

2 possible amplitude levels
$\times$ 8 possible phase shifts
= 16 options

With sixteen possible options, you can represent any possible combination of four data bits. To put it another way, at each phase-shift point, the information contained in four data bits may be transmitted at one time. Using a carrier with 600 frequency changes per second (baud), this results in a transmission rate of 2400 bits per second.

A modem designed for 2400-bps operation usually includes separate circuits for 300-bps and 1200-bps operation. Even though we've added new modes of operation, the modems must still be able to handle each of the old modes. The higher the operating speeds, the more sensitive the modems are to noise and interference from the telephone lines. For example, a phone line that is acceptable at 1200 bps may present many problems at 2400 bps.

9600 BPS and Beyond

Some of the latest modems use data-compression techniques, in addition to QAM, to achieve transmission rates of 9600 bps. At present, there are several competing "standards" for 9600-bps modems. When you set up an interface using 9600-bps modems, you must be sure that the modems at both ends of the link are compatible.

These high-speed transmission techniques are expensive and complicated because the modems are forced to use the public telephone system. However, there is a better solution on the horizon. A *coaxial cable*, of the type used in cable-TV installations, can handle a very wide bandwidth, and thus can be used to carry digital information at very high speeds. At some point in the future, we may be using the cable-TV network to carry high-speed computer signals.

Supervising Modem Operations

Modem Operating Modes

When a modem operates in "half-duplex" mode, characters typed on the computer are transmitted to the

other end of the link. This is a "one-way" operation. Before the other end of the link can answer, it must wait for the first unit to stop sending (Fig. 14-12A).

Most microcomputer modems can operate in the "full-duplex" mode. This means that information can flow both ways at once. This is illustrated in Fig. 14-12B.

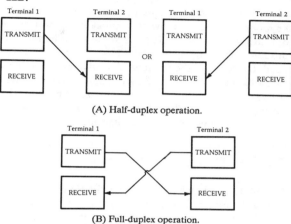

(A) Half-duplex operation.

(B) Full-duplex operation.

Fig. 14-12. Modem operating modes.

Modem Software

Many modems used with microcomputers are "smart" modems. This means that they have some on-board intelligence. A "smart" modem includes an on-board microprocessor, which can set up the modem and supervise its operation. When the smart modem is in the "on-line" state, it is connected to the telephone line and is ready to send or receive data. In the "command" state, the modem is ready to accept commands from the operator. The operator would use the "command" mode to reconfigure the modem—changing the operating speed, for example.

Hayes Microcomputer Products was an early leader in the modem business, and most "smart" modems are advertised as "Hayes compatible." Hayes® modems use a standard command set, and many other modem manufacturers have adopted these commands. The Hayes command set is sometimes called the "AT" command set, since the commands begin with the prefix "AT."

As the smart modem receives a string of characters, it is prepared to recognize command characters and act on them. For example, using the Hayes command set, you would send the modem a string of three "plus" signs (+++) from the keyboard to shift from "on-line" mode to "local command" mode.

To switch back to "on-line" mode, you would send the characters, "AT O." Let's say that you want to set up the modem to dial a telephone number using "pulse" dialing. To do this, you would use the command "+++" to shift the modem to "command" mode, and then you would send the code "AT P."

It is possible to supervise a modem using just these commands, by typing them on the computer keyboard by hand. However, most microcomputer operators use *communications software* to handle the modem. The software produces the "AT" codes needed to control the modem. The software also takes care of other jobs, such as saving and retrieving files, storing telephone numbers, etc. Just as important, the software organizes the whole process with a series of menus, smoothing out the "user interface."

Modem Control Circuits

Fig. 14-13 is a block diagram of a simple modem. This particular modem has separate circuits for both 300-bps and 1200-bps operation. The modem has two modulator-demodulator ICs—one for each of these operating modes. During the "modulation" process, the incoming data are added to a carrier and transmitted down the telephone line. When the modem receives a signal, the incoming data are mixed with the carrier from the other end of the phone line. During "demodulation," the carrier is separated from the incoming data.

The *Scrambler* and *Descrambler* circuits in the diagram are included to prevent a peculiar problem that can occur when the modem tries to send certain combinations of data bits. The problems can occur when the modem tries to send a continuous series consisting of the bit-pair "01"; i.e., "01–01–01." This signal corresponds to a phase shift of 0°, and it would confuse the timing recovery circuits. To prevent this, the "scrambler" changes some of the data bits. The "descrambler" circuit is synchronized with the scrambler and can reconstruct the original data from an incoming "scrambled" signal.

As the output from the modem travels over the phone line, it picks up "noise." A *Receive Filter* is included to "clean up" the incoming signal. A *Transmit Filter* conditions the outgoing signal, producing a smooth analog signal with the bandwidth required by the phone lines.

This particular modem has an automatic speed-sensing circuit. When this circuit detects a 600-Hz carrier on the incoming line, it knows that the modem at the far end of the link is using PSK coding. The circuit automatically switches to the modulator-demodulator for this type of input.

The modem interfaces to the phone line through a 600-ohm 1:1 matching transformer. Telephone lines sometimes carry dangerous "spikes" of high voltage, so the modem may be protected by one or more varistors. Most modems have a separate power supply, but some are powered by the phone line.

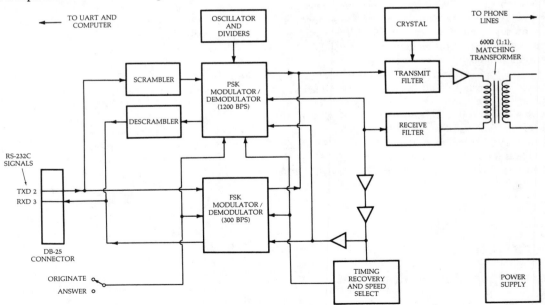

Fig. 14-13. Block diagram of a simple modem.

A "smart" modem will be more complicated than the unit we have shown here. A modem of this type will be designed around a small microprocessor IC.

Modem Service Problems

The network of phone lines is a tempting target for lightning. A lightning strike can cause a very large voltage "surge" in the phone lines. This type of surge can be powerful enough to "cook" most of the components in a modem. There is not much point in trying to fix a modem that has received a powerful surge.

One way to avoid this problem is to unplug the modem from the telephone system when you're not using it. Some direct-connect modems are protected by one of the "varistors" we described in Chapter 14. You can also buy a "surge protector" for use in stopping any high voltages on your incoming phone line. Inmac sells one unit for about $60.00.

Many communications problems are not caused by the modems, but by the telephone network. The phone network is a huge system, with lines running into almost every home and office in the United States, and with other branches reaching around the world. Unfortunately, some parts of this system are not very healthy. The worst problems occur when the local line to your home or office is noisy. Noise can introduce false characters as you send or receive data. If you plug in a phone and listen to the line, you can often hear the noise yourself—it is usually a crackling or frying sound. Noisy phone lines are usually caused by bad grounding or loose connections. Both problems are aggravated by wet weather. The phone company will eventually repair a noisy line, but you may have to be insistent.

Sometimes the noise may be caused by bad connections within your own building. This is your responsibility; the phone company will not help you here. Problems can arise if too many devices are plugged in to the same phone line. Each telephone or modem has a "ringer equivalency number." This number indicates how much load a device places on the telephone line. On any single phone line, the total of the ringer equivalency numbers should be no more than 5.0.

When you make a long-distance call, the phone company may use any one of several transmission methods—microwave link, fiber-optic cable, or even satellite. Some of these methods may give better transmission results than others. For example, cable and satellite links can include time delays which may confuse modems. Today, each of us can decide which

long-distance company we wish to deal with. If you have trouble getting a "clean" long-distance line, try using another long-distance carrier. The phone companies do not like to advertise this, but you can switch from one long-distance carrier to another at will, without applying in advance. For example, in our office, when we dial a long-distance number without any special codes, we're automatically connected to AT&T. However, when we dial the prefix "10222" first, the call will be handled by MCA. In order to use this system, you do not have to sign anything in advance—a bill will appear in the mail eventually. The long-distance carriers will give you these access codes if you ask for them.

The faster the modem, the more sensitive it will be to noise problems. Sometimes you can use a noisy line successfully if you slow down the transmission rate. For example, if you experience problems at 1200 bps, try operating at 300 bps. If you are transmitting a text file, a noisy line might result in a few altered characters. The person at the other end of the link should be able to locate these errors and repair them quickly. However, noise can cause serious problems when you try to send other types of files, particularly programs or data files. Let's say that you transmit a program, and the noise changes a few of the characters. This can change the meaning of several of the commands in the program. There is no way of predicting how the altered program will behave.

Most communications software packages include a solution to ths problem. Earlier in this chapter, we described the X Modem protocol, which uses the signals ACK and NAK to control data transmission. By using a format like X Modem, you can protect yourself from errors caused by noise.

In general, the electronic circuits in modems are quite reliable. The parts outside of the modem, including the cables and connectors, cause a higher proportion of the failures. Also, users tend to place modems in precarious positions. Sometimes, an inept worker will trip over the modem's cable and pull the unit off of the desk and onto the floor. This can crack the modem's circuit board. If the crack is large, the modem will not operate at all. A small crack can cause a "make and break" connection and can result in intermittent errors. The 600-ohm 1:1 matching transformer is a heavy part. If the modem falls, the destructive forces seem to focus around the transformer, so look for a problem there. The RS-232C cable usually plugs into a DB-25 connector in the rear of the modem. If someone uses too much force while inserting or removing a cable, the DB-25 connector can start to pull away from the circuit board. Check the base of the connector for bad connections.

The servicing picture for modems is a bit unusual, because modems are licensed by the FCC. The government insists that only a manufacturer or a licensed service agent can repair modems. The bureaucrats don't want poorly repaired modems "polluting" the public telephone lines. If an unauthorized person works on a modem, the unit's certification is voided, and it is illegal to use the repaired modem until it has been recertified. This means that you will not be able to make repairs on a modem, unless you are authorized to do this by the FCC. If your modem fails, you will have to send it back to manufacturer, or find a local dealer. For this reason, we will concentrate on the functions the FCC allows us to perform—diagnosing and localizing problems.

Troubleshooting Modems

We will begin this section by describing four diagnostic tests. Whenever you encounter a problem with a modem or an RS-232C link, we suggest you start by running through these four tests. As we said, the FCC will not allow you to actually make repairs on a faulty modem. In this section, like before, we will use key numbers (14.1.1, 14.2.2, etc.) to refer to specific paragraphs.

14.1.1 Test Number 1
A serial interface checklist.

Many interfacing problems are caused when the two ends of the serial link are not matched. Each end of the link must be expecting the same type of signals. Before testing the hardware, check these items:

- Which unit is the terminal (DTE) and which unit is the communicator (DCE)?

- If both are DTE or DCE, have you installed a null modem between them?

- What type of handshaking will be in use?

  1. DTR/DSR
  2. RTS/CTS
  3. X-ON/X-OFF

- Are both ends expecting the same bit rate (i.e., 300 bps, 1200 bps, etc.)?

- Are both units expecting the same word length (7-bit or 8-bit ASCII)?

- Is parity enabled?

- Have you chosen odd or even parity?

- If the computer has multiple output ports, is the correct port assigned (i.e., LPT1, PR#2, etc.)

14.1.2 Test Number 2
A local loopback test.

Many modems have a "self-test" mode that allows you to test them quickly. During the "loopback" test, signals from the modem's transmitter are fed back into the receiver. The modem should be disconnected from the computer when you run this test. During the self-test, when you press a key on the keyboard, the character is converted by the computer, sent through the RS-232C cable (if any), and sent out by the modem. Next, the signal is picked up by the receiver, demodulated by the modem, converted back to RS-232C mode, and displayed by the computer. This one test allows you to check all of the important circuits in your computer and modem.

To make the test, set the modem switches to "originate," "self-test," and "full-duplex." To test an acoustic modem, you must use the handset of the telephone as part of the test loop. Set the handset in place and dial one digit on the phone to get a quiet line without the dial tone.

When using this "self-test" option on direct-connect modems, the test loop is made inside the unit. (This is why we call it a "local" test.) If you have a Hayes-compatible modem, use this command to set up the self-test:

AT S16=1 C1 D

The characters "AT" signal the modem that you are sending it a command. By setting (storing) a "1" or "0" in register 16 in the modem, you can turn the self-test on or off. "S16=1" turns on the self-test. "C1" forces the carrier detect circuits to turn on before they detect a carrier from the other end of the phone line. The "D" character starts the test. Now, anything you type on the keyboard should be looped back and displayed on the monitor. The code listed above tests the "originate" section of the modem. To test the "answer" section, type in:

AT S16=1A

On units without the "self-test" feature, you can connect the test loop yourself by connecting pins 2 and 3 in the RS-232 connector.

What if the modem fails this test and does not "loop back" the test characters? You must determine whether the problem is in the modem, or in the circuits in the computer which generate the RS-232C signals. One simple way of doing this is to borrow another modem, "swap" it with the suspect unit, and see if the symptoms disappear. If the borrowed modem works correctly, this means your first modem is faulty. If the borrowed modem does not work, look for a problem in the RS-232C circuits. See Section 14.1.4.

14.1.3 Test Number 3
Testing an RS-232C interface with a breakout box.

The "breakout box" is a test instrument which allows you to see the status of each of the lines in the RS-232C interface. See Fig. 14-14. The breakout box has two DB-25 connectors, so it can be plugged "in-line" with the RS-232C cable. Some breakout boxes are powered by the RS-232C lines, but these boxes tend to "load down" the signals. The better boxes are powered by separate batteries. A very simple breakout box might cost less than $50.00, while a more elaborate model will cost about $150.

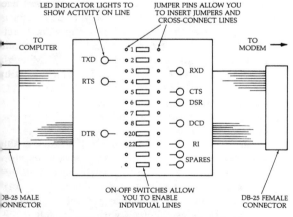

Fig. 14-14. Diagram of a breakout box.

The breakout box shown in the diagram of Fig. 14-14 has a series of LED indicators. Each LED indicates the status of one of the important lines of the interface. On the better breakout boxes, these LEDs turn red to indicate "high," and green for "low." On an in-expensive box, the LEDs might indicate the "high" state only.

A row of on-off switches runs down the center of the box. You must turn a switch "on" to enable one of the RS-232C lines. This allows you to choose which lines will be active. A series of jumper pins are also included. By inserting jumpers across these pins, you can cross-connect different lines.

A breakout box can reveal problems with the RS-232C interface very quickly. The box is most useful for detecting problems with the "handshaking" signals. For example, let's say that the RS-232C interface seems to be "hung-up," and signals are not passing through. You plug in the breakout box, and you notice that the LED for RTS (Request To Send) is lit. However, the LED for CTS (Clear To Send) is not lit. This suggests that the computer is prepared to interface, but for some reason, the modem is not. You can focus your troubleshooting activities on the modem. The same situation can arise with DTR (Data Terminal Ready) and DSR (Data Set Ready). If DTR is "high" and DSR does not answer, look for a problem in the modem.

If the modem appears to be operating correctly, and the problem seems to be in the interfacing circuits in the computer, try the RS-232C loopback test described in the next section.

14.1.4 Test Number 4
An RS-232C loopback test.

It is possible to execute a loopback test on the RS-232C circuits alone, with the modem disconnected. The trick is to convince the RS-232C interface that it is still talking with the modem. Get a DB-25 connector and install jumper wires as follows:

Connect	To	Resulting Connection
pin 2	pin 3	"transmit data" to "receive data"
pin 4	pin 5	"request to send" to "clear to send"
pin 4	pin 6	"request to send" to "data set ready"
pin 20	pin 8	"data terminal ready" to "data carrier detect"
pin 20	pin 22	"data terminal ready" to "ring indicator"

You may have to modify these connections for your system. Once you have installed the jumpers, turn off the computer and fit the special DB-25 connector in place on the serial connector. Turn on the computer again. Now, any character that you type on the keyboard should "loop back" and be repeated on the monitor. If your equipment passes this test, you know that the RS-232C circuits in the computer are working correctly.

Problem Checking

14.2.1 Symptom 1
Intermittent bad characters.

Whenever you have an intermittent problem with a modem, start by trying the "self-test" described in Section 14.1.2, above.

Many problems that are blamed on modems are actually caused by the telephone lines. You can check for this problem by listening to the line yourself. If you're using an acoustic modem, just pick up the telephone handset and listen. If you have a direct-connect type of modem, use a Y-connector to connect a phone to the line that the modem is using.

If just the long-distance portion of a connection is noisy, you can get around this by hanging up and calling back. You will probably get a different circuit. If the local line directly to your phone is noisy, every call you make may be affected. The noisy line must be repaired by the telephone company. Check all of the connections at your end of the phone line. Be sure each of the wires is connected to the proper point, and each of the connections is clean and tight. If your line is consistently noisy, call the phone company and have them track down the problem. Don't accept anything less than a clean line.

Once the RS-232C interface between the computer and the modem is set up and working, it should not give you much trouble. If the modem develops an intermittent problem, check the cables and connectors in this link, as described in Chapter 7. Look for bent pins, corroded contacts, etc.

At the computer's end of the RS-232 link, you will find a set of serial interface circuits. On the Apple II, IBM PC, Mac II, and some other computers, these circuits are mounted on removable cards. If possible, swap the suspect interface circuits for a set of circuits that are known to be good. The serial interface is often built around a UART or ACIA chip. If you have an intermittent problem in the interface circuits, check the signals at this chip.

14.2.2 Symptom 2
No "Ready" indicator.

Start by making sure that the modem is getting power. Many modems use a supply that includes a separate plug-in transformer. This transformer should supply low-voltage AC (5–12 V) to the power connector. Check the cables, connectors, and the power switch according to the instructions given in Chapter 7. Check the rest of the power circuitry inside the modem according to the instructions given in Chapter 16.

If you have an acoustic-coupled modem, is the telephone handset in the correct position? Is the modem mistakenly set on "self-test?" When you communicate with a central computer network, your modem should be set to "originate." At other times, you and the operator at the other end of the link must agree on which unit will "originate" and which will "answer."

Try a "self-test." We described this test in Section 14.1.2.

Check to see if the RS-232C interface is active. To do this, you may use a "breakout box," as described in Section 14.1.3. You may also use an oscilloscope or voltmeter to check each of the control lines. By watching the state of these lines, you should be able to tell if your modem is "hung up" at a particular point. For example, if your system uses line 8 (carrier detect), and this line shows a negative voltage (false), you know the modem can't find the carrier. Maybe the carrier is missing, or perhaps the fault is inside the modem, but at least you know where to start. Check to be sure you have "true" signals on lines 20 and 6 (TERMINAL READY and DATA SET (COMMUNICATOR) READY, respectively). If line 4 (REQUEST TO SEND) is "true," and line 5 (CLEAR TO SEND) is "false," you know that the modem is holding up the action for some reason.

Modems can't take much physical abuse. On acoustic modems, an operator can push the handset down into the couplers with too much force. This can break traces on the circuit board under the couplers. On a direct-connect modem, it is possible to plug the cables into their connectors with too much force, breaking some of the traces at the base of the connectors. Check the circuit board carefully for signs of mechanical damage. See the "Circuit Board" discussion given in Chapter 7.

If the signals coming from the computer seem incorrect, check the serial interface circuits inside the computer. On Apple IIs, IBM PCs, Mac II computers, and other models, the serial interface circuits are mounted on removable circuit cards. If possible, substitute a good interface card for the suspect unit and see if the symptoms disappear.

The serial interface may be supervised by a single UART or ACIA IC. Check the signals around this IC.

Chapter Review

In this chapter, we have examined two groups of related circuits. The UART takes parallel data from the computer and converts it to serial data in the RS-232C format. The RS-232C interface can be set up to operate with just three lines—TXD, RXD, and GND. However, other lines may be used for "handshaking," including DTR/DSR and CTS/RTS. One software handshaking protocol uses "X-ON" and "X-OFF" characters instead.

The modem circuits "modulate" and "demodulate" the RS-232C signals so they can be sent over the telephone lines. Different modem principles may be used, depending on the operating speed of the link. Faster modems tend to have more trouble when using noisy phone lines.

When troubleshooting these circuits, determine whether the problem is in the RS-232C serial-to-parallel circuits, or in the modem circuits. For a quick check of the modem, try a local loopback test. To check the RS-232C circuits, use a breakout box. Always be alert for handshaking problems.

Review Questions

1. You are receiving a file over a modem, and you suddenly begin to receive many incorrect characters. You hang up, call back, and retransmit the file with no problems. Can you think of a cause for this?

2. You want to "down-load" a program from the local user's group, using your modem. Should you take any special precautions?

3. A modem is not able to transmit characters. You try a local loopback test. The characters you type on the keyboard are not returned to the monitor. You try the test with a different modem, and this time the characters are returned. What does this tell you?

4. In the example in Question 3, you reconnect the first modem and install a breakout box in the cable between the computer and the modem. The breakout box shows you that DATA TERMINAL READY (DTR) is "high" and DATA SET READY is not. What does this tell you?

5. A modem stops working. You open the case and notice that a number of ICs seem to be blackened. Can you suggest a reason for this?

15

Monitors and Displays

Introduction and Objections

In this chapter, we will discuss the principles and circuitry behind the "cathode-ray tube" monitor. We will also touch on two less-common types of displays—the "liquid-crystal display" and the "gas plasma display." As you will learn, the typical monitor is a complex piece of equipment. The circuitry inside a monitor is quite different from the circuitry in a computer, because the monitor relies on analog principles, rather than digital principles. This means that the test instruments and troubleshooting procedures used will also be different.

Most of the components in a modern monitor (Fig. 15-1), except for the picture tube, are solid-state components. As a result, most modern monitors are much more reliable than were the earlier tube-type television sets.

There is one factor that helps the technician who is trying to service a monitor—the monitor is a visual display device. When something is wrong with a monitor, the display on the screen will often help in localizing the problem. Later, at the end of the chapter, we have shown the characteristic displays for some common monitor problems.

For the beginner, a monitor is a relatively difficult piece of equipment to service. Most computer equipment uses digital principles. Generally, any point

Fig. 15-1. Typical color monitor. *(Courtesy Amdek Corp.)*

in a digital circuit is either "on" or "off." Thus, it is relatively simple to tell whether a digital circuit is working. If a digital circuit is processing signals at all, you can usually assume that it is working correctly.

Most of the circuitry inside a monitor uses analog principles, and various points in the analog circuitry are not simply "on" or "off"—the signal levels often fall in between. Therefore, it is not enough to know whether an analog circuit is working, you must also know whether the circuit is handling these intermediate signal levels correctly. Also, because the monitor circuits use these analog principles, they require different test equipment than that used for digital circuits. The trusty TTL logic probe will not be of much help if you must repair a monitor. Instead, you must use a different set of tools.

We will begin this chapter by describing the operation of the *monochrome* or *black-and-white* monitor. Then, the following section will cover color monitors. Next, we'll look at the circuits in the computer which drive a typical monitor, and the last part of the chapter will include instructions for testing, aligning, and troubleshooting monitors. When you finish this chapter, you should understand how monitors work. Then, when you encounter a faulty monitor, you should know how to localize the problem.

Before we move on, we must add an important note about safety. Monitors can be dangerous to the inexperienced technician. Some of the circuits in a monitor carry very high voltages. For example, in a color monitor, the picture tube may use a voltage as high as 35,000-volts DC! This high voltage can be very dangerous. In this chapter, we've tried to outline the main safety dangers.

This book is intended to be used as a classroom text, and many students will someday have to work with monitors. For these reasons, we have included servicing information on monitors. However, we don't want to encourage any beginners to work with monitors without adequate expert supervision. Get the help of an experienced person before you begin working on a monitor.

IF YOU ARE AN INEXPERIENCED TECHNICIAN, WORKING ALONE AND UNSUPERVISED, DON'T WORK ON MONITORS!

Monochrome Monitors

A monochrome monitor is very similar to a black-and-white television set, although the television set has some additional circuitry which is not found in the monitor. The TV will have a tuner and an intermediate frequency (IF) stage for handling the high-frequency signals from the antenna tuner. In most other respects, the two units are the same.

Picture Tube Operation

The image on a TV or monitor is traced on the "picture tube," or "cathode-ray tube" (crt), by a single beam of electrons (Fig. 15-2). The beam is created by an "electron gun" located at the rear end, or "cathode," of the picture tube, as shown in Fig. 15-2A. The inside surface of the front of the picture tube is given a strong electric charge—15,000 volts or more on a monochrome monitor—and the electrons in the electron beam are attracted toward the front of the picture tube by this strong charge. The inside of the picture tube is coated with a special "phosphor" material, which glows when it is struck by the beam of electrons. Thus, as the electrons pass through the front of the tube, they cause a point on the picture tube to glow.

On a monochrome monitor, the electron beam may trigger a green, orange, or white light, depending on the type of phosphor used. The electron beam is not turned on all of the time. Instead, it is *modulated* (switched on and off) to create a picture. When the beam is turned on, the electrons strike the phosphor layer, creating a bright dot. The electron beam strikes each point on the phosphor coating for a very short time, but the phosphor continues to glow for a moment after the electron beam passes. Then, when the beam is turned off, the electrons do not strike the phosphor, so that point on the screen remains dark.

The electron beam in the crt is scanned rapidly across the screen in a zig-zag pattern, as shown in Fig. 15-2B. The electrons in the beam have a negative charge. This means that the beam can be repelled by magnets having a negative charge and attracted by magnets with a positive charge. Several powerful electromagnets are mounted at the rear end (the neck) of the picture tube. By changing the currents through these "sweep" magnets, the electron beam can be aimed by the circuitry.

To begin the "painting" of a picture, the electron beam scans across one horizontal line, moving from left to right (Fig. 15-2B). At the end of the scan line, the beam is turned off. The sweep magnets then return the beam to the left side of the screen, and move it down a bit to begin the start of the next line. The electron beam continues this process until it reaches the bottom of the screen. When the beam has completed the last line, it *retraces* (returns) to the upper left-hand corner of the screen (Fig. 15-2C). During this "vertical retrace," the beam is turned off.

After the retrace, the beam does not begin painting a completely different picture. Rather, it begins tracing a new set of lines between the horizontal lines of the last picture. The old picture lines and the new lines

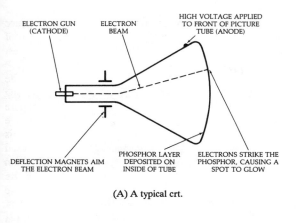

(A) A typical crt.

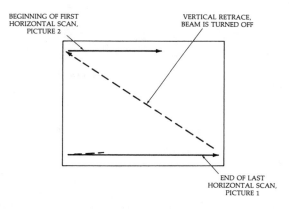

(C) Vertical retrace.

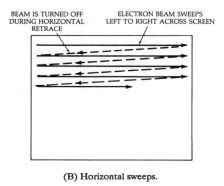

(B) Horizontal sweeps.

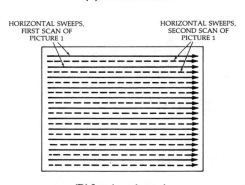

(D) Interleaved scanning.

Fig. 15-2. Picture tube operation.

are interleaved, as shown in Fig. 15-2D. To paint a complete image, the beam actually scans the entire screen twice.

We have just described a *raster scan* monitor. The complete pattern of interleaved traces is called the *raster*. On some newer models, succeeding screens are not "interleaved." This is the most common type monitor used for microcomputers. Some advanced monitors and some video games use the *vector scan* principle. The raster scan monitor creates a lighted field (the "raster") and then writes data on that field. On a vector scan monitor, the circuitry traces just those lines which are part of the picture. The monitor does not bother to paint a complete raster. This is illustrated in Fig. 15-3.

Monochrome Monitor Signals

Fig. 15-4 shows the type of signal which might be sent to a monochrome monitor. The illustration shows the signal sent during two of the horizontal scans. During each scan, the beam is turned on and off, or "modulated," to create the picture. At the end of the scan, a horizontal sync pulse triggers the horizontal sweep circuits, which then return the electron beam to the left side of the monitor screen.

The monitor covered in this discussion requires 262 passes of the electron beam to paint a complete screen. When the beam reaches the bottom of the display screen, a vertical sync pulse is included in the signal. This triggers the vertical sweep circuits, which begin the vertical retrace.

Three different kinds of information are carried in the type of signal shown in Fig. 15-4. The horizontal sync pulses, the vertical pulses, and the actual video information are all carried by a single signal. This type of signal is called "composite" video.

Monitor Control Circuits

Let's look at the circuits which process the composite

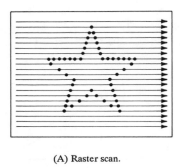

(A) Raster scan.

(B) Vector scan.

Fig. 15-3. Raster and vector scan images.

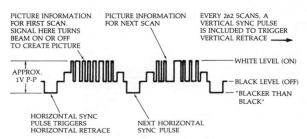

PICTURE INFORMATION FOR FIRST SCAN. SIGNAL HERE TURNS BEAM ON OR OFF TO CREATE PICTURE

PICTURE INFORMATION FOR NEXT SCAN

EVERY 262 SCANS, A VERTICAL SYNC PULSE IS INCLUDED TO TRIGGER VERTICAL RETRACE →

APPROX. 1V P-P

WHITE LEVEL (ON)

BLACK LEVEL (OFF)

'BLACKER THAN BLACK'

HORIZONTAL SYNC PULSE TRIGGERS HORIZONTAL RETRACE

NEXT HORIZONTAL SYNC PULSE

Fig. 15-4. Monochrome monitor signals.

video signal and translate it into a picture on the screen. Fig. 15-5 is a simplified block diagram of a monochrome monitor. The composite video signal is brought in to a sync amplifier and separator. Here, the sync pulses are conditioned and separated from the video data. The stream of video data contains the instructions for switching the electron beam on and off to create dots on the picture-tube screen. This stream of signals is amplified, and passed on to the crt tube.

The vertical sync pulses are separated and sent to an oscillator circuit. (An "oscillator" is a circuit that switches quickly back and forth between two states.) The oscillator produces a regular train of pulses which can be used to control the timing of other parts of the circuitry. Thus, the vertical sync pulses trigger the activity of the vertical oscillator, and keep the oscillator operating in time with the rest of the circuits. The vertical oscillator circuit and the associated amplifiers control the vertical movement of the electron beam on the crt screen. The signal from this circuitry causes the beam to scan down the screen, and then jump back to the top of the screen during the vertical retrace.

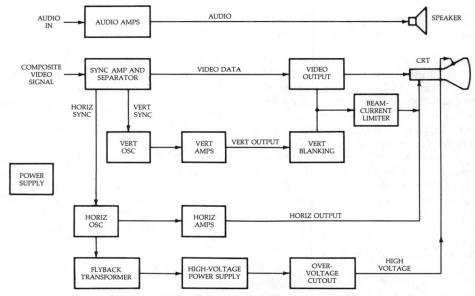

Fig. 15-5. Block diagram of a monochrome monitor.

The horizontal sync pulses are used to synchronize a second oscillator, and the horizontal circuits are used to control the horizontal movement of the beam on the screen. These circuits cause the beam to scan across the crt screen from left to right, and then retrace back to the left side of the screen.

Different monitors may use different horizontal and vertical scanning speeds. A monitor must be matched with the driver circuits so that both parts of the system use the same scanning signals. "Multiscan" monitors are available, however, which are adaptable and thus can handle many different scanning speeds.

As we said earlier, the anode of the picture tube requires a high voltage—about 15,000 volts for a monochrome monitor. This high voltage is usually developed in a chain of components that begin at the horizontal oscillator. The high voltage is often developed by a special component part called a *flyback transformer* (Fig. 15-6). Sometimes, however, a device called a *voltage tripler* may be used instead. The high-voltage output is conditioned by the high-voltage circuits and is passed on to the picture tube. A safety circuit is designed to check the output of the high-voltage circuits, and turn off the monitor if the voltage becomes too high.

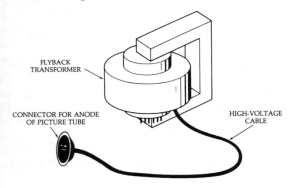

Fig. 15-6. Flyback transformer.

The power-supply circuits in any monitor are probably much like the circuits we describe in Chapter 16. There are some important differences, however. The circuits inside the monitor often use a higher voltage than the +5-V DC level you would find inside a computer. On a modern solid-state monitor, this "B+" voltage may be +10 V or higher. Do not use a logic probe inside a monitor until you have tested the voltages with a VOM.

A monitor's power supply usually includes a self-protecting "foldback" feature. A regulating circuit holds the output current at a constant level. If the monitor tries to draw too much current, the regulator

will drop the output voltage to hold the current within the allowed limit. If a short circuit causes a very large current drain, the regulator may cut off the output completely.

Color Monitors

The monochrome monitor just described has a single electron gun, and the inside of the picture tube is coated with a single type of phosphor material. In contrast, a color monitor has three separate electron guns, and the inside of the picture tube is coated with dots of three different phosphor materials. One of the phosphor materials glows red when it is struck by electrons, another type of phosphor glows green, and a third type glows blue. Dots of each of the phosphor types are clustered together, as shown in Fig. 15-7. By striking these dots with different amounts of energy, it is possible to create a full range of colors. For example, when a dot of red phosphor material and a dot of blue phosphor are both struck by strong electron beams, they glow at the same time and produce a violet image. When all three dots are struck at the same time, they produce a white image. Other colors are created by sending a strong signal to one type of phosphor, and weaker signals to the other phosphors.

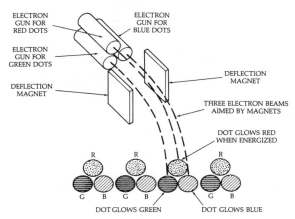

Fig. 15-7. Basic principle of a color monitor.

As we said, the picture tube in a color monitor has three separate electron guns. One gun provides the electron beam which strikes the red phosphor dots, and the two other guns handle the signals for the green and blue phosphor dots. The three electron beams are controlled by the same deflection magnets, and are scanned across the picture tube at the same time. The voltage at the front of the picture tube (the anode) on a color monitor is usually quite high (about 35,000 volts).

The color monitor also has to handle three separate streams of video information—one for each of the three electron guns. All three signals may be mixed with the horizontal and vertical sync pulses, and combined into one "composite" signal. This is illustrated in Fig. 15-8A. A "composite video" color monitor includes demodulation circuits which can separate the red, green, and blue signals from this composite signal. The color information is coded into the composite signal using two variables. The strength or "amplitude" of the incoming signal is changed. The second variable is the phase relationship between the incoming signal and a reference. In order to reconstruct the color information, the demodulator circuits must compare the phase of the incoming signal with phase information from the circuit that originally generated the signal. This phase-reference information is coded right into the composite video signal. Following each horizontal sync pulse is a "color burst" signal. The color burst synchronizes the phase-detection circuitry in the monitor, and provides the necessary phase reference (Fig. 15-9).

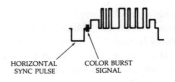

HORIZONTAL SYNC PULSE   COLOR BURST SIGNAL

Fig. 15-9. Signals to a color monitor.

In an RGB-type monitor, each of the three color signals has a separate input. This is shown in Fig. 15-8B. Sometimes the sync pulses have a separate input line, and sometimes they are mixed with one of the color signals.

The simplest type of RGB monitor can only display eight colors. On this "TTL" type of monitor, each of the three guns is either "on" or "off." On a more expensive "analog" RGB monitor, each of the three guns can be turned on or off, or can be operated in a range of middle values.

Video Driver Circuits

Much of the signal-processing work of the video system is done inside the computer. Sometimes this circuitry is mounted on a separate interface or adapter card, which can be plugged into the computer's main circuit board. Usually the video circuitry is mounted directly on the main circuit board.

Fig. 15-10 shows a special type of read-only memory called a *character generator ROM*. This device takes ASCII-coded characters from the computer, and produces a dot pattern that can be used to control the beam on the crt. ASCII is the standard coding system for letters and numbers. Each character is given a separate 7- or 8-bit code. ASCII codes are used at several points in the computer system. (ASCII codes are listed in Appendix D.)

When the computer wants to display a certain character on the monitor, it sends the ASCII code for that character to the character generator circuits. Decoder circuits interpret the ASCII code, and refer to a memory location in the character generator ROM. In our illustration in Fig. 15-10, the computer is preparing to display a line of text and has reached the letter "T." The memory spaces in the ROM hold a dot pattern which will create this letter on the screen. Where the ROM has stored a digital "1," the electron beam will be turned on and the monitor will create a dot. Where the ROM has stored a "0," the beam will be turned off.

In the example given, the complete letter "T" will require $5 \times 7 = 35$ dots. But the electron beam can only create one horizontal row of dots at a time. This means that the letter "T" must be sliced into seven

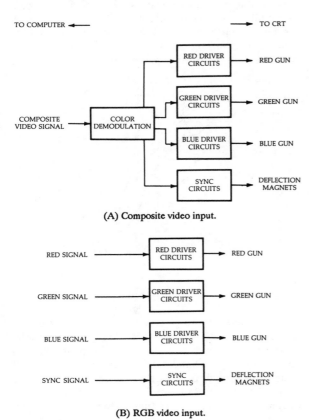

TO COMPUTER ◄——   ——► TO CRT

RED DRIVER CIRCUITS ——► RED GUN

GREEN DRIVER CIRCUITS ——► GREEN GUN

COMPOSITE VIDEO SIGNAL ——► COLOR DEMODULATION

BLUE DRIVER CIRCUITS ——► BLUE GUN

SYNC CIRCUITS ——► DEFLECTION MAGNETS

(A) Composite video input.

RED SIGNAL ——► RED DRIVER CIRCUITS ——► RED GUN

GREEN SIGNAL ——► GREEN DRIVER CIRCUITS ——► GREEN GUN

BLUE SIGNAL ——► BLUE DRIVER CIRCUITS ——► BLUE GUN

SYNC SIGNAL ——► SYNC CIRCUITS ——► DEFLECTION MAGNETS

(B) RGB video input.

Fig. 15-8. Color signal inputs.

horizontal lines of one dot each. To paint the complete letter, the beam will have to make seven passes, moving down one line each time.

On a signal from the scan-line counter, each horizontal "slice" of the letter is sent to a shift register.

"0s" can be used to switch the electron beam on or off, and thus create a dot pattern.

Fig. 15-11 shows how the character generator ROM is used in a complete video driver circuit. The circuitry shown here is located inside the computer, and

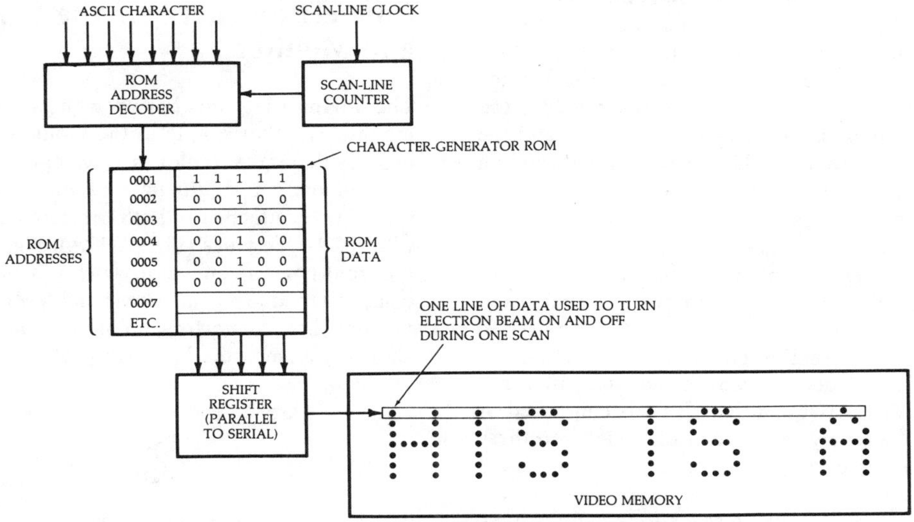

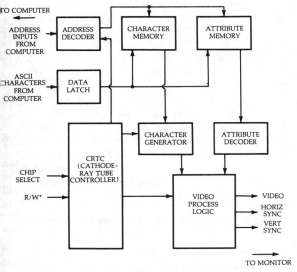

Fig. 15-10. A character generator ROM.

This register converts the parallel data from the ROM to serial data which may be stored in the video memory. The "slices" from this character are stored with "slices" from the other characters in the line of text. When the transformation is complete, the video memory holds a whole line of characters, each "sliced" into horizontal lines. These horizontal lines of "1s" and

produces signals for a monochrome monitor. The characters to be displayed, coded in the ASCII format, arrive at the data latch. At the same time, an address code arrives on the address lines. Based on this address, the decoder decides whether the incoming data represent a character to be printed, or a character's "attributes." On many computer systems, each character has a matching "attribute" code. The "attribute" carries special information on how the character should be displayed. Depending on the computer system, the attribute might indicate that the character should be shown in flashing type or in dimmer-than-normal type. When the attribute calls for reverse type, the character will be displayed as a light letter on a dark background.

Incoming characters are sent to a character memory space. Incoming attributes are sent to a separate attribute memory area. Usually, a computer will have enough video memory to store several full screens or "pages" of characters. This allows the display to scroll up or down easily, without having to read in a new line of characters for each new line of the display. The memory space for this is often called a "frame buffer." Sometimes a section of the computer's main memory is set aside for video memory. In a computer of this type, the video memory is stored in a certain range of memory addresses. Sometimes the video memory is stored in separate RAM ICs.

Fig. 15-11. Video driver circuits.

The characters are held in the video memory until the computer is ready to display them. To begin this process, the characters are converted into horizontal "slices" of dot patterns by the character generator ROM, as we've just described. A set of decoder circuits interpret the matching attributes. The "slices" of dot patterns from the characters are sent, along with the decoded attributes, to the video processing circuits. These circuits produce the outputs that are sent to the monitor. These outputs include the horizontal sync pulses, the vertical sync pulses, and the video signal, which contains the dot-pattern information used to switch the electron beam on and off.

This whole process is usually controlled by a large IC called a *cathode-ray tube controller* (CRTC). The CRTC performs several important jobs. One section of the CRTC handles the video memory, producing the correct memory addresses needed to call up the desired characters. Another section generates the sync pulses. The CRTC also includes a scan-line counter and scroll logic circuits. The activity of the CRTC is controlled by several "registers." By writing control codes into these registers, the computer can change the CRTC's functions.

The image on the screen tends to fade quickly, so the CRTC must repaint the whole screen about 30 times a second. Each time it does this, the CRTC must have access to the video memory. The main microprocessor must also have access to the video memory so it can change the characters displayed on the screen. The system must be designed so that both the CRTC and the microprocessor have enough time to access the video memory. There are several ways of doing this. Sometimes, the microprocessor is connected to the video memory during the horizontal and vertical retrace periods. The CRTC does not need access to the memory during these periods.

Some microprocessors use a two-phase clock signal (often labeled $\phi1$ and $\phi2$). On systems of this type, the CRTC is given access to the video memory during one clock phase. The microprocessor is connected to the video memory during the other phase. In a third scheme, access to the video memory is controlled by a separate *direct memory access* (DMA) controller.

If the driver circuits are designed to be used with a color monitor, there must be a way of generating the color signals. There are several ways of doing this. One arrangement uses a memory device called a *color lookup table*. The outputs from the lookup table device are connected to three digital-to-analog converters. Each converter handles one of the color outputs—red, green, or blue. The inputs of the lookup table receive digital signals which represent particular colors. Based

on these inputs, the table produces digital outputs for each of the digital/analog converters. The converters then produce the three analog signals used to supply color information to the monitor.

Connections Between the Computer and Monitor

The wiring that runs between the computer and the monitor is rather simple. If the monitor is using a composite video signal (color or monochrome), the signal is carried over a single pair of lines. The wires will probably be attached to both the computer and monitor with RCA-type plugs (Fig. 15-12A). Fig. 15-12B shows a different type of connector which is also used to carry a composite video signal. The signal level on any of these "composite" connectors, color or monochrome, will be about 1 volt, measured peak-to-peak.

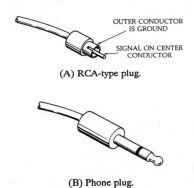

(A) RCA-type plug.

(B) Phone plug.

Fig. 15-12. Composite video connectors.

On some monochrome adapter cards, the horizontal and vertical sync pulses are separated from the video data signal, and sent over separate lines. Fig. 15-13A shows the 9-pin connector used with this interface.

An RGB color monitor will have at least three separate inputs. If the RGB unit has only three inputs, then the sync signals are carried along with one of the color inputs (often the green input). If the RGB unit has more than three inputs, one of the wires carries just the sync pulses. Fig. 15-13B shows how the RGB outputs may be routed through a DB-9 connector.

Television Sets Used as Monitors

Some inexpensive computers use regular television sets as video display devices. In computers of this type, the

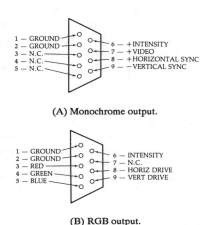

(A) Monochrome output.

(B) RGB output.

Fig. 15-13. A DB-9 connector.

video information is used to modulate a *radio frequency* (RF) signal. This RF signal is then fed into the tuner of the TV, just as if it were a signal coming in from an antenna. Inside the set, the desired signal is separated from the RF carrier. (It is "demodulated.") The

following stages of the set operate in much the same way as the circuits in a monitor.

Liquid-Crystal Displays

If you have a digital watch, you are already familiar with the appearance of a liquid-crystal display. The characters displayed are usually black, and appear against a silver or lighted background. Fig. 15-14 illustrates the operating principle behind this type of display. Some "laptop" computers use a similar display. Fig. 15-14A shows how the display panel is constructed.

The display uses a special liquid containing small crystals of a material which is sensitive to electromagnetic force. These crystals are free to move in the liquid. The liquid material is sandwiched between two glass plates, with a grid pattern of conductive material etched on the inside of each glass plate. The conductors on the two plates run in different directions, as shown in Fig. 15-14B. Below the lower glass plate is a mirror. Some "electroluminescent" displays have a light source here, instead.

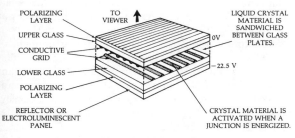

(A) Display panel construction.

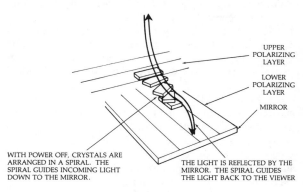

WITH POWER OFF, CRYSTALS ARE ARRANGED IN A SPIRAL. THE SPIRAL GUIDES INCOMING LIGHT DOWN TO THE MIRROR.

THE LIGHT IS REFLECTED BY THE MIRROR. THE SPIRAL GUIDES THE LIGHT BACK TO THE VIEWER

(C) Panel section is turned off.

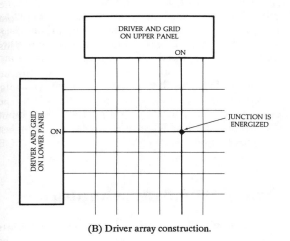

(B) Driver array construction.

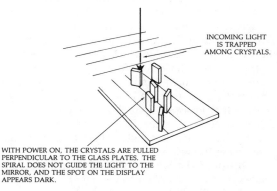

WITH POWER ON, THE CRYSTALS ARE PULLED PERPENDICULAR TO THE GLASS PLATES. THE SPIRAL DOES NOT GUIDE THE LIGHT TO THE MIRROR, AND THE SPOT ON THE DISPLAY APPEARS DARK.

(D) Panel section is turned on.

Fig. 15-14. Liquid-crystal display.

· On the outside surface of each **glass plate** is a polarizing layer. Each layer is designed to pass light that is "polarized" in a certain way, and reflect light which is polarized in other ways. The two filters are 90° out of phase. To put this another way, the **upper filter** will only pass light that is polarized in one direction, which we will call a "north/south" direction. The lower filter will only pass light that is polarized, with respect to the first filter, at a 90° angle, or in an "east/west" direction.

Fig. 15-14B shows the grid of conductors on the upper and lower glass panels. How can the circuits "turn on" a specific point on the display? This happens when one conductor on the upper panel is energized and another conductor on the lower panel is also energized, both at the same time. The point where the two conductors cross is then "turned on."

Fig. 15-14C shows the liquid material at rest. Incoming light with the correct polarity is allowed to pass through the upper polarizing layer. When the power is off, the crystals arrange themselves in a "spiral staircase" pattern, as shown in Fig. 15-14C. This spiral guides the incoming light, and rotates it 90°. This rotation is just enough to align the light with the second polarizing layer. To put it another way, "north/south" light has become "east/west." The light passes through the second polarizing layer and strikes the mirror. This light is then reflected, and passes back up the spiral and out to the viewer. When a certain location is not energized, the viewer sees the mirror at the back of the display.

Fig. 15-14D shows what happens when a particular part of the display is energized. The crystals are pulled perpendicular to the glass plates. This breaks up the spiral, so the incoming light is not rotated and passed to the lower polarizing filter. Instead, the incoming light is trapped among the crystals. That spot on the display appears to be dark.

On one type of display, the conductors on the upper glass plate are grounded and the conductors on the lower plate receive −22.5-volts DC. On the newer "supertwist" displays, the crystals twist the incoming light by about 240°, rather than the 90° twist we have shown in the illustration. This results in a higher contrast and a better image. Some displays do not use a mirror to reflect light through the display. Instead, they replace the mirror with a light source. Sometimes an "electroluminescent" panel is placed behind the display. In other units, the display is back-lighted by one or two small fluorescent bulbs. These fluorescent bulbs typically use 100-volt AC at 400 Hz.

Most of the work required to drive an LCD display is usually handled by a single IC. This "LCD driver" chip includes many of the functions of the monitor interface circuits that we decribed earlier. One block of the driver IC handles the job of character generation, for example. Other blocks provide memory spaces for the incoming characters and their attributes. Rather than producing signals for individual dots, as a controller circuit for a crt might, the LCD driver IC scans through the whole display—row by row.

LCD displays are generally quite reliable. Even on a "good" display, a few of the intersection points may not be operating. If a display panel is cracked, the LCD material can leak out and the whole display will have to be replaced. If a whole row or column of the display stops operating, check the LCD driver IC and any latches or amps that drive that row or column.

Gas Plasma Displays

Fig. 15-15 illustrates the operating principle of a *gas plasma display*. A mixture of argon and neon gasses is sandwiched between two glass plates, as shown in Fig. 15-15A. A pattern of conductors is etched on the inside of each glass plate. Fig. 15-15B illustrates how a particular location on the display is turned on. One conductor on the upper panel is energized, and another conductor on the lower panel is energized. At the point where the two conductors cross, the gas is broken down or "ionized." The voltage difference between the two conductors is about 200-V DC, and this is enough to strip away some of the electrons from the gas molecules. These free electrons are able to carry an electrical current from one conductor to the other, and this current causes the gas to glow. A gas plasma display is usually controlled by a driver IC, similar to the LCD driver we've just described.

Gas plasma displays tend to be quite reliable. One type of display lists a "Mean Time Before Failure" of 30,000 hours of operation. This works out to about 3 years of continuous operation! But, if the glass panels are cracked, the gas will leak out and the display will have to be replaced. Often, a few of the locations on a display will not work.

Most displays will have a few locations which do not work. On occasion, a whole row or column of locations will stop working. This points to a problem with either the driver IC, or with the latch or amp for the affected row or column.

Troubleshooting Monitors

Modern monitors are fairly reliable, and should not

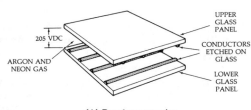

(A) Panel construction.

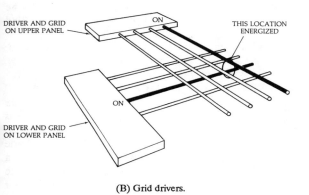

(B) Grid drivers.

Fig. 15-15. Gas plasma display.

require a lot of servicing. However, sometimes a monitor will fail completely, and will not produce any image at all. This is often caused by a problem in the high-voltage circuitry. The flyback transformer is often a particularly weak point.

Over time, the phosphor material on the inside of the picture tube will wear out, and it will not produce as bright an image. A very worn picture tube will produce an indistinct or "fuzzy" image. If this happens, the picture tube must be replaced. It takes several years for a monitor to reach this point, and the replacement tube is usually expensive, so it may not be cost-effective to replace the tube.

If a monitor is constantly turned on, and is always displaying the same image, that image may become "burned" into the phosphor. If you must leave the computer on, you can protect yourself against this problem by turning down the "brightness" control so that the screen is completely dark. Be sure your co-workers know that the computer is still on. Also, you can use a "screen saver" program, which is a memory-resident routine that automatically darkens the screen if the computer is not used for a few minutes.

Over time, some of the circuits in a monitor may drift out of alignment. Because a monitor is an analog

device, it is sensitive to the gradual changes that can occur as components age. For example, a capacitor may change in capacitive value as it ages, and the driver circuits for the deflector magnets may begin to produce slightly less output. This can cause the electron beam to be slightly "misaimed." As we said before, the phosphor material on the inside of the picture tube may become less responsive. Also, any analog circuit in the monitor may "drift" out of alignment. A circuit may continue to work, but not as well as it did earlier, and, over a long period of time, a number of small changes in the circuitry may gradually degrade the performance of the whole monitor. However, many of these circuits can be realigned. We will discuss this in a moment.

Some special tools are required if you intend to work on monitors. For safety reasons, you should always use an *isolation transformer*. This device can protect you from a dangerous "hot chassis" situation. We will describe this problem in a moment. Also, a *Variac* may be necessary, in order to repair monitors with short-circuited parts. We will describe the use of such a component in the next section. The use of a *leakage current tester* is also important for safety. A *degaussing coil* is necessary when realigning a monitor.

The high voltages in a monitor cannot be sensed directly with a conventional VOM. But, many VOMs will accept a special high-voltage probe. The high-voltage probe may plug into a special jack on the VOM, or it may be connected to a separate adapter box. And, some special VOMs are designed specifically for high-voltage use, and can read the high voltages directly.

Using a Variac

A monitor usually includes some self-protective circuitry to limit the current output from the power supply. If a short circuit develops, the circuitry will try to draw more and more current from the power supply. If this happens, the self-protective circuits will "fold back" the current output to keep it within the allowable limits. If the overload is serious enough, the protective circuits will cut off the power completely. This presents the service technician with a "Catch 22" situation: You can't diagnose the problem until the power supply is working, and you can't get the power supply working until you have repaired the problem.

The solution is a special type of adjustable transformer called a *Variac*. The output of a Variac is an AC voltage which may be varied from 0 V up to 120 V, or higher. To use a Variac, place it in the AC line between the monitor and the AC outlet. Start by setting the Variac to produce an output of 120-V AC. Turn on the monitor and see if it operates. If it does not, gradually adjust the output of the Variac to a lower voltage. At some point, the monitor should begin operating. This occurs because, at the lower AC voltage, the damaged circuits demand less current from the power supply. The monitor may not operate normally, but at least you'll be able to see which parts of the unit are operating. Sometimes a **Variac** will be combined with an isolation transformer in a single unit. B&K Precision sells a combination unit for about $150.

Special Safety Notes for Monitors

Monitors and television sets present special dangers. We discussed these dangers in Chapter 2, but we'll repeat our comments here. As we said, some sections of a monitor use very high DC voltages. These areas are shown in Fig. 15-16. The circuitry in a monitor has to generate a very high voltage to pull the electron beam from the rear of the picture tube to the front surface. A small monochrome (B&W) monitor might require 12,000 volts for this. On a larger color monitor, or a color TV, the voltage could be as high as 35,000 volts or more.

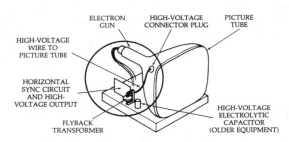

Fig. 15-16. Monitor danger areas.

The high voltage in a monitor is usually created in the same part of the circuitry that generates the horizontal synchronization pulses. A part called a "flyback transformer" is often used. The high voltage is carried from the horizontal circuits, through a special high-voltage wire, to a plug near the front of the picture tube. The high-voltage circuits inside a monitor can give you a dangerous shock! As long as the monitor is mounted inside its case, none of this high-voltage circuitry can hurt you.

Before you work on a monitor, you must deenergize the high-voltage circuits. Some of the parts inside a monitor can hold a dangerous charge, even if the unit has not been used for several days. Start by

connecting a jumper wire to the metal frame around the front of the picture tube. Fasten the other end of the wire to a screwdriver. Slip the end of the screwdriver under the rubber cap covering the anode connection on the picture. This will drain off most of the charge on the tube.

Next, remove the anode lead from the picture tube. Touch the tip of the screwdriver to the inside of the anode socket. However, even though you have discharged the picture tube once, the charge may build again over a period of time. To prevent this, connect a jumper wire from the anode of the tube to the chassis. (Be sure to remove the jumper before you turn on the set.)

Monitors may contain some large capacitors, and these can also hold dangerous charges. Before you work on this kind of equipment, discharge the large capacitors. Refer to the discussion given in Chapter 2 and also see Fig. 15-17.

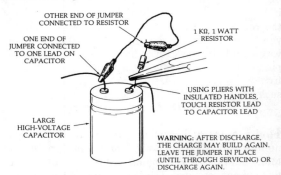

Fig. 15-17. Procedure for discharging high-voltage capacitors.

You can't measure these very high voltages directly with a normal voltohmmeter as the high voltages would burn out the meter. Instead, you'll have to use a high-voltage meter or a special high-voltage probe.

There is another danger involved in working on monitors. If the high voltage for the picture tube is allowed to rise too high, the monitor can begin to produce X rays. Actually, *all* monitors produce small amounts of X rays, but if the set is operating normally, the output is very low. However, as the voltages rise, the output of X rays rises very quickly. X rays can damage your body. If you receive a large dose of X rays, you may face a higher risk of cancer and other medical problems. But, even if the X rays do cause some damage to your body, medical problems may not be apparent for many years. A sloppy technician may take chances with X rays and not show any ill effects for years. Since you can't see or feel X rays, you cannot tell if a monitor is producing them. But, if you find that the high voltage is much higher than specified, you have to assume that the monitor is producing X rays.

Monitors have protective circuits which are designed to keep the high voltage within design limits and shut the set down if the voltage rises above specification. However, if a monitor is not working correctly, or if an inexperienced technician has altered the circuitry, the safety circuits in the set may be bypassed, and the unit may be generating lots of X rays. If you suspect a problem like this, don't leave the unit turned on for very long. Any X rays present will come out of the front of the monitor, so don't stand in front of it. Be sure the high-voltage safety circuits are working properly before you move on to other parts of the unit.

There is a vacuum inside the picture tube on a monitor or TV. If you break this tube, the glass will *implode* (collapse inward) with a lot of force. An imploding picture tube can throw bits of glass all over the room. You should not have a problem as long as you leave the tube in the chassis, and don't hit it hard with a tool or a part. If you have to remove or replace a picture tube, handle it very carefully. Once the tube is free of the chassis, place it face down on a soft surface, such as a folded towel.

Hot Chassis Conflicts

Many monitors are designed with a "hot chassis." On this type of unit, one side of the AC line is tied directly to the chassis. This type of monitor has a two-prong plug. The plug is "polarized" so that the prongs cannot be reversed when the plug is inserted. (On a polarized plug, one of the prongs is larger than the other.) As long as the AC outlet has been wired correctly, and the unit does not have any internal problems, this type of arrangement should be safe. However, safety problems can occur when you're using two pieces of equipment (one of them has a hot chassis), and either the AC outlet or one of the sets has been wired incorrectly.

Let's say that you're working on unit A, a monitor. You plug the AC cord into an outlet, but you don't know that the wires on this outlet have been reversed. (Fig. 15-18.) The wire that was **meant** to be "hot" is actually grounded, and the wire that was meant to be GROUND is actually "hot." The monitor still works, because it still has 120-V AC.

As we said, this particular monitor has a "hot chassis." If you look closely at our sketch in Fig. 15-18, you'll see that one side of the AC line has been connected directly to the chassis (the metal frame) of the monitor. (The name is a bit misleading. The chassis

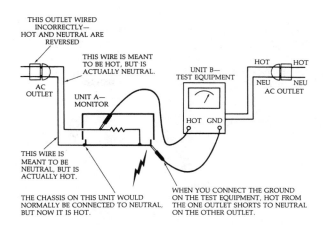

Fig. 15-18. The "hot chassis" conflict.

is called "hot" because it is tied to one side of the AC line. When the unit is wired as designed, the chassis is usually connected to the GROUND side of the AC line.) In this example, the chassis was meant to be grounded, but since the wiring in the AC outlet is reversed, the chassis is now tied to the "hot" side of the AC line.

Nothing unusual happens until you start using unit B, your test equipment. Unit B is plugged into an outlet that has been wired correctly. The grounding lead on the test equipment runs back to the ground side of the outlet. As part of your test set-up, you'll usually want to attach the ground from the test instrument to the ground on the monitor. As soon as you touch the test unit's ground to the hot chassis, you've got a direct short circuit. The "hot" 120-V AC current from one outlet is shorted to the ground on the other outlet. Sparks fly and fuses blow.

Now suppose that you don't know the chassis is hot, and you touch it with your finger. You've made yourself part of the circuit. It's just as if you'd shoved your finger into a light socket. If all AC outlets and monitors were wired correctly, you'd never have to worry about this problem. However, you can never trust AC outlets without checking them. Also, since the monitor is damaged, remember that this damage might result in the monitor having a "hot" chassis.

When servicing monitors, always use an "isolation transformer" to defend yourself against problems of this type. During servicing, the isolation transformer (Fig. 15-19) is connected between the monitor and the outlet. This is a 1:1 transformer, so it doesn't change the voltage. The transformer still produces 120-V AC at the outputs, but both sides of this AC are independent of ground. In the example shown in Fig. 15-18, if we had connected an isolation transformer between the monitor and the outlet, it would have prevented a short circuit. Commercial isolation transformers often include **some overload** protection and other features. B&K Precision sells a small isolation transformer for about $60.00.

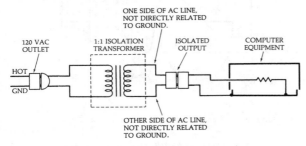

Fig. 15-19. Using an isolation transformer.

Leakage-Current Checks

Once a monitor has been reassembled, be sure that none of the exposed metal parts are "hot." You can be sure of this by checking for any current leakage from these parts to ground. If one of the components is faulty, current can leak from the component to a screw or other part on the case, causing that part to be hot.

A "cold leakage-current check" is performed with the monitor unplugged, as shown in Fig. 15-20A. Place a jumper across the prongs of the AC plug. Turn on the AC power switch on the monitor. If all of the components are all right, and you have reassembled the monitor correctly, there should be a high resistance from each of the exposed metal parts to ground. If you detect a low resistance to ground anywhere, the exposed part may be "hot" when the monitor is turned on. (On a "hot chassis" set, some of the internal parts will be "hot," but this is normal. You should be sure that all *exposed* parts are safe.) The most accurate way of testing for this problem is with a special resistance-measuring device called an "insulation tester." Connect one lead of the tester to the jumpered AC plug. Touch the other lead to any exposed metal parts on the case. Be especially sure to check any exposed metal parts which have a return path to the chassis. **The allowable resistance will fall within a certain range. For example, on one type of color monitor, the leakage resistance should be more than 300 kilohms and less than 5 megohms. Any resistance value outside this range indicates that something is wrong inside the monitor. The allowable resistance limits are different from one monitor to the next—check your documentation.

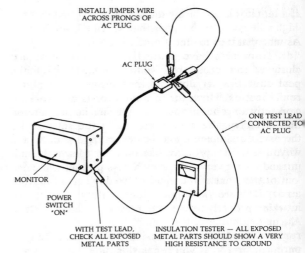

(A) Cold leakage-current test.

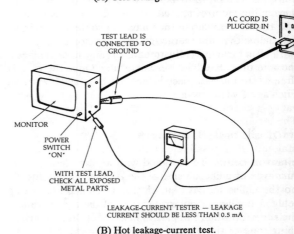

(B) Hot leakage-current test.

Fig. 15-20. Leakage-current tests.

A "hot leakage-current check" is made with the monitor turned on (Fig. 15-20B). Plug the monitor's AC cord into an outlet. Do not use an isolation transformer. Turn on the monitor's power switch. For this test, you will need a special type of current-measuring device called a "leakage-current tester." Clip one of the test leads to an earth ground. With the other lead, check each of the exposed metal parts. Be especially careful to check any exposed part with a return path to the chassis. Any leakage current should be less than 0.5 mA. If you measure a greater current, something is wrong inside the monitor. Do not give the monitor back to the customer until you have located the problem.

Alignment Procedures

As we explained earlier, the circuits in a monitor may "drift out of alignment." Over time, many small changes can cause the whole monitor to begin performing poorly, but many of the circuits can be realigned. However, a complete realignment is a complicated process and differs from one monitor to the next. You will need some specific documentation on the particular monitor you are servicing. In this section, we'll try to give you an overview of the alignment process.

Over time, the picture tube gradually accumulates stray electrical charges. These charges can interfere with the normal operation of the picture tube. At the beginning of the alignment process, you must remove these stray charges. The tool used for this purpose is called a "de-gaussing coil." To use a coil of this type, turn off the monitor, plug in the coil, and hold it near the front of the picture tube. Slowly move the coil around the edge of the tube. As you do this, the coil will redistribute the charges on the picture tube.

The "purity" adjustments allow you to fine-tune the aim of each of the electron beams. At the rear of the picture tube are several small magnets, as shown in Fig. 15-21. (The exact locations of these magnets may vary, so check the documentation for your monitor.) The magnets which control purity are often mounted on two plastic rings. By moving the rings, and the attached magnets, it is possible to adjust the alignment of the electron beam. To make this adjustment, start by turning down the blue and green outputs as much as possible. The monitor should have controls which will let you do this. Turn up the red output as much as possible. Loosen the deflection yoke clamp, and push the deflection yoke as far backward (away from the front of the CRT) as possible. Adjust the rings until the red beam appears in the center of the screen. Move the deflection yoke back into position. The whole screen should have a uniform red color. Clamp the deflection yoke in position and reset each of the color controls to a normal position.

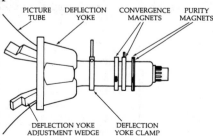

Fig. 15-21. Alignment adjustment points.

The next step is the "convergence" adjustment. For this adjustment, you will need a way of generating a test pattern. If you have the right software, you can use a computer to generate test patterns. Many diagnostic packages offer this option. You can also use the type of test-pattern generator that is used on television sets, as long as the generator has outputs which are compatible with your monitor. When making the convergence adjustment, use a pattern of small white dots or a crosshatch pattern of fine lines. If the monitor is out of alignment, some of the dots may not be white. By adjusting the convergence magnets, you should be able to get a uniform pattern of white dots.

On some monitors, the convergence magnets are locked in place, and you cannot make adjustments. Other monitors include wedges which hold the deflection yoke in position, as shown in Fig. 15-21. Use these wedges to adjust the yoke if the convergence is bad at the outer edges of the screen.

Other alignment adjustments are possible. Check the documentation for your particular monitor.

Troubleshooting and Documentation

Documentation is helpful in any kind of troubleshooting work, but it is especially important when you are troubleshooting monitors. Sometimes, the cause of a problem is obvious. For example, if you open the case and see that the flyback transformer is blackened and smoking, you don't have to look much further. Generally, it requires more effort to find the faulty parts, and good documentation can be a big help. As we said earlier, a monitor is an "analog" device. When working with analog circuits, it is not enough to know that a circuit is functioning—you must also know if the circuit is functioning *correctly*. Good documentation will show you the voltage levels you should expect to find at key test points. The COMPUTERFACTS series published by Howard W. Sams & Company even includes pictures of the waveforms you should find at the test points. To use these illustrations, check each of the test points with an oscilloscope. Compare the actual waveforms found with the illustrations, and you should be able to locate the circuits that are not working correctly. A good documentation package will also help you to locate parts inside the monitor, and will list the part numbers in case you must get replacements. Good documentation also often includes alignment instructions. Since alignment procedures vary a bit from one monitor to another, this information can be very important.

When troubleshooting monitors, as in any kind of troubleshooting work, try to substitute **as** often as possible. If you are troubleshooting a **monitor**, start by substituting the monitor itself. If the problem disappears, you know that the computer is all right, and the problem lies inside the suspect monitor. What if the second monitor shows the same trouble symptoms? This points to a problem in the circuits in the computer which are producing the signals for the monitor.

On the IBM PCs, and some other computers, the video circuits are mounted on removable "adapter cards." If it looks like the troubles might be in the computer, substitute a good adapter card and see if the symptoms disappear. If they do, look for a problem on the original adapter card. Even if the computer does not use removable circuit boards, you may be able to substitute some of the more important ICs. For example, you may be able to swap both the character-generator ROM and the CRTC chip. If the monitor begins working correctly, you know that one of these ICs is faulty.

The display on the monitor screen can often indicate the cause of the problem. In Fig. 15-22, we have shown some abnormal monitor displays. Using code numbers, we will refer to a section which includes troubleshooting instructions for that symptom. By checking Fig. 15-22 and referring to the block diagram given in Fig. 15-5, you should be able to localize the cause of the problem. If you are working with a color monitor, refer also to Fig. 15-8.

> WARNING! Some sections of television sets and monitors carry very high voltages. These voltages are very dangerous. Don't work inside of monitors or television sets unless you understand the exact nature of the risks involved! Be sure to read the safety warnings of this chapter carefully!

15.1.1 Problem 1
Symptom: Screen is dark.

This symptom can occur if the monitor is not getting any power. The AC source at the outlet may be dead, or the monitor's power supply may be faulty. As we explained earlier, a short circuit outside of the power supply can cause the supply to "fold back" to protect itself. In order to check a problem of this type, you will need an adjustable transformer called a "Variac." See the section of this chapter that discusses using a Variac.

The screen may also be dark if the monitor is not generating an electron beam, or if the beam is not being

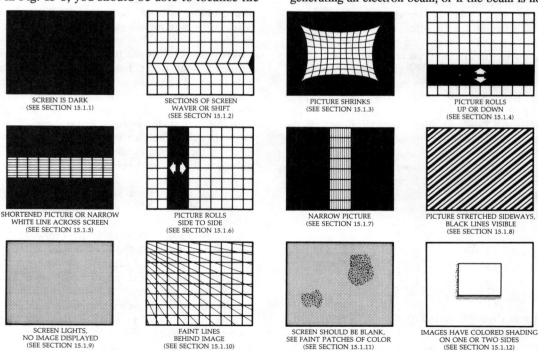

SCREEN IS DARK (SEE SECTION 15.1.1)	SECTIONS OF SCREEN WAVER OR SHIFT (SEE SECTON 15.1.2)
PICTURE SHRINKS (SEE SECTION 15.1.3)	PICTURE ROLLS UP OR DOWN (SEE SECTION 15.1.4)
SHORTENED PICTURE OR NARROW WHITE LINE ACROSS SCREEN (SEE SECTION 15.1.5)	PICTURE ROLLS SIDE TO SIDE (SEE SECTION 15.1.6)
NARROW PICTURE (SEE SECTION 15.1.7)	PICTURE STRETCHED SIDEWAYS, BLACK LINES VISIBLE (SEE SECTION 15.1.8)
SCREEN LIGHTS, NO IMAGE DISPLAYED (SEE SECTION 15.1.9)	FAINT LINES BEHIND IMAGE (SEE SECTION 15.1.10)
SCREEN SHOULD BE BLANK, SEE FAINT PATCHES OF COLOR (SEE SECTION 15.1.11)	IMAGES HAVE COLORED SHADING ON ONE OR TWO SIDES (SEE SECTION 15.1.12)

Fig. 15-22. Some typical monitor symptoms.

scanned across the screen. Check the high-voltage circuits and the horizontal output circuits.

15.1.2 Problem 2

Symptom: Sections of the picture waver or shift.

This is often caused by bad filter capacitors in the monitor's power supply. Over time, these capacitors may begin to break down and allow some "noise" into the monitor's circuitry. See Chapter 16.

15.1.3 Problem 3

Symptom: Picture shrinks.

Something is causing the deflector circuits to reduce their output. The electron beam is not pulled towards the edges of the screen with as much force, so the picture is concentrated in the center of the screen. Sometimes the picture shrinks for just a moment. This can be caused by low voltage at the AC outlet. If the picture becomes smaller, and then stays that way, check the power supply and the horizontal output circuits. For information on the power supply, see Chapter 16.

15.1.4 Problem 4

Symptom: Picture rolls up or down.

Try adjusting the "vertical hold" control. The vertical sync and vertical output circuits are supposed to keep the picture from rolling vertically. If these appear to be all right, check the sync separator circuits.

The monitor must be designed to use the type of sync signals produced by the driver circuits. Different video arrangements use sync signals of different frequencies.

15.1.5 Problem 5

Symptom: Picture is shortened, or there is a narrow white line across the screen.

Try the "vertical size" adjustment. The monitor may have a weak vertical output. Check the vertical oscillator and the vertical output circuits.

15.1.6 Problem 6

Symptom: Picture rolls from side to side.

Try adjusting the "horizontal hold" control. Check the

horizontal sync and the horizontal output circuits. If these appear to be working, check the sync separator circuits.

The monitor must be designed to use the type of sync signals produced by the driver circuits. Different video arrangements use sync signals of different frequencies.

15.1.7 Problem 7

Symptom: Narrow picture.

The monitor has a weak horizontal output. Check the horizontal oscillator and the horizontal output circuits. Also, check the power supply feeding the horizontal output circuits.

15.1.8 Problem 8

Symptom: Picture is stretched sideways; black lines are visible.

The picture is out of sync. Check the horizontal oscillator and the output sections. Also check the sync separator circuits.

15.1.9 Problem 9

Symptom: Screen lights, but no image is displayed.

The monitor is displaying the "raster," so you know that several parts of the unit are working—the power supply, and the high-voltage, horizontal, and vertical circuits. For some reason, the signal is not reaching the electron beam and switching it on and off. Check the video output and the sync separator circuits.

15.1.10 Problem 10

Symptom: Faint green or white lines are behind the picture.

The "black level" setting may be too high. Adjust this control.

15.1.11 Problem 11

Symptom: When screen should be blank, you see faint patches of color.

The monitor is out of alignment. One or more of the electron beams are not aimed correctly. See the section of this chapter that discusses alignment procedures.

15.1.12 Problem 12

Symptom: Letters or images have colored shading on one or two sides.

The monitor is out of alignment, One or more of the electron beams are not aimed correctly. See the section of this chapter that discusses alignment procedures.

Chapter Review

In this chapter, we've outlined the operating principles behind the most common types of monitors. The circuitry in a monochrome monitor sweeps an electron beam across the screen, and turns the beam on and off to create a picture. A color monitor uses similar principles, except that it uses three electron guns, instead of one.

We also examined the circuits inside the computer which drive the monitor. The "character-generator" IC converts coded ASCII characters into dot patterns. The "cathode-ray tube controller" (CRTC) organizes these dot patterns, and sends them to the monitor.

The circuits in a monitor use analog principles, so they tend to become less efficient over time, rather than fail completely. The "alignment" process can correct for many of these changes. When troubleshooting a monitor, use the screen display to help determine the cause of the problem. Fig. 15-22 shows some of the most common symptoms.

Always beware of the high-voltage areas inside a monitor. Use an isolation transformer to protect yourself from possible "hot chassis" conflicts.

Review Questions

1. A customer brings you a faulty monitor. You turn on the unit and you see a single bright dot in the center of the screen. Can you suggest a cause for this?

2. What are the dangerous high-voltage areas inside a monitor?

3. Why should you use an isolation transformer when working with monitors?

4. What is the correct way of discharging the voltage at the anode of the picture tube?

5. A faulty monitor appears to be rolling both vertically and horizontally at the same time. What does this tell you?

6. You are watching a monitor, and the picture shrinks for a moment, and then returns to normal size. What has happened?

7. A customer brings you a monitor that is not working. You check the fuse, circuit breaker, etc., but you can find no obvious cause for this. What is the next step?

8. Why is it bad practice to leave the computer turned on when it is not in use?

16
Troubleshooting
Power Supplies

Introduction and Objectives

In any digital equipment, the power supply has an important job. The power supply must take power from a 120-volt AC source, and reshape it into one or more low-voltage DC outputs. (The abbreviation "AC" stands for *alternating current*, and "DC" means *direct current*.) Digital circuits require smooth, even power, so each of the power outputs must have good regulation and filtering.

Many types of computer problems may cause the power supply to stop working. Sometimes the problem is in the power-supply circuits themselves, but this is not always the case. Often a problem occurs on the circuit boards, "downstream" of the power supply. A short circuit in one of these other circuits can "drag down" the output from the power supply. The power supply may then turn itself off, as a protective measure. Thus, the power supply may appear to be dead when the problem actually is not in the power-supply circuits at all. Whenever you troubleshoot a power-supply problem, you must first determine whether the problem is in the power-supply circuits, or in one of the other circuits.

In the first part of this chapter, we will explain the principles behind *linear* and *switching* power supplies. Next, we will include some important safety notes. Power supplies can carry dangerous amounts of

electricity, so you must work carefully. In the section on troubleshooting, we will tell you how to determine whether the problem is in the power-supply, itself, or in one of the circuit boards. If the power supply itself is faulty, it may not operate at all, so you will not be able to make test measurements. We will describe some ways of defeating the self-protective circuits, so that you can get the power supply working temporarily, and can make repairs. The last part of the chapter includes some troubleshooting instructions for three common trouble symptoms.

Operating Principles

Fig. 16-1 shows a "linear" type of power supply. At the left of the illustration, 120-V AC comes into the supply through the AC plug. A fuse is included in the line to protect the computer equipment. If a short circuit develops, the circuitry may try to draw too much current. The power supply might try to keep up with this increased demand, and the large current could cause parts to overheat. Before this can happen, the fuse will open, cutting off the 120-V AC.

One common type of fuse consists of a short glass tube, with metal contacts at each end. (This type of fuse was illustrated earlier in Chapter 7, in Fig. 7-32.) The

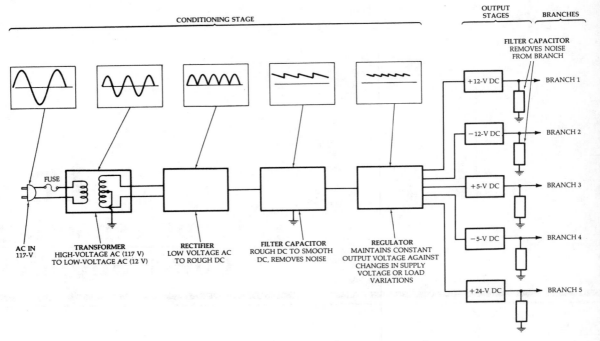

Fig. 16-1. Block diagram of a "linear" power supply.

metal contacts are connected by a center conductor, made from a metal with a low melting point. All of the electricity used by the equipment must flow through this fuse. As long as the current is within specifications, the center conductor will be able to handle the current. When an overload causes a large current to move through the fuse, the center conductor overheats and melts.

When a fuse blows, you can tell something about the nature of the problem by checking the condition of the glass tube. If the inside of the tube is blackened, and you can't see any trace of the center conductor, you know that a serious short circuit has occurred. If the center conductor is still in place but simply is broken in the center, the circuit problem created less of an overload. (We showed these conditions in Fig. 7-32.)

Instead of a fuse, a circuit breaker may be used in the equipment. A circuit breaker is a special switch which opens when the current passes a preset limit. When a circuit breaker trips, you can usually use a "reset" switch to set the breaker back to its original condition. The circuit breaker is usually mounted on the rear of the equipment, and the "reset" switch often has a small red button. Many circuit breakers can only trip a few times before they must be replaced.

The 120-V alternating current is sent through a transformer, which provides a low-voltage AC output.

Some transformers include a protective device called a *fusible link*. A fusible link acts like a normal fuse, opening up if the transformer draws more than the rated maximum current. If a transformer does include a fusible link, the link will probably be wrapped right in with the windings of the transformer wire. To test the link or to replace it, you will have to unwrap some of the tranformer windings. It may be easier to replace the transformer.

In the "rectifier" section, the low-voltage AC is converted to a DC voltage. Fig. 16-2 shows how a rectifier operates. The rectifier shown is a "full-wave" type, because it uses all of the energy available in the AC input. The rectifier assembly is made of four diodes arranged in a "bridge." You will recall that a diode will conduct electricity in one direction, but not the other. Fig. 16-2B shows how the rectifier operates during the "positive" part of each AC cycle. Two of the diodes conduct electricity, and a positive pulse is produced on the DC wiring. Fig. 16-2C shows the rectifier during the "negative" part of the AC cycle. During this phase, the other two diodes conduct electricity. Notice that the output current still flows in the same direction. At this point, the AC input has been converted into an uneven DC output.

A filtering section is used to smooth out this uneven DC signal. Usually, the filter includes one of

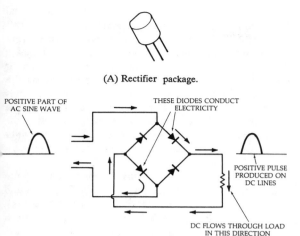

(A) Rectifier package.

(B) Positive portion of AC cycle.

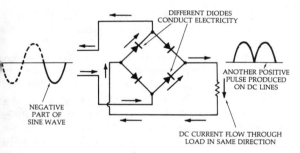

(C) Negative portion of AC cycle.

Fig. 16-2. A full-wave bridge rectifier.

more capacitors. A capacitor may be connected between the DC line and ground. A capacitor may also be used in combination with a resistor or coil. The value of the capacitor and other parts are chosen carefully to give the filter circuit a certain *timing constant*, or TC. This TC measures hows fast the circuit responds to changes in the voltage level. If the circuit has just the right timing constant, it can act to smooth the output voltage, and once the voltage leaves the filter stage, most of the variations or "ripple" should be removed. The AC has been converted into a smooth DC.

When a capacitor fails, it often creates a short circuit directly to ground. This usually blows a fuse, or announces itself in some other way. A capacitor can also develop an open circuit, although this is less common. In this case, the capacitor will not drain off the AC, and the output from the power supply will be very noisy. Occasionally, the capacitor will lose some of its capacitance. Some of the AC signal will be allowed

to remain with the DC, creating a signal which is noisier than it should be.

When an electrical load is connected to a power supply, the voltage produced by the supply tends to drop. In computer applications, the DC voltages must be very stable. The "voltage regulator" stabilizes the DC output, regardless of load. We described how to test a voltage regulator at the end of Chapter 8.

Once the circuitry has produced a smooth regulated DC, this voltage can be distributed to the rest of the circuitry. Computers usually require more than one type of DC voltage. Most of the ICs in computer equipment operate on +5-V DC. Some types of memory chips require other voltages (+12 V, −12 V, −5 V). Electromechanical parts, such as solenoids, often use higher DC voltages (+24-V DC). As you can see in Fig. 16-1, the basic DC output is divided into several "branches" to produce each of the these outputs. Each branch often has its own filter capacitors.

In the drawing of Fig. 16-1, you will notice that several different DC outputs are derived from one basic DC power supply. Sometimes a transistor is used to "boost" the DC for a particular branch. Devices called *voltage doublers* may also be used. Sometimes the basic DC supply is high (+12 V) and the desired branch output is lower (+5 V DC). In this case, a regulator may be used to produce the lower voltage.

The +5-V DC output usually has the best filtering and regulation. Some computer equipment will not operate if the +5-V supply varies by more than 0.1 volt (+4.9- to +5.1-volt DC). Because of this, the +5-V DC branch of the supply may have its own regulator and special filters. Sometimes the voltage on one of the other branches (+12-V DC, +24-V DC) may not be regulated at all.

Some very small computers and some peripheral equipment (such as modems) will use a variation of this arrangement. The transformer may not be mounted with the rest of the power-supply components. Instead, the transformer may be mounted in a small molded plastic unit which plugs into the 120-V AC outlet. This transformer produces a low-voltage AC output (about 10-V AC), which is then routed to the computer or peripheral. The power-supply circuits in the computer then handle the other steps in the process, producing a smooth DC output.

We have just described a *linear* power supply. Many types of computer equipment use a *switching* type of supply, which is somewhat different (Fig. 16-3). A "switching" power supply includes a full-wave rectifier, which produces an uneven DC output, In the next stage, this uneven DC is "chopped" by an oscillator circuit and converted back to AC at a high frequency.

The high-frequency AC output from the oscillator can now be processed by a transformer. Different "taps" on the transformer take off the AC voltages which will be turned into the DC values required: 5-V AC, 12-V AC, etc. Each of these AC voltages is then rectified, filtered, and regulated to produce a clean DC voltage. The output from the +5-V supply is then connected, through a "feedback" loop, back to the oscillator circuit. When the voltage from the +5-V supply rises or drops a bit, the oscillator circuit will act to correct the output.

The switching type of power supply has a high tolerance for changes in the voltage on the 120-V AC line. The 120-V AC is converted to DC, and then "chopped" to a much lower AC voltage. This means the input voltage can vary quite a bit from 120-V AC. The "chopping" process also makes this type of supply resistant to electrical noise on the 120-V AC line.

A switching power supply also often includes a protective or "foldback" circuit. This circuit is designed to limit the current flow, and protect the other parts of the computer equipment. The foldback circuit constantly senses the amount of current being produced by the power supply. If a short circuit occurs, and the circuits try to draw too much current, the protective circuit "folds back" and limits the maximum current produced. If the current draw is too great, the protective circuits may cut off the output if the power supply senses a "no load" condition. This can be troublesome when you try to disconnect the power supply from the circuit boards. You may have to add a "dummy" load to induce the power supply to work.

The power supply is usually contained in a metal box. The metal box both acts as a shield and intercepts any electromagnetic noise produced by the power-supply circuits. On many computers, the box containing the power supply is riveted shut to discourage amateur technicians. Also, the box is usually mounted on the bottom of the computer case, because the power-supply components are heavy. The various outputs (+5-V DC, +12-V DC, etc.) are usually connected to the rest of the equipment via one or more connectors. From the power connectors, the various voltages are routed to the rest of the equipment.

The +5-V DC supply has the most complicated distribution system, since both +5-V DC and ground must be provided to every IC on the circuit board(s). You can usually find +5 V and ground on the largest circuit traces on a circuit board. (These large traces are often routed around the outer edges of the PC board. The traces are large because they must carry relatively large currents.)

The power supply in a typical microcomputer produces several low DC voltages—usually +5-V DC, +12-V DC, and −12-V DC—and, perhaps, some other voltages. The power supply in a dot-matrix or daisy-wheel printer will produce the voltages listed, and, in addition, may also produce one or two higher DC voltages to power the drive motors and solenoids. Some disk drives will have their own small power supplies, and some will be powered by the computer. However, most monitors will have separate supplies. Besides the low voltages, the power supply in a monitor will also produce a high-voltage "B+" output to the horizontal

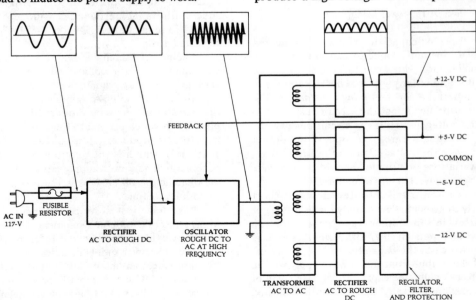

Fig. 16-3. Block diagram of a "switching" power supply.

sync circuits. All of these power supplies are similar, and the troubleshooting procedures are basically the same.

Battery-Type Power Supplies

Many "portable" or "luggable" computers can be powered by batteries. A few of the tiny hand-held computers use conventional dry-cell flashlight-type batteries. Most of the more expensive portable computers use *nickel-cadmium* (NiCad) *cells.* A battery-powered computer will have simpler circuits than those shown in Fig. 16-1 and Fig. 16-3, since the batteries produce a low-voltage DC, and the transformers and rectifiers are not necessary. However, the DC outputs from a battery-powered supply will still be regulated and filtered.

By using the computer incorrectly, it is possible to damage a NiCad cell so that it will not hold a full charge. NiCad cells work best when they are charged completely, then used until they are almost run down, and then recharged again. If you drain just the first part of the charge in a NiCad cell, and then allow the cell to stay in that state for a while, the cell may lose its ability to take a full charge. You do not "save" this type of battery by not using it. You do not want to damage the NiCad cell, since a replacement may cost $50.00 or more.

If you have a computer that uses NiCad cells, and you know you will not be using the unit for a while, remove the battery. If you leave the cell in place, be sure to use the computer every two weeks or so. Even if you do not use the computer to do any work, turn it on for two or three hours daily to drain down the battery.

If a NiCad cell is damaged, it is sometimes possible to rescue the cell. Charge the cell as completely as possible, and then use the cell until it is almost completely drained. Recharge the cell again. Repeat this cycle two or three more times.

A NiCad cell can be permanently damaged by a short circuit. A short can cause the interior of the battery to overheat, and this can increase the pressure inside the cell's case. The case is made with a weak point which ruptures to release the pressure. It may not be immediately obvious that the case has ruptured. The contents of the battery can cause a white or greenish corrosion on the battery terminals, and this may be your first indication that something is wrong. If you observe this symptom, replace the battery and clean the terminals. (A very small amount of white corrosion on the terminals is normal.) If your computer has a NiCad type of battery, be sure to check the terminals for corrosion every six months.

Many small computers, including the IBM PC, include a "real time" clock. This clock is always running, even when the main 120-V AC power is turned off. While the AC power is shut off, the clock is powered by a small dry-cell battery. This battery also powers a small amount of RAM memory, which records some important information about the configuration of the computer—memory size, type of display adapter, type and number of disk drives, settings for the modem and printer ports, and so on. If the battery ever fails, this special RAM memory will lose power, and the configuration information will be lost. Dry-cell batteries usually last for two or three years or more, so for most computer users, this is not a pressing problem. However, as the current generation of computers grows older, we will be seeing this problem more frequently. The fix for this problem is simple—replace the battery before it dies. You should do this while the main 120-V AC power is turned on, so the memory in RAM will not be lost. Advanced Concepts Research makes a device that warns you when the battery begins to run down.

The "dry-cell" type of battery does not require any special handling. However, if you allow a dry-cell battery to wear out, and then leave the battery in place for a long time, it can corrode the battery contacts inside the computer.

Sometimes the special RAM is powered by a lithium battery. On some small industrial computers, a lithium cell may be used to power a whole circuit-card full of RAM. This allows the computer to retain large amounts of information, even after the main power is turned off. Lithium batteries can easily last for five years or more. But, batteries of this type require some special handling. Lithium is a very soft metal, with chemical properties that make it well-suited for batteries. However, lithium has a nasty side as well. The solid lithium can burn, and it will produce explosive gasses when it is exposed to the open air. Never heat or burn a lithium battery.

Troubleshooting Procedures

It may not be cost-effective to repair a faulty power supply. If you have a common computer, such as an IBM PC or an Apple II, you should be able to find a replacement supply easily. For example, Jameco Electronics sells a replacement power supply for an Apple IIe for about $35.00. A brand-new replacement for an IBM-AT costs about $90.00 from the same source. When replacement parts are this inexpensive, and can be delivered in two days via air freight, it probably does not pay to invest a lot of effort in repairing a faulty supply. Try to buy a power supply which has been approved by Underwriter's Laboratory, Inc.

Some computers, including the IBM PC line and the Apple II series, allow the user to add plug-in circuit cards. This gives the operator a lot of flexibility, but it also creates the potential for power-supply problems. Each circuit card that you add draws some additional power. If you add several cards, they **can try** to draw more power than the power supply can produce. This usually causes the power supply's output voltage to drop. When computer circuits are forced to operate on a low voltage, they become unreliable. A temporary solution to this type of problem is to remove some of the extra cards, and reduce the load on the power supply.

A better solution to the problem is to install a replacement supply which can produce more power. If you have a common type of computer, you should be able to find a more powerful supply. Power supplies are rated in *watts*, which represents the maximum amount of power they can produce. On the replacement supply, each of the outputs should be able to produce as much, or more, current than the original. Be sure that the replacement part will fit inside the computer's cabinet, and that it uses the same connectors as the original.

As we said earlier, a problem which appears to be caused by the power supply may actually be caused by a fault in another part of the computer. Your first step should be to determine whether the problem is in the supply itself, or out among the other circuits. One way of doing this is to substitute a new unit for the main power supply. If the replacement supply operates the computer, you know there is a problem in the original supply. The power supply is usually held in place by just a few screws, and is connected to the other circuits via a plug-in connector. Of course, to use this substitution method, you must have a spare supply on hand.

If you do not have a spare power supply, you will have to try another method. When a short circuit develops, the power supply normally "folds back" quickly. This protects the circuitry in the computer or other equipment, but it makes your troubleshooting work more difficult. You're confronted with a dead power supply, and you can't find the cause of the problem. It's a "Catch-22" situation: You can't fix the power supply until you get the unit working, and the unit won't work until you fix the problem. One way of dealing with this is to start disconnecting branches of the power system. When you disconnect the faulty branch, the power supply *may* start to operate normally. If this happens, you can then track down the problem in that branch. Also, an adjustable transformer (sometimes called a Variac) will help you deal with this situation. We have described the use of this tool in Chapter 15 and in Section 15.1.1. The discussion is repeated again in Section 16.1.1.

The "foldback" circuits protect the power supply if the computer tries to draw too much current. Other circuitry can protect the supply if the load is removed, and the computer does not draw enough current. This means that if you simply disconnect a power supply for the rest of the circuits, the supply may still not operate. If you encounter a supply of this type, you must connect resistive loads (similar to the loads presented by the normal circuitry) to the unit. You can do this by connecting resistors across each of the outputs, or by using small light bulbs. We'll discuss this procedure in Section 16.1.1.

In any case, it is good practice to test a power supply while it is under load. When a power supply is under no load, or under a light load, it may appear to be working correctly. The trouble symptoms may appear only when the power supply is placed under a heavier load.

We'll assume that you've localized the problem to the power supply itself. When power-supply components fail, the failure is often spectacular. The bad component may produce sparks, smoke, and bad odors. The typical power supply presents a classic "chain" of components: transformer to rectifier to regulator to filter, etc. You should be able to use the troubleshooting techniques we outlined in Chapter 7. Start by checking a point in the middle of the "chain." For example, if the signal at the input of the regulator is all right, you know that everything "upstream" of that point is working. You can then concentrate on the components which follow the regulator. Work your way along the chain until you find the faulty circuitry, and then hunt for the specific component that has failed.

And what if the problem is out among the other circuits in the computer? This situation is very common, and troubleshooting this type of problem can be more complicated. As we said, the +5-V DC supply is routed to every IC on every circuit board. Because the +5-V DC supply reaches so many of the component parts, it is most likely that most problems will occur with this supply line. One of the +5-V circuit traces may develop a short circuit to ground, or it may short to another circuit trace. Any one of the ICs may also develop a short circuit inside its case, as we explained in Chapter 8.

Safety and Safety Warnings

Dangerous amounts of electricity are present in some sections of the power supply. Remember that the power supply is plugged into 120-V AC house current. At 120 volts, the house current certainly has enough voltage to be dangerous. If you create a short circuit, the system can supply current up to the limit allowed by the fuse or circuit breaker on that circuit, usually about 20 amperes. This means that the AC house current can deliver a lot of power—more than enough to kill you.

Whenever you must work inside the power supply, turn off the equipment and pull the AC plug. Turn on the equipment only while you are making test measurements, and then turn it off again.

Normally the 120-V AC will be carried just to the first stage of the power supply. In Fig. 16-4, we have shown the parts which carry this dangerous current. In a "linear" supply, the 120-V AC is carried to a transformer and changed to a lower voltage. From that point on, since the voltage is reduced, there is less of a shock hazard. You are also protected by the fuse or circuit breaker inside the computer equipment. In a "switching" type of supply, the 120-V AC might go through several stages before it is converted to low-voltage DC. Always assume that the first few stages of any power supply carry dangerous voltages.

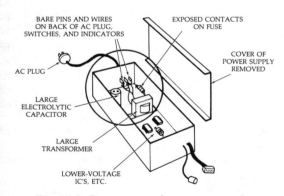

Fig. 16-4. Danger areas in a power supply.

The power supply in a typical small computer is mounted inside a metal box. This limits the amount of radio interference that the unit produces. The dangerous 120-V AC areas usually are safely enclosed within this metal box. You normally should not have to open this box, but if you do, remember that you're entering a dangerous section of the computer. Be careful not to touch any bare metal parts which might be carrying 120-V AC. If you have good documentation,

and you understand how the power supply is laid out, you can determine whether a part carries 120-V AC or not. However, if you don't have any service literature, or if you don't really understand how the power supply is designed, use this rule:

> ## ASSUME ALL THE PARTS IN THE POWER SUPPLY ARE "HOT."

If you're not sure whether a part is energized or not, you can always check it with a voltmeter. However, if a part is using a high voltage (400 V and up), you won't be able to check it with a normal voltmeter. Use a voltmeter designed for high voltage, or add a special high-voltage probe to your standard voltmeter.

Capacitors

Some equipment includes large capacitors. A typical large electrolytic capacitor is contained in a metal can, and it looks something like a salt shaker. If a capacitor handles 120-V AC, it can store quite a charge, and the capacitor can hold this charge even after you have turned off the equipment.

Before you start to work on a unit containing a large capacitor, be sure to discharge the capacitor. You can do this by creating a short circuit between the leads. See Fig. 16-5. Use a jumper and a 1-kilohm, 1-watt resistor to short-circuit the two leads on the capacitor. Hold the resistor with a pair of pliers having insulated handles. Before you discharge the capacitor, be very careful not to touch either of the capacitor leads with your fingers. After being discharged, the charge may build again. Leave the jumper in place until you are through servicing, *or* discharge the capacitor again frequently.

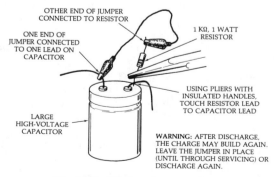

Fig. 16-5. Discharging capacitors.

Typical Service Problems

In the next section of this chapter, we'll consider three common trouble symptoms. Section 16.1.1 covers the most common power-supply problem—no output from one or more power-supply stages. Section 16.1.2 covers the problem of electrical "noise" or incorrect voltage levels in the power supply, and Section 16.1.3 deals with a power supply that is putting out a voltage which is slightly high or low.

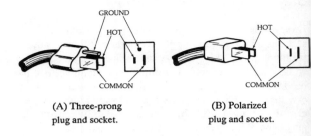

(A) Three-prong plug and socket. (B) Polarized plug and socket.

Fig. 16-6. Typical AC plugs and sockets.

16.1.1 Problem 1

Symptom: No power in one or more sections of the equipment.

Whenever a computer or a peripheral is completely dead, the problem is most likely to lie in the power-supply circuits. Start by checking the obvious—is the equipment plugged in? If the equipment is connected to a power-distribution strip or line filter, is that plugged in? Do all the connectors fit tightly? Are they pushed all the way into the sockets?

The metal prongs on the end of the plug may have been damaged by someone stepping on them, etc. If this has happened, gently bend the prongs back into position, and test the plug for a tight fit in the socket. Plan on replacing the damaged plug as soon as possible. Don't let anything interfere with a clean, reliable source of power for your equipment. (Be sure to turn off the equipment before you move the plugs and check connections. If the equipment is on while you're moving connections, it may receive temporary voltage peaks and other abnormal signals that could cause damage.)

Most computer equipment uses a three-prong plug, as shown in Fig. 16-6A. Two of the prongs carry different sides of the AC supply. The smaller of the two prongs is supposed to be "hot," while the other prong is "neutral." If the AC outlet has been wired incorrectly, these assignments could be reversed. The third prong is supposed to be a "safety ground," but this third prong may not be connected. (You can't assume that your AC circuits were wired correctly.) You can check an AC outlet quickly with an "outlet tester." We described this tool in Chapter 5. You can also use a VOM to check an AC outlet, as shown in Fig. 16-7.

A less common socket/plug arrangement is the two-prong "polarized" plug (Fig. 16-6B). This arrangement doesn't include a third conductor for ground. Instead, the plug is designed so that it can only

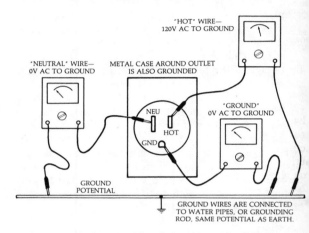

Fig. 16-7. Checking for correct AC wiring.

be plugged in one way. One prong is smaller than the other—this is the "hot" lead. For several years, building codes have required electricians to install wall sockets that match these polarized plugs. You can create a problem when you use a three-prong-into-two "cheater" connection. With these intermediate connectors, it is possible to get the "hot" and "neutral" conductors reversed. Some equipment is designed to detect this, and will not operate until you reverse the plug in the socket.

Normally, the chassis of any equipment is supposed to be grounded. But, if the equipment has been plugged into an AC outlet which has been wired incorrectly, the chassis of the equipment may be "hot" (Fig. 16-8). However, the equipment may work correctly, in spite of this. You won't know there's a problem until a part inside the equipment fails, or until you make a mistake while servicing the equipment. Either of these cases can result in a connection between the "hot" chassis and ground, causing a lot of current to flow, and possibly resulting in a dangerous shock to someone.

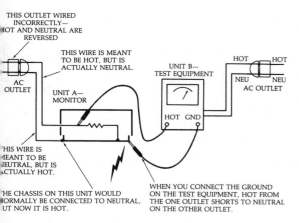

Fig. 16-8. The "hot chassis" conflict.

Before you start to work on a power supply, always check to be sure that the equipment **has been** grounded properly, and that the **chassis ground** is actually connected to the "neutral" wiring at the AC outlet. This is especially important when the equipment you are repairing has a two-pronged "polarized" plug. On equipment of this type, use an "isolation transformer" in the AC line (Fig. 16-10).

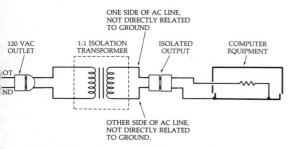

Fig. 16-9. Using an isolation transformer.

Some power-distribution strips have built-in circuit breakers or fuses. Be sure the fuse has not burned out, or the circuit breaker has not been tripped. If you suspect a fault or bad connection in the power-distribution strip, bypass it by plugging the equipment directly into a wall socket. Sometimes the computer equipment will be plugged into a combination unit, which includes a distribution strip plus a circuit that filters electrical "noise" from the AC source. Depending on the specific model, this unit may also include some kind of current-overload protection. Check the unit by bypassing the filter and plugging the computer equipment directly into a wall socket.

Now, let's look inside the power supply itself. The power-supply circuits are usually located near the rear or side of the equipment, near the entrance of the cable that runs to the wall socket. The circuits are often placed inside a shielded metal box to reduce interference with nearby radios and TVs. Some power supplies include power-supply transformers, and some of these include fusible links in their primary windings. Use your voltohmmeter, set to read OHMS, to check for continuity in the transfomer windings. We explained how to do this in Chapter 7.

All the power supplies used in computer equipment have some kind of built-in protection against current overloads. Some models include a small circuit breaker that cuts off power when the computer draws too much current. Look for a red button or pin on the back of the unit. Usually, these circuit breakers ask you to *"Push to Reset."* If your computer has such a circuit breaker, reset the breaker and see if the computer begins to operate normally. If the computer does begin to work, you may have fallen victim to a very brief electrical transient from the AC line. We explained this problem in detail in Chapter 5. It is also possible that the computer will operate for a moment, and then quit again. This points to a problem in the power supply or in the circuits served by the supply.

Any time that a circuit breaker trips, it points to an unhealthy condition inside the equipment. Sometimes you can get the equipment to operate again by running it until the circuit breaker trips, waiting a bit, resetting the breaker, and then operating until the breaker trips again. Don't try to operate this way. Find the cause of the problem. Incidentally, many circuit breakers are designed to cycle for just a few times. If you try to reset the breaker very many times, you will quickly wear out the part.

Some computers use fuses to protect the power supply. Look for a small black cap labeled "Fuse" on the back of the unit. Unscrew this cap, and you will find a small glass-and-metal fuse. We described this device in Chapter 7. In some models, the fuse is mounted inside the case of the equipment, on one of the circuit boards. Check the fuse and replace it, if necessary.

At this point, you have tried all of the easy options. There is probably a short circuit or a bad component somewhere in the system. Many power supplies can protect themselves by using a "foldback" procedure. When a power supply having this feature senses an overload, it shuts itself off. The supply continually retests the lines, but does not produce any output until the problem is corrected. In some power supplies, you can actually hear a whistle or a series of "clicks" as the supply retests the lines.

While this "foldback" feature does protect the computer very well, it makes troubleshooting more difficult. During a "foldback," the whole computer appears to be dead. You cannot take test readings, so how do you locate the problem? One simple solution is to substitute a whole new power supply. The supply is usually mounted in a metal box, and is held in place by a few screws, so if you have a spare supply, it is a simple matter to remove the original and install the replacement. Then, if the equipment begins to operate normally, you know the problem was in the original power supply.

If you do not have a spare supply, you will have to take another direction. You can start disconnecting the various "branches" of the power-distribution system from the power supply. Once you've disconnected the branch that includes the faulty component, the power supply will stop the "foldback" process, and you should find a normal supply of power to the other parts of the computer. You can use this same strategy whenever you want to troubleshoot part of the power-supply system: Cut off the bad part of the system and the rest of the system should begin working normally.

Often the voltage outputs are carried to the rest of the computer via a plug-in connector. By unplugging this connector, you can disconnect the power supply from all of the branches at once. But this can create another problem. Many power supplies will not operate unless they are connected to a load of some sort. To check this possibility, you must connect "dummy loads" on each of the outputs (Fig. 16-10).

Look up the specifications for the power supply. The specs should list the maximum currents for each of the voltage outputs. For example, the power supply on an Apple II lists these outputs:

+5 V	2.5 A
−5 V	250 mA
+12 V	1.5 A
−12 V	250 mA

Your job is to connect resistors which will allow these same currents to flow. Actually, there is no need to allow the absolute maximum currents to flow—40% of maximum is fine for our purposes. You can use Ohm's law to choose the resistor:

$$\text{Resistance} = \frac{\text{Voltage}}{\text{Current}}$$

We will choose a resistor which will allow about half of the maximum current to flow:

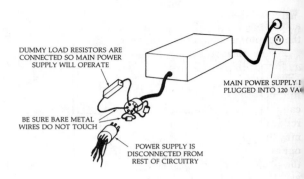

Fig. 16-10. Installing dummy load resistors.

$$\text{Resistance} = \frac{\text{Voltage}}{0.50 \times \text{Current}}$$

To choose a resistor for the +5-V supply on the Apple II, the calculation would be:

$$\text{Resistance} = \frac{5 \text{ volts}}{0.50 \times 2.5 \text{ Amps}}$$

$$= 4 \text{ ohms}$$

The actual value of the resistance is not critical as long as you do not allow more than the rated maximum amount of current to flow. In this example, we could use a 5-ohm resistor, and this would allow about 40% of the maximum current to flow. Be sure to use a resistor which can handle the power that will be dissipated. Use the formula:

$$\text{Power} = \text{Voltage} \times \text{Current}$$
$$= 5 \text{ V} \times (2.5 \text{ A} \times 40\%)$$

In this situation, you could use a 10-watt brick resistor for the +5-V supply. You can probably use 1 watt resistors for the other supplies. Remember, this is a temporary test setup. Do not operate the power supply this way for more than a minute or so, while you take your voltage readings. Do not allow the leads of one resistor to touch the leads on another, or you may create a short circuit.

On a computer with removable circuit cards, you can disconnect some of the circuits by simply unplugging the cards. Turn off the computer, retest each of the supply voltages again, and see if the power supply is working normally. If it is, look for a problem in one of the cards you just removed. If not, turn off the equipment, replace one card, turn on the equipment, and test again. When you finally replace the faulty card, the symptoms should reappear.

An adjustable transformer (also called an *autotransformer* or a *Variac*) can be very helpful at this point. As we explained before, the main power supply is folding back because the circuitry in the computer is calling for too much current. When the input voltage is reduced, the demand for current from the other circuits may be reduced and the power supply may begin operating again. Connect the autotransformer between the power supply and the source of 120-V AC current, as shown in Fig. 16-11. Turn the control on the autotransformer down as far as possible, so the output is 0-V AC. Now turn up the control gradually. At some point, the power supply should begin operating. The supply will continue operating until the current output from the power supply becomes too high. Turn the control back down a bit so the supply starts operating again and continues operating.

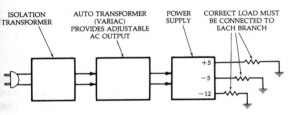

Fig. 16-11. Using an autotransformer to avoid feedback.

Using one of the methods described above, you may be able to get the main part of the power supply working. Next, you've got to find the problem that caused the supply to fold back. Fig. 16-12 shows how the power supply divides into separate sources, each of which supplies a particular voltage to different sections of the equipment. Once you have the main part of the power supply operating, you must find out how many of these separate outputs are working correctly. Let's say that you have a system with four separate power outputs, as shown in Fig. 16-12. Check the output voltage from each section. Use a voltohmmeter, set to the 12-V DC scale. In some cases, the output wires will run into a plastic plug-in connector, and you can take your readings from the pins on the connector. In other equipment, the power-supply outputs will go directly to traces on the circuit boards. In this case, test pins will probably be provided. For ground connections, use one of the test points we described in Chapter 7, in the section entitled "Find Good Test Points."

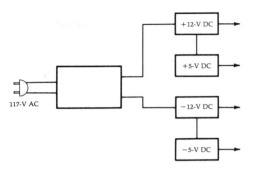

Fig. 16-12. Power supply divides into four sources.

How do you interpret the readings from these stages? Fig. 16-13 summarizes this information. If all of the output voltages are dead, the problem may lie in the main part of the power supply, in the section between "AC IN" and the output stages (Fig. 16-13A). As we explained earlier, it is also possible that the supply is "folding back" because of a short circuit somewhere on the circuit boards. Before you begin working on the main supply, you must eliminate this possibility.

If two output stages are dead, look for a situation where an output stage is tied to another, as shown in Fig. 16-13B. The problem cuts the output from the "master" stage, so the "slave" loses power too.

What if you find the voltage missing from just one output, as shown in Fig. 16-13C? Don't start working on that output stage just yet—the problem could be in the circuits served by that output.

Each of the output stages supplies a certain voltage to all of the parts of the equipment that require that particular voltage. For example, in equipment that uses the common "transistor-transistor-logic" (TTL) circuits, every IC in the equipment will use the +5-V DC source for its basic operating power. Every IC is connected electrically back to that single power source, as shown in Fig. 16-14. This also means that a problem involving any +5-V DC line to any one of the ICs can disturb the power supply to all the rest of the ICs. You must determine if the fault is in the power supply itself, or is out among the various devices that are served by that power source.

The basic strategy is this (Fig. 16-13C):

1. Shut off the equipment.

2. Disconnect one of the power supply branches, just after it leaves the output stage.

3. Turn on the power again, and see if output has returned to normal.

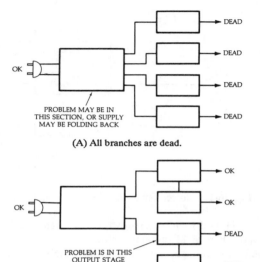

(A) All branches are dead.

(B) Two branches are dead.

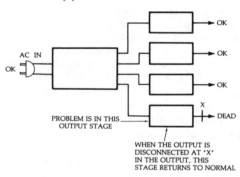

(C) One branch is dead.

Fig. 16-13. Troubleshooting power supplies.

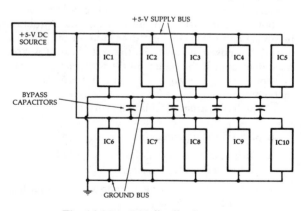

Fig. 16-14. +5-V distribution system.

With a voltmeter, test on the upstream side of the break and see if the voltage for that stage has returned to normal.

If the output does come up to specifications, you know that the problem is out in the equipment, somewhere among the components that require that particular voltage. The problem, perhaps a short circuit, is "drawing down" the output from that particular stage. When you disconnect the branch from the supply, you remove the problem, and the power supply can then begin operating normally.

On the other hand, if the power supply does not return to normal, you will then know that the problem lies in another output stage and branch, or perhaps in the main part of the power supply. Move on to another output stage and disconnect the circuits from the power supply there as well. Continue until the power supply begins operating normally (indicating that you've found the branch with the problem), or until you've disconnected all of the branches.

On most equipment, each branch of the power supply feeds directly into traces on the circuit card. You may be able to use a schematic to identify the traces that are connected to each branch. Unfortunately, the most common +5-V DC power-supply traces are usually not included on schematics. If this is the case, you'll have to follow the traces across the circuit board.

Fig. 16-15 shows how to proceed. Turn off the equipment and disconnect one branch at a time. (The procedure for cutting and repairing a trace on the circuit board was illustrated in Fig. 7-7 in Chapter 7. Refer to it, if necessary). If a test pin is provided, disconnect the line downstream of the test pin so you can use that pin to take voltage readings. With a voltmeter, check the reading on the upstream side of the break and see if it has returned to normal. When you are through troubleshooting, be sure to reconnect each of the branches that you've disconnected.

Let's say that you have determined that the problem is definitely in the main supply. One of the components is probably "shorted." This means that it has failed in such a way that it passes current straight through from the DC source to ground. If a component is "shorted," it will usually carry too much current and will overheat. Turn off and unplug the equipment; then, carefully touch each of the components in the section of the power supply which you suspect. (The "touch test" procedure was illustrated in Fig. 7-10 in Chapter 7.) You may also want to use a tool like the Thermoprobe.

Some components are designed to be hot, even while operating normally. These will have large metal tabs (heat sinks) to carry away the excess heat. If a component without a heat sink feels really hot, check it carefully.

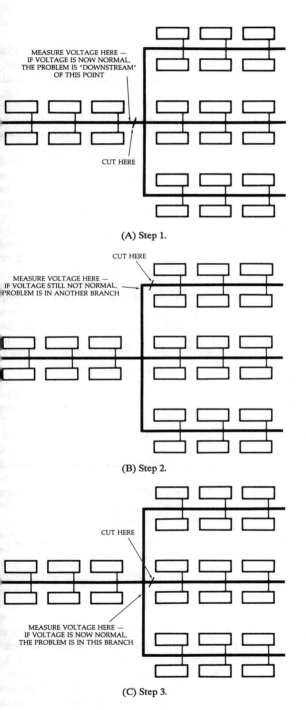

MEASURE VOLTAGE HERE —
IF VOLTAGE IS NOW NORMAL,
THE PROBLEM IS "DOWNSTREAM"
OF THIS POINT

CUT HERE

(A) Step 1.

CUT HERE

MEASURE VOLTAGE HERE —
IF VOLTAGE STILL NOT NORMAL,
PROBLEM IS IN ANOTHER BRANCH

(B) Step 2.

CUT HERE

MEASURE VOLTAGE HERE —
IF VOLTAGE IS NOW NORMAL,
THE PROBLEM IS IN THIS BRANCH

(C) Step 3.

Fig. 16-15. Checking the +5-V distribution system.

It is possible that more than one component is

bad. For example, in the linear power supply diagram shown in Fig. 16-1, if one of the diodes in the rectifier is shorted, it can cause the large filter capacitor located downstream to fail.

If the "touch test" doesn't reveal anything, use an oscilloscope to check the voltage and waveforms in each section of the power supply. Use the "chain troubleshooting" procedures we outlined in Chapter 7. In that chapter, we also included some specific test procedures for each of the components you'll find—the rectifier, regulator, capacitor, etc.

What do you do when the problem is not in the supply itself, but is somewhere among the ICs and foil traces on the circuit board? Where do you begin? Start by checking the circuit board for obvious problems. Look for a crack in the circuit board—it might cause an intermittent open circuit. Check for any spattered solder or solder balls. Loose solder can cause a short circuit to ground. These checks were also described in Chapter 7.

If you can't find an obvious mechanical problem, there's a good chance that the cause is a short circuit inside an IC. A low-resistance path may have developed inside an IC, allowing a direct connection between the power-supply branch and ground. Because of this short-circuit, the power supply can never put out enough power to get the voltage up to specification. But how do you tell *which* IC is bad?

At this point, it may be time to take the board to a service shop. However, the technicians there probably won't bother to troubleshoot further—they'll just swap boards. From this point on, troubleshooting by yourself can be quite time-consuming. You may also have to make several cuts in the foil traces on the circuit board. We should warn you, however, that if you cut the traces on one of the circuit boards, the manufacturer may not allow you to trade it in for credit. On the other hand, you could find the problem quickly. This is a decision point—the choice is up to you.

Let's assume that you want to continue troubleshooting on your own. Remember, this is a power-supply problem. You're not trying to determine if a component is processing information correctly, only whether it is "working" or "not working." This simplifies your detective work considerably.

Let's take a closer look at each of the branches that might be involved. The branch that supplies +5-V DC power is the most extensive, and also the one most likely to give you a problem. It serves every single IC on the board, as shown in Fig. 16-14. In a typical arrangement, the +5-V DC system breaks into several subbranches. One of these subbranches may feed a particular section or group of ICs.

The +5-V DC system includes many very small

"bypass" capacitors, connected from the positive voltage to ground. These "caps" are included to drain off any high-frequency noise which may be induced in the +5-V system, and any of these tiny "caps" may short-circuit to ground. It can be time-consuming to check all of these parts.

The current tracer is an ideal tool for tracking down a problem of this type. (We described this tool in Chapter 7.) There are actually several types of current tracers, but all of these instruments can show you the point where a circuit is shorted. One type of tracer produces a series of "beeping" tones, and the "beeps" grow louder when you move the probe closer to the point of the short. Another type uses a flashing LED, and the flashing rate may either speed up or slow down. Some tracers cannot detect the current flow unless the current is constantly changing direction (an AC current). To use a tracer of this type, you must sometimes "inject" a pulsing signal with a logic probe.

In Fig. 16-16, we show how to use a tracer to locate a short circuit. In the first part of the figure (Fig. 16-16A), we are moving the tracer from left to right. The signal from the tracer is growing stronger, so we know we haven't passed the point of the short. In Fig. 16-16B, the signal is still growing stronger. In Fig. 16-16C, however, the signal is growing fainter, so we know we've passed the short circuit. The IC shown in the center of the drawing is probably faulty.

The distribution systems for the +12-V DC and −5-V DC systems will be much simpler to troubleshoot than the system used for the +5-V DC system. Normally, these voltages go only to the RAMs and to certain peripherals.

A few printers use higher DC voltages to drive motors and solenoids. The distribution systems for these voltages will also be simple.

If you do not have a current tracer, you must continue with the strategy of cutting off different parts of the branch until the remaining parts begin to behave normally again. (Fig. 16-15 illustrated this process.) As shown in Fig. 16-15A, it is best to cut a circuit trace upstream of the point where the traces branch out. In the illustration (Fig. 16-15A), this has the effect of disconnecting three of the branches of the distribution system. Next, we check the voltage just upstream of the break. If the voltage returns to normal, we know that the faulty part is downstream of the break. Repair the break, and move on to another point. In Fig. 16-15B, we have made a break farther downstream, cutting off one of the branches. Again, we check the voltage upstream of the break. In this illustration, the voltage does not return to normal. This tells us that the problem is not downstream of this point. Again, we repair the break and move on. In Fig. 16-15C, we have cut off another

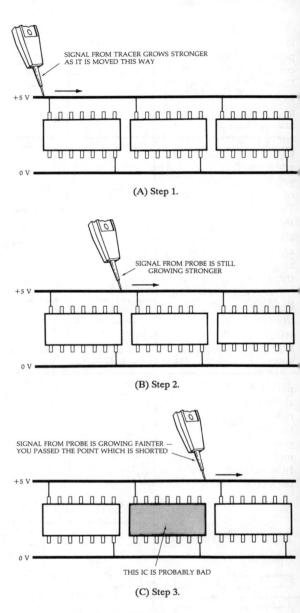

(A) Step 1.

(B) Step 2.

(C) Step 3.

Fig. 16-16. Using a current tracer.

branch. This time, the voltage upstream of the break does return to normal. Now we know that the faulty component is located somewhere downstream of the break. By continuing this process, it is possible to track down the bad component. As you work, remember to reconnect each break after testing. If you forget to do this, the section of the branch downstream of the break will not be "live," so the following test(s) will not be valid.

There are other test methods which do not involve cutting up the circuit board. For example, it is possible that one of the RAMs is shorted. The computer may be able to operate without most of the RAMs. If this is the case, you can test for shorts in some of the RAMs without instruments. Check the manual for your computer, and identify the RAMs that are essential to keep the computer running. These will contain memory space for the "stacks" used by the CPU. The essential RAMs usually have the lowest addresses. Leave these essential RAMs in place. Before you remove any of the other RAMs, review the section of Chapter 8 that discusses "Special Handling for ICs." Turn off the computer. Unplug each of the nonessential RAM ICs, and set them aside in such a way that will allow you to return them to the same sockets. Turn the equipment on and check the power-supply voltages again. If the voltages are normal, then you've localized the problem to one of the RAMs.

To find out which particular RAM is bad, turn off the equipment again, replace four of the RAMs, and then turn the equipment on again. If the trouble has returned, then the problem lies in one of the four chips that you just replaced. Continue this process until you've identified the faulty RAM chip.

If this process doesn't reveal the problem, perhaps one of the other ICs is faulty. Many of the ICs should be mounted in sockets, which will allow easy removal and replacement. You could proceed by simply removing each IC and checking the power supply, until you find the bad IC. This method will work, but you must work carefully to avoid damaging one of the ICs. In equipment where the ICs are soldered directly into the circuit board, this is not much of an option.

16.1.2 Problem 2

Symptom: Electrical "noise" in the power supply.

The power supply is supposed to take power from an AC source and produce a smooth DC power output. Much of this smoothing action is done by capacitors. A capacitor will hold back a DC voltage, but will let an AC signal pass. In many applications, a capacitor is used to allow AC, or another rapidly changing signal, to escape to ground. A capacitor used in this way is called a *filter cap*. If one of these capacitors changes value or fails, some or all of the AC signal may not be removed from the DC voltage. The resulting "ripple" component can cause many different kinds of problems

in the computer equipment. If the ripple is bad enough, some sections of the equipment may interpret each ripple variation as a digital pulse. The equipment won't work at all if this is happening. If the ripple is less serious, it may cause only intermittent problems.

In Figs. 16-1 and 16-3, we illustrated the filtering arrangements in two kinds of power supplies. The supply shown in Fig. 16-1 has a large filter capacitor following the conditioning section, with a separate smaller capacitor included in each output stage. Use an oscilloscope to check the performance of each of these smaller capacitors. To do this, check the voltages produced by each of the different output stages. At each stage, you should see a fairly smooth, clean output, as shown in Fig. 16-17A. If the output shows some ripple, as in Fig. 16-17B, check the filter capacitor for that output stage—it may be faulty. If all the outputs show some ripple, check the large capacitor at the downstream end of the conditioning stage.

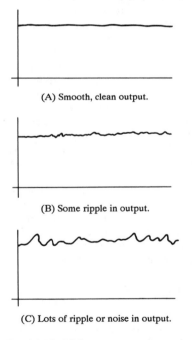

(A) Smooth, clean output.

(B) Some ripple in output.

(C) Lots of ripple or noise in output.

Fig. 16-17. Noise on power outputs.

Some kinds of electrical "noise" can't be blamed on the filter capacitors. Various "transients" and "spikes" in the AC source can be powerful enough to force their way through all the filters and get into the computer. We discussed this problem in Chapter 5.

16.1.3 Problem 3

Symptom: One voltage output is slightly high or low.

As you test the voltages from the various output stages of a power supply, you may notice that one supply voltage is consistently high or low. There may be several possible causes for this. It is possible that the voltage on the AC line is low. During a "brownout," the AC line may be producing only 110-V AC or less. This low input voltage can cause the DC voltages inside the computer to drop.

Some computers are designed to allow you to install plug-in circuit cards. Each of these cards adds to the load on the power supply. If you have added too many cards, the power output may be marginal, particularly on the +5-V supply. The +5-V output may be adequate most of the time, but may drop a bit when the computer is unusually busy. If this is the case, install a power supply which can supply more current.

When a component develops a short circuit, it generally develops a very low-resistance path. This causes a large current to flow to ground. As a result, the main power supply "folds back," and you know about the problem rather quickly. Sometimes, however, a short circuit can develop which has a higher resistance. The faulty part may be drawing much more current than it should, yet it still may not be directly shorted to ground. This condition can load down the power supply, causing low voltages throughout the system.

A component that is shorted like this will draw much more current than normal. As a result, the bad part will probably be much hotter than its neighbors. Check the temperature of each IC on the circuit board, either using the "touch test" we described in Chapter 7, or using a tool like the Thermoprobe. If the computer will still operate, you may also be able to use a software diagnostic program. For example, if the bad IC is one of the RAMs, a memory-testing program may be able to find the bad part.

Some circuits allow you to adjust the output voltages. The adjustment is often made by adjusting a small "trimmer pot" with the tip of a screwdriver. Refer to the manual for your equipment.

A component called a "voltage regulator" is supposed to keep the supply voltage stable and compensate for the effects of loading. If no adjustment is provided, or if the voltage is more than slightly out of specification, check this component. We've listed some tests in the section on "Voltage Regulators" discussed at the end of Chapter 8.

Chapter Review

In this chapter, we have explained the operating principles of the *linear* and *switching* power supplies. As you troubleshoot power supplies, refer back to the block diagrams shown in Fig. 16-1 and Fig. 16-3.

Power supplies can be dangerous to the inexperienced technician. The 120-V AC house current has enough voltage, and can deliver enough current, to be very dangerous.

When a computer system appears to be completely dead, you can't assume that the power supply has failed. The power supply may be turning itself off as a defense against problems in other parts of the system. Your first task is to try to get the power supply working again so you can track down the problem. You can do this by substituting another power supply, or by disconnecting the supply from the rest of the equipment. In order to get the power supply to operate, you may have to install *dummy load resistors* or use an *autotransformer*.

If you determine that the problem lies in the power supply itself, you can use traditional "chain" troubleshooting techniques. If the problem has been caused by a short circuit or a bad part on one of the circuit boards, the repair may be more complex. A *current tracer* will be a big help. You can also proceed by cutting off various parts of the system until the voltage outputs return to normal.

Review Questions

1. Which sections of a power supply may be dangerous?

2. You think a transformer may be faulty. With an ohmmeter, you check the resistance through the transformer coils. You find an open circuit on the input coil. Can you think of a reason for this?

3. A piece of equipment fails, and you remove the fuse and inspect it. The center conductor of the fuse is completely gone, and the inside of the glass case is blackened. What does this tell you?

4. There is a short circuit somewhere on a circuit board. You determine that there are no faults from the circuit traces to ground. Is there another possible cause for the short circuit?

5. With an oscilloscope, you find "noise" or "ripple" in the +5-V DC output. Can you suggest a possible cause?

17

Advanced Troubleshooting

Introduction and Objectives

What do we mean by the term "advanced" troubleshooting? As we explained earlier, many service shops depend on a "board-swapping" strategy. In shops that use this system, any trouble symptom is diagnosed to the point where the technician knows which circuit board to replace. The faulty board is then returned to the manufacturer for repair. Before the board can be repaired, however, someone must determine exactly which component has failed. This is called "component-level" troubleshooting. Servicing at this level generally requires better test equipment and more expertise on the part of the technician.

We have already given you many of the important "building blocks" you will need to perform component-level troubleshooting. For example, the "chain troubleshooting" techniques we explained in Chapter 7 are essential to component-level troubleshooting. In the second part of Chapter 7, we described some tests for common discrete components—resistors, capacitors, transistors, and so on. In Chapter 8, we described some troubleshooting techniques for circuits which use ICs. In the second part of that chapter, we listed test techniques for many common ICs. If you have mastered the topics covered in those chapters, you already have many of the skills you will need for this type of work.

Using those techniques, you will be able to handle *most* troubleshooting situations. However, there are several factors which can call for special techniques. Many circuits operate too quickly to be checked with simple instruments. Other circuits perform complex functions which cannot be checked easily. For example, all of the address and data lines around the CPU are very active. With simple tools, you can determine that a particular line is active, but you can't tell exactly what is happening on that line. In many situations, the basic "go/no-go" information will be adequate. However, there are times when you must have detailed information. It may not be enough to know that a device is functioning—you may have to know if it is functioning correctly. You need special test instruments which can provide this information.

In this chapter, we will take a quick look at some tools and techniques which can help you with this more advanced type of troubleshooting.

Deeper Understanding of the Circuits

Throughout this book, we have used an approach which does not require the troubleshooter to have an absolute understanding of the circuitry under test. Instead, the troubleshooter can concentrate on "blocks" of circuit elements. Simple "go/no-go" tests are used to check the individual components. In most cases, this approach will allow you to make repairs. However, there are cases when you will need more detailed information on the circuitry. It is easy to forget that the activity of every single bit is carefully planned. When you get down to the most detailed level, every circuit follows a specific sequence of operations: Step A leads to step B, and then to steps C, D, E, etc.

There are several ways of getting this detailed information. Sometimes the manufacturer has invested in a detailed technical manual which includes step-by-step descriptions of the circuitry. The relevant section of the manual may be called the "Technical Reference" or "Theory of Operation." Sometimes the circuit descriptions may be rather cursory. The manual may tell you that a certain circuit exists, and not give you much more information. In a good manual, however, you should find a very detailed description.

There are some other sources of information which you should not overlook. Some applications are fairly standard from one piece of equipment to the next. For example, let's say that a piece of equipment uses a certain kind of CPU chip. You may not be able to get detailed information on the equipment itself, but you should be able to find out about the CPU. This may give you most of the information you need, since the CPU handles all of the most important signals. Detailed data sheets on CPU chips and other ICs are available from the IC manufacturers.

Finally, it may be possible to contact someone who knows about the circuitry. For the price of a few telephone calls, you may be able to locate a manufacturer's engineer or technician who understands the circuit in question. If you are lucky, you can sometimes track down the person who actually designed the equipment.

It can sometimes take a lot of effort to develop this detailed information. Is the knowledge worth the effort? The answer depends on your particular situation. Detailed knowledge is certainly helpful if you must often work with a particular circuit. This would be the case if you work for a manufacturer and are involved in testing a particular part of the equipment. At the other end of the scale, the general technician must work with many different types of equipment and does not have time to focus on any one circuit.

Machine-Language Programming

This is a technique which can be helpful in certain troubleshooting situations. An understanding of machine-language programming can also help you to understand the operation of the CPU more clearly. In this brief discussion, we don't have the time or space to tell you how to program in machine language. However, we can give you a general idea of what is involved. In the future, you may want to explore further on your own.

Most computer programs use a "high-level" language, such as BASIC or COBOL. These languages are easy for programmers to understand and work with. They are necessary when programmers are trying to design complicated software routines. Regardless of the type of higher-level language used, the CPU itself always works with a much more basic set of instructions, called *machine language*. The machine-language instructions are expressed as digital "1s" and "0s." To put this another way, the machine-language instructions are the actual digital inputs handled by the CPU IC. When you are dealing with machine language, you are working with the most basic level of logic in the computer system.

Let's say that you want to add two numbers. Using the higher-level language, BASIC, the programmer might use just two program lines to tell the CPU to add these numbers:

Program Line	Instruction
100	8 + 15 = X
105	PRINT X

Before the CPU can execute this instruction, however, it must be translated into a series of simpler machine-language instructions. Here is how this same function might be handled by a machine-language program:

Memory Location	Instruction	Mnemonic	Function
100	A9	LDA 08	Load 08 in the accumulator
101	08		
102	69	ADC 0F	Add 15 (0F in hex)
103	0F		
104	20	JSR FDDA	Go to a subroutine and display the result
105	DA		
106	FD		

The program is stored in a continuous series of memory locations. In this example, these locations are 100 through 106. The next column represents the actual instructions presented to the CPU. Normally, these instructions are carried over the **data lines** from memory. The instructions shown here are represented as hexadecimal numbers. (If you are not familiar with these numbers, see Appendix D.) As we said, these numbers represent the actual digital inputs on the data lines. For example, the instruction represented by the hexadecimal number A9 would produce this sequence of "1s" and "0s" on the CPU's data lines:

1010 1001

If you could halt the CPU and check the data lines with a logic probe, you could actually see this instruction going into the CPU.

Notice that one command may require two or three lines of memory. A complete **address** is represented in two sections, with the least-significant part of memory listed first. In our table, the next column lists the "mnemonics." These are abbreviations which describe the functions performed by the instructions. For example, the mnemonic "LDA" stands for the instruction "Load the Following Value in the Accumulator." (The accumulator is a temporary memory space in the CPU.) The last column describes how the program is meant to operate.

There are two ways that this type of **information** might be useful to you as a programmer. If you understand the functioning of the equipment at this level, you can use your test instruments to follow the actual "1s" and "0s" through the system. You are able to work directly with the digital values handled by the system—you are not separated from the electronic reality by several layers of logic. This knowledge can also be helpful when either the computer or software is not functioning. If you understand the functioning of the system on this basic level, you can generate your own test signals and stimulate parts of the system as needed.

Programming in machine language can be confusing at first, and not everyone is comfortable with the meticulous type of work required. The CPU contains several different temporary memory spaces called "registers." As the CPU processes information, the various bits are moved from one register to another. The machine-language programmer must keep track of the status of each of the registers. Several different schemes are used to refer to addresses. These arrangements are convenient for the engineers who design the CPU's, but can be confusing to the beginner.

Timing Considerations

There are many cases where the relative timing of signals is important. Often several signals must act together to perform a certain function. For example, Fig. 17-1 shows some of the signals which might reach a memory IC during a "write" operation. This type of

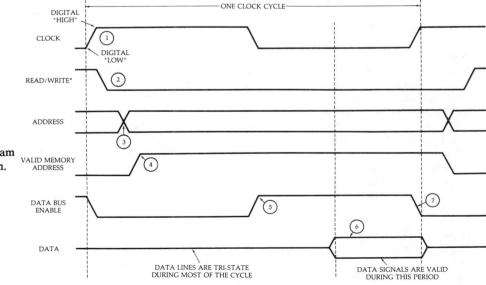

Fig. 17-1. Timing diagram for a "Write" operation.

sketch is called a "timing diagram." The **time** scale moves from left to right. Each vertical **"slice"** of the diagram represents one moment in time. **Actions which** are aligned vertically happen at the same time.

Now let's take a closer look at the sketch. The top line (point #1) represents the "clock" signal. This signal is generated by the clock circuits, and is used to synchronize many different parts of the computer system. This illustration shows the activity during one clock cycle (one positive pulse and one negative pulse). The whole clock cycle might occur in one **microsecond** or less, so you can see that all of the activity shown here happens very quickly.

When the CPU is ready to write to memory, the "Read/Write*" line is held "low" (point #2). (The asterisk after the word "Write" indicates **that** this signal is "true" when it is "low.") **On the timing** diagram, you can see that Read/Write* is held low during the whole period of the writing action,

When the CPU writes to memory, it must specify the address of the memory location to be written to. This address is presented on the address lines. As you can see by the diagram, this happens a moment after the Read/Write* line goes low (point #3). A moment later, the "Valid Memory Address" line goes "high" to show that the address chosen is part of **the** memory area (point #4).

Once all of the address lines have stabilized, the CPU can send the data for storage in memory. When the CPU is ready to do this, it holds the "Data Bus Enable" line "true" (point #5). A moment later, the actual data bits are placed on the data lines (**point #6**). During most of the cycle, the data lines are held in the TRI-STATE status, and are neither "high" nor "low." On the timing diagram, this state is indicated by the line drawn between the high and low levels. When the data bits are actually written, each data line is held high or low, as shown by the waveforms in the diagram.

The diagram in Fig. 17-1 shows the kind of complicated timing interrelationships you can find between different signals. One action is followed by another and another. For the equipment to work correctly, these actions must take place in a specific sequence, and within a specific time range.

Generally, you will not have to be too concerned with timing relationships. These are usually worked out by the engineers at the time the equipment is **designed.** From a troubleshooting point of view, you should only be concerned if a signal is missing or late. For example, let's say that the data bits are delayed a moment (point #6), so that they arrive after the "Data Bus Enable" line has dropped back to "low" (point #7). If this happens, the memory ICs will not be able to read the data bits. The data bits could be delayed by a latch or

other part which is "hung up" or is not working as quickly as it should.

There are other kinds of servicing problems which may be related to timing considerations. You may recall that "dynamic" RAMs must be constantly "refreshed" or they will not be able to retain data. If these "refresh" signals are weak or do not arrive on time, the memory ICs may become unreliable.

Some digital circuits produce signals which pass too quickly to be sensed by other circuits. The solution to this problem is a device called a *pulse stretcher*. This type of circuit takes a very fast input signal and produces a longer output pulse. This idea is illustrated in Fig. 17-2A. If a pulse-stretcher circuit stops working, it can create problems for other circuits "downstream." Refer to Fig. 17-2B. If the output pulses are too short, the following circuits may not be able to work with the pulses.

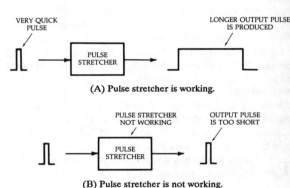

(A) Pulse stretcher is working.

(B) Pulse stretcher is not working.

Fig. 17-2. Diagram of a pulse stretcher.

Some circuits use devices called *debouncers* to condition the inputs from a switch. When a mechanical switch is closed, the contacts often "bounce" several times before making a clean contact. Many digital circuits are fast enough that they are able to "see" each of these bounces, and they interpret each bounce as a separate unit. The operation of a debounce circuit is shown in Fig. 17-3. If a debounce circuit is not working correctly, the circuits "downstream" may receive the "bouncing" output from the switch. This is illustrated in Fig. 17-3B.

If you are working with a simple device like a pulse stretcher, you may be able to do some useful troubleshooting using simple tools. However, if you are working with more complicated timing relationships like the set of signals shown in Fig. 17-1, you will need more sophisticated tools. The test equipment must provide a way of displaying several signals at the same time, so that you can see how they behave in relation to

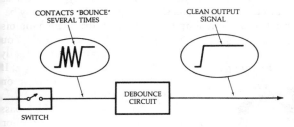

(A) Correct circuit operation.

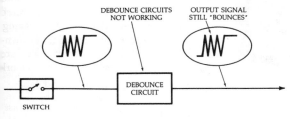

(B) Circuit not working properly.

Fig. 17-3. Diagram of a debounce circuit.

each other. The equipment must also be able to "hold" the display for a while, so you can examine the signals and understand what they are doing.

Professional Tools

Full-time technicians use a variety of professional tools to help them solve special troubleshooting problems. Some troubleshooting problems are difficult because the circuits being tested are very active, or handle signals very quickly. Special tools are necessary to "freeze" the complicated signals so the technician can examine them closely.

Other special tools are used to simplify the troubleshooting process. These devices can be used to test ICs and other components, even if the worker has no understanding of the circuitry. It is ironic that some of these "professional" tools are designed to be used by entry-level or uneducated workers. In the next part of this chapter, we'll describe a few of the more common professional tools.

Component Testers

In Chapter 7, we listed some simple tests for resistors, capacitors, transistors, and other "discrete" components. Most of these tests could be perfomed with a simple VOM. These simple test techniques are suitable when the technician has plenty of time to spare. However, a professional technician needs a way of testing components quickly and reliably, and several special test instruments have been designed to fill this need.

Also, in Chapter 7, we described a simple "transistor tester." More expensive versions of this device perform the same basic functions, but are more convenient to use. The more elaborate transistor testers can also check some of the less-common types of transistors.

If you are using a standard VOM, you can check a capacitor for a short circuit or open circuit, but you cannot check the capacitive value. For most troubleshooting work, you do not need to know the capacitance of a part. As long as the part is doing its job, the troubleshooter is generally satisfied. However, in lab work, and in some special troubleshooting situations, you may sometimes need to know the exact capacitance of a part. To handle this job, you will need a "capacitance meter." You can use the meter to make either in-circuit or out-of-circuit tests. To make an in-circuit test, you connect the meter's positive and negative leads to the suspect part and turn on the meter. To make an out-of-circuit test, you can plug the capacitor into a socket on the front of the meter. Some of the newer VOMs have this feature built in.

The most capable type of testing tool is the *Component Tester* shown in Fig. 17-4. This tool is somewhat similar to an oscilloscope, in that it has a CRT-tube display, and produces a trace on the front of the screen. To test a component, the tester produces an AC test signal. This signal is then connected to the part being tested, and the unit traces the behavior of the suspect part as the AC voltage varies. The Component Tester can make in-circuit or out-of-circuit tests.

Fig. 17-5A shows the results you might see when testing three different values of resistors. The basic trace shape (waveform) produced when testing a resistor is a single diagonal line. As you can see, the angle of the line changes as the resistance of the part is changed.

In Fig. 17-5B, we show the patterns you might see when testing three different capacitors. When testing capacitors, the basic trace shape is an oval or oblong. Again, the size and angle of the pattern changes as the capacitive value of the part is changed.

Fig. 17-5C shows the traces you might see when testing transistors. In order to make this test, the unit decreases the current to the "base" of the transistor in a series of steps.

The tester may also be used to check circuits in which several different components have been combined in series or parallel (Fig. 17-5D). The complicated trace images result when the individual traces for each of the components are combined.

There are several ways that this type of tester may be used. In troubleshooting work, the tester may be used to make a simple "go/no-go" test. This type of

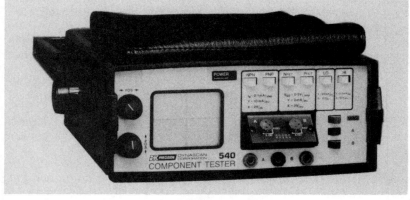

Fig. 17-4. Component Tester.
(Courtesy B&K Precision.)

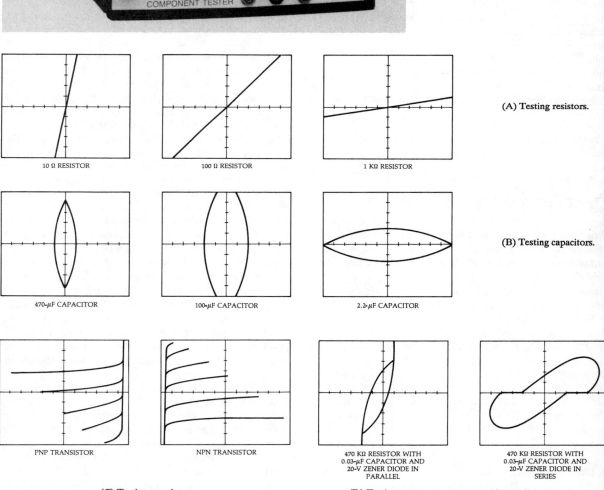

(A) Testing resistors.

10 Ω RESISTOR   100 Ω RESISTOR   1 KΩ RESISTOR

(B) Testing capacitors.

470-μF CAPACITOR   100-μF CAPACITOR   2.2-μF CAPACITOR

PNP TRANSISTOR   NPN TRANSISTOR   470 KΩ RESISTOR WITH 0.03-μF CAPACITOR AND 20-V ZENER DIODE IN PARALLEL   470 KΩ RESISTOR WITH 0.03-μF CAPACITOR AND 20-V ZENER DIODE IN SERIES

(C) Testing transistors.   (D) Testing components connected in parallel and series.

Fig. 17-5. Waveforms found when using the component tester.

tester often has two separate display channels. The unit may be set up to switch the display back and forth from one channel to the other. One channel may be set up to show the activity at a part which is known to be good. The second channel may be set up to check the part which is suspect. The tester will display the display shape first for one component, and then for the other. By comparing the display shapes, the operator can tell if the suspect part is working correctly. This type of test does not require much expertise on the part of the operator. The Component Tester is quite expensive, so it is not often used in field work. This kind of "A/B" test is sometimes used to make the quality-control checks at the end of a manufacturer's assembly line.

The Component Tester may also be used in design work. In Fig. 17-5C, we showed the characteristic display shapes for two transistors. When designing new circuits, engineers often need to know the details of the operating characteristics of a part. For example, it is sometimes necessary to match transistors which have the same "gain," or ability to amplify current. It is simple to do this by comparing the display shapes on a Component Tester.

Logic Clips

A logic clip is similar in appearance to the IC test clip described in Chapter 6. See Fig. 17-6. The lower end of the logic clip fits over the pins of the IC being tested. A series of LEDs along the top of the logic clip indicates the logic state of each pin. By feeding known signals into an IC, watching the output on the logic clip, and comparing the results with a truth table, a technician can tell if the IC is working correctly.

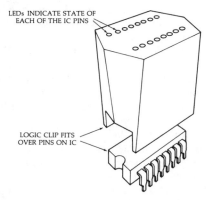

LEDs INDICATE STATE OF EACH OF THE IC PINS

LOGIC CLIP FITS OVER PINS ON IC

Fig. 17-6. A logic clip.

Each LED produces the same indications you would get from a logic probe. For example, an LED

might be green when its test point is a digital "high," and red when the point is "low." In fact, you can think of this tool as a series of logic probes, grouped together. The clip is powered by the circuit being tested. When the unit is first clipped in place, it automatically identifies the "+5-V DC" and "ground" pins. Each clip is designed to work with ICs with a certain number of pins (8 pins, 14 pins, 16 pins, etc.). A logic clip costs about $150.

The logic clip is small and convenient to use, so it is suitable for use in field servicing. The clip indicates the state of each of the outputs but, in order for this information to have meaning, the technician must know which inputs are being presented to the IC. Sometimes, it is possible to depend on the equipment being tested to generate useful signals. This is only possible if the IC under test is performing a simple job, or is handling signals which change slowly. In some cases, the technician can write a short "loop" program that will cause the computer to produce useful test inputs. It is also possible to generate one or more test inputs using logic probes. The logic clip is especially helpful when checking simpler ICs which contain a few gates. However, if the IC is handling signals which are changing quickly, or if the part requires many different test inputs, the logic clip may not not be so useful.

Logic Comparator

This device provides a convenient way of checking a suspect IC against an IC which is known to be good. We have shown one type of comparator in Fig. 17-7. To use the comparator, the technician attaches a test lead to the IC which will be tested. An identical IC, which is known to be good, is placed inside the comparator. Next, the technician turns on the computer or other equipment, and operates it normally. The various signals flow through both the IC on the circuit board and the identical IC on the comparator. The comparator tells the technician if the two ICs seem to be behaving differently. If the comparator notes any differences, the technician knows that the part being tested is faulty.

The *logic comparator* is compact and convenient for use in the field. Since this unit makes a simple "go/no-go" test, it does not require any expert knowledge on the part of the operator. A technician can simply check all of the ICs on a circuit board, one at a time, until the faulty part is revealed. In order to use a comparator, the technician must have samples of each IC type on hand. One model of logic comparator sells for $700.

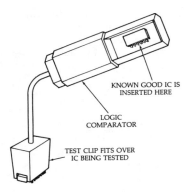

KNOWN GOOD IC IS
INSERTED HERE

LOGIC
COMPARATOR

TEST CLIP FITS OVER
IC BEING TESTED

Fig. 17-7. A logic comparator.

Signature Analyzer

If you were to watch the activity of any given point in the computer system, you would see a "stream" of data flowing past that point. In most troubleshooting work, it is not necessary to know all of the details of the data stream. We want to know if the circuit is working correctly, so all we really need to know is whether the data bits in the stream are correct. To put this another way, it is the "correctness" of the bit stream which is most important to the technician.

The *signature analyzer* is a tool which gives a technician a convenient way of comparing complicated "streams" of data. This device uses a mathematical conversion to "compress" a stream of data into a single four-digit number. In order for the analyzer to be useful, the test point must first be checked while the circuit is working correctly. During this first test, the signature analyzer will produce a four-digit number which summarizes the bit stream past the test point. When the equipment fails, the technician can return to the test point and run the test again. Again the analyzer will produce a four-digit code called a "signature." This number will usually be expressed as a hexadecimal number, and it will usually include some of the special hexadecimal numbers, "A" through "F." A typical signature might be something like "213A" or "BB05." (If you're not familiar with hexadecimal numbers, see Appendix D.) The actual value of the four-digit signature is not important. The signature number is used only as a testing device to compare the activity of the circuit at two different times. If the original signature and the signature taken during troubleshooting do not match, the operator knows that the signal at the test point is not normal. Using this type of

"go/no-go" test, the technician can check whole blocks of circuitry. The signature analyzer can be very helpful when used with the *chain troubleshooting* techniques we described in Chapter 7.

In order for a test to be valid, the bit stream examined during the second test must be exactly the same as the bit stream used when the original signature was taken. The equipment being tested must be executing the same program in each case. The two test periods must also start and end at exactly the same points. Usually, the equipment being tested will generate signals which can be used to begin and end the test period.

During the test period, the analyzer breaks the bit stream into many short "slices" or samples. (This process is similar to the sampling procedure used to digitize the outputs from musical instruments.) Next, the analyzer checks the data from each of the samples. If the signal is a logic "high" during a particular sample, it is given a value of "1," and a "low" is given a value of "0." The "1s" and "0s" are then used to calculate the four-digit code number. The sampling rate is usually tied to some other signal in the system. For example, the output from the clock may be fed into the analyzer, and used to determine how often the analyzer will record a new sample.

The signature analyzer has been promoted as offering a way of providing "idiot-proof" servicing. The advantage of this method is that the technician does not have to know much about the equipment being tested. All he or she must do is compare the number produced by the signature analyzer with a number produced earlier. However, this level of performance can be expensive—a signature analyzer may cost $1000 or more.

Generally, a signature analyzer is not much help unless someone has done some preparatory work. When the device is first designed, someone must go through the equipment and take signatures at the important test points. These signatures are then included in the documentation, as shown in Fig. 17-8. The equipment to be tested is usually designed to produce the special signal required by the analyzer; i.e., sampling rate, start of test, and end of test.

In some cases, signature analysis can be used, even if the equipment has not been specifically prepared for this. The technician can generate signatures by taking readings from identical equipment which is working correctly. As we said, the analyzer requires inputs to set the sampling rate, start of test, and end of test. Some analyzers can be set up to use inputs generated by the equipment being tested. For example, one of the "clock" signals might be used to set the sampling rate.

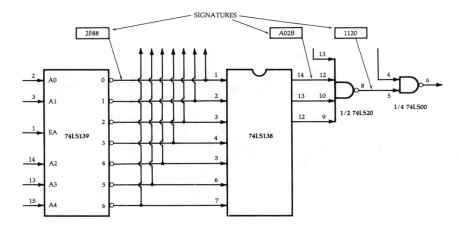

Fig. 17-8. Schematic and signatures for signature analysis.

Logic State Analyzer

We mentioned earlier that the timing between different signal elements is important. The *logic state analyzer* can be used to display the logic states of many different signals at the same time. This type of analyzer takes a "snapshot" of the activity on many different test points. Usually, the analyzer is set up to record the activity on all the address lines and all the data lines. Sometimes, the analyzer may also be set up to check for activity on a few of the more important control lines.

The analyzer can only record this activity during a limited sampling period. The sampling period is usually begun when the analyzer receives a signal on a special "trigger" input. The test period ends when the analyzer runs out of space in memory.

Different logic state analyzers may present this information in different ways. Sometimes, the signal levels are represented as digital "1s" and "0s" on a screen or a printout. We have shown this type of display output in Fig. 17-9A. This same information can be presented in a more compact form using hexadecimal numbers, as shown in Fig. 17-9B. Other analyzers present the information in graphic form, as shown in Fig. 17-9C.

A logic state analyzer can cost $5000 or more. Most field service situations do not require a very detailed analysis of the circuitry, so the logic state analyzer is not used much outside of the laboratory. This type of tool is most useful to design engineers. Often the logic state analyzer is brought into action after the engineers build the prototype of a circuit, and then discover "bugs" in the design. This tool is particularly helpful in running down problems in the relative timing of different signals.

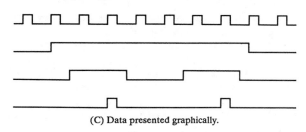

(A) Data presented as digital "1s" and "0s."

ADDRESS	DATA
$0000	$00
$02CD	$01
$02CE	$02
$02CF	$03
$02D0	$04

(B) Data presented as hexadecimal numbers.

(C) Data presented graphically.

Fig. 17-9. Displays from a logic state analyzer.

IC Tester

Many different devices are available for making in-circuit and out-of-circuit tests on ICs. We have shown one kind of tester in Fig. 17-10. This type of device is different from the logic comparator because it does not require the technician to have a known-good spare of the IC being tested. The typical tester is supervised by an on-board microprocessor. This CPU can run a series of different test routines for each of the different ICs to

Fig. 17-10. Programmable IC Tester.
(Courtesy B&K Precision.)

be tested. Sometimes, these test routines are permanently stored in ROM, and sometimes they are down-loaded from a larger computer.

The procedure for an out-of-circuit test of an IC is quite simple. The technician places the suspect IC in a special socket on the tester, or attaches a test clip to the IC. The tester then produces a series of test inputs, checks other resulting outputs, and tells the operator whether the part is working properly. The better testers use a special *zero insertion force* (ZIF) socket for the IC being tested. The technician can insert and remove ICs from this type of socket without damaging the IC, or without wearing out the socket.

An in-circuit test is a bit more demanding. To begin the test, the technician connects the test clip to the IC as it sits on the circuit board. Some of the pins of the IC will be connected to +5 V or ground. On a simple tester, this will make the IC appear to be bad, but the better testers can overpower these inputs temporarily. Several of the IC's pins may be connected together, so the tester must be able to recognize this and make adjustments.

An expensive tester usually is provided with a "library" of test routines for most common ICs. If a particular IC is suspect, and is not included in the library, some testers allow the technician to make an on-site test. First, the technician checks an identical IC in a circuit which is working properly. The IC tester "learns" the pattern of responses from this "known-good" IC. Next, the technician tests the suspect IC. When used in this way, the IC tester is similar to the logic comparator we described earlier.

A good IC tester can be very helpful to the beginning technician because it does not require a lot of detailed knowledge about the circuitry. If the suspect IC is listed in the tester's memory, the operator can usually

call up the test routine by pressing a few keys. The tester makes a simple go/no-go test. If the test results are "no-go," the technician can replace the suspect chip. With enough persistence, a beginner can go through a whole circuit board, one IC at a time, until the bad part is revealed. In the hands of an expert, the IC tester can find a problem even more quickly.

A simple IC tester may cost $250 or more. Units of this type are small and are convenient enough to be used in the field. A more capable model may cost much more, but it is more likely to be used in the lab. From time to time, various electronics magazines present plans for simple IC testers. Bill Green described a useful tester in the November 1987 issue of *Radio-Electronics*.

CPU Stimulator

Some technicians use a sample device called a "no-op" tester. This device operates by "forcing" a particular instruction onto the data lines of the CPU chip. This instruction causes the CPU chip to count upward through all of the possible addresses, and this creates a characteristic "test pattern" on the address lines. The "no-op" tester is hardwired so that only one instruction can be forced onto the data lines.

Other types of CPU stimulators are available which are much more versatile. To use one type of stimulator, you remove the CPU and plug a test connector into the empty socket. The stimulator has a series of switches which allow you to set the state of each of the address lines, each of the data lines, and some of the control lines. When a particular switch is open, the appropriate data or address line is held high, forcing a digital "1" onto the line. When the switch is closed, the line is connected to ground, holding the line low and forcing a digital "0." Control signals can be forced in the same way. "Debounce" circuits are included for the signals to the control lines.

A device like this makes it possible to move through a test sequence step-by-step and check the activity of the circuits at each step. This type of testing is very helpful when a system is completely dead. The test signals are generated by the stimulator, so it is not necessary for the CPU to operate. This test technique is sometimes used when engineers are developing a prototype and are trying to get a circuit to run for the first time.

There are some limitations on this technique, however. For one thing, the system is not much help when testing dynamic RAMs. In order to retain memory, dynamic RAMs must be constantly "refreshed." When the CPU is out of action, the "refresh" signals are not generated, so the DRAM does not retain memory. But, while the actual memory locations may not retain data, all of the other signals associated with the RAM will be working. The address lines, data lines, and memory control signals will all be functional. RAMs are tested more easily using diagnostic software.

The other limitation is purely practical. On a computer with a 16-bit address bus, 8-bit bus, and 10 or 12 control lines, the stimulator may have 36 or more switches. Each time you make a "step" in the program, you may have to adjust most of these switches. This is a cumbersome process, and it is easy to lose your place in the procedure.

If the computer is operating, it is often possible to step through a program without using hardware control. Some utility programs allow you to do this under control of software. After each step, you can use your logic probe to check the status of various parts of the system. (The old "dinosaur" computers had this capability built in. A switch on the front panel allowed the operator to step through the program, and a row of indicator lights showed the status of the address and data lines, and the important registers in the computer. This is why early computers were always shown with rows of blinking lights.)

Disk-Drive Exerciser

This device performs the same function as the disk exerciser programs we described in Chapter 6. However, this type of exerciser is a stand-alone unit. This allows the technician to test a disk drive even if a computer is not available. The complete unit includes a power supply and the outputs to the drive. By setting switches or typing in commands, the technician can command a disk drive to step in, step out, write a test pattern, etc.

Tools of this type are expensive, and are generally found only in shops that work with many disk drives each day.

Chapter Review

In this chapter, we have discussed some of the concepts and tools used in advanced troubleshooting. In the industry, "advanced" troubleshooting is generally taken to mean "component-level troubleshooting." In the earlier chapters, we have given you the basic concepts and skills necessary to troubleshoot to the component level.

Every digital circuit behaves in a predictable way. If necessary, you can learn all of the details of a circuit's functioning. In some troubleshooting situations, the relative timing between signals is important. The easiest way of understanding the relationship between signals is with the use of a "timing diagram." Some test instruments can display many signals at the same time.

In the last part of the chapter, we reviewed some special troubleshooting tools. The "logic comparator" or "IC tester" allows the technician to check complicated ICs, either in-circuit or out-of-circuit. The "logic state analyzer" allows the technician to examine many different signals at once. The "signature analyzer" can be used to make "go/no-go" tests at prepared test points in the equipment. Many of these tools are too expensive for the field technician, and will mainly be found in design labs.

A

Resistor Color Code

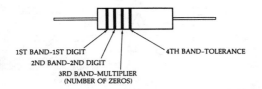

1ST BAND-1ST DIGIT
2ND BAND-2ND DIGIT
3RD BAND-MULTIPLIER
(NUMBER OF ZEROS)
4TH BAND-TOLERANCE

BLACK-0
BROWN-1
RED-2
ORANGE-3
YELLOW-4
GREEN-5
BLUE-6
VIOLET-7
GRAY-8
WHITE-9

FRACTIONAL MULTIPLIERS
GOLD-MULTIPLY BY 0.1
SILVER-MULTIPLY BY 0.01

TOLERANCE:
NO BAND ± 20%
SILVER ± 10%
GOLD ± 5%

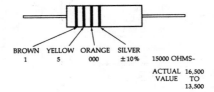

BROWN	YELLOW	ORANGE	SILVER
1	5	000	±10%

15000 OHMS-

ACTUAL 16,500
VALUE   TO
         13,500

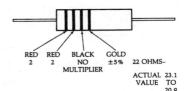

RED	RED	BLACK	GOLD
2	2	NO MULTIPLIER	±5%

22 OHMS-

ACTUAL 23.1
VALUE   TO
         20.9

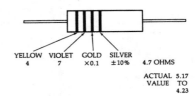

YELLOW	VIOLET	GOLD	SILVER
4	7	×0.1	±10%

4.7 OHMS

ACTUAL 5.17
VALUE   TO
         4.23

B

Manufacturers' Logos

LOGO	MANUFACTURER/ADDRESS
AM	**Advanced Micro Devices** 901 Thompson Place Sunnyvale, CA 94088 (408) 732-2400
ANALOG DEVICES	**Analog Devices** One Technology Way Norwood, MA 02062 (617) 329-4700
ANALOGIC	**Analogic Corporation** 8 Centennial Drive Peabody, MA 01961 (617) 246-0300
BECKMAN	**Beckman Instruments** 2500 Harbor Boulevard Fullerton, CA 92634 (714) 773-8603
BURR-BROWN BB	**Burr-Brown** P.O. Box 11400 Tucson, AZ 85734 (602) 746-1111
CHERRY SEMICONDUCTOR	**Cherry Semiconductor Corp.** 2000 South County Trail East Greenwich, RI 02818-0031 (401) 885-3600
C	**Commodore Semiconductor Group** 950 Rittenhouse Road Norristown, PA 19403 (215) 666-7950
	Cybernetic Micro Systems P.O. Box 3000 San Gregorio, CA 94074 (415) 726-3000
	Cypress Semiconductor 3901 N. First Street San Jose, CA 95134 (408) 943-2600
	Data General Corp. 4400 Computer Drive Westborough, MA 01581 (617) 366-1970
DATEL	**Datel** 11 Cabot Boulevard Mansfield, MA 02048 (617) 339-9341
EG&G RETICON	**EG&G Reticon Corp.** 345 Potrero Avenue Sunnyvale, CA 94086 (408) 738-4266
XR	**EXAR Integrated Systems** 750 Palomar Avenue Sunnyvale, CA 94088-3575 (408) 732-7970
FAIRCHILD A Schlumberger Company	**Fairchild** 10400 Ridgeview Court, Box 1500 Cupertino, CA 95014 (408) 864-6250
FERRANTI	**Ferranti** 87 Modular Avenue Commack, NY 11725 (516) 543-0200
FERRANTI interdesign	**Ferranti/Interdesign** 1500 Green Hills Road Scotts Valley, CA 95066 (408) 438-2900

LOGO	MANUFACTURER/ADDRESS
FUJITSU	**Fujitsu Microelectronics, Inc.** 3320 Scott Boulevard Santa Clara, CA 95054-3197 (408) 727-1700
GI	**General Instrument** 600 W. John Street Hicksville, NY 11802 (516) 933-3379
GOULD Electronics	**Gould Semiconductors** 3800 Homestead Road Santa Clara, CA 95051 (408) 246-0330
GTE	**GTE Microcircuits** 2000 W 14th Street Tempe, AZ 85281 (602) 968-4431
	Harris Semiconductor P.O. Box 883 Melbourne, FL 32901 (305) 724-7000
	Hitachi America, Ltd. 2210 O'Toole Avenue San Jose, CA 95131 (408) 435-8300
HONEYWELL	**Honeywell** 1150 E. Cheyenne Mountain Blvd. Colorado Springs, CO 80906 (303) 577-3580
HUGHES AIRCRAFT COMPANY	**Hughes Aircraft** 500 Superior Avenue Newport Beach, CA 92658 (714) 759-2349
	Hybrid Systems 22 Linnell Circle Billerica, MA 01821 (617) 667-8700
DDC	**ILC Data Device Corp.** 105 Wilbur Place Bohemia, NY 11716 (516) 567-5600
inmos	**INMOS Corp.** PO Box 16000 Colorado Springs, CO 80935 (303) 630-4000
intech ADVANCED ANALOG	**Intech/Advanced Analog** 2270 Martin Avenue Santa Clara, CA 95050 (408) 988-4930
intel i	**Intel** 3065 Bowers Avenue Santa Clara, CA 95051 (408) 987-8080
INTERSIL	**Intersil** 10600 Ridgeview Court Cupertino, CA 95014 (408) 996-5000
ITT semiconductors	**ITT Semiconductors** 7 Lake Street Lawrence, MA 01841 (617) 688-1881
Jameco ELECTRONICS	**JAMECO ELECTRONICS** **1355 SHOREWAY ROAD** **BELMONT, CALIFORNIA 94002** (415) 592-8097

LOGO	MANUFACTURER/ADDRESS
LSI COMPUTER SYSTEMS	**LSI Computer Systems** 1235 Walt Whitman Road Melville, NY 11747 (516) 271-0400
	Lambda Semiconductor 121 International Drive Corpus Christi, TX 78410 (512) 289-0403
LT LINEAR	**Linear Technology** 1630 McCarthy Boulevard Milpitas, CA 95035-7487 (408) 432-1900
3M	**3M/Electronic Products Division** P.O. Box 2963 Austin, TX 78769 (512) 834-6708
MN	**Micro Networks** 324 Clark Street Worcester, MA 01606 (617) 852-5400
mii	**Micropac Industries** 905 E. Walnut Street Garland, TX 75040 (214) 272-3571
M	**Micro Power Systems** 3151 Jay Street, Box 54965 Santa Clara, CA 95054-0965 (408) 727-5350
	Mitel Semiconductor P.O. Box 13320, Kanata Ontario, Canada K2K 1X5 (613) 592-5630
	Mitsubishi Electronics America 1050 E. Arques Avenue Sunnyvale, CA 94086 (408) 730-5900
MMI	**Monolithic Memories** 2151 Mission College Boulevard Santa Clara, CA 95054 (408) 970-9700
Thomson Components/ MOSTEK	**Mostek** 1310 Electronics Avenue Carrollton, TX 75006 (214) 466-6000
M	**Motorola** 5005 E. McDowell Road Phoenix, AZ 85008 (602) 244-7100
NS	**National Semiconductor** 2900 Semiconductor Drive Santa Clara, CA 95051 (408) 721-5000
NCR	**NCR** 8181 Byers Road Miamisburg, OH 45342 (513) 866-7217
NEC	**NEC Electronics, Inc.** 401 Ellis Street Mountain View, CA 94039-7241 (415) 960-6000

LOGO	MANUFACTURER/ADDRESS
OKI JAPAN	OKI Semiconductor, Inc. 650 N. Mary Avenue Sunnyvale, CA 94086 (408) 720-1900
OEI	Optical Electronics P.O. Box 11140 Tucson, AZ 85734 (602) 624-8358
MATSUSHITA	Panasonic (Matsushita) 1 Panasonic Way Secaucus, NJ 07094 (201) 348-7000
PLESSEY	Plessey Solid State 9 Parker Street Irvine, CA 92718 (714) 472-0303
PMI	Precision Monolithics, Inc. 1500 Space Park Drive Santa Clara, CA 95052-8020 (408) 727-9222
Raytheon	Raytheon Semiconductor 350 Ellis Street Mountain View, CA 94039-7016 (415) 968-9211
RCA Solid State	RCA Route 202 Somerville, NJ 08876 (201) 685-6000
Rockwell	Rockwell International 4311 Jamboree Road, P.O. Box C Newport Beach, CA 92658-8902 (714) 833-4700
SAMSUNG Semiconductor	Samsung Semiconductor, Inc. 5150 Great America Parkway Santa Clara, CA 95054 (408) 434-5400
	Sanyo Semiconductor Corp. 7 Pearl Court Allendale, NJ 07401 (201) 825-8080
seeQ	SEEQ Technology, Inc. 1849 Fortune Drive San Jose, CA 95131 (408) 942-1990

LOGO	MANUFACTURER/ADDRESS
	SGS Semiconductor 1000 E. Bell Road Phoenix, AZ 85022 (602) 867-6100
signetics	Signetics 811 E. Arques Avenue Sunnyvale, CA 94088-3409 (408) 991-2000
SG SILICON GENERAL	Silicon General 11861 Western Avenue Garden Grove, CA 92641 (714) 898-8121
SSi	Silicon Systems 14351 Myford Road Tustin, CA 92680 (714) 731-7110
B	Siliconix 2201 Laurelwood Road Santa Clara, CA 95054 (408) 988-8000
S	Solitron Devices, Inc. 8808 Balboa Avenue San Diego, CA 92123 (800) 327-8462
② SPRAGUE	Sprague Electric 115 N.E. Cutoff Worcester, MA 01613-2036 (617) 853-5000
SPRAGUE SOLID STATE	Sprague Solid State 3900 Welsh Road Willow Grove, PA 19090 (215) 657-8400
	Standard Microsystems 35 Marcus Boulevard Hauppauge, NY 11788 (516) 273-3100
	Supertex 1350 Bordeaux Drive Sunnyvale, CA 94088 (408) 744-0100
TELEDYNE PHILBRICK	Teledyne Philbrick 40 Allied Drive Dedham, MA 02026-9103 (617) 329-1600

LOGO	MANUFACTURER/ADDRESS
	Teledyne Semiconductor 1300 Terra Bella Ave., Box 7267 Mountain View, CA 94039 (415) 968-9241
	Texas Instruments P.O. Box 401560 Dallas, TX 75240 (214) 995-2011
TRW	TRW Semiconductors P.O. Box 2472 La Jolla, CA 92038 (619) 457-1000
TFK	AEG-Telefunken Corp. P.O. Box 3800 Somerville, NJ 08876 (201) 722-9800
	Thomson-CSF Components Corp. 6203 Variel Avenue, Unit A Woodland Hills, CA 91367 (818) 887-1010
	Toshiba America, Inc. 2692 Dow Avenue Tustin, CA 92680 (714) 832-6300
WESTERN DIGITAL	Western Digital 2445 McCabe Way Irvine, CA 92714 (714) 863-0102
Xicor	Xicor 851 Buckeye Court Milpitas, CA 95035 (408) 432-8888
Zilog	Zilog, Inc. 210 Hacienda Avenue Campbell, CA 95008-6609 (408) 370-8000

Courtesy Jameco Electronics, 1355 Shoreway Road, Belmont, CA 94002.

C
Manufacturers' IC Numbering Systems

JAPANESE STANDARD TRANSISTORS

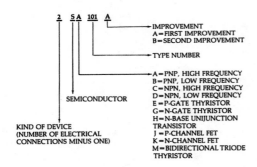

2 S A 101 A

IMPROVEMENT
A = FIRST IMPROVEMENT
B = SECOND IMPROVEMENT

TYPE NUMBER

A = PNP, HIGH FREQUENCY
B = PNP, LOW FREQUENCY
C = NPN, HIGH FREQUENCY
D = NPN, LOW FREQUENCY
E = P-GATE THYRISTOR
G = N-GATE THYRISTOR
H = N-BASE UNIJUNCTION TRANSISTOR
J = P-CHANNEL FET
K = N-CHANNEL FET
M = BIDIRECTIONAL TRIODE THYRISTOR

SEMICONDUCTOR

KIND OF DEVICE
(NUMBER OF ELECTRICAL
CONNECTIONS MINUS ONE)

ADVANCED MICRO DEVICES

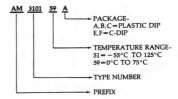

AM 3101 59 A

PACKAGE-
A,B,C = PLASTIC DIP
E,F = C-DIP

TEMPERATURE RANGE-
51 = −55°C TO 125°C
59 = 0°C TO 75°C

TYPE NUMBER

PREFIX

INTEL

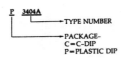

P 3404A

TYPE NUMBER

PACKAGE-
C = C-DIP
P = PLASTIC DIP

FAIRCHILD SEMICONDUCTOR

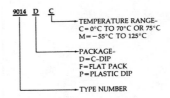

9014 D C

TEMPERATURE RANGE-
C = 0°C TO 70°C OR 75°C
M = −55°C TO 125°C

PACKAGE-
D = C-DIP
F = FLAT PACK
P = PLASTIC DIP

TYPE NUMBER

INTERSIL

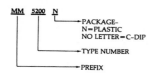

IM 5603 C DE

- PACKAGE-
  DE=C-DIP
  PE=PLASTIC DIP
- TEMPERATURE RANGE-
  C=0°C TO 75°C
  M=−55°C TO 125°C
- TYPE NUMBER
- PREFIX

NATIONAL SEMICONDUCTOR

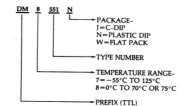

DM 8 551 N

- PACKAGE-
  J=C-DIP
  N=PLASTIC DIP
  W=FLAT PACK
- TYPE NUMBER
- TEMPERATURE RANGE-
  7=−55°C TO 125°C
  8=0°C TO 70°C OR 75°C
- PREFIX (TTL)

MONOLITHIC MEMORIES

MM 5200 N

- PACKAGE-
  N=PLASTIC
  NO LETTER=C-DIP
- TYPE NUMBER
- PREFIX

SIGNETICS

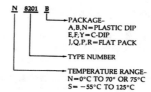

N 8201 B

- PACKAGE-
  A,B,N=PLASTIC DIP
  E,F,Y=C-DIP
  J,Q,P,R=FLAT PACK
- TYPE NUMBER
- TEMPERATURE RANGE-
  N=0°C TO 70° OR 75°C
  S=−55°C TO 125°C

HARRIS SEMICONDUCTOR

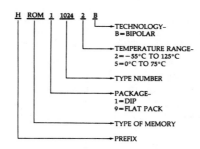

H ROM 1 1024 2 B

- TECHNOLOGY-
  B=BIPOLAR
- TEMPERATURE RANGE-
  2=−55°C TO 125°C
  5=0°C TO 75°C
- TYPE NUMBER
- PACKAGE-
  1=DIP
  9=FLAT PACK
- TYPE OF MEMORY
- PREFIX

TEXAS INSTRUMENTS INCORPORATED

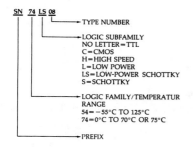

SN 74 LS 08

- TYPE NUMBER
- LOGIC SUBFAMILY
  NO LETTER=TTL
  C=CMOS
  H=HIGH SPEED
  L=LOW POWER
  LS=LOW-POWER SCHOTTKY
  S=SCHOTTKY
- LOGIC FAMILY/TEMPERATUR
  RANGE
  54=−55°C TO 125°C
  74=0°C TO 70°C OR 75°C
- PREFIX

MOTOROLA SEMICONDUCTOR PRODUCTS

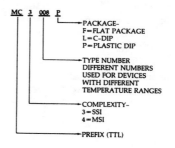

MC 3 008 P

- PACKAGE-
  F=FLAT PACKAGE
  L=C-DIP
  P=PLASTIC DIP
- TYPE NUMBER
  DIFFERENT NUMBERS
  USED FOR DEVICES
  WITH DIFFERENT
  TEMPERATURE RANGES
- COMPLEXITY-
  3=SSI
  4=MSI
- PREFIX (TTL)

D
Hexadecimal-Decimal-ASCII Conversion

At many points in the computer system, letters and numbers will be represented as "ASCII" codes. ASCII is an acronym for *American Standard Code for Information Interchange*. Table D-1 shows all the standard ASCII codes and their associated characters. (These characters can be displayed using PRINT characters CHR$(*n*), where *n* is the ASCII code.) Each character may be represented by a decimal number, or a number written in the "hexadecimal" numbering system. For example, the decimal code for the letter "A" is the decimal number 65. The "hexadecimal" code for the same letter is "$41."

The hexadecimal numbering system is based on the number 16. This numbering system runs from 0 to 15, with the numbers above 9 being represented by the letters A (=10), B (=11), C (=12), D (=13), E (=14), and F (=15). When the number "1" appears in the first place in a two-digit number (i.e., 10), it means "1 × 10." When the number "1" appears in the first place of a two-digit hexadecimal number, it means "1 × 16." Hexadecimal numbers are often written with a dollar-sign prefix: $10, $FF, etc.

Hexadecimal numbers are useful because they are easy to convert into the binary "1s" and "0s" used by computer equipment. Here is the pattern for a 4-bit binary number:

2^3	2^2	2^1	2^0	= Power of two
8	4	2	1	= Place value
0	1	0	0	= Binary 4

The hexadecimal number $41 can be represented by 8 data bits. To convert this number to its binary form, you convert each digit separately. Each hexadecimal digit becomes a 4-bit binary number. Thus, four bits represent the first digit (4) and four more bits represent the second digit (1). For example, the binary equivalent of $4 is 0100, and 1 equals 0001. Here is the complete conversion for the capital alpha character A:

decimal	65	
hex	$4	1
binary	0100	0001

The conversion of the lowercase alpha character l is:

decimal	108	
hex	$6	C (decimal 13)
binary	0110	1101

Why is this important? If you can convert from ASCII and hexadecimal codes to binary notation, you

318

can determine the exact patterns of the signals that will appear on the data lines. For example, let's say that a computer should be sending the letter "A" to a printer.

If you know how to make these conversions, you can determine that the signals on the data lines should be 0100 0001.

Table D-1 Code Conversion Chart

Hexa-decimal	Decimal	ASCII Value	ASCII Character	Hexa-decimal	Decimal	ASCII Value	ASCII Character
$00	00	000	(null)	$32	50	050	2
$01	01	001	☺	$33	51	051	3
$02	02	002	☻	$34	52	052	4
$03	03	003	♥	$35	53	053	5
$04	04	004	♦	$36	54	054	6
$05	05	005	♣	$37	55	055	7
$06	06	006	♠	$38	56	056	8
$07	07	007	(beep)	$39	57	057	9
$08	08	008	■	$3A	58	058	:
$09	09	009	(tab)	$3B	59	059	;
$0A	10	010	(line feed)	$3C	60	060	<
$0B	11	011	(home)	$3D	61	061	=
$0C	12	012	(form feed)	$3E	62	062	>
$0D	13	013	(carriage return)	$3F	63	063	?
$0E	14	014	♫	$40	64	064	@
$0F	15	015	☼	$41	65	065	A
$10	16	016	►	$42	66	066	B
$11	17	017	◄	$43	67	067	C
$12	18	018	↕	$44	68	068	D
$13	19	019	‼	$45	69	069	E
$14	20	020	¶	$46	70	070	F
$15	21	021	§	$47	71	071	G
$16	22	022		$48	72	072	H
$17	23	023	↨	$49	73	073	I
$18	24	024	↑	$4A	74	074	J
$19	25	025	↓	$4B	75	075	K
$1A	26	026	→	$4C	76	076	L
$1B	27	027	←	$4D	77	077	M
$1C	28	028	(cursor right)	$4E	78	078	N
$1D	29	029	(cursor left)	$4F	79	079	O
$1E	20	030	(cursor up)	$50	80	080	P
$1F	31	031	(cursor down)	$51	81	081	Q
$20	32	032	(space)	$52	82	082	R
$21	33	033	!	$53	83	083	S
$22	34	034	"	$54	84	084	T
$23	35	035	#	$55	85	085	U
$24	36	036	$	$56	86	086	V
$25	37	037	%	$57	87	087	W
$26	38	038	&	$58	88	088	X
$27	39	039	'	$59	89	089	Y
$28	40	040	(	$5A	90	090	Z
$29	41	041	)	$5B	91	091	[
$2A	42	042	*	$5C	92	092	\
$2B	43	043	+	$5D	93	093	]
$2C	44	044	,	$5E	94	094	^
$2D	45	045	-	$5F	95	095	_
$2E	46	046	.	$60	96	096	`
$2F	47	047	/	$61	97	097	a
$30	48	048	0	$62	98	098	b
$31	49	049	1	$63	99	099	c

Table D-1 (cont.). Code Conversion Chart

Hexa-decimal	Decimal	ASCII Value	ASCII Character	Hexa-decimal	Decimal	ASCII Value	ASCII Character
$64	100	100	d	$9C	156	156	£
$65	101	101	e	$9D	157	157	¥
$66	102	102	f	$9E	158	158	P₊
$67	103	103	g	$9F	159	159	ƒ
$68	104	104	h	$A0	160	160	á
$69	105	105	i	$A1	161	161	í
$6A	106	106	j	$A2	162	162	ó
$6B	107	107	k	$A3	163	163	ú
$6C	108	108	l	$A4	164	164	ñ
$6D	109	109	m	$A5	165	165	Ñ
$6E	110	110	n	$A6	166	166	ª
$6F	111	111	o	$A7	167	167	º
$70	112	112	p	$A8	168	168	¿
$71	113	113	q	$A9	169	169	⌐
$72	114	114	r	$AA	170	170	¬
$73	115	115	s	$AB	171	171	½
$74	116	116	t	$AC	172	172	¼
$75	117	117	u	$AD	173	173	¡
$76	118	118	v	$AE	174	174	«
$77	119	119	w	$AF	175	175	»
$78	120	120	x	$B0	176	176	░
$79	121	121	y	$B1	177	177	▒
$7A	122	122	z	$B2	178	178	▓
$7B	123	123	{	$B3	179	179	│
$7C	124	124			$B4	180	180	┤
$7D	125	125	}	$B5	181	181	╡
$7E	126	126	~	$B6	182	182	╢
$7F	127	127	⌂	$B7	183	183	╖
$80	128	128	Ç	$B8	184	184	╕
$81	129	129	ü	$B9	185	185	╣
$82	130	130	é	$BA	186	186	║
$83	131	131	â	$BB	187	187	╗
$84	132	132	ä	$BC	188	188	╝
$85	133	133	à	$BD	189	189	╜
$86	134	134	å	$BE	190	190	╛
$87	135	135	ç	$BF	191	191	┐
$88	136	136	ê	$C0	192	192	└
$89	137	137	ë	$C1	193	193	┴
$8A	138	138	è	$C2	194	194	┬
$8B	139	139	ï	$C3	195	195	├
$8C	140	140	î	$C4	196	196	─
$8D	141	141	ì	$C5	197	197	┼
$8E	142	142	Ä	$C6	198	198	╞
$8F	143	143	Å	$C7	199	199	╟
$90	144	144	É	$C8	200	200	╚
$91	145	145	æ	$C9	201	201	╔
$92	146	146	Æ	$CA	202	202	╩
$93	147	147	ô	$CB	203	203	╦
$94	148	148	ö	$CC	204	204	╠
$95	149	149	ò	$CD	205	205	═
$96	150	150	û	$CE	206	206	╬
$97	151	151	ù	$CF	207	207	╧
$98	152	152	ÿ	$D0	208	208	╨
$99	153	153	Ö	$D1	209	209	╤
$9A	154	154	Ü	$D2	210	210	╥
$9B	155	155	¢	$D3	211	211	╙

Table D-1 (cont.). Code Conversion Chart

Hexa-decimal	Decimal	ASCII Value	ASCII Character	Hexa-decimal	Decimal	ASCII Value	ASCII Character
$D4	212	212	⊨	$EA	234	234	Ω
$D5	213	213	⊫	$EB	235	235	δ
$D6	214	214	⊓	$EC	236	236	∞
$D7	215	215	╫	$ED	237	237	φ
$D8	216	216	╪	$EE	238	238	ε
$D9	217	217	⌐	$EF	239	239	∩
$DA	218	218	⌐	$F0	240	240	≡
$DB	219	219	■	$F1	241	241	±
$DC	220	220	▬	$F2	242	242	≥
$DD	221	221	▮	$F3	243	243	≤
$DE	222	222	▯	$F4	244	244	⌠
$DF	223	223	▬	$F5	245	245	⌡
$E0	224	224	α	$F6	246	246	÷
$E1	225	225	β	$F7	247	247	≈
$E2	226	226	Γ	$F8	248	248	°
$E3	227	227	π	$F9	249	249	·
$E4	228	228	Σ	$FA	250	250	·
$E5	229	229	σ	$FB	251	251	√
$E6	230	230	μ	$FC	252	252	η
$E7	231	231	τ	$FD	253	253	²
$E8	232	232	Φ	$FE	254	254	■
$E9	233	233	Θ	$FF	255	255	(blank 'FF')

E

Dealer/Manufacturer Addresses

Apple Programmers and Developers Association
(hardware information on Macintosh computers)
290 S.W. 43rd Street
Renton, WA 98055
(206) 251-6548

Ames Supply
(Fedron, printer adjustment tools)
169 Msgr. O'Brien Highway
Cambridge, MA

B & K Precision
(test instruments)
6460 W. Cortland Street
Chicago, IL 60635
(312) 889-8870

Beck-Tech
(schematics of Macintosh computer)
41 Tunnel Road
Berkeley, CA 94705
(415) 548-4054

Black Box Catalog
(cables, connectors, data switches, test instruments)
P.O. Box 12800
Pittsburgh, PA 15241
(412) 746-5530

Digi-Key
(variety of parts)
P.O. Box 677
Thief River Falls, MN 56701
(800) 344-4539

Dysan (Xidex)
(alignment diskettes)
Sold through electronics chains:
Kielrulff Electronics
Arrow Electronics
Hall-Mark Electronics

E Z Hook
(special test connectors)
P.O. Box 450
Arcadia, CA 91006

Fordham Radio
(test instruments, tools, parts)
260 Motor Parkway
Hauppauge, NY 11788
(800) 645-9518

Heathkit
(test instruments)
Benton Harbor, MI 49022
(800) 253-0570

Inmac
(computer accessories, cables, switches)
P.O. Box 58031
Santa Clara, CA 95052-8031
(800) 826-8180

Jameco Electronics
(ICs, parts, tools, subassemblies)
1355 Shoreway Road
Belmont, CA 94002
(415) 592-8097

JDR Microdevices
(ICs, cables, subassemblies,
test instruments)
110 Knowles Drive
Los Gatos, CA 95030
(800) 538-5000

MCM Electronics
(transistors, flyback transformers,
tools, test instruments)
858 E. Congress Park Drive
Centerville, OH 45459-4072

Pomona Electronics
(test connectors)
P.O. Box 2767
Pomona, CA 91769-2767

Projector Recorder Belt
(Thermoprobe, test instruments and chemicals, parts)
Rt. 3, Highway 59
Whitewater, WI 53190-0176
(800) 558-9572

Radio Shack, a Division of Tandy Corp.
(electronics parts and tools)
Many local stores.

Vortron, Inc.
(IBM PC diagnostics)
107 South Meadowview
Washington, IL 61571

Windsor Technologies
(diagnostic software and ROMs for IBM PCs)
130 Alto Street
San Rafael, CA 94901

F
Symptoms and Possible Causes

Main Computer—Computer Starts Operating Correctly, Then Stops

Possible Cause	Check	See Section
Computer is processing a long program.	Blinking cursor appears on screen. Let computer run for a while.	
Computer has initiated a garbage-collection routine.	Let computer run for a while.	
Computer is processing an endless loop or has stopped.	Try the Reset key or boot the computer	
Transient from power line.	Run original copy of the software again.	Chapter 5
Bad copy of software.	Try a backup copy of the same software.	
Bad copy of DOS.	Load a different copy of the DOS.	
Problem in one of the peripherals or removable circuit cards.	Strip down to minimum working system.Remove as many circuit cards as possible (power off).	Floppy disk drives, Chapter 10; Hard disk drives, Chapter 11; Dot-matrix & daisy-wheel printers, Chapter 12; Laser printers, Chapter 13; Modems, Chapter 14; Monitors, Chapter 15
Hardware problem in main computer.	Try diagnostic programs.	Chapter 16
Low voltage from power supply.	Measure output voltages.	Chapter 16

Main Computer—Computer Starts Operating Correctly, Then Stops (cont.)

Possible Cause	Check	See Section
Bad filtering noise from power supply.	Check for noise at each output.	9.2.1
No Clock signal to CPU.	Check with logic probe	9.2.2
No Reset signal to CPU.	Check with logic probe	9.2.3
Problem with data or address lines.	Use logic probe, diagnostics.	
Faulty CPU IC.	Replace.	

Main Computer—Makes Intermittent, Random Errors

Possible Cause	Check	See Section
Transient problem.	Run original copy of the software again.	Chapter 5
Bad copy of software.	Try a backup copy of the same software.	
Environmental problem.	Fault related to time of day, temperature, nearby equipment switching on or off, etc.	Chapter 5
Bad memory IC.	Run diagnostic software.	Chapter 9
Bad filtering, noise from power supply.	Check for noise at each output.	Chapter 16
Faulty CPU IC.	Replace.	

Main Computer Seems Dead

Possible Cause	Check	See Section
Failed power-on indicator.	Bulb or LED.	
Problem in one of the peripherals or removable circuit cards.	Strip down to minimum working system. Remove as many circuit cards as possible (power off).	Floppy disk drives, Chapter 10; Hard disk drives, Chapter 11 Dot-matrix and daisy-wheel printers, Chapter 12; Laser printers, Chapter 13; Modems, Chapter 14; Monitors, Chapter 15
Power supply problem.	Measure output voltages	Chapter 16
No clock signal to CPU.	Check with logic probe.	9.2.1
No reset signal to CPU.	Check with logic probe.	9.2.1
Problem with data or address lines.	Logic probe, no-op tester.	9.2.3
Faulty CPU IC.	Replace.	

Main Computer—At Power On, Garbage On Screen

Possible Cause	Check	See Section
Transient from power line.	Try reset key. Turn computer off, wait 60 seconds, turn on again	Chapter 5
Problem in one of the peripherals or removable circuit cards.	Strip down to minimum working system. Remove as many circuit cards as possible (power off). Try reset again.	Floppy disk drives, Chapter 10; Hard disk drives, Chapter 11; Dot-matrix and daisy-wheel printers, Chapter 12; Laser printers, Chapter 13; Modems, Chapter 14; Monitors, Chapter 15
Power supply problem.	Measure output voltage.	Chapter 16
No clock signal to CPU.	Check with logic probe.	9.2.1
No reset signal to CPU.	Check with logic probe.	9.2.2
Problem with data or address lines.	Logic probe.	9.3.3
Problem with video driver circuits	Inspect, test.	Chapter 15
Faulty CPU IC.	Replace.	

Game Controller Problems

Possible Cause	Check	See Section
Joystick jammed, broken.	Open case, inspect, replace.	9.2.5
Bad cable or connectors.	Clean, tighten connections. Ensure continuity through each wire in the cable. Substitute cable.	Cables and Connectors, Chapter 7
Worn, dirty switches and potentiometers.	Inspect, test, replace or clean with tv tuner cleaner.	Testing Switches & Potentiometers, Chapter 7

Keyboard—Hit Any Key, No Response

Possible Cause	Check	See Section
Computer is executing a long program or garbage collection routine.	Let computer run for several minutes or hit reset key.	Cables and Connectors, Chapter 7
Bad cable or connector.	Clean, tighten connections.	Inspect, test.
Faulty keyboard decoder IC.	Ensure continuity through each wire of the cable. Substitute cable.	9.2.4

Keyboard—Hit a Key, Two Characters Appear on Screen

Possible Cause	Check	See Section
Modem.	Both your terminal and terminal at other end of data link are set so both echo the characters you send.	Chapter 14
Dirty, corroded key switches.	Clean or replace switches.	9.2.4
Faulty keyboard decoder IC.	Check, replace.	9.2.4

Keyboard—Intermittent Problems

Possible Cause	Check	See Section
Bad cable or connector.	Clean, tighten connections.	Clean or replace switches
	Ensure continuity through each wire of the cable. Substitute cable.	9.2.4
Dirty, corroded key switches.	Cables and Connectors, Chapter 7	9.2.4
Faulty keyboard decoder IC.	Check, replace.	

Floppy Disk Drive—Drive Will Not Operate

Possible Cause	Check	See Section
Jammed disk.	Try to remove the disk.	
Loose part jamming the mechanism.	Open case, inspect.	
Broken drive belt.	Inspect, check belt.	10.3.4
No power to drive motor.	Drive motor.	10.3.3
Bad cable or connectors.	Clean, tighten connections. Ensure continuity through each wire in the cable. Substitute cable.	Cables and Connectors, Chapter 7
Fault in interface circuits. (Computers with removal cards)	Substitute another interface card.	10.3.15
Fault in control circuits in the drive itself.	Substitute the suspect drive. Swap drives 1 and 2.	10.3.15
Fault in control circuits.	Ensure drive motor is on and signal present in cable.	10.3.1, 10.3.15

Floppy Disk Drive—Drive Will Not Format a Disk

Possible Cause	Check	See Section
Slow drive motor.	Motor speed adjustment.	10.2.1
Drive out of alignment.	Alignment procedure.	10.2

Floppy Disk Drive—Intermittent Read or Write Failure

Possible Cause	Check	See Section
Dirty read/write head.	Clean the head, try the original disk again.	Maintenance, Chapter 10
Hardware or software error indicated by error statement.	Check the namual for your equipment. See if the error statement is helpful.	10.1.4
Interchange problem.	Look for a pattern. One drive will not read disks written on another drive. One or both drives need alignment.	
Bad disk—hard error.	Inspect for mechanical damage. Substitute another disk with a copy of the same program or file. Use a utility to check the suspect disk for bad sectors.	
Bad disk—soft error.	Substitute a backup copy of the same program or file.	
Software problem.	Look for a pattern. Try other software. Does the error appear in several programs?	
Bad cable or connectors.	Clean, tighten connections. Ensure continuity through each wire of the cable. Substitute cable.	Cables and Connectors, Chapter 7
Fault in interface circuits. (Computers with removable cards.)	Substitute another interface card.	10.3.15, Fig. 10-11
Fault in control circuits in the drive itself.	Substitute the suspect drive. Swap drives 1 and 2.	10.3.15
Fault in read circuits.	Fault occurs only during read.	10.3.9
Fault in write circuits.	Fault occurs only during write.	10.3.10
Environmental problems.	Fault related to time of day, temperature, nearby equipment switching on or off, etc.	Chapter 5
Power-supply problem.	Noise, bad ground.	Chapter 16
Incorrect motor speed.	Adjust motor speed.	10.2.1
Drive out of alignment.	Alignment procedure.	10.2
Fault in control circuits.	Check for correct signals through the cable.	10.3.15

Floppy Disk Drive—Disk Will Not Slide In or Out

Possible Cause	Check	See Section
Mechanical parts slightly out of alignment.	Open and close door a few times, try again.	
Head remains loaded.	Boot computer, use Reset key.	
Mechanical eject—bent part.	Open case, inspect.	10.3.13
Auto eject—bent part.	Open case, inspect. Check for bad solenoid.	10.3.13
Faulty motor-driven ejector.	Inspect ejector.	10.3.13

Floppy Disk Drive—Drive Operates, but Will Not Read

Possible Cause	Check	See Section
Dirty Read/Write head	Clean the head, try the original disk again.	Maintenance, Chapter 10
Hardware or software error indicated by error statement.	Check the manual for your equipment. See if the error statement is helpful.	
Bad copy of Disk Operating System.	Substitute a backup copy, try again.	10.1.4
Bad disk—hard error.	Inspect for mechanical damage. Substitute another disk with a copy of the same program or file. Use a utility to check the suspect disk for bad sectors.	
Software problem.	Look for a pattern. Try other software. Does the problem appear as you use different programs?	
Bad cable or connectors.	Clean, tighten connections. Ensure continuity through each wire in cable. Substitute cable.	Cables and Connectors, Chapter 7
Fault in interface circuits. (Computers with removable cards.)	Substitute another interface card.	10.3.15, Fig. 10-11
Fault in control circuits in the drive itself.	Substitute the suspect drive. Swap drives 1 and 2.	10.3.15
Worn head-load pad.	Inspect load pad.	Periodic Inspection, Chapter 10
Drive select problem.	Check for drive-select signal through the cable.	10.3.1, 10.3.5
Faulty read circuits.	Check for read-data signals through the cable.	10.3.1, 10.3.9
Drive out of alignment.	Alignment procedure.	10.2
Fault in control circuits.		10.3.15

Floppy Disk Drive—Damaged Files on Disk

Possible Cause	Check	See Section
Recoverable fault on disk.	Recovery procedures.	10.3.16

Floppy Disk Drive—Head Oscillates at Track 0

Possible Cause	Check	See Section
Faulty Track-zero detector.	Test detector.	10.3.11
Faulty Track-zero logic.	Check circuit.	10.3.11

Floppy Disk Drive—Drive Turns Slowly, Noise from Drive

Possible Cause	Check	See Section
Faulty or jammed disk.	Try to remove disk.	
Loose part jamming the mechanism.	Open case, inspect.	
Loose, slipping drive belt.	Inspect, check tension.	10.3.4
Inadequate power to drive motor.	Ensure correct power is available. Check voltages through the cable.	10.3.2
Bad cable or connectors.	Clean, tighten connections. Ensure continuity through each wire in the cable. Substitute cable.	Cables and Connectors, Chapter 7
Motor speed needs adjustment.	Run motor-speed test software.	10.2.1
Mechanical problem—drive motor and spindle.	Raw data test. Inspect drive motor and spindle.	10.2.7, 10.3.2

Floppy Disk Drive—Drive Operates but Will Not Write

Possible Cause	Check	See Section
Hardware or software error indicated by error statement.	Check the manual for your equipment. See if the error statement is helpful.	
Disk is write-protected.	Inspect write-protect notch.	
Bad disk—hard error.	Inspect for mechanical damage. Substitute another disk and try to write again. Use a utility to check the suspect disk for bad sectors.	
Software problem.	Look for a pattern. Try other software. Can the drive write while under control of these other programs?	
Bad cable or connectors.	Clean, tighten connections. Ensure continuity through each wire of the cable. Substitute cable.	Cables and Connectors, Chapter 7
Fault in interface circuits. (Computers with removable cards)	Substitute another interface card.	10.3.15, Fig. 10-11
Fault in control circuits in the drive itself.	Substitute the suspect drive. Swap drives 1 and 2.	10.3.15
Drive out of alignment.	Alignment procedure.	10.2
Faulty write-protect circuit.	Inspect components, test the circuit.	10.3.8
Faulty write circuits.	Inspect components, test the circuit.	10.3.10
Fault in control circuits.	Check for write-gate and write-data signals through the cable.	10.3.1, 10.3.15

Floppy Disk Drive—Head Will Not Step In or Out

Possible Cause	Check	See Section
Fault in stepper logic or stepper motor.	Inspect mechanism, test circuit.	10.3.6

Floppy Disk Drive—Drive Cannot Read a Disk Written on Another Drive

Possible Cause	Check	See Section
One drive is out of alignment.	Alignment procedure.	10.2

Hard Disk Drive—Damaged Files on Disk

Possible Cause	Check	See Section
Recoverable fault on disk.	Recovery procedures.	Recovering Data from a Hard Disk, Chapter 11

Hard Disk Drive—Intermittent Read or Write Failures

Possible Cause	Check	See Section
Identifiable error.	Look up error statement. Check self-diagnostics.	
Break in cable, bad connector.	Continuity through cable.	Cables and Connectors, Chapter 7
	Signals through cable.	11.2.1
Bad connection on card connector.	Check card connections.	
Problem on interface card.	Substitute card.	
Problem with one circuit on card with duplicate circuits.	Connect drive to second circuit.	
Low voltage or electronic noise.	Check power-supply output voltages.	Chapter 16
Internal drive causes overheating.	Install fan.	
Internal drive overloads power supply.	Install more powerful supply.	
Worn bearings.	Check for noise from drive.	
Worn Read/Write heads.	Bit-shift test.	11.2.8
Weak Read/Write output.	Read circuits. Write circuits.	11.2.4 11.2.5
Faulty index detector circuits.	Check index detector.	11.2.7

Hard Disk Drive—Head Oscillates at Track 000

Possible Cause	Check	See Section
Faulty Track 000 circuits.	Track 000 system.	11.2.6

Hard Disk Drive—Unusual Noise From Drive

Possible Cause	Check	See Section
Worn bearings, damaged head.	Return to manufacturer.	

Hard Disk Drive—Head Will Not Step In or Out

Possible Cause	Check	See Section
Identifiable error.	Look up error statement. Check self-diagnostics.	
Break in cable; bad connector.	Check continuity through cable. Check signals through cable: "Step," "Direction."	Cables and Connectors, Chapter 7 11.2.1
Bad connection at card connector.	Check card connections.	
Problem on interface card.	Substitute card.	
Problem with one circuit on card with duplicate circuits.	Connect drive to second circuit.	
Faulty signals to stepper motor.	Check signals to stepper motor	11.2.3
Faulty signals to voice coil.	Check signals to voice coil.	Solenoids, Chapter 7
Mechanical problem.	Return drive to manufacturer.	

Hard Disk Drive—Drive Operates, Will Not Write

Possible Cause	Check	See Section
Identifiable error.	Look up error statement. Check self-diagnostics.	
Break in cable; bad connector.	Check continuity through cable. Check signals through cable: "Write Gate," "Write Data," "Write Enable."	Cables and Connectors, Chapter 7 11.2.1
Bad connection at card connector.	Check card connections.	
Problem on interface card.	Substitute card.	
Problem with one circuit on card with duplicate circuits.	Connect drive to second circuit.	
Worn Read/Write heads	Bit shift test.	11.2.8
Weak or absent write signals.	Check write circuits.	11.2.5

Hard Disk Drive—Drive Operates, Will Not Read

Possible Cause	Check	See Section
Identifiable error.	Look up error statement. Check self-diagnostics.	
Break in cable, bad connector.	Check continuity through cable. Check signals through cable: "Read Gate," "Read Data," "Read Clock," "Read Enable."	Cables and Connectors, Chapter 7 11.2.1
Bad connection at card connector.	Check card connections.	
Problem on interface card.	Substitute card.	
Problem with one circuit on card with duplicate circuits.	Connect drive to second circuit.	
Worn Read/Write heads.	Bit shift test.	11.2.8
Weak or absent read signals.	Check read circuits.	11.2.4

Dot-Matrix or Daisy-Wheel Printer—Produces One or More Incorrect Characters—Intermittent Problem

Possible Cause	Check	See Section
Software problem.	Look for a pattern. Try other software. Does the error appear in several programs?	
Interface problem.	Printer starts normally, then produces many incorrect characters, or printer loses a number of characters.	12.2.9
Bad cable or connectors.	Clean, tighten connections. Ensure continuity through each wire of the cable. Substitute cable.	Cables and Connectors, Chapter 7
Mechanical problem.	Open printer, check for loose parts, etc.	
Bad internal connection in printer.	Internal cables. Reseat circuit boards.	
Loose conductive material moves, causes shorts.	Open printer, inspect	
Faulty carriage-drive mechanism.	Inspect.	12.2.1
Faulty platen-drive mechanism.	Inspect.	12.2.3
Power-supply problem.	Check output voltage levels. Check for noise in outputs.	Chapter 16
Environmental problem.	Fault related to time of day, temperature, nearby equipment switching on or off, etc.	Chapter 5
Disk drive not reading or writing correctly.	Swap disk drive.	Chapter 10 & Chapter 11
Computer makes errors.	Swap computer.	Chapter 9
Faulty interface.	Check signals through cable.	12.2.9
Faulty control circuits in printer.	Check signals at printer CPU.	12.2.10

Dot-Matrix or Daisy-Wheel Printer—No Print Action, but Front Panel Indicators Light

Possible Cause	Check	See Section
On-line/local switch.	Set to on-line.	
Printer stopped to protect itself.	Error or alarm indicators. Is paper out, ribbon out, cover open?	
Carriage has moved beyond normal limits.	Open cover, check carriage position.	
Interface problem.	Set printer to on-line; try a self-test.	12.2.9
Bad cable or connectors.	Clean, tighten connections. Ensure continuity through each wire in the cable. Substitute cable.	Cables and Connectors, Chapter 7
Power-supply problem.	Output voltages.	Chapter 16
Faulty control circuits in printer.	Signals at printer CPU.	12.2.10

Dot-Matrix or Daisy-Wheel Printer—Incomplete Characters

Possible Cause	Check	See Section
One print wire not working (dot-matrix).	Line of dots missing across page.	12.2.5
Print hammer strikes off-center (daisy-wheel).	Left or right edge of each character is too light.	12.2.6
Daisy wheel dirty.	Enclosed areas in characters filled in. Clean.	
Ribbon high or low.	Bottom or top of all characters chopped off. Characters half red, half black.	12.2.8

Dot-Matrix or Daisy-Wheel Printer—Weak Printing

Possible Cause	Check	See Section
Ribbon worn.	Swap ribbon, try again.	
Ribbon jammed.	Inspect ribbon path, jammed cartridge	
Ribbon advance mechanism jammed.	Inspect	12.2.8
Impression control set for light impression.	Check setting.	
Printhead out of alignment.	Inspect.	12.2.4, 12.2.6
Platen loose.	Inspect.	12.2.3
Worn daisy wheel.	Inspect, substitute.	
Weak print hammer.	Inspect.	12.2.7
Incorrect signals to printhead (dot matrix).	Check duration of pulses.	2.2.5

Dot-Matrix or Daisy-Wheel Printer—Printer Completely Dead, No Fan, No Indicators

Possible Cause	Check	See Section
No AC to printer.	Ensure printer is plugged into live socket. Is fuse good?	
Faulty power supply in printer.	Check output voltages.	Chapter 16

Dot-Matrix or Daisy-Wheel Printer—Printer Starts Normally, Then Stops

Possible Cause	Check	See Section
Printer stopped to protect itself.	Error or alarm indicators: paper out, ribbon out, cover open.	
Interface problem.	Set printer to local; try self-test.	12.2.9
Bad cable or connectors.	Clean, tighten connections. Ensure continuity through each wire in the cable. Substitute cable.	Cables and Connectors, Chapter 7
Low voltage from power supply.	Measure voltages.	Chapter 16
Noise through power supply.	Test with oscilloscope.	Chapter 16
Environmental problems.	Fault related to time of day, temperature, nearby equipment switching on or off, etc.	Chapter 4
Faulty control circuits in printer.	Signals around printer CPU.	12.2.10

Dot-Matrix or Daisy-Wheel Printer—Carriage Does Not Move

Possible Cause	Check	See Section
Mechanical problem.	Open printer, inspect.	
Faulty stepper motor, drive circuit.	Inspect, test.	12.2.1

Dot-Matrix or Daisy-Wheel Printer—Carriage Moves, No Printing

Possible Cause	Check	See Section
Mechanism jammed.	Open printer, inspect.	
Broken cable to carriage printhead.	Inspect	
Mechanical problem in printhead.	Inspect.	12.2.5, 12.2.7
Power-supply problem.	Measure output voltages.	Chapter 16
Faulty control circuits in printer.	Check signals at printer CPU.	12.2.10

Dot-Matrix or Daisy-Wheel Printer—Letters Are Part Red, Part Black

Possible Cause	Check	See Section
Ribbon high or low.	Adjust mechanism.	12.2.8

Dot-Matrix or Daisy-Wheel Printer—Uneven Print Density

Possible Cause	Check	See Section
Platen too low.	Top of each letter too light.	12.2.3
Platen too high.	Bottom of each letter too light.	12.2.3
Platen out of square.	Type becomes lighter as it nears one edge of the page.	12.2.3
Print hammer strikes off-center (daisy-wheel printers).	Left or right edge of each character is too light.	12.2.6

Dot-Matrix or Daisy-Wheel Printer—Printer Operates Slowly

Possible Cause	Check	See Section
Printhead overheated.	Shut off printer, allow head to cool, try again.	
Faulty temperature sensor.	Test.	
Mechanical problem causing drag.	Inspect mechanisms.	

Dot-Matrix or Daisy-Wheel Printer—Printing Action, but No Printed Characters on Page

Possible Cause	Check	See Section
Ribbon jammed.	Inspect ribbon path. Is cartridge jammed?	
Ribbon advance mechanism jammed.	Inspect.	12.2.8

Dot-Matrix or Daisy-Wheel Printer—Paper-Feed Problems (Tractor Feed)

Possible Cause	Check	See Section
Paper mounted incorrectly on drive pins.	Number of pins showing above and below the perforation line.	
Paper mounted too loosely/too tight between tractors.	Distance between tractors.	
Bent parts in tractor mechanism.	Inspect.	

Dot-Matrix or Daisy-Wheel Printer—Paper-Feed Problems (Friction Feed)

Possible Cause	Check	See Section
Friction adjustment set too loose.	Setting.	
Friction springs worn, not enough force.	Tension, alignment.	
Paper drags on guides.	Inspect paper path, allow correct clearance.	
Printhead catches left edge of paper.	Move paper to left so printhead is always over paper.	

Dot-Matrix or Daisy-Wheel Printer—Paper Does Not Advance

Possible Cause	Check	See Section
Jammed mechanism.	Remove case, inspect.	
Faulty drive motor or circuit.	Inspect, test.	12.2.3

Daisy-Wheel Printer—Print Wheel Will Not Stop Spinning

Possible Cause	Check	See Section
Faulty head-driver circuits.	Inspect, test.	12.2.7

Daisy-Wheel Printer—One Missing Letter

Possible Cause	Check	See Section
Missing arm on daisy wheel.	Replace daisy wheel.	

Laser Printer—No Printing; White Page

Possible Cause	Check	See Section
No DC bias on developing cylinder.	Image development check.	13.2.1
No ground to photosensitive drum.	Remove cartridge and check connections.	Fig. 13-3
Drum not turning.	Check movement of drum.	13.1.2
Cartridge out of toner.	Replace cartridge.	
Laser beam is blocked.	Inspect beam path.	
No transfer corona.	Inspect transfer corona wire. Check corona voltage.	Fig. 13-2

Laser Printer—Black Page

Possible Cause	Check	See Section
No primary corona.	Inspect primary corona wire. Check for corona voltage.	Fig. 13-2
Laser permanently on.	Check control circuits.	Chapter 13
Damaged beam detector.	Inspect beam detector.	Fig. 13-5

Laser Printer—Horizontal Black Lines

Possible Cause	Check	See Section
No beam detect signal.	Inspect detector.	Fig. 13-5

Laser Printer–Black Page with White Horizontal Lines

Possible Cause	Check	See Section
No beam detect signal.	Beam detector.	13.1.13, Fig. 13-5

Laser Printer–Random Dot Patterns

Possible Cause	Check	See Section
Incorrect signals from host computer.	Try self-test.	Control Circuits, Chapter 13
Faulty control circuits.	Printer CPU.	

Laser Printer–Smeared Print

Possible Cause	Check	See Section
No fusing action.	Heating action of rollers. Fusing lamp. Fusing temperature controls.	Fig. 13-2
Static charge eliminator teeth bent.	Inspect teeth.	Fig. 13-3
Incorrect type of paper.	Use correct paper.	Chapter 13

Laser Printer–Repeating Marks on Paper

Possible Cause	Check	See Section
Dirt or mark on a roller.	Measure distance, calculate diameter, inspect and clean roller.	13.1.12

Laser Printer–Very Light Print

Possible Cause	Check	See Section
Cartridge is out of toner.	Remove cartridge, rock it, and replace it.	Fig. 13-2
No transfer corona.	Inspect transfer corona wire. Check for corona voltage.	Fig. 13-2
No DC bias on developing cylinder.	Check for DC bias.	Fig. 13-3

Laser printer–Left or Right Side of Page Is Blank

Possible Cause	Check	See Section
Laser scanning to one side.	Large mirror over photosensitive drum.	Fig. 13-5

Laser Printer—Page Is Out of Registration; Distorted Print

Possible Cause	Check	See Section
Drive rollers worn or dirty.	Inspect, replace.	
Drive gears worn or clogged.	Inspect, replace.	

Laser Printer—Slightly Light Print

Possible Cause	Check	See Section
Cartridge running out of toner.	Remove cartridge, rock it and replace it.	Fig. 13-2
Faulty cartridge sensitivity switches.	Check switches.	Switches, Chapter 7
Erase lamps not working.	Check lamps.	Fig. 13-3

Laser Printer—Dark Blotches

Possible Cause	Check	See Section
No primary corona.	Inspect primary corona wire. Check for corona voltage.	Fig. 13-2

Laser Printer—Vertical White Streaks

Possible Cause	Check	See Section
Dirty mirror above photosensitive drum.	Inspect, clean.	Fig. 13-5
Dirty transfer corona assembly.	Inspect, clean.	Fig. 13-3
Cartridge running out of toner.	Remove cartridge, rock it, and replace it.	Fig. 13-2

Monitor—Shortened Picture or White Line Across Screen

Possible Cause	Check	See Section
Vertical size adjustment.	Adjust.	
Weak vertical output.	Check vertical oscillator and vertical output circuits.	Fig. 15-5

Monitor—Images Have Colored Shading on One or Two Sides

Possible Cause	Check	See Section
Monitor out of alignment.	Alignment procedure.	Chapter 15

Monitor—Faint Lines Behind the Picture

Possible Cause	Check	See Section
Black level setting	Adjust.	

Monitor—Picture Stretched Sideways, Black Lines Visible

Possible Cause	Check	See Section
Picture out of sync.	Horizontal oscillator and horizontal output sections.	Fig. 15-5

Monitor—Narrow Picture

Possible Cause	Check	See Section
Weak horizontal output.	Horizontal oscillator and horizontal output circuits.	Fig. 15-5

Monitor—Picture Rolls Side-to-Side

Possible Cause	Check	See Section
Horizontal hold adjustment.	Adjust.	
Horizontal sync and horizontal output circuits.	Check circuits.	Fig. 15-5

Monitor—Picture Rolls Up or Down

Possible Cause	Check	See Section
Vertical hold adjustment.	Adjust.	
Vertical sync and vertical output circuits.	Check circuits.	Fig. 15-5

Monitor—Screen Is Dark

Possible Cause	Check	See Section
No power to monitor.	AC outlet, plug, fuse, circuit breaker.	Chapter 16
Short circuit causing "foldback."	Use variac.	Chapter 16
No electron beam.	Picture tube, high-voltage circuits, scanning circuits.	Chapter 15

Monitor—Screen Lights, but No Image Displayed

Possible Cause	Check	See Section
No modulation to electron beam.	Video output and sync separator circuits.	Fig. 15-5

Monitor—Sections of Picture Waver

Possible Cause	Check	See Section
Bad filter capacitor in power supply.	Check capacitor.	Chapter 16

Monitor—Picture Shrinks

Possible Cause	Check	See Section
Faulty power supply.	Check output voltages.	Chapter 16
Beam not deflected outward.	Horizontal and vertical outputs.	Chapter 15

Modem—No Ready Indicator

Possible Cause	Check	See Section
No power to modem.	See if modem is plugged in.	Cables and Connectors, & Switches, Chapter 7; Chapter 16
Handset reversed in holder (acoustic-modems).	Check position of handset, reverse if necessary.	
Modem set to incorrect mode.	Check mode setting. (One modem should be set to originate, other to answer.)	
Fault in modem.	Try self-test.	14.1.2
Problem with RS-232C interface.	Check for correct signals through RS-232C cable.	14.1.1
Mechanical damage to modem circuit board.	Inspect circuit board.	Circuit Boards, Chapter 7
Faulty modem IC.	Check, replace.	Modem Control Circuits, Chapter 14
Fault in serial interface circuits in computer.	Remove, replace circuits (computers with removable circuit cards). Inspect, replace UART IC.	Interface Circuits, Chapter 14

Modem—Intermittent Problem

Possible Cause	Check	See Section
Fault inside modem.	Try modem self-test.	14.1.2
Noisy phone line (long-distance section).	Listen to line (line bad only on one call), hang up, call back.	
Noisy phone line (local section).	Listen to line (line bad on all calls), call phone company.	
Bad cable or connectors.	Clean, tighten connections. Ensure continuity through each wire in the cable. Substitute cable.	Cables and Connectors, Chapter 7
Faulty modem IC.	Check, replace.	Modem Control Circuits, Chapter 14
Fault in serial interface circuits in computer.	Remove, replace circuits (computers with removable circuit cards). Inspect, replace UART IC.	Interface Circuits, Chapter 14

G

COMPUTERFACTS™
Index

COMPUTERFACTS™ are available for the following types of microcomputers and peripheral equipment. Each package includes complete schematics, parts location charts, parts lists, IC pinout diagrams, and test instructions.

Listing complete through December 1987

EPSON
FX-80 (Printer).................CP7/008940
FX-100 (Printer)...............CP11/008950
FX286E (Printer)...............CP32/009013
LQ1500 (Printer)...............CP22/008981
MX-80FT III (Printer)...........CP1/008904
MX-100 (Printer)................CP2/008908
QX-10 (Computer).............CSCS4/008923
RX-80 (Printer).................CP9/008945
LQ1500 (Printer)...............CP22/008981

FRANKLIN
ACE 1000 (Computer)...........CC6/008917

HITACHI
CM1216D (Monitor).........CMT11-2/008993
CM1406C (Monitor).........CMT11-1/008993
CM1481 (Color Monitor).......CMT1-1/008905

IBM
5152-002 (Printer)...............CP3/008913
5151 (Monochrome Monitor)....CMT4-1/008916
5153 (Color Monitor).........CMT4-2/008916
PC 5150 (Computer/Disk Drive).CSCS-2/008914
PC Jr Model 4860 (Computer/
    Disk Drive)..................CSCS8/008943
PC-XT Model 5160-086
    (Computer/Disk Drive).....CSCS10/008967
QUIETWRITER I,II (Printer)......CP30/009010

LEADING EDGE
MODEL M (MP1676L)
    (Computer/Disk Drive)......CSCS16/008990

MITSUBISHI
M4851 (Disk Drive)............CD11/008992

NEC
PC-8023A-N (Printer)...........CP10/008948
PC-8025A (Printer).............CP5/008931

OKIDATA
EN3211, OKIMATE 20
    (IBM Version) (Printer).......CP34/009015
GE8232 (Printer)..............CP26/09000
ML82 (Printer).................CP23/008977
ML92 (Printer).................CP20/008985

OSBORNE
OCC-1, OCC-1A (Computer
    /Monitor/Drive).............CSCS-1/008909

PANASONIC
CT-1310M (Color Monitor).....CMT1-2/008905
CT-1320M (NMX-GLA)
    (Color Monitor)...........CMT5-1/008929
CT-1350MG (NMX-KS-1)
    (Color Monitor)............CMT2-1/008910
CT-1920M (Color Monitor).....CMT6-1/008922

PC'S LIMITED
TURBO PC
    (Computer/Disk Drive).......CSCS18/008991

QUME
QUMETRAK 142 (Disk Drive)....CD16/009007

RADIO SHACK
FD501 (Disk Drive).............CD14/008997
TRS 80 (Level II) (Computer/
    Monitor/Expansion)..........CSCS3/008933
TRS 80 III
    (Computer/Monitor/Drive)......CSCS5/008942
TRS 80 Model 4 (Computer/Disk Drive/
    Monitor)..................CSCS13/008976

TRS 80 DMP-120 (Printer).........CP6/008935
TRS 80 (26-1160/61)(Disk Drive)...CD7/008936
TRS 80 (26-1164A)(Disk Drive)....CD5/008934
TRS 80 (26-3002)(Color Computer).CC13/008946
26-3136 & 26-3134
    (Color Computer).............CC15/008970

RANA
ELITE I (Disk Drive)............CD3/008918
ELITE III (Disk Drive)...........CD1/008902
ELITE II (Disk Drive)...........CD2/008907

SANYO
AVM 196 (Color Monitor)......CMT6-2/008922
AVM 255 (Color Monitor)......CMT9-2/008986
MBC 550 & 555
    (Computer/Disk Drive).......CSCS11/008972

SHUGART
SA455 (Disk Drive).............CD10/008987

SINCLAIR
ZX-81 (Computer)..............CC14/008969

SPERRY
HT (PC10)(Computer/Disk Drive)CSCS20/009017

STAR
DELTA 10 (Printer).............CP19/008973
GEMINI 10X (Printer)...........CP13/008955
GEMINI 15X (Printer)...........CP16/008959
NX10 Version 2 (Printer).........CP35/009025
RADIX 10 (Printer).............CP31/009012
SG-10 (Printer).................CP25/008996

TANDON
TM100-2/2a (Disk Drive).........CD8/008966

TANDY
1000SX (Computer/Disk Drive)..CSCS19/009006

TEAC
FD-54A (Disk Drive)...........CD15/009009
FD-55BV-75 (Disk Drive)........CD17/009008

TEXAS INSTRUMENTS
TI99/4A (Computer)..............CC-2/008901

TIMEX
TS 1000 (Computer).............CC14/008969

ZENITH
ZVM-121 (Monochrome Monitor)CMT2-2/008910
ZVM-122A/123A (CHASSIS 12ZM2ZX)
    (Monochrome Monitor).......CMT5-2/008929
ZVM-131 (Color Monitor).....CMT8-2/008939
ZVM-135 (Color Monitor).....CMT7-2/008932
ZF-151-52
    (Computer/2 Disk Drives)......CSCS6/008956
ZFA-161-52 (Computer/
    Monitor/2 Drives)............CSCS9/008949

COMPUTERFACTS	Prices
Computer Systems (CSCS)	$39.95
Computers (CC)	$21.95
Printers (CP0	$24.95
Disk Drives (CD)	$21.95
Monitors (CMT)	$21.95

Howard W. Sams & Company

H
Answers to
Review Questions

Chapter 2

1. Don't touch the razor until you unplug it! The water may conduct electricity and give you a dangerous shock.

2. The shock can cause your heart to stop or can interfere with your breathing.

3. The rubber pad provides insulation for extra protection against shock if you make a mistake.

4. The parts near the AC switch may carry 120-volts AC. Watch out for any uninsulated parts in this section of the power supply.

5. A "hot chassis" is possible when a device has a two-prong plug. Prevent problems by using an isolation transformer.

6. It is not safe to work when you're tired or rushed.

7. The necktie could become caught in the moving parts of the printer. Take the tie off or tuck the end of the tie into your shirt.

Chapter 3

1. After the first few days, computer equipment is usually quite reliable for the first year. The dealer is not taking a big risk.

2. If you leave the equipment turned on, this will accelerate the appearance of any problems. You should know about any problems before the warranty period is up.

3. RAM memory is more reliable than floppy disk memory. The floppy disk drive has many mechanical parts, and these tend to drift out of alignment.

4. A simple IC is usually more reliable than a RAM IC. The devices inside a RAM must be very small, and thus are more likely to fail.

5. Answer is D—all of the above.

Chapter 4

1. Service contracts offer the dealers high profits with low risk.

2. The equipment tends to be quite reliable during the first year of operation.

3. The local dealer may not want to service the computer you bought from a discounter. Some dealers are forced by the manufacturer to provide servicing.

4. Working as quickly as possible, this will take at least a week. The job is more likely to take three weeks or more.

5. If you hide facts from the technician, he or she will take more time to find the problem, and your bill will be higher.

Chapter 5

1. Cold weather causes dry air in heated areas, and this can cause static charges to collect.

2. Perhaps the equipment was damaged by a large "spike" caused by lightning.

3. Check for a large motor or other device which is turned off every day at this time.

4. Arrange better shielding for your computer or a better antenna system for your neighbor. You might try shielded cables on your system, or a shielded lead-in wire on your neighbor's antenna system.

5. A fiber-optic link is a good choice for a "noisy" environment like this.

6. These devices include small capacitors on the inputs, and these can easily be damaged by static charges.

7. All of the cooling vents should be unobstructed. If the vents are blocked, the equipment may overheat, and some of the components may fail.

8. Dirty heads cause intermittent Read/Write errors.

9. A magnetic paper-clip holder should not be allowed in the same room with a computer. The magnetized clips may damage floppy disks.

10. This is the question you will have to answer if you ever encounter this situation. It is very important to have a reliable system of backups.

Chapter 6

1. If you have a messy bench, it is easy to knock things over, lose parts, and cause accidental damage.

2. You can't use the $1/4$-watt resistor, because it has a power rating lower than the rating of the original part. When placed in service, the $1/4$-watt resistor would eventually burn out.

3. Don't count on a "near replacement" transistor. Sometimes, the replacement has values which are not "near" those of the original part.

4. This is a common 7400-series IC, so you should be able to find a replacement easily. The 74S74 probably will use more power. In most cases, you should be able to use this part.

5. Some current tracers will not work unless there is a changing current in the line under test.

6. For this type of part, you must get an exact replacement from the manufacturer of the printer.

7. Depending on the brand, a local dealer may sell you a replacement. If the computer is a common type, you may be able to buy a replacement from a mail-order outlet.

8. Use just a drop of thread-lock compound. If you cover the whole screw, you will never be able to remove the part.

Chapter 7

1. The transistor is completely short-circuited, and must be replaced.

2. A damaged capacitor may explode when power is first turned on.

3. The capacitors tend to fail first.

4. The motor must be replaced.

5. Stray voltages can creep into the system, if the grounding point is located far from the test point.

6. Not necessarily. The power supply may be "folding back" to protect itself. One of the ICs or other parts may be short-circuited.

7. Try driving the printer through the second serial port.

8. The blackened case tells you that the fuse has experienced a large over-current. Look for a "dead short."

Chapter 8

1. Not necessarily. One of the ICs "downstream" of this point may also be bad.

2. Sometimes you can take +5 V and ground from large traces on the circuit board. These voltages are also available on the pins of each IC.

3. When an output line is broken inside the IC, the output line appears to be "floating." The part which still has the correct signal is inside the IC, so you can't detect it.

   If the break is outside the IC, the part of the line downstream of the break will appear to be "floating." The part upstream of the break will show normal signals.

4. The trace never varies from 0 V. Use a VOM or logic probe to test. Use a current tracer to find the short.

5. Use a logic pulser and probe. If pulses on one line appear on the next line, the two lines are shorted.

6. Use the probe to test the input line and the output line. The signal on the output line should be the opposite of the signal on the input line.

7. To test a complicated interface IC, substitute an IC which is known to be working.

8. To test a RAM chip, use a diagnostic software program.

Chapter 9

1. Don't assume that the printer is faulty. The problem could lie in one of the computer circuits which drive the printer. Run your own tests.

2. The software affects all parts of the system. When troubleshooting, always eliminate the software as a possible cause of the problem.

3. Press the "Reset" key, or turn the computer off, and then turn it back on again.

4. It is unlikely that many RAMs would fail at once, unless the unit has been damaged by lightning. Perhaps one of the address or data lines is faulty.

5. These three groups of signals run to all parts of the computer. Since these systems are so extensive, any problems are most likely to occur here.

6. Check for signals on the pins of the CPU chip, or on the pins of the card-slot connectors.

7. The "Reset" signal is not being generated in the first place, or it is being interrupted before it can reach the CPU chip.

8. This symptom is probably caused by dirty or corroded key contacts.

9. The mouse "ball" tends to pick up dirt and transfer it to the rollers.

10. People become excited while playing video games, and tend to damage the game controllers.

Chapter 10

1. The customer may have removed the card while the power was turned on.

2. The bearings in the motor or drive spindle may be wearing out.

3. Perhaps the index detector is not working. The index system may also include a "debounce" circuit, and this may not be working.

4. The switch may be damaged, or the line may be shorted to +5 V or ground.

5. This symptom could be caused by a bad power supply. It is also possible that the drive is never being "selected."

6. It may be cost-effective to buy a whole new drive.

7. The door mechanism is often used to "load" the Read/Write head.

8. You may be able to recover the erased file if you have not used the disk since you made the mistake. However, this is not of critical importance if you made a backup disk.

Chapter 11

1. A hard disk drive should never be moved while it is operating. This practice invites a "head crash."

2. You must return the drive to the manufacturer for servicing. You cannot open a hard drive unless you have access to a "clean room."

3. The Read/Write head may be worn, and may be producing weakened signals.

4. Try to buy a copy of the manual for your disk drive. You might also try to get a schematic.

6. Simply edit in the corrections using the word-processing program.

7. When the system is working with a faulty copy of DOS, anything can happen. Your data may be "corrupted."

8. "/M" selects files which have been modified since a given date. "/A" appends these files onto the end of a string of backups. It you use "/M" without "/A", you must be careful to specify the date of your last master backup. If you do not, the completed backup may not include updated versions of all of the files.

Chapter 12

1. The problem is located inside of the printer itself.

2. For some reason, the printer is saying it is busy. The buffer in the printer may be full, or one of the interlock switches may be open. It is also possible that the printer has developed a fault which holds the "busy" line "true."

3. This client may be using off-brand ribbon cartridges, and these cheap ribbons may not have the correct lubrication.

4. The printer has a red/black ribbon, and the ribbon has slipped out of position. Check the vertical positioning of the ribbon.

5. The characters on the daisy wheel may be worn.

6. The data lines to the printer will be connected to one of the peripheral interfaces (lines PA0 through PA7 or PB0 through PB7).

7. The print wire is bent, or the head of the wire has been enlarged. The damaged wire cannot retract back into the printhead. The head should be replaced.

8. The ink orifice is probably plugged. There is usually a way of increasing the pressure behind the orifice to unplug it.

9. With a loose carriage belt, the printer will not be able to position the carriage accurately.

10. Check the transistor that drives the faulty print wire.

11. The printhead may be overheating, and the printer may be slowing down as a protective measure.

Chapter 13

1. The problem is located in the printer itself.

2. The interlock switch turns off the laser when you open the cover. If you bypass this switch, you may look at the laser light and damage your eyes.

3. Laser cartridges are sensitive to light and humidity. The cartridges should be kept wrapped until they are used.

4. For some reason, the printer is not "painting" the page image of -100-V dots on the drum. Check the primary corona and the laser system.

5. No. You must use a type of toner that is specifically compatible with laser printers.

6. The fusing section is not doing its job.

7. It sounds as if something is preventing this printer from operating. Check the signals at the printer's CPU chip.

8. The cartridge is low on toner. Plan to replace the cartridge.

Chapter 14

1. This symptom can be caused by temporary noise on the phone line.

2. You must be sure that you have received the program accurately. Use a protocol like "XMODEM" to check each bit of the incoming file.

3. The problem is located inside the first modem.

4. For some reason, the modem is not ready to operate. The line may be shorted in a "false" condition.

5. The modem may have been damaged by a large "spike" caused by a lightning strike.

Chapter 15

1. The electron beam is not being deflected vertically or horizontally.

2. Beware of the high-voltage areas near the horizontal oscillator and the picture tube. Watch out for parts which may carry 120-V AC. Beware of any large capacitors.

3. Many monitors are designed with a "hot chassis." The isolation transformer reduces the shock hazard possibility.

4. Connect a jumper wire to the chassis frame around the picture tube. Fasten the other end of the wire to a screwdriver, and slide the tip of the screwdriver under the rubber cover of the high-voltage anode lead to discharge it. Then, remove the anode lead from the picture tube and again touch the end of the screwdriver to the inside of the anode socket.

5. The picture is "out of sync" both horizontally and vertically. Perhaps there is a problem in one of the circuits that handles both sets of sync signals.

6. A temporary low-voltage condition on the AC lines reduced the deflection voltages for the electron beam.

7. The power supply is probably "folding back" because of a short circuit somewhere in the set. Use a variac to get the unit working.

8. The image may "burn" into the phosphor material on the screen of the monitor.

Chapter 16

1. Beware of any exposed parts near the AC switch or the fuse.

2. This transformer may have a "fusible link" in the input coil. It may be simplest to replace the part.

3. This fuse experienced a severe overload. Check for a "dead short."

4. Any of the ICs or capacitors may be shorted.

5. One of the filter capacitors is not doing its job.

Index